Counseling and Psychotherapy

An Existential-Humanistic View

THIRD EDITION

Dugald S. Arbuckle

BOSTON UNIVERSITY

Allyn and Bacon, Inc.
Boston

Library of Congress Cataloging in Publication Data

Arbuckle, Dugald Sinclair, date.
    Counseling and psychotherapy.

    Edition for 1961 published under title: Counseling; an introduction.
Editions for 1965–1970 published under title Counseling; philosophy, the-
ory, and practice.
    Includes bibliographical references and index.
    1. Counseling. 2. Psychotherapy. 3. Existential psychology.
4. Humanistic psychology. I. Title.
[DNLM: 1. Counseling. 2. Psychotherapy. BF637.C6 A667c]
BF637.C6A67   1975   158   74-23738

ISBN 0-205-04634-7

    The author wishes to thank authors and publishers who have permit-
ted him to use extracts from copyrighted sources.
    Angelo V. Boy and Gerald J. Pine, Client-Centered Counseling in the
Secondary School (Boston: Houghton Mifflin, 1963), copyright 1963 by Angelo V. Boy and Gerald J. Pine.
    Angelo V. Boy and Gerald J. Pine, The Counselor in the Schools, 2nd
ed. (Boston: Houghton Mifflin, 1968), copyright 1968 by Angelo V. Boy and
Gerald J. Pine.
    Robert R. Carkhuff and Bernard G. Berenson, Beyond Counseling and
Therapy (New York: Holt, Rinehart and Winston, 1967).
    © Copyright 1969 by Rahe B. Corlis and Peter Rabe. Reprinted from
Psychotherapy from the Center, by Rahe B. Corlis and Peter Rabe, by per-
mission of Intext Educational Publishers.
    Reprinted from The Art of Existential Counseling, by Adrian van
Kaam, published by Dimension Books, Inc. Copyright © 1966.

TO PENELOPE

Contents

Contents

Preface

While this book is a revision of *Counseling: Philosophy, Theory and Practice* (Second Edition), it is in many ways a new book both in content and in tone. About one-half of the pages are new, about one-quarter have been modified and changed, and the remainder are about as they were. The major additions to the book are to be found in Part Two, "Theories of Counseling," in which there are five new chapters, and in Part Four, "The Counselor," in which there are significant additions and deletions.

The book reflects my own movement and growth in the direction of an existential-humanistic philosophy of life and living. I do not see the book as one on existential-humanistic counseling, but rather an existential-humanistic viewpoint of the broad field of counseling and psychotherapy. While the book, professionally, is geared more to the school milieu, it is actually written for anyone who is involved in a human relationship with others, in either a personal or a professional sense. I would like to think of it as a book about people living and learning and growing together in the direction of greater individual freedom.

I have learned some exciting things from books, but mostly I have learned from the people with whom I have worked and lived and played. They are to be found throughout the pages of this book, and I thank them for the riches they have given to me.

DSA

PART ONE

The Philosophy of Counseling

Chapter **1**

A Philosophical Base for Counseling

The actions of all humans are reflective of their philosophical bases of life and living, even though some people, possibly most, find it very difficult to articulate just what their philosophy might be. Let us look in this chapter, then, at what I would consider to be an existential-humanistic version of life and living, with particular stress on its implications for counselors and therapists.

INDIVIDUAL FREEDOM AND INDIVIDUAL RESPONSIBILITY

In the last decade there has been great stress on the "rights" of individuals, especially those individuals who happen to be members of minority groups. Much of this, of course, reflects long overdue pressure for social and human justice, and no decent human being can take issue with this. Nor can one be too critical of the highly emotional, and often almost irrational, tone of some of what is said and written. But this irrationality often tends to cloud the real social and human issues, and very rarely in the "demands" for individual rights and freedom does one find the essential ingredient without which there can be no individual freedom—namely, individual responsibility.

Let me note what I would consider to be a few of the elements which are crucial to this central issue of individual freedom and individual responsibility:

1. Every human being is, to a high degree, an obviously conditioned product of an environmental milieu, which, at any point in

3

time, is itself a product of conditioning. The black man who is considered to be inferior to a white man is no less a product of conditioning than is the white man; the woman who accepts her function as service to a man is as conditioned as is the man; the devout religionist who has found "the" God is as victimized by his culture as is the man he wishes to convert; the man of fifty years who feels that because of his age he is finished is no more the victim than the culture which consigns him to the scrap heap.

What is usually overlooked is the reality that the greatest enemy of the black man who has accepted the myth of his inferiority is not the white man who has conditioned him to believe this, but the black man who has allowed himself to accept it. The enemy of the woman who is a second-class citizen is not the man who has pressed it upon her, but the woman herself who has accepted it. The victim of the religious bigot perpetuates his condition by accepting the act of bigotry rather than opposing it. The man of fifty is doomed to a life of nothingness because he will not rise above the pressures and say, with certainty, to himself, "For me, this is not so."

Very simply, the major struggle in the battle for individual freedom is the struggle of me against me, the struggle in which I try to extricate myself from the conditioning that has taught me I am what I am not, that I cannot be who I can be. The victim, not the oppressor, is the major enemy to be overcome. The struggle is with the inner, rather than the outer forces. The black man who accepts his inferior status, the woman who is willing to walk two paces behind the man, the individual who meekly bows to the bejeweled religious bigot, the man who is willing to retreat into a blob-like existence because "they" say he is finished—*these* are the real enemies of individual freedom.

2. The reality of outside negative pressures often clouds the equal reality that basic individual change comes from the inside out, not from the outside in. Of course there *is* prejudice; there *is* cruelty; there *is* betrayal; there *is* a vast array of negative behaviors of human toward human. The primary issue for me, however, is what can I do to change the behavior of me toward me; the secondary issue is what can I do to change the behavior of others toward me. One of the peak experiences in living occurs when the human being begins to realize that as he changes his attitudes and his behavior toward himself, so he changes the attitudes and behaviors of others toward him. When others begin to realize that this unique individual actually determines the *meaning* of what happens to him, then what happens is quite different than when it is clear that this person is, basically, a non-person covered by a human exterior.

This is, probably, one of the major errors of the more dog-

4

matic behavioral scientists who, functioning as therapists, assume that changing the outside environment or the outside individual behavior will change inside individual attitudes. The folly of this action is surely seen by the wastage of vast sums of federal monies in a vain attempt to change attitudes and behaviors by changing the outside environment. Slums are the products of people. Most American slum areas were once pleasant places, or they were new areas which were quickly turned into slums. This was done by people who were quite capable of making them into something else.

The last decade has seen billions of dollars go into the destruction of old buildings, and the building of new ones, with the naive assumption that a change of buildings would remove a slum from the landscape. The new buildings, of course, became slum dwellings within months, since nothing had been done to change the attitudes of the people who lived there. I can remember over one hundred bright-eyed young university students volunteering to spend a day cleaning up an apartment building. While the students scrubbed and swept and removed the feces and urine and slop and garbage in the halls and yards, the producers of the feces and urine and slop and garbage sat, with glazed and wondering eyes, watching them. The students departed, leaving a relatively clean building. A week later it was back to its usual condition. Some individuals appear to have an absolute faith that we can change people by changing things around them, while totally ignoring the humans who have created the situation.

The environment may well be dreadful beyond imagination, but the human *can* surmount it, the human can become its master. If one does not believe this simple reality, it is difficult to see how anyone can talk about individual freedom. If so-called individual freedom is dependent on the other, then obviously it is no more than the cruel illusion described by Skinner. (Skinner himself, interestingly enough, does not appear to accept the idea that *his* individual freedom is dependent on others.) If, on the other hand, we can help the individual to become more independent of the culture which surrounds him and more dependent on himself, then change will move from within to without. Change in the life and living of any person, is not, of course, entirely his own product; but the responsibility for change belongs on the shoulders of the person who is undergoing change.

3. Individual responsibility is the creator of individual freedom, rather than the other way about. One cannot be granted freedom any more than one can have his freedom taken away by some other person. Freedom is not of the stuff to be granted or removed at the whim of the other. Freedom is within, and it becomes the basic

5

core of those who have accepted the responsibility for the direction of their own lives.

A responsible mother with five children should expect to be greeted by an employer in exactly the same manner as a father with five children. If the mother makes it clear that "my children come before my job," however, she should not expect to be treated in the same manner as a man or woman who would not feel this way, no matter how praiseworthy her statement might be. The mother made the choice of being a mother of five children, and the mother made the decision that her children came before the job. It is hardly responsible behavior on her part to blame the employer for actions directly related to decisions made by her. The employer is not a representative of a social service agency.

The reality, of course, is that women who become mothers do quit their jobs more frequently than men who become fathers, and that a working woman will quit her job when her husband moves more readily than a working man will quit his job when the woman gets a chance of a better position elsewhere. Thus the employer is being quite rational when he views the advent of motherhood in a somewhat different light than the advent of fatherhood. It is the mother and the father, by their actions, who create this situation, not the employer.

I can think of two examples of this behavior. An academic department in a university hired a woman in the fall. During the year, she impressed everyone with her professional competence, and her rapid professional advancement was certain. Her fiancé, however, was graduating a year later, and was looking for a job in another part of the country. Instead of the man, who had no job, joining the woman and looking for a position in the area where she was employed, she gave up her position after one year and left to look for a position near him. In another case, a department hired a woman who made it clear that she wanted the position very much and helped her husband get a position in a neighboring institution. The husband, however, changed his mind and turned down his position. His wife wanted very much to stay, but being conditioned to be "the good wife," she quit her job and went with him. Much time and effort and money were spent in the process of screening and interviewing these women, and the time and the effort and the money were wasted. These women, and tens of thousands like them, must accept the responsibility of having much to do with the attitude of employers, male and female, toward potential female employees. At the same time, the employer must accept the responsibility of making a decision about a person which may be overwhelmingly based on his experience with other people, and this is obviously unfair to the individual. Yet, even if it is unfair, it is also understandable. The man who believes in hiring ex-convicts to give them another chance and then is robbed three times in a row by his new employees will, eventually, say "No" simply because the person who is applying for the job is an ex-convict.

4. Too frequently, too, in the "freedom" literature, we find indignant statements regarding bigotry and prejudice when the so-called "evidence" is no evidence at all. For example, one cannot call a university department sexist because there are few women on the staff. If there is a ten to one proportion of male applicants over female applicants, one could expect there would be a ten to one proportion of males over females on the staff. The fact that there is only one woman for every ten men who can be considered for a position is because men *and* women have accepted a certain role for women in society—a role which is now, happily, being challenged.

Unfortunately, in this battle for equality, the whole concept of responsibility is often overlooked. If a woman expects to be considered for a position in the same light as a man, then the expectations of her should be the same as for the man. If women expect equal treatment from an employer (which they should), then they should assume that the employer is justified in having equal expectations of them.

On the other hand, the fact that a female professor with the same professional qualifications is paid less than a male is very definite evidence of sexual prejudice, as long as the woman accepts the same job expectations. If she does not, of course, then the difference in salary is a valid difference related to a difference in contribution. Even here, though, a major reason for the differentiation is the fact that many women will refuse to speak up about the inequalities regarding salaries. I was a member of a committee investigating possible sexual prejudice at a private university, and we were dismayed to find that the vast majority of women who gave us information insisted on its being treated as confidential, and they refused to appear in person to state their cases. Here again, they were their own greatest enemies. They refused to accept responsibility for action on their own behalf and, instead, passed the responsibility on to a committee.

The same irresponsibility is seen among many university students. They complain endlessly about the inane and ridiculous pattern of formal education, but accept no responsibility for doing anything about it. Instead, they use the universal cop-out—"After all, we're only students"—which is exactly the same as "After all, we're only women" or "After all, we're only black people." Students will often say they would like to do something about a certain situation,

7

but they can't run the risk of getting an "F" in a course or being thrown out of a program. This illustrates the sad illusion that one can somehow achieve freedom without risk, without possibly having to pay for the step one takes toward greater individual freedom. But risk and freedom go together. The security of freedom is not the lack of risk, but rather the calm certainty about one's ability to cope with risk, and to maintain one's self no matter what may come from the outside.

Actually, the risk factor more often than not is really the creation of the timid mind rather than some outside condition. Risk does not actually refer to action taken, but rather to the attitude of the person taking the action. I have noted many times that involved individuals see less risk than individuals who do nothing. It is not that the risk is different in the sense of what might happen, but the risk-taker is more certain about his ability to deal with what might come. He thus tends to view the possible consequences as much less threatening.

The more fearful and irresponsible person is one who sees the risk as something over which he has no control, something totally in the hands of others. On the other hand, the person who accepts individual responsibility is a freer individual and, in a way, lessens the risk because he is the one who determines the meaning of that risk.

5. A responsible and free individual is one who has narrowed the gap between attitudes and behaviors. As a genuine and congruent person, his behaviors accurately reflect his attitudes. He is open, and what he does is a direct reflection of what he believes. In our culture, however, the young soon learn that outer behavior is more important than inner feelings, and that many behaviors must be suppressed because they are not acceptable to the outer world. The suppression of these behaviors, in turn, affects and distorts the original attitudes. A child may feel good about masturbation—a natural feeling—but he is soon taught that he must never do this because it is "bad." He represses the behavior, and his original good feeling becomes one of guilt. In due time he may even be able to totally repress the original natural feeling—with even more disastrous results. He is no longer consciously aware of who he really is. Of such stuff is psychosis made!

There are many common day-by-day examples of this accepted dishonesty with self. When we meet or telephone someone, we learn that we are supposed to say, "How are you?" even though in most cases we care not at all about the condition of the other's health. I have found that when I reply, "Okay," but do not ask the other person how he is, he usually says, "Okay." If I ask why he said that, the result is some degree of discomfort. If, when he says, "How are you?" I ask, "Do you care?" this causes even greater discomfort!

Attitudes, of course, are often highly superficial too, and a mark of the irresponsible person is that he not only wants to know what behaviors are acceptable, but he also wants to have the "right" attitudes. It is fashionable, for example, in a race relations group, to have all the white members hang their heads and say, "Yes, we are all racists." They obviously don't believe what they say, and sometimes I have asked such people why they appear to be so cheerful when they say, "I am a racist," as if it were something amusing. If they really believe this, and react in this way, then an honest expression would be "Yes, I am a racist, and I enjoy being a racist." I also find that when I ask such an individual to describe some of his racist behavior, he usually has great trouble in doing this. He has even more trouble when I say, "Well, since you can't think of any of your behavior being racist, how come you say you are a racist?" Another way to cause a commotion in such a group is to indicate, if you are a white person, that you do not think you are a racist, or if you are a black person, to indicate that you think you are a racist. There are certain attitudes we are supposed to have and certain attitudes we are not supposed to have. We learn not to show the attitudes we are not supposed to have and to show the attitudes we are supposed to have, whether we own them or not. To be at least mildly socially schizophrenic is almost a cultural necessity if one is interested in getting ahead!

In a responsible and free individual, behaviors will accurately reflect attitudes, and the behavior thus tends to be acceptable and pleasing to the person himself. If his own behavior is causing him stress and strain, we can assume that the problem is the attitude that produces the behavior rather than the behavior per se.

Behavior therapy tends to work backwards, trying to modify the behavior without paying too much attention to the attitude that produces it. Most behaviors that are causing unhappiness are, in a sense, needed. I can think of a woman, for example, who was seemingly very "unhappy" about what she felt was her very strange behavior. When she would come in contact with a man who was attractive to her, she would dress and look and behave in the worst possible way so that invariably the man did not stay around very long. On the other hand, when she would meet a rather repulsive man she would become seductive and attractive and inviting, and very often end up in bed with him. Her basic desire and need was to degrade and hurt herself and to behave in such a manner as to satisfy herself that she was a worthless creature. This attitude was far more dominant than her desire to overcome her unhappiness resulting from this behavior. When she began to be able to look at herself openly, to begin to question her negative attitudes about herself, she began gradually to feel better about herself, to believe that she was worthy of happiness. Her change of behavior was a natural outcome of her change of attitude. Exercises in trying to change her behavior would have been futile because, in a real sense, she needed to behave as she did. When she no longer needed to behave this way, her behavior changed without any attempt being made to change it.

6. Another thought is that the literal meaning of freedom and responsibility changes as the culture changes. Neither freedom nor responsibility can be considered to be some kind of absolute, totally unaffected by cultural changes. It is never "I am free" versus "I am not free," but rather "Have I stretched the boundaries of my freedom, distinguishing between the restrictions I have imposed upon myself, and the restrictions that others have imposed upon me?"

Technology may potentially raise the level of outer restrictions, but it may also force a higher level of individual responsibility. Contraception, for example, has forced women to become more responsible for their sexual behavior, especially in the matter of pregnancy. The woman can no longer say that the last thing in the world she wanted to do was get pregnant, but it was God's will or it just happened. It is definitely not God's will, and if it just happens it is because after all, it is her body, not that of the man which becomes pregnant.

With the easing of abortion laws, the woman must also accept the responsibility for giving birth to a child. This is now her choice. No woman need get pregnant if she doesn't want to, and no woman need give birth to a child if she doesn't want to. The simple facts of contraception and a change in the social attitudes toward abortion have modified dramatically the degree to which the woman must accept responsibility for a significant part of her life, and thus move closer toward being a truly free individual.

7. And, finally, a responsible individual is one who has no need to impose himself or his ideas on others. One of the saddest aspects of the radical student movement was, and is, its irresponsible denial of individual freedom. This is viewed, by some students and faculty, in a strange and twisted fashion, as their "right." A professor who has been one of the leaders of the radical student movement during the last decade once calmly told me, during a confrontation, that as long as he knew that his cause was just, he would feel free to do what had to be done to me if I stood in his way. This,

from a supposedly educated professor, in the name of individual freedom!

Another aspect of this neurotic behavior is a form of book-burning that is enthusiastically supported by certain professors and students. A bibliography that contains the names of books which do not meet with the approval of these self-appointed censors must be edited. If not, the professor will face picketing, class disruptions, and various other kinds of harassment because he refuses to go along with the newly anointed saviors of the human mind.

Research too, becomes prostituted, and any research that comes forth with implications or conclusions that do not meet with approval must be suppressed and the researcher done away with. This is a common practice, of course, of the autocratic mind, and it has been with us for centuries. In some Western universities today, however, it is those who supposedly support freedom against autocracy who practice this peculiar form of tyranny. In the last few years, for example, a number of researchers have come up with studies dealing with the relationship of racial and genetic factors to intelligence. These individuals have been accused of racism, and little or no attention is paid to the validity and reliability of the research. This is very much akin to the way certain individuals interpret the purpose of religious research—namely, to prove that there is a God, since, of course, there *must* be a God! Similarly, it would appear that research on intelligence *must* prove that sex, race and religion are insignificant variables.

If the purpose of research is to prove that what we know is true is true, then we are back in the Dark Ages, and the open, questioning, critical mind is the enemy to be done away with. But those who feel this way are surely the enemies of individual freedom. There is much more that we do not know than we know, and research, to be worthy of the name, must imply an openness of the mind. This means, obviously, that there may be implications and conclusions that will challenge some of our cherished ideas which we cling to like the sucking blanket of our infancy.

Thus, individual freedom, without which life is nothing but a play upon a stage, will remain an elusive will-o'-the-wisp if we see it as something which is *my* right, but granted to me by others, or as something that I have the right to remove from others. Individual freedom comes only to one who accepts individual responsibility for his life and living, and has no need to impose his pattern on others. It is created by such people for themselves, and it can never be taken away. Such people do not wait upon death to find their happy life, their Valhalla. They live it every day.

11

HUMAN VALUES

A value is not something that exists apart from a person. Values are human products, and they exist only in the human community. Since they are human products, they are subject to change with people, with places, with times—a reality which many people find difficult to accept. Equally difficult to accept is the concept that for all of us there exists a hierarchy of values, and that sometimes one "value" must be sacrificed for another—e.g., we may accept as a value "Thou shalt not kill," but we will go to war and kill other humans if we feel our cause is just. We know, of course, that the "others" who are trying to kill us are going to war because they know that their cause is just!

Values may be looked at in different ways. Wrenn, for example, comments:

> *"Value" can mean what one desires, or it can refer to what one should desire. In the first sense, values are human preferences. They are descriptive and normative; they are the way people are. These values change with social conditions and are a normal dimension of social conditions. In a second sense, values are goals or standards, what people ought to be. These values are resistant to change because in one's thinking they are often endowed with a sense of changelessness. These values may be lofty and provide appropriate goals. On the other hand, they may be totally unrealistic and a dead weight upon change.*[1]

Rogers refers to the description by Morris[2] of "value" as a term that we use in different ways. "Operative value" refers to the tendency of any living beings to show preference, in their actions, for one kind of object or objective rather than another. It need not involve any cognitive or conceptual thinking. "Conceived value" is the preference of an individual for a symbolized object. Usually in such a choice there is anticipation or foresight of the outcome of behavior directed toward such a symbolized object. Then there is "objective value," which refers to what is objectively preferable, whether or not it is in fact sensed or conceived of as desirable.[3]

The personal philosophy of the counselor or therapist obviously has a major impact on the way in which he views human val- level intellectual prowess.

1. C. Gilbert Wrenn, *The World of the Contemporary Counselor* (Boston: Houghton Mifflin, 1973), p. 6.
2. Charles Morris, *Varieties of Human Value* (Chicago: University of Chicago Press, 1956).
3. Carl R. Rogers, *Freedom to Learn* (Columbus, Ohio: Charles E. Merrill, 1969), p. 241.

ues and their place in the process of counseling. A humanistic point of view is offered by Bühler and Allen when they say that

> a fundamental tenet of humanistic psychology is the pursuit of values, which are seen as inherently needed by humans. This pursuit receives its directives from the self, which is considered a central core system, continually present in nuclear form from the beginning of the individual's life. In this theory there is a decisive divergence with psychoanalysis, which regarded the pursuit of values as a secondary goal—a goal pursued under the pressures of society when the individual's drives could not otherwise be satisfied.[4]

Boy and Pine also offer a humanistic point of view when they comment:

> Counseling, then, is a relationship in which the counselor provides the client with a communicating atmosphere that gives the client the opportunity to become involved in the discovering, processing, and synthesizing of values.[5]

Rollo May reveals the values of an existential therapist when, in talking about a dream, he makes the following comment:

> But the context of existential therapy would be very distinct; it would always focus on the questions of how this dream throws a light on this particular patient's existence in this world, what it says about where he is at the moment and what he is moving toward, and so forth. The context is the patient not as a set of dynamisms or mechanisms but as a human being who is choosing, committing, and pointing himself toward something right now; the context is dynamic, immediately real, and present.[6]

While some counselors might cringe at the thought, it is fairly clear that all human beings, including counselors, feel that certain values are "better" than other values. The extent to which the values of the counselor should, or do, become emulated by the client, has been a center of controversy for many years, and will likely continue to be for many years to come. Attitudes range all the way from the older version of client-centered therapy, which appeared to totally

4. Charlotte Bühler and Melanie Allen, *Introduction to Humanistic Psychology* (Monterey, Cal.: Brooks/Cole, 1972), p. 63.
5. Angelo V. Boy and Gerald J. Pine, *The Counselor in the Schools: A Reconceptualization* (Boston: Houghton Mifflin, 1968), p. 35.
6. Rollo May, in Jack C. Huber and Howard L. Millman (eds.), *Goals and Behavior in Psychotherapy and Counseling* (Columbus, Ohio: Charles E. Merrill, 1972), p. 243.

remove the counselor and his values from the client, to the brash-
ness of Ellis and his rational-emotive therapy, in which the values of
the therapist were clearly presented as being anywhere from somewhat to totally superior to those of the client!

It is clear that any involvement of the counselor with another
human will mean the transmission of the values of the counselor to
that other human. I may not impose or even directly state my values
to a client, but if we are intimately involved with each other, then the
client will soon understand where I am. Counselors are not impartial
(that is, if they are human), and one might ask just why counselors
should try to hide the attitudes they have from the client. This does
not mean that the counselor should give a long speech about his
attitudes at the beginning of every session, but it does question the
veracity of the counselor painfully trying to pretend that he has no
values whatsoever, while all the time he is obviously exhibiting his
values by his behavior.

Most counselors would agree with Pietrofesa, Leonard, and
Van Hoose when they say, "The overriding factor, once again, is that
the counselor does not impose his values upon the counselee."[7] And
yet, this point may well be academic. If the counselor does not have
institutional authority, then he can truthfully feel and say that he
does not have the power to impose his values on the client. He can
impose his values only to the degree that the client allows him to do
so, and the authentic counselor should be one who does not need to
impose his values on anyone. This is probably the crucial point—that
as a counselor, I do not have the need to impose my values, and thus
I can feel free to express my values. On the one hand, I can say to the
drug-addicted client, "No, of course I cannot *make* you get off
drugs," but I can also say, "Of couse I would like to see you kick the
habit—I like you enough so that I don't like to see you killing yourself."

As counselors become more involved with others, it would
appear to be inevitable that they will be setting themselves, and their
values, up as models, at least to be considered, if not to be emulated.
Thus the ethical questions "Who am I?" and "What are my values?"
become even more crucial. This need for a total involvement in human problems is voiced by Kelly:

*Our professional ethics should rather incorporate the serious
business of actively and constructively confronting and dealing*

7.   John J. Pietrofesa, George E. Leonard, and William Van Hoose, *The Authentic
Counselor* (Chicago: Rand McNally, 1971), p. 75.

*with the desperate (and sometimes not so desperate) human
problems in our society with intelligence, skill, and courage.*[8]

One must be careful too, that in the pell-mell rush for "involvement" we do not totally abandon any concern with the values
that produce the behavior to which we are reacting. While it is futile
to attempt to teach children to be happy, it is nonsense to assume
that by conditioning children to smile when they are supposed to
smile they are thereby happy. Any philosophy of human behavior
that remains as a concept, and nothing else, obviously does nothing
to change human behavior. Sprinthall is correct when he says, "Humanism as a concept does not solve either the value question or the
ethical one as a basis for guidance."[9] Unfortunately, his remedy is to
propose another concept, developmental psychology, by means of
which children will learn the virtues of personal development and
understanding. A human being cannot determine his values if he has
not experienced, any more than one can write about his philosophy
of life if he has not lived.

Humanism, or developmental psychology, or any other methodology or philosophy will have little impact on human behavior if it
remains in the realm of academic discussion and never gets into the
testing ground of *process*. The existential-humanistic counselor is
very much involved, and methodology is an inaccurate way of describing the involvement of the counselor. The *manner of involvement*, however, does differ. The existential-humanistic counselor
will put primary stress on values and causes, rather than on symptoms and overt behavior. The child who does not make friends, for
example, will be helped to look *inside to discover just why* he does
not make friends, and if, possibly, he can live a happy and satisfying
life without making friends. The stress is from the inside out, rather
than the outside in.

With the stress on the "why," it is most unlikely that a client
or a group of people involved with an existential-humanist counselor, would feel personal fulfillment and satisfaction simply by
doing their thing. A person who looks deeply at himself is not satisfied with behavior which degrades his self or the self of others. I
agree with Carkhuff's description of humanism, but unlike him, I
have never associated it with a "pseudo-democratic idealism":

*For me, humanism reflects man's reaching up to new heights to
actualize his resources. I distinguish this from the kind of*

8. Eugene W. Kelly, Jr. "The Ethics of Creative Growth," *Personnel and Guidance
Journal*, 51:171–175 (November, 1972).
9. Norman A. Sprinthall, "Humanism: A New Bag of Virtues for Guidance," *Personnel and Guidance Journal*, 50:349–356 (January, 1972).

pseudo-democratic idealism that I have come to know as humanism, in which man is leveled down in an equalizing process, never being asked to do "more" or "better" but only to do "his own thing."[10]

Unfortunately, however, many counselors still believe that somehow, in some way, values can be taught. An opinion voiced by Mueller some years ago would probably be acceptable to many counselors:

In discipline the counselor is teaching emotional stability, moral judgment, self reliance and self control. . . . The balance between force and sympathy is achieved by first exhausting every resource of counseling and persuasion and only then turning to punitive action.[11]

There would appear here, again, to be a concept of a detachment of the human act from the person, the idea that values are some form of appendices that one "learns" by being taught. There is an absence of the feeling that values, being a part of the person, can only come through an experiencing and a living and a human relationship. Close human contact with a patient and compassionate person may help another person to free himself so that he, too, may move in the direction of patience and compassion. He may thus "learn," from a counselor, from a teacher, from a friend, but he has not been taught. History would surely bear witness to the futility of the attempt by one person to "teach" his value system to another person.

Most counselors would probably agree with Samler when he says, "It ought not to be irreligious to propose that if value commitment and promulgation work in bringing about lasting client change in desirable direction then it provides its own justification."[12] The questions that do remain, however, are "what value commitment?" and "what desirable direction?"

Ferree also leaves these questions unanswered, and he raises what would appear to be a contradiction, when he calls for "a clear commitment on the part of the counselor to certain values which he in turn seeks to foster in his counselees," indicates that the counselor is to "promote in his counselee what is not already there," and

---

10. Robert R. Carkhuff, "Credo of a Militant Counselor," *Personnel and Guidance Journal,* 51:237–242 (December, 1972).

11. Kate H. Mueller, *Student Personnel Work in Higher Education* (Boston: Houghton Mifflin, 1961), pp. 356–357.

12. Joseph Samler, "An Examination of Client Strength and Counselor Responsibility," *Journal of Counseling Psychology* 9:5–11 (Spring, 1962).

states that "it may involve deliberate effort on the part of the counselor to change the basic nature of the person."[13] Can the counselor actually have such values as "tolerance and respect for others and a capacity to listen well," and at the same time seek to foster values in his client? Can one be acceptant while he is seeking to eliminate from the individual certain values that are not of the "right" kind? These are difficult questions, but they must be faced by the counselor who feels that it is essential that he be involved with his clients and with the society in which they all reside.

In a way, Lowe has provided an answer to this question when he says:

We conclude that differences in value orientations cannot be resolved, each orientation having adherents whose beliefs should be respected. We suggest that each counselor have an understanding of the values both of himself and others and that his values be known by all who are personally affected by his professional behavior.[14]

Simply by being the person he is, in a close human relationship, the counselor is making obvious some of his own value patterns. The fact that he is always acceptant of generally unacceptable material, the fact that he does not criticize, measure, or evaluate, the fact that he centers his attention on the client, the fact that he shows unwavering patience and kindness—these are surely a display of the person, and are almost certainly transmitted in some degree to the client, who, more likely than not, will hold the therapist in trust and admiration. This situation is well described by Rosenthal:

It may be that the therapist communicates his values to the patient in many unintended, subtle ways, even when trying to avoid doing so. The patient, who is often sensitized to the therapist's every word and inflection, may be able to receive these communications, and because of his trust, admiration, and respect, may permit himself to be influenced by them.[15]

It is pointless for the counselor to strive to achieve for the client something, some answer, some right path or goal that is external to the client, and possibly to the counselor. This is almost like the counselor's cheating on his income tax returns and then trying to

13. George Ferree, "Psychological Freedom as a Counseling Objective," *Counselor Education and Supervision,* 3:13–18 (Fall, 1963).
14. C. Marshal Lowe, "Value Orientations—An Ethical Dilemma," *American Psychologist,* 14:687–693 (November, 1959).
15. D. Rosenthal, "Changes in Some Moral Values Following Psychotherapy," *Journal of Consulting Psychology,* 19:431–436 (December, 1955).

convince the client who has been cheating on exams that the virtue of honesty is something that he should practice. Actually, this "virtue" is real for neither client nor counselor, and it is unlikely that any change is going to take place in either one. On the other hand, we might hypothesize that if the counselor is a "no-cheating" sort of fellow, in his living-being, regardless of any words, then he will see no point in trying to press this on the client. And the client, in turn, might possibly internalize, or at least let stir around inside him, the idea that this might be something worth incorporating so that it becomes a part of his being. People who believe feel no particular pressure to convince others that they should believe the same way. It is likely that the evangelist is very concerned with who he is and where he is going, and that this is why he continually tries to convince others that they should follow him. He neither respects nor trusts the other to find his own right way. If his religion includes compassion and gentleness and love toward his fellow man, he spends his time preaching it rather than practicing it.

The concept that one can separate a person from his values is a very common one in counseling. It is almost as if one could view a human act and the person who commits it as two separate entities. One might feel that the act of robbery, the taking away of another person's belongings so that one can further his own interests, is questionable. But when a counselor is relating with another fellow human who has committed the act of robbery, he cannot divorce the person from the act. Part of the person is the fact that he has committed a robbery, and since we accept the client as he is, the unrelated fact of robbery, or what the counselor may think about it, has no relation to the therapeutic interaction whatsoever. It is the person, all of him, with whom we are concerned, and the various bits and pieces, by themselves, mean nothing. The existential-humanistic counselor, however, would not view acts at any time as detached from human beings, so that a question such as "Well, do you mean that you don't think that robbery is bad?" really isn't a question because robbery, per se, really doesn't mean anything. It is only when it becomes a part of an individual's human behavior that it means something.

While we could agree that the counselor might as well admit that he has his own values, it is important to distinguish between those values that are a part of the makeup of the inner self of the counselor, and are shown in his patience, his compassion and his acceptance of the client, and values of judgment and evaluation. The counselor who feels that "robbery," per se, is "bad," is not actually very far removed from the counselor who feels that the client who has robbed is "bad," who in turn is not too far removed from the individual who feels that the person who has robbed is bad and should therefore be punished. While such individuals may be being existential in the sense that they are saying, "You, and you alone, must be responsible for your deeds," they are not existential in the sense that they are not getting close to, or being understanding of, the existential self. They may be observing it, but they are not living it.

Curran expresses more of a trust in the person-in-being when he indicates that we should seek a personal integration that is also an integration with the whole civilization that has produced us. This might then

> *free us from the more recent, possibly Kantian, ethical concept that all personal values must be imposed from without, which has come not to mean either by parents, society or even more threatening and dangerous, by the state. It would restore again the possibility of starting out . . . on a thrilling personal pursuit of oneself in a fierce and independent search for reasonable self-values and yet allow that one would ultimately come by this process, not to violent rebellion and anarchy, but to ancient and secure traditional values.* [16]

This might represent a somewhat theistic existential point of view, in that while Curran trusts the individual to determine for himself how he will move and when and where he will move, he believes that there are, somehow, already established answers and values that the individuals will come to find. The individual does not develop and create his own answers, but moves toward preestablished answers. In this case, in Curran's mind, these are likely established by some deity or God. Curran also indicates the interesting concept that somehow the "ancient" values are more "secure," and, we can assume, somehow better, than more recent values. Were the ancient and traditional values of the Romans more secure, and better, than some of the values that were being advanced by a heretic named Christ? Were the ancient and traditional values of the Greeks more secure than those of the heretic Socrates? The nontheistic existentialist would probably feel, with Curran, that the individual must find his own way. With Curran, he would have faith that the individual could find his own way. But he would differ with Curran in that he would have no preconceived concept of where the individual might end, or what his values might become. They might be like those of yesterday, or they might be like those of tomorrow, but man lives his

16. Charles A. Curran, "Some Ethical and Scientific Values in the Counseling Therapeutic Process," *Personnel and Guidance Journal,* 39:15–20 (September, 1960).

life, and creates his values. He never goes back to what once was, although he may become like what once was.

In a sense, Curran would seem to have his "man" attempting to discover preexistent truths and values, to somehow become congruent with what already is, and in this sense, of couse, he is expressing the view of determinism. For him, what is, was, but for the existentialist, what is, is. Life is today, now, not yesterday, and we move away from yesterday, not toward it, even though we may yearn for this return to the womb.

In a later volume Curran continues to stress this abandonment of self to the unknown Other:

> While we may affirm then a Total Other, it is by a faith commitment and the gift of self that genuine religious experience is made possible. We have seen that such acceptance of an abandonment to the enigmatic in another is basic to any real human commitment and relationship.[17]

One cannot discuss values and freedom, and living, without also taking into consideration that closely allied experience that eventually comes to all—death. The free man of the existentialist, the human being who is never merely a victim of a predetermined culture, the person-in-being who is the maker of his values, being free to live, is also free to die, and it would seem that no person can really be free to live if he is afraid to die. Feifel expresses this feeling when he comments that

> the willingness to die appears as a necessary condition for life. We are not altogether free in any deed as long as we are commanded by an inescapable will to live. . . . Life is not genuinely our own until we can renounce it.[18]

Sartre relates freedom with death when he says, "The very act of freedom is therefore the assumption and creation of finitudes: if I make myself, I make myself finite and hence my life is unique."[19]

May, too, feels that the confronting of death gives the most positive reality to life itself.[20] It makes the individual existence real, absolute and concrete. The contemplation of suicide is one way that many people have faced the reality that they literally hold their lives

17. Charles A. Curran, *Religious Values in Counseling and Psychotherapy* (New York: Sheed and Ward, 1969), pp. 48–49.
18. Herman Feifel, in Rollo May (ed.), *Existential Psychology* (New York: Random House, 1961), p. 71.
19. Jean-Paul Sartre, *Existentialism*, translated by B. Freeman (New York: Philosophical Library, 1947), p. 545.
20. Rollo May, in Jack C. Huber and Howard L. Millman, *op. cit.*, p. 240.

in their hands, and that death is available at any time to any human. On this point May makes the interesting comment, "I am doubtful whether anyone takes his life with full seriousness until he realizes that it is entirely within his power to commit suicide."[21]

It is ironic, and sad, that one of the basic feelings that many individuals learn from their "religion" is fear, particularly fear of death. Feifel, for example, found, in a study of his patients, that the religious person, as compared with the nonreligious person, was personally more afraid of death.[22] There must be untold millions of Christians who spend much of their lives trying to guarantee their entry to Heaven, but, since they feel that they are not the ones who control their destiny, are never quite sure whether God is approving or disapproving. They thus seek as much as they can in the way of assurances that there is a Heaven, and that they, and a few of their chosen fellows, are the ones who will be there. The old and hoary joke about each group in Heaven having to be segregated behind walls so that they might not discover that there are other peoples in Heaven too is not a joke to many. Many "devout" Christians cannot accept doubt and uncertainty as a part of their religion. They must know, particularly about the rewards and punishments of the hereafter, and this might logically tend to make them somewhat self-centered in their actions toward others. The one who does not know about the future, and will, with certainty, face this uncertainty, even to the point of dying to defend a fellow human, is indeed showing a far higher level of altruism and compassion.

The existential man would live his life of freedom and responsibility and would not have to "know" about what happens after death. If his reason conflicted with some religious fairy stories, he would not be too disturbed since his life is now, and he would live this the best he could. The rest he could accept, without fear, as the unknown.

Kaufmann, however, feels that not one of the existentialists has grasped the most crucial distinction that makes all the difference in facing death, and he quotes Nietzsche in *The Gay Science*: "For one thing is needful: that a human being attain his satisfaction with himself—whether it be by this or by that poetry and art; only then is a human being at all tolerable to behold."[23] It would appear, however, that this is just what the existentialist does believe: The person is as he is; satisfaction must come from within; man is able to be free; man is able to choose and so, to himself, becomes "tolerable to

21. *Ibid.*, p. 256.
22. Herman Feifel, in Rollo May (ed.), *op. cit.*, p. 68.
23. Walter Kaufmann, *The Faith of a Heretic* (New York: Doubleday, 1961), p. 383.

behold." Whether he is tolerable to others is of secondary importance. He must first be tolerable to himself, and it would surely seem that most people who are intolerable to themselves are the ones who find others intolerable. One person becomes a heretic to another person because that person has not yet learned the life of the free man and is thus afraid.

For the counselor, then, several points might be noted on this question of human values:[24]

1. It is surely obvious that one can hardly be a human being without values. Indeed, the values of the person *are* the person, although one may argue that at any one moment the values that a person is exhibiting are not necessarily the authentic values of that person. But for the moment they are his values, and they are the best answer to the questions, "Who is he? What is he like?" It is interesting to note that one of the earlier criticisms of the so called "nondirective" counseling of Carl Rogers, was that the very concept of nondirection by the counselor meant that the counselor possessed no values. One may wonder about the values of an individual which are such that another person who says, "I do not direct or advise or tell the other how to live his life" is assumed to possess no values whatsoever! The very statement of deep feeling of the lack of either ability or right to direct the way of life of another is a very definite indication of a value that is a part of the individual. So, of course, is the feeling that one could not have any values if one were not quite certain about how others should live their lives!

2. Thus being alive, being a member of the human species, being homosapiens means that one does possess values, and the rather simple question "Where do these come from?" is not quite as simple as it appears. To a tremendous degree, of course, our values are the values that we have learned, and we usually learn them from the people and the organizations that have most control and most influence over us. A clergyman once took some offense when I commented that for the vast majority of us, our race, our nationality, our sex and our religion were but accidents of birth. He had no concern about the first three, but he was bothered by the thought that religion too, might be no more than an accident of birth! Many American Christians have calmly accepted their role as the superior ones, although their values are such that some Christians are assumed to be more superior than others. Some probably feel that one is not a really *real* Christian unless one is a Catholic, or maybe a Baptist, or maybe a Seventh-Day Adventist. Then of course, color of skin is

---

24. *See* Dugald S. Arbuckle, "Values, Ethics and Religion in Counseling," *National Catholic Guidance Conference Journal,* 13:5–17 (Fall, 1968).

sometimes important, and until recently the white Christian felt that he was just a little bit better Christian than his brother whose skin was dark. Then too, our Christian values have showed in our attitude toward male and female Christians. Women have minimal power in most organized Christian churches, and while our values wouldn't let us say so, we have tended to regard them as second-class citizens. Imagine the shock of some of our brethren if, on getting to heaven, they were welcomed by a God who had a dark skin and who was obviously a female! We, however, at least have the virtue of consistency in that the devil is usually portrayed as a light-skinned male!

All of this, of course, is intellectual madness. And indeed, our conditioning has often moved us in the direction of madness. The dreadful and the bestial things that man has done to man over the centuries he has learned to do, but he was not destined to do. And the question must be: How much do we allow ourselves to be the victims of our culture? To what extent are we passively acceptant of the dogma of yesterday as being the light of tomorrow, which will surely mean that there will be no tomorrow? The blind, unthinking, irrational obedience to dogma, religious or no, can lead to nothing but destruction.

3. But the question then arises: Are these values, these conditioned products, the real basic human values of the particular human being? It would seem reasonable to assume that the more one learns that he cannot be who and what he is, the more artificial he becomes as a person. His whole being exemplifies a lack of congruence; he cannot be open and spontaneous and honest. His life becomes, possibly, somewhat like the beginning counselor who cannot let himself go, and must carefully surround himself with methodology and technique. He will say that he does what he does because he is thus and so. There is a high level of security in this procedure, since one never need accept responsibility for what one does. The price one pays, of course, is heavy, and the face of such a person does not reflect the inner man, but is rather the mask which has been molded in the desired contours: desired, that is, by others rather than by the self.

A clash will come if this inner self rebels against the conditioned front, and very often this is what the client is saying when he comes to see the counselor. "I am not who I wish to be, and I want to do something about it." As Johnson says, "Cultural values may, however, contradict real experienced values, and thus the individual is thrown into conflict."[25] The struggle is one in which the person

25. Ernest L. Johnson, "Existentialism, Self-Theory, and the Existential Self," *Personnel and Guidance Journal,* 46:53–58 (September, 1967).

tries to become more trusting of his own experiencing, his own feelings; the meanings he gives to actions and situations are closer to being *his* meanings rather than those of someone else. Such a person is open to continual change, and he has no need to hold blindly to any values. In this sense he does not have a value *system*, because there is no system. His values are open to change as he lives and experiences, deeply, his life. He is free to allow his experiences of living to modify and change his self, and he has no preconceived concepts into which his experiences must fit. There is thus honesty toward self, rather than alienation from self, and individual freedom becomes a reality.

SOME PHILOSOPHICAL CONCEPTS

Each counselor, as a member of the human species, should ask of himself, "What are the philosophical concepts on which I base my operation as a counselor?" This is the answer which I would give to that question:

1. A basic tenet is that man is the determiner of the culture. This in no way detracts from the obvious fact that man is, to a tremendous degree, a conditioned product of his culture. But man came first, and it is man who produces the culture. Cultural change does not just happen; it is a human product. Thus man *can* be one who has some say in his fate, or he *can* be one who, willy-nilly, accepts his role as the product of a kindly or vengeful culture. With the more pious this culture is often seen in terms of a supernatural deity (it is God's will), whereas with the more secular it is simply seen as fate (that's the way it is). A less determined and more existential view would see man as having to accept his responsiblity of choice and decision. Attitudes toward race and religion and sex and ethnic background may mean that one person is the recipient of more human abuse than is another, but this does not mean that that individual cannot have some say in how he feels and what he does about that which others do to him. No human can ever, with total accuracy, say, "I did it because I had to." Somewhere along the line one has to agree that a choice was made, and in this case the choice was to do what "I didn't want to do"; it is never accurate to say straightforwardly, "I didn't want to do it." One never has to do what one does not wish to do; it is very simply a question of what penalty one is willing to pay for doing what one wishes to do. A more accurate statement than "I didn't want to do it," would be "I was unwilling to pay the price for doing what I wanted to do, and for this reason I am

doing what I am doing." Very often, of course, the price that one refuses to pay is minimal—the loss of a pay raise, getting a low grade instead of a high grade, criticism instead of praise from one who might have been a friend; occasionally the price may be major, such as jail or death.

Such a philosophy, of course, makes life more Spartan, since one cannot easily rationalize one's behavior toward one's fellows. When one comfortably says, "Well, I can see that I dislike my white (or black) brothers because of my conditioning," the existential reply is: "So what? What are you going to do now? Are you going to keep on disliking them because of your conditioning, or are you going to ask yourself how stupid can you be? No one *has* to dislike someone just because of a difference in the color of his skin. Are you going to accept the responsiblity of either staying the way you are, or making some change in your attitude? You *do* have a choice. What is it going to be?"

Man, then, cannot excuse himself because of a harsh Nature or a capricious God. He is born with certain assets and certain liabilities, and one must be cautious about assuming that what appear to be many assets and liabilities, or vice versa, are actually so. It is not what one *has* that is the major determiner of the future for the vast majority of mankind, but rather *what one does* with what one has, and this ability to deal with one's life is an indication of a high level of individual freedom.

2. If one is nothing but a victim of the culture, to be tossed hither and thither by the whims of nature, then any concept of individual freedom is, of course, simply a happy illusion. On the other hand, if one conceives of human freedom as an individual matter, to be determined by each individual, then total freedom, for each human being, is a real possibility. It is a goal which may never be achieved, but it is a worthy goal toward which one might dedicate his life. When I am the one to determine the extent to which I am free, then the oppressor, either subtle or manifest, can never chain me, even though I may be shackled. The other may have the external power to kill me, but never to totally destroy me.

Children soon learn from their parents, from the school, and from the church, that freedom is an external matter which is determined by someone else, and that they thus have no control over their individual freedom. It would seem to be of crucial importance that the school, while accepting the legal and practical dependence of the child, helps him to develop individual freedom within the very real limitations which surround him. A child may be forced to experience a certain educational curriculum, but he does have the freedom to affect, in some way, just what he gets out of that educational experience. A child may have little or no control over the kind of teacher he happens to have, but he can control his reactions to that teacher, and the individual freedom of some children is such that they can actually learn from a poor teacher. Such a child is one who is having some effect on what is learned, rather than being totally dependent on the teacher.

The freedom, then, to become, the freedom to be, is the real freedom, and for this, of course, the individual must be willing to pay a price. In some societies, such as that of the United States, the price the individual must pay is often quite modest, because other generations have already paid a heavy price. But even in the United States and other so-called "free" countries, one must be willing, if necessary, to pay a very high price for the maintenance and strengthening of one's individual freedom. Such a person is free to live and free to die, he is free to love and free to hate, he is free to experience sorrow and free to experience ecstasy. Despite all the uncontrollable factors which push in and upon him, he is the one who determines the extent to which he is free, and in this way, of course, he will always be free. He is the maker of the culture, not its victim.

3. The worth and the dignity of the human individual is an obvious addition to these two basic tenets. The government is the servant and the organized voice of the people, not its master. In a free society one obeys a law simply because this is a rule or a regulation of human behavior which the majority of the citizens have found to be desirable. In a truly free society there will obviously be a minimum of such laws, since a truly free individual will have no need to impose himself on others or do things which will be obviously destructive to a large number of his fellows. The more autocratic the society, the more laws that are necessary to control the population, and the mark of a decaying free society is the increase in the number of laws, usually stressing what one cannot do.

Even in a relatively free society such as that of the United States, the individual still must come first. In a sense, in a "free" society the individual owes the state nothing, nor, of course, does the state owe him anything. In the long run the law of one's conscience must take precedence over the law of the land, and in the decade of the 1960's in the United States a significant number of responsible citizens, who had contributed much to their fellow man, deliberately violated the laws of the land because they could not, in all conscience, obey those laws. Possibly the most ironic commentary on the 1970's will be that this was the decade when those in high positions who had zealously pursued the lawbreakers of the 1960's were themselves jailed because they broke the laws they had described as sacred! Hopefully, the 1970's will not become the decade when the rights of the human individual become even more subordinated to the rights of the organization.

For the school counselor and the teacher this tenet simply means that the child comes first. The school is there for the benefit of the child; its purpose is to serve him, not to enslave him. The only reason for the existence of a school is the children who populate it. The positive development of each child, as an individual, should be the goal of the school, rather than the mass production of a number of human robots, which is the necessary goal of any school in an autocratic society.

4. Philosophically, it would seem that we can make more out of our lives, that we can live our lives more fully, if we live in a world of today rather than a world of yesterday or tomorrow. For some humans, life would appear to be predominantly based on what has gone, and we hear much about "how it used to be," or "the good old days," or "when I was young." All of this is understandable, but it is wasteful of life, since what is gone *is* gone, and, in a way, this living in yesterday is a culturally acceptable form of schizophrenia. It is a running away rather than a running back. It is a refusal to face the only real issues of living—namely the issues of now and today. The individuals who live for tomorrow are much the same, and their life today is as if there were no today, only a tomorrow. A powerful motivator of this attitude has been the Christian religion. It has tended traditionally to place more importance on life in the next world rather than life in the only world we will know during our lifetime—the one we live in now. The Hebrew prophets would appear to have been more concerned with the life of man on earth today than were the Christian apostles, and in the some two thousand years of the Christian church, it has hardly shown a consistent concern with the lot of man on this earth, today. Indeed, it has frequently allied itself with a corrupt and autocratic state to impede the development of individual man.

This existential concept of stress on life today does not mean that one ignores the lessons of the past, nor does he ignore the fact that man will have a tomorrow. But the only life we know on this earth is the life we live today, and it is this life which should be the center of attention. It is of little point to say that there is racial and religious prejudice in America because of thus and so which happened some time ago. Nor do the pious meandering platitudes that "things will be better in the next century if we will just be patient and wait" mean much to the victim of prejudice. The time we live in is today, now, and for each one of us the basic question is not "What did you do yesterday?" or "What do you plan to do tomorrow?" but rather "What are you doing *now*?"

5. While we all know, in a cognitive sense, that we are creatures of mind and emotion, we often appear, particularly in educational institutions, to ignore this as a philosophical tenet of operation. As one goes up the educational ladder, emotions would appear to be considered to be of less and less importance in the learning process. The university student is generally considered, by the great majority of professors, as a cognitive creature, capable of reacting in a totally rational manner to all issues, questions, and problems, intellectual or otherwise. Thus teaching becomes more important than learning, and the university teacher is acceptable as long as he knows what he is talking about; whether he is able to communicate and thus help the student to learn something would often appear to be of minimal importance. The result is that a good grade often bears little relationship to the ability to think and reason, with feeling, but it indicates rather a high-level ability to retain data, often quite meaningless.

If a human being is accepted as a creature of mind and emotion, then the teacher and the counselor are as sensitive to what the child feels as they are to what the child thinks. When the teacher screams, "Sit down and learn your lesson," it is surely obvious that the child is learning a lesson, but not the lesson that the teacher has insisted he must learn. All counselors are doubtless aware of situations in which the client has, for example, come to understand intellectually the absurd reasons behind his feelings of guilt, but still feels guilty. Despite Albert Ellis, one does not think oneself out of certain basic and well-entrenched human feeling. One must experience the feeling before one can change the feeling. The ineffectiveness of simple knowing in problems of human behavior is well illustrated by the racial and religious prejudice of those who, in an intellectual sense, "know better," but still carry with them strong feelings of prejudice toward others. Thus, if human behavior is to change for the better, if man is to realize his full development as a self-actualized creature, a basic tenet of operation must surely be the acceptance of man as a creature who feels as well as thinks. Indeed, the progress of mankind is probably more dependent on what one feels about what he thinks than what he thinks about what he feels. The ability of man to offer a nonpossessive and nondemanding love to his fellow man is a better indication of his membership in the human species than is his high-level intellectual prowess.

Chapter 2

Religion, Science and Humans

Historically, the philosophic questions such as "Who am I?" and "What is life?" and "Why am I here?" have been intrinsically related to religion, and increasingly, as technology moves to become our master, they are questions related to science. Einstein was a great scientist, but he was very concerned about what his findings would do to our life and living. Skinner, today, is a psychologist and a scientist, but his theories and ideas have shaken the worlds of philosophy and religion rather than science. Thus it would seem fitting that counselors and therapists should be aware of their beginnings—religion and science—even though one might say that organized religion and science have not been noted historically for their dedication and commitment to the welfare of mankind.

How, then, are people viewed by religion and by science?

RELIGION AND HUMANS

People, in their present form, have been around for some time. Louis S. B. Leakey, by the time he died, had upped that time to some thirteen million years. It is likely that for an important segment of that time people practiced what might loosely be called religion, although the religion of yesterday tends to become the superstition of today. One cannot help but wonder, too, about the chauvinism even of deities, since practically all our great religious figures are males! On the more recent pages of history four great religious leaders appeared within less than two thousand years of each other. From an anthropological point of view, Moses, Mohammed, Christ, and Buddha were all born, and lived, and died within the same day, and one must assume that man's development must have had something to do with their joint appearance on the earthly scene. In the several centuries since their day, a significant proportion of the world's organized religions has become centered around these four giant figures, and as long as man has need to differentiate and separate his identity from that of his brother, it is likely that "I am a Jew" and "I am a Christian" will be enough to separate one from another. It is likely, too, that the debate and the dissension and the violence that have grown out of the attempt to answer the question of just who these men were, and what they believed, what they said, and what they did, will continue for some time. It may be just as well for organized religion that tape recorders were not available several thousand years ago. Human beings being what they are, we can assume that there would be some discrepancy between these people as they actually were and the images of them that have been developed.

The Greeks looked at life rationally, and the Greek citizen could have his religion and his reason. The Christian religion, however, was based on faith, and even more important for the future of man in the centuries that lay ahead, he *had* to believe or be guilty of heresy. For much of the Western world, philosophy became *religious* philosophy. It was concerned with the other world rather than with this world, and with man's relation to God rather than with man. Aquinas became the official Christian spokesman for the separation of reason from faith, and truth was that which came from God, rather than the product of reason.

Science, at least as we know it today, was a rather modern upstart, and it has been engaged in an almost constant struggle with organized religion. The counselor, particularly one of somewhat humanistic leanings, may periodically find himself in line of fire from both sides! In many ways, this struggle has been primarily one of faith (believe what I tell you) against reason (believe what your mind says is true); a struggle of truth against truths; a struggle of the absolute against the relative; a struggle of answers against questions. Ironically enough, both religion and science have expressed their love of man and their concern for him, yet both would appear to have been concerned generally with bits and pieces of him, although they may, of course, have felt that these bits and pieces were man. Thus, in the Western world, the Christian church has generally exerted no great social effort for the benefit of man, and has appeared more concerned with getting him into the next world than with helping him in the current world, which is the only one that man can know. The Church has always been concerned about the soul of man, but it has too frequently ignored the rest of him. Religion and science have struggled against each other, and yet, so often, neither appeared to have known and understood the real existential living-in-being man. To the Church he was a soul, preparing for the glory to come; to the scientist, he was a set of behaviors to be examined. For both, he was someone to be controlled and manipulated and directed for the good of someone other than himself. To both, he was one who could not be trusted. Freud was antireligious, and yet the psychological body of man, as developed by Freud, bears a striking resemblance to the spiritual body of man of the Church of the day.

The stresses and strains that are shaking the Christian church today are directly related to the increasing involvement of many members of the clergy in the human and social issues of the day. As the Church becomes more concerned with people and their problems, it becomes more humanized and thus is more subject to criticism and attack. When a prince of the Church, clad in magnificent robes, carried on the backs of his subjects, makes some statement about the afterlife, that is one thing; when an aged celibate man, whose own sexual life has been definitely atypical, tries to tell a healthy young couple about their proper sexual behavior, that is something else again!

Although Tillich was later to argue that the man whose will is in bondage must have the power of self-determination, since a being without the power of self-determination has no capacity for decision at all,[1] organized religion has generally shared with science a deterministic view of man. Thus while science may talk about "natural laws" being lawful and determined, religion will talk about "universal truths" being ultimately determined by some divine will or some supreme supernatural being. In both situations, man is obviously not in control; he is being controlled.

It would probably be safe to say that most religions—those of Moses, and Buddha, and Christ, and Mohammed—were at least to some extent a protest of man against his suppression and his misery and his fear and his anxiety. They were movements, and all of the major original religious figures, known and unknown, were heretics against the current ruling order. Christ and Socrates shared the same fate, and they were guilty of the same offense, heresy against the state. It is ironic that the revolutionary individualism of Christ should have become symbolized so quickly by the dogma and con-

---

1. Paul Tillich, *The Protestant Era* (Chicago: University of Chicago Press, 1948).

servatism of an organized church named after him. Kaufmann points this out when he says:

> *What is ironical . . . is that Jesus' dissatisfaction with all for-*
> *mulas and rules should have given way within one generation,*
> *to an attempt, not yet concluded, to determine the most precise*
> *dogmas.*[2]

And again:

> *The point is not just that religion tends to become repulsive*
> *when it prospers, or that religion is at its best in times of perse-*
> *cution . . . but whether religion is a pious name for conformity*
> *or a fighting name for non-conformity. The men who con-*
> *ducted the Greek heresy trials, the Inquisition, and the witch*
> *hunts, who went on crusades and to holy wars, were conform-*
> *ists, men of the crowd, true believers. The Hebrew prophets*
> *were not.*[3]

Religion and the Church need not, of course, be synonymous, and one might pose a reasonable argument as to why "religious" and "religion" need not be linked. Most individuals, growing up in a "re-ligious" culture, generally assume that if one is religious he must have a denominational title, and they would probably be disturbed if someone said, "Yes, I think I'm religious, but I don't know that I fit any particular title or name." For many citizens, agnostic and atheis-tic mean the same thing, and both are nasty words! Most, too, would probably think that one's devoutness is measured by the extent to which he accepts the dogma of the particular creed that he pro-fesses, although very rarely would this dogma have anything to do with man's relations with man. Affiliation with a particular denomi-nation often tends to encourage and facilitate withdrawal and segre-gation, and the building of parochial walls. This, in turn, tends to make it more difficult to see all men as one's brothers, just as does the stress on any differences between men. There is no particular difference in the element of the denial of one's fellows when one is told, "Don't ever forget you are an American, not an Indian," or "a white man, not a black man," or "a Jew, not a Baptist." They are all equally vicious, and it is particularly tragic when, in the name of religion, one must learn to spurn and suspect, and if necessary to kill, one's fellows. "Love" is a word that organized religions have used profusely, but they have practiced love less frequently.

On the other hand, man as seen by various people who prob-

---

2. Walter Kaufmann, *The Faith of a Heretic* (New York: Doubleday, 1961), p. 233.
3. *Ibid.*, p. 264.

ably consider themselves religious, in a current cultural sense, is by no means the same fellow. We may contrast, for example, this somewhat broad perspective of religion of Progoff:

> *The psychological dimension of religion is the dimension of lived experience in which religion is not a dogma but a fact of life and of accomplishment for persevering effort.*[4]

with this astonishingly parochial version of one who happens to be a psychoanalyst:

> *The historical defect in human psychological understanding has been spanned by the vision of religion; the historical inadequacy of human responsibility has been remedied by the heroic in military life. Without religion, society would have lost its capacity for faith; without military life men would have failed to give embodiment to hope and its accompanying social morality.*[5]

On the other hand, Curran, who is a man of the cloth, also feels that man must search for his own answers.

> *It would restore again the possibility of starting out . . . on a thrilling personal pursuit of oneself in a fierce and independent search for reasonable self-values and yet allow that one would ultimately come, by this process, not to violent rebellion and anarchy, but to ancient and secure traditional values.*[6]

Curran is existential in that he would see man taking the lonely road of choice in search of his self, and the measure of his existentialism might be seen in the extent to which he would freely allow man to make his search, and to move in directions that might not be toward those "ancient values" that Curran apparently feels *must* be there.

It is often difficult too, to try to determine just what is meant by the often vague and somewhat amorphous term "God." In much of the culture, God has become a requisite, and for many Americans, God is something of a status symbol. Fromm has a related thought when he says:

> *If there is anything to be taken seriously in our profession of God, it is to recognize the fact that God has become an idol.*

4. Ira Progoff, "The Psychological Dimension of Religion," *Journal of Existential Psychiatry*, 3:166–178 (Fall, 1962).
5. Paul Rosenfels, *Psychoanalysis and Civilization* (New York: Library Publishers, 1962), pp. 34–35.
6. Charles A. Curran, "Some Ethical and Scientific Values in the Counseling Therapeutic Process," *Personnel and Guidance Journal*, 39:15–20 (September, 1960).

Not an idol of wood or stone like our ancestors worshiped, but an idol of words, phrases, doctrines. . . . We consider people to be "religious" because they say that they believe in God. Is there any difficulty in saying this?[7]

Many counselors would see God as being in the person, and of the person. Wheelis comments:

But freedom is not fortuity, does not war with continuity, means only that we make out of past and present something new, something which is not a mechanical unfolding, and cannot have been foretold, that no law limits how far we may go, how wide, how deep. We are gods because we create.[8]

Sartre, who could hardly be considered to be denominationally "religious," says:

The best way to conceive of the fundamental project of human reality is to say that man is the being whose project is to be God. . . . To be man means to reach toward being God. Or, if you prefer, man fundamentally is the desire to be God.[9]

The more one feels that counseling is related to, or aligned with, philosophy, the more likely it is that he feels it is also related to religion; whereas the more he feels that counseling is an empirical science, the more likely it is that he will question the necessity of counseling's becoming involved with religion. On the other hand, most counselors would agree with Becker when he writes:

Thus psychology and religion, which entered into a state of legal separation during the early part of this century in order to allow psychology to thrive as a science unfettered by doctrinal restraints, have fallen in love again, and are at least cohabiting if not fully married to each other because of the influence of psychotherapy on psychology.[10]

Certainly the basic principles of operation of the counselor often appear to bear a remarkable resemblance to the basic principles of the operation of the Christian and Jewish cultures. Statements regarding the integrity and rights of the individual are found

7. Eric Fromm, *Beyond the Chains of Illusion* (New York: Pocket Books, 1962), p. 169.
8. Allen Wheelis, "To Be a God," *Commentary*, 36:125–134 (August, 1963).
9. Jean-Paul Sartre, *Existentialism and Human Emotions* (New York: Wisdom Library, 1957), p. 63.
10. Russell J. Becker, "Links Between Psychology and Religion," *American Psychologist*, 13:566–568 (October, 1958).

as often in religious literature as they are in counseling literature. In fact, it would almost seem that if John Smith, Christian, and Mart Cohen, Jew, were to *practice* to the nth degree the basic principles of their religions as regards their relationship with their fellow men of all faiths and sizes and colors, then there might not be much difference between their relationship with another human being and the relationship between a counselor and a client. It is when one gets to what people actually do, in the name of their religion, or supposedly because of their religion, or for their religion, that one might say "Well, if this is what you must be or if this is what you must do—and if this is synonymous with your religion, then there is a big gap between the practice of your religion and the practice of counseling."

In an article on this subject Cole has this to say:

> *If this interest in psychotherapy does no more than muzzle the minister its worth will be beyond measure. The contrast between the approaches of parson and psychiatrist to troubled human beings is sharp and cutting. The psychotherapist, even if he is a psychoanalyst, the most directive of the new secular priesthood, listens and listens and listens, with an angelic fear of treading too heavily on an already trampled psyche. He waits for weeks before he essays a highly tentative diagnosis and he allows the patient to come to his own insights into the nature of his problems and their solution. The minister, dealing with the same individual, talks and talks and talks!*
>
> *The minister wants to persuade the troubled parishioner to see his problem in terms of a particular theological formulation. And that is precisely what the analyst does not want. . . .*
>
> *Thus, if the psychotherapeutic binge now being enjoyed by the clergy does no more than influence them to talk less and listen more, the results will be startling. Further, if ministers can learn the importance of focusing on how people feel rather than on what they say, then counseling will be more effective. For the Bible is at one with the new depth psychology in regarding all human behavior, including conversation, as symptomatic, as springing from the inner wells of emotion. "As a man thinketh in his heart, so is he."* [11]

What Cole is saying here is not that religion is in the way of counseling, but rather that some individuals who are called clergy-

11. William Graham Cole, "Couch and Confessional," *Nation* (September 20, 1958), pp. 147–150.

men operate, in the name of religion, in ways that could hardly be called therapeutic.

Mann stresses another problem of the religious counselor when he says:

> In the meantime, the clergyman employed in clinical work will have to stand guard against his own need to trespass upon the apparent theological insufficiencies of the patient. Otherwise, he will reap the bitter fruits of his compulsion: a rebellious patient who will not return for counseling, or a submissive devotee who has temporarily buried his pathology under the superficial signs and symbols of religion.[12]

Because in recent years the role of the clergyman as a counselor has been increasingly stressed, counseling is becoming a familiar term to those preparing to become clergymen, rabbis, or priests. On the other hand, if the counselor is primarily a clergyman it means that he may view his function as a counselor in a somewhat different light than does the professional secular counselor. On the Catholic side of this question, for example, Bier says:

> As a Catholic, I consider this care to be first of all of a spiritual nature and to be exercised through the spiritual ministrations of the priest. . . . A clergyman would think of himself as being dedicated principally to the religious care of those entrusted to him.[13]

And Moynihan has this to say:

> Pastoral counseling primarily involves education and re-education, a realization of how a problem may be solved through the means at hand in a given religion, be it prayer, the sacraments, conferences and retreats, whereby a new outlook on life is reached, new motivations are reached, and the basis of character modification through a change of will is developed. The primary function of the pastoral counselor is the care of the souls entrusted by ecclesiastic jurisdiction to his ministration, and since this is a spiritual function, the means he employs will be primarily spiritual.[14]

Judaism has not moved into the area of pastoral counseling to the same degree as has Christianity, one of the reasons being that a

12. Kenneth W. Mann, "Religious Factors and Values in Counseling: A Symposium," *Journal of Counseling Psychology,* 6:255–274 (Winter, 1959).
13. William C. Bier, "Goals in Pastoral Counseling," *Pastoral Psychology,* 10:10 (February, 1959).
14. James F. Moynihan, "The Counselor and His Religion," *Personnel and Guidance Journal,* 36:328 (January, 1958).

rabbi is viewed somewhat differently from the priest or the clergyman. First and foremost they are teachers. This is the essence of
their being. In light of this situation, the obvious problem of the
rabbi as a counselor is expressed by Schnitzer:

*The usual and accepted role of the rabbi may not be readily
adapted to the requirement of the professional counselor who
listens and helps people to help themselves.*[15]

It is in the Protestant area that pastoral counseling has probably found its greatest support. Fairly typical of the comments of
Protestant clergymen would be those of Hiltner:

*Broadly speaking, the special aim of pastoral counseling may
be stated as the attempt by a pastor to help people help themselves through the process of gaining understanding of their
inner conflicts. Counseling is sometimes referred to as emotional re-education, for in addition to its attempting to help
people with a problem immediately confronting them, it should
teach people to help themselves with other problems.*[16]

And Wise adds the thought:

*Counseling is essentially communication and as such it is es-
sentially a two directional process. It is not what the counselor
does for or to the counselee that is important; the important
thing is what happens between them. The pastor needs to know
himself as well as the dynamic processes of personality as they
find expression in the counselee.*[17]

Even in these few examples of the expressed attitudes of clergymen who are leaders in the area of pastoral counseling, there are
noticeable differences between the secular counselor and the clerical
counselor.

There are many traits and characteristics that are usually associated with organized religion and, to a greater or lesser degree,
with those who are the spokesmen for religion. Let us look at some
of these traits that would appear to be somewhat contradictory to a
philosophy of counseling, and that might be considered to hinder the
development of a therapeutic relationship between counselor and
client.

1. The desire to convert and to change—usually to the religion of the counselor, and to his particular denomination of that

15. Jeshaia Schnitzer, *New Horizons for the Synagogue* (New York: Bloch Publish-
     ing Co., 1956), p. 16.
16. Seward Hiltner, *Pastoral Counseling* (New York: Abingdon Press, 1949), p. 19.
17. Carrol A. Wise, *Pastoral Counseling: Its Theory and Practice* (New York: Harper
     and Row, 1951), p. 63.

religion—is a trait of many clergymen, if not an outright obligation that the clergyman has to his particular church. Many religious denominations even have particular orders whose primary purpose is to convert people to see the truth and the light. "The truth and the light," of course, are the way the particular denomination sees them, even though quite a different truth and light from those accepted by another religion. Whether an individual who feels within him a burning responsibility to persuade all people to feel and to think the way he does could be considered a counselor is a question. Such a setting would surely contradict the concept of the acceptance of the right of the individual to be as he is and to hold the values that he holds, the right to be a free man and to develop his own system of values. It may be a moot theological question whether the "true" Christian, or whether the X denomination—which, in its own mind, represents the "true" Christianity—can operate in a philosophical area such that they would, in effect, be saying that other Christian denominations, or other non-Christian religions, might have the true answers. If this is the case, one might push a little further and say, "Well, since, you do not *know* if you have answers, and since others might be just as right as you, then what difference does it make what denomination of Christian I might be, or whether I am a Christian at all, or instead a Jew or a Buddhist?" What it boils down to might be the simple question: Can a good and devout Christian say that he might, in later years, in a later period of the world's history, be shown to be quite wrong in his religious beliefs? Certainly Church leaders appear to find no problem in disagreeing with the Church's earlier pronouncements regarding, say, Galileo and Bruno, the question of the sun or the earth as the center of the universe, and the question of evolution.

Actually, there would appear to be little difference between those who would speak of relative truths and the more theologically oriented who feel that there is a God's truth, but are willing to accept the possibility that the current version of *the* truth may not be the correct godly version. If the Church of earlier years had accepted this philosophy, there would have been little reason for it to jail Galileo and burn Bruno. This too, of course, would remove from the Church the major reason for the existence of heresy; at least one could hypothesize that the doubter might be closer to God's truth than the devout! The acceptance of the possibility of human (if not godly) error also removes the major reason for the existence of different branches and denominations of religions. Thus, as the leaders of the Eastern and the Western branches of the Catholic church meet and talk with each other, and cautiously say, "We should not be so far apart—we are not *that* different," they are doing what is also being done by various Protestant denominations, by Protestants and Catholics, and by Christians and Jews. And the closer they become, of course, the more absurd their centuries-long self-segregation becomes. And it may be, eventually, that there will be no point in saying to a man, "I am a Methodist" or "I am a Catholic" or "I am a Jew." All one will need to say is "I am a human being, and you are my brother."

Certainly many of the concepts of religion are quite akin to those of counseling. The Judeo-Christian heritage stresses the worth and the dignity of the individual man, and it puts on the shoulders of man the responsibility for his actions.

Curran describes some of the relationships between counseling and religion as "parallels." The first parallel is the commitment of self of both the counselor and the religious person. The second parallel has to do with communion—the religious person "communes" with God, whereas the client and the counselor "communicate" together. A third parallel relates to the urge of the religious person to "do better" for himself because of the love and acceptance and understanding of him by God; so too the client is urged to movement and growth because he knows he is understood and accepted, and is thus freer to become.[18]

White speaks much like a counselor when he says:

We Catholics ask of psychotherapy, not to make us good, not to tell us what to do or not to do in order to be good, nor to make us "normal" in accord with any given norm, however estimable; but only to help us to achieve greater freedom through a better knowledge of our necessities and compulsions. We must decline to be "made" anything by psychotherapy; we want to be helped to be able to make or mar ourselves.[19]

On the other hand, the *meaning* of religion, like that of every other aspect of living, must be measured by what it does rather than by what it says. If the Christian counselor who, when some topic about religion is being discussed, feels toward his Jewish client, "*I* am right," then he is probably saying not only "*You* must be wrong," but also, "*I* must be right." The problem, then, rests: Is it possible to be accepted by your church as a good and devout and faithful member, and be able to say to yourself, "I think I'm right, but it doesn't really matter too much if it turns out that I am wrong, and you are right, as well you might be." If he can feel this way, then it might be

18. Charles A. Curran, "Religious Factors and Values in Counseling: A Symposium," *Journal of Counseling Psychology*, 6:266–270 (Winter, 1959).
19. Victor White, *God and the Unconscious* (London: Harvill Press, 1953), p. 166.

possible for him to be completely acceptant of an individual whose value system, as well as religion, differed sharply from his own. If he cannot feel this way, it would be rather difficult for him to accept another individual when he is saying to himself, "You are, of course, quite wrong."

2. Another area where counseling and religion might find themselves to be uneasy bedfellows is in dealing with the question of sin, original or otherwise. A generally accepted psychological tenet is that it is not so much the actual "sinning," but the acceptance of the belief that we have sinned that causes problems and troubles of the mind. A person may become neurotic not because of his sins, but because he feels that he has sinned. Is the person who wears a hair shirt, or scourges himself, or pays penance, indicating the depth of his religious belief, or is he rather indicating his lack of capacity to accept himself as he is? And does he thus appease himself by doing something to atone for his sins, and, in the meantime, do nothing whatsoever to really change this self that is such that he must continue to sin, and to punish himself for sinning?

Lee and Pallone, in discussing the clash between counseling concepts and the Catholic concept of morality, make the comment that, "Nowhere can this clash be more clearly seen than in the case of the client whose problems are materially (as contrasted to formally) sinful (e.g. masturbation)."[20] The word "sinful," however, is a human value judgment, whereas masturbation is a physical act. Must the Catholic counselor, for ever and ever, operate on the belief that masturbation, no matter by whom, under what circumstance, is an act of sin? The psychotic patient, who, for quite obvious psychological reasons, openly masturbates in front of a group of visiting experts; the little child, who in his exploring, discovers how to have a pleasant physical feeling, and thus masturbates; and the disturbed girl, who after every sexual encounter with a man, can only find sexual satisfaction by masturbation—*must* the counselor actually believe that all of these people are guilty of sin? Then, too, one might wonder what leeway one has in a definition of sin. Curran, for example, does not think of sin as worthlessness, but rather as the absence of desirable goodness.[21] Even here, of course, there is judgment, and it is someone else who has made the blanket judgment that a certain act does not indicate "desirable goodness." Curran, too, shows an acceptance of what might be described as both a religious and psy-

20. James Michael Lee and Nathaniel J. Pallone, *Guidance and Counseling in the School* (New York: McGraw-Hill, 1966), p. 99.

21. Charles A. Curran, "Religion—Its Relation to Counseling," in Dugald S. Arbuckle (ed.) *Counseling and Psychotherapy: An Overview* (New York: McGraw-Hill, 1967), pp. 62–63.

chological dogma when he states: "There is in man the mystery of evil: a tendency toward disorder and even viciousness."[22] It is not so much that such dogma is right or wrong, it is simply that judgments have been made without empirical evidence one way or the other. In the first example a descriptive term is given to a physical act; in the second example a statement is made about human behavior. Since such statements are accepted by some, not by others, cannot the counselor at least be open, and not be compelled to believe? How can the counselor communicate to the client "You must determine the meaning of life for yourself," if he cannot allow himself this freedom, but feels, "I must believe, because I was told it is so."

It might be, too, that one should distinguish between the social and the religious mores of a Judeo-Christian society. Can we compare the feeling of sinfulness that the Jew might have in committing adultery (which would also be breaking a social law), and that which he might feel because he did not eat kosher foods (which would be a religious custom, limited only to those Jews who accepted this particular concept)? Every counselor has had as clients individuals who are highly disturbed because they cannot intellectually accept some of the "sinful" acts of their religion as being sinful, and yet who cannot dismiss them. They may be torn between being what they feel is intellectually dishonest but secure, or being intellectually honest and uneasy. The Jew who eats nonkosher foods, the Catholic who uses contraceptive devices, the Mormon who drinks coffee, the Seventh-Day Adventist who works on Saturday—these individuals are sinning according to their religion, but not according to their society. If a person accepts such acts easily or rejects them easily, then he has no problem; but the unhappy one is the person who can do neither.

There are even good citizens who almost seem to be being scared into heaven because they are afraid that if they do what they want to do, then they will go to hell. Preparing for heaven in this manner seems a most unhappy way of spending one's years on earth; and yet there is a strong segment in nearly every religious denomination—more in some than others, of course—where a basic tenet seems to be "You have sinned, and only by living the life that we say you should live will you have any chance of ever seeing the promised land." Surely, this is rather a negative way to do good. Are we good to our neighbors only because of our guilt feelings? It would seem that an ideal and realistic society will be one where such authoritarian and autocratic means for control are not necessary. We know, as a matter of fact, that such means of control are actually

22. *Ibid.*

useless, and in the long run no control at all. In a free and democratic society, the individual accepts his responsibility for his own behavior without any pressures, subtle or otherwise. He does not steal his neighbor's belongings because he has *no need to steal*, even though he may have a very real need for his neighbor's belongings.

As long as a person can be acceptant, however, of his particular religion's "sins," and not do what he is not supposed to do, or if he can, on the other hand easily reject them as sins, then he has no psychological trouble. If, however, these sins begin to be imposed as sins on others who do not see them as sins, what then? Laws preventing the sale of merchandise on Sunday or preventing the dissemination of information on contraceptive devices are good examples of supposedly "social" laws that are actually religious laws, and are imposed on some who do not accept them as religious laws.

If a person believes too that he is basically a sinful creature, through no fault of his own other than having been born, then he begins his life as a guilty creature. This, too, would seem to be an insecurity-breeding way of introducing the young to life—the idea that a person must somehow get off his back sins for which he has no responsibility, other than by being a human being. Does man have potential for good and a tendency to evil, or does he have, to start, potential for good and potential for evil, but tendency, if there must be tendency one way or the other, for good rather than evil? This latter point, however, would be in the realm of belief. The empiricist might well say that man, at the beginning, has his various potentialities, but he has no tendencies until he is born, or at least, to play it safe, until he is conceived.

The problem of sins and sinning may also raise problems for the theologian as a counselor, since a client, in talking with a clergyman about sins he has committed, knows that the clergyman must consider them sins, and therefore cannot be acceptant of them. Hence the client will assume, almost certainly, that the clergyman cannot be acceptant of him as a person. This situation is illustrated by a statement by Moynihan, who says, "While the pastoral counselor cannot permit anything which is contrary to the laws of God and nature, what he may legitimately permit is the opportunity for the client to talk out any kind of situation or motivation which may have led him to contemplate such a course of action."[23] This point of view indicates that the pastoral counselor must surely be in a somewhat conflicting situation, and that his acceptance is of the most limited type. If the Catholic pastoral counselor does not feel free as

23. James F. Moynihan, "Symposium: The Counselor and His Religion," *Personnel and Guidance Journal,* 36:327–331 (January, 1958).

an individual to accept the decision of the Catholic client to use contraceptive devices, if the Jewish pastoral counselor does not feel free as an individual to accept the decision of his Jewish client to eat nonkosher foods, if the Methodist pastoral counselor does not feel free as an individual to accept the decision of his Methodist client to use alcoholic beverages, if the Mormon pastoral counselor does not feel free as an individual to accept the decision of his Mormon client to drink coffee, and if all four feel that as the arm of their respective churches they must be nonacceptant of the client's right to do these things, then surely their acceptance is most limited, and surely, as therapists, they are handicapped.

Such a situation, of course, occurs to some extent with every counselor, since clients frequently discuss various deviations which are not acceptable, and might even be considered criminal, by their culture; and the client may have some beginning uneasiness as to the extent to which the counselor will be acceptant of him and his actions. Thus a lesbian client once said to me, "I feel okay talking to you like this when I think of you as a counselor, but when I think of your title as professor of education, I don't feel so good!" At least the client may not know how the secular counselor feels about these things; but he does know, in his own mind at least, that the theological counselor is the arm of a powerful organization that says, "This is a sin that you should not have committed."

Mowrer has spoken out in defense of sin as being of therapeutic value:

> Therefore, we can and should show him all the love and charity within our souls, and do not need in the least to play a punitive role. But this is very different from saying that we should dispute or brush aside his assertions of guilt or minimize the reality of his need for deliverance. Several members of the group expressed the conviction that much of our present would-be therapeutic effort is useless and even harmful because we so actively oppose the patient's own most substantial psychological realities and his brightest prospects for change and recovery, i.e., his conviction of guilt and sense of sin. Perhaps the patient is not so wrong, not so "crazy" as some of our own theories have been![24]

3. Another problem that finds its way into any discussion of religion and counseling is that concerned with morality and virtue. If religion thinks of itself, as it appears to, as the custodian of man's

24. O. Hobart Mowrer, "Judgment and Suffering: Contrasting Views," *Faculty Forum,* No. 10 (October, 1959).

moral values, then it is speaking in terms of absolutes, a stand thaι poses a knotty set of problems in a nation where there are many religions, and therefore many sets of values, each set being somebody's "absolutes." Roessler has some interesting comments on this subject. In comparing a personal morality with a "codified" morality, he writes as follows:

> *Personal morality is defined in positive terms. Feelings become a reliable guidance to action which enhances and enriches both self and others. . . . By contrast, codified moralities are most often preponderantly prohibitions, because they are frequently based on a pessimistic view of man's nature . . . .*
>
> *Like good law, such morality is centered in the needs of men rather than in the sometimes arbitrary demands of institutionalized codes. Because it is so centered, it is tailor-made . . . .*
>
> *It is a morality of dynamic rather than static quality, changing with ever-changing circumstances and the ever-changing person. It is ceaselessly fluid, completely or almost completely adapted to the requirements of the complex moment . . . .*
>
> *Personal morality is morality without absolutes. . . . Another characteristic of personal morality is its tolerance for the behavior of others . . . .*
>
> *The person capable of choice . . . does not function in spite of circumstances but because of them and in concert with them . . . .*
>
> *It seems to me that codified moralities may have a predominantly negative effect on self-realization and thereby on society. If they are characterized preponderantly by an absence of "roots in man's nature," if they are inherently inflexible and narrow, if they are absolute—then they will serve neither the needs of the individual nor those of the society comprised of individuals. Fortunately for man, such systems either die because of their lack of pragmatic value, or they are ignored in action as they deserve to be.*[25]

This probably points to one of the dilemmas that religion faces when it begins to be involved in the problems of man's behavior. Neither man nor his society, nor the needs of the individual man nor those of the collective society, have much resemblance to what they were several thousands of years ago. The "moralities" of then do not fit the "moralities" of today any more than the sins of yesterday are the sins of today. We may argue that they should be, but if we go on

25. Robert Roessler, "A Psychiatrist's View of Morality," *Humanist,* 18:333–339 (November–December, 1958).

the basis of the way man operates, then he simply does not accept them. If we assume that there should be some relationship between a man's behavior and his morality, then those individuals who are most closely related to a religion or to a church should be our most moral citizens (in the sense of being acceptant of their responsibility toward their neighbors, their love of their fellow man, and their defense of the rights of others). I know of no evidence to indicate that this is so. Theoretically, one might assume that among the graduates of religious schools there should be less in the way of immoral behavior, but there is no evidence to indicate that this is so. We might assume that the person who goes to his synagogue or church every Sunday should be a better man than the one who does not; but, again, there is no evidence that this is so.

Indeed, one of the sadder aspects of the revelations of governmental corruption has been the extent to which those involved, were, in the eyes of society, "good" men. They dressed properly, they belonged to the right organizations, they used good English, they believed in law and order, and they were, usually, devout churchgoers!

The counselor is very much concerned with love and acceptance, and with his ability to love and accept an individual client. The client finds in the counselor an individual who may gradually help him to feel, "I *really* am being accepted—me—as I am." Although he may not say it to himself, somewhere in his feelings may possibly come a sense that he is experiencing a non-wanting and a nondemanding love from a counselor who wants nothing from the client. This is surely the love that was preached by the great and original men of many religions, and it is the love that must encompass man's morality. But it is the love that man over the centuries has really believed that he was getting from his religion; or did he feel rather that he was being measured and judged, and then possibly forgiven, but not loved? It might even be that what we are saying is: Has the Christian, over the centuries, been Christian, and has the Christian church, over the centuries, been Christian? Has it really practiced what is written in the books? Has it been moral in its concern for the welfare of the individual man, or has it been more concerned with the welfare of the Church as a massive organization? On this point Becker writes:

> It need hardly be argued that the patience involved in spending
> 50 or 100 or 200 hours with a single individual plus the depth of
> permissiveness, acceptance and respect involved in the thera-
> pist's capacity to be open to the emotional complexities of an-
> other person's life provide a new definition of what "caring"

45

for another person means, of what charity or true "love"
means, of what creative personal relationships may be, of what
the ethical demands of religion upon daily living are. . . . What
we have in the evolving field of psychotherapy is a new concep-
tion of the ethic of love and a new understanding of the worth
of persons that has grown up largely outside of organized reli-
gion.[26]

Just as nationalistic and racial dogma teaches superiority, and thus the inferiority of those of other nationalities and races, so often does religious dogma teach the inferiority of others. If the Catholic church is the sole possessor of "absolute truth," it is very clear that the majority of mankind does not possess the truth. Although the scholarly theologian might not agree, many Jewish children, I believe, are taught from the *amidah,* as part of their religious dogma, that they are the selected, if not the chosen people. The Mormons are taught that black people represent those unhappy individuals who are paying for their sins, and they can thus never become members of the ruling circle of the Mormon church. These are beliefs which deny to others the right of individual dignity and freedom. They are representative of the conditioned value structure of the individuals who, against their own reason and rationality, feel that they *must* hold to them in order to be true to the faith.

Thus it is probably correct to say that clergymen and counselors are both *concerned* with the morality of man, but that different religions represent different codified systems of morality, whereas the counselor tends to operate on a basis of personal morality. Thus there is no clash of an absolute with another, one truth with another, a clash that surely must occur if the counselor feels and believes that *his* set of truths and moral values is the only *true* set of truths and moral values.

4. Another question that involves religion and its role in counseling has to do with the extent to which religion stands for authority and the control of human behavior rather than the acceptance of human behavior. There would probably be general agreement that religion has been a major factor in the control of human behavior over the centuries, and probably most people would agree that some form of control has been necessary. If, however, we talk in terms of the development of a free and democratic society, and think of the counselor as one who operates in a free and democratic society, with the rights of the individual paramount in his mind, there will possibly be a clash between the individual and the church trying to im-

26. Russell J. Becker, *op. cit.*

pose its controls for what it sincerely believes is the good of the individual. Ostow refers to the various devices by means of which behavior can be influenced, and the way in which organized religion has made use of these devices. One method is imitation, the lives of saints and religious heroes being described in religious literature for the express purpose of inviting imitation. Second is by the communication of affect, accomplished on an individual-to-individual basis, by congregations worshipping together and sharing the same feelings, by religious rituals, by sacred objects, by religious art. Religion also intervenes in the pursuit of instinctual gratification, and thus exercises control by promising rewards for good behavior and threatening frustration and injury for bad behavior. The invoking of obedience is a primary concern of religion, and God and his surrogates are seen as parental figures who require and deserve obedience, while human beings are seen as refractory children. Religion also exploits human susceptibility to signs of vulnerability, and weakness, innocence, humility, and suffering are displayed constantly. Ostow refers too to the encouragement, by religion, of a controlled regression, whereby the individual becomes more compliant to religious authority and hence to religion's effort to control human behavior to the end of social stability.[27]

Thus, as clergymen become more involved in counseling, this is a problem that they must face. If they basically represent an organization that is trying to control human behavior, then they enter the counseling relationship with a handicap, just as do the teacher, the policeman, the judge. All of these may be splendid people, consciously concerned with the improvement of the human lot, but they cannot function completely as counselors because they have other obligations that clash with their basic obligation, as counselors, to the individual.

5. A final issue of some concern to the problem of counseling and religion is the matter of faith and belief. Traditionally, a therapist has been thought of as a man of science, whereas a clergyman has been considered to be a man of faith. It might be, however, that in recent years each one has been affected somewhat by the other, with the clergyman beginning to become more of a man of science and the therapist beginning to become more of a man of faith—a movement that has probably been good for all concerned. It should not be unempirical to say that the counselor who does not have faith in the capacity of his client to find an answer to his problems is not going to have much success in helping the client to find the strengths

27. Mortimer Ostow, "The Nature of Religious Controls," *American Psychologist*, 13:571–574 (October, 1958).

that the counselor does not believe exist. The person with strength is the one who has faith in himself, and the individual should originally derive this solidarity from his parents. If he does not, the counselor in a school system is probably the next person who will have the job of trying to help him to achieve some confidence in himself; but the counselor himself *must believe* if he is ever to help the client to believe.

There is no question about the fact that religion has traditionally given the individual a faith, but it may be that this in too many cases was a faith in somebody else's doing something for him and looking after him. Although such a faith may have led to stability of a sort, it gave the individual strength deriving from his belief in the strength of someone or something else. A responsible member of a free society must come to have faith in himself, and man's greatest rationalization throughout the ages has probably been the statement, "It is God's will." It has been, in a way, a comforting thought, but man would never have pulled himself out of the caves if he had accepted all of his misfortunes as God's will, never to be tampered with. Man became a forward-moving creature when he could really look at himself, blame himself for his own mistakes, and at the same time have confidence in his capacity to move ahead. Thus the counselor needs more faith—faith in the capacity of the individual client to actually learn to move ahead. The clergyman needs the same sort of faith—possibly less of the faith in someone else—and more faith in himself, not just as an arm of the church, but as a human being with human responsibilities toward his fellows that may even transcend his responsibilities toward his church.

On the other hand, all of this need not in any way detract from the therapeutic possibilities of faith, since faith in one's self often comes from faith in someone else. Throughout the ages, miracles have been testimony to the faith. It is not so much *what* one believes in, as it is that one deeply *believes* that something positive, or negative, will happen. Converts are sometimes good examples of the power of faith; a Jew who becomes a Catholic may find tremendous new strengths because of his faith in his new religion, while at the same time a Catholic who becomes a Methodist, and a Methodist who becomes a Jew will also find tremendous new strengths in their respective new religions. It is obviously not the religion, per se, that has the effect, but rather what the individual sees in it.

Another example of the power of faith is seen in various experiments, in which placebos containing inert substances have been given to some patients as having curative powers, while the same substance is given to other patients as something that has doubtful curative powers. The general procedure has been used in a variety of ways, and in most cases there is a significant difference in the improvement of those individuals who *have a belief in what they are taking*. The druggist could likely substitute placebos in half of his aspirin bottles, and it would be doubtful if those who benefit from aspirin would benefit any less.

These then, would appear to be some of the issues that face the counselor who is also involved in religion, either as a lay individual or as a theologian. Organized religion has already moved into the field of counseling, and discussions of issues such as those raised in this section are becoming commonplace in seminaries and schools of theology. Both counseling and religion, and thus, in the long run, man, should benefit from this rapprochement.

SCIENCE AND HUMANS

Science, like religion, is a rather large word, and takes in a rather broad area. One may wonder whether man, as an existential being, has greater likelihood of growth under the autocracy of religion or under the autocracy of science—or, possibly, in a humanistic, existential society in which man is viewed as the center and the reason for being. Some might ask, of course, whether humanism and existentialism cannot exist in a religious or a scientific society, or in a society that is religious-scientific, if such a thing is possible. It would certainly seem that in somewhat modern Western times, the Greek society was one in which man reached a high point of being. His existential being was realized to a high degree, and he was seen as a reasoning man, living on this earth. In the many dark centuries that followed, however, man all but disappeared. He was viewed by the Christian church as a soul, with faith as the primary asset and reason as the primary sin. His purpose on earth was not to live, but to prepare for the hereafter. With the Renaissance, the light began to shine once again on reason, and science began the movement that is accelerating to this day. Increasingly, however, to science man became a thing, and as medicine graduated from the barber pole to the status of a profession it too saw man as a part of a thing—namely, a disease. The psychologist, striving for status, kept within the scientific fringe, and tended to see man as a problem. It is somewhat intriguing to note that the basic underlying theme of today's "new," "dynamic" "revolution in psychiatry" is the dawning realization that it is just possible that man is a total being after all—he is not a soul, or a thing, or a disease, or a problem. He is a total existential being, and he should be considered as such.

There are those few voices, too, which indicate that if we are to talk about the human being in a total sense, then we cannot just talk in scientific terms. Bergman, who is a psychiatrist, feels that we have much to learn from the Navajo Indians, who in the medicine man unite the three professions of medicine, law, and theology. He states:

The biochemist psychiatrists, I suppose, are grappling with some of the hardest scientific-technical problems of medicine, but sooner or later they will succeed in eliminating major mental illnesses, leaving the rest of us with only the universal nuttiness and misery of human life to take care of. How will we do it? Not, I think, as scientists or even as priests of science, but somehow as healers—like the medicine men.[28]

Bergman also believes:

The value judgments inherent in the definition of the relationship of man to man and of man to nature will be more explicit than we make them at present and will no longer be obscured by scientism, because we are ashamed of being non-scientific or subjective.[29]

Huxley is another person who has consistently questioned the narrowness of science in its relationship to humanity. Some years ago he stated:

Systematic reasoning is something we could not, as a species or as individuals, possibly do without. But neither, if we are to remain sane, can we possibly be without direct perception, the more unsystematic the better, of the inner and outer worlds into which we have been born.[30]

Keen, in talking about Oscar Ichazo and the Arica Institute, says:

The new religion is challenging the psychological approach to understanding and curing human disease. It is offering both a new anthropology and a new therapeutic which begin with the assumption that psychology is a manifestation of the disease for which it purports to be the cure.[31]

28. Robert L. Bergman, "Navajo Medicine and Psychoanalysis," *Human Behavior*, 2:8–15 (July, 1973).
29. *Ibid.*
30. Aldous Huxley, *The Doors of Perception and Heaven and Hell* (New York: Harper and Row, 1963), p. 77.
31. Sam Keen, "Oscar Ichazo and the Arica Institute," *Psychology Today*, 7:66 (July, 1973).

50

In the psychological fraternity these voices represent a minority, but particularly since the decade of the 1960's, a rapidly increasing minority which might eventually become the major voice in psychology and in counseling. Anything philosophic or nonscientific is still, however, highly suspect among psychologists and, likely, among most counselors and therapists. Some years ago the negative reaction to a philosophic version of the counselor was indicated in two letters written in reply to an article by Rogers called "Persons or Science? A Philosophical Question."[32] One of the letters states:

> *Rogers' article was painful in its implication for those who are now struggling for scientific method to clarify our present state of development. It could be more harmful to the graduate student who is looking for leadership in this field. How can such an integration as Rogers' which reifies science, glorifies mute feelings of ignorance by calling them personal subjective values, and abounds in infallible premises be looked upon as typical of the clinician's or psychologist's viewpoint . . . .* [33]

Another letter writer, commenting on the same article, says:

> *Comment on Rogers' article is irresistible, yet difficult and saddening. . . . Yet what graduate student could get by with such talk of "the essence of therapy," "the subjective and the objective person," "the scientific versus the experimental viewpoint," etc.? . . . The greatest disservice that Dr. Rogers does for psychotherapy seems to be his insistence on something mystical in the therapeutic process. There is nothing mysterious about the source of this mysticism. . . . There is another trace of mysticism in his seeming naïveté about learning. What happens in therapy, he says, is a type of learning that cannot be taught. . . .* [34]

In the article that evoked the above comments Rogers had pointed out some of the basic questions of the scientist as compared with those of the experientialist. The questions asked by the scientist might be as follows:

1. How can you know that this account, or any account given at a previous or later time, is true? How do you know that it has any

---

32. Carl R. Rogers, "Persons or Science? A Philosophical Question," *American Psychologist,* 10:267–278 (July, 1955).
33. Letter in "Comment," by George F. Castore, *American Psychologist,* 11:154–155 (March, 1956).
34. Letter in "Comment," by Richard A. Lake, *American Psychologist,* 11:155 (March, 1956).

relationship to reality? If we are to rely on this inner and subjective experience as being the truth about human relationships or
about ways of altering personality, then Yogi, Christian Science,
dianoetics, and the delusions of a psychotic individual who believes himself to be Jesus Christ are all true, just as true as this
account.
2. Any experience that can be described at all can be described in
operational terms. Hypotheses can be formulated and put to test,
and the sheep of truth can thus be separated from the goats of
error.
3. Implicit in the description (by the experientialist) of the therapeutic experience seems to be the notion that there are elements in it
that *cannot* be predicted—that there is some type of spontaneity
or (excuse the term) free will operative here. Why not at least *aim*
toward uncovering the causes of all *behavior*?
4. Why must the therapist challenge the one tool and method that is
responsible for almost all of the advances that we value—namely,
the method of science?

In reaction to these thoughts of the scientist, Rogers has the therapist responding as follows:
1. Science has always to do with the other, the object. It never has
anything to do with the experiencing me.
2. Because science has as its field the "other," the "object," everything it touches is turned into an object. This has never presented
a problem in the physical sciences, but in the biological sciences it
has caused certain difficulties. It is in the social sciences, however, that it becomes a genuinely serious issue. It means that the
people studied by the social scientists are always objects. In therapy, both client and therapist become objects for dissection, but
not persons with whom one enters a living relationship.
3. When science transforms people into objects, it has another effect. The end result of science is to lead toward manipulation. If
we know how learning takes place, we use that knowledge to
manipulate persons as objects. It is not too strong a statement to
say that the growth of knowledge in the social sciences contains
within itself a powerful tendency toward social control, toward
control of the many by the few. An equally strong tendency is
toward the weakening or destruction of the existential person.
When all are regarded as objects, the subjective individual, the
inner self, the person in the process of becoming, the unreflective
consciousness of becoming, the whole inward side of living life, is
weakened, devalued, or destroyed.
4. Is not ethics a more basic consideration than science? In the physical sciences it took centuries for the ethical issue to become cru-

cial. In the social sciences the ethical issues arise much more quickly because persons are involved. But in counseling the issue arises most quickly and most deeply. We should think long and hard before we give up the values that pertain to being a person, to experiencing, to living a relationship, to becoming, that pertain to one's self as a process, to one's self in the existential moment, to the inward subjective self that lives.

This article is not recent, but it has been referred to at some length because it poses this problem of the counselor and the scientist as succinctly as any with which I am familiar, probably because its author is the one who has raised this problem as an issue more than any other contemporary counselor. In pondering how to solve this dilemma, Rogers concludes his article by saying "If I am open to my experience, and can permit all of the sensing of my intricate organism to be available to my awareness, then I am likely to use myself, my subjective experience, *and* my scientific knowledge, in ways which are realistically constructive."

Over a decade later, Carkhuff and Berenson expressed much the same feeling when they referred to counseling as an

approach that emphasizes a process culminating in a moment-to-moment, fully sharing process—a process born not only of the emotional resources of both parties to the relationship, but also of the deepest and broadest understanding of existing knowledge, and complemented by anything that will work for the client.[35]

Patterson refers to something totally different from this, when, in discussing the counselor's responsibility in rehabilitation, he effectively describes what is all too often thought of as the scientific method in counseling.

He determines *the eligibility of clients as clients and the feasibility of their rehabilitation; he* appraises *the client's vocational potential and the probability of his success; he* evaluates *the suitability of various jobs; he* interviews *the client* toward realistic *(as defined by himself) goals; he* develops *a vocational rehabilitation plan with all its parts; he* carries out *the plan, implementing and administering its various aspects; he* makes referrals *to related services. One might ask: What is the client doing all this time? Too often he is literally doing nothing, except what he is told to do by the counselor.*[36]

35. Robert R. Carkhuff and Bernard G. Berenson, *Beyond Counseling and Therapy* (New York: Holt, Rinehart and Winston, 1967), p. 233.

36. C. H. Patterson, "The Counselor's Responsibility in Rehabilitation," *Journal of Rehabilitation*, 23:7-11 (January–February, 1958).

The possible reason that the client is doing nothing is that he is viewed as an object, a piece of material, to be manipulated by the counselor who has the knowledge and the know-how not possessed by the client. Patterson wrote this as a protest against the all too prevalent concept of vocational counseling, but surely it describes frighteningly what happens when the client becomes lost as a person, as a human being, and is treated as one who is not to be accepted and understood as he is, but who, rather, must be manipulated and modified until he becomes another faceless creature.

But an existential-humanistic counselor should not confuse a scientific fact with a faith or a belief, nor need he be defensive about that which is not scientific or factual, even though the newer version of science is more inclusive of the total human being. He does not have to *know* about that which cannot be known; he does not have to find a *rational* explanation for that which is not rational; and he can go beyond the realm of the mind without demanding guarantees that he will safely return.

The function of science is to determine what is, and, as a result of this determination, to predict what might be. Such a scientific prognosis is based on evidence and facts; it is not concerned with values, with what ought to be. Generally this has not been a problem for the medical doctor, since man's physical body is not concerned with what ought to be either. A leg is smashed; there are certain proven techniques which have shown themselves to be superior over others in the mending of the broken leg. The leg does not ask, "Why should I mend?" or "What difference will it make if I do mend?" or "How did I come to get into this situation which resulted in a broken leg?" Thus as long as the medical doctor functioned as a surgeon, he could well be scientific. But as soon as he began to work with the owner of the leg, a human being who had a mind, his organic scientific knowledge began to fail him.

This circumstance probably posed no problem for the earlier medical doctor, who actually knew very little other than how to use his few skills and dispense his few medicines; however, if he was an intelligent individual, concerned with human values, then he probably functioned very much as a philosopher and a counselor. When Freud appeared on the scene with the first studied presentation of counseling and psychotherapy, it was presented as a science, although Freud was probably thinking of the dangers of the "too scientific" approach when he said, "Cases which are thus destined at the start to scientific purposes and treated accordingly suffer in consequence; while the most successful cases are those in which one proceeds, as it were, aimlessly, and allows oneself to be overtaken by any surprises, always presenting to them an open mind, free from any expectations."[37] Freud was no doubt influenced by his medical background, and with his generally antireligious point of view, it is little wonder that there was not much in the way of a philosophical approach to his psychotherapy. It should be noted, too, that then as now philosophy tended to be related to religion. While this is obviously true, it is not correct to assume, as some theologians do, that in order to be a philosopher one must be allied with a denominational religion. Some of the greatest minds in philosophy have been, and are, looked at with some suspicion by the more orthodox of their brethren, and the narrowness of philosophical breadth of some individuals may be correlated with their concept of religion as a set of dogmas, mostly telling man what not to do.

Thus, in a way, man moved into the study of the psychological and philosophical nature of man, with very little in the way of knowledge about the former, and a general bias or suspicion toward the latter. To some degree this condition still holds today, with the psychologist, as the newcomer in the field, taking on many of the characteristics of the medical profession, even while he strives with might and main to prove that he is different, as obviously he is.

The theologian has not generally been considered to be very scientific, being, rather, a man of faith. As he moves into the therapeutic arena, however, will he tend to become more scientific, and if he does, what will this attitude do to his faith? Although one might agree with Walters that "existential anxiety is properly the object of priestly concern, while pathologic anxiety is the concern of the psychotherapist,"[38] I cannot accept the implication that existential anxiety is not the concern of the psychotherapist. This very example might be an excellent indication of the difference between the counselor and the psychotherapist as scientists and as philosophers. If the counselor is concerned only with the pathological, and this is often thought of as the logical concern of the medical doctor and the clinical psychologist, then he can probably remain as the empirical scientist. Once, however, he becomes concerned with the more "existential" aspects of anxiety (and how could one be a counselor without having this concern?), then he has entered the realm of philosophy. Certainly it is not man's acts that cause him stress and strain so much as it is the guilts, the anxieties, the fears, the frustrations that have come to be associated with these acts. An individual is not disturbed by the physical act of masturbation until he learns that it is

37.   Sigmund Freud, "Recommendations for Physicians on the Psychoanalytic Method of Treatment," *Collected Papers, II* (London: Hogarth Press, 1925), pp. 326–327.

38.   Orville S. Walters, "Metaphysics, Religion and Psychotherapy," *Journal of Counseling Psychology*, 5:243–252 (Winter, 1958).

bad for him to masturbate, or that something dreadful will happen to him if he does; one is not distressed about hating a miserable parent unless one has learned that one is supposed always to love one's parents; one is not concerned about killing one's fellows as long as he knows that they are his enemy and must be killed, and that he will be rewarded for the act. These are surely matters of values that bring in questions about who we are, what we are around for, what is right, and what is wrong. And these are questions for which it is difficult to pose clear-cut empirical answers. One might be scientific in his attempts to evaluate what happens as a result of his counseling, what might happen if he does this instead of that, what happens if a certain variable (difficult to isolate in the social sciences) is introduced, and so on; but how scientific can one be in actual relationship with the client? And this, after all, is what counseling is.

Certainly the organic aspects of counseling can be scientific. Neither the patient nor the medical doctor is in the realm of philosophy when both are involved in a brain lobotomy or an electroshock, or in the injection of various drugs. Here one can be somewhat pragmatic, and on the basis of statistical evidence, say that he will proceed thus and so with this helpless patient, with no involvement on his part; and he knows the statistical odds that this, instead of that, will happen.

The traditional case-study approach, revered by social workers, might also be considered to be somewhat scientific, since it tends to be an investigation of what is, without the personal involvement of the client, and without the personal involvement and intrusion of the values and ideas and thoughts and feelings of the counselor, other than those that are based on evidence. Again, however, when the social worker becomes a counselor, she is no longer working *on* a case, but *with* a human being, and again the question arises. How scientific can you be in the actual close personal relationship between client and counselor, or does the very "scientificness' of one's approach render you less effective?

Many of the techniques and methods of counseling might logically be described as scientific. Thus, diagnosis is an empirical means of assessment of an individual or his problems. The whole process of analysis and interpretation can really be defended only on the basis of a scientific validation of their use. Thus it would probably be correct to say that counseling, as it is allied with or descended from medicine or psychology, will tend to have a strongly scientific tinge; and certainly many counselors, in their descriptions of counseling, would refer to it as "the science of. . . . "

Probably all counselors would agree that if counseling is to have the status of a profession, then its practitioners cannot say that they operate on faith and intuition, or that they need no evidence of whether the client is better or worse off because of their ministrations. This is surely the road to quackery, and counseling already has more than its share of quacks. On the other hand, if one thinks of counseling as basically a human relationship between two individuals, rather than as things the counselor does with or to the client during the relationship, then he enters the realm of the more subjective, the realm of human feelings.

One may wonder, too, if even the science of physics is as exact as it might appear to be, in that while it may be laws of nature that are being examined and studied, it is *man* who is involved in the examining. He sees what he sees, and what he sees depends on certain assumptions and suppositions. As May says:

> *Every scientific method rests upon philosophical presuppositions. These presuppositions . . . determine not only how much reality the observer with this particular method can see . . . they are indeed the spectacles through which he perceives, but also whether or not what is observed is pertinent to the real problem, and therefore whether the scientific work will endure. It is a gross, albeit common, error, to assume naively that one can observe facts best if he avoids all preoccupation with philosophical assumptions. All he does, then, is mirror uncritically the particular parochial doctrines of his own limited culture. The result in our day is that science gets identified with isolating factors and observing them from an allegedly detached base—a particular method which arose out of the split between subject and object made in the seventeenth century in Western culture and then developed into its specialized compartmentalized form in the late nineteenth and twentieth centuries.*[39]

Much the same thought is expressed by Rogers:

> *Science exists only in people. Each scientific project has its creative inception, its process, and its tentative conclusion, in a person or persons. Knowledge—even scientific knowledge—is that which is subjectively acceptable. Scientific knowledge can be communicated only to those who are subjectively ready to receive its communication. The utilization of science also occurs only through people who are in pursuit of values which have meaning for them.*[40]

39. Rollo May, *Existence* (New York: Basic Books, 1961), p. 149.
40. Carl R. Rogers, *On Becoming a Person* (Boston: Houghton Mifflin, 1961), p. 216.

And by Walters:

*The therapist usually conceives of himself, and is often repre-
sented as the detached, dispassionate scientist. A more realistic
view would see him as an involved participant with an interest
in the outcome, following a sectarian psychotherapeutic doctrine or combination of doctrines, the selection, and practice of
which are tinctured by his own basic philosophy of life.*[41]

Einstein was also thinking of the human aspect of science
when he wrote:

*For the scientific method can teach us nothing else beyond how
facts are related to, and conditioned by, each other. . . . Yet it is
equally clear that knowledge of what is does not open the door
to what should be.*[42]

As was Burtt:

*In its most general historical meaning the word "science" sim-
ply denotes the search for some orderly pattern in the world
around us; its aim is to conquer the contingency and chance
that initially confront us wherever and as far as it can. But it is
evident when we think about it that this aim, merely as such, is
quite ambiguous and indeterminate. Many different kinds of
order are discoverable; in fact, everything that one experiences
is related with some measurable degree of regularity to an in-
definite number of other things. Accordingly, what sort of order
is discovered depends primarily on the sort that scientists ag-
gressively look for, and what they look for depends in turn on
the further ends which, consciously or unconsciously, they
want their explanations to serve.*[43]

All of these reflections of dissatisfaction with the traditional
perception of "science" were but a faint indication of the revolution
that was to come in the decade of the 1960's. It was in this decade
that a mutiplicity of methods and techniques and procedures by
which we could transform ourselves began to appear, and this movement shows no signs of diminishing in the decade of the 1970's. In all
of these movements, many heavily influenced by Eastern thought,

41. Orville S. Walters, "Metaphysics, Religion and Psychotherapy," *Journal of
Counseling Psychology,* 5:243–252 (Winter, 1958).
42. Albert Einstein, *Out of My Later Years* (New York: Philosophical Library, 1950),
pp. 21–22.
43. E. A. Burtt, "The Value Presuppositions of Science," in Paul C. Obler and Herman A. Estrin (eds.), *The New Scientist: Essays on the Methods and Values of
Modern Science* (New York: Anchor Books, 1962), p. 282.

the center of attention was not the human body *or* the human mind but the whole total being, the gestalt, and all the mental and physical functions that are a part of it. The stress was on the *soma,* and somatology began to be a somewhat less suspect term!

Science has been an "observe, examine, predict" sort of procedure, and it has always been from the outside in. It has been *you* or *them* looking at *us* or *me,* under their terms with their methods of observation and measurement, and this is why traditional psychology, as a science, has simply missed the whole man. Indeed, psychology has generally been quite unaware of the whole man, and has operated as if his existence was no more than a myth. Thus, scientific reality has always been *your* perception of me, never *my* perception of me, and what *I* can do for and with me has been relatively unimportant compared with what *you* can do to and for me. As Hanna says:

> *All of these things become possible, not because of the confirmations and discoveries which are coming from somatic science, but because the growing millions of humans who are thrusting somatology into such prominence are also those who are learning that a wholistic vision of man supplies the only antidote for the unwholeness of man. After centuries of third-person exploration of the powers and structures of the environing universe, we have now entered an era of exploration of the powers and structures of that corresponding universe: the somatic centrum which is the explorer.* [44]

Every scientist, man or woman, is a human being, but the denial of their own wholeness, and the wholeness of others, is a very strong part of the scientific tradition, and the resistance to somatology is strong. Traditions die hard, and it is strange to think that one of the hardest tasks of the human being is to come to believe that he really is the whole, gestalt being that he is! The 1970's may be the decade in which this now established reality may become acceptable to people generally, and even to the scientific community!

44.   Thomas Hanna, "The Project of Somatology," *Journal of Humanistic Psychology,* 13:3–14 (Summer, 1973).

PART TWO

Theories of Counseling
and Psychotherapy

Chapter 3

Theories of Counseling
and Psychotherapy

The moment one begins to peruse the literature on the subject of theories of counseling, he is immediately enmeshed in a semantic maze, and there is a high level of confusion about such ordinary terms as schools, methods, techniques, and theories; personality, learning, and growth; philosophy and theory. In this section I have placed major stress on existential and humanistic counseling on the one hand, behavioral counseling on the other hand, since I see these two theories as having sharply different philosophical connotations about the nature of man and the meaning of life and living. Various other theories will be examined in terms of their relationships to these two major theories. A separate chapter will be devoted to groups and group counseling, since I see these as a particular kind of extension of the various theories of counseling.

It might be pointed out, too, that we are currently in a period of "theory explosion," in which new "theories" appear continually on the counseling stage. Like plays, some catch on and stay around, for at least a while, while others are very short-lived.

It is often difficult to distinguish "kinds" of counseling from "theories" of counseling, and in this chapter I would like to look at various kinds of counseling before discussing theories of counseling, and then presenting my own theory about theories.

KINDS OF COUNSELING[1]

I think of "kinds" of counseling in a more pragmatic, functional sense, whereas "theories" refers to the more theoretical base upon which counselors are supposed to develop their method of operation. This section will examine the more traditional kinds of counseling, and question the extent to which there are kinds of counseling as distinguished from kinds of counselors.

1. One of the first kinds of counseling is that which might be described as involving basically "well" people, as contrasted to the opposite kind, which involves "sick" people. The literature on developmental counseling stresses its concern with well rather than sick people, and it is the opposite of what is referred to as crisis counseling. Those who support this point of view, however, are not always consistent. Shertzer and Peters, for example, refer to developmental counseling as the "enhancement of an already adequately functioning person," but almost immediately add that it is also concerned with those who have problems that interfere with classroom learning.[2] In a similar manner, Zaccaria refers to the preventive and positive approach of developmental guidance, but then, in describing the modern concerns of education, he sees the future as bringing an intensification of "these problems."[3]

Thus it would appear that the developmental counselor, like other counselors, is going to talk with individuals who have problems and concerns and difficulties, even though these individuals are not sick. This would then mean that most of the people who are described as "mentally ill" would fit into this category; since they are not sick in a disease or injury sense, they do not need a hospital in a medical sense, nor do they need medical treatment. They do need help in learning how to be different, in learning how to become the person they want to become. This is a concept being accepted not only by school counselors, but by both the M.D. and the Ph.D. psychotherapists.

Glasser, for example, in what he describes as Reality Therapy, refuses to accept the concept of mental illness, and he feels that the whole development of mental hygiene is stalled because the psychiatric approach stresses mental illness rather than responsibility.[4]

1. Dugald S. Arbuckle, "Kinds of Counseling: Meaningful or Meaningless," *Journal of Counseling Psychology*, 14:219–225 (May, 1967). Copyright 1967 by the American Psychological Association. Reprinted by permission.
2. B. Shertzer and H. J. Peters, *Guidance: Techniques for Individual Appraisal and Development* (New York: Macmillan, 1965), pp. 38–49.
3. J. S. Zaccaria, "Developmental Guidance: A Concept in Transition," *School Counselor*, 13:226–229 (May, 1966).
4. W. Glasser, *Reality Therapy* (New York: Harper and Row, 1965), p. 155.

English, a psychoanalyst, assumes that getting well means taking responsibility for self, and refusing as far as possible to be abused by persons or fate.[5]

Van Kaam's version of psychotherapy from an existential point of view is very similar. He views therapeutic care as being fertile only to the person who wishes to grow, and for this reason the approach to psychotherapy must be entirely different from that of medicine.[6]

Few would question the overt directiveness of Ellis' rational psychotherapy, but he too, departs from the medical model.[7] Hummel has some difficulty in defining what might be called another "kind" of counseling, namely, "ego counseling," but he does see it as being with persons who are relatively free of crippling neurotic defenses.[8]

Thus while medically oriented psychotherapists such as English and Glasser still use the terms "patient" and "hospital," as do psychologically oriented psychotherapists such as Ellis, they, like Van Kaam and Hummel, are all generally talking about well human beings and the learning process. They are not talking about sick people and medical treatment.

2. The word "cognitive" also appears frequently as a means of describing a kind of counseling. Williamson, in discussing the trait-factor theory in counseling, sees counseling as a highly personalized and individualized assistance to the individual in his effort, cognitively, to discover his capabilities and the opportunities that exist in school and in vocations.[9] O'Hara sees vocational counseling in much the same way, when he talks about counseling as a dialogue between relatively well-adjusted people, which presumes enough openness to warrant a dialogue.[10]

On the other hand, in describing the "cognitively flexible" counselor, Sprinthall, Whitely, and Mosher say, "Counseling in this

5. O. S. English, "Changing Techniques in Psychotherapy," *Voices*, 2:91–98 (Fall, 1966).
6. Adrian van Kaam, "Counseling and Psychotherapy from the Viewpoint of Existential Psychology" in Dugald S. Arbuckle (ed.), *Counseling and Psychotherapy: An Overview* (New York: McGraw-Hill, 1967), pp. 45–46.
7. A. Ellis, "Rational-Emotive Psychotherapy" in Dugald S. Arbuckle (ed.), *Counseling and Psychotherapy: An Overview* (New York: McGraw-Hill, 1967), pp. 78–95.
8. R. C. Hummel, "Ego Counseling in Guidance: Concept and Method," *Harvard Educational Review* 32:463–482 (Fall, 1962).
9. E. G. Williamson, "Vocational Counseling: Trait-Factor Theory," in B. Stefflre (ed.), *Theories of Counseling* (New York: McGraw-Hill, 1965), p. 212.
10. Robert P. O'Hara, "Counseling and Vocational Psychology" in Dugald S. Arbuckle (ed.), *Counseling and Psychotherapy: An Overview* (New York: McGraw-Hill, 1967), p. 112.

framework is concerned with both the thoughts and the feelings of the clients"[11] while from a behaviorist point of view, Michael and Meyerson say, "Behaviorally oriented counselors agree that telling people what is wrong and what they 'should' do is an ineffective procedure."[12]

Thinking and feeling, of course, go together, and all counseling has a place for the cognitive. Surely the counselor who in answer to the client's squirming question, "Where is the men's room?" says, "You feel you would like to go to the men's room," is as guilty of questionable behavior as the counselor who says, "You should go out with John because he's more suited for you," when the client asks, "Which guy should I go out with?" If a client can absorb a rational statement, there would seem to be no reason why the counselor or anyone else, assuming that he has a rational answer, should withhold it from him. On the other hand, wisdom is a good deal more than the mere accumulation of knowledge. Wisdom is in and of the human system, whereas knowledge may have little or no relationship to one's day-by-day living. As Kierkegaard put it, "To exist and to know are two very different things."[13]

3. The degree of humanness in counseling would appear to be another measure of the kind of counseling that one might practice. While developmental counseling and behavioral counseling appear to be pretty much the same thing, the behavioral "counselor" would appear to be one who sets up the experiences which will affect the behavior of the individual rather than the one whose own personal involvement with the individual is the principal factor affecting behavior. The developmental counselor, it would appear, retains somewhat more of his humanness than does the behavioral counselor! Blocher, for example, sees the goal of counseling as the formation of an integrated structure of values and ideas, together with a repertory of coping behaviors.[14] Shoben elaborates on what would appear to be a somewhat similar description when he refers to counseling as "a developmental experience in which attempts to solve problems and arrive at decisions are the events out of which, through reflec-

11. N. A. Sprinthall, J. M. Whitely, and R. L. Mosher, "Cognitive Flexibility; A Focus for Research on Counselor Education," *Counselor Education and Supervision* 5:188–197 (Summer, 1966).

12. J. Michael and L. Meyerson, "A Behavioral Approach to Counseling and Guidance" *Harvard Educational Review*, 32:382–403 (Fall, 1962).

13. S. Kierkegaard, *Concluding Unscientific Postscript*, translated by D. F. Swenson and W. Lowrie. (Princeton, N.J.: Princeton University Press, 1941), p. 18.

14. Blocher, *op. cit.*, p. 9.

tion and the process of 'working through,' personal growth takes place."[15]

Krumboltz uses the term "behavioral counseling" only as a reminder that all counseling is designed to affect the behavior of the client, but he puts minimal stress on the counselor as a gestalt human being, and on counseling as the human relationship between two humans, when he says, "As we learn more about what activities can be used to bring about the types of behavior changes that clients request, then we as counselors will be better able to fulfill our professional responsibilities."[16] The same minimal stress of the humanness of man and the human relationship in counseling is seen when Michael and Meyerson state: "The heart of the behavioral approach in counseling is that the environment must be manipulated so as to allow strong reinforcing consequences to become attached to the behavior that is desired."[17] Similarly, while Sprinthall, Whitely, and Mosher agree that the counselor himself is an important dimension in the counseling process, they also state: "While human qualities may indeed be relevant to counseling, the authors' view is that particular counselor behaviors are a more relevant criterion of counselor effectiveness."[18]

Truax, on the other hand, while acceptant of the evidence of the effectiveness of behavior therapies on human behavior, holds that "man is both a whole being and also a collection of habits and behaviors; that his total being can be seen as a product of the interplay between the molar self and the specific acts and habits that fill in the mosaic of daily living."[19]

Thus one could say that as a developmental or behavioral counselor one is interested in and involved in the development of change in the client, who is viewed as a person who is capable of changing, or of being changed by certain experiences. These experiences might, or might not, involve the counselor in a human relationship with the client. Some behaviorists would likely see the counselor as one who might devise a machine that would produce the experience that would in turn create change in the client. In this sense, Skinner and Pavlov could both be called counselors, as could

15. E. J. Shoben, Jr., "The Counseling Experience as Personal Development," *Personnel and Guidance Journal*, 44:224–230 (November, 1965).

16. John D. Krumboltz, "Behavioral Counseling: Rationale and Research," *Personnel and Guidance Journal*, 44:383–387 (January, 1965).

17. J. Michael and L. Meyerson, *op. cit.*

18. N. A. Sprinthall, J. M. Whitely, and R. L. Mosher, *op. cit.*

19. C. B. Truax, "Some Implications of Behavior Therapy for Psychotherapy," *Journal of Counseling Psychology*, 13:160–170 (Summer, 1966).

any behavioral scientist who is interested in creating change in the human being, even though he might never have any human contact with the person who is being changed.

4. The "kinds" of counseling that have probably been with us the longest are those described as "vocational counseling" and "educational counseling." The immediate question, of course, is the extent to which these are discrete kinds of counseling, or should be considered as basically counseling with a vocational or educational bent. In describing what the counselor does in one kind of counseling, Ohlsen says the counselor should listen to the client, help her to look at herself, help her to explore what else she needs to know about herself, help her to make a decision, help her to identify what appeals to her the most.[20] In describing another kind of counseling, Lair states that it centers on the one-to-one relationship, is concerned with change in the individual who wishes to alter behavior that is unsatisfactory to him, and with specific change in the overt behavior of the student in a particular direction.[21] Ohlsen is referring to occupations and jobs and colleges, while Lair is referring to academic and intellectual performance. It seems that they could be just as easily switched so that Ohlsen could be describing academic counseling instead of vocational counseling, while Lair could be describing vocational counseling instead of academic counseling. Actually, they are both primarily describing counseling, and the vocational counselor described by Ohlsen is an individual who possesses more in the way of knowledge and information about jobs and colleges than other counselors. Educational counseling, on the other hand, at least as described by Lair, is very much counseling, since the problems of the underachieving student are overwhelmingly psychological, and can hardly be solved by the counselor's possession of academic information. As a counselor, I could see where I might have to refer a student who came in seeking specific information about jobs and colleges, since I do not have this information, but I would see no such problem with the student who came in because of his unsatisfactory academic and intellectual performance.

5. In the last few years, a rash of books, scores of papers and articles, and a professional journal have appeared on the subject of elementary school counseling, and one might at least assume that this would imply that elementary school counseling was a different kind of counseling from secondary school counseling. This, however, is anything but the case, and one could easily substitute "secondary"

20. Merle M. Ohlsen, "Vocational Counseling for Girls and Women," *Vocational Guidance Quarterly,* 17:124–127 (December, 1968).
21. George Scott Lair, "Educational Counseling: Concern of the School Counselor," *Personnel and Guidance Journal,* 46:858–863 (May, 1968).

for "elementary" in nearly everything that is written on the subject. The primary difference, of course, is that the counselor would be working with younger children rather than older children, and he would be working in a school setting with teachers who differed somewhat from those in a secondary school. Other than this, however, it is fairly clear that the counselor is involved in very much the same professional activity regardless of whether he is operating in an elementary school, a secondary school, or a college.

The preliminary statement, for example, of a joint ACES-ASCA committee on the elementary school counselor came up with the not very revolutionary statement that a counselor should be a member of the staff of each elementary school, and that the three major responsibilities of this counselor should be counseling, consultation, and co-ordination.[22] Numerous papers come forth with what would appear to be rather glaringly obvious statements. Mayer concludes that counseling can and should be the central role of the elementary school counselor.[23] Mayer (in another journal, with Munger) reinforces his earlier conclusion by again concluding that counseling "can and should be the central role of the elementary school counselor."[24] Foster found that five types of educators—elementary school teachers, elementary school administrators, elementary and secondary school counselors, and counselor educators all perceived counseling type activities as the most important function of the elementary school counselor.[25] Nelson concluded that the elementary school counselor is first a counselor with children, and second, a consultant to the adults who affect children.[26] Dinkmeyer comes to similar conclusions when he describes the elementary school counselor's primary functions as counseling, consultation, co-ordination, and the development of in-service training in guidance for classroom teachers.[27] Thus, other than the differences in the specifics of one's occupational task, there would appear to be general agreement that one cannot describe elementary and secondary

22. "The Elementary School Counselor," *Personnel and Guidance Journal,* 44:658–661 (February, 1966).

23. G. Roy Mayer, "An Approach for the Elementary School Counselor: Consultant or Counselor," *School Counselor,* 14:210–214 (March, 1967).

24. G. Roy Mayer and Paul F. Munger, "A Plea for Letting the Elementary School Counselor Counsel," *Counselor Education and Supervision,* 6:341–346 (Summer, 1967).

25. Carl M. Foster, "The Elementary School Counselor: How Perceived," *Counselor Education and Supervision,* 6:102–107 (Winter, 1967).

26. Richard C. Nelson, "The Preparation of Elementary School Counselors: A Model," *Counselor Education and Supervision,* 6:197–200 (Spring, 1967).

27. Don Dinkmeyer, "Elementary School Guidance: Principles and Functions," *The School Counselor,* 16:11–16 (September, 1968).

school counseling as two discrete kinds of counseling. This is reinforced by a study by Danielson from which he concludes that "there was nothing to indicate a distinct elementary school counselor personality."[28]

Thus, in a functional sense at least, I would feel that counseling *is* of a different kind if one tends to stress the "well" concept of clients rather than the "sick" concept of patients, if one operates in a basically cognitive fashion rather than in an affective and emotive manner, and if one stresses the humanness of people rather than the behaviors of individuals. On the other hand, it is difficult to distinguish as discrete kinds of counseling the educational versus the vocational and the elementary versus the secondary.

The satire that is most near the truth is the one that bites hardest. Dunlop has analyzed, tongue in cheek, different types of counseling (as well as the techniques commonly used by each type) and has divided the field into nine categories.[29] Unfortunately, even the most hilarious of his examples are only too familiar. Indeed, some counselors (but not, I hope, many!) may actually get the feeling that they are looking in a mirror when they read them.

The critical question, then, may not be the somewhat meaningless "What kind of counseling do you practice?" but rather "What sort of person are you?" If the goal of the intelligent counselor is to effect change in the client so that the counselor, or the state, or the church, may more easily control and direct and manipulate him, then the counselor's actual practice of counseling may be somewhat different than if his goals are viewed as helping the individual to move toward self-determination and individual freedom. If the intelligent counselor could, with honesty, say to the client, "I have no goals for you, but I hope you will let me be with you so that I may be of some help as you try to formulate and do something about your goals," he would likely function as a counselor in a different manner than if he had a precise goal in mind for the client. On this point, Dreyfus wonders whether therapists are not reinforcing the self-as-object views of man, and whether the personality characteristics of behavior therapists are different than those of the more relationship-centered therapists.[30] The evidence indicates that school administrators are different kinds of people than school coun-

28. Harry A. Danielson, "Personality of Prospective Elementary School Counselors: Implications for Preparation," *Counselor Education and Supervision*, 8:99–103 (Winter, 1969).

29. Richard S. Dunlop, "Letters and Comments," *Personnel and Guidance Journal*, 47:71–77 (September, 1968).

30. See Edward A. Dreyfus, "Humanness: A Therapeutic Variable," *Personnel and Guidance Journal*, 45:573–579 (February, 1967).

selors, and we could assume that it is likely that counselors who are the I-like-to-do-things-to-people type are different from those who are the I-like-to-help-people-to-grow-on-their-own-terms variety. If individual freedoms were suddenly to be drastically reduced in this country, it is interesting to wonder which psychologists and therapists would become the most effective manipulators and controllers working in the service of the new state. It is unlikely that the answer would lie in the kinds of counseling practiced, but rather in the kinds of humans represented by various counselors and therapists.

On the other hand, some counselors might be ineffective in achieving their goals, whatever they might be, because as individuals they are the significant variable, rather than the various techniques or methods which they might be using. Truax hypothesizes that the "high condition" therapists are more effective because they are more potent positive reinforcers, and because they elicit a high degree of positive effect in the patient, while "low condition" therapists are ineffective and produce deteriorative change in patients because they are noxious stimuli who serve primarily as aversive reinforcers.[31]

There would thus seem to be two points of difference which stand out in the discussion of kinds of counseling and kinds of counselors, and both of these have been brought into sharp focus by the increasing stress on behavior therapies.

1. Is the crucial element in counseling the human relationship between the counselor and the client, or does counseling also include anything that might be done to the client to induce change, including certain actions in which the counselor might have no personal involvement with the client? If the latter, it would seem that counseling then becomes meaningless as a term and almost anyone who might be described as a change engineer would be a counselor. As a medical doctor, I might know that anxiety can be lessened by the use of a certain drug, which may be purchased at a drugstore, and I tell this to a patient. As a teacher, I find out that the attention span of children is maintained at a higher level if every hour at least five minutes is given to relaxation and movement. As a war-minded autocrat, I find that people can become more acceptant of war and violence by having it continually portrayed on all the communication media as necessary and desirable. Anyone could obviously add endlessly to this list, but surely such individuals could not be called counselors or psychotherapists. Thus, because the counselor is involved in change, I hope we do not muddy the waters either by insisting he is not involved in change at all, or by saying that everyone

31.   C. B. Truax, *op. cit.*

who is involved in the development of change in others is a counselor. Most "behavior therapies" I would not see as therapies, but rather as means and methods, primarily those of conditioning and reconditioning, of changing behavior. This could be in the direction desired by either the individual concerned, or by others who feel they are more capable, and who also feel that it is ethically more desirable that they determine for the other what his better behavior might be. They are means by which someone does something to another person, or for another person. The human relationship between the doer and those who are the recipients of the action is a minimal factor, and may not even be a factor at all. Dreyfus has classified behavior therapies with medical model therapies because they all stress the importance of techniques and the ministration of some form of specific treatment with but minimal attention to the role of the relationship to the treatment process.[32] It is the particular ministration, it is felt, that produces the change.

2. If, then, we could limit counseling to that experience in which the human relationship between counselor and client is the major aspect of the experience, then the kind of counseling that might be more generically described by the degree of humanness of the counselor and the client is the major factor in the relationship. What the counselor does—his techniques, his methods, his various procedures, would be important only in the sense that they are reflective of the person of the counselor, and of his objectives. The kind of counseling would then be described through the description of the counselor, and the basic question determining the kind of counseling he practices would be his degree of humanness. On the one hand the counselor might see his function, and the purpose of his relationship, in much the same way as the behavioral engineer would, only the significant variable would be the human relationship. His purpose would be to change the individual into some predetermined "better" pattern, and this would likely be in terms of someone else's decision as to what a member of a society should be like. It might be to help to condition a number of individuals to become more interested in being nurses, because society is lacking in qualified nurses; it might be to help individuals to become happier with eating a new kind of food developed from algae from the sea. Its purpose, in effect, would be the dehumanization of the human race, so the humans would become more literally things and objects, and patterns of behavior, with no particular individual rights or individual freedoms or individual choices. Life would become comfortable, but empty. Anxiety, unhappiness, loneliness, hostility—all would be

32.   Edward A. Dreyfus, *op. cit.*

reduced or removed. We would, in other words, no longer be living as *human* beings, but rather as conditioned sets of behaviors.

On the other hand, the counselor might see the purpose of his human relationship as the enhancement of the individual, the development and the flowering of the individual as a free human being, one who is able to live the life of the human; one who does not need certainty, one who does not have to have guarantees of happiness and joy. Man would be the determiner of his direction, and the counselor would be one who would help the client, as a free individual, to accept the responsibility for his own determination of the direction his life might take. It would be a life with risk and with tension, but it would be living. It would be a life of uncertainty, but it would be the life of the free man, responsible in his humanness to himself, and for himself. Such a free man would be capable of caring and being concerned for the other. Such a counselor and such a client could never become the victims of the culture, because they would have accepted their responsibility as makers of the culture. Thus, the degrees of the counselor's humanness, the extent of his dedication to the individual freedom of man, to the dignity and the worth of man—these are possibly the crucial questions which will determine the kind of counselor, and automatically, the kind of counseling, in which we are involved.

THEORIES OF COUNSELING

Table 1 illustrates the somewhat traditional systems of counseling and psychotherapy as described by six authors. These theories fairly accurately reflect theories of counseling up until about the mid-1960's, and more will be said about what happened after that period later on in this section. I have attempted here to show the relationship that each of these descriptions bears to the other, and I refer to the name of the theory or system or school, and the names of the individuals who are associated with it.

Patterson has referred to five basic theories of counseling and psychotherapy:[33]

1. Psychoanalytic. (Patterson, like other authors, tends to distinguish between Freud and "the others" who may be known as psychoanalysts. He refers to Bordin and Alexander, and Adler, Fromm, Horney, Jung, Rank, Sullivan, and French.)

33. C. H. Patterson, *Theories of Counseling and Psychotherapy* (New York: Harper and Row, 1966), pp. 13–487.

2. Existential Psychotherapy. (Major attention is paid to Frankl and his logotherapy, and reference is made to May and van Kaam.)
3. Rational approaches to counseling. (The major theorists referred to are Williamson, Thorne, and Ellis.)
4. Perceptual-Phenomenological approaches to counseling. (Discussed here is Kelly's psychology of personal constructs and counseling, Grinker's Transactional approach, and Rogers' Client-Centered Therapy.)
5. Learning Theory approaches to counseling. (Here Patterson discusses the conditioned reflex therapy of Salter, psychotherapy by reciprocal inhibition of Wolpe, the reinforcement theory and counseling of Dollard and Miller, the reinforcement theory and counseling of the Pepinskys, Rotter's social learning approach and the inference theory approach of Phillips.)

Carkhuff and Berenson also mention five theories of counseling, which they refer to as potential preferred modes of treatment.[34] It is interesting to note how these compare with Patterson's theories:

1. Psychoanalytic, which they describe by the term "the illusive suicide." (Here they discuss Freud, and mention as neo-Freudians, Adler, Fromm, Horney, Jung, Rank, and Sullivan.)
2. The Existential approach, which they describe by the term "man for each other." (The major name mentioned here is May.)
3. The Trait-and-Factor approach, to which they affix the term, "chance, not choice or change." (This is their major departure from Patterson, but I have placed it in the same column as Patterson's "rational," since it is the rational and cognitive approach of the vocational counseling theorists. The names mentioned, too, are those of vocational counseling theorists—Super, Ginzberg, Tiedeman, Roe, Holland, Tyler, and Hoppock.
4. The Client-Centered approach, described as "apparency in search of a person." (The counselor discussed here is Rogers.)
5. The Behavior Modification approaches, or "to act or not to act." (Four of the contributors are those mentioned by Patterson—Dollard and Miller, Wolpe, and Salter, and others are Eysenck, Bandura, and Krasner and Ullmann. Thus it may be noted that four of the "behavior modification" theorists of Carkhuff and Berenson are the "learning" theorists of Patterson.)

Ford and Urban describe ten systems of psychotherapy,[35] but

34. Robert R. Carkhuff and Bernard G. Berenson, *Beyond Counseling and Therapy* (New York: Holt, Rinehart and Winston, 1967), pp. 63–131.
35. Donald H. Ford and Hugh B. Urban, *Systems of Psychotherapy* (New York: Wiley, 1963), p. 712.

six of these are what others have referred to as psychoanalytic, one is existential, one is client-centered, and two are either learning theory or behavior modification. Thus the ten systems may be described as follows:

1. Psychoanalytic. (The six systems described here are the psychoanalysis of Freud, the ego analysis, Adler's subjectivistic system of individual psychology, the will therapy of Rank, the character analysis of Horney, and Sullivan's theory of interpersonal relations.)
2. Existential analysis.
3. Rogers' client-centered psychotherapy.
4. The learning theory psychotherapy of Dollard and Miller and the reciprocal inhibitor psychotherapy (behavior modification) of Wolpe.

It may be noted that there is no equivalent here of the rational approach of Patterson and the trait-and-factor approach of Carkhuff and Berenson.

Blocher describes six models of counseling theory,[36] and these can be fitted into four of Patterson's theories:

1. Psychoanalytic. (While Bordin is used as the author to illustrate this approach, it can be taken without saying that Freud would rank as *the* person. A second model which would fit in this category, according to other authors, is described as the social psychological model, and the theorists referred to are Adler, Fromm, Horney and Sullivan.)
2. The rational-emotive model of Ellis.
3. The client-centered model of Rogers.
4. The behavioral counseling model of Skinner, Meyerson and Michael, and Krumboltz, and the teacher-learner model.

It may be noted here that the major missing theory is the existential.

Holland refers simply to three theories of psychotherapy,[37] but his three, again, can be fitted into four of the five described by Patterson:

1. Psychoanalytic. (Holland divides psychoanalytic theory into two: Freudian and neo-Freudian, the latter being used to incorporate

---

36. Donald H. Blocher, *Developmental Counseling* (New York: Ronald Press, 1966), pp. 25–44.
37. Glen A. Holland, *Fundamentals of Psychotherapy* (New York: Holt, Rinehart and Winston, 1965), pp. 3–34.

TABLE 1. Kinds of Psychotherapy

1. Patterson	2. Carkhuff and Berenson	3. Ford and Urban	4. Blocher	5. Sahakian	6. Holland
1. Psychoanalytic—Bordin, Alexander and Adler, Fromm, Horney, Jung, Rank, Sullivan, French	1. Psychoanalytic—Freud Neo-Freudian—Adler, Fromm, Horney, Rank, Sullivan	1. Psychoanalysis—Freud	1. Psychoanalytic—Bordin	1. Psychoanalytic—Freud	1. Freudian
		2. Ego-Analysts	2. Social-psychological—Adler, Fromm, Horney, Sullivan	2. Analytic psychology—Jung	2. Neo-Freudian—Rank, Adler, Jung, Horney, Sullivan, Fromm, Alexander, Klein, Reich, Rosen, Szasz
		3. Subjective—Adler		3. Individual psychology—Adler	
		4. Will therapy—Rank		4. Humanistic psychoanalysis—Fromm	
		5. Character analysis—Horney		5. Neo-Freudianism: The Sociological School—Horney	
		6. Inter-personal relations—Sullivan		6. Interpersonal theory—Sullivan	
2. Existential—Frankl, May, van Kaam	2. Existential—May	7. Existential analysis		7. Self-actualizationism—Maslow	
				8. Organismic psychology—Goldstein	
				9. Personalistic psychology—Allport	

3. Rational—
   Williamson, Thorne, Ellis

4. Perceptual phenomenological—
   Kelly, Grinker Rogers

5. Learning theory—
   Dollard and Miller, Wolpe, Rotter, Salter, Phillips, Pepinskys, Krasner and Ullmann, Skinner, Michael and Meyerson

3. Trait-and-factor—
   Super, Ginzberg, Tiedeman, Roe, Holland, Tyler, Hoppock

4. Client-centered—
   Rogers

5. Behavior modification—
   Dollard and Miller, Wolpe, Eysenck, Salter, Bandura, Krasner and Ullmann, Reyna

3. Rational-emotive—
   Ellis

4. Client-centered—
   Rogers

5. Teacher Learner

6. Behavioral counseling—
   Skinner, Krumboltz, Michael and Meyerson

8. Client-centered—
   Rogers

9. Learning theory—
   Dollard and Miller

10. Reciprocal inhibition—
    Wolpe

10. Factor theory psychology—
    Cattell

11. Phenomenological—
    Rogers

12. Stimulus-response psychology—
    Dollard and Miller

13. Factor theory psychology—
    Eysenck

14. The Sociometric approach—
    Moreno

15. Stimulus-response psychology—
    Mowrer

3. Psychological psychotherapies—
   Ellis

   Rogers

   Dollard and Miller, Wolpe, Rotter, Salter, Thorne, Bach, Moreno, Johnson, Wolberg, Brammer and Shostrom

Rank, Adler, Jung, Horney, Sullivan, Fromm, Alexander, Klein, Rosen, Reich, and Szasz.)

2. Holland's third theory he refers to as psychological psychotherapies. (This includes, from Patterson's categories 3, 4, and 5, the rational-emotive theory of Ellis, the client-centered theory of Rogers, and the learning theory or behavior modification theories of Dollard and Miller, Rotter, Wolpe, and Salter, plus the work of Thorne, Bach, Moreno, Johnson, Wolberg, and Brammer and Shostrom.)

Again, it may be noted here that the major missing theory is existentialism.

Sahakian has edited a book which contains twenty theories on the psychology of personality.[38] Fifteen of these would appear to fit the five theories of counseling and psychotherapy as described by Patterson. Another author, of course, might obviously make a different selection:

1. Psychoanalytic. (Six theories which would appear to fit this category are described. These are the psychoanalysis of Freud, the analytic psychology of Jung, the individual psychology of Adler, the humanistic psychoanalysis of Fromm, the neo-Freudian sociological school of Horney, and the interpersonal theory of Sullivan.)

2. Existential. (Fitting into this category would appear to be the self-actualization theory of Maslow, the organismic psychology of Goldstein, and the personalistic psychology of Allport.)

3. The factor theory psychology of Cattell would appear to be closely related to the rational or trait-factor theories of counseling.

4. The phenomenological theory of personality of Rogers is another name for the client-centered theory of counseling.

5. The learning theory or behavioral modification theory is represented by the learning theory of personality of Dollard and Miller, the two-factor learning theory of personality of Mowrer, the factor theory psychology of Eysenck, and the sociometric approach to personality of Moreno.

These various theories are, I think, fairly representative of the current concepts regarding theories of counseling and psychotherapy. Several points of interest may be noted in examining the picture that they present:

1. There would appear to be five basic theories of counseling and psychotherapy, with the psychoanalytic holding its place as the

38. William S. Sahakian (ed.), *Psychology of Personality: Readings in Theory* (Chicago: Rand, McNally, 1965).

oldest and the most dominant. The existential might be considered to be the "newest" of the traditional, and it is distinctive in that it is often considered to be more of a philosophy than a psychological theory. It may be noted, too, that "humanistic" does not appear at all.

While behavior theories are often trumpeted as the "new wave," they have actually been around for a long time, as have learning theories. Rational counseling and client-centered counseling have also by now earned the description of "traditional."

2. Learning theories and behavior modification theories overlap to the extent that they are almost synonymous. Nor should this be surprising, since learning produces behavior modification, or looking at it the other way, behavior modification results from learning. Four names that fairly consistently appear as learning theorists or behavior modification theorists are Dollard and Miller, Volpe, and Salter.

3. While the existential and client-centered phenomenological theories have much in common, they are usually described as two different theories. It may be noted that Rogers is very frequently considered to be much the same, both as a person and in his thinking, as Maslow, May and van Kaam.

4. The trait-and-factor theory is predominantly the product of vocational counseling theorists, and it tends to appear most frequently in the vocational counseling literature. It is the rational and cognitive approach which tends to be descriptive of vocational counseling.

5. There is obvious disagreement as to just who, with of course, the exception of Freud, belongs in the psychoanalytic camp. Adler, for example, is described as holding to a theory of neo-Freudian psychoanalysis, of individual psychology, and of social psychology. Ansbacher and Ansbacher suggest that since the position of "neo-Freudians" (that is, stressing social relations rather than biological factors, the self rather than the id and the superego, self-actualization rather than the sex instinct, the present rather than early experiences) is much closer to Adler than to Freud, they should be called neo-Adlerians rather than neo-Freudians.[39] Such individuals would be Alexander, French, Fromm, Fromm-Reichmann, Horney, Kardiner, Mullahy, Sullivan and Thompson. Adler himself says:

> But I never attended one of his lectures, and when this group was to be sworn in to support the Freudian views I was the first

39. Heinz L. Ansbacher and Rowena R. Ansbacher, *The Individual Psychology of Alfred Adler* (New York: Harper and Row, 1956), pp. 16–17.

79

to leave it. No one can deny that I, much more than Freud, have drawn the line sharply between Individual Psychology and psycho-analysis.[40]

6. It is interesting to note that Blocher refers briefly to existentialism as a philosophical base for counseling, but not as a theory of counseling. The word does not even appear in the index of Holland's book.

7. Over the years, at least five theorists have become irrevocably linked to the theories they have created. To most students of counseling and psychotherapy Freud *is* psychoanalysis, Ellis *is* rational-emotive psychotherapy, Rogers *is* client-centered counseling, and Dollard and Miller *are* learning theory. There are many others, of course, but these would seem to stand out, and few would argue that their prominence is not justified.

These, then, are the most traditional theories of counseling and psychotherapy, but in the decade of the 1960's and continuing into the decade of the 1970's they have been vastly expanded, and the divergence between the existential-humanistic on the one hand, and the behavioral-deterministic on the other would appear to have been sharpened. Before looking at this in more detail, let me present my theory about theories.

A THEORY ABOUT THEORIES

Regardless of the differences in viewpoints about counseling and the counseling process, and methodologies and kinds of counseling, and even purpose of counseling, there is general agreement that we are talking about people and their behavior, and the means and the processes by which people change their behavior and their selves. We are also talking, then, about personality and about learning, and any discussions of counseling theories must take into account theories of personality and theories of learning.

Some individuals question the very existence of such a thing as a discrete counseling theory. Chenault, for example, says:

Counseling theory is necessarily more than a relationship of personality theory to counseling practice. Yet these approaches to counseling which are called counseling theory do not fit the existing definitions of theory in the behavioral sciences. With

40. Alfred Adler, *Social Interest: A Challenge to Mankind* (New York: Capricorn Books, 1964), p. 254.

the exception of the Pepinskys' contribution, there is really no such thing as counseling theory.[41]

Landsman feels that "the uses of theory in the orderly world of science as it is generally known seem to bear little relationship to the uses of personality theory as known in counseling and guidance broadly considered."[42] Wolberg sounds equally skeptical when he says, "'Theories' proposed for these many hundreds of types of procedures have all been based on speculation, and speculation is a self-serving business."[43] Carkhuff would probably agree with all of these criticisms, but he proposes what he would consider to be a more valid way of developing a theory of counseling. He says:

We are suggesting then, a central core of dimensions shared by all counseling and therapeutic processes, complemented by a variety of potential "preferred modes of treatment," given a relevant interaction of counselor, client, and contextual variables.[44]

A "theory" is a somewhat intellectualized term for a concept or an idea that has gradually been worked out by an individual on the basis of work and experimentation and reading and meditation. If it is to be considered to be scientific, it has followed the precepts of observe, predict, test. It is tentative, and it may be disproved. It is an intelligent working frame of reference that can be used until something better comes along. Unfortunately, however, most counselors, if they hold to a theory at all, follow one developed by someone else, and few individual counselors follow the "observe, predict, test" concept in the development of their own personal theory.

Everyone pays homage, of course, to the idea that each counselor should develop his own theory of counseling. Indeed, there would be general agreement with Shoben, who talks about counseling theory as a "personal trait"[45] and Boy and Pine, who say that "the role that a counselor assumes is basically an extension of his essence as a person."[46] Peters and Bathory are also referring to a self

41. Joann Chenault, "Counseling Theory: The Problem of Definition," *Personnel and Guidance Journal*, 47:110–114 (October, 1968).
42. Ted Landsman, "Personality Theory and Counseling," in Dugald S. Arbuckle (ed.), *Counseling and Psychotherapy: An Overview* (New York: McGraw-Hill, 1967), pp. 166–170.
43. Lewis R. Wolberg, *Short-Term Psychotherapy* (New York: Grune and Stratton, 1965), p. 68.
44. Robert R. Carkhuff, "Counseling Research, Theory and Practice—1965," *Journal of Counseling Psychology*, 13:467–480 (Winter, 1966).
45. E. J. Shoben, Jr., "The Counselor's Theory as Personality Trait," *Personnel and Guidance Journal*, 40:617–621 (March, 1962).
46. Angelo V. Boy and Gerald J. Pine, *The Counselor in the Schools* (Boston: Houghton Mifflin, 1968), p. 44.

theory when they say, "Theory will only evolve out of working at the problem of conceptualizing and identifying school counseling approaches."[47]

Hipple describes the structural factors to be considered in constructing a personal philosophy and theory of counseling as being the nature of man, learning theory, behavioral change, goals of counseling, role of the counselor, and responsibilities to society.[48]

The development of a so-called "theory for me," however, while it is highly commendable, is also fraught with danger. The development of a theory to defend one's practice is as questionable as the development of a practice on the strength of a theory developed by someone else. Van Kaam is correct when he says, "Theories of personality and psychotherapy should supplement rather than supplant my understanding,"[49] but this assumes, of course, a high level of "understanding." Landsman offers a word of caution to those who develop their own theory of counseling:

> The counselor notes a phenomenon of behavior in his practice, creates a theory, and then proceeds to govern his counseling practices entirely by the untested theory. The bright-eyed devotions of the early orthodox psychoanalysts and the militant nondirective therapists both illustrate this sinful temptation.[50]

As does Brammer:

> There are also what I call the "lazy" eclectics. In their state of inertia they pick and choose among the theories largely what their whimsey dictates is attractive at the moment without regard to depth, consistency, or system.[51]

The acceptance of a theory, in this case a self-determined learning theory to determine the actions of the counselor, is illustrated by O'Hara when he says, "If we teach the student to make increasingly more adequate vocational differentiations and integrations, then our theory says that the result will be more adequate vocational responses."[52] This would seem to put theory as the deter-

47. Herman J. Peters and Michael J. Bathory (eds.), *School Counseling Perspectives and Procedures* (Itasca, Ill.: F. E. Peacock Publishers, 1968), p. 80.
48. John Hipple, "Development of a Personal Philosophy and Theory of Counseling," *School Counselor*, 16:86–89 (November, 1968).
49. Adrian van Kaam, *The Art of Existential Counseling* (Wilkes-Barre, Pa.: Dimension Books, 1966), p. 157.
50. Landsman, *op. cit.*, pp. 166–170.
51. Lawrence M. Brammer, "Teaching Counseling Theory: Some Issues and Points of View," *Counselor Education and Supervision*, 5:120–131 (Spring, 1966).
52. Robert P. O'Hara, "A Theoretical Foundation for the Use of Occupational Information in Guidance," *Personnel and Guidance Journal*, 46:636–640 (March, 1968).

miner of the actions of client and counselor rather than their moment-by-moment experiencing of each other. Much the same
"trapped by the theory" attitude seems to be evinced by Miller when
he says, "A learning theory approach, as described here, clearly
leads to the types of controlling procedures that are practical for the
teacher and parent."[53] These two latter quotes illustrate perfectly
what Corlis and Rabe were talking about when, in describing the
counseling encounter, they said that "its occurrence will be instantly
altered, if not limited by the introduction of a prearranged focus
which in this case is supplied by a personality theory."[54] The fact
that they are referring to a personality theory instead of a learning
theory should not make any difference, unless we believe that personality refers to humans and learning refers to nonhumans!

A number of practicing counselors and therapists were asked
to react to two brief questions about counseling theories, and, as
would be expected, their replies vary greatly.[55] The following is a
summation of their reactions to the first question, which was: Do
you have a counseling theory?

Albert Ellis: "Yes, I do have a theory of counseling. It simply
states that human individuals are not upset by the events that occur
to them (whether these occur in the past or the present) but by their
cognitive evaluations of these events." Ellis feels, for example, that
failing at a certain task is not the problem, but the problem arises
when the individual then calls himself "a Failure with a capital F; a
pretty worthless person." Such feelings, says Ellis, "are dogmas and
categorical imperatives that cannot be substantiated; that cause
enormous harm in terms of feelings of worthlessness, anger, grandi-
osity, and low frustration tolerance; that result in self-fulfilling negative prophecies; and that would better be changed or minimized if
the individual is to lose his disturbed symptoms. They can quickly be
revealed to the client by the therapist; the client can be clearly
taught how to challenge and question them; he can be shown how to
work against them in actual practice in his real life; and he can be
persuaded to relinquish them."

Dana Farnsworth did not react directly to the question, but
enclosed several publications which he felt would describe his basic
ideas about counseling. My assumption from reading these materials
(and from personal knowledge) is that Farnsworth, like many other

53. Adam W. Miller, Jr., "Learning Theory and Vocational Decisions," *Personnel and Guidance Journal*, 47:18–23 (September, 1968).
54. Rahe B. Corlis and Peter Rabe, *Psychotherapy From the Center* (Scranton, Penn.: International Textbook Co., 1969), p. 2.
55. These comments resulted from personal communications from Albert Ellis, Dana Farnsworth, John Krumboltz, John Warkentin, Angelo Boy, and C. H. Patterson.

therapists, thinks more in terms of the philosophy of his operation and the way in which he operates, rather than holding to any particular theory.

C. H. Patterson: "I believe that every counselor's practice is related to his theory of counseling. However, a counselor's practice may not be related to his verbalized theory; that is, the counselor may not be aware of or have verbalized the actual theory upon which he operates. . . . This matter of style, it seems to me, is the source of confusion about theoretical differences, and probably of the idea that every counselor should develop his own individual theory. I have always considered this as an illustration of a lot of the nonsense which many writers and counselor educators propagate. It is logically inconsistent to believe that there are as many different and equally effective theories as there are counselors. . . . In fact, apparently different theories are effective not because of their unique elements, but because in practice they include the basic common elements of all theories."

John Krumboltz: "Whether I have a 'theory' of counseling depends on your definition of the term. I prefer less elegant terms like 'approach' or 'framework.' But if you are writing a book on theories of counseling, I would not want behavioral counseling to be left out just because I avoid the word 'theory.'" Thus it would appear to me that Krumboltz does not have a theory, but he has, rather, a rationale for operating the way he does as a counselor. He has found something, through experimentation, that makes sense to him, and appears to be effective, but he is not bound to anything. I realize, of course, that Krumboltz is often described as a client-centered counselor. I am not sure, however, that Krumboltz is any less "client-centered" than I am, or that I am any less "behavioral" than he is!

John Warkentin: "I was rather taken aback that you seemed to assume that 'everyone has a theory of counseling.' If you mean by this term a general attitude or life style within the therapist, that I certainly do have. If you mean by a theory of counseling some philosophical principle, which brings my thinking and feelings into a coherent systematic unit, I do not have such a theory at all. In fact, when I hear people lecture on such a coherent 'theory of counseling' I sometimes wonder if they could be having delusions of grandeur. Whatever my life style is, it is continually changing. A high compliment I recently got from a 'patient' with whom I worked for three years was to the effect that I had improved more than she had. In other words, a 'theory of counseling' seems worthless to me as a philosophical concept unless it is one which is revised every few weeks."

84

Angelo Boy: "I've reached a conclusion that I do not possess a theory of counseling. What others may call a theory of counseling I prefer to call a process model of the counseling relationship. I cannot theorize how man does, or should, adequately interact with man—I just go ahead and do it in the moment of the interaction. Therefore, counseling is the active extension of a theory; but this theory is not of counseling, but of the self and the nature of man. I begin with my theory regarding myself and the nature of man, and counseling becomes the process whereby I express my theory regarding myself and the nature of man. How a counselor counsels is but an extension of the self, and the self of Angelo Boy is his theory; and Angelo Boy contemplates himself, his nature, and the nature of man, and what he is becomes his theory. What he does in counseling is a process extension of the theory which he himself is. But I cannot call this a theory of counseling—it is a theory of the self which finds expression in the interactive process called counseling.

"When I counsel, then, I am but a process extension of what I am internally. Therefore, there is no theory of counseling (for me); counseling is a process by which I express me, and my attitude toward man."

These reactions are, I think, fairly representative of experienced practicing counselors and therapists, and as much as anything else they seem to demonstrate the personal aspect of counseling. Ellis says he has a theory and Boy says he does not, but Ellis just as much as Boy is indicating his personal belief and his personal mode of operation. In a way, whether one "has a theory" or not seems to be more a matter of semantics than of practice. Some would probably say that Warkentin had an eclectic theory of counseling! It may be noted too, that in terms of the theories that are discussed in the next section, two of these contributors would be described as psychoanalytic, one would be a behaviorist, one a rational-emotive counselor, and two would be client-centered counselors!

I had also asked a second, more pragmatic question, as to what the counselors did and did not do, what they said and did not say, that reflected their personal adherence to a theory. None of the contributors really answered this question, and it was not until I was reading their reactions that it struck me as to why they possibly could not answer the question. It may be that loving and counseling share a great deal in common. If one were to ask, "What did you do when you were in the process of loving that person?" the description of a physical act or a few spoken words would really tell nothing at all about the real depth of the loving that was taking place. So it is in counseling: what one says tells little or nothing about what is really happening, and the depth of the counseling process has to be measured in terms of the mingling and the mixing of the two human beings involved in a relationship with each other.

This also tends to imply an existential-humanistic aspect of all theories of counseling, even though it may be stoutly denied by some. Counselors and therapists, whether they be Freudians, Rogerians, gestaltists, behaviorists or whatnot cannot deny their own humanness, nor can they deny the impact of their own person on the other individual. They may wear their professional mask, and use the language and the behavior that they feel their model demands, but their person still comes through, and the more they try to follow a model, the more likely it is that the image that comes through is that of a non-person person.

What then, can one say in attempting to develop, at least a concept, if not a theory, about counseling theories?

1. There would appear to be little or no evidence to indicate that a conscious and intellectual awareness and understanding of a counseling theory is necessary for effective counseling. Indeed, one might wonder if the possession of a theory, personal or borrowed, is a hindrance more than a help. Possibly one of the reasons for the effectiveness of many lay therapists is that their minds and their emotions are not cluttered up with theories which tell them what they must do! Since they do not have any "our theory tells us" attitude, they do not expect anything, and they might thus fit the description of the phenomenological therapist given by Corlis and Rabe when they say:

> He must allow himself to receive what he might not expect, what he might not understand. He must allow the patient to unfold what no theory can predict with individual accuracy: the unique self.[56]

On the other hand, one might assume that for the secure person, for the whole person, a theory would be no more than a guide, and it would not take precedence over one's knowledge and understanding, it would not take precedence over what one's sense and one's sensitivity indicates is the reality of the situation. A theory should not bind the therapist the way religious dogma all too often controls the intellect of the individual. Possibly the crucial difference is that between the understanding of theories and the way they may relate to one's human involvement, and the dogmatic adherence to a theory, come what may.

I recently had two students, who were under some stress, talk to me about their therapists. The two students did not know each

56.   Rahe B. Corlis and Peter Rabe, op. cit., p. 2.

other, and it happened that the therapist for one of them called himself a "client-centered counselor," while the other described himself as following "the Carkhuff model." Both students could have been talking about the same person, for their complaints were the same. They felt totally frustrated by their inability to get the counselor to come from behind his mask and show himself to be human. Both counselors likely felt that they were being professionally correct, and yet they were being humanly inadequate because they simply could not expose their self to the self of the client. When there is obvious anger in the counselor, the client deserves something better than a "You're getting angry because you feel I'm angry" or "Let's examine the meaning of your question" to his question, "Why are you getting angry at me?" The client, in this case, is the rational one—it is the counselor who is being irrational!

2. One may develop a theory on the basis of long years of practice, marked by observation and prediction and testing. This was the route of Freud and Rogers, and one might say it is for the select few who blaze the unknown pathways. It may be noted too, that Freud was not, and Rogers is not, the slave of his theory. They made it; it did not make them. Far too many counselors, however, at least among those who have a theory, base their practice on their theory, or rather on someone else's theory which they have adopted. It is interesting, too, to note that most of the better-known vocational counseling theorists are not practicing counselors, but the theories they develop are intended for practicing counselors. We thus have theoreticians without a practice, and practitioners without a theory. It may be that the former will be potentially more damaging than the latter.

3. A theory of counseling cannot be isolated from either theories of learning or theories of personality. While there is somewhat of a tendency to relate personality theory more in the direction of the emotive, and learning theory more in the direction of the rational and the cognitive, this need not be so. Indeed, it should not be so, since personality theory and learning theory are both centered in the human individual, and man is a creature of both mind and emotion. It is difficult to see how one can become involved in personality theory and ignore learning theory, and the opposite is equally true. Thus a counseling theory, in a sense, cannot avoid being the child of personality theories and learning theories.

4. One cannot separate a viable counseling theory, at least as it applies to the individual counselor, from the person of the counselor, for the very simple reason that it is the person of the counselor that is involved with the client, not his theory. Thus it is absurd to talk about a counselor "following" a certain counseling theory, un-

less this theory is deeply reflective of his total person. A counseling theory which is functionally meaningful must be reflective of the philosophical base of the counselor.

An exception to this would be those theorists and counselors who view humans in a nonhuman sense. Certainly one might argue that the above does not apply to a counselor who can adequately be replaced by a teaching or learning machine, or to a client who is a predictable set of behaviors. A consistent operational theory could be developed about such a counselor and about such a client. In my experience, however, I have for some reason been unable to find such a client or such a counselor. In fact, the clients and counselors who come closest to being such creatures are those who are most in need of counseling and psychotherapy. They are the ones who are perilously close to having been destroyed by their society. They are not the whole people; they are not the free people. Their humanity has *almost* (but never more than almost) been destroyed. They have become the victims rather than the creators of their culture.

But still, they are *humans,* and a machine which is quite obviously a machine is potentially less damaging in a human relationship than a human being who must operate very much like a machine. It is a sad experience for a client who is struggling to expand his own humanness to come face to face with a counselor who is afraid of his humanness. Such counselors may be found swearing allegiance to every kind of theory of counseling.

5. Any counseling theory must be open to experimentation, modification, and possible proof of error. One of the saddest of sights is to see a supposedly secure, professionally competent counselor vehemently defending a theory. A theory should need no defense. The proof, surely, should be in the pudding. The question is the pragmatic one: For you, does it make functional sense, does it work? This sort of thing is reminiscent of the ancient theologians telling Galileo that they couldn't see what they could see because they weren't supposed to see it. By the time an idea becomes a theory, there should have been a great deal of experimentation, which is why most ideas do not get to the theory stage, but continuing experimentation should be part and parcel of any theory. A theory should be considered as the best we have at the moment, but it should never be taken to mean that it will be the best for all of the tomorrows that follow today.

Chapter 4

Existential-Humanistic Counseling

While I see existential as being basically humanistic, and thus use the term "existential-humanistic," the literature generally refers to these as separate entities. Thus, in this chapter, I will look first at existentialism and its characteristics, then at phenomenology, which I feel is closely related to both existentialism and humanism, and finally at humanistic counseling.

Writing *about* existential counseling is difficult, and, in a sense, quite contradictory, since the basic core of existential counseling is related to the *experiencing* of the *person now*. Here, as elsewhere in the book, I am sharing my personal perception of existential-humanistic counseling, as well as writing about it.

EXISTENTIAL COUNSELING

The philosophy of humanity that is reflected in existentialism can hardly be described as new, and much of our history reflects the struggle between humanistic, idealistic perceptions of people, and the more scientific, pragmatic, everything-can-be-measured-and-predicted picture of mankind. It should be noted, too, that the existential counselor is a practitioner as well as a philosopher, and the views of the existential counselor are not as pessimistic or as nihilistic as those of the early European existential philosophers.

Existentialism is, however, primarily an European product, and it is philosophic rather than psychological in nature. It is true too, that the current psychological involvement in existentialism has

been primarily brought about by practicing counselors and psychotherapists rather than by psychological theoreticians. There are also,
of course, many differences among the major figures of existentialism, such as Sartre, Heidegger, Kierkegaard, Jaspers, and Frankl,
and the range of religion that they represent extends from atheist to
theologian.

Here are a few of Sartre's thoughts on existentialism:

*... by existentialism we mean a doctrine which makes human
life possible, and, in addition, declares that every truth and
every action implies a human setting and a human subjectivity.*[1]

And again:

*Not only is man what he conceives himself to be, but he is also
what he wills himself to be after this thrust toward existence.
... Man is nothing else but what he makes of himself. Such is
the first principle of existentialism.*[2]

And again:

*There can be no other truth to take off from than this: I think,
therefore I exist.*[3]

For Sartre, man is free, man *is* freedom. If we accept the concept that existence does precede essence, then there can be no determinism. Man can be what he will.

The existentialist is antideterministic in that he sees the person as transcending both himself and his culture. May describes existential thought in this way:

Existentialism means centering upon the existing *person; it is
the emphasis on the human being as he is* emerging, becoming.
*... Traditionally in Western culture, existence has been set
over against* essence, *the latter being the emphasis on immuta-
ble principles, truth, logical laws, etc. that are supposed to
stand above any given existence.*[4]

Maslow is speaking about the existential self as he describes
his authentic person as one who

*not only transcends himself in various ways; he also tran-
scends his culture. He resists enculturation. He becomes more*

1. Jean-Paul Sartre, *Existentialism and Human Emotions* (New York: Wisdom Library, 1957), p. 10.
2. *Ibid.*, p. 15.
3. *Ibid.*, p. 36.
4. Rollo May, *Existential Psychology* (New York: Random House, 1961), p. 16.

detached from his culture and his society. He becomes a little more a member of his species and a little less a member of his local group.[5]

Van Kaam describes a basic aspect of existentialism when he says:

Existential psychology . . . insists on the free responsibility and the spontaneous creativity which remain the unique and fundamental characteristics of existence. It retains awareness of the limits of freedom revealed by deterministic psychologies, yet it transcends determinism by its recognition of man's radical freedom.[6]

And again:

The main characteristic of the human existant is that he exists, literally stands out in a world of meaning. Subject and world, self and world are correlatives . . . the counselee is best understood from his personally lived and experienced universe.[7]

Lyons comments that "existentially one always begins within human subjectivity; it is the given framework and source,"[8] and Howland states: "To put it in existential terms, a part of being always consists of 'having been.' 'Having been' is a kind of immortality in that it can never be destroyed or taken away."[9]

The self, the person-in-being as seen by the existentialist, is not one who is subject to empirical prediction and control. Ostow expresses this anti-deterministic concept when he says:

If religion, then, has failed to obtain complete control over human behavior, if its effect is merely one of influence and modulation, it is not because of poor technique, but because of the ultimate independence of the human spirit and the essential autonomy of the instinctual apparatus.[10]

5. *Ibid.*, p. 55.
6. In a statement at an Arden House conference, January, 1963.
7. Adrian van Kaam, "Counseling from the Viewpoint of Existential Psychology," *Harvard Educational Review*, 32:403–415 (Fall, 1962).
8. Joseph Lyons, "The Problem of Existential Inquiry," *Journal of Existential Psychiatry*, 4:142 (Fall, 1963).
9. Elihu S. Howland, "Nostalgia," *Journal of Existential Psychiatry*, 3:197–204 (Fall, 1962).
10. Mortimer Ostow, "The Nature of Religious Controls," *American Psychologist*, 13:571–574 (October, 1958).

As does Frankl:

A real person is not subject to rigid prediction. Existence can neither be reduced to a system or deduced from it.[11]

Freedom is the core of existential thought. This may be expressed as Sartre's consciousness as freedom, Jasper's existence as freedom, Kierkegaard's self as freedom, or Tillich's concept of man as freedom. They are all saying the same thing—that I am free, that where I go and what I do depends on me, not on the forces outside of me or even on the forces which I may have internalized as a part of me. I, and I alone, always have the ultimate choice, and this choice I am free to make. The very fact that one is alive means that he has the potential to be free, but one is never free to live, of course, until he is free to die.

Effectively expressing this point of view is Rogers when he talks of freedom as essentially an inner thing, something that exists in the living person quite aside from any of the outward choice of alternatives which we so often think of as constituting freedom.[12] And Frankl:

. . . everything can be taken from a man but one thing: the last of the human freedoms—to choose one's own attitude in any given set of circumstances.[13]

And Buber:

He who forgets all that is caused and makes decisions out of the depths . . . is a free man, and destiny confronts him as a counterpart of his freedom. It is not his boundary, but his fulfillment.[14]

And May:

No matter how great the forces victimizing the human being, man has the capacity to know that he is being victimized, and thus to influence in some way how he will relate to his fate. There is never lost that kernel of the power to take some stand, to make some decision, no matter how minute.[15]

11. V. E. Frankl, "On Logotherapy and Existential Analysis," *American Journal of Psychoanalysis*, 18:28–37 (No. 1, 1958).
12. Carl R. Rogers, "Learning to Be Free," an unpublished paper.
13. V. E. Frankl, *From Death Camp to Existentialism* (Boston: Beacon Press, 1955), p. 65.
14. M. Buber, *I and Thou* (Edinburgh: T. & T. Clark, 1937), p. 53.
15. Rollo May, *op. cit.*, p. 41.

This movement toward freedom is also the core of the therapeutic process, and May is really describing the process of counseling when he says:

*The patient moves toward freedom and responsibility in his
living as he becomes more conscious of the deterministic experiences of his life. . . . As he becomes more conscious of the
infinite deterministic forces in his life, he becomes more free.
. . . Freedom is thus not the opposite to determinism. Freedom is
the individual's capacity to know that he is the determined one
. . . and thus to throw his weight on the side of one particular
response.*[16]

Although determinism may be a fact of the physical world, it
is man who completes that world, and it is man who makes of the
world whatever reality he may wish it to become. Thus the growth
that occurs in counseling might be considered to be the process, the
experience, and the learning to be free. Rogers refers to the qualities
of a growth-facilitating or freedom-promoting relationship as being:

1. The element of congruence—the therapist being what he is. The
   feelings the therapist is experiencing are available to his awareness, and he is able to live them and be them and communicate
   them if need be.
2. The counselor's warmth and acceptance of what is in the client—
   the counselor's willingness to be whatever feeling is going on in
   him at the moment—the unconditional positive regard.
3. Empathic understanding—the sensing and perceiving of the feelings from the inside, as they seem to the client.[17]

Freedom may not be the opposite of determinism, but one
does not find the concept of freedom in a deterministic society. The
existentialist would feel that the individual may live in a physical
world which is, in a sense, determined, but the human individual, the
existential self, the spirit of man is not bound by any set of determined chains. Man basically *is* free, and any man can come to learn
and to grow and to become the free person he is. This is the purpose
of counseling—to help the individual to loose himself from his deterministic shackles and to come to realize and to see what he has
always had—choice and freedom.

Being free is difficult, and one cannot be free without continually running the risk of losing one's person. The struggle to be free,

16. Rollo May, "Freedom and Responsibility Re-examined," unpublished paper giv-
    en at 1962 APGA Convention, Chicago.
17. Carl R. Rogers, *On Becoming a Person* (Boston: Houghton Mifflin, 1962), pp.
    61–62.

too, is often much more intense and complicated at the inner self-level than is the struggle against overt and obvious forces of oppression. If education results in real understanding, it can widen one's horizon of freedom, and the counselor must be concerned about the extent to which the educational experience helps to free each child.

Although one could hardly be both deterministic and existential, neither can be considered as absolute terms. Skinner might be considered to represent the deterministic end of a continuum, where man would appear to be a nothing, manipulated and controlled for the furtherance of the ends of some faceless and unknown "group," whereas Sartre would represent the other end of the continuum, which would see man as supreme, responsible for his own actions, answerable only to himself. Such a man lives in a world in which things and events have not been determined by him, but the human self is the determiner of the reaction to these events, and the human self will determine the manner and the mode in which man will live and grow and die.

The existential view of man could not accept the concept that the ends might justify the means, since the human person and his world of reality cannot be separate, and they are not tomorrow, but today. Thus, the world of work for the child is a very real world of work. However, it is not something in the vague future; it is today. A "stay-in-school" campaign will seem a little pointless to a child when, from his reality, nothing has changed, either in his view of the world or in its view of him.

Nor would the existentialist help to maintain, for the child, the myth of equality, at least in the sense that every young American child has the same chance. Even worse, of course, is the attendant myth that inequality and difference are synonymous with inferiority. Having a dark skin instead of a white skin, being a male instead of a female, having an IQ of 90 instead of 140, these may be very real outer restrictions, but the existentialist operates with what *is,* and thus, in a very real sense, helps to change what is. Excellence is within the reach of all, but excellence is an inner concept of self, and it is the excellence that is missing in many of our fellows because we have alienated them from us, and we have helped them to come to believe that they are small people. They have not transcended their culture, and their fight against it seems hopeless, because they have become enculturized and entrapped by it.

Choice, too, becomes an inner, relative matter. The child who can be helped to choose really freely to stay in school has immediately removed from himself some of the restrictions and impositions of that school, even though there has been no outer change of either curriculum or teachers. The very fact of choice is freedom, and this immediately changes the outer world around us. Man may live in a determined world, but he is not determined. Choice of a job, after all, in the sense of "I want to be able to choose any job I want" has always been an illusion. It is unfortunate that some American children come to view freedom and choice as "something I can do to someone," rather than as a continuing struggle by one to maintain his integrity and his responsibility. For many children, choice becomes more and more restricted, but the real restriction comes in the sense that they have allowed themselves to come to believe that they are determined victims of a determined world. Freedom and choice have nothing to do with outer restrictions. They are an inner matter, a matter of the self—of the spirit, if you will. The man who kills is usually less free than his victim; the man who hates is less free than the man who loves.

In education, the existential view is being expressed by Mathewson when he says that "in the form of education which emphasizes development of individual potential and adaptability, narrow forms of information acquirement may cease to remain at the center of the educational target,"[18] and by Murphy, who comments that "the teacher must help the learner to believe in his own individuality and his capacity to learn."[19] Vanderberg also points out an existential view in commenting that education is the process of becoming oneself, that freedom is restricted when pupils are treated as objects, and that the authentic teacher thinks only in terms of the interactions of individuals who have achieved different degrees of becoming themselves.[20]

CHARACTERISTICS OF EXISTENTIAL COUNSELING[21]

I would think that there are several crucial characteristics which distinguish existential counseling from other theories or methodologies:

1. The basic issue in the discussion of any "kind" of counseling, including existential counseling, has to do with the nature of

18. Robert H. Mathewson, *Guidance Policy and Practice* (New York: Harper and Row, 1962), p. 374.
19. Gardner Murphy, *Freeing Intelligence Through Teaching* (New York: Harper and Row, 1961), p. 47.
20. D. Vanderberg, "Experimentation in the Anesthetic Society: Existential Education," *Harvard Educational Review*, 32:155–187 (Spring, 1962).
21. Dugald S. Arbuckle, *Counseling Today and Tomorrow* (Washington: American Personnel and Guidance Association, 1972). Copyright 1972 by the American Personnel and Guidance Association. Reprinted by permission.

humanity and the relationship of humans to the culture they have produced. The behavioral and deterministic view sees humans as conditioned sets of behaviors, and their life and living can thus be predicted and controlled, for good or evil. On the other hand, the world of the existential counselor is subjective rather than objective, and humans are streams of consciousness and experiencing, and thus cannot be predicted and measured and controlled.

When Osipow and Walsh describe what they call "facilitative-effective" counseling, I would see this as being very much akin to existential counseling. They say that this viewpoint "has the higher human objective of facilitating normal development and individual creativity. . . . its counseling activities encourage the client to look inward and develop, through verbalized introspection, insights into his behavior that can be used to foster growth." In contrast to this, the "interventionistic-cognitive" counselor focuses "on the development of methods to identify causes of client ineffectiveness, peer performances or discomfort, and toward the elimination of undesired behaviors and the introduction of new and more effective behaviors by means of learning principles."[22]

The existential counselor would also feel that when Maslow refers to humanistic qualities such as boldness, courage, freedom, spontaneity, perspicuity, integration, and self-acceptance,[23] he is talking about qualities that can be developed, by each one of us, from within.

Rogers raises a very pertinent point when he comments:

The issues of personal freedom and personal commitment have become very sharp indeed in a world in which man feels unsupported by a supernatural religion, and experiences keenly the division between his awareness and those elements of his dynamic functioning of which he is unaware.[24]

Hitt described the behavioral model in this way:

Man can be described meaningfully in terms of his behavior; he is predictable; he is an information transmitter; he lives in an objective world; he is rational; he has traits in common with other men; he may be described in absolute terms; his charac-

22. Samuel H. Osipow and Bruce W. Walsh, *Strategies in Counseling for Behavior Change* (New York: Appleton-Century-Crofts, 1970), p. 19.
23. A. H. Maslow, *Toward a Psychology of Being* (Princeton: Van Nostrand, 1962) p. 136.
24. Carl R. Rogers, *Freedom to Learn* (Columbus, Ohio: Charles E. Merrill, 1969), p. 260.

teristics can be studied independently of one another; he is a reality; and he is knowable in scientific terms.[25]

As contrasted with the existential model:

Man can be described meaningfully in terms of his consciousness; he is unpredictable; he is an information generator; he lives in a subjective world; he is irrational; he is unique alongside millions of other unique personalities; he can be described in relative terms; he must be studied in a holistic manner; he is a potentiality; and he is more than we can ever know about him.[26]

Another way of looking at it might be to say that existential counseling views a human as being basically an inner rather than an outer person. Our inner self is our real self, and to a greater or lesser extent our outer behavior reflects the kinds and the degree of our conditioning. The greater the gap between the two, the more artificial our life becomes. Ideally, the *me* that I reflect to *you* should be the phenomenal me with which *I* live. In a very literal sense, the level of the actualization of my self will be minimal if there is a great discrepancy between the me that I present to me, and the me that I present to you. The extent to which you, of course, can be open to receive the me that I am communicating to you is affected by the degree and the kinds of conditioning to which you have been subjected.

Behavioral counseling, too, would appear to consistently separate the culture from the people who have created it, as if somehow the culture, impinging upon, modifying, and controlling human beings, was separate and apart from those human beings. Skinner, in talking about the improvement of culture by people, comments that "the ultimate improvement comes from the environment that makes them wise and compassionate,"[27] but at the same time he says, "The man that man has made is the product of the culture that man has devised."[28] It would seem to me that Skinner is simply saying that the environment, the culture, is people, past and present. Thus when someone agrees, rationally, that he is racially prejudiced, what he is saying is that people, past and present, have taught him to be that way. It would seem that a logical counselor reaction to this would

25. William D. Hitt, "Two Models of Man," *American Psychologist,* 24:651–658 (July, 1969).
26. *Ibid.*
27. B. F. Skinner, "Beyond Freedom and Dignity" *Psychology Today,* 5:37–80 (August, 1971).
28. *Ibid.*

be, "Well, how about you, now? Is this you, is this the way you want to be, and if it isn't what will you do about it?"

Skinner is partially correct when he says that "the individual remains merely a stage in a process that began long before he came into existence and will long outlast him."[29] But the past, nevertheless, is still people, and my life, *for me,* is not "merely" a stage, since it is the only life that I now experience. Thus I must accept responsibility for the degree to which the dogmas of the past shackle me, limit my freedom, and make me blind to the reality of the existence of my self and my fellow humans. All of us can try to come closer to understanding and being open to experiencing who we are, but this continuing struggle is a basic part of our existence. Indeed, it *is* our existence. It is hard to peel off the layers, not only of our own span of living, but also those which have been squeezed into us and onto us over the centuries.

2. It is fairly obvious that another crucial difference between existential counseling and the more behaviorally oriented therapies has to do with this question of objectivity and subjectivity. It is likely, too, that this is one of the reasons for the difficulty in communication, since the existential counselor tends to view the behaviorist in a subjective way, while the behavioral counselor is equally puzzled, and sometimes irked, as he views the existentialist through what he perceives as his objective eyes. It may possibly be like the problems that would arise if a poet and an engineer tried to develop a love affair. They might respect each other, but they would have a very difficult time in getting together, both literally and figuratively!

Barclay is discussing phenomenology, but he is talking about the world of the existential counselor when he says "the world of subjective phenomena and facts, as contrasted with the world of scientific and objective reality."[30] Dreyfus is talking in the same vein when he says, "The counselor must expose himself, and, therefore, cannot maintain the scientific objective attitude of the physical scientist. He cannot view the client as an object to be manipulated, exploited and explored."[31] So too, are Schell and Daubner when they say:

> The realistic counselor should help his client perceive his problem situation as it "really" is and as it appears to others. The phenomenalist counselor cannot do this; instead, he can only

29. *Ibid.*
30. James R. Barclay, *Foundations of Counseling Strategies* (New York: Wiley, 1971), p. 15.
31. Edward Dreyfus, "The Counselor and Existentialism," *Personnel and Guidance Journal,* 43:115–120 (October, 1969).

try to enter the client's subjectivity and to help him deepen and enrich his unique perception of the problem situation.[32]

Kemp discusses this inner subjective world of the self, the *Eigenwelt,* as presupposing self-awareness, self-relatedness, and self-transcendence, possessed only by human beings. He describes this as the potential for grasping what something, such as a snow-topped mountain, a ballet, or a personal relationship, means to us. "In our false attempt to be more scientific, more truthful," he says, "we lose the sense of reality in our experiences."[33]

The existential counselor helps the individual to develop a sharper awareness, a keenness, a sensitivity to what is going on around him and in him. In a way, the senses of such a person become more highly developed—a mountain is more than rock and snow, drenching rain is not just water, a flower is more than a yellow object. Even more important is the sensitivity to all of the ways in which a fellow human tries to communicate with us—sometimes desperately trying to tell us something that so often we do not hear. This is touching the reality of our experience.

A thread here too, is *believing,* and certainly believing is subjective. It is often the object of the scorn, and the amusement, of the scientist who sees himself, and the world, in what he actually *believes* is an objective manner. While he might say that he knows, his moment-by-moment life and living is overwhelmingly affected by what he *believes* he knows. A startling and tragic example of this mistaken impression of the infallibility of supposed knowledge is to be found in a book on Robert S. McNamara and his Vietnam adventure by Trewhitt.[34] McNamara, a brilliant man, had the best that was available in the technology of the day, and he applied it. His predictions were scientifically sound, his analysis logical and correct. He knew, without doubt, what would happen in Vietnam when certain procedures and pressures were applied. But what he knew would happen didn't happen, and I would think that this was because he was too much of an objective man. He discounted the irrationality of human beings, and his own inability to be aware of, let alone control, the multiplicity of variables that are to be found in each human being. The Vietnamese, possibly, were like the British of 1940. They were the only ones who didn't know that they were beaten and that their cause was hopeless! Both *believed* otherwise.

---

32. Edith Schell and Edward Daubner, "Epistemology and School Counseling," *Personnel and Guidance Journal,* 47:506–513 (February, 1969).

33. C. Gratton Kemp, "Existential Counseling," *Counseling Psychologist,* 2:2–30 (Fall, 1971).

34. Henry L. Trewhitt, *McNamara: His Ordeal in the Pentagon* (New York: Harper and Row, 1971).

3. The subjectivity of existential counseling is related to another aspect, namely, the stress on the experiencing of me, now, rather than the talking about me yesterday or tomorrow. Many individuals, sadly, live their lives without ever becoming open to this human experience. If I am a highly defensive person who cannot risk looking at me, I will probably talk about others yesterday or tomorrow; with more certainty I may talk about others today; if I am still more certain I may talk about me yesterday or tomorrow; and if I am beginning to feel capable of taking a risk, if I feel I may be worth something, I may even go beyond talking about me now, but actually experience me, now. This would mesh into the ideas of Kell and Mueller, who say that

> we think it is rare that significant changes in human behavior occur without an effective experience. Change in behavior in regard to other humans, the interpersonal dimension, as we understand it, almost invariably calls for an affective, and often, conflicted experience. [35]

This movement toward the experiencing of self now is not, of course, limited to the period of counseling. Indeed, if the only time this ever took place was during the counseling period, the prognosis would be somewhat dismal. Clients may talk, with much feeling, about changes they have experienced as occurring in them. I can remember a young woman who had been seeing me for a year, coming in, flushed and excited and pleased, sort of bursting out, "You know, I've been having the craziest feelings this week—I'm actually coming together—and I'm scared—because I'm going to let go of what I used to need and had to hang on to, but I don't need it now—but it's real scary letting it go" and her whole person expressed her excitement and her joy and her fear.

Or a man, who had been seeing me for a year and a half, who came in tightlipped and hostile, and almost immediately accused me of betraying him, and thus making it clear that he was originally right in feeling that he could never trust anyone, even me. I did not try to convince him he was wrong, but tried rather to help him to accept the responsibility for either trusting me or not trusting me. He left, still tight-lipped, and I wondered if I would see him again. A letter I received a few days later told me what happened. Halfway home he became so overcome with feeling that he pulled off to the side of the road and wrote me a letter. The letter indicated that his

---

35. Bill L. Kell and William J. Mueller, *Impact and Change: A Study of Counseling Relationships* (New York: Appleton-Century-Crofts, 1966), p. 66.

reaction to me was his last attempt to somehow get back to the way that he was, to use me as the rationale. My putting the responsibility on his shoulders helped him to see what he was doing, and now the past was really gone, and he could move ahead.

Or a session where the client was a woman who had never been able to feel anything but revulsion, even though her head did not agree with her body, toward men, because of several dreadful childhood experiences with men, especially with her father. At the end of the session, as we both stood up, we moved spontaneously toward each other, and held each other tightly. It was tender and it was loving, and it was real. She had experienced something she had never been able to allow herself to experience before.

4. The experiencing of the client cannot take place without the involvement of the counselor as a person, as a fellow human being, and thus the person of the counselor is of crucial importance in existential counseling. Such counselors could hardly be acceptant of behavior modification as described by Madsen and Madsen: ". . . behavior modification means changing behavior by rewarding the kind you want to encourage and ignoring or disapproving the kind you want to discourage. Used with understanding, it is an effective caring way to control behavior in school."[36] Such a "counselor" would sound very much like one of the controllers of the future as perceived by Skinner, who says that "we must delegate the control of the population as a whole to specialists—to police, priests, teachers, therapists, and so on, with their specialized reinforcers and their codified contingencies."[37]

A lesson of history, of course, is that too often, shortly after we have "delegated" control of a part of our lives to others, we awaken to discover that we have lost control. Man can be individually free if he is willing to accept the responsibility that comes with freedom. If he does not, it is clear that the world of controllers described by Skinner will indeed become our fate. If we, for example, continue to spew forth children, as unfortunate accidents of the sex act, into an overpopulated and uncaring world; if we continue to blindly pollute and destroy the environment that is part of our life; if we eat up our limited natural resources as if they would continue forever; if we accept the horrors of war as one of those things that cannot be avoided—then indeed, we will soon be in the hands of the controllers. We will continue to exist, but we will not live. But we do have the choice. We can live the life of individual freedom if we are

36. Clifford K. Madsen and Charles H. Madsen, Jr., "What Is Behavior Modification?" *Instructor,* 8:44–48 (October, 1971).

37. B. F. Skinner, *op. cit.*

capable of accepting it. Skinner feels that homo sapiens is not capable of accepting this responsibility. I do. It's as simple as that.

Krumboltz and Thoresen are, of course, correct when they say that behavioral counselors are human beings like any other counselors, and they are equally concerned about the welfare of the client.[38] Nonetheless, the behavioral counselor does tend to stress method and techniques over the person, and he feels free to use any techniques which will achieve the desired behavioral goals. As Krumboltz and Thoresen say, "If one technique does not work, he tries something else."[39] There is not here the personal exposure and involvement of the counselor with the client such as that implied by Jourard when, in talking about clients, he says that

> they have become so estranged from their real selves that they are incapable of making these known to their associates in life. I don't see how we can reacquaint our patients with their real selves by striving to subject them to subtle manipulation.[40]

In some ways, I would think of the behavioral counselor or the behavioral engineer as being somewhat like a surgeon. He can have a tremendous impact on us—indeed, he can be the determiner of whether we live or die—but he need have no personal contact with us, since he is concerned only with our behavior, just as the surgeon is concerned only with the physical body. Human intimacy is difficult and complicated enough with anyone, but certainly one who controls us is hardly one with whom we can comfortably and honestly become intimate. We do not sleep easily with those who hold our destiny in their hands.

The existential counselor, on the other hand, is intimately involved in a personal human experience with another person. It is essential that such a counselor have a clear understanding of the meaning of this human involvement, since intimacy is usually initiated for self-satisfaction, rather than for the satisfaction of the other. If I am to become intimately involved with a client it behooves me, for the sake of the client as well as for my own sake, to have a clear understanding of just why I am doing what I am doing.

Intimacy also implies that the counselor is experienced in life and living, and not just a personally removed scholar of life and living. There are confrontations in existential counseling—verbal, physical, personal. In a very literal sense, there will be a transference

38. John D. Krumboltz and Carl E. Thoresen, *Behavioral Counseling* (New York: Holt, Rinehart and Winston, 1969), p. 3.
39. *Ibid.*
40. Sidney Jourard, *The Transparent Self* (Princeton, N.J.: Van Nostrand, 1964), p. 74.

of feelings from the client to the counselor and from the counselor to the client. These feelings are part of the humanness of the counselor and the client, and they are faced and shared. They are not analyzed to determine their real meaning by the personally aloof expert, as in the more traditional psychoanalysis, nor are they considered to be a form of resistance to be worked out under the direction of the therapist.

The human involvement of the existential counselor as a person also means that he must share some of the responsibility for what happens. It would seem inevitable that the existential counselor, possibly more than any other kind of counselor, would serve as a model of a human being for the client. This, needless to say, is a very grave responsibility, but it should be faced and accepted as a reality of existential counseling.

PHENOMENOLOGY

Phenomenology is mentioned here because, from my phenomenological frame of reference, its implications are much more existential than they are behavioral and deterministic. Its stress on the immediate experience, and the phenomenological reality as being what I see and interpret that experience to mean, is surely existential. On the other hand, Barclay sees a difference when he says that "in phenomenology, meaning is prior to, or at least embodied in the nature of being, existentialism is a philosophy that focuses on experiences and experiencing."[41]

But phenomenology and existentialism both stress the inner subjective world of the person. Reality is what I perceive and experience rather than what the scientifically objective observer might diagnose it as being. Laing, as he wonders about who is really "mad" in our society, is stressing this inner world of reality.[42] Our immediate experiencing, our existence, this is what is stressed as being our existential reality.

Phenomenological psychology is by no means new, and in a way it grew up with psychology. Descartes, in the early seventeenth century, was probably the first phenomenological psychologist, and his approach was simply to study the mind through the immediate experience as it appears at the conscious level. This was, of course, long before the unconscious became postulated as the major aspect

41. James R. Barclay, op. cit., p. 329.
42. R. D. Laing, The Politics of Experience (New York: Ballantine Books, 1967).

of the mind, and the maker of human behavior. A century later, in Ireland, Berkeley was arguing much the same way—that is, that perception is reality, that what we perceive is real. Many consider Husserl, the German philosopher, to be the one who developed the concept of phenomenology.

In more recent times, Rogers in his 1942 book, *Counseling and Psychotherapy*, was describing a phenomenological approach to counseling. In a 1949 book, *Individual Behavior*, Snygg and Combs gave a detailed presentation of the phenomenological approach. In a later, revised edition, they refer to the phenomenological approach as seeking

> to understand the behavior of the individual from his own point of view. It attempts to observe people, not as they seem to outsiders, but as they seem to themselves.[43]

Combs and Snygg would also appear to be deterministic in their phenomenological approach to human behavior, although their means of determinism would not be the same as those of empiricist Skinner or therapist Freud. They say, ". . . let each one of us look at his behavior as we actually see it at the moment we are behaving. At once, we find lawfulness and determinism."[44] And again, "The concept of complete determinism of behavior by the perceptual field is our basic postulate. . . . All behavior . . . is completely determined by, and pertinent to, the perceptual field of the behaving organism."[45]

However, although phenomenologists Combs and Snygg would apparently feel that what one does, what one sees, what one chooses, and where one goes—in fact all human behavior—are determined by the phenomenal or perceptual field, they would not likely say yes to the question raised by Levine and Kantor, who ask: "Is man only a hapless and hopeless organism, a servant to his surroundings and a prisoner of his passions?"[46] They do say, however, that man is "neither so completely responsible for his behavior as the first view . . . nor, on the other hand so willy-nilly at the mercy of his environment as the second. . . . He is part controlled by and in part controlling of his destiny."[47] In this regard they agree with Shoben, who is critical of what he feels to be an oversimplification of

43. Arthur W. Combs and Donald Snygg, *Individual Behavior* (revised) (New York: Harper and Row, 1959), p. 17.

44. *Ibid.*, p. 17.

45. *Ibid.*, p. 20.

46. L. S. Levine and R. E. Kantor, "Psychological Effectiveness and Imposed Social Position," *Personnel and Guidance Journal*, 40:418–425 (January, 1962).

47. Combs and Snygg, *op. cit.*, p. 310.

determinism into a fatalism of events and a neglect of the self-determining quality of human character.[48]

One can be phenomenological in his approach and still be deterministic, whereas one cannot be deterministic and existentialist. There would seem, however, to be little difference between the concept of the phenomenal self and that of the existentialist self, since both operate within the perceptual field. Combs indicates his own feeling of the primacy of the *self* over the *field*, which is, of course, the opposite of the deterministic point of view, when he says that "the perceptual field is usually organized with reference to the behaver's own phenomenal self," and that "the phenomenal self is both product of the individual's experience and product of whatever new experience he is capable of."[49] The degree of determinism, however, depends on the primacy of the field over the self. If one feels that one's actions are determined by the phenomenal field, of course, he has no choice, and he can hardly be held "responsible" for his actions. Combs would seem to at least be somewhat acceptant of this deterministic concept when he describes the term "conflict" as

> *a term of external description. It is an outsider's description of what he observes. The behaver himself does not experience conflict. He experiences threat to self maintenance from one or more differentiations of his self which he is unable to accept at that moment . . . may . . . even be described by the individual as "conflict." In so doing, however, he is making an external observation of his behavior just as any outsider would.*[50]

May apparently feels no necessity of a phenomenological concept also being deterministic and thinks of phenomenology, the first stage in the existential psychotherapeutic movement, as being the endeavor to take the phenomena as given.[51] Nor does Rogers, who sees a goal of human development:

> *as being a* basic congruence *between the phenomenal field of experience and the conceptual structure of the self . . . the establishment of an individualized value system having considerable identity with the value system of any other well adjusted member of the human race.*[52]

48. E. J. Shoben, "New Frontiers in Theory," *Personnel and Guidance Journal* 32:80–83 (October, 1953).

49. Combs and Snygg, *op. cit.*, p. 146.

50. *Ibid.*, p. 185.

51. Rollo May, *Existential Psychology* (New York: Random House, 1961), p. 26.

52. Carl R. Rogers, *Client-Centered Therapy* (Boston: Houghton Mifflin, 1951), p. 532.

Again, however, it is important to note that Rogers's "unconditional acceptance" is not dependent on the "considerable identity" of the value system of the self with the value system of some other "well adjusted" members of the human race. This *may* or *may not* happen, but it is the self, the transcendent self, the self-in-being, that is the determiner of the congruence.

Thus we might even say that it may be that an acceptance of the phenomenological field theory of human behavior might make it easier to see determinism as the fate of mankind; yet, on the other hand, the existentialist accepts the phenomenological concept without in any manner feeling that this means the dominance of the field in which the self operates over the self. In fact, one could hardly hold to an existential concept without being acceptant of the basic phenomenological approach to reality and to the self.

HUMANISM AND COUNSELING

One might well assume that all counseling, since it is concerned with humans and their well-being, would be "humanistic." But when the reality of a human is what he is observed to be by others, with no consideration given to how he is perceived to be by himself, then counseling cannot be considered to be humanistic. Humanism stresses the phenomenological self, and thus existential and client-centered counseling mesh closely with humanistic psychology. While any counselor might correctly describe himself to be humanistic, the theoretical models of existential and client-centered counseling are those which fit most closely the perception of humans in humanistic psychology. I refer to "existential-humanistic" to stress the humanistic aspect of my existential viewpoint.

In psychological circles, humanism is often equated with a nonscholarly, anti-intellectual stance. Some psychologists scorn humanistic psychology as a sort of refuge for those psychologists who have nothing to contribute in the more rigorous and demanding world of the clinic or the research laboratory or the halls of academe. To be professionally respectable, it would almost seem that one must avoid being called a humanist, and must never even be found associating with such people.

In public circles, humanism is even more onerous. Anyone espousing humanism is suspect of being antireligious, anti-God, and anti-country.

Politically, humanists are assigned far to the left. They are seen, at best, as socialists, but more likely as Communists, Marxists, or members of some revolutionary organization.

Religiously, humanism is related with the more open, nondogmatic religious groups, with noninstitutional religion, or with those individuals who have left the theological fold. By professional psychologists, and by the public generally, humanistic psychology is considered to be, at best, offbeat, personally suspect, and intellectually indefensible.

One extreme produces another, and humanistic psychology, as a protest against the nonhumanness of psychology yesterday and today, has its share of quackery and extremism. There are those "humanist psychologists" who would appear to have a total distrust and contempt for anything intellectual. Thinking is taboo, and it is not a part of what one does to learn how to live the good life. They too, however, ignore the reality of the integration of the experiential and the cognitive in the human being. For them, one only feels. For the extremists on the other side, one only thinks.

The fact that the experiential and the cognitive, the heart and the head, feeling and thinking have been placed in an either-or position is in itself a most anti-intellectual set. It is, in a way, an experiential expression of human feeling rather than a cognitive product of rational thinking. No human being can think without feeling, nor can he feel without thinking. We are all gestalt beings and, like it or not, we do consist of an integrated whole. As in society, of course, we are individually involved in a constant battle to segregate the parts of the integrated whole.

This at-point-of-conception integration is immediately affected by our cultural conditioning. Children soon begin to show differences in the extent to which their feeling and their thinking function as an integrated whole. By the time one has spent many years in our institutional organizations, such as the home, the church, and the school, the balance has become one-sided. While the culture may consider both feelings and the intellect as suspect, there is generally the suppression of the feelings to a much greater extent than there is a suppression of thinking. One might say with some justification that there is not too much in the way of the encouragement of the feelings. Schools do not too often ask, "What do you think about that?" but they consider a question such as "What do you feel about that?" as having no place in a school. The school may be a place for the development of the intellect, but many would say it certainly is not a place for the development of the person! Thus, the child who comes to school soon learns that he is really a head, supported by several useful but not very important appendages.

Yet, one might argue that the very suppression of the experiential is in itself an experiential act. Much feeling obviously goes into any act of suppression. The feelings remain operational, even though they may be suppressed and unconscious. The fact that my feelings do not show outwardly does not mean that I am not being affected by them. At a more surface, conscious level, I might know that I am frightened, even though I can control my feelings of fear so that there is no display of fear. At a deeper level, when the likelihood of my immediate demise is good, I may be able to say, with conscious honesty, "I am not afraid to die." Feelings that would interfere with my being able to feel and say that I am not afraid to die have been relegated to a back room somewhere in my mind, and replaced by "It is an honor and good and courageous to die," but feelings—the old, and possibly more honest, as well as the new—are all still operational as I present a picture, to myself as well as to others, of the calm, cool, fearless individual, ready to die if need be, with no betrayal by emotions which do not fit my picture of such an individual.

So, too, the person who is professionally known as a scholar, because of his intellectual production, feels as well as thinks. The unwritten product of Skinner and Ellis is generally considered to be more cognitive and less experiential than the product of, say, Rogers and May. But whatever the product of the four men has been, it is a product of their thinking as well as their feelings. While Ellis stresses the rational in his rational-emotive therapy, his views on the supremacy of the intellect over the feelings are very much a product of his own feelings as well as his thinking. Skinner, too, both feels and believes, as well as thinks about the behavioral status of the animal known as man. Indeed, if we are to be intellectually honest, we should never say, "I think that . . ." or "I feel that . . ." What we should say is what really is happening, namely, "I feel and think that . . ."

I can remember Skinner, at a dinner conversation, making a comment about the behavior of another individual (who was not with the group) that he obviously considered to be normal and natural and acceptable. He delivered the comment with the degree of feeling that he might have evinced saying, "It has been quite a cold day." Another person at the table, however, reacted with some display of feeling to this statement, obviously regarding the behavior as unusual and somewhat immoral. The content was the same, but the feeling reaction was quite different, and therefore, the meaning was different.

Beyond Freedom and Dignity was the product of a human being with a brilliant mind, but with a mind nonetheless affected by feelings. In this sense, it was no different from *Love and Will*. B. F.

Skinner and Rollo May both think and feel, no matter how much they may stress one or the other.

In our society, however, and in the institutions which reflect it, the stress is on the development of our intellect rather than our awareness. For practically all of us, our awareness and our sensitivity—to ourself, to others, and to the environment that is part of us— is underdeveloped. For some, of course, one could correctly say that it is quite obvious that the intellect has hardly reached a high level of development. Scientific thinking reasonably enough demands a rigorous mind. But science, over the years, has done little to differentiate between humans and things, people and objects, the physiology and the psyche. Thus, the rigorous scholarly examination of people is an examination of humans by nonhumans with skills and methodologies adapted to the measurement of nonhumans. *Thinking about* is the scholarly and acceptable way, while *feeling with* is subjective and unacceptable.

Students of psychology are disciplined to know about feeling, but not to feel about knowing. Man, in the mind of science, is an inanimate object, not different from the clothing that covers his back. Scholars, even more than the general public, are upset by the suggestion that there may be something beyond what we do know or ever will know. Witches and ghosts and seeing beyond the now or traveling in someone else's body are hardly subject to rigorous statistical treatment. They are not considered by psychologists to be serious subjects for scientific investigation because they do not lend themselves to objective study.

I cannot learn about myself and about others unless I am open to myself and to others, and being open means being open to my feelings and to my thinking. For example, I may learn "about," but I cannot learn the meaning *of* love by reading books *about* love, or by learning forty-seven positions for sexual intercourse or by thinking in celibate isolation on a mountaintop. Nor can I learn the meaning of love by performing the sex act, or frolicking naked with others, or by squatting, semiconscious, in the lotus position for two days, or by gazing fixedly at various parts of my, or others', anatomy.

Nor will any of these actions result in my learning the gestalt meaning of anxiety or fear or loneliness or anger or despair. I can learn about, but I cannot learn humanness without (a) some experiential involvement with humans and their behavior, (b) being open enough to allow what is happening to sift through me, (c) thinking and questioning and wondering about what is happening, and (d) adding knowledge to complete the gestalt whole.

Experiencing, as an isolated "high," is cathartic, but seldom therapeutic. The confessional of the Catholic church was a good catharsis for the faithful, but I know of no evidence to indicate that it did much to change human behavior. We must think about how we are feeling and feel our thinking if behavioral change is to take place.

Feeling, of course, especially feeling me about me, me about others, and others about me, is potentially much more risky than thinking. Our head is more capable of rationalizing than is our heart. Possibly this is why we are so capable in our objective world of things, like the technology that allows us to get to the moon, and the knowledge that allows us to do remarkable things with the human physiology. Yet, on ordinary little things that are obviously totally irrational and senseless, and should, therefore, be practiced only by idiots, we do very poorly. We continue to have war, and poverty, and racial/religious/sexual prejudice, and drugs. Indeed, practically all of our human woes today are not because we do not know, not because we lack the requisite knowledge. We cannot use what we know because the psychology of learning has overwhelmingly insisted that humans are not human. The experiential side of learning-growth, development, self-actualization has been almost totally ignored. Thus, we stagger toward human oblivion, loaded with knowledge, the misuse of which may yet kill all of us. The cry of the humanist psychologist is to let us try, somehow, as possibly a last-ditch effort, to get the humanness back to humans before the time has passed.

While humanism is considered to be anti-intellectual, I would like to note a few examples of the highly irrational behavior that is practiced by intelligent, thinking people who are considered to be the best products of our system:

1. The irrational stress on what is considered to be rationality and scholarliness is evident in most professional psychological publications. Editors pay homage to a paper they consider to be "scholarly," which usually is a bloodless, nonhuman statistical view of research. Often this is on the most minute of topics, buttressed by footnotes and references. A controlled statistical study on the effect on clients of counselors crossing the left leg over the right, instead of the right over the left, would probably take precedence over a piece by Laing on "Why I Think Counselors Are Crazy" or Carl Rogers writing on "Meditations on B. F. Skinner." These would be devoid of statistics and footnotes, and they would reflect the authors' thinking and feeling. Such subjectivity is always highly suspect in any scholarly psychological journal.

There is a place, of course, for empirical research in the study of man and his behavior. But too often such research seems to ignore the reality of homo sapiens. Indeed, it usually insists that human beings fit their research on human beings into an already-established narrow pattern.

Many of the most interesting, challenging, creative papers that I have read either were rejected for publication, or were not submitted for publication because it was obvious that they would be rejected. The author, after all, is very often much more experienced and scholarly in what he writes about than are those who reject his production. In an ironic sense, the professional subjectivity and bias of editors and members of editorial boards take precedence over the professional subjectivity of the author. And appointments to membership on editorial boards is, as anyone who has been involved in national organizations knows, more a matter of professional politics than it is of professional competency.

Not uncommon statements in rejection of a paper are "I don't agree with him" or "I think this word is a better choice than the one that he used" or "I have evidence which is contradictory to his" or "I don't like what he says" All of these, surely, could hardly be called scholarly reasons for rejection. I have read them all!

In many ways, writing for publication in professional journals becomes a sort of sad game of trying to guess what the particular bias of the editorial board might be. This is what determines what is published in a journal rather than the quality or worthiness of what is presented. In many ways writing a paper for professional publication is like writing a dissertation. One writes to fit an already established norm, and to please those who established it, rather than developing a creative, individual product of experiencing and thinking. It becomes a sort of "democratic" process in which the majority determines what is acceptable and what is not.

Much of the content of many exciting and challenging books would never be published in professional psychological journals. They reflect the thinking and feeling and experiencing and questioning of human beings. They are far more scholarly presentations of man and his behavior than the dryasdust treatises that grace the pages of the most professional journals.

Even the *kind* of writing becomes stereotyped. Humor or any other personal display is frowned upon. The person of the author must be totally removed from that about which he writes. If Freud were to return from the dead with a piece entitled "What It's Like Over There," it would likely be rejected as being too subjective. Nor can an author ever use a personal pronoun such as "I" or "we." It must be "the author" or "the writer." Even when I quote myself, it is considered better form to say, "In 1968 Arbuckle wrote that . . . " rather than "In 1968 I . . . "

111

Certain words, too, are taboo. A significant proportion of the youthful population knows only one word to describe the sex act. I, for example, was fifteen years of age before I discovered that there were other words that meant the same thing as "fuck." It was usually used not as a "dirty" word, but simply a word that was used to describe a particular function. But even if we are writing about the verbalizations of a population for whom "fuck" is a common ordinary word, we must substitute some other term or write, "you f——ing rat!" Obviously a word is "dirty" to a certain group of people only because they have put it in that category, but they could be more open to the fact that many other people do not look at it in the same way. Surely it is the intent of the word that makes it cruel and obscene rather than the word per se. "I enjoy fucking" would seem to be a reasonable statement coming from most healthy people, while "People like you are all stupid" is an insulting phrase.

2. Professional conventions, where supposedly scholarly activities take place, are another example of idiotic happenings. Hundreds of people sit in hot, stuffy rooms to hear, or give the impression of hearing, someone read a paper that is frequently a doctoral dissertation and that, from this point on, will mercifully be heard no more. They internalize only the odd sentence, and as they stumble out they buy, or are given, the paper that was read. Sometimes they come to hear a "name," but most names in psychology are not too good on the public platform. When an incomprehensible paper is combined with a droning monotone the result is a stupefied audience who will later speak of having heard Dr. Jondidtus, although they can't even remember the subject of his talk.

For many, the most meaningful intellectual part of a convention is an evening in someone's room with interesting people who argue and debate about issues and ideas and happenings. This is one place where people revert back to their human state and, possibly, learn something.

Those programs where there is to be a discussion or some other involvement of the audience (not just the usual "Are there any questions?" when the time is up) attract conventioneers like a water hole does a desert traveler. But they are few in number, and true scholars consider them to be unworthy of visiting, other than to observe how dreadfully unintellectual they are.

3. The school, of course, where children are supposed to learn, is probably our greatest example of irrationality masked under the guise of education. There is little learning in formal education because formal education is in almost every way the antithesis of learning. It punishes creativity and originality (straight A students are seldom among the most creative) and it stresses memorizing the

product of others' thinking rather than developing the ability of each individual to think. It rarely starts with *who* the student is, *where* he is, *who* he wants to be and *where* he wants to go, but rather imposes its version of where to start, what to do, how to do it, and where to go. Counter to all laws of learning, it is compulsory and repressive. It almost invariably stands for and represents yesterday, very rarely today and tomorrow. Worst of all, many of the people who make up the school staff are more often than not simply human machines who pass on the knowledge that has been created by someone else. The school is not an exciting laboratory for the creation and discussion of the new by involved and motivated human beings, but rather a processing center, tended by technicians. Most of what happens in the school, as far as the formal education part of it is concerned, could be done more effectively and accurately by machines. It would seem reasonable to assume that machines will soon replace the non-human humans unless they somehow regain their humanity.

The school's major function would sometimes appear to be custodial, and one might almost believe that children are very dangerous creatures who must be tightly controlled lest they wreak havoc on our established institutions of civilization. Just how such dangerous creatures are going to be prevented from wrecking our society when it is their turn to control it, is never quite made clear. We do a splendid job in the school of helping children to learn irresponsibility by treating them as irresponsible creatures. We stoutly refuse to consider them as young, but nonetheless responsible, human beings who need help in expanding their level of responsibility by being given experiences in responsibility.

In half a century our society has moved ahead thousands of years on an anthropological scale. But the school has barely kept pace with an ordinary sixty-five years. Indeed, it has hardly moved at all. If one looks at life and living in 1910, and compares it with today, the change is fantastic. If the person of 1910 were suddenly transported into today, it is doubtful if he could long stand the show and successfully readjust to a totally new world. If, however, he happened to be transported into a school, the shock would be minimal, since any changes would be minor. The man of 1910 would likely feel quite comfortable in the school of 1972!

The research, past and present, on the effects of the school on the development of the individual, is depressing. It tends to indicate that counter to the great American dream, the school, other than giving to a person a piece of paper which may open some doors, has little effect on what happens to the individual. We triple teachers' salaries, cut the size of classes, have esoteric school buildings and furniture and overwhelmingly expensive gadgets, compensatory programs, integration, busing—but none of it has much effect. True, our modern teachers have more years of formal education, but considering what this is, it probably makes them even less effective as human beings capable of being involved in learning experiences with other human beings.

The bits and pieces of formal education have changed little. We still have examinations, given by teachers and professors who could not likely pass their own examinations, let alone those of their colleagues. I can remember an ego-deflating experience in which my name was one of five responses on a multiple-choice question. I took the exam, but did not think that I was the right answer to the question. It turned out that I *was* the right answer, and when I mildly protested to the test-makers, they said they knew better than I did. On another occasion, a student dared me to take a final examination that he had from a professor who strictly followed the textbook. I took the exam, and my failure was a blow, since the textbook being used was one that I had written!

And, of course, school is a place where you either pass or fail, with various levels of passing but only one level of failing. I have never heard a rationally defensible reason why a student of any age must ever "fail." If a child cannot yet read at a certain level at a certain time, why not accept the simple reality that the child may need more time and more help and more understanding to get to a certain level of reading? If I do not do too well in one ski class, I will try one where the technique is not so advanced, but I do not get an "F" stamped on my forehead. Why, then, should I have to run the risk of "failing" if I attempt to learn how to read or master the intricacies of certain chemical compounds?

Equally irrational is the time pressure in school. Even while we preach individual differences and respect for the individuality and integrity of the child, the student must learn something within a certain period of time or he has failed. Is it not more rational to see school as a happy place where individuals, young and old, are helped to learn what they want to learn at their own pace? And why shouldn't students be able to leave school for a while if they wish to sample non-school life, and return when and if they wish, without any stigma, to begin again where they are at, not where they were at?

Nor do we believe in individual differences for teachers, and most teachers react violently to the mildest of suggestions that they measure and evaluate children every day, and yet they insist that it is impossible to determine what makes a good teacher. At the same time, they insist that every teacher be considered to be a good teacher, and be paid accordingly. Thus, teachers apparently consider both children and teachers all to come from the same mold, one quite undistinguishable from the other.

The five-day week, 180 school days a year, with numerous holidays, is, considered rationally, quite ridiculous. It is a throwback to our pioneer days when few children got beyond grade five, because the outside world needed them and provided them with a much better education than they could get in school. The latter still applies, but the former, unfortunately, is no longer the case. At the turn of the century, the ninety percent who dropped out of school had somewhere to drop to! The act of dropping out of a meaningless school experience is quite rational. It is what we do to the children who have had the good sense to drop out that is irrational and inhuman.

Humanism, then, views mankind very much in an existential manner, and it is phenomenological in the sense that the phenomenological world of the individual is the world of reality for the individual, but it is not phenomenological in a deterministic way. This forward-looking, existential-humanistic concept of human beings as free, self-evolving, self-actualizing *beings* would appear to me to be the best base on which to build the practice of counseling and psychotherapy.

The basic human problem is never the overt issue, but the individual concept of the degree to which that issue controls and dominates and determines his life. Deprivation becomes crucial and controlling only when it is of the *inside* as well as of the outside. In a way, the counselor would help the child who is having difficulties in school to make his school experience more real, not in the sense that it would become any more pleasant, but rather that it is there, and he is there, and he can make reality out of the unpleasant as well as the pleasant. One does not have to run; one runs only because one chooses to.

While this counselor may be the provider of information, he is not the sort of counselor described by the United States Department of Labor,[53] who would appear to be overwhelmingly a center of information. I would question the effectiveness of information in actually helping a child who is already alienated from his group, one who has the outer characteristics of failure, and who has likely come to believe them, one who is hostile and afraid of self. This person, surely, needs the warmth of human closeness; he needs acceptance of him as he is; he needs to live close to security and freedom so that he can eventually come to know, and to believe that they are within his grasp too.

53. *Counseling and Employment Services for Youth* (Washington, D.C.: Department of Labor, November, 1962).

Nor would he be the sort of counselor described by federal manpower employment legislation, in which the counselor both "counsels" and "selects." One of these actions would seem to contradict the other.

Counseling is not helping the client either to adjust to society or to fight it. It is helping him come to see who he really is, and what he has and what he does not have; what he can do easily, what he can do with difficulty, and what he probably cannot do at all. This might, I suppose, be called self-actualization, and the person comes to see that the struggle for being is really the struggle to have people take him as he is, rather than accepting the culture's version of him. This obviously is a process of living and experiencing; it is a far cry from the rather simple telling and directing, and since it involves a good deal of personal sharing, we can assume that the counselor himself must be one who sees himself as a free human being, one who has personally achieved a high level of self-actualization.

Thus the counselor, as a human being, is more important than the counseling, just as every child and adult is more important as a human being than the title that purports to describe him. Whatever the current status of the client might be, he still has strength, he still has the potential for freedom, and although many things on many fronts must be done to help him, the counselor is the one who, now, *should* be able to offer him what he needs most. This is a close sharing of a human relationship with one who has for him a high regard; one who can offer him acceptance, but one who has no guarantees, no answers; one who can help him to see freedom, but freedom with risk; one who can help him to come to see that freedom and self-integrity are the same thing, that they are within the grasp of each of us, and that we are the ones to determine whether we wish to hold them tightly or let them fall.

Existential-humanistic counseling is an intimate and very real human experience between two human beings, one of whom has not yet experienced his inner self as much as the other. But both individuals are equal in their humanness and their sharing of each other, and both have the same goal of the expanding of individual freedom, so that a person can move toward freedom and choice and self-responsibility, and thus be alive until the moment he dies.

Chapter 5

Behavioral Counseling

Behavorial counseling sees itself as possibly the most scientific of counseling methodologies, and it is acceptant of the scientific version of a determined humanity in a determined world. A human usually appears to be a rather hapless and helpless creature, fated to be buffeted around during a rather miserable existence by various forces—the id, the culture, and others—over which he has no direction and no control. Orwell paints his society as an example of what might happen to man,[1] but Skinner's version is painted objectively as the inevitable fate of man. As a determinist, Skinner assumes that behavior is lawful and determined. As his hero says:

> ... democracy ... isn't, and can't be, the best form of government, because it's based on a scientifically invalid conception of man. It fails to take account of the fact that in the long run man is determined by the state. A laissez-faire *philosophy* which trusts to the inherent goodness and wisdom of the common man is incompatible with the observed fact that men are made good or bad, and wise or foolish by the environment in which they grow.[2]

This is the world of the empirical scientist, and in it the existential man, the living being, is nowhere to be seen. A counselor with such a concept would probably be acceptant of the statement by Michael and Meyerson that "the phenomenon with which counselors deal, then, is behavior."[3]

1. George Orwell, *1984* (New York: Harcourt, Brace, 1949).
2. B. F. Skinner, *Walden Two* (New York: Macmillan, 1948), p. 273.
3. Jack Michael and Lee Meyerson, "A Behavioral Approach to Counseling and Guidance," *Harvard Educational Review,* 32:383–402 (Fall, 1962).

117

Behavioral counseling is somewhat like an older individual who has been around for some time, but whose person and ideas have suddenly been rediscovered. The research and the literature, in the past few years, is extensive, and so too are the claims made by behavioral counselors. This has resulted in a good deal of passion and emotion in both the criticism and defense of behavioral counseling, and this has often made an objective view somewhat difficult. This chapter will attempt to pull together some of the literature, both pro and con, and look at some of the basic counseling issues which are part of behavioral counseling. These issues, which are also those of the existential-humanistic counselor, center on the place of the counselor as a person in the counseling relationship, the goals of counseling, client-counselor responsibility, the scientific status of counseling, the question of human values, and the degree of client-counselor control of the counseling relationship.

THE PERSON OF THE COUNSELOR

There is little doubt that in behavioral counseling the involvement of the counselor as a fellow human being in the counseling relationship is considered to be of little importance. Bijou, for example, sees the counselor as a behavioral engineer, and his function is "to arrange and rearrange the environment in order to bring about desired changes in behavior."[4] Osipow and Walsh see the counselor as a facilitator in the learning process. They say, "The counselor is concerned with the relationship between environmental changes that foster changes in behavioral responses."[5]

Reyna feels that the behavior therapist does not need for his procedures a strictly private situation, and he goes on to say, "It is predicted that in the conditioning therapies the identity of the therapists will prove to be less important than the nature of the administered procedure."[6]

This lack of involvement of the counselor as a human being is disturbing to those who view counseling as an intense and intimate

4. S. W. Bijou, "Implications of Behavioral Sciences for Counseling and Guidance," in John D. Krumboltz (ed.), *Revolution in Counseling* (Boston: Houghton Mifflin, 1966), p. 44.
5. Samuel H. Osipow and W. Bruce Walsh, *Strategies in Counseling for Behavior Change* (New York: Appleton-Century-Crofts, 1970), p. 13.
6. L. J. Reyna, "Conditioning Therapies, Learning Theory, and Research," in Joseph Wolpe, Adrian Salter, and L. J. Reyna, *The Conditioning Therapies* (New York: Holt, Rinehart and Winston, 1969), p. 78.

human relationship between two individuals. Laing, for example, states:

> Behavior therapy is the most extreme example of such schizoid theory and practice that proposes to think and act purely in terms of the other without reference to the self of the therapist or the patient, in terms of behavior without experience, in terms of objects rather than persons. It is inevitably, therefore, a technique of non-meeting, of manipulation and control.
>
> Psychotherapy must remain an obstinate attempt of two people to recover the wholeness of being human through the relationship between them.
>
> Any technique concerned with the other without the self, with behavior to the exclusion of experience, with the relationship with neglect of the persons in relation, with the individuals to the exclusion of their relationship, and most of all, with an object-to-be-changed rather than a person-to-be-accepted, simply perpetuates the disease it purports to cure.
>
> And any theory not founded on the nature of being human is a lie and a betrayal of man. An inhuman theory will inevitably lead to inhuman consequences—if the therapist is consistent.[7]

Jourard also stresses the person of the therapist:

> The psychotherapists whom we consider great—I have argued—are great not because of their theories, which are efforts to scientize existential courage and enlightenment—but they are great because their lives were threatened by some aspect of facticity and they learned how to tame, to transcend it, and could teach others how to be free and upright. . . . The plethora of oversold theories and techniques in individual and group therapy, in encounter groups and in primal screaming, in gestalting, rolfing, yoging, meditating, to me is evidence of arrogance and false prophecy. Look at the prophet, not his methods and words, to see if he knows how to live.[8]

Gardner sees behavior modification as the application of the techniques and findings of experimental psychology and the psychology of learning to clinical problems. He sees the behavior modifier as being concerned with a particular maladaptive behavior pattern, individual reinforcement preferences and hierarchies, and

7. R. D. Laing, *The Politics of Experience* (New York: Ballantine Books, 1967), p. 53.
8. Sidney Jourard, "Prophets as Psychotherapists and Psychotherapists as Prophets," *Voices,* 7:11–16 (Fall, 1971).

current and future desirable behavior repertoires. He also feels that with these concerns the individual becomes lost.[9] He says:

> However, when transferred to interactions between people, this attitude of objectivity prevents the behavior therapist from utilizing what may be his most important, unique, and irreplaceable attribute—himself. Deprived of the experience of dealing with clinical problems by using his personal warmth, sensitivity, and intuition, the therapist cannot grow. Therapeutic failures are attributed to errors in the program, or failures to specify the proper reinforcement contingencies, etc., and never in the therapist himself. Such procedures can be devastating to the therapist. . . . it is only when the behavior modifier dares to abandon his objectivity, to deal with man as a whole human being functioning within a complex convoluted social system, and to recognize and accept the basic underlying nature of all men, that he can begin to grow.[10]

It should be noted too, that the existentially, humanistically oriented counselors are not questioning the use of techniques—which, of course, are almost certainly a part of any kind or method of counseling. But it is the place, and the importance, of the techniques that causes concern. In contrast to the behavioral counselor's deliberate and planned use of a technique as a means of changing behavior, the existential counselor would see "techniques" as evolving from the real-life, human experiencing of the client and the counselor. Thus technique, in one approach, is a means of manipulating people as well as objects; in the other, it is part of an evolving human experience, a product of that experience.

Dreyfus raises another point which would question the behavior of the behavioral therapist when he says, "In counseling, technique in and of itself does little regarding change within the client. It is only what one does with the technique and how one views the material evoked through it that allows change to occur."[11]

The person of the counselor is also stressed by Kell and Mueller:

> Both affective and cognitive dimensions enter into an effective counseling process. However, we wish also to emphasize that we think it is rare that significant changes in human behavior

---

9. James M. Gardner, "Can Behavior Therapists Grow?" *Voices*, 6:16–20 (Fall, 1969).
10. *Ibid.*
11. Edward A. Dreyfus, *Youth's Search for Meaning* (Columbus, Ohio: Charles E. Merrill, 1972), p. 11.

occur without an effective experience. Change in behavior in regard to other humans, the interpersonal dimension as we understand it, almost invariably calls for an effective, and often, conflicted, experience. [12]

Pietrofesa, Leonard, and Van Hoose imply the necessity of counselor involvement in counseling when they stress the need for self-understanding by the counselor:

Counselors, since they are concerned with the self-actualization of their clients, must make a thorough study of themselves and their own progress toward self-actualization. They should understand their personality needs, the level they are functioning at, and the defense mechanisms they use to preserve the self concept. [13]

Van Kaam stresses the person of the counselor and the client when he says:

If I reduce the gift of my person to such intellectual and generalized information, I am not fully and really present. I am only there as a factual intellect or an objective informant. The appeal of a whole person can be answered only by the presence of a whole person. [14]

And again:

If I am a good counselor I will penetrate first into behavior and experience as it manifests itself and only then ponder how existing theories of personality may illumine this experience without distortion. I should remain open for the possibility that such scientific theories should be corrected, expanded or renewed to keep in touch with behavior as given in reality today and as faced by me in the counseling situation. Theories of counseling and psychotherapy should supplement rather than supplant my understanding. [15]

Thus there would seem to be little question that the behavioral counselor stresses methods, techniques, procedures far more than he does the more subjective and complicated involvement between two human beings who meet in a relationship called counseling.

12. Bill L. Kell and William J. Mueller, *Impact and Change* (New York: Appleton-Century-Crofts, 1966), p. 85.
13. John J. Pietrofesa, George E. Leonard, and William Van Hoose, *The Authentic Counselor* (Chicago: Rand McNally, 1971), p. 147.
14. Adrian van Kaam, *The Art of Existential Counseling* (Wilkes-Barre, Pa.: Dimension Books, 1966), pp. 21–22).
15. *Ibid.,* p. 157.

Matheny, of course, is correct when he says, "Engineering experiences for the counselee's benefit may not imply less counseling interaction with him."[16] It *may* not, but the techniques and methods used by the existential-humanist counselor *and* client are an outgrowth of the relationship, and are incidental rather than planned. For the behavioral counselor, they *are* the counseling process, and they are planned and determined by the counselor.

GOALS OF COUNSELING

Krumboltz and Thoresen refer to counseling goals as having to be goals desired by the client, goals that the counselor is willing to help the client to achieve, and goals such that it is possible to assess the extent to which they have been achieved. The counselor is viewed as one who is free to use any technique, the only test being the pragmatic question, "Does it work?"[17] In another publication, Krumboltz adds to the above criteria for counseling goals by indicating that they should be capable of being stated differently for each individual client, and that the goals of counseling should be compatible with, though not necessarily identical to, the values of the counselor.[18]

Hosford describes the goals of behavioral counseling in this way:

> *First, the goal should describe in behavioral terms the desired outcome; i.e., it should specify what the client should be able to do differently as a result of the counseling. Second, the objectives should be formulated in such a way that the counselor has some idea as to which procedures and techniques he might employ to promote this desired behavior.*[19]

Barclay, however, sees behavioral counseling goals as being primarily centered in the counselor:

> *... a set of individual goals in counseling are related to specific behavioral objects. In this sense, behaviorism is task-oriented in that the goals and procedures of counseling are related ei-*

16. Kenneth Matheny, "Counselors vs. Environmental Engineers," *Personnel and Guidance Journal*, 49:439–444 (February, 1971).
17. John D. Krumboltz and Carl E. Thoresen, *Behavioral Counseling* (New York: Holt, Rinehart and Winston, 1969), pp. 1–30.
18. John D. Krumboltz, "Behavioral Goals for Counseling" in Samuel H. Osipow and W. Bruce Walsh (eds.), *Behavioral Change in Counseling: Readings and Cases* (New York: Appleton-Century-Crofts, 1970), pp. 22–23.
19. Ray E. Hosford, "Behavioral Counseling—A Contemporary Overview," *Counseling Psychologist*, 1:1–33 (1969).

*ther to the reduction of certain behavioral deficits or maladap-
tive behaviors, or the building up of a set of new and appropriate behaviors. . . . In nearly all cases behavioral counseling
seems to work best in a setting where the behaviors desired can
be precisely identified. . . . In other words, the behavioral counselor often brings to the counseling process a more precise idea
or notion of what constitutes effective human social behavior
in a given setting, and this judgment, rightly or wrongly, appears to be references in relationship to cultural expectations.*[20]

Michael and Meyerson make it quite clear that when they talk
about "goals" they mean goals of the *counselor* for the *client:*

*Parents, educators and guidance workers make no bones about
their earnest intention to create and maintain the "good" behavior that is valued and approved of by the culture and to
eliminate "bad" behavior to the maximum degree of which
they are capable.*

*. . . For most of those to whom society entrusts the guidance
of others influencing or inducing people to behave in ways that
society says are "good" ways is an accepted goal, and the critical question is "How can we 'motivate' a person so that he does
behave, 'wants' to behave, and 'enjoys' behaving in good
ways?"*[21]

The behavioral scientist would probably subscribe to the
above, possibly with some variations, but in general he would tend
to feel not only that man lives in a lawful and determined world, but
that man is a bit of that lawful and determined world. Man is the
product of his culture, and any such ideas as freedom and choice are
subjective and sentimental myths. Man is "fated" to be what he is,
and there is little or nothing that he can do about it. Man becomes
another creature, or possibly not even a creature, but rather another
thing, to be manipulated and directed by someone to do something
for somebody. The manner in which one becomes a manipulator instead of the manipulated is also determined. This is a sort of womb-
to-tomb philosophy of life, in which man has given up the risks of
freedom, and instead has accepted, as inevitable, the security of the
autocrat. In a way, it accepts what Fromm has described as the authoritarian ethic, which

*denies man's capacity to know what is good or bad; the norm
giver is always an authority transcending the individual.*

20. James R. Barclay, *Foundations of Counseling Strategies* (New York: Wiley,
1971), pp. 72–81.
21. Jack Michael and Lee Meyerson, *op. cit.*

. . . Materially . . . authoritarian ethics answers the question of what is good or bad primarily in terms of the interests of the authority, not the interests of the subject.[22]

It would, of course, be extremely naive to assume that one can live his individual life, in the company of other individuals, past, present, and future, without being affected by them. It is equally obvious that, to a great extent, we live in a determined world. But there is a vast difference between the individual who knows and feels and believes that he *is* the master of his fate, that in the long run he *can* choose, even though, because of circumstances, that choice might be infinitesimally small, and the individual who has not this conviction. Man always, even in the most oppressive of circumstances, possesses the small, thin wedge of freedom, and if we feel that education is a process or a means by which one can become what he is, and if we believe that learning is growing into greater depths of freedom and creativity, then the counselor must surely be one who does not accept the concept of the determinism of man. The counselor, we could hope, would be sympathetic to the protest of Scher when he says:

Life for most of us so-called normals is a constant struggle to scorch the feelings of richest life, to render ourselves unconscious, stamp out individuality, and all in the name of normality. Better a bit more abnormality than this living death we call normal living.[23]

If the counselor is willing to accept the deterministic concept of the nature of man, and of course many are, it would seem that he must be willing to accept his function as that of a manipulator of the individual for the predetermined "good" of some current body or organization of people who are no longer individuals. It would also seem that he must, in some respects at least, be the enemy of the free man, since he is surely saying to man that he has no rights as an individual, that he has no integrity as a human personal entity, that his only purpose is, like the cows in the field, to serve the predetermined state.

Such a determined counselor would see his function as helping the client to adjust and fit more comfortably into the already established societal order, and in this sense he could probably work as comfortably in a totally autocratic country as in a country with a relatively high degree of individual freedom. He would not likely

22. Erich Fromm, *Man for Himself* (New York: Rinehart and Winston, 1947), p. 10.
23. Jordon M. Scher, "Vivacity, Pathology, and Existence," *Journal of Existential Psychiatry*, 3:205–210 (Fall, 1962).

agree with Carkhuff and Berenson, who see society as the enemy, when they say:

> Society is not organized to free man's creative potential but rather to maintain or render man impotent or maintain him with minimal potency. . . . In its rules and regulations and in the role models which it presents for emulation, society replaces the individual experience with a collective experience. Man cannot create with someone else's experience.[24]

One might be excused for some degree of skepticism when behavior therapists stress, as they usually do, the idea that the behavior goals to be achieved must be those determined by the client. If the goals of the client must mesh with those of the counselor, then surely the counselor is saying, "You can only expect me to help you as long as your version of where you want to go and who you want to be are acceptable to me." This attitude severely limits the extent to which the client is free to determine *his* goals in the counseling process, and as Barclay indicates, the goals of the counselor are directly related to cultural expectations. If, in addition to this, the behavioral counselor accepts the position of Skinner that there is no such reality as individual choice,[25] then the role of the client in determining the goals of counseling would appear to be most limited! All of this, too raises the question of control.

CONTROL

The imposition of counselor values on the client certainly carries with it the implication of counselor control over the client. We can assume that the client knows very little about kinds of techniques that might 'be used, and that these will be determined by the counselor. It is unlikely, however, that the counselor, being a human being despite his protestations of scientific objectivity, can remove *his* goals for the client from *his* determination of the means by which these goals are to be achieved. The goal of a sixteen-year-old girl, for example, might be to sleep with boys without getting pregnant. The behavioral counselor who feels that sixteen-year-old girls shouldn't sleep with boys is going to have a difficult time in helping this girl achieve her desired goal. Might it be possible that what he will do is

24. Robert R. Carkhuff and Bernard G. Berenson, *Beyond Counseling and Therapy* (New York: Holt, Rinehart and Winston, 1967), p. 219.
25. B. F. Skinner, "Beyond Freedom and Dignity," *Psychology Today,* 5:37–80 (August, 1971).

suggest techniques by which the girl might have less need to sleep with boys and thus have less likelihood of becoming pregnant?

The total lack of involvement of the client in the choice of methods to attain goals is made clear by Osipow when he says, "At the same time, the *choice of method* used to attain goals, once agreed upon, does legitimately remain in the province of the professional, since, presumably, he is the one who is expert in such matters."[26]

Reyna also leaves little doubt as to who is in control: "The behavior therapist expresses this when he explicitly defines the goals of therapy, and then arranges conditions so as to alter emotional responses to indicated situations."[27]

There would seem to be equal certainty in the minds of Wolpe and Lazarus as to who is in control when they say, "Just as the unlearning of the experimental neurosis is completely in control of the experimenter, so the overcoming of a human neurosis is within the control of the therapist through techniques quite similar to those used in the laboratory."[28] And again:

The truth is that the grade of acquiescence required is the same as in any other branch of medicine or education. Patients with pneumonia are ready to do what the medical man prescribes, because he is the expert. The same is the case when psychotherapy is the treatment required.[29]

These words surely make clear the extreme degree of control of the therapeutic process by the counselor. It should be stressed again, too, that control is not so much a matter of technique or method as it is the *attitude* of the therapist. The attitude of Wolpe and Lazarus is shown by the words they use—they see the client as acquiescing; psychotherapy is a branch of medicine or education; pneumonia and anxiety are only different kinds of diseases; the doctor with a pneumonia patient has the same level of control over what happens as has the therapist with a client suffering from extreme anxiety; and, apparently, the physical self is no different from the psychological self!

Allen questions the concept of some behaviorists regarding

26. Samuel H. Osipow, "Some Ethical Dilemmas Involved in Behavioral and Client-Centered Insight Counseling," in Samuel H. Osipow and W. Bruce Walsh (eds.), *op. cit.,* p. 77.

27. L. J. Reyna, *op. cit.*

28. Joseph Wolpe and Arnold A. Lazarus, *Behavior Theory Techniques* (London: Pergamon Press, 1966), p. 17.

29. *Ibid.,* p. 23.

the lack of choice, but he has no question regarding the matter of control:

> Operant conditioning is not then to be considered to be a mechanical process. Rather, it assumes the existence of such unmechanistic phenomena as choice and anticipation. The "behavior modifier" generally arranges the circumstances in such a manner as to provide the subject with an effective enticement to behave "more constructively." Unsurprisingly the subject tends to elect to behave in this fashion with the expectation of securing the relatively more congenial consequences as a result.[30]

By their own statements, and their own counseling behavior, it would seem likely that behavioral counselors would generally agree with Carkhuff and Berenson when they say:

> The behavior therapist must be willing to dictate the procedure and direction of therapy. The client influences the process only with his responses to treatment.[31]

There might, however, be some slight disagreement with their description of the behavior therapist:

> The therapist is thus seen as a programmed therapy machine or computer which administers specific reinforcement schedules to the response system of a machine-like patient.[32]

Humans who are totally comfortable in controlling the destiny of other humans are usually characterized by an almost absolute certainty about the rightness and the effectiveness of their ways. Haley, in a tongue-in-cheek piece, says:

> A therapist is likely to present a method of therapy which he says has worked effectively with x percent of patients, it has been taught to vast numbers of students, and it is superior to any method yet evolved. Such a presentation is typical of a Behavior Therapist.[33]

Wolpe and Lazarus, however, are dead serious when they say practically the same thing: "A point that must be given the strongest

---

30. Thomas W. Allen, "Adlerian Interview Strategies for Behavior Change," *Counseling Psychologist*, 3:40–48 (1971).
31. Robert R. Carkhuff and Bernard G. Berenson, op. cit., p. 91.
32. Ibid., p. 88.
33. Jay Haley, "How to Criticize Your Fellow Therapists," *Voices* 6:16–20 (Special Issue, 1970).

emphasis is that *behavior therapy is effective in all neuroses,* and not only in unitary phobias."[34]

The same calm and somewhat chilling certainty is evinced by Skinner when he says that "we must delegate control of the population as a whole to specialists—to police, priests, teachers, therapists, and so on, with their specialized reinforcers and their codified contingencies."[35]

This would appear to me to be a very crucial human issue. If, in the counseling relationship, it is someone else who determines where I go and what I become, then what about the question of the degree of *my* responsibility *for* my behavior?

RESPONSIBILITY

The degree to which the client is in control over what is happening to him in the therapeutic process is obviously related to the extent to which he can accept responsibility for his behavior. Wolpe and Lazarus reflect the feeling and belief of the behavioral counselor that any concept of individual choice is pure fantasy when they say, "Since the patient has had no choice in becoming what he is . . ."[36]

If the client has had no choice in becoming what he is, up to the point of meeting with the therapist, then it would be safe to assume that he will continue to have no choice in what happens. He will continue to be the victim of various manipulating forces, including the therapist. I would think that it would be rather difficult, under these circumstances, to stress the responsibility of the client for any change in his behavior. The client would have every reason to accept the irresponsibility of his behavior as being the product of forces beyond his control.

This attitude is quite contrary to Glasser's reality therapy, which stresses the responsibility of the client. As Glasser puts it:

> We never sympathize with, or excuse him for anything he does, nor do we let him excuse himself. We never agree that his irresponsibility is justified no matter how much he may have suffered at the hands of others.[37]

The behavior therapist tends to stress the "what" rather than the "why"[38] and Glasser agrees with this, thereby, I would think, being somewhat inconsistent. Glasser makes the comment: "'Why'

34. Joseph Wolpe and Arnold A. Lazarus, *op. cit.,* p. 11.
35. B. F. Skinner, *op. cit.*
36. Joseph Wolpe and Arnold A. Lazarus, *op. cit.,* p. 16.
37. William Glasser, *Reality Therapy* (New York: Harper and Row, 1965), p. 32.
38. Patricia Jabukowski-Spector and Carlton E. Beck, *Philosophical Guidelines for Counseling* (Dubuque, Iowa: W. C. Brown, 1971), p. 336.

implies that the reasons for the patient's behavior make a difference in therapy, but they do not."[39] The "why," I would think, makes no difference if, like the behavioral therapist, one stresses the utter irresponsibility of the client. One might wonder, however, how the therapist, being subject as a fellow human to the same basic forces which have conditioned the client, is not equally irresponsible. On the other hand, if one stresses the responsibility of the client for his actions, *now,* then the question of "why," which is a moral issue involving values, must become part of the picture.

Keen speaks to this point when he says, "The behavior therapies confuse symptoms and causes and forget that persons have life histories."[40] I find it difficult to see how I can determine the level of my responsibility or irresponsibility if I do not ask myself why I am doing what I am doing.

If the feeling of a client, for example, is one of guilt over his responsibility for the death of another person, surely the question "Why did you do what you did?" is crucial. If, as a drunken driver, I run over and cripple a little child for life, my psychological problem is quite different than if, in a struggle with a man who is trying to kill one of my children, I kill him. The moment the therapist stresses the responsibility of the client for his behavior, he is bringing in moral and ethical issues. And moral and ethical issues, and science, sometimes clash.

BEHAVIORAL COUNSELING, HUMAN VALUES, AND SCIENCE

Since behavioral counseling sees itself as the "scientific" approach to counseling, a further examination of this question seems appropriate, even though I have already referred to the place of science in counseling.

The importance of being empirical, scientific, factual is overwhelmingly evident in the writings of behavioral counselors. Thoresen, for example:

Behavioral is used here to convey efforts to use systemically both theoretical and empirical knowledge from experimental work in psychology and related disciplines. Behavioral further emphasizes the use of the empirical case approach, i.e., experimental study of the single case.[41]

39. William Glasser, *op. cit.,* p. 32.
40. Sam Keen, "Janov and Primal Therapy," *Psychology Today,* 5:43–89 (February, 1972).
41. Carl E. Thoresen, "Comment," *Personnel and Guidance Journal,* 49:608–610 (April, 1971).

Fullmer, too, makes this feeling quite clear:

Behaviorists use criterion measures for their referents. The advantage of criterion measures is immediately evident because a definitive measure is possible. This gives the further advantage of preciseness in measures taken as data in relation to a specific defined criterion instead of a norm ambiguously defined. This type of model fits research criteria with greater precision than any normative data model available for the standard and classic therapies.[42]

And again:

If a technique works, the behavioral counselor sees no need or purposes served by such inferences as why a technique works. . . . We mean that a technique works whenever the behavior changes.[43]

Rachman also stresses the same point:

Behavior therapy . . . has developed out of established psychological theories and has a large body of experimental evidence on which to proceed. The therapeutic process and its outcome are both open to quantification. It permits precision and a systematic planning of the treatment required in individual cases.[44]

Many counselors, on the other hand, feel that this stress of the behavioral counselor on his scientific status is no more then a futile attempt to avoid his own subjective humanness. Rogers, for example, in discussing the action taken by a boy who is finally able to reach out his hand to a girl, stresses meaning and value and humanness:

Perhaps a behaviorist could account for the reaching out of his hand by saying that it was the result of intermittent reinforcement of partial movements. I find such an explanation both inaccurate and inadequate. It is the meaning *of the decision which is essential in understanding the act.*[45]

42. Daniel W. Fullmer, *Counseling: Group, Theory and System* (Scranton, Pa.: International Textbook Co., 1971), p. 49.
43. *Ibid.*, p. 215.
44. S. Rachman, "Behavior Therapy" in Bernard G. Berensen and Robert R. Carkhuff (eds.), *Sources of Gain in Counseling and Psychotherapy* (New York: Holt, Rinehart and Winston, 1967), p. 78.
45. Carl R. Rogers, *Freedom to Learn* (Columbus, Ohio: Charles E. Merrill, 1969), p. 268.

London feels that it is quite impossible for the therapist to avoid the question of values:

> No matter how much he specifies his goals or limits his attack to the alleviation of clear cut symptoms, the fact remains that some symptoms of dysfunction are sources of psychological distress precisely because they are rooted in what may equally well be seen as systems of meaning.[46]

Allen reflects much the same feeling when, in reacting to a paper on behavioral counseling, he says:

> For, by Hosford's own account, behavior counselors do make inferences which transcend the realm of directly observable behavior. It is simply that they obdurately refuse to acknowledge this fact in their pronouncements.[47]

It is interesting to note that in a book on the science of astronomy, Whitney tends to stress the people who made the discoveries and evolved theories as much as the discoveries and theories themselves.[48] He believes that the basic human sources of scientific creativity are irrational rather than rational, and that if we are to understand the making of science, we must first understand the complex human nature of the men and women who make it.

Kemp feels: "In our false attempt to be more scientific, more "truthful," we lose the sense of reality in our experiences."[49] Breger and McGaugh are skeptical of the scientific claims of the behavior therapists, and they even suggest that those psychotherapies which seek justification in learning theory may actually be devoid of any tangible scientific content.[50] Lowe doubts that science can be kept free of personal values, and he comments: "Many physicists now believe that man's perceptions of what has hithertofore been considered an objective world of nature are in fact determined by psychological processes closely akin to what I describe here as personal values."[51]

46. Perry London, *The Modes and Morals of Psychotherapy* (New York: Holt, Rinehart and Winston, 1964), pp. 123–124.
47. Thomas W. Allen, "Purpose Is Alive and Well and Living in the Empty Organism," *Counseling Psychologist*, 1:72–81 (1969).
48. Charles A. Whitney, *The Discovery of Our Galaxy* (New York: Afred A. Knopf, 1971).
49. C. Gratton Kemp, "Existential Counseling," *Counseling Psychologist*, 2:2–29 (1971).
50. Louis Breger and James L. McGaugh, "Critique and Reformulation of 'Learning Theory' Approaches to Psychotherapy and Neurosis," *Psychological Bulletin*, 63:338–358 (May, 1965).
51. C. Marshal Lowe, *Value Orientations in Counseling and Psychotherapy* (San Francisco: Chandler Publishing Co., 1969), p. 217.

Goodman makes an interesting comment on this science-versus-values debate:

The behavioral sciences are really part of the humanities, yet they continually, and erroneously, try to model themselves after predictive sciences, which are technological. The role of the behavioral sciences is like that of the literary critic. A literary critic doesn't seek to produce a poem. Rather he takes an ongoing situation and says: "It can run a little more smoothly if we fix this little piece here and fix that little piece there." They should come on like humanist critics rather than as a priori or empirical system-builders. [52]

Preciseness and exactness are of understandable importance to the scientist, but it is also scientific to determine the degree to which we can be precise and exact about that which we are examining and attempting to measure. On this issue, as on others, the behavioral counselor, like the existential counselor, at some point *believes* what he thinks. He believes the evidence he has produced or discovered, since no scientific mind would ever say, "I now have the answer and need search no more."

Rationally, man's belief should be weighted by empirical evidence, but man is a creature of rationality and irrationality. Counselors, behavioral and existential, are homo sapiens. They will likely continue to be irrational and subjective, thereby showing their humanness, even though some insist that they are rational and objective.

It is likely that some of the negative reaction to behavioral counselors is because of their insistence on their own omnipotence, and their certainty regarding the scientific infallibility of their pronouncements regarding behavioral counseling. This is unfortunate, since it tends to obscure the real contribution of behavioral counseling to the entire field of counseling. I am quite sure, for example, that much of the negative reaction to Skinner is simply because many people, including professional counselors, do not like the sound of what he is saying!

Out of all of this I would have several tentative reactions to behavioral counseling, all, of course, subject to change at any time, since, as a non-behavioral type, I am *not* too certain about what I am saying:

1. Behavioral counseling is not the answer, any more than primal screaming is *the* answer, but it has a place in the total counsel-

52. Robert Glasgow, "A Conversation with Paul Goodman," *Psychology Today,* 5:62–96 (November, 1971).

ing process. Behavioral counseling is obviously sufficient for certain behavioral problems, but it is insufficient and inappropriate for much of the trauma which bedevils the human species.

2. The basic characteristic of behavioral counseling is involving the client in an experience, determined by the counselor, for the purpose of modifying the behavior of the client. The counselor is viewed as the professional expert. The client has the same degree of involvement in what happens as has a hospitalized patient suffering from a disease or an injury. The counselor "cures" the client of his problem.

This, in turn, means that the human relationship between the client and the counselor is relatively unimportant and incidental to the curing of the problem, unless, of course, this is part of a planned experience. The counselor is not involved in a human-with-a-human sense, but he is, rather, the concerned and caring professional whose skill and understanding provide the experiences that will solve the client's problems. The client is not in control of what happens.

3. This also means that the client accepts little or no responsibility for what happens in the counseling process, nor is there any stress on his responsibility. In fact, the behavioral counselor does not believe in the reality of client choice, and he continues the conditioning process which is the client's life. Thus the counselor accepts the irresponsibility of the client and the professional responsibility of the counselor for effectively modifying the client's behavior. The modified behavior is behavior that meets the approval of the counselor.

4. The behavioral counselor sees himself as a scientist involved in a scientific enterprise, namely, the modification of human behavior. Human behavior *is the human,* that is, homo sapiens is a multiplicity of intertwined and complicated sets of behaviors, produced by eons of conditioning by the environment. Since science is amoral, we can assume that counseling, for the behavioral counselor, is amoral, and human values are not involved in the counseling process. Counseling is a scientific process. Its purpose is to change human behavior, and this change is measurable.

5. The goals of behavioral counseling appear to be generally limited to the cure of the symptoms which are causing distress. This is a laudable objective, but it is limited, even though the curing of the symptom may mean, without doubt, the modification or alleviation of the cause. But the gestalt human being, as one who is immeasurably more than sets of behaviors, is considered to be a subjective fantasy, and humanness is an immeasurable, and therefore meaningless, term.

Chapter 6

Groups and Group Counseling

One of the major aspects of the explosion of the decade of the 1960's in the field of counseling and psychotherapy was the stress on groups. For some, groups became the answer to anything and everything. They became part of the quick cure for any kind of problem that might have troubled human beings, and it seemed that almost anyone could, overnight, or at least over a weekend, become an expert leader or facilitator of a group.[1]

This stress on groups continues in the decade of the 1970's, and it is important that we distinguish between the quackery that has become a part of the group movement, and the tremendous contribution to human growth and development that has been provided by the experiences of humans in groups. In this chapter I would like to share a few thoughts on groups and the learning process, take a look at sensitivity and encounter groups, and then look at some questions regarding theories of group counseling.

GROUPS OF HUMANS AND THE LEARNING PROCESS

Two writers have made comments that are most applicable when discussing groups and the learning process. Corsini, for example:

From where I stand, groups are aimed at any one or any combination of three gains: (a) intellectual—such as greater under-

1. See William R. Coulson, *Groups, Gimmicks and Instant Gurus* (New York: Harper and Row, 1972) and Bruce L. Maliver *The Encounter Game* (New York: Stein and Day, 1973).

134

standing of ourselves, (b) emotional—such as better feelings about ourselves, and (c) behavioral—such as better and more competent behavior.[2]

And Lakin:

One may emphasize "interpersonal intimacy" (as does Coulson), but in doing so exclusively, we put such a premium on it as to foster "faking it" or obscuring other vital elements of interpersonal experiences in groups. On the other hand, if a group is too intellectual, too detached from its emotional experiences, it becomes a sterile exercise. The productive balance is difficult to establish, but it must be sought nevertheless. It depends on a good mix of the personal, the idiosyncratic, the egocentric and the collective or communitarian. It depends upon using all of oneself, one's intellect, one's emotionality, etc.[3]

When a group of people have come together for some purpose, the leader or teacher or facilitator operates on the assumption that the members of the group wish, in some way, to learn something. It would not be unreasonable to assume that individuals who are in a group where the subject of learning has been described as "groups" would have some personal motivation to learn something about groups.

If this first basic assumption is incorrect, then the first task would appear to be to somehow separate those who wish to learn something about groups from those who do not. Some time might be taken with the "do nots" to attempt to find out what it is they do want, since we must assume that by taking the time and paying the money that is necessary to become a member of the group, they must want to learn *something*. It may then be found that some of the original "do nots" could still remain within the context of the group and learn their something; others would likely have to leave the group or accept the reality that they would not learn their "something" within the group. We could assume that if these people accepted this responsibility, they would not expect to become the recipient of some symbol that implied that they had learned something about groups.

So now we have a group of people who have said, "Yes, I wish to learn something about groups." Several problems immediately arise. The members of the group, being individuals, do not all learn best in the same way. "Learning" may be viewed in a quite different

---

2. Raymond J. Corsini, "Issues in Encounter Groups: Comments on Coulson's Article," *Counseling Psychologist*, 2:28–34 (1970).
3. Martin Lakin, "Response to Coulson," *Counseling Psychologist*, 2:34–38 (1970).

manner by the leader and by different members of the group; the leader may feel strongly that people do not learn by following the procedures by which certain members of the group feel that they do learn; attitudes on the place of the experiential and the cognitive in the learning process will differ markedly among members of the group; the emotional status of the members of the group, including the leader, may differ widely, so that a very heavy personal involvement might be desired by some, feared by others; the knowledge level of members of the group may differ widely.

I would think that an effective leader will, among other things, be knowledgeable in his area of study. He will also be open and flexible, and will not feel rigidly committed to any particular structure or methodology or technique. He should, however, provide the initial structure and communicate to the members of the group just what this structure is.

If an individual feels that the proposed structure is not the best for him, it is his responsibility to communicate this to the leader and to other members of the group. It would also not seem unreasonable to assume that this person would accept the responsibility of indicating a procedure by which he could learn more effectively. Since there are many and varied "This is the way I would like it . . ." views, each person cannot expect the leader and other members of the group to follow the procedure he may wish to set up for himself. The leader, too, may feel that he would be compromising himself if he did what certain members of the group might want him to do. He could well *understand* what they wanted and why they wanted it, but he would be inconsistent if he did what they wanted.

I feel strongly, for example, that the primary function of the leader is not to supply information and answers to human problems. Much information and many cognitive answers (few of which really make much difference, since there are no "answers," per se, to human problems) are available on the written page. Rather, the leader should facilitate and encourage members of the group to share with each other thoughts and feelings about issues and about themselves. I feel that I can contribute most by sharing my thoughts and feelings and experiences as reactions to questions, issues and feelings as initiated by members of the group.

I feel, too, that the content of a discussion is often important primarily as a means of facilitating discussion, since it is the discussion, rather than what is being discussed, that results in learning. We learn more about counseling and learning and human behavior and communication by being a participating member of a group than by personally removed reading about these subjects. Thus, I do not feel comfortable being the "answer man" because I do not see myself as having answers for others, and even if I did, I cannot see this as helping individuals learn more about humans and their behavior. I like to share ideas and thoughts and feelings, sometimes with some heat, but always, I hope, with an open mind. I have to be personally involved to learn, and I believe deeply that this applies to all humans, not just to me.

Basically, I see myself as one involved in helping others to learn in a way they want to learn, and in this way I learn too. "Teaching" rarely results in learning, either for the teacher or for the one who is being taught, because it seldom involves the one who is supposed to learn in doing what he wants to do.

In a group persons can learn if (a) they add to their store of knowledge by reading and listening and experiencing, (b) they accept responsibility for their own learning, and for helping others in the group to learn, (c) they are willing to share their thoughts and feelings with other members of the group, (d) they are willing to take some risk of being rebuffed, hurt, embarrassed, criticized, (e) they continually work on being open to what others are communicating without putting a value judgment on what is being communicated, and (f) they are sensitive to the dynamics of the group and see the group itself as a means by which they can learn much about humans and their behavior.

SENSITIVITY GROUPS AND ENCOUNTER GROUPS

One might assume that in any group of people getting together there should be sensitivity and there should be encounter, but these terms have come to have a particular kind of meaning for a particular kind of group. I see such a kind of a group as being relatively unstructured, providing a climate of maximum freedom for personal expression, exploration of feelings, and interpersonal communication. Emphasis is upon the interaction among the group members, in an atmosphere where everyone is encouraged to drop his mask and defenses and relate more openly and directly with other members of the group. Individuals come to know themselves and each other more fully than is possible in the usual social or professional relationships. The climate of openness generates trust, which enables members of the group to test out different behaviors and to relate more effectively with other human beings in everyday life.

Maximum growth occurs for both the group and the leader when the leader participates as a person, sharing himself with the others, rather than as an aloof expert.

There is more stress on the affective than the cognitive. The aim is to help the individual become a more effective human being, one who can be honest with himself and with others, and thus become a more helpful and positive member of his society. It encourages human growth and the expansion of individual freedom.

It is true, of course, that millions of individuals desperately seek immediate answers for that for which there is no answer, and in the last few years encounter groups and sensitivity groups have become a means by which charlatans may prey upon their unhappy fellow humans. On the other hand, a professionally competent facilitator or leader is one who has carefully examined, among other things, his own motivation for involvement. Such an individual would have great respect for the integrity of each member of the group. He would consider human privacy to be the keystone of individual freedom, and would nurture it rather than despoil it.[4]

The self-exposure that often occurs in a group has been misrepresented and misunderstood by many of the critics, or it may be, of course, that their criticism has reflected their own fear of self-exposure. It is easy to use certain examples, and if one were to do this about religion, for example, one could assume that religion consists of meetings where psychotic evangelists deliver from the clutches of the devil a group of fearful, ignorant people, for, of course, a price. Life everlasting, described in great detail, can be assured as long as one does what one is told by those who, in some mysterious manner, have been anointed by God. Psychology, too, might easily be assumed to be some totally mechanistic procedure by which unfortunate human beings are programmed to do what Big Brother wants them to do, or possibly a kind of mumbo-jumbo witch-doctor-like procedure in which strange incantations and actions are guaranteed to cure the sufferer of anything from dandruff to suicidal tendencies.

I am sure that I reflect the feelings of many humanistic psychologists involved in group work when I say that I am very skeptical of the positive value of some of Bindrim's methods, such as "crotch-eyeballing,"[5] nor do I find joy in all of Schutz's statements and methods.[6]

But exposure of the self to the self *is* the guts of therapy. How

4. See Dugald S. Arbuckle, "Comment on Silber's 'Encountering—What,'" *Center Magazine*, 4:75–77 (September/October 1971) and Dugald S. Arbuckle, "Koch's Distortion of Encounter Group Theory," *Journal of Humanistic Psychology*, 13:47–51 (Winter, 1973).

5. P. Bindrim, "A Report on a Nude Marathon," *Psychotherapy: Theory, Research and Practice*, 5:180–188 (1968).

6. W. Schutz, *Joy* (New York: Grove Press, 1967).

am I ever going to know who I am if I cannot be open to myself? And most people *can* be helped by other concerned and caring humans to get closer to who they really are, and thus become a more authentic person, although many people fear this openness to self—for very good reasons. We are all, to a greater or lesser degree, encrusted with masks which obscure our real shape and form. All too often the mask of courage covers the real fear, the mask of loving covers the anger, the mask of patience covers the irritation. This fear, this anger, this irritation must be faced if one is ever to get to a deeper and more meaningful level of life and living.

It is the facilitator or leader who accepts the responsibility of helping a person to remove the masks, and this responsibility requires professional competence. The facilitator is not just a member of the group, and he has certain professional responsibilities that are not those of other members. If he did not, why call him the "facilitator"? The client or group member may share much with the therapist or facilitator, but the latter has a different kind of responsibility than does the former, even though he may be very much a part of the group.

Rogers gives a generally acceptable comment regarding groups when he says:

> *I trust this chapter has made clear that the whole movement toward intensive group experience in all its forms has profound significance, for both today and tomorrow. Those who may have thought of the encounter group as a fad or phenomenon affecting only a few people temporarily would do well to reconsider. In the troubled future that lies ahead of us, the trend toward the intensive group experience is related to deep and significant issues having to do with change.*[7]

The openness and acceptance of the group provides a means for the expression of feelings which have long been bottled up, and the tears that sometimes flow are tears that should have been shed long ago. As in an individual therapeutic relationship, a person can come to express and look at feelings that were hidden, and experience a love and acceptance from those around him as he is finally able to become more honest with himself. The private monster that has bedeviled an individual for a long time sometimes becomes no more than a harmless ghost when one can finally share it with a small group of fellow humans who obviously care very much for him. A peak human experience is to share part of one's private life

7. Carl R. Rogers, *Carl Rogers on Encounter Groups* (New York: Harper and Row, 1970), p. 167.

with another human or humans, and to realize that one is being accepted with respect and with dignity. The masquerade that we may practice in ordinary life will soon be revealed in an individual or group experience for what it is.

The individual who, in a group setting, uses words without any depth of meaning soon has his own level of superficiality pointed out to him. The superficial "I love you" is more likely to be used when an individual enters a group experience; when he leaves he may use the words less frequently and more accurately in relation to his actual ability to love another person. It is society that degrades the human being, and as part of that process degrades the meaning of beautiful words. The existential-humanistic facilitator tries to help the person to once again find the beauty that is his so that, as part of his behavior, he will never need to use words of beauty in a gross and ugly fashion.

People sometimes see the exposure that may occur in groups as indecent and immoral. They see "indecent" verbal exposure as the use of certain words, and "indecent" physical exposure as being measured by the extent to which one's body is covered with clothing. From a human and intellectual point of view this is naive, and from a psychological point of view it is absurd. Words are not indecent per se. Any words, used under certain circumstances, with certain meanings, directed at certain individuals, can be indecent and cruel and inhumane and dirty. When a white teacher cuts a struggling black student with a "Well, of course I couldn't expect a person like you to do any better," the words are indecent and dirty. When the black student, who may have been the recipient of hundreds of such incidents, replies with a "Fuck you," his words are quite reasonable and not the least indecent!

When a group of people in a commune swim naked together, there is more beauty than indecency in what they do. The right to privacy is, of course, a basic tenet of individual freedom, but anyone involved in psychotherapy is acutely aware of the price that humans pay for not being able to share with caring fellow humans feelings that should have been shared and held out and looked at a long time ago. It is too frequently our social indoctrination that makes what is clean dirty, and what is honest dishonest, and what is ordinary and normal and human dreadful and evil.

The encounter group, the sensitivity group, group counseling—I would see them as the same thing. Their basic purpose is to help a person to grow and develop, to realize his potential, to expand the boundaries of his freedom, to live. The methodologies and procedures that are used are as varied as the leaders and facilitators, and they are obviously reflections of these leaders and facilitators, both personally and professionally.

THEORIES OF GROUP COUNSELING

Any reader can find some literary contribution to support his own beliefs regarding the existence or lack of existence of various theories of group counseling. Zimpfer, for example, does not believe there is yet a true theory of group counseling. He says:

There probably cannot be a single theory of group counseling. There are too many philosophical positions about the nature of man, too many psychological bases for human growth and development and the ways by which change is effected, too many variations in counselor personality and style of functioning interpersonally, and too many possible ways for groups to form and develop uniquely for a singular group counseling theory.[8]

While Beymer is showing concern about confrontation groups, he could be referring to group counseling generally when he says:

Clearly we stand in need of such a reappraisal of group processes today, but it is difficult to make a specific request for clarification and revision because no single individual or small number of individuals is responsible for these ideas.[9]

On the other hand, many writers refer to various theoretical orientations to group counseling. Dinkmeyer and Muro, for example, refer to the socioteleological approach, which views man as a decision-making being whose actions have a social purpose; the behavioral approach, which operates on the premise that most human behavior is learned; the transactional groups, which are concerned with three ego states—parent, adult and child; group-centered counseling, which emphasizes a humanistic and existential approach; and the T-Group approach, which is a specialized approach used to develop sensitivity by the National Training Laboratories.[10] Gazda uses a somewhat different approach, and refers to theo-

8. David G. Zimpfer, "Some Conceptual and Research Problems in Group Counseling," *School Counselor*, 15:326–333 (May, 1968).

9. Lawrence Beymer, "Confrontation Groups: Hula Hoops," *Counselor Education and Supervision*, 9:75–86 (Winter, 1970).

10. Don C. Dinkmeyer and James J. Muro, *Group Counseling: Theory and Practice* (Itasca, Ill.: F. E. Peacock, 1971), p. 69.

ries indirectly in discussing the orientation of group counselors. He refers to those who were influenced by group guidance as reflecting a vocational guidance orientation, preferring a leader-centered and topic-centered approach with an emphasis on educational and vocational counseling; the group counseling theorists and practitioners who have been influenced by the discipline of group psychotherapy tend to emphasize the rehabilitative or adjustive (personal-social) qualities of the process; those who have come from a background of study and/or practice in the group dynamics movement tend to develop, emphasize, and deal with the group themes or goals; those who have evolved from the group work and social case work disciplines bring to their groups a combination of group dynamics emphasis with a psychoanalytic orientation; child guidance-oriented counselors who reflect an Adlerian theoretical influence; the Human Potential Movement, which emphasizes body contact and nonverbal "games," but also stresses positive verbal reinforcement techniques and deemphasizes responding to or recognizing negative behavior.[11]

Then there are the few bold theorist-practitioners who spurn the established theories and develop one to fit their own practice. Fullmer is one of these. His "theory" of group counseling is based on the following belief:

> *Human behavior is created anew within the context of the group. The behavior is all-at-once, the symbol of the personal experience. The motivation for behavior is the need to express a meaning defined by the perception of the relationship in the individual's personal experience of the moment. The behavior set is the symbol used in communicating to significant other persons. Feedback and confrontation from others completes the process. When all of the antecedents and consequences are considered in the context of a group life event, the necessary parameters and rules for understanding "what is happening" do exist.*[12]

On the other hand, the theoretical orientation of many group counselors is quite obvious when they talk about goals and methods. The existential orientation of Kemp, for example, is quite obvious when he talks about goals and methods of group counseling:

> *The goals in group counseling are not visualizable but are generally understood to be the satisfaction of emotional needs.*

11. George M. Gazda, *Group Counseling: A Developmental Approach* (Boston: Allyn and Bacon, 1971), pp. 14–15.
12. Daniel W. Fullmer, *Counseling: Group Theory and System* (Scranton, Pa.: International Textbook Co., 1971), p. 48.

Critical thinking is focused in the emotional content of inter-personal and intrapersonal relationships and frequently concentrated on the "here and now", that is, what is occurring in the group at the time.

Problem solving is only incidentally related to ideational situations. Instead it is focused on understanding of emotions and the resolving of emotional conflicts. There is occasional decision making in relation to self-understanding and understanding of others. Listening takes place on all levels and is especially significant as interpreter of the emotional state and as an aid to understanding.

There is considerable emotional involvement directly related to the satisfaction of needs. . . . Interactions are those of clarifications, reflections, summarizations, syntheses, and nonverbal supportive gestures, questioning is minimal and generally member-to-member.[13]

The behavioral orientation of Thoresen is obvious when he refers to the counselor as an applied behavioral scientist and indicates that the conduct of relevant research depends primarily on using a theoretical framework that encourages, indeed demands, empirical studies.[14] His description of group counseling is not quite the same as that of Kemp:

Counseling in groups should be defined as those activities specifically selected (and then empirically assessed) to help two or more clients engage in actions that will bring about clearly stated and mutually agreed upon changes in each individual's behavior. . . . Group counseling should not be limited by definition to certain problems or certain prescribed goals e.g., self understanding and self acceptance.[15]

Nor does the above quite agree with Gordon and Liberman when, in discussing various schools of thought in group psychotherapy, they say: "The common denominator reflected in these flavorings and schools of thought is a turning toward humanistic conceptions of self-actualization."[16]

13. C. Gratton Kemp, *Foundations of Group Counseling* (New York: McGraw-Hill, 1970), p. 63.
14. Carl E. Thoresen, "Comment," *Personnel and Guidance Journal,* 49:608–610 (April, 1971).
15. *Ibid.*
16. Myron Gordon and Norman Liberman, "Group Psychotherapy," *Personnel and Guidance Journal,* 49:611–617 (April, 1971).

It is equally obvious that Rogers is reflecting his phenomenological, client-centered orientation when he says:

*The group . . . is . . . relatively unstructured, choosing its own
goals and personal directions. The experience often, though not
always, includes some cognitive input—some content material
which is presented to the group. In almost all instances the
leader's responsibility is primarily the facilitation of the expression of both feelings and thoughts on the part of group
members. Both in the leader and in the members there is a focus on the process and dynamics of immediate personal interactions.* [17]

Dinkmeyer is reflecting his theory of counseling when he says:

*Group counseling is particularly valuable when man is under-
stood as an indivisible, social, and decision-making being
whose actions have a social purpose. Man's problems are primarily social. It is within the group that the individual can
identify and find his place. At the same time, his behavior expresses his goals and social intentions.* [18]

And, as a final example, the behavioral bent of Mayer, Rohen,
and Whiteley is quite obvious when they say:

*Group counseling appears to offer an excellent environment
for the creation of dissonance through the aid of segments of
social learning theory. In such a setting more than one model is
provided for each student to listen to, observe, and interact
with. As a result of this interaction among members contradictory items of information are likely to be introduced in the
group. Furthermore, group counseling provided several potential sources of reinforcement that could be used to aid clients
in behavioral change.* [19]

The goals and the methods of group counseling would appear
to be very much related to the theoretical orientation of the group
leader, and this orientation applies equally well to either individual
or group counseling. The goals and the methods of Kemp and Thoresen and Rogers are different because they are based on theories of

17. Carl R. Rogers, *op. cit.*, p. 6.
18. Don C. Dinkmeyer, "Group Counseling Theory and Techniques," *School Counselor*, 17:148–152 (November, 1969).
19. G. Roy Mayer, Terrance M. Rohen, and A. Whiteley, "Group Counseling with
Children : A Cognitive Behavioral Approach," *Journal of Counseling Psychology*, 16:142–148 (May, 1969).

counseling that view man and his nature and his purpose in living in quite different ways, and these theories are based on *belief* rather than empirical evidence.

GROUP COUNSELING THEORIES AND GROUP COUNSELING PRACTICE

It would seem fairly clear that there is no such thing as *a* theory of group counseling, but that most counseling theoreticians use their particular theory of counseling, with certain modifications to adjust to the dynamics of the group, as their theory of group counseling. In other words, such people as Fullmer, Rogers, Kemp, Thoresen, and Dinkmeyer are quite obviously Fullmer, Rogers, Kemp, Thoresen, and Dinkmeyer whether they are referring to individual counseling or group counseling.

When we look at some of the experiments and studies in group counseling, however, there is usually no clear-cut indication other than in behavioral counseling that the experimenter is putting into practice a particular theory of counseling. In some studies it is made clear that *no* particular theory is being followed. Prediger and Baumann, for example, report on a study in which group counseling was one of the procedures used. They indicate that no specific theoretical approach was used, and they describe the process as the free and confidential expression of feelings about adjustment problems at home and in the school.[20]

But then, one might say, every counselor involved in group counseling *must* be following some theoretical approach even if he makes no reference to it or shows no particular concern about it. The most obvious way to search for the theoretical orientation of the researcher is to examine the indicated goals and purposes of the study, and the actual process of what is referred to as group counseling. It is fairly clear, from the studies that I have examined, that the goals of group counseling are usually determined *by the counselor* before the participants in group counseling are brought together.

Yunker gives an example of this when, in talking about group counseling for children in primary grades, he says:

Counseling groups enable the counselor to both effectively meet the social and developmental needs of children and simulta-

20. Dale J. Prediger and Reemt R. Baumann, "Developmental Group Counseling," *Journal of Counseling Psychology,* 17:527–533 (November, 1970).

neously encourage a more comprehensive guidance approach within the early elementary grades.[21]

In a similar manner Nelson indicates that the goals of group counseling, as described to children who might participate, are to help them to become involved in deep listening, to help one another talk, to discuss problems or concerns, and to discuss feelings.[22]

While the students may have some degree of latitude as to whether or not they wish to join the group, it seems fairly clear that it is the counselor who determines the group from which the participants may be chosen, and that the goals have already been determined before the group is made up. Anderson, for example, talks about an experiment in group counseling in drug awareness with a group of drug abusers.[23] But it was school personnel who compiled a list of suspected drug abusers, and it was the counselor who determined that one of the goals was to increase the drug awareness of these children.

Youthful participants in group counseling, after all, have little choice as to whether they want to attend school or not. When school personnel and parents of the children make clear their feelings that this would be a good thing for the child, the element of choice becomes very narrow indeed!

Other than in behavioral group counseling studies, there is usually a vagueness as to what happens, or just what is done under the rubric of "group counseling." Sometimes, when the researcher expresses his feelings about what he is doing, one gets some picture of the theoretical orientation. An example of this would be Ainsworth, when, in talking about a group counseling experience with some girls, she says:

> *The most difficult thing for me to learn and remember was that my imposition or manipulation of the people in the group would be detrimental to their growth. If I pressed them into encounters or tried to fulfill my expectations of what a group should be, I would be controlling them and demonstrating my lack of faith in their potential.*[24]

21. John A. Yunker, "Essential Organizational Components of Group Counseling in the Primary Grades," *Elementary School Guidance and Counseling,* 4:172–179 (March, 1968).

22. Richard C. Nelson, "Organizing for Group Counseling," *Personnel and Guidance Journal,* 50:25–28 (September, 1971).

23. Sonia Anderson, "Group Counseling in Drug Awareness," *School Counselor,* 19:123–126 (November, 1971).

24. Marti Ainsworth, "The Small Group—A Movement Assured," *School Counselor,* 19:232–236 (March, 1972).

More often than not, however, there is little evidence of any particular theoretical orientation, and, it is difficult to determine just what is meant by "group counseling." Usually, it appears that the counselor sets up a certain goal, and then determines some way by which he hopes this goal may be achieved. Generally, the process would appear to consist of an open discussion, with an acceptant and understanding counselor, where students are encouraged to express their feelings without any risk of penalty.

Winder and Savenko describe a group counseling program which attempted to reduce the alienation that keeps youth within the poverty-failure cycle. They state that the major technique used by the counselors was the establishment of appropriate patterns of group behavior. These patterns were achieved through the effects of the counselor's own behavior.[25]

Dodson decided to have "sibling sessions" with the purpose of becoming better acquainted with pupils and understanding their home situations better. The sessions were structured but informally conducted, and "conversation flowed uninhibitedly."[26] Patsau reports a study in group guidance in which a teacher felt that if a class of her children were given an opportunity to voice some of their concerns, they could be freed not only to settle down to learning, but also to increase their awareness and understanding of each other within their peer group. In the sessions the children discussed personal concerns that made it difficult for them to concentrate on their work.[27]

Finney and Van Dalsem describe an experiment in which underachieving gifted students were given group counseling to see if it would have any effect on their grades.[28]

A somewhat similar study by Creange reports on the effects of group counseling on underachieving grade nine students. Group counseling is defined somewhat vaguely as a dynamic process that provided group members with opportunities to explore feelings and attitudes.[29] In a study by Apostal and Muro of the effects of group

25. Alvin E. Winder and Nicholai Savenko, "Group Counseling with Neighborhood Youth Corps Trainees," *Personnel and Guidance Journal,* 48:561–567 (March, 1970).
26. Anna G. Dodson, "Group Guidance: Sibling Sessions as a Means of Establishing Rapport in an Inner City Elementary School," *Elementary School Guidance and Counseling,* 6:104–107 (December, 1971).
27. Christine Patsau, "An Experiment in Group Guidance with the Whole Class," *Elementary School Guidance and Counseling,* 5:205–214 (March, 1971).
28. Ben C. Finney and Elizabeth Van Dalsem, "Group Counseling for Gifted Underachieving High School Students," *Journal of Counseling Psychology,* 16:87–94 (January, 1969).
29. Norman C. Creange, "Group Counseling for Underachieving Ninth Graders," *School Counselor,* 18:279–285 (March, 1971).

counseling on counselors in training, the process is described by indicating that counselor activities were aimed at promoting self-understanding through reinforcement of member-to-member interactions.[30]

Andersen and Binnie refer to a "group vocational guidance experience" designed to effect the educational and vocational goals and plans of the students.[31] The experience appeared to consist of the giving out of material, the administration of a test, and a series of discussions. The effects of group guidance on sex education are described by Kelly. The population here consisted of "slow learners," and the goal was to help the students explore their attitudes, including those toward sexuality.[32] An open discussion appeared to be the procedure followed. Watson refers to "group work" with principals, in which a number of principals met as a group to work out mutually agreed-upon problems. Certain techniques and procedures were used as part of the series of group discussions.[33]

All of the studies reported above might accurately be described as attempts to change and modify behavior. However, there are an increasing number of group counseling studies which are explicitly referred to as behavior modification. These studies tend to be more precise and sharper in describing goals and procedures and results. Even more than the above-reported studies, they tend to ignore the person of the counselor, who does not appear to be a part of the experiencing of the members of the group. It is apparently assumed in these behavioral experiments that it would make no difference if the group leader happened to be Carl Rogers or Albert Ellis or John Krumboltz or Adrian Von Kaam or Dugald Arbuckle. This attitude is hardly reflected by Corsini when, in talking about encounter groups, he comments that "in a group, the subject of the group is the therapist. It doesn't matter so much what the gimmicks are, who is in the group; *what the members are studying and what they learn is the therapist.*"[34]

Hinds and Roehlke refer to a group counseling experiment

30. Robert A. Apostal and James J. Muro, "Effects of Group Counseling on Self Reports and on Self Recognition Abilities of Counselors in Training," *Counselor Education and Supervision,* 10:56–63 (Fall, 1970).

31. Dale G. Andersen and Arthur A. Binnie, "Effects of a Group Vocational Guidance Class with College Community Students," *Vocational Guidance Quarterly,* 20:123–126 (December, 1971).

32. Gary F. Kelly, "Group Guidance on Sex Education," *Personnel and Guidance Journal,* 49:809–814 (June, 1971).

33. Darge H. Watson, "Group Work with Principals: Implications for Elementary Counselors," *Elementary School Guidance and Counseling,* 3:234–241 (May, 1969).

34. Raymond J. Corsini, *op. cit.,*

with children whose specific behaviors interfered with classroom learning. Counseling involved the use of positive and negative reinforcement to increase adaptive behaviors and decrease interfering behaviors.[35] The purpose of the research of Hedquist and Weinhold was to compare the effectiveness of two group behavior counseling approaches in increasing the verbal assertive responses of anxious and socially unassertive students. The specific treatments which were used were described in detail.[36] Kelly and Mathews report on a study to investigate the effectiveness of short-term group counseling on the school behavior of children identified as behavior problems. The group discussions had a content focus, a process focus, and embraced a small number of specific techniques, including direct behavior modification.[37] A study by Tosi, Swanson, and McLean examines the effects of group counseling with nonverbalizing elementary schoolchildren. Social reinforcement (praise, encouragement, etc.) was used within a group modality.[38] McBrien and Nelson report on the use of two commonly used group procedures (a play group and a discussion group) as a strategy for changing sociometric status among primary grade children.[39] Although neither the terms "group counseling" or "behavior modification" are used in this study, it is a report of the modification of behavior using procedures which have been described in other reports as either group guidance or group counseling.

From all of these reported studies, then, several tentative conclusions might be drawn regarding group counseling:

1. There is no such thing as *a* theory of group counseling, any more than there is *a* theory of counseling. Only the most parochial and uneducated of group counselors would claim that they have at last found a theory of man and his behavior that equips them to practice group counseling *the* way it should be practiced.

2. Most of those individuals who might be called "practicing

35. William C. Hinds and Helen J. Roehlke, "A Learning Theory Approach to Group Counseling with Elementary School Children," *Journal of Counseling Psychology*, 17:49–55 (January, 1970).

36. Francis J. Hedquist and Barry K. Weinhold, "Behavioral Group Counseling with Socially Anxious and Unassertive College Students," *Journal of Counseling Psychology*, 17:237–242 (May, 1970).

37. Eugene W. Kelly, Jr., and Doris B. Mathews, "Group Counseling with Discipline Problem Children at the Elementary School Level," *School Counselor*, 18:273–278 (March, 1971).

38. Donald J. Tosi, Carl Swanson, and Pat McLean, "Group Counseling with Non-Verbalizing Elementary School Children," *Elementary School Guidance and Counseling*, 4:260–266 (May, 1970).

39. Robert J. McBrien and Randolph J. Nelson, "Experimental Group Strategies with Primary Grade Children," *Elementary School Guidance and Counseling*, 6:170–174 (March, 1972).

theorists" practice their theory of counseling regardless of whether they are involved in a counseling relationship with an individual or a group of individuals. Some follow an established theory, others develop a theory that fits their particular practice of counseling.

3. Most of the reported studies place surprisingly little emphasis on the dynamics of the group. One might assume that the basic purpose of group counseling, above and beyond the economy of time and money and human effort, would be that the group itself, and its impact on each of its members, is the crucial difference between individual counseling and group counseling. More often than not in the reported studies, however, it would appear that the group is a means by which a counselor can do with, or to, nine children, what he might otherwise have done with, or to, one child.

4. In most of the studies, no mention is made of counseling theory. Sometimes, the theory of the counselor is fairly obvious in the way in which he describes the goals and purposes of the experiment. The description of the actual process of group counseling is also a means by which the practice of a theory may be noted. In most studies, however, the process is usually described in such vague language that it is very difficult to see its relationship to any theory of counseling.

5. The exception to the above statement are those studies which are described as behavior modification. In these, it is usually quite clear that this is an experiment in behavior modification. The goals and the process are defined clearly, as are the results, or lack of results, of the study. The behavioral group counselor, in keeping with his practice of individual counseling, places minimal stress on the person of the counselor in the group counseling process.

6. In practically all of the studies, it is quite obvious that the objectives of group counseling are determined by individuals other than the recipients of group counseling. The members of the group are sometimes involved in the actual process, but even here it would appear that, more often than not, what happens has been determined before the process starts. The authority, the control, the direction—these are *not* in the hands of the members of the group involved in the group counseling process, but rather have been determined by those who have planned the group counseling and who are the controllers of what happens.

Chapter 7

Other Theories of Counseling

Some readers may feel that I have been somewhat negligent in relegating what they consider to be an important theory of counseling to a few paragraphs in a chapter on "Other Theories." However, the major purpose in looking at other theories in this chapter is to see their relationship to the existential-humanistic or behavioral model, rather than looking at them in any great detail. The "other theories" that I mention are obviously the ones that I consider to be most important on the current scene.

CLIENT-CENTERED COUNSELING

As has already been indicated, client-centered counseling would appear to be closer to the existential-humanistic model than any other theory of counseling. Indeed, whatever changes have taken place over the years in client-centered counseling are in the direction of existential counseling. One might say that client-centered counseling has become more existential.

Titus, for example, describes existentialism thus:

Existentialism is an emphasis on the uniqueness and primacy of existence in the sense of the inner, immediate experience of self-awareness. . . . The most meaningful point of reference for any person is his own immediate consciousness.[1]

1. Harold H. Titus, *Living Issues in Philosophy* (New York: American Book Co., 1959), p. 292 (4th ed., 1964).

This would not appear to differ much from Rogers' description of the counseling relationship:

> I launch myself into the therapeutic relationship, having a hypothesis, or a faith, that my liking, my confidence, my understanding of the other person's inner world will lead to a significant process of becoming. . . . I enter the relationship . . . as a person. . . . I risk myself. . . . I let myself go . . . my reaction being based (but not consciously) on my total organismic sensitivity to this other person.[2]

In a somewhat similar manner, May describes the existential approach to psychotherapy:

> [I]t is not a system of therapy, but an attitude toward therapy, not a set of new techniques but a concern with the understanding of the structure of the human being and his experience that must underlie all techniques.[3]

This appears to be what therapist Gendlin described over a decade ago:

> As I express my present feeling and my vague images of what may be happening between us now, a very personal quality enters into my expressions. I am giving words to my ongoing experiencing with him. There is a quality of personal risk and openness in my saying these things. . . . The client lives in a responsive context made up of my person and my openly expressive interaction with him. Yet, his side of the interaction might be quite tentative, implicit, until he wishes to make it explicit as his.[4]

Gendlin also described what he then referred to as "recent modifications" in client-centered therapy: (1) Basic therapist attitudes, rather than any specific "client-centered" behaviors, are essential therapeutic factors. (2) Genuine spontaneity and expressiveness of the therapist are needed—an undefensive transparency and genuineness of the therapist as the person he is, free of professional or personal artificiality. (3) Experiencing (the preconceptual feeling process) constitutes therapy rather than verbal self-expression.[5]

I would not see these as being too different from the "condi-

2. Carl R. Rogers, "Learning to be Free," unpublished paper.
3. Rollo May, "Freedom and Responsibility Re-examined," unpublished paper given at 1962 APGA Convention, Chicago.
4. Eugene T. Gendlin, "Client-Centered Developments and Work with Schizophrenics," Journal of Counseling Psychology, 9:205–213 (Fall, 1962).
5. Ibid.

152

tions" set up by Rogers in the earlier years. However, the changes described by Hart are very definitely a movement in an existential direction. He describes these in a table:

TABLE 1.   Periods in the Development of Client-Centered Psychotherapy.[6]

	Functions of the Therapist	Personality Changes
Period i Nondirective Psychotherapy 1940–1950	Creation of a permissive noninterventive atmosphere; *acceptance* and *clarification*	Gradual achievement of *insight* into one's self and into one's situation
Period II Reflective Psychotherapy 1950–1957	*Reflection* of feelings, avoiding threat in the relationship	Development of congruence of self concept and the phenomenological field
Period III Experiential Psychotherapy 1957–1970	Wide range of behaviors to express basic attitudes. Focus on the client's experiencing. Expression of the therapist's experiencing.	Growth in the process continuum of inter- and intra-personal living by learning to use direct experiencing.

It would thus seem that increasingly the client-centered counselor and the existential therapist are talking much the same language when they discuss human beings, the person-in-being, the counseling relationship, the process of becoming, and the meaning of reality and freedom. It would seem to me, however, that the basic characteristics of client-centered counseling are the same today as they were several decades ago. The major change, it would appear, is the increasing extent of counselor involvement and counselor exposure.

Major characteristics today, and several decades ago, are:

1. The crucial factor in counseling is the establishment of a human relationship that is characterized by such terms as warm, acceptant, empathic, congruent and nonjudgmental. This is possible

6. Joseph Hart, "The Development of Client-Centered Therapy," in J. T. Hart and T. M. Tomlinson (ed.), *New Directions in Client-Centered Therapy* (Boston: Houghton Mifflin, 1970), p.4.

only if the counselor can reflect these attitudes as a part of his person, rather than as a learned technique or procedure.

2. This relationship itself is the major part of the growth experience.

3. An individual has the capacity to modify and change his perceptions, and this can occur when a threat-free relationship is established with another person. Every human individual has the potential for self-growth, self-development, and self-actualization. The counselor helps the client to be who he can be.

4. A person's behavior is directly related to his perceptions of the moment. Reality for the client is what is perceived by the client about the client and about others, not what is perceived by the counselor or others. My self *is* the self of which *I* am aware.

5. The stress is on the immediate situation rather than the past. Thus there is minimal need of testing and diagnosis to determine where the client *was*. What counts is where the client *is*—now.

6. The stress in the relationship is put on feelings rather than thinking, but the feelings of the counselor are more of a factor today than they were originally.

7. Client-centered counseling was so named because the entire attention was on the person of the client, and it is in this area that the greatest change has taken place. The counselor is becoming more involved in the relationship with the client as the other human being, and this means, of course, that there is more likelihood of counselor direction, even though this may not be the purpose of the counselor. Client-centered counseling is still *client*-centered, but it is more counselor-involved. And the more the counselor becomes part of the relationship the more likely it is that he will influence the outcome of that relationship.

All of this, of course, is what is theoretically so. In my experience, most counselors who call themselves client-centered counselors still function like the earlier model. The major technique continues to be reflection of feeling, and this includes clarification, reformulation, and summarization. It also includes interpretation, if, that is, we think of interpretation as meaning the counselor's perception of what the client, in a feeling sense, is communicating to him. That is, a client might say, "I love my mother very much," while an accurate reflection of *feeling,* which is also an interpretation, would be "You feel angry, even though you say you love her." It should be noted, too, that this reflection and/or interpretation is highly verbal, and the person of the counselor is relatively uninvolved and unexposed.

REALITY THERAPY

I would see reality therapy, the product of William Glasser,[7] as being very much akin to behavior therapy, with one major and very significant difference. Glasser, while he is a psychiatrist, tends to view the people with whom he works not as being sick, but rather as having not learned, or having lost the ability they did have, to be responsible for their own behavior. Inmates in institutions are irresponsible rather than mentally ill. Glasser sees the therapist as first having to become so involved with the patient that the patient can face reality and see how his behavior is unrealistic; the therapist must then reject the behavior which is unrealistic but still accept the patient and his involvement with him; and finally, the therapist must teach the patient better ways of fulfilling his needs within the confines of reality, and thus accept responsibility for his own behavior. All of this sounds very much like Ellis' rational-emotive psychotherapy, the major difference being that Glasser tends to stress a deeper counselor-client relationship than does Ellis.

As in behavior therapy, reality therapy is centered in learning theory, and the new ways of behavior that are learned promote further behavioral change. It is the initial change in behavior that starts the process, thus the attitude of the patient changes regardless of whether or not he understands his old ways. Insight is not viewed as an important or necessary ingredient for behavior change.

Since it is believed that the reasons for the behavior do not make a difference in changes in behavior, in reality therapy there is stress on the "what" rather than the "why." In all of these aspects, reality therapy might be considered to be simply a somewhat restricted version of behavior therapy.

The crucial difference, however, is that the basic ingredient of reality therapy is the fact that the patient is held responsible for his behavior, and that he is helped to learn that his inappropriate behavior is irresponsible. Thus the message communicated to the patient is that he does have a choice—to move in the direction of more appropriate behavior and thus be more responsible, or remain with his current behavior and accept his irresponsibility.

At the same time, however, it is the therapist who determines, to a great extent, just what "appropriate" behavior might be. Patients are patients because they deny the reality of the world around them. They must learn to face this reality, and, at the same time, learn how to satisfy their needs. Thus appropriate behavior, it would

7. William Glasser, *Reality Therapy* (New York: Harper and Row, 1965).

appear, is behavior that is more in keeping with the demands of society, which, in turn, is viewed as "reality." While the reality therapist refers to the facing up to the reality of the world around the patient, the implication is that the therapist provides the patient with experiences so that he is more acceptant of the reality of the therapist and of society in general. The young man who is considering leaving high school would probably be considered to be unrealistic and irresponsible, guilty of inappropriate behavior.

Thus there is a contradiction. The reality therapist does stress the responsibility of the client to become more responsible by developing more appropriate behavior, but the meaning of "reality" and "appropriate" would appear to be determined by the therapist, not the patient. The reality therapist is unlike the behavior therapist in that he does hold the patient responsible for his behavior, but he is like the behavior therapist in being very much in control of any determination of the future behavior of the patient.

PSYCHOANALYTIC THERAPY

While the psychoanalysis of today has changed somewhat from the psychoanalysis of Freud's day, it still retains the same characteristics.[8] It is a pessimistic view of humanity, and it is a behavioral view. The therapist is still the expert, and he operates in the same way as a medical doctor with a sick patient. The person coming to see the therapist, is, indeed, viewed as a sick patient. The doctor is in control, and the patient has little choice as to what is done to him and what happens to him. The personal relationship between the patient and the therapist is of minimal importance.

The basic characteristics of the psychoanalytic point of view are as follows:

1. Humans would appear to be basically unhappy, unfree, and evil creatures, governed by aggressive instincts.

2. More than any current form of psychotherapy, psychoanalysis stresses the past as being crucial for the present, and the intellectual understanding of this past is essential.

3. The goal of the therapist is to maintain a balance between internal instincts and impulses (the id, which is amoral and unconscious) and social restrictions (the superego, which is the moral

8. See A. A. Brill, *The Basic Writings of Sigmund Freud* (New York: Random House, 1927); Sigmund Freud, *Beyond the Pleasure Principle* (London: Hogarth and the Institute of Psychoanalysis, 1924); Sigmund Freud, *The Future of an Illusion* (New York: International Psychoanalytic Library, No. 15, 1943); Harry J. S. Guntrip, *Psychoanalytic Theory, Therapy and the Self* (New York: Basic Books, 1971).

voice of society, imposed upon the individual from the moment he is born). The ego attempts to maintain a balance between the two, and man thus spends his life trying to reduce his tensions. It is assumed that the therapist has done a better job of this on himself than has the patient.

4. In the more traditional psychoanalysis, the developing sexuality of the individual, from infancy onward, was considered to be the central factor of his developing personality. The developmental history of the individual was considered to be psychosexual in nature, and pathology was related to the blocking and thwarting of the sexual instinct in the early years. Currently, more stress is placed on the total developmental history of the individual, with less on the psychosexual.

5. The therapist uncovers, interprets and integrates the unconscious repressed material which dominates the individual's life and living. Traditionally, this was done primarily through free association, but currently there is more direct involvement of the therapist. The relationship is stressed more, and some therapists even feel comfortable facing a patient who is sitting up instead of lying on a couch!

6. The approach of the therapist tends to be rational and cognitive rather than affective and emotive, even though Freud, in stressing the irrationality of man, took sharp issue with the scientific thinking of his day.

Thus the psychoanalytic approach would basically appear to be pessimistic. Man is doomed to live out his life struggling to maintain a balance among forces which are not of his making. He is the victim rather than the creator of his culture. It has been said that Galileo struck the first hammer blow against the smug security of man when he pointed out that the earth we lived on was not the center of the universe; Darwin continued it when he raised the suggestion that, rather than being the superior creatures of God's creation, man had evolved out of some much more lowly forms of life; and Freud hammered the nails in the coffin of man's self-esteem when he made him a creature of his psychosexual instincts!

RATIONAL-EMOTIVE PSYCHOTHERAPY

Although the term that Albert Ellis uses to describe his particular mode of therapy is "rational-emotive,"[9] it is overwhelmingly ra-

9. See Albert Ellis, *Reason and Emotion in Psychotherapy* (New York: Lyle Stuart, 1962) and Albert Ellis, "Rational-Emotive Psychotherapy," in Dugald S. Arbuckle (ed.), *Counseling and Psychotherapy: An Overview* (New York: McGraw-Hill, 1967).

tional. The rational therapist believes that what we feel depends on what we think, and that we are capable of thinking our way out of our negative and harmful feelings. The major function of the therapist is to teach, in a dominant, directive manner, using any kind of effective technique—challenging, confronting, prodding, manipulating. The patient is taught how to get rid of his anxiety as an irrational feeling for which he has little or no responsibility. The stress is on intellectual insight and understanding.

The rational therapist, like the behavioral therapist, sees himself as teaching the patient more appropriate modes of behavior. Unlike the behavioral therapist, however, he sees much of this behavior as being inborn. Thus irrational thinking and behavior is a natural human state. Since the patient is not to blame for his irrational behavior, he cannot be expected to accept responsibility for it. In this sense, he cannot be considered to be irresponsible because of inappropriate behavior which may be damaging to himself or to others.

Needless to say, the dominating teacher-therapist is in control. The patient would appear to have as little to say as to what happens and where he goes as would the sick patient of the medical doctor or the inappropriately behaving client of the behavioral counselor. Just as in reality therapy it is the therapist who determines what is realistic and what is unrealistic, and in behavior therapy it is the therapist who determines what behavior is appropriate and what is inappropriate, so in rational therapy it is the therapist who determines what is rational and what is irrational. These words—realistic, appropriate, rational—are synonymous, and they all spell out therapist control, domination and direction.

Rational therapy, like most modern therapies, stresses the present rather than the past. There is a difference, however, in that it is not so much the event or the behavior of the present that is stressed, but the patient's view or idea or perception about the event or the behavior. This, according to the rational therapist, is what causes the problem. Thus the pregnant teenaged girl who is feeling guilty is taught that it is quite irrational to feel guilty. When she then comes to accept the irrationality of her feelings, she will be able to make some logical, rational decisions as to what she is going to do about her pregnancy. It is not the event but how we feel about the event that creates the neuroses. Since our feeling is due to either innate factors or environmental factors over which we have no control, it is irrational for us to feel poorly about ourselves.

With this stress on directive teaching and rationality, it is obvious that the person-to-person relationship between patient and therapist is of minimal importance. The relationship is that of student to teacher or patient to doctor. One person, the expert, knows what is wrong and what should be done about it; the other person feels something is wrong, but doesn't know *what* is wrong, or what should and could be done about it.

Summing up, then, the basic points about this theory of counseling are:

1. What we feel depends on what we think; thus thinking should take precedence over feeling. Our security is measured by our ability to think our way out of our negative and harmful feelings.

2. It is not the event, but our cognitive evaluation of the event that causes our troubles and stresses and strains.

3. The major function of the therapist is to teach the client (to persuade, to challenge, to prod) to change his irrational views. The client is taught to view scientifically his irrationality.

4. It is the present situation that is important, not the past. Ideas about events, past and present, are more important than the events themselves.

5. The client-counselor relationship—the experiencing—these are not considered to be important aspects in rational-emotive therapy.

6. It is assumed that the client has the ability, with the assistance of the counselor, to look rationally at his irrationality. It is assumed he can think about his feelings.

THE NEW THERAPIES

In this day of rapid change it is obviously hazardous to write about anything as being "new," since by the time written words become published words the "new" might have become "old!" However, it would seem to me that what happened in counseling and psychotherapy in the latter half of the 1960's, and continued in to the 1970's might truly be called revolutionary. It was Carl Rogers who, in the early 1940's, loosened us from the shackles of the medical model in psychotherapy, but it took another twenty years before the real explosion took place. While behavioral counseling has been referred to as revolutionary, I cannot see it in this way, since it is predominantly the reestablishment of already questioned perceptions about humanity and human behavior. Nor can I see reality therapy or rational-emotive therapy as being revolutionary in any basic sense, and psychoanalysis, needless to say, should be interesting primarily in a historical sense!

Thus while client-centered is by now an established form of therapy, it did make the first major break with the medical model of psychotherapy and establish a base for the revolution that was yet to come. But it is the existential-humanistic model of counseling and psychotherapy that is most open to the new ideas and methods, because it places a high value on creative and transpersonal experience, on the expanding and altering of states of consciousness, and on the developing of a sharper awareness of the gestalt being and the world in which he resides. Krippner and Murphy, in discussing parapsychological issues, say:

> However, the fact that they are discussed, and the fact that existential considerations form the underlying philosophical basis for humanistic psychology, provides a common ground for communication between the two disciplines. Furthermore, humanistic psychologists would be, in general, more open-mined to the novel theories of causation put forward than would most behaviorists or psychoanalysts.[10]

While the new therapies stress the individual in a total sense, they do not ignore the reality that all of us live within some form of societal structure—even if we reside in a small commune. Jaffe refers to the several techniques and values of the new therapies as follows:

1. Focus on immediate experience and feelings;
2. Expressiveness of interior experience;
3. Powerful, positive support from a small group;
4. A socializing forum for the redefinition of social norms, values, and finally, behavior.[11]

He also refers to an alternate model of counseling as consisting of:

1. Contact: rapport, mutual contract, support, helping relationship, sharing with others;
2. Awareness: expressive therapy, encounter, Gestalt; exploration of interior experience;
3. Strategy for action: understanding life situation, changing relationships, altering environment, redefining self and goals.[12]

---

10. Stanley Krippner and Gardner Murphy, "Humanistic Psychology and Parapsychology," *Journal of Humanistic Psychology,* 13:3–24 (Fall, 1973).
11. Dennis T. Jaffe, "A Counseling Institution in an Oppressive Environment," *Journal of Humanistic Psychology,* 13:25–46 (Fall, 1973).
12. *Ibid.*

I realize that there might be some debate over my choice of "new" therapies. What follows is no more than a thumbnail sketch of my version of the major new therapies of the 1970s:

Gestalt Therapy.

While the term "gestalt" has its own meaning, it is likely that the name of Fritz Perls will continue to be considered to be almost synonymous with gestalt therapy.[13] In a technique sense, gestalt therapy might be considered to be behavioral, but its basic view of the person is existential-humanistic.

The stress is on the here and now, and the past or future is viewed as a means of escaping from the reality of now. The client has the potential to function in a responsible manner, and it is the responsibility of the therapist to help the client to recover what he already has.

The provision of opportunities is considered to be more effective than verbal explanation, and this means that a major tool of the therapist is manipulation of both the client and the environment. This, in turn, means that there is a great variety of "gestalt" techniques. For example, if a client is referring to a difficult relationship with his wife, he might be asked to sit in a different chair and *become* his wife, and a discussion might then take place with the client changing chairs as he alternates between being husband or wife. A client who views himself as having conflicting roles may be asked to take turns being each of his two beings. If a client has a fear of cats, he might be asked to become the cat as the cat faces the person. In experiencing a dream, one might be asked to become various parts of the dream—one might become the door of a cabin, the cup from which one drank some hot tea, and so on.

The therapist deliberately manipulates the circumstances so that the patient is forced to face the meaning of the affective relationship between the therapist and himself. The therapist, for example, might point out certain bodily movements of the client, and wonder about their meaning, thus almost forcing a more immediate intimacy between client and therapist. Nonverbal communication is viewed as being more authentic than verbal communication, and there is a good deal of stress on the immediate person-to-person relationship between client and therapist.

13. See Fritz Perls, *Gestalt Therapy Verbatim* (Lafayette, California: Real People Press, 1969) and Fritz Perls, *In and out the Garbage Pail* (Lafayette, California: Real People Press, 1969); Jean Fagan and Lee Shepherd (eds.), *What is Gestalt Therapy?* (New York: Harper and Row, 1973).

Interestingly enough, while the gestalt therapist views manipulation as a major technique, he is opposed to interpretation because, it is felt, this implies that the therapist knows more about the client than the client knows about himself. This would appear to me to be somewhat contradictory, since while the therapist may be less verbally interpretive, he nevertheless sets up experiences that help the client to develop new meanings about his behavior. I would consider this to be a sort of back-door kind of interpretation.

Needless to say, there is no question that there is therapist direction and therapist control, since manipulators must be manipulating a person with some goal in mind. At least I hope that the gestalt therapist does not manipulate blindly, praying for the best!

Primal Therapy

Primal therapy is referred to as an accidental discovery of a therapist who became interested in the screams that seemed to occur among his clients at a certain stage in their therapy. Arthur Janov came to regard the scream as the product of central and universal pains that resided in all neurotic individuals, and he referred to these as Primal Pains.[14] I would see the following as the basic characteristics of primal therapy:

1. Primal therapy is an intensive, short-term, emotional experiencing.

2. Much stress is placed on the early years, and the pains that developed as the child became "armored" in his relationships with his parents must be relived and experienced.

3. Primal therapy is involved with internal processes, as contrasted with conditioning therapies, which concern themselves with overt behavior.

4. The activities which make basic changes in an individual must flow from his feelings, and this flow must occur from the inside out.

5. When a person can come to experience his primal wants and needs without the fear of losing love, he is then experiencing his "being."

6. Warmth has little to do with insight, because primal therapy is not a therapy of relationships. Insightfulness cannot be taught, any more than feeling can be taught. It is the feeling that is the teacher.

7. The primal definition of love is letting someone be what he

14. Arthur Janov, *The Primal Scream* (New York: Putnam, 1970).

162

is. This can happen only when needs are fulfilled. From the point of view of the primal therapist, eclecticism can be an inverted solipsism, in which almost anything can be true because nothing is.

While Janov claims that primal therapy is the newest of the new, and the superior answer for the neuroses of humanity, it is obvious that the theories and practice of psychoanalysis are not totally ignored, and the contributions of Wilhelm Reich[15] are also incorporated into primal therapy. The history of psychotherapy gives enough evidence to warrant some skepticism about claims for the superiority of any methodology or technique!

Transactional Analysis

In the last decade or so the initials T.A. have come to stand for transactional analysis, which was brought to public attention by two books by Eric Berne[16] and further publicized by Thomas A. Harris.[17] Transactional analysis looks at human communication as a transaction between people where things are being exchanged—ideas, words, feelings—at both a verbal and nonverbal level, although the verbal exchange seems to be stressed more than the nonverbal.

Berne saw any human interaction as being between three basic ego states—parent, adult, child—and Harris elaborated on the four basic life positions as being (1) I'm OK: You're OK; (2) I'm not OK: You're not OK; (3) I'm not OK: You're OK; (4) I'm OK: You're not OK. The one ego state of one person is always reacting to one ego state of the other person, and the reaction of one person to the other is very much dependent on the ego state that is communicated by the other person. Thus the woman, who traditionally has been taught to react as the child, may say to her husband, "John, don't you think we should go and see a movie tonight?" and this encourages him to react as he has been taught, as the adult or parent, "No, Mary, I have read the reviews and I don't think we should go."

Therapy helps the individual to use the three ego states in a more appropriate fashion. At times it is natural and human to react as the child, or the parent, or the adult, and as one becomes more aware of one's being, the ego state that is communicated will be reflective of the secure human being—it will be an accurate and

15. Wilhelm Reich, *The Function of the Orgasm: The Discovery of the Orgone* (2nd ed.) (New York: Farrar, Straus and Giroux, 1961).
16. Eric Berne, *Transactional Analysis in Psychotherapy* (New York: Grove Press, 1961) and Eric Berne, *Games People Play* (New York: Grove Press, 1964).
17. Thomas A. Harris, *I'm OK-You're OK* (New York: Harper and Row, 1967).

163

healthy reflection of the person, rather than being a non-natural conditioned response.

Transactional analysis can, however, become "gimmicky," and it can become an objective, technological version of the human being, in which the person is seen as one of three ego states, but never as a gestalt human being, a complicated person who cannot be measured in terms of this, or this, or that. We live in a technological world, and there is a real danger that transactional analysis may create an acceptance of this narrow world and never help us to go beyond to a vastly expanded awareness of the self.

Biofeedback as Therapy

Human beings, more in the East than the West, have long hypothesized that the mind has power ever the body, that the mind controls our bodily functions. There have been amazing reports of yogis in India being able to affect heartbeat, salivation, bodily temperature; being able to survive with little oxygen and to prevent the production of a blister by a burn or the flow of blood from a cut. From all of this one can hypothesize that it is what our mind tells us about ourselves that produces much of what we know as physical disease, and if the mind can generate problems which produce diseases, why then cannot the mind reverse the procedure when the patient is helped to become aware of what he is doing to himself?

Earlier evidence indicated that it definitely was possible to gain voluntary control over internal bodily functions, but the question of how this happened remained a mystery. The assumption of biofeedback techniques is that certain responses are made when information, or biofeedback, is received by the organism. These responses are modified and corrected, depending on the feedback, until the organism determines that the desired goal has been reached. Normally, we are not aware of this feedback information, and it is modern technology that has solved this problem. Electronic instruments are used to amplify changes in the body such as occur in blood pressure, heart rate and muscle contractions. These changes give signals in external instruments. On repetition a person can come to identify the signals of internal changes and thus come to learn to control them.

While biofeedback therapy is, in a way, the training of one's self to modify and control internal physiological processes, it has also increased interest in cognitive control of bodily processes through yoga, Zen, meditation and hypnosis. It has also raised the prospect that one can train oneself to open up creative, imaginative aspects of one's thoughts, to expand one's conscious awareness.[18]

A brochure describing a biofeedback program states that biofeedback training is helpful for the alleviation of migraine headaches, general tensions or anxiety, high blood pressure, and some insomnia problems. It also cautions that biofeedback training is most likely to be effective when combined with other kinds of therapy. Another brochure describes a biofeedback monitor, which features brain-wave detection, GSR or skin-resistance monitoring, heartbeat detection, and a built-in sensor test.

As in all of the newer therapies, the positive outcomes of biofeedback therapy are sometimes overshadowed by the grandiose claims made by some converts. Schwartz gives a reasoned, professional view when he comments:

> Biofeedback, if used in conjunction with other medical and psychological techniques, may be useful with certain patients. However, in the face of specific biological and environmental constraints, I am somewhat pessimistic about its application to chronic physical disease, particularly in the absence of other therapeutic procedures. . . .
>
> Even if "direct" voluntary control of certain bodily functions proves to have little therapeutic value, biofeedback per se can still serve an important function—to signal both the therapist and the patient that the patient is currently thinking, feeling, or doing specific things that are detrimental to his physical or emotional health. . . . By means of immediate, augmented feedback (with its associated increased bodily awareness), the patient may be able to learn new ways of coping behaviorally with his environment, or he may be able to alter his life-style in such a way as to keep his physiological processes within safer limits.[19]

Biofeedback stresses mind *and* body, rather than the older mind *or* body, and it has existential-humanistic implications in that it provides evidence that *I* can control my body, and thus *I* am the one who can determine, to a great extent, what happens to my body. *I* can effect my inner as well as my outer limits.

18. Theodore X. Barber, Leo V. DiCara. Joe Kamiya, Neal E. Miller, David Shapiro, and Johann Stoyva (eds.), *Biofeedback and Self-Control* (Chicago: Aldine-Atherton, 1971).

19. Gary E. Schwartz, "Biofeedback as Therapy: Some Theoretical and Practical Issues," *American Psychologist,* 28:666–673 (August, 1973).

Psychomotor Therapy

Diane and Albert Pesso are the cofounders of psychomotor therapy[20] and some would say they *are* psychomotor therapy. Albert Pesso believes that we have strong primal feelings and needs that have been repressed in our childhood, and that it is these repressed feelings that cripple much of our day-to-day living. Not only, in psychomotor therapy, is there an acting out of the feeling, but there is a reaction, and then an interaction, to the feeling. Thus a "negative accommodator" may be chosen to represent a feared parent, and while there is no touching, the negative accommodator will cry, scream, groan, and if necessary die in an accurate reaction to the actions of the client. This, however, produces feelings of guilt, so that a "positive accommodator" is also necessary. This person represents the ideal parent who will offer as much love and support as is needed, and eventually the negative parent is replaced by the ideal parent.

Again, here, in a very physical and emotionally involved sense, there is an existential-humanistic stress on helping a person to come to be the person he really is, to get rid of the feelings that have inhibited his growth so that needs can be satisfied in a healthy manner. It is a realization of the true self of the person.

Arica

The Arica Institute was created by Oscar Ichazo, and while some would see it as a religion, Arica would prefer to be seen as an experience that is spiritual, but not a religion. Functionally, the training consists of hundreds of exercises representing a great variety of yogas, gestalt, meditations, massage, encounter and others.

Arica stresses the oneness of humanity, and our ability to go far beyond the limited view of consciousness that is typical of the Western world—and Western religion. This Oneness applies in all ways, so that there is no humanity *or* God, or science *or* religion, or faith *or* reason. They—and we—are all one. This is stress on the inner basic Being—my answers to my difficulties come from within, not from without. As Ichazo says:

When we turn away from our primal perfection, our completeness, our unity with the world and God we create the illusion

20. Albert Pesso, *Movement in Psychotherapy: Psychomotor Techniques and Training* (New York: New York University Press, 1969) and Albert Pesso, *Experience in Action: A Psychomotor Psychology* (New York: New York University Press, 1973).

*that we need something exterior to ourselves for our comple-
tion . . . man . . . can find no real happiness until he returns to
his essence, that is until he reaches what Buddhism called nir-
vana or the Void.*[21]

Transcendental Meditation

Transcendental Meditation, which consists basically of twenty minutes of meditation each morning and evening, has won an astonishing number of converts in recent years in the United States and in
the West, although, as is often the case, the Eastern "way to life"
somehow does not seem to find as many converts in its native land!
The meditator closes his eyes, sits upright, and silently repeats a
"mantra." The mantra, which has more sound than meaning, and
comes usually from Hindu holy books, is supposedly geared to fit the
person, and becomes the individual's personal and secret possession,
not to be told to outsiders.

The father of TM is Maharishi Mahesh Yogi, and his disciples
include not only the young, but businessmen, academicians, and
even a general of the U.S. Army. The relative ease of transcendental
meditation is no doubt one of the reasons for its popularity, but there
is also an impressive array of scientific evidence of what TM does for
blood pressure, lactate levels in the blood, oxygen consumption, and
a general stablizing of the nervous system. All of this, of course, may
be a better argument for the power of faith in a procedure than it is
for the procedure itself, but it can hardly be faulted if the results are
positive. The best-known supporter of TM, John Lennon, of Beatle
fame, is now its best-known detractor, although this probably says
no more than that John Lennon has changed more than TM has
changed!

Psychosynthesis

Robert Assagioli first presented his conception of psychosynthesis in
a doctoral thesis in the year 1910, so some might wonder what in the
world is "new" about psychosynthesis. In the United States, however, it is only recently, with the advent of a more existential-humanistic version of psychology and psychotherapy, that psychosynthesis
has become one of the better-known therapies.

21. Sam Keen, "A Conversation about Ego Destruction with Oscar Ichazo," *Psychology Today*, 7:64–72 (July, 1973).

While Assagioli sees important differences between existentialism and psychosynthesis, I would see him as one of the earlier existential humanists, taking issue with the then dominant form of psychotherapy, namely, psychoanalysis. Psychosynthesis, is, literally, the expansion of the psyche, the expanding of the consciousness, the moving toward being part of a greater whole. This is what I hear Assagioli saying about psychosynthesis:[22]

1. The stress is on the whole person, the gestalt being. The living person, now, is what is being considered, and one works to expand the health of the person, and to remove those obstacles which have prevented the attainment of even greater health.

2. The primary asset of the therapist is himself, and the human aspects of his personality are as important as, if not more important than, the professional aspects.

3. Each individual is considered to be unique, and this means that there is no one technique. The techniques that are used depend on the people who are involved, the place, and the time. This human uniqueness applies to therapist as well as to client, and thus the interplay between therapist and client is considered to be more important than the use of any particular technique. This, in turn, means that there is active involvement of both client and therapist with each other.

4. For some individuals, a biological synthesis, that is, the harmonious development of all the normal human functions, is all that is needed. For others, however, more than this personal psychosynthesis is needed, and there must be a more spiritual transpersonal self-realization.

5. Assessment is stressed rather than diagnosis, and in assessment the therapist should ascertain what functions are underdeveloped, repressed, and neglected, but also what functions are overdeveloped. Synthesis, too, does not mean the abolition of differences, but rather a balancing and uniting at a higher level.

Assagioli does not see the differences between existential therapy and psychosynthesis to be great, but he does point out certain differences:[23]

1. In psychosynthesis much greater stress is placed on the will as an essential function of the self, and various techniques are used to arouse, strengthen, develop, and direct the will.

22. From a personal conversation with Robert Assagioli in Florence, Italy, in July, 1972, and from Vin Rosenthal, "The Gentle Synthesizer: An Interview with Robert Assagioli," *Voices*, 9:18–26 (Fall, 1973), and from Roberto Assagioli, "Jung and Psychosynthesis," *Journal of Humanistic Psychology*, 14:35–55 (Winter, 1974), and Roberto Assagioli, *The Act of Will* (New York: Viking Press, 1974).

23. Robert Assagioli, *Psychosynthesis* (New York: Viking Press, 1965), pp. 5–6.

2. The direct experience of the self, of pure self-awareness, independent of any content of the field of consciousness and of any situation in which the individual might find himself, is considered in psychosynthesis to be a true phenomenological experience, an inner reality.

3. There is not only a recognition of the positive, creative, and joyous experiences which may occur along with painful and tragic ones, but these lived experiences are actively fostered and induced through the use of various methods and techniques.

4. The experience of loneliness is not considered in psychosynthesis either ultimate or essential. It is a stage, a temporary subjective condition.

5. In psychosynthesis there is a deliberate use of a large number of active techniques for the transformation, sublimation, and direction of psychological energies; the strengthening and maturing of weak or undeveloped functions; the activation of superconscious energies and the arousing of latent potentialities.

6. Finally, there is a conscious and planned reconstruction or re-creation of the personality, through the cooperation and interplay of the therapist and the client.

Probably the basic core of psychosynthesis is the belief of Assagioli that life is universal, that it is a continuing movement toward a unity that is being shaped within us. This is, as he says, the supreme synthesis.[24]

Parapsychology

Studies in parapsychology, or at least the clairvoyance aspect of parapsychology, were being conducted by J. B. Rhine over forty years ago at Duke University. In these studies individuals would be asked to name cards that were placed face down in front of them, and certain individuals would have correct answers far in excess of any laws of chance. Today, with increased interest in altered and changed states of consciousness, parapsychology is at least being investigated, if not accepted, as a branch of psychology.

Telepathy is another form of parapsychology, in which one person has an extrasensory perception of the thoughts and experiences of another person. The ability to foretell the future is also being looked at with more seriousness, and this obviously raises questions about the very nature of time. The past, the present, and the future may not be quite as distinct from each other as we have assumed.

24. *Ibid.,* p. 31.

Research is also being conducted on the possibility of the existence of some form of energy currently unknown to us. This is at least a possible explanation for the apparent ability of some individuals such as Uri Geller to move inanimate objects. A friend of mine, for example, swears that he saw Geller, in one room, bend a spoon lying on a table in another room! This ability, called psychokinesis, is also under serious investigation.

Probably the oldest form of parapsychology is psychic healing, and it is likely that everyone has known, or heard of, some individual who was incurably ill suddenly recovering for no apparent reason. Kirlian photography has shown the existence of coronas around human fingers, and these coronas change in size and shape and color as the individual's feelings change. This at least tends to imply that there is some unknown flow of energy between two people such as a client and a therapist, or between a healer and a patient. Is this what happens when a Christian Scientist "reader" reads to an afflicted person?

All of these aspects of parapsychology raise more questions than answers. The more gullible will unquestioningly embrace any explanation that is offered, while the more rigid will scoff at all of this as utter nonsense. What we do know about parapsychology, however, is that certain things (that cannot be rationally explained at the present time), do happen, certain things that cannot be done are done, and certain behaviors that are impossible become possible. Hopefully, we will remain open to the possibility that life as we know it now is a view through one window, and there are many windows yet to be opened, presenting to our startled eyes as yet undreamed-of realities.

In all of these newer therapies discussed here the going back to one's self is a common theme, as is the looking to one's inner self to find the way of life rather than depending on some outer source. But more than anything else, the newer therapies, and I have mentioned only a few, are causing us to look more deeply at ourselves. They are helping us to be less smug about ourselves, and to be more responsible human beings. And if each one of us can come to believe that the answers for *me* must lie within *me*, then only good can come to the society of which we are a part.

PART THREE

The Counseling Process

Chapter 8

The Nature of Counseling

It is clear that there is no paucity of theories and kinds of counseling, and it is equally clear that they are being added to at an increasing rate. There is an equal and continuing divergence regarding the "why" of counseling, and the number of gurus who have found the way, the answer, increases at an astonishing rate. Many, if not all, professional and lay gurus have an absolute certainty about the virtue of their way, and they have no trouble in finding evidence to support their way. Let us look in this chapter at the "why's" of counseling, and then at what the evidence says about the effectiveness of counseling.

THE PURPOSES OF COUNSELING

Most counselors would see the broad aim of counseling as change: change in attitudes and change in behavior. The counselor might see himself as involved with the client in a cognitive, information-sharing sort of relationship, or in a more therapeutically centered relationship, but in both cases the goal would be change in the client. Krumboltz sees the three behavorial goals of counseling as altering maladaptive behavior, learning the decision-making process, and preventing problems.[1] Blocher refers to behavioral changes being assumed in terms of new coping behaviors acquired within con-

1. John D. Krumboltz, "Behavioral Goals for Counseling," *Journal of Counseling Psychology,* 13:153–159 (Summer, 1966).

structs such as commitment, competence, consistency, and control.[2] In a report of a fairly typical study on the effects of vocational counseling, Hewer refers to ultimate employment in a chosen vocation as the goal in the study being reported.[3] Holland simply says, "The ultimate reason for seeking psychotherapeutic assistance is an unfavorable balance between unpleasant and pleasant feelings. . . . It becomes the responsibility of the psychotherapist to recognize, interpret, and attempt to change the nature of emotional experience,"[4] Thus, regardless of the argument over counseling being synonymous with or different from psychotherapy, or counseling as a rational and cognitive, rather than an emotional therapeutic experience, there is general agreement that the counselor is one who is involved in helping the client to change his attitudes and his behavior, and thus, in a sense, become a different kind of person.

While there is general agreement that the broad goal of counseling and psychotherapy is change of behavior, there is by no means similar agreement on the question of changes to what kind of behavior, and who is the one who is in control of the changing of behavior. The goals and the behavior of counselors and therapists have often been the subject of biting comments. Some years ago Lecky made a comment that many would say is equally valid today:

> *Thus the psychoanalytic pursuit of unconscious complexes with no stated goal except to destroy them, suggests the superstitious fervor of the witch burner, and psychiatry in general may be thought of as engaged in a moral crusade against the demon Neurosis.*[5]

When one pauses to wonder just what the objectives of counseling *are,* he is struck by the fact that his list of answers is usually smaller and more difficult to arrive at than when he wonders what his objectives *are not.* Such a circumstance is understandable, since a good deal of the professional education of the counselor has to do with unlearning rather than learning. Much of what he has learned as a citizen of his community will not make him effective as a counselor, and much of what he has learned professionally, whether he be

---

2. Donald H. Blocher, *Developmental Counseling* (New York: Ronald Press, 1966), p. 232.

3. Vivian H. Hewer, "Evaluation of a Criterion: Realism of Vocational Choice," *Journal of Counseling Psychology,* 13:289–294 (Fall, 1966).

4. Glen A. Holland, *Fundamentals of Psychotherapy* (New York: Holt, Rinehart and Winston, 1965), p. 202.

5. Prescott Lecky, *Self Consistency* (New York: Island Press, 1951), p. 186.

a theologian, a medical doctor, or a teacher, will help him even less. White, for example, states that

> when a person acts in the capacity of therapist, his goal is not to dominate or persuade, but simply to restore a state of good health. . . . A therapist has nothing to sell and nothing to prescribe.[6]

It is likely that the goals and objectives expressed by individuals for other people are reflective rather of the needs of the person who expresses the goals than of the people for whom we supposedly have the goals. Often when parents talk about goals for their children, there is no question that the children and their needs have little to do with these goals. They are an expression of the needs of the parents, which may, of course, also be the needs of the children. When the teacher talks about objectives for her pupils, these again are the objectives of the teacher for someone else; often they make little sense to individual children, since they ignore the child completely.

The professional counselor, however, when thinking about goals must be thinking in terms of client satisfaction, not counselor satisfaction. The important question is not whether the counselor will feel better if the client decides to get a divorce, but rather whether this is what is best for the client. Similarly, the teacher may feel happy if the child decides not to run away from home, but leaving home could be the better answer to the problems of the child. We might, therefore, seriously question the objectives of counseling if they are the objectives of the counselor rather than the objectives of the counseling experience as it will apply to a certain individual. Indeed, one may raise the rather intriguing question of whether or not the counselor should have any specific objectives for the client; whether, rather, he should hold to broad general objectives of counseling, which may become more specific as the counselor helps the client to become more realistically oriented in the search for his own goals.

There will be little agreement on the objectives of counseling as long as such objectives are those of the counselor, although evidence tends to indicate that there is more agreement on objectives among counselors who have a high level of professional preparation (such as indicated, say, by having a doctorate in the field and being a Fellow of the American Psychological Association, or a Diplomate of

6. Robert W. White, *The Abnormal Personality* (New York: Ronald Press, 1948), p. 314.

175

the American Board of Examiners in Professional Psychology) than
there is among counselors who have little in the way of professional
preparation. Even with professional counselors, however, one has to
step carefully before making any blanket statements about the objectives of counseling. This has been brought out most effectively in
an article by Walker and Peiffer. They point out, most logically, that
we can hardly think in terms of self-adjustment, since a psychotic
patient might well have reached a stage of adjustment in purely private terms; nor can we accept client contentment, since we cannot
defend the position that all schizophrenics are unhappy or that all
sexual psychopaths are sad.[7]

Each person must speak from his own personal frame of reference, no matter how sensitive he may be to the other person's frame
of reference. Each person's verbalizations will also tend to be at least
somewhat indicative of his own particular professional background,
and one of the difficulties of communication in counseling may be
owing to the many different professional groups involved in it. Thus
when we discuss the "why" of counseling, our differences may not
be as great as they appear, and even when we talk about what we do,
the discrepancies may not be as large as they would seem to be. The
student of counseling is continually faced with the danger of superfi-
cially "accepting" some goal or objective of counseling, and only by
examining himself in operation can he come close to determining
whether or not this goal is even remotely related to his total person.
Our basic goals of living, and our basic attitudes toward others, are
revealed by what we do, not by what we say. Goals, too, are human,
so we should talk in terms of the goals of the counselor, not of counseling.

Rogers, the original "client-centered" counselor, or at least
the original Rogerian, shows his intensive involvement with the
"other" in all his writings. More than most counselors, he tends to
speak through his clients, and one of his books, a compilation of
articles written over a ten-year period, illustrates the extent to which
he is centered on the client.[8] When he says that the outcome of
therapy is "a more broadly based structure of self, an inclusion of
greater proportion of experience as a part of self, and a more comfortable and realistic adjustment to life,"[9] he is describing a very
personal, operational objective, which he illustrates in his counseling.

Some counselors illustrate an existential-humanistic attitude,

7. Donald E. Walker and Herbert C. Peiffer, Jr., "The Goals of Counseling," *Journal of Counseling Psychology,* 4:204–209 (Fall, 1957).
8. Carl R. Rogers, *On Becoming a Person* (Boston: Houghton Mifflin, 1961).
9. *Client-Centered Therapy* (Boston: Houghton Mifflin, 1951), p. 195.

when, in talking about objectives, they appear to stress more doing something *with* the client than *for* him; experiencing and living with him, rather than discussing and explaining to him, thus stressing the affective rather than the cognitive; a concern with the total existential being, today, rather than parts of him, yesterday; a high level of confidence in the self-actualizing ability of the individual; a nondeterministic view of man as the maker of his culture.

When Boy and Pine describe the goal of client-centered counseling, they are talking about *their* goal as counselors, and what they actually do:

> *to help the student become more mature and more self-actu-ated, to help the student move forward in a positive and constructive way, to help the student grow toward socialization by utilizing his own resources and potential. . . . The counselee's perceptions change, and as the result of newly acquired insights there is a positive reorientation of personality and living for the counselee. The counselor's focus is more on the affective than on the cognitive components of behavior.*[10]

When they describe the goals of the clinical counselor, however, they are on less certain, less personal ground. We might say that they are being less affective, but more cognitive, in the sense that they are using descriptions of the counseling activities of others who have been called, by some, "clinical counselors":

> *. . . to help the counselee "feel better," i.e., to help the counselee accept himself, to diminish the disparity between real self and ideal self; and "to help persons think more clearly in solving their own personal problems." The counselor must be concerned with feelings and affect as prerequisite to clear thinking. The objective is to help the counselee arrive at the point where he understands himself not only affectively but also rationally or intelligently. At this point he needs external information to understand himself in terms of other persons around him. Man is essentially striving to become a rational, problem-solving organism.*[11]

Byrne discusses goals in an existential sense, with possibly one notable exception:

> *The counselor's goal, firmly based on the human worth of the individual, regardless of education, intelligence, color, or back-*

10. Angelo V. Boy and Gerald J. Pine, *Client-Centered Counseling in the Secondary School* (Boston: Houghton Mifflin, 1963), p. 43.

11. *Ibid.*

*ground, is to use his technical skills (a) to help each counselee
attain and maintain an awareness of self so that he can be
responsible for himself, (b) to help each counselee confront
threats to his being, and thus to open further the way for the
counselee to increase his concern for others' well being, (c) to
help each counselee to bring into full operation his unique potential in compatibility with his own life style and within the
ethical limits of society.* [12]

The somewhat clashing aspect of this description is Byrne's
reference to the counselor's using his "technical skills." Existentially, it is rather difficult to think of a close and intimate human
involvement, such as that between counselor and client, in which the
counselor *uses* technical skills. The counselor gives of himself, and
part of that self may be a technical skill.

Hora also talks in an existential sense, with the stress on self-
realization:

*. . . health is being what one really is . . . the psychotherapeutic
process aims at bringing about this authenticity in a human
being. . . . It consists of a realization of the attainment of the
open mind. . . . The open mind . . . is attained by the realization
of the closed mind.* [13]

Others also indicate their own personal concept of man and
his nature, as viewed from their particular frames of reference, when
they write about the goals and objectives of counseling. Tyler, for
example, feels that "the psychological purpose of counseling is to
facilitate development,"[14] while Shoben thinks of values as he
writes, "At any rate, perhaps the crucial learning that occurs in psychotherapy is the acquisition of a functional, critically held, and personally relevant system of human values."[15]

It is interesting to note that in a later revision of her book,
Tyler shows a more existential attitude when she states that the
purpose of counseling "is to facilitate wise choices of the sort on
which the person's later development depends."[16]

12. Richard Hill Byrne, *The School Counselor* (Boston: Houghton Mifflin, 1963), pp. 19–20.
13. Thomas Hora, "Psychotherapy: Healing or Growth," *Annals of Psychotherapy*, 4:9; Monograph Number 5 (1963).
14. Leona Tyler, *The Work of the Counselor* (New York: Appleton-Century-Crofts, 1961), p. 17.
15. Edward J. Shoben, "The Therapeutic Object: Men or Machines," *Journal of Counseling Psychology*, 10:264–268 (Fall, 1963).
16. Leona Tyler, *The Work of the Counselor* (New York: Appleton-Century-Crofts, 1969), p. 13.

Thorne feels that, from the viewpoint of the counselor, the main objective of personality counseling is to protect and secure mental health by preventing or modifying pathogenic etiologic factors productive of maladjustment or mental disorder. The prime obligation of the counselor, he feels, is to help people to live happier and healthier lives by psychological methods of healing and reeducation.[17]

Sullivan states his position as follows:

The interviewer must discover who the client is. . . . And, on the basis of who the person is, the interviewer must learn what this person conceives of in his living as problematic, and what he feels to be difficult. . . . [That] the person will leave with some measure of increased clarity about himself and his living with other people is an essential goal of the psychiatric interview.[18]

Williamson describes the objectives of counseling by stating that "the counselor assists the student to choose goals which will yield maximum satisfaction within the limits of those compromises necessitated by uncontrolled and uncontrollable factors in the individuals and in society itself."[19] He also feels that the counselor "should be prepared to assist the student to solve, choose, master, learn, and deal with situations and problems of a wide variety."[20]

Hadley feels that "the most essential goal [of psychological counseling] is to aid the individual in his efforts to achieve an effective relationship with his environment,"[21] while Alexander maintains that the aim of psychoanalysis "is to effect permanent changes in the personality by increasing the ego's integrative power . . . to change the ego by exposing it to conflictful repressed material."[22]

The Committee on Definition of Division 17 of the American Psychological Association describes the objectives of counseling by stating that the counseling psychologist contributes to the following:

(a) the client's realistic acceptance of his own capacities, motivations, and self-attitudes, (b) the client's achievement of a reasonable harmony with his social, economic and vocational en-

17. F. C. Thorne, "Principles of Personality Counseling," (Brandon, Vt.: Journal of Clinical Psychology, 1950), p. 89.
18. Harry S. Sullivan, *The Psychiatric Interview* (New York: Norton, 1954), p. 18.
19. E. G. Williamson, *Counseling Adolescents* (New York: McGraw-Hill, 1950), p. 221.
20. *Ibid.*, p. 219.
21. John M. Hadley, *Clinical and Counseling Psychology* (New York: Alfred A. Knopf, 1958), p. 26.
22. F. Alexander, *Fundamentals of Psychoanalysis* (New York: Norton, 1948), pp. 275–276.

179

vironment, and (c) society's acceptance of individual differences and their implications for community, employment, and marriage relations.[23]

Although these authorities may use different terms such as counseling, therapy, and psychiatry, and although they may use different methods of description, they are all likely describing the same basic process, and their differences reflect a personal difference rather than the differences, say, between those who might be called counselors or psychologists or psychiatrists.

Counseling is very much a human expression, and it is likely, indeed it is to be hoped, that differences will remain. It is also to be hoped, of course, that the "believer" can accept the reality that there actually exist other people who believe and think in different ways, which may well be more effective than his way!

In the more recent literature, for example, we may note Hoover quoting Lester Fehmi as saying:

Behaviorism controlled psychology for such a long time that if you couldn't really see something and pick it up and touch it, it didn't exist. Yet we all know that there are real things attributed to the "mind" that you can't see and that are very important.[24]

Such a comment would likely sound rather dreamy and wishy-washy to Hendricks, Ferguson, and Thoresen, who, in describing a counselor-education program, comment:

Conspicuously absent from the Stanford program is the attitude that counseling is a mystical enterprise practiced by saintly persons whose warmth and understanding are exceeded only by their charisma. (However, as soon as we define the components of charisma and find that charisma helps clients change, we may include it in our training program.)[25]

One might wonder if the Stanford program has defined the components of humanism, love, and compassion, or are these excluded from the program until scientific data show their worth!

In another example Mahrer and Pearson stress the concept that psychotherapy is basically a human relationship rather than

23. Reported by C. Gilbert Wrenn, "Status and Role of the School Counselor," *Personnel and Guidance Journal,* 36:175–183 (November, 1957).

24. Eleanor Links Hoover, "Alpha, the First Step to a New Level of Reality," *Human Behavior,* 1:8–15 (May-June, 1972).

25. C. G. Hendricks, Jeffrey G. Ferguson, and Carl E. Thoresen, "Toward Counseling Competence: The Stanford Program," *Personnel and Guidance Journal,* 51:418–424 (February, 1973).

some form of medical or psychological treatment, and it is through this relationship that one can attain a higher level of humanness.[26] On the other hand, Malcolm, in a paper on drug abuse, appears to feel that one of the evils of drug use is that the subject believes "that everyone must be free to determine for himself the quality and course of his own life."[27] He also makes the comment:

The counter-society contains a great variety of people. The immature, the mentally disturbed, the socially disadvantaged, and the sociopathic all may be attracted to it for diverse reasons.[28]

It is true, of course, that such people do form a part of what might somewhat loosely be called the "drug culture." It would be equally accurate, however, to describe our business and political culture as being made up of chronic liars, social schizophrenics, cheats, and bigots!

There are human and personal differences as counselors and therapists talk about their objectives of counseling, and there are the same differences when they discuss those things that *should not* be considered as goals or objectives. These differences, however, tend to be reduced when the primary professional function of the individual is counseling or psychotherapy. If, for example, we talk with school counselors rather than schoolteachers, counseling psychologists rather than clinical psychologists, psychiatrists rather than medical doctors, existential therapists rather than existential philosophers, the level of agreement rises markedly. I can probably safely say that a number of counselors share with me the feeling that the following might be considered some of the "should not's" among counselor objectives:

1. Considering the multi-disciplined background of counseling, it is not surprising that many counselors still talk of the "solution of the client's problems" as one of their objectives. After all, teachers have solved problems for children, medical doctors have told patients what their trouble was, and what they, the doctors, would do to alleviate that problem, and psychologists have probed the psyche to help us to determine how the conscious might better guide the unconscious. Humphries, Traxler, and North make what would still be, for many school counselors, a perfectly acceptable statement when they say that "in counseling, the immediate goal of

26. Alvin R. Mahrer and Leonard Pearson (eds.), *Creative Developments in Psychotherapy*, Vol. 1 (Cleveland, Ohio: Press of Case Western Reserve, 1971).
27. Andrew I. Malcolm, "Drug Abuse and Social Alienation," *Today's Education*, 59:29–31 (January, 1970).
28. *Ibid.*

the counselor and counselee is to arrive at the most satisfying solution as quickly as possible."[29] Still, many counselors would also feel that most individuals become clients because they have not learned to solve their own problems; while assistance in the solution of a problem may afford temporary relief, it does not help the individual to do something about changing the causes of his problems. Thus the assistance that might be given to an individual toward learning how to solve his own problems would seem to be a more valid objective than the actual solution of a specific problem. In most cases, of course, the personal problems of a human being cannot be *solved* by another person, even if the latter is aware of the real problem. Since the client himself is quite frequently unaware of his basic problem, it is unlikely that the counselor would have this awareness, although this in itself would not usually mean too much. It would be unlikely that any professional counselor would feel that he could solve for the client problems which might be expressed by such statements as "I feel so lonely and worthless, I don't know what to do, and you've just got to tell me what to do to get rid of this awful feeling," or "I just hate him . . . I hate his guts, and I know I shouldn't feel this way because he is my father; but I do, and I don't know what to do about it," or "Sure it's time that I burst loose—I'm sick and tired of being tied down by my wife, but I need your advice on just what I can do about it," or "I shouldn't have to compete and excel and be better than my husband, but it seems that I just have to, and I wonder why," or "My sister's whining and crying is driving me crazy, and I can't see how I can stay in that house until I graduate, but what can I do?"

These are a few statements made over the space of a short time to one counselor by several of his clients. They are not unusual, certainly, but would any reader of these words feel that he could solve even the immediate problems of these clients, as they have expressed them?

2. We may also question the idea that a primary goal in counseling is to make the client happy and satisfied, although this depends on how one views happiness and satisfaction. A human being may be helped, through counseling, to take a risk and make a choice that may result in pain and failure; another may decline a well paying position because he now realizes that, although he could have easily satisfied his employer, he would not have satisfied himself. Thus while counseling may, in the long run, help the client to develop in himself a deep and personal satisfaction with self, any sort

---

29. J. A. Humphries, A. E. Traxler, and R. D. North, *Guidance Services* (Chicago: Science Research Associates, 1960), p. 345.

of overt and immediate happiness and satisfaction is a by-product, rather than a primary objective. Indeed, as a result of counseling the client may become less smug, less self-centered, and more concerned with the world around him. He may be helped to move toward such a stage of security that he does not have to be happy all the time to feel that all is well. He may become secure and solid enough so that he can accept a certain degree of unhappiness and sorrow and despair as a normal part of living, rather than something to be avoided at all costs. It might even be safe to say that the one who pursues happiness—his own happiness, that is, as a major objective of his life—is not revealing a high degree of security and stability.

3. Making society happy and satisfied with the client is an even more unacceptable goal. Indeed, it could hardly be called an objective of either counseling or mental health, although it is true that increasingly in our culture adjustment seems to be measured by the extent to which an individual gets along with the group, is acceptable to the group, and is eventually absorbed by the group. While adjustment may have to be related to the culture, since the individual does not live alone, it might be that real security is something that is a good deal deeper, more internalized, and thus independent of the whims and the likes or dislikes of the passing crowd. The secure individual will not be independent just to be independent. He will not stand up, alone, just because standing up alone gives him a special thrill and a feeling of independence. If it must be, however, that in order to be true to himself he must stand up and be counted, he will do so; and in such a case, whether he stands alone or has the entire group with him will be of little consequence.

A goal of counseling might be to help the individual attain a stage of development at which he can look honestly at himself, and eventually a point where he can derive some element of satisfaction in what he sees. He might, indeed, be able to say to himself, deeply, and with meaning, "I can certainly be a lot better than I am, but all in all, I am not too bad. I can afford to hold my head high, even though others may think I am nothing." This is the sort of person who will be less dependent on the group. He will draw his strengths from his inner self. This is the man who may make society very unhappy with him. He is no organization man, and he may utter truths that others would rather ignore. He will accept the fact that he has to live within the mores of his society, but he will not feel that his very life depends on the adulation and approval of that society. The goals of counseling, at least as I see them, do not include the concept that the counselor must somehow help the client to become a passive, acceptant, agreeable fellow who resembles a vegetable much more than an independent human being.

If, on the other hand, one accepts the concept of a completely determined state of being, then it would seem that we have no choice, and each man must become a simple pawn, the victim of his culture, to do as it demands. The counselor in such a world would also, of course, be the inanimate voice of the state. Any concept of the existential being, of the self-actualization of the individual, of the inner integrity of the person, of the potential for human growth—all of these would be naive illusions. While we may hope that this would not be the view of the counselor, there is no doubt that it is the view of many individuals. A statement, for example, that smacks remarkably of *1984*[30] and *Walden Two,*[31] or the writings in journals like *Pravda,* is seen in a booklet written for school counselors by the Orientation Group, USAF, Wright-Patterson Air Force Base, Ohio, entitled *The Struggle for Men's Minds.* There appears in the introduction a quotation from Samuel Johnson. It reads as follows:

> *Every society has a right to preserve public peace and order, and therefore has a good right to prohibit the propagation of opinions which have a dangerous tendency. . . . Every man has a physical right to think as he pleases; for it cannot be discovered how he thinks. He has not a moral right, for he ought to inform himself, and think justly. But, Sir, no member of society has a right to teach any doctrine contrary to what the society holds to be true.*

This is not a statement that one would expect to find in a document published by a service that is dedicated to defend the freedom and integrity of every individual American.

4. Another common but questionable idea is that an objective of counseling should be to persuade the client to change certain decisions and choices in favor of those that are "right." The professional counselor approaches the client not with a bag of answers, but rather with an open and understanding mind that respects the integrity of his client to the extent of believing that he has the right to make his own decisions and choices; and whether or not these would be the decisions and choices of the counselor is of no importance. The professional counselor cannot have preconceived notions and ideas regarding choices and decisions to be made by the client. Many teachers, for example, find it extremely difficult to accept the idea that a student has the right to say nasty things about a faculty mem-

30. George Orwell, *1984* (New York: Harcourt, Brace and World, 1949).
31. B. F. Skinner, *Walden Two* (New York: Macmillan, 1948).

ber to a counselor, if the student feels secure enough, or harried enough, to make such a statement. The preconceived notion here is that all children are supposed to be respectful toward adults, no matter how miserable these adults may be, just as all nurses are supposed to respect all medical doctors, all students to respect all teachers, all privates all officers, and so on. But respect is obviously an attitude that one person develops toward another person because of his feelings toward that person, and people cannot be "told" to feel a certain way. Thus the counselor does not plan and decide for the client, since he honestly does not know what is best for him. His function is to help the client to decide what is best for *him*, not for the counselor, or society, or anyone else, although there will very often be a close relationship among all of these.

It is difficult to talk about the specifics of goals or objectives of counselors who are involved in the counseling process, since the more specific one becomes, the more personal he is. There would seem, however, to be several general points on which counselors and therapists tend to agree when talking about objectives:

1. Any "objective" is affected by the humanistic feeling that man is, basically, a capable, self-determining creature. This is not determined by any particular title that the counselor may give to his counseling, and it applies equally well to those who may call themselves Adlerians or Freudians or Rogerians, or clinical counselors, or eclectic counselors, or client-centered counselors, or rational counselors. The methods or procedures of the individual counselor may differ, but their views of man tend to be somewhat alike. They are optimistic, and although some might scoff, they would appear to have some degree of faith in the fellow man. Certainly they trust him far more than do most of his fellows.

2. Most counselors would probably feel that another somewhat general objective is that of working with the client to help him to move toward a greater level of self-acceptance and self-understanding. He learns, one might say, to be. An individual cannot change himself if he refuses to recognize and accept himself as he is. Such a person spends his life in a futile attempt to convince himself that he is what he is not. Understanding, for the counselor, is a good deal more than just an intellectual statement. True understanding implies self-acceptance, and this understanding will likely come through a reliving, an experiencing, a feeling, rather than through an intellectual step-by-step process.

Much of one's behavior, for example, such as aggressiveness, hostility, promiscuous sexuality, may be part of a vain attempt to convince oneself of one's maleness, an attempt to flee from the latent homosexual tendencies that the individual has learned. The

185

sneering and contemptuous remarks that may be directed at higher education generally, at a college degree, or toward a particular university may indicate the individual's struggle to avoid the acceptance of his own unimpressive intellectual competence. As children grow, they soon learn that they should not be what they are, they should not think what they think. The growing adolescent girl will find it difficult to accept calmly and securely her six feet of height; in another culture, it might not be a problem, but in America it is. A child may soon learn, from his parents and from his teachers, that lack of intellectual competence is not good; since he can do nothing directly about it, he will almost certainly, if he is to survive, find ways to compensate. He may learn too, that he cannot be "poor," and that he must have the ambition to be better than his parents. Sometimes changes are possible, but since the individual is not changing because he wants to, the psychological and physical price that he has to pay is too high. More often than not, however, an actual direct change is not possible, and the individual is placed in the impossible position of having to be what he cannot be. It is unfortunate that the school does not do more to help the child to accept what he is and work with what he has, rather than pretend that he can do what he cannot or that he has what he has not. Such a pretense tends to drive him even deeper into the rut of unacceptance, and to set the pattern for years of frustrated striving and avoidance of his real self.

A move toward greater self-acceptance also means that the individual tends to decrease the discrepancy between his real self and his ideal self. Seeing himself as he really is, he is more likely to think in terms of realistic goals rather than fantastic fantasies. Yet some people do become adept at satisfying the cultural demand without any real personal change. A good example is the way in which some school people get around the need for a higher degree. They do not want to become more educated; in some cases they are not capable intellectually of doing any legitimate graduate work. But since they must have a degree, they in effect buy one.

Generally, however, a person who has moved to a greater stability will not try to be a college professor if he is of low intellectual capacity; if he has a small physique, he will not strive vainly to be a football hero; if he lacks an understanding of music and has no real interest in it, he will cease trying to pretend that he is lover of the opera and all things cultural; if his income is modest, he will not try to convince himself that somehow his fairy godmother will appear and help him to maintain the standard of living that he feels he must pretend he can afford. He will, in effect, come fairly close to accepting himself as he is. In this frenzied culture most children will need assistance if they are to develop into this very stable sort of fellow.

3. A somewhat related goal has to do with the development of a greater level of honesty, particularly honesty toward self, in the client. An essential quality of the counselor is his congruence and his honesty, both toward the client and toward himself. In a human relationship with such an individual, the client may come to have less need to pretend that he is what he is not. The counselor does not buoy the client up with false support, and indeed, if he tries, the client is usually quite aware that such support is false. What man who has lost a hand believes that "things will be just as they were before"? What child who has been forced to repeat a grade believes that "this will really be much better than it was last year"? What girl who has been jilted by her one and only love believes that "you'll soon get over this and forget that it ever happened"? What child who has to go back and live with a brutal parent believes that "things will be much better now"? People have a habit of giving support that is not really honest, although they do not do so deliberately with malice in mind.

On the whole, we live in a culture where we do not call a spade a spade, particularly if the spade happens to be an unpleasant one. We like to pretend that what should be is. Although everyone must live to some degree in the realm of fantasy, such a practice can get to a point where it begins to make living somewhat difficult. It is nice—and it may sometimes be good—to feel that if we believe long enough, what we believe will come true. But we are on psychologically dangerous ground if we assume that we can wish things away, since this very attitude usually indicates that we are carefully avoiding the real basis for our problems. The counselor should not help the Jewish student to believe that it is just as easy for him to get into an American college as it would be if he were a Catholic or a Protestant; it is not. The counselor should not increase the unreality of the black student's dreaming by giving him the idea that it is just as easy for a black student to get a job as it is for a white one; it is not. Acceptance of the reality—and including here an acceptance of the reality of all of the factors involved (a Jewish student may not get into a certain college simply because his grades are too low; a black applicant may not get a job because he does not have the required education and skill)—is not passivity and hopelessness, or bitterness, but it is the first step toward doing something about reality.

It is important to note, too, that the counselor *can* be honest because of his own high level of self-actualization, because of his own level of being. He feels no personal pressure to take sides, to agree or disagree, to tell the client what is right and what is wrong,

187

to encourage or discourage. He can be easily acceptant of the fact that in most human differences what is right for one may be wrong for another. He is aware that the husband who talks about his wife's negative qualities and his plans for a divorce *may* be right about her and about his plans; he *may* be. The student who talks about his miserable teachers and parents *may* also be right on all counts. But the counselor is not the judge, he is not the chooser of sides; by remaining impartial he is more likely to be able to help the client to achieve a realistic outlook on his life and on the lives of others.

4. Objectives should be based on client need, not counselor need. Although any professional worker, including a counselor, should like what he is doing, an even more basic question for those people whose work is with other human beings has to do with the effect of what he does on the recipient of his efforts. Counseling cannot be justified on the basis of satisfactions that accrue to the counselor; it can only be justified on the basis of its effect on the client. More often than not, when the counselor feels, "That was a very good session," it doubtless was a good session; but ultimately the only true measure of the effectiveness of the session is found in the behavior of the client. Since every person exhibits himself in what he does and what he says, the counselor must be sure that he is not functioning in a certain manner simply to satisfy some of his own frustrations and unmet needs, rather than to benefit the client. Too frequently the defense of a supposed method or technique is a defense of the self. The rigid type of counselor, who cannot accept the idea that there are "other ways," unconsciously indicates that what he does is very much for his own satisfaction rather than that of the client. There is a marked resemblance between the father who says, "I don't want to beat you, but I'm doing it for your own good," the teacher who says, "The only way to gain the respect of the child is to bear down on him so that he'll know who's boss," and the counselor who says, "This client-centered stuff is a lot of nonsense. I've tried it and it never works for me." The father, the teacher, and the counselor are all giving a display of self, rather than showing their professional and learned skills and understandings. The father who beats his child, the teacher who happily bears down, the counselor who dismisses any contradictory point of view—their actions must be taken to bolster self. If the results are positive for the client, it is a fortunate accident rather than the result of any professional action.

Thus there is a very real point to the argument that counselor preparation should include experience in counseling under supervision and, indeed, personal counseling of the student counselor himself, so that he may become more aware of the extent to which he is becoming a counselor to satisfy his own needs regardless of the effects on the client. When the counselor can benefit the client as well as satisfy his own needs, all is well, but certainly every counselor should have an awareness of the extent to which he is possibly harming the client in his attempts to satisfy his own needs. The low level of professional competance required of school counselors at the present time almost surely means that many school counselors are working almost entirely for self-satisfaction, with very little in the way of professional evidence to back up their actions and their deeds. "I like my work" is not always a valid criterion to use in measuring one's effectiveness.

THE EFFECTIVENESS OF COUNSELING[32]

In attempting to look at the effectiveness of counseling, it would seem reasonable to first question the research methodology itself, which has pretty much tended to imitate the time-honored scientific practices followed in the physical sciences and in medicine. Most counselors tend to follow this scientific model, if any at all, when attempting to discover the results of their work. There have been scores, probably hundreds of studies, for example, on the effects of various "kinds" of counseling, on the questionable assumption that one could actually isolate, as a precise measurable variable, such a thing as "client-centered counseling," or "rational counseling," or "vocational counseling," or "trait-and-factor theory approach," and so on. Even more questionable, of course, is the related assumption that we can isolate the human beings, client and counselor, who are involved in the counseling process. Thus we might debate the accuracy of the evidence on the results of a certain "kind" of counseling, in which a number of "counselors" are involved with a number of "clients." In a somewhat curious contradiction, we insist as counselors on the uniqueness of the human individual, and yet, in our research, we seem to find no difficulty in lumping him as one of many faceless members of a group. In actuality, could we not say that there is only one "Rogerian," one "Freudian," and one "Adlerian?" Even then, however, all we could say would be that thus and so appears to have happened to an individual *after* a human relationship with Rogers, but we still would not necessarily know if this was *because* of the relationship with Rogers. The unfortunate difficulty

32. Dugald S. Arbuckle, "Counseling Effectiveness and Related Issues," *Journal of Counseling Psychology,* 15:430–436 (September, 1968). Copyright 1968 by the American Psychological Association. Reprinted by permission.

with "controls" in most of our research is that they are viable human beings, and even if we found six humans who appeared to be exactly the same, had three of them had a series of contacts with Rogers while three others did what they would usually do, we still would not *know* that the reason for the greater change in the three individuals who experienced counseling with Rogers was that contact with him.

When we have been involved in research with human beings, and their behavior, we have generally followed a pattern which was set up for things and objects, and if the assumption of the behavioral scientist that man is a set of behaviors is correct, then this pattern is reasonable enough. If the assumption is not correct, however, and many *believe* (do not know) that this is the case, then perhaps we should try to devise some means of research which will operate on the assumption of the uniqueness of man as a human being, with humanness as his unique quality. On this point, Bergin suggests:

> *The best way to capitalize on the ferment and promise in this area is to foster clinical innovation, evaluation of practice, and a continuing ability to move toward the new and the valuable. If this means recasting the scientist-practitioner model in new terms of innovating practice and naturalistic inquiry rather than an integration of traditional practice and physics-style research, so be it. The old model has done its job and now holds back the development of a more viable psychological profession.* [33]

Thus it may be that the individual counselor must become involved in research in which he at least controls the variable of himself, in that he will generally be consistent in his inconsistencies. One will not say, "I follow the trait factor theory in my vocational counseling because it gets results," because this doesn't really mean anything. Rather one might say, "I must try to find out the results of my involvement with certain students, in what I describe as vocational counseling geared to the trait factor theory." Counselors should, as Sanborn suggests, ask themselves what behavioral characteristics they are looking for in students who go through their school,[34] although it might be better to try to help students to develop the behavioral characteristics that they consider to be desirable rather than those set up by the counselor. There might, at least, in this way be some degree of research accuracy, but whether certain characteristics of students, years after they have left school,

33. Allen E. Bergin, "An Empirical Analysis of Therapeutic Issues," in Dugald S. Arbuckle (ed.), *Counseling and Psychotherapy: An Overview* (New York: McGraw-Hill, 1967), p. 208.
34. Marshal P. Sanborn, "Following My Nose Toward a Concept of a Creative Counselor," *School Counselor*, 14:66–73 (May, 1966).

could be credited to the effect of the school, let alone the effect of an individual counselor, might be held in some doubt.

In the book edited by Mahrer and Pearson not only is there some skepticism about what therapists are doing and accomplishing in psychotherapy, but questions are asked regarding the needs and motivations of people who become counselors and psychotherapists.[35]

Different researchers, too, very frequently disagree with the validity of each other's research. The periodic publication of such criticism represents only a small part of the actual disagreement. Representative of this conflict is a statement by Mills and Mencke, who, in referring to a previously published paper, stated, "On the basis of the above noted methodological errors, the findings of the Demos and Zuwaylif article seem to be in serious question, and cannot be accepted as representing differences between effective and non-effective counselors."[36]

While there is increasing evidence that the effective practice of counseling and psychotherapy is related to such ingredients as congruence and genuineness, nonpossessive warmth, and empathic understanding, there is also evidence that at least implies that many programs of counselor education do not consider these as the basic ingredients around which a counselor education program should be built. Studies by Bergin and Solomon,[37] and by Melloh,[38] for example, indicated no relationship between the level of empathic understanding provided in counseling and such measures as grade point average and practicum grades. In fact, the students who were most effective received the lowest grades in their training programs!

Adding to the skepticism about the effectiveness of counselors and counselor education programs is the fact that there is evidence which implies that lay personnel may be just as effective as professionally trained counselors and psychotherapists. Golann and Magoon, for example, describe an experiment from which they conclude that psychotherapeutic services can be provided in a school setting by carefully selected and specially trained individuals who do not need professional degrees.[39] Carkhuff concludes that the evi-

35. Alvin R. Mahrer and Leonard Pearson, *op. cit.*

36. David H. Mills and Reed Mencke, "Characteristics of Effective Counselors: A Reevaluation," *Counselor Education and Supervision,* 6:332–335 (Summer, 1967).

37. A. E. Bergin and Sandra Solomon, "Personality and Performance Correlates of Empathic Understanding in Psychotherapy," A.P.A. Convention, Philadelphia, 1963.

38. R. A. Melloh, Accurate Empathy and Counselor Effectiveness (unpublished doctoral dissertation, University of Florida, 1964).

39. Stuart E. Golann and Thomas M. Magoon, "A Non-Traditionally Trained Mental Health Counselor's Work in a School Counseling Service," *School Counselor,* 14:81–85 (November, 1966).

dence available today "indicates that the primary conditions of effective treatment are conditions which minimally trained non-professional persons can provide."[40] In describing their own training program, Carkhuff and Berenson point out that the most potent therapists were individuals who were "either thrown out of their graduate training programs or led a very tenuous graduate school existence."[41] Patterson even goes so far as to suggest that psychologists may abandon the practice of counseling and psychotherapy, the reason being "that it is below the professional dignity of a psychologist with a doctorate to engage in something which can be done just as well by someone with a bachelor's degree, or perhaps even less."[42]

These studies do not, of course, refer only to the effects of psychotherapy in a clinical or medical setting. They hold just as true for schools and the children in them. Hill and Grieneeks, for example, report a study from which they conclude "If academic counseling is positively affecting performance it is not being reflected when the criterion measure chosen is grade point average."[43] A study by Gonyea indicated that there was a negative relationship between the extent to which counselors developed the "ideal therapeutic relationship" and the degree to which their clients reported themselves to be improved.[44]

In practically every issue of the "On the Other Hand" section of *Contemporary Psychology* authors clash swords with reviewers who have dared to question the accuracy of their published research. These same reviewers, when the roles are reversed, react in exactly the same way!

In a major contribution to the scientific literature, Bergin and Strupp not only question the current theories and methodologies and schools, but express doubt that the question of effectiveness of counseling can have any meaning. Basically, they feel that until there is greater collaboration between therapists and researchers in pinpointing the means of change, there will be little chance of accurate measurement of the effectiveness of counseling.[45]

40. Robert R. Carkhuff, "Training in the Counseling and Therapeutic Practices: Requiem or Reveille," *Journal of Counseling Psychology*, 13:360–367 (Fall, 1966).
41. Robert R. Carkhuff and Bernard G. Berenson, *Beyond Counseling and Therapy* (New York: Holt, Rinehart and Winston, 1967), p. 14.
42. C. H. Patterson, "What Is Counseling Psychology?" *Journal of Counseling Psychology*, 16:23–29 (January, 1969).
43. Arthur H. Hill and Laurabeth Grieneeks, "An Evaluation of Academic Counseling of Under- and Over-Achievers," *Journal of Counseling Psychology*, 13:325–328 (Fall, 1966).
44. G. Gonyea, "The Ideal Therapeutic Relationship and Outcome," *Journal of Clinical Psychology*, 19:481–487 (December, 1964).
45. Allen E. Bergin and Hans H. Strupp, *Changing Frontiers in the Science of Psychotherapy*, (Chicago: Aldine-Atherton, 1972).

192

It is interesting to note, too, that the major criterion of change is often what the client feels rather than what the client does. While there is an obvious relationship between what I feel and what I do, the more pragmatic and realistic measure of positive growth is my action rather than my thought. I may come to feel more certain about my bias toward certain individuals, or my anxiety about my cheating on my income tax may be reduced greatly, or I may come to lose my feeling of uneasiness about lying over certain matters. In all of these cases I feel better, but in the meantime my level of prejudice, my cheating, and my lying continue to increase. Thus it would seem that behavior is a more valid criterion of the effectiveness of counseling, at least if we are to think of counseling effectiveness as being related to our behavior with others.

At any rate, as a profession ages, one could presume that it develops more precise answers to the question, "What is the result of what you do?" In the case of counseling, however, we might wonder if we have more evidence now questioning the effects of counseling than we have supporting the positive effects of counseling!

In many ways Rogers was one of the first to challenge and question the effectiveness of at least traditional psychotherapy, and those who attacked him indicated rather clearly that they had little in the way of empirical evidence to back up their statements about the effects of their particular brand of psychotherapy. It is likely that at least part of the violence of the reaction against Rogers was because he was presenting at least some evidence as to what happened to clients with whom he was involved, whereas his opponents could give little other than their opinion.

Probably the major gadfly in the side of all counselors and psychotherapists, however, was Eysenck. In an article published some years ago, he presented evidence which resulted in his flat statement that "the figures fail to support the hypothesis that psychotherapy facilitates recovery from neurotic disorder."[46] A few years later Levitt presented evidence which caused him to come to a similar conclusion regarding children. He said, "It is concluded that the results of the present study fail to support the view that psychotherapy with 'neurotic' children is effective."[47]

In an earlier book Bergin presented compelling evidence questioning the efficacy of psychotherapy, and in a statement which sums up much of what he presents, he says, "Most controlled studies of psychotherapy reveal no significant effect of treatment."[48] Cark-

46. H. J. Eysenck, "The Effects of Psychotherapy: An Evaluation," *Journal of Consulting Psychology*, 16:319–324 (August, 1952).
47. E. E. Levitt, "The Results of Psychotherapy With Children," *Journal of Consulting Psychology*, 21:189–196 (June, 1957).
48. A. E. Bergin, *op. cit.*, p. 177.

huff does much the same thing in several chapters in a book edited by Berenson and himself, and their statement is that "there are no professional training programs which demonstrated their efficacy in terms of a translation to constructive behavioral gains in clients."[49] Needless to say, Carkhuff also felt that *his* way did produce significant gains, and the "Carkhuffian model" is now subject to the same criticism which he earlier leveled at other models!

Stuart has presented a strong argument against the traditional methods of psychotherapy. He feels that concentration on pathology as having to fit psychiatric descriptions of pathology not only does little to change behavior, but is almost certainly a guarantee of failure.[50]

Another research problem is that any measures of the effectiveness of counseling must be related to the purposes of counseling as they are perceived by the counselor. On this point Boy and Pine comment:

> *Measuring the outcomes of counseling is basically a matter of measuring human behavior and personality, for if counseling has been successful, then positive behavioral changes have taken place. But objectively measuring behavioral changes is extremely complex and involves first selecting objective evaluative criteria.*[51]

There is no question that determining, with some degree of scientific exactness, the specific outcomes of the counseling of *a* counselor with *a* client is fraught with much difficulty. If we hold to the concept that each human being is unique, obviously the complexity of the human relationship varies with each counselor and each client, and the existentialist would feel that the total examination of man, piece by piece, is impossible. The behaviorist would not agree with this, and Eysenck would appear to be fairly well satisfied that counseling and psychotherapy have no effect whatsoever on human behavior.[52]

In many of the current journals, the research being reported has taken place in an educational milieu, and the criteria that are used are usually the achievement of the individual in this educational setting, or some modification in his attitudes, concepts and

49. B. G. Berenson and R. Carkhuff, *Sources of Gain in Counseling and Psychotherapy* (New York: Holt, Rinehart and Winston, 1967), p. 7.
50. Richard B. Stuart, *Trick or Treatment: How and When Psychotherapy Fails* (Champaign, Ill.: Research Press, 1970).
51. Angelo Boy and Gerald J. Pine, *Client-Centered Counseling in the Secondary School* (Boston: Houghton Mifflin, 1963), p. 234.
52. H. J. Eysenck (ed.), *Handbook of Abnormal Psychology* (New York: Basic Books, 1960), pp. 697–725.

general behavior. For example, Spielberger, Weitz, and Denny report, as a result of a study, that anxious college freshmen who regularly attended group counseling sessions showed more improvement in their academic performance than students who were not counseled or did not regularly attend counseling.[53] Ivey reports that "there is some indication in this study that students who receive more intensive and long-term counseling are more likely to improve their marks than those who receive short-term counseling."[54] Baymur and Patterson, referring to an underachieving high school population, state that "a comparison of the two counseled groups with the two noncounseled groups indicated that they differed significantly in Q-sort adjustment score change . . . and in increase in grade point average."[55]

Similar positive growth of a group of high school children with behavior problems who had experienced counseling, as compared with the lack of growth of those who had not, was indicated in a study reported by Arbuckle and Boy.[56]

In somewhat different words, Broedal, Ohlsen, Proff, and Southard reported the same thing with a population of gifted underachieving high school students.[57]

On the other hand, Searles reports as a result of his study that three-interview counseling does not appear to have any significant effect on the first-semester academic achievement of superior freshmen in a small liberal arts college,[58] while Goodstein and Crites state that there was no evidence, from their study, that vocational educational counseling, as it is usually conducted, leads to greater academic achievement by low ability college students.[59]

53. Charles D. Spielberger, Henry Weitz, and J. Peter Denny, "Group Counseling and the Academic Performance of Anxious College Freshmen," *Journal of Counseling Psychology*, 9:195–204 (Fall, 1962).
54. Allen E. Ivey, "The Academic Performance of Students Counseled at a University Counseling Service," *Journal of Counseling Psychology*, 9:347–352 (Winter, 1962).
55. Feriha B. Baymur and C. H. Patterson, "A Comparison of Three Methods of Assisting Underachieving High School Students," *Journal of Counseling Psychology*, 7:83–90 (Summer, 1960).
56. Dugald S. Arbuckle and Angelo Boy, "An Experimental Study of the Effectiveness of Client-centered Therapy in Counseling Students with Behavior Problems," *Journal of Counseling Psychology*, 8:136–139 (Summer, 1961).
57. John Broedal, Merle Ohlsen, Fred Proff, and Charles Southard, "The Effects of Group Counseling on Gifted Underachieving Adolescents," *Journal of Counseling Psychology*, 7:163–170 (Fall, 1960).
58. Aysel Searles, Jr., "The Effectiveness of Limited Counseling in Improving the Academic Achievement of Superior College Freshmen," *Personnel and Guidance Journal*, 40:630–633 (March, 1962).
59. Leonard D. Goodstein and John O. Crites, "Brief Counseling with Poor College Risks," *Journal of Counseling Psychology*, 8:318–321 (Winter, 1961).

One might safely assume that a change in academic achievement is the result of some behavioral change or modification in the individual, and this, of course, might occur because of some modification of the environmental milieu. Braaten, for example, concludes that in "successful" client-centered therapy there is a highly significant movement in the verbal communications of the client from nonself to self.[60] In another study, Williams concludes that educational-vocational counseling restores a normal level of adjustment and degree of congruence among the client's perceptions of himself, his ideal self, and other persons.[61] After a long-range "eight years after" follow-up study, Merenda and Rothney appeared satisfied that intensive counseling with high school students resulted in more favorable attitudes and behaviors.[62] The conclusion of a study reported by Sorensen is that a few counselor-initiated interviews do not produce sufficient change in the classroom behavior of low-ability high school students to result in grade improvement.[63] Gonyea reports that vocational counseling with college students does not appear to be a factor in significant change in the appropriateness of vocational choice.[64]

These studies, which are probably fairly representative of the research being conducted on the effectiveness of counseling, are all, to a greater or lesser degree, vulnerable. Since the object of investigation is the human being, they operate with a multiplicity of unknowns, and every study is subject to a series of "ifs" and "buts." This in no way detracts from their value, but all results should be taken as highly tentative, subject to possible drastic change at any time.

It has already been pointed out that what one feels about what has happened does not necessarily indicate what one will do, but client feelings about counseling do at least give an immediate perception. Here are some examples of what clients say about counseling and psychotherapy. An adult male client says:

I think I learned, for one thing—I learned to trust someone with information. It gives me a good feeling to trust, and to allow myself to experience the feelings that go along with the verbal-

60. Leif J. Braaten, "Non-Self to Self in Client-Centered Psychotherapy," *Journal of Counseling Psychology*, 8:20–24 (Spring, 1961).
61. John E. Williams, "Changes in Self and Other Perceptions," *Journal of Counseling Psychology*, 9:18–30 (Spring, 1962).
62. Peter F. Merenda and John W. M. Rothney, "Evaluating the Effects of Counseling—Eight Years After," *Journal of Counseling Psychology*, 5:163–168 (Fall, 1958).
63. Mourits A. Sorenson, "Counseling Marginal Students on Classroom Behavior," *Personnel and Guidance Journal*, 40:811–812 (May, 1962).
64. George G. Gonyea, "Appropriateness of Vocational Choices of College Students," *Journal of Counseling Psychology*, 10:269–275 (Fall, 1963).

ization. It's one thing to be able to speak in a detached and specific manner about some specific subject—some particular problem. But it's another thing entirely to be able to allow yourself the luxury of indulging in all the same feelings that should go along, that are natural concomitants of this particular problem, or whatever it is.

Another adult male client:

And it was quite clear, Dr. San, that I couldn't accept myself as I was, so I had to construct someone that I could like and accept. I introjected how others felt about me, and God knows how much of this is left. All I know is—and it's kind of amazing—I remember clearly the feeling—I don't know why I couldn't tell you—but it—was a kind of good-bye. I realize that one of my characters, one of my favorite characters, was leaving—and I felt sad and resentful.

A number of junior high school boys and girls comment in this way about the effects of counseling:

"It's made me confident—sort of better able to do things."
"It's made me less afraid—I don't fear new people or new things."
"It has enabled me to face the issue of being dominated."
"It made me realize that I'm not sick."
"It enabled me to stop fighting things in my life which were, really, now that I look at them, pretty unimportant."
"It enabled me to realize that my progress depends more on me than on the teacher."
"It has helped me to become more clear about my future."
"It has made me realize that I don't have to always be in a state of anger—always suspicious of people."
"It has helped me be less nervous and tense when I'm in school."
"It has helped me to improve my school work because—well—I'm not fighting school anymore."

When asked "How do you feel about the effects of counseling?" a number of clients replied in the following manner.
A female said:

How Do I Feel? Through the help given me in these sessions of therapy, I have been able to get on an even keel again. The permissive atmosphere which was established allowed for an outpouring of feelings and emotions from the past and present such as I had never experienced before. This left me free to concentrate on regaining control of myself, and I learned how

197

to help myself over any bad spots which come along. I don't know what the future will bring, but in the past three weeks I have succeeded in throwing off a life which I had grown to hate but had allowed to become a habit which could not be shaken. I know I have many more problems to face and temptations to resist, but somehow I feel I have gained the strength to face life squarely and accept what it has to offer.

All this I was not able to do with medical and spiritual help, so I feel client-centered counseling was most successful in my particular case. I also feel I can return again if necessary. It's wonderful to feel like a human being again and to be able to face people again.

A male client said:

How Do I Feel? Although I do not feel that we have fully worked through the problems at the present time, several positive things have happened. The anxiety about my school work has been reduced to the point where I could at least do some studying—although it has been neither adequate nor very efficient. Secondly, the recurring thoughts have receded to the point where I have them only occasionally and for not very long and where I can inhibit them. This has resulted in a very great drop in my anxiety, because, although intellectually I know that this is sheer nonsense, emotionally I have been very afraid of becoming mentally ill, and of losing control of my thought processes. Just a few meetings were enough to reduce this fear very markedly. With that, my irritability at home decreased.

A female client said, simply:

Did I gain anything yet—honestly—No—just more analyzing myself and more confusion.

Another, feeling more growth, said:

I have gained a greater understanding of myself, and, indirectly, others. I think I know myself better—can understand my reactions to situations in a better light. I surely feel more at ease—at peace even.

Comments of other clients were:

As a client now, I see myself as a person who has a much greater understanding of himself . . . why he has the need to behave in a particular fashion; however, there still is this need in some areas which, though understood, has not been fully accepted as to its origin; appearingly the acceptance of the why, at the moment, is too threatening to me. Intellectual understanding is one thing, acceptance of this understanding on the emotional level is something else. I feel now that, though I still have feelings of inadequacy, I have become free in part from much of the painful life that has little or no purpose and thus lacks the solid satisfaction that endures . . . the needs which are insatiable and lending to a circular form of existence can only supply one with a moment or two of satisfaction which then dies in the wake of the insatiable need itself; satisfaction that endures is derived from living which implies growth, not existing. At the moment I have great hopes or better said, "Great Expectations" which have been formed by a realistic understanding and partial acceptance of me; the "Great Expectations," however, in my case, are somewhat different from Pip's in that mine are associated with a greater understanding and acceptance of myself, and thus the freedom to grow in the direction of man's potential goodness . . . to approximate as closely as possible my potential, which is living.

and:

I really don't know. I do know that I am trying to accept myself and others. I still have many fears and superstitions. My problems on sex and religion are being solved.

Some other client reactions to psychotherapy:

". . . it has meant the beginning of the most dynamic experience—being alive."

"For the first time in my life it seems that I'm not locked into some predetermined series of actions."

"I do not now feel that I am utterly committed to a bad choice."

". . . it opened me to life."

"I have found the way to give without sense of depletion."[65]

Possibly a comment of Axline is as good as any to describe how counseling can be effective. In talking about Dibs, one of her young clients, she says:

Yes, Dibs had changed. He had learned how to be himself, to believe in himself, to free himself. Now he was relaxed and happy. He was able to be a child.[66]

65. Rahe B. Corlis and Peter Rabe, *Psychotherapy from the Center* (Scranton, Pa.: International Textbook Co., 1969), pp. 128–130.
66. Virginia M. Axline, *Dibs: In Search of Self* (Boston: Houghton Mifflin, 1964), p. 181.

Still, the nagging question must remain. Was this the effect of a procedure known as psychotherapy and counseling, or was it the result of an intense human experience between a small boy and a woman named Virginia Axline? Or is this, after all, the real description of counseling and psychotherapy?

If counseling and psychotherapy are precise and measurable techniques, procedures, methodologies, which are used under controlled conditions to produce behavioral change in a definable and measurable creature known as a human being, then the effectiveness of these procedures can be measured accurately, if they are not now being measured accurately. But if counseling and psychotherapy accept the relationship between involved people as a reality, and as an inescapable aspect of counseling and psychotherapy, then the accurate prediction of effectiveness is as far away now as it was decades ago.

This debate has been going on for a long time. The recent literature, despite the certainty and dogmatism of some researchers, would indicate that the argument is in a state of good health, and has a long life ahead of it!

Chapter 9

The Counseling Experience

In this chapter, the counseling experience will be considered primarily by observation of what actually happened in a series of counseling sessions with a number of clients and a number of counselors. Excerpts from various counseling sessions with different students and different clients will be used to illustrate certain phases and aspects of the counseling process. Extensive use will be made of John Bin, a high school client; Tom Ril, an adult client; the five clients, Carl, Jane, Jack, Edna, and Richard, in Evraiff's casebook;[1] and a number of other high school clients.

     The clients presented here are basically ordinary, normal human beings facing problems of living. The children are in school, and if one is willing to accept the professional title of counselor, he should be professionally competent enough to work with them in a counseling relationship. The adults are individuals who were in school and received little assistance and little help when they needed it. The counselors would probably use a variety of names to describe their counseling. The counselors also represent a range of experience, from those with a doctoral degree in the field and many years of professional counseling, including counseling of private clients, to student counselors who are almost at the beginning stage.

THE SETTING FOR COUNSELING

One of the realistic problems that faces any counselor is the setting, the environment, the situation for counseling. While the situation

1. William Evraiff, *Helping Counselors Grow Professionally* (Englewood Cliffs, N.J.: Prentice-Hall, 1963).

varies from school to school, it is probably safe to say that most schools still provide a poor setting for counseling. Even in new schools the provisions that are being made for counseling facilities have not improved as much as have the facilities for other aspects of the school program, such as, for example, the teaching of foreign languages. Facilities that can be used in the education of counselors, such as counseling rooms with sound equipment for monitoring and recording, and one-way mirrors, are, other than in a few schools and laboratory institutions, practically nonexistent. Many schools have reached the point where they admit the need for a counselor, but they still do not see why he has to have anything different in the way of facilities than the teacher. This is particularly so in those schools where "counseling" is still seen as a friendly chat, or the offering of some advice by a person who, even though he may have the title "counselor," is still seen as a teacher, and who, in fact, very likely actually *is* a teacher masquerading in a counselor's clothes!

The attitudinal setting is usually reflected by the physical setting. The low esteem and the complete lack of understanding of the meaning of counseling are often reflected in some schools by the fact that there is next to nothing in the way of physical facilities. Counselors may not have offices. Often, if they do, there is no secretarial service or protection, so that privacy is impossible.

Tape recorders are still considered a luxury in many schools, and there are many school counselors who have yet to hear what they sound like, and what they say, when they "counsel." Videotape is even more of a rarity.

In some schools where the actual facilities are fairly good, they are rendered ineffective by being placed cheek to jowl with the administrative offices. A student who may want to see a counselor to talk about his desire to bash the principal or perform some dastardly deed upon a teacher will naturally shy away from coming if he sees the offices together, assuming, reasonably enough, that there is a close connection between the people who are in the offices. I was once in a counselor's "office" that formerly was an anteroom to the principal's office, and the only way to the latter was to go through the former. The few clients who came to see the counselor naturally spoke in low tones, were wary of what they said, and kept a weather eye cocked on the principal's door.

If a school has a counseling suite, it should be away from the administrative offices. This is important even as a symbol of the fact that the counselor and the principal are two quite different individuals with quite different functions and responsibilities. It is important too, to have the counseling suite away from the main flow of traffic, to have a pleasant waiting room, with a secretary, to have individual counseling rooms, as well as counselors' offices, and to have at least one exit door that opens only one way. If a client has been under some stress and emotion, he naturally does not want to have to parade past many curious eyes, or to step out into a corridor swarming with fellow students.

I have recently been in several fairly new schools where the upper half of the walls of the counselors' offices were glass, giving both client and counselor somewhat of a fish-in-a-fishbowl feeling. I have been in another school where the principal insists that the counselors keep the doors of their offices open, to convey to the students the impression of counselor friendliness!

The need for privacy, whether from other eyes or from telephones, is obvious. The office should not be austere, not should it be a living room, although school counselors would say that while there might be some danger of the former type of office in a school, there never would be any danger of the latter type. The client, after all, will probably feel more comfortable if he has a choice of one or two comfortable chairs, and possibly even the choice of some sort of divan or couch.

Thus, in a school, at least, the counselor must face the fact that he may be hired to function as a counselor in an institution that has little understanding of and even some hostility toward counseling, and in which the physical facilities for effective counseling simply do not exist. If the counselor, by being an effective counselor with students and parents and colleagues, can come to modify the first part of this problem, then the second part may work out without too much difficulty.

The rehabilitation counselor in a state agency of a veterans' affairs office often has much the same impossible surroundings, in that his "office" may consist of his desk and two chairs in a large room shared with a dozen other counselors, similarly equipped. Indeed, the physical setting for so many counselors, in a variety of areas, is such that we must assume that privacy is something that many still consider an unnecessary luxury in counseling! Actually, of course, it is an absolute necessity for effective counseling, and little can be done without it.

PREPARATION FOR THE COUNSELING SESSION

The degree of preparation for the first counseling session with a new client depends on the degree of sophistication and experience of the counselor, his own particular concept of his function as a counselor, and, of course, the amount of time available. It is also true, of course, that sometimes the counselor has no chance to prepare anything, even if he wants to, since the client appears suddenly and unannounced.

If the counselor sees himself as the interpreter of test data, we can assume that he will make himself familiar with the client's test data before seeing the client. If the counselor sees his function as the presenting of information regarding what college or what job would best fit the client he is going to see, he will probably want previous information about the client so that he can accumulate accurate information for him. If, on the other hand, the counselor sees himself not so much as the provider of information, but rather as one involved in a human helping relationship with another individual, the purpose, and the need, of information changes somewhat.

Many counselors of a more diagnostic orientation would probably feel the need of information about the client so that they could understand him better and thereby work more effectively with him. Another counselor would work with the client as he presents himself, and since he does not see himself as doing something for or to the client, he would see little or no need of previous information about him. Generally, such counselors would feel that their understanding of the client was also based on the frame of reference as it is presented to them by the client, and thus they need no previous information to develop their concept of the client's frame of reference. Some of the counselors have worked with previous information, and some with none. John Bin and Tom Ril presented themselves as they were. Their counselors had no previous information about them, other than that they wanted to see them. Other counselors referred to here had perused all the information they could about the client before they saw him.

THE ESTABLISHMENT OF RAPPORT

Rapport might be described as the ideal relationship that is developed between the client and the counselor, a relationship that is easy and comfortable and free, where each person can be honest, and in which the client can learn to be. There are many factors, some out of the control of the counselor, that might affect the kind of relationship that is established.

1. Long before the counselor ever sees the client, factors are at work that may make it easy or difficult for the counselor to establish rapport with his client. In the school situation particularly, the

child gradually develops a picture of the school and the people who work in it. Although it is sometimes a very positive and pleasant picture, the odds are that the disturbed children who come to see a counselor will be those individuals who have built up a picture of the school as at best a rather unpleasant place, and at worst a regular hell-hole. The people who work there may be regarded in an equally negative manner, although, over a period of time, individual teachers and counselors may gradually come to be accepted by troubled children as different from the run-of-the-mill teacher and counselor.

Generally, however, the school counselor can assume that many of the children who have problems will regard him with suspicion, and it will be the actions of the counselor, rather than his words, that may gradually dispel this suspicion. Needless to say, of course, if the school "counselor" thinks of himself as a stool pigeon for either the school administration or the culture generally, the justifiable suspicion of the child will only be reinforced. Many of the clients described here had good reason to be skeptical about the motives of anyone who was connected with the school system.

2. The establishment of rapport will also be affected by the manner in which the client happens to appear in the counselor's office. If he appears because he has something weighing on his mind, and he feels that a talk with someone in the counseling office might be beneficial, the establishment of a good relationship will be a much simpler matter than if he has been brusquely sent down to the counselor's office to be "straightened out" or disciplined in some manner. The latter sort of situation will increase the difficulties, but one must not imply that it creates an impossible situation for the counselor. An acceptant counselor can still be acceptant even in an autocratic school; and acceptance of the client's feeling that coming to the counselor's office is a lot of nonsense is no different from acceptance of the feeling that the experience might be something that would be good for him.

The client may, on the contrary, have too good an opinion of what the counselor can do for him. If he has been led to believe that the counselor is a medicine man who has all the answers to any problems that may beset him, it is likely that very soon, even in the first counseling session, he will be disturbed to find that the counselor cannot do any of the things that were expected. Most children have come to expect domination and control and direction from school personnel. Even in counselor education departments, most student counselors take this counselor education domination for granted, and are somewhat disturbed if it is not forthcoming. Though they may, of course, pay no attention to the attempted domination, they nevertheless expect it, and thus some students may at first find the acceptant counselor "queerer" than the more old-fashioned Napoleonic type, because they are more accustomed to the latter. If the counselor is capable of helping the student to work through this confusion, the relationship that can then be established may be most worthwhile; but it is at this point that the relationship between the counselor and the client sometimes founders. The counselor should remember, of course, that if he has a forced clientele, the number of clients will be determined as much by the neuroticism of the teachers as by the neuroticism of the clients. A neurotic teacher will probably see a good deal of what the mental hygienist would consider normal behavior as indicative of a disturbed child; so the more disturbed the teacher, the more the counselor may expect to find healthy children trooping to his office "to have something done about their behavior."

The counselor's problems may also be affected by the manner in which the appointment was made. If the client talked to a secretary, for example, was she kindly and understanding, or brusque and impatient? Did she give him the feeling that his meeting with the counselor would be a nice experience, or did she imply that it would be unpleasant, and probably a waste of time for both client and counselor? Did he first hear about the counselor from a friend, and, if so, what was the picture he got? If he is a voluntary client, it is likely that the picture he got was a good one—possibly too good, since if he received a negative picture he would not have come voluntarily. He may, of course, be a quite unwilling client, going to see a counselor about whom he has a very unhappy picture. He may have met the counselor in the hall, spoken to him, and formed his impressions on the basis of this brief meeting.

3. The immediate impression that the client receives when he opens the counselor's door is also going to affect him. He should see a reasonably comfortable office, with such things as curtains on the windows, pictures on the walls, comfortable chairs, some evidence of a library, and the professional competence of the counselor. He should also be able to sit down without having a desk between himself and the counselor.

Needless to say, the client will also notice the other person in the room. The greeting of the counselor should be warm, but not effusive. The counselor who rushes around the desk, seizes the hand of the client in a death grip, gives an intimate squeeze on the shoulder, and smiles his biggest smile before his "I'm AWFULLY glad to see you" would be enough to scare me as a potential client right out of the office! Overtness is next to aggressiveness, and the super-gregarious counselor must surely pose a threat to many clients. On this point it is obvious, of course, that the uneasiness of the counselor is a paramount factor in the establishment of rapport with the client, and the beginning counselor, particularly, is going to experience sessions when he feels threatened and insecure. It is well if he is in a situation where he can work this out with the assistance of some other counselor, and it is nothing that need alarm him, since even the experienced counselor periodically runs into situations that shake him.

4. The client may sometimes immediately challenge his acceptance by the counselor, and what happens will have an important effect on their future relationship. A school counselor may find a client whipping out a cigarette, and the counselor's acceptance of this can be indicated by passing an ashtray to him. Obvious and studied verbal insolence is another means by which the counselor may be tested, and the counselor's capacity to accept such behavior is a good measure of his professional competence and personal security.

5. The more a counselor is attuned to the feelings of the client, the less of a problem the lack of understanding of the intellectual content of what he says will be. Some counselors may be somewhat disturbed when in the first few minutes of the beginning session the client mumbles several statements that are unintelligible. Generally speaking, it is better to refrain from asking for a repetition of certain statements, since the meaning of what has been said will usually become obvious anyway. If the counselor has to ask repeatedly for clarification, the counseling session will degenerate into a "teacher-asking-what-do-you-mean" sort of thing, a situation that will not usually help in the establishment of a good counseling relationship. If the client continually talks so softly that the counselor cannot hear him, the latter should gently point out that it is rather difficult to hear what is being said—although even here there is some question as to whether or not the counselor should take this step.

The counselor may sometimes hear a word, but lack the understanding of what it means. In this case, it is better to let the client continue. The counselor may eventually pick up the meaning of the word either by listening to a tape, or by hearing it again and using a dictionary. If he has to stop the client from an expression of feeling and say, "Pardon me, but what does that mean?" he is letting himself in for several potential difficulties. For one thing, the client may assume that the counselor must be a rather ignorant fellow if he does not understand the meaning of a word. It may also be that the intellectual explanation of the word will prove embarrassing to the client. Finally, an intellectual discussion is not the purpose of a counseling session, and there is no reason why an individual cannot function as a counselor, reacting to the feelings of the client, even though he does not understand the exact meaning of a word that is being used.

At the college level the counselor may sometimes have as a client a psychology student who is trying to impress himself with both the erudite state of his own mind and the lack of intelligence of his counselor; to this end he will deliberately use many long and complicated words quite new to the counselor. When this is obviously happening, the counselor may react to what is actually going on, and the verbalization may then develop into a more fruitful investigation, by the client, of just why he has to try to convince himself that he is more intelligent than the counselor. It is not, of course, of any importance whether the client actually is, or is not, more intelligent than the counselor; but it is of some importance to help the client to discover why he must feel as he does.

The counselor who must know the meaning of each word—and former teachers tend sometimes to be this way—may also find himself in difficulty with adolescent clients who insist on using a language all their own. Even if the counselor makes a valiant effort to find out just what some of the terms actually mean—and often even the adolescents themselves do not know—there will be further frustration in that the current language, like popular tunes, is in a constant state of flux. Thus the best thing the adult counselor can do is abandon any attempt to "know" the meaning, and rather concentrate on understanding the feeling behind the words that are being used. Possibly the real test comes when the counselor tries to establish a counseling relationship with a client who speaks another tongue. If these two can get together, it is certainly not on the basis of an intellectual understanding of what they are saying to each other!

Taping poses something of a problem for some counselors in some schools, although the major difficulty is often the counselor's own uncertainty about what to do. In clinical or laboratory situations this is less of a problem, and in an increasing number of schools taping is taken as a matter of course by the students, although this is an ethical issue that cannot be dismissed lightly. Many counselors, particularly in schools, do feel that a tape hinders the establishment of rapport somewhat during the first session, and will withhold the use of a tape, usually bringing up the subject toward the end of the first session, and then using it, if satisfactory to the client, from the second session on.

All of these items may prove to be initial problems for the student counselor as he becomes involved in the establishment of rapport with the client in the initial counseling session. But in the long run the extent to which they prove to be continuing problems will be a measure of the counselor's professional competence and personal integrity. For some of the counselors depicted here, the establishment of rapport is still a major difficulty, as they struggle to find themselves, whereas others no longer have to *try,* and thus the relationship is better.

WHAT HAPPENS IN THE BEGINNING SESSION

The beginning session is more likely to be a testing ground for the client, and even for the sophisticated counselor there is the element of the unknown—neither person really understands the other, although the client may know about the counselor, and sometimes, of course, the counselor may know about the client. It is likely that some counselors want to know about the client in order to bolster their own feeling of security when, for the first time, they meet him.

Buchheimer and Balogh describe three phases of the beginning session: the statement of the problem, exploration, and closing and planning for the future.[2] These are reasonable enough, and very often do occur, although the student counselor should not assume that the client always follows this timetable! Some clients, for example, will spend more than the first session evading the problem in a variety of ways; some counselors will not give the client a chance to look at his problem, but will provide one for him; some clients will press the counselor for answers, for his version of who they are and what they should do; some clients will sit passively and take no overt action, verbal or otherwise; some clients will leave at the end of the first session without any plans for the future.

Often, at the beginning of a counseling session, clients do not go into any particular specific detail as to why they are coming to see a counselor. Sometimes, of course, the counselor does not give the client much of a chance. In Evraiff's book, for example, this is what happened with Carl:

Co.: Carl, I'm Mr. Williams.
Cl.: Glad to meet you, Mr. Williams.
Co.: Nice to know you. I see you had a little trouble last week.
Cl.: Right.[3]

2. Arnold Buchheimer and Sarah Carter Balogh, *The Counseling Relationship* (Chicago: Science Research Associates, 1961), p. 15.
3. William Evraiff, p. 17, dialogue entries C1–S2. © 1963. Reprinted by permission of Prentice-Hall, Inc., Englewood Cliffs, N.J.

When Jane's counselor, early in the first session, asked her what she would like to talk about, she replied:

I'm kind of sick of talking about myself, first of all, because I've had, I don't know what I should say, trouble, I guess, is the closest thing to it. Not with the police, not with anyone like that, but with my own self, and maybe with my family.[4]

Many students come to a counselor after having been told that the counselor will give them tests or supply them with information that will be helpful to them. Jack's counselor prods him with a question about his thoughts about a future job, but all he gets is:

Well, so far about, ah, the only thing I've really thought of is welding. My father's one and I can weld a little bit. Be a good job. And, ah, I've thought of flying, something like helicopters, that would be a good job.[5]

Edna, a twelve-year-old, gives a not uncommon reaction to the counselor who presses her by asking her what she would like to discuss:

I don't know, I don't know what to discuss.

and, as her next comment:

Well, I'll, do you want me to tell you how old I am, or where I live, or something like that?[6]

Richard reacts much the same way, when the counselor comes forth with the usual "would you like to tell me . . ." bit:

I don't know what to tell you.[7]

These reactions could be expected from individuals who are very likely in need of help, but frequently, when a referred child arrives at the counselor's office, his immediate feeling is that he is there because someone else told him he should be there. His problem, as he sees it, is the person who referred him, rather than the issue or action for which he was supposedly referred!

These junior high school clients (Cl) are all self-referred, and

4. *Ibid.,* p. 74.
5. *Ibid.,* p. 167.
6. *Ibid.,* p. 227.
7. *Ibid.,* p. 317.

we could expect that they would wish to talk about their problems, at least as they see them, without any urging by the counselor. If, on the other hand, they had been sent to the counselor so that "he could do something about you," it is unlikely that they would have expressed themselves so easily. These are the beginning comments:

Co.: Hi, Ted, come in.
Cl.: Thanks.
Co.: What's up . . .
Cl.: Well, I wanted to see you about whether or not I should quit school.

. . . .

Co.: Hi, Jane, how are things going?
Cl.: They're not . . . things are at a standstill . . . everything's so boring.
Co.: Uh-huh . . .
Cl.: Sometimes I wonder whether I'm ever going to be happy in life. I mean . . . well . . . I seem to need excitement. I can't be content with any kind of routine.
Co.: Things have to be happening in my life in order for me to be content . . .
Cl.: Yeh. . . . I just sort of need excitement . . .

. . . .

Cl.: Hi . . .
Co.: Hi, Jim . . . you wanted to talk with me . . .
Cl.: Yeah . . . I want you to help me get out of the foster home I'm in. I'm just about fed up with the way I'm treated. What am I, an animal?
Co.: You've just about had it, eh?

. . . .

Co.: Hi, how are things going?
Cl.: Pretty good.
Cl.: Pretty good . . . but not as good as they could be . . .
Cl.: Yeah, that's right. Brother, I've gotten . . . ah . . . I've gotten into a lot of trouble and my parents are going to kill me when they find out.

. . . .

Co.: Hi, come on in—have a chair . . . what's new?
Cl.: Oh . . . well . . . ah . . . nothing much, I guess . . . except I'm not friendly with Ruth any more . . . we had a fight . . . I called her some awful names . . . and we really hurt each other and well . . . I . . . uhmm . . . I don't feel too good about the whole thing . . . it's stupid . . .
Co.: It bothers me . . . I'm not happy about what happened between me and Ruth . . .
Cl.: Yeah . . . that's why I came down to see you . . . I thought if I could talk about the fight I might feel better . . . you know . . . blow off some steam . . .

. . . .

Co.: Hi, come on in. . . . You made an appointment to see me . . . what's on your mind . . .

Cl.: Well, I wanted to talk to you about math. . . . I'd like to change my math class.

Co.: Uh . . . huh . . .

Cl.: I'm not doing even fair work now . . . in fact, right now, as far as I'm concerned, math rots . . .

Co.: (Silence) . . .

Cl.: I'm fed up with math . . . and with . . . him . . .

Jane's counselor engages in a "getting to know you" sort of conversation:

Cl.: It's nice here.

Co.: We've got the fan going. We're trying to make it more comfortable.

Cl.: Mm-hmmm.

Co.: On the sheet, as I mentioned before, you can take that home and finish it, and, uh, if you do come back you can bring it back or mail it back, whichever you prefer.

Cl.: Mm-hmm.

Co.: Tell me, did you have a rough time getting down here?

Cl.: Not rough, but whenever I ride the bus I just get all excited about whether I'm going to get off on time and . . .

Co.: Oh, and you just made the mistake of going up on the third floor.[8]

Jack's counselor overelaborates on the equipment, and shows his own nervousness:

Co.: Hello, Jack; sit down. Picked a warm day to come down, didn't you?

Cl.: Mm-hmm (looking around). Two-way mirror, huh?

Co.: Yeah, that's right. Did she tell you about it? So that if there are people studying to come here to observe, they can do that. That makes you a little uneasy about it?

Cl.: Yeah.

Co.: Well, if there are any, there's no one around today, and if there are people who come, they will be people who are studying advanced work in college, and they're not much interested in you or me, as persons, it's just the way the counseling goes. So that's a little comfort, maybe. (Pause) It's kind of strange, isn't it, the first time?

Cl.: Yeah (Pause).

Co.: Can you tell me a little about what you, ah, came down for?[9]

8. *Ibid.*, p. 72, dialogue entries S1–C8.
9. *Ibid.*, p. 166, dialogue entries C1–C7.

Edna is not too eager to talk with her counselor:

Co.: Hello, Edna. How are you today?

Cl.: All right.

Co.: Do you mind the heat very much?

Cl.: No.

Co.: Did you come all by yourself?

Cl.: Yes, Ma'am.

Co.: Would you like to put your umbrella in the corner so you can be comfortable? And your purse you can put on the table or somewhere. Would you like to talk to me today about something? Would you like to discuss things with me? (Short pause)

Cl.: I don't know, I don't know what to discuss.

Cl.: Well, maybe you could tell me something about yourself so I'd know you better. How would that be?

Cl.: Well, I'll, do you want me to tell you how old I am, or where I live or something like that?[10]

Richard's counselor pushes and probes and dominates at the start:

Co.: Make yourself comfortable. Would you like to tell me a little bit about school and the trouble you are having?

Cl.: I don't know what to tell you.

Co.: Uh-huh. You understand the set-up here at the counseling center?

Cl.: Uh-huh.

Co.: Who was it that suggested that you come down?

Cl.: My mother.

Co.: She's concerned about how you are doing in school? Is that the reason she suggested it, or what?[11]

By the end of the first session, all of these clients had indicated their willingness to return. However, one should be cautious in interpreting just what this might mean. It could mean that the client felt that at last he had found an adult who would listen to him, and with whom he felt easy and comfortable, or it might mean that he felt he had found someone who would answer his problems for him, or it could mean that he felt he was supposed to return, and he was willing to do whatever the authority figure suggested.

10. *Ibid.*, p. 227, dialogue entries C1–S10.
11. *Ibid.*, p. 317, dialogue entries C1–C7.

Some points that might be noted in the first counseling session:

1. The client is likely going to be testing the counselor to see if he fits into his preconceived image of him. If he does, this may be good or bad, depending on the image the client has of the counselor.
2. While some beginning sessions may prove to be also concluding sessions, the counselor can usually operate on the assumption that his primary function in the first session is to establish a positive climate so that the client may wish to return for further consideration of his difficulty.
3. The beginning session, like other sessions, belongs to the client, not the counselor, and the counselor's behavior should carry this message to the client.
4. If the aim of the counselor is to establish at least the beginning of a genuine human relationship, he will feel that he has no obligation to any methodology or technique, that his obligation is rather to his self-integrity.
5. Toward the end of the session the counselor can indicate his interest in the return of the client without implying that the client has no choice and should return because he, the counselor, wants him to return. Some counselors give the impression of aloofness and lack of concern, whereas others imply that the client must return regardless of how he might feel.

THE INNER FRAME OF REFERENCE

Counseling, at least in an existential-humanistic sense, cannot take place unless there is an involvement between client and counselor, and it has to be a certain kind of involvement if growth is to take place. The unique characteristic of the counseling involvement is that it is centered on the client, and the counselor is one who is sensitive to, aware of, and able to operate within the frame of reference of the client. He can accept as reality the client's perception of reality, a reality which is often quite different from that of the counselor. Although I may not be able to see the knife that the client says is sticking in his back, that knife is very real and the pain is very real. It may be a "knife" that the client has put in his back and can remove from his back, but it is nonetheless as real as a knife that someone else physically put in his back!

214

The ability to operate within the world of the client should not be confused with the extent of counselor intervention and direction. The counselor who thinks he is being Carl Rogers by mumbling "Hmm . . ." is as far away from the client as the counselor who thinks he can be Freud by saying, "Now let's get into more about your sex life."

Here, then, are a few examples of attempts of the counselor to become involved in the world of the client:

Sometimes it's hard to grow up. You get the feeling that you should act more grown up, but still, in a way, you'd rather remain a little girl.

. . . .

One day the foster home seems OK . . . another day you hate it. You wish you could have the same feelings about it instead of one day liking it and the next day hating it.

The counselor may sometimes become so involved with the other's frame of reference that he will use the first person. Needless to say, the counselor could hardly be genuine if he was using this as a "technique":

These tests concern me, they sort of make me worry—it seems that they might have some influence on my schooling. . . . And I'm hoping that they won't have any influence, that they won't count as much as I sometimes think they will.

. . . .

I wish that people would allow me to make my own decisions. . . . I'm old enough to decide what's best for me.

The use of the first person, however, is no guarantee that the counselor is operating within the client's frame of reference. A long counselor statement, first person or no, is more likely to be an intellectual summation from the counselor's frame of reference. For example:

In other words it bugs me that everybody sort of thinks the worst of kids today when they aren't any different and they don't do any different than the kids of my parents' generation, or kids who even lived before that. I kind of feel there's nothing wrong in having a good time. My parents had their good times. . . . Why can't I without people getting so worried?

215

Many counselors will fluctuate back and forth from the client's frame of reference to the counselor's frame of reference. Note this counselor:

Co.: What subject do you think you're failing in?

Cl.: Literature.

Co.: Would you like to talk about that or how you feel about it?

Cl.: Well, I never read nothing and I don't like to read.

Co.: There's something about reading in general that has made you dislike it?

Cl.: Yeah . . .

Co.: Doesn't it kind of hinder your work in school?

Cl.: Well, I just read enough to get by and that's about it.

Co.: Just enough to get by.

Cl.: Yeah . . .

Co.: How do you feel about that?

Cl.: (Pause) What do you mean "How do I feel about that"?

Co.: About getting by all the time.

Cl.: I don't know.

Co.: You don't feel anything.

Cl.: Uh-huh . . . As long as I get it done I don't care.

Sometimes the conversation would appear to be geared entirely to the counselor's external frame of reference. Jack's counselor, for example, in session eight comments as follows:

Co.: I think an important thing here is that this turning it off in school, this is what happens to the school work, in some cases.

Cl.: Yeah.

Co.: This is the first real talk we've ever had.

Cl.: Yeah.

Co.: I wish we could go on.

Cl.: I'm about talked out though.

Co.: I think you're just starting now.

Cl.: Maybe we've just started on the subject, but I'm about talked out for today.

Co.: (Laughs) Yeah, I mean for today, but for the future maybe we could find out some other ways to get rid of this tension, this anger, so that it wouldn't interfere with your school work.[12]

12. *Ibid.*, p. 206, dialogue entries C338–C346.

So the extent to which the counselor operates within the client's frame of reference varies. The student counselor must determine what is *real* for him and *effective* for the client. If he can manage to combine these two, he is probably better off than most counselors!

LEARNING TO BE FREE

A basic and crucial part of the counseling experience is the gradual experiencing of being free. The individual can become, in an atmosphere of security, a little more honest, both with himself and with others. This learning to be free is often painful, and although it is cathartic, there may be despair and hostility and frustration. These are feelings the client comes to be able to experience, and to live with, and to go beyond. They are necessary if there is to be growth and movement. We might assume that the more a person, young or old, has lived a lie, the more violent some of these expressions will be, whereas the moderately stable, ordinary child, living through his developmental problems, periodically needs some assistance so that he can maintain his high level of honesty and genuineness. Here are some junior high school children who are receiving such assistance from their counselors. They are learning to express, and to look at, their selves.

Anxiety may be detected here:

If he ever calls my mother I'm sunk—she'll never believe it wasn't my fault.

. . . .

I just wish she'd leave me alone . . . every time I go in her room I get a feeling like . . . well, as if I had a piece of lead in my stomach.

. . . .

I just go blank. Whenever someone says tests to me I just freeze. If someone tested me on my name I don't think I'd remember it—just because it's a test.

These children express frustration:

It's nice to be able to talk about this problem, but what can I do about it? Nobody at school can help me, you can't do anything, and I can't do anything. What's the use of even discussing it? All we're doing is running into a stone wall.

. . . .

*What makes me mad though . . . the teachers just keep put-
ting on your report card "capable of doing better." How do they
know? That's what I can't figure out. How do they know you're
capable of doing better if you think you're doing your best now?*

. . . .

*I wish I could get through to him. I wish I could make him
listen and understand. I keep trying to make contact with him
but he doesn't seem to care. It's as if I were a chair or a lamp . . .
like I'm not alive . . . and all I want him to do is pay attention,
to listen and understand. Even if he can't, if he'd only try.*

These clients express overt hostility:

*Sometimes I wish I could choke him or push him downstairs. I
sometimes just want revenge for what he's done to me.*

. . . .

*I'll pay her back—somehow-somewhere-sometime—I'll let her
know that she can't treat me like a piece of dirt.*

. . . .

*Who does he think he is? If he thinks he can insult my mother
like that and get away with it he's crazy. When I see him after
school today I'm going to deck him. . . . I'll shove my fist right
down his throat. . . . I don't care who sees me.*

These are periods when this client feels despair.

*I feel terribly defeated, especially in the morning. All the
dreams one makes . . . I just have to discard them and come
down to earth . . . and try to accept things gracefully and with
a measure of composure. . . . I'll never be able to . . . (pause) . . .
and yet, having admitted these things, you can sometimes turn
around and prove them wrong.*

*I guess I have to go through a period of hating her . . . and
after that maybe I can see her as she was. Now I hate her guts
most of the time . . . the poor, neurotic, shrill, demanding
woman. She did an incalculable amount of damage, and the
pathetic thing is that in a way I think she knew it.*

This client can also be free to be honest about his feelings
about the counselor, and they are not always positive:

*I experienced a distinct chill when I left here last week. . . .
(Long pause.) May I smoke?*

. . . .

If you'd been a close friend I might have said, "He's just being bitchy, so forget it. . . ." But this is a very special relationship we have, and I'm extremely sensitive to anything you might say—quite sensitive. . . .

And here in session five a client shows that he is beginning to learn to be free:

Cl.: I grew up too damn fast. My body matured but my mind didn't. I was easily led. I wanted to show my muscles. I wanted to show how tough I was. Sometimes I slip back, but I think . . . well . . . I think my mind is starting to understand things. I'm starting to say to myself,"Who do you think you are?" I never said that before. I always thought I was somebody.

Co.: You feel that you're gaining in maturity, and this is a good feeling for you.

Cl.: I'm not saying that I enjoy school all the time. I mean . . . you know . . . there are things around here that are chicken. Ah, I can never change those things . . . but I am learning. I mean I'm starting to enjoy it more than I dislike it. But the thing that I really dislike . . . you know . . . those few teachers. They think they're better than other people. They look down at me. They think they're better than everybody else. Boy, that's a bad way to feel because nobody is better than anyone else.

Co.: Those teachers who feel that they're better than other people kind of bother you.

Cl.: Sure they do. I can't see that. Why in hell should they think that way? What makes them think that way? One thing I don't understand is why teachers don't respect certain classes and certain kids . . . I mean, who do they think they are. . . . (Pause) . . . Well, I guess time's up for now. So long, Mr. Del.

Co.: So long, John.

And so the client comes to learn to experience his feelings, and to live with them, and after experiencing them, he learns, too, that somehow they are no longer the same. The ghosts are not quite the ghosts they were, the faces are not as threatening as they were, and the new face I see—the me—is stronger and more pleasing.

GROWTH AND MOVEMENT

As the person moves and grows, things become better—the individual himself becomes better, and somehow other people become better too. All is by no means, of course, sweetness and light, but the individual does gain the strength to be who he is. Often in the counseling hour the client may be talking, in a somewhat intellectual sense, about what has happened rather than what is happening, but often, too, what he is expressing is his feeling of an ongoing process. He is not simply saying positive words because they sound good, or because he feels this is what he is supposed to say; his words are truly expressive of what is, as well as he can perceive it, and experience it, happening.

Here are some comments from various high school students:

I find that I'm becoming more interested in reading just because I don't have to be angry any more.

You know, I could go on blaming others for things that have gone wrong in my life, but when I really look at it . . . I mean honestly look . . . well, I could have avoided a lot of trouble simply by using my own head.

In the past I've always reacted with anger when somebody was mad at me . . . seems that's pretty threatening for me and I have to defend myself. It must be that I've been insecure all my life, not having any real affection or love from my dad. I just have to defend myself when I'm around him or anybody like him.

Sometimes I think I enjoyed being afraid . . . but you know, I don't have to be scared if I don't want to. Before I thought that being afraid was the only way I could ever be.

Let's face it—I can stand up or I can crawl. Now I figure that once I begin to crawl, that crawling becomes a way of life; but if I stand, then standing can become a way of life. Right now I prefer standing.

This client expresses his feelings of growth toward self-actualization and freedom:

And yet for some strange reason it doesn't . . . I can . . . can feel the failure of it . . . it was a failure . . . and yet it . . . ah . . . it doesn't . . . I don't seem to have taken it as hard as I thought I was going to . . . I don't understand it . . . I wish it was otherwise . . . I don't know. . . .

As does this client:

Sitting right here now . . . I feel more like myself—whatever myself is I don't know—but I and me are both right here together—right here right now . . .

 I don't have to go outside of me . . . I can stay right here and be me . . . I have less faces to meet the faces . . . but you see,

when you drop the masks—and I haven't dropped them com-
pletely . . . but enough to know what it feels like to do it . . .
there is a sense of loss, of not belonging anymore . . . my posi-
tion in relation to other people is changed : . . . I sort of feel . . .
not all the time . . . but some . . . something is over and done
with . . . and now . . . now I can look ahead . . . reach out. . . .

And this client:

I've been learning to communicate more in the last few months
. . . with more people . . . to take a little chance—and that pays
off, you see, and you take another little chance . . . and the roof
doesn't fall in on you after all . . .

And movement and growth can be painful, as in these ex-
changes with the counselor:

Co.: Are you saying, Mr. Ril, that it's difficult to feel without wondering
what's behind this—why is this—and it's difficult to accept this feeling . . .

Cl.: (Long pause) . . . I guess the . . . I guess I'm crying because one by one
I've had to destroy the illusions . . . and it's hard to give them up . . .

Co.: They've been important . . . but now you're saying good-bye to them
. . .

Cl.: Yeah . . . yes . . . uh . . . yes, I guess so . . .

And again:

Cl.: . . . and I suppose that's why I want to cry . . .

Co.: I want these big things . . . excellence . . . but I can't . . . I won't be in
first place. . . .

Cl.: No, I won't be in first place . . . there's a wide gap between fact and
fancy . . . (long pause) . . . boy, it's a long fall. . . .

Co.: . . . back to the company of other humans . . .

Cl.: To hell with them . . . I don't care . . . about most humans . . . I care
about me . . .

Co.: Uh . . . huh . . .

Cl.: Their concern is their concern, not mine . . . (long pause) . . . that
sounds conceited, doesn't it . . . but I don't care . . . that's how I feel . . .

Cl.: You care more about you . . .

Cl.: I do . . . I do . . . I do . . . but I want to separate caring from an excessive
preoccupation . . . you see . . . there is a difference there.

And again:

Cl.: I just couldn't accept the whole thing, so I had to rearrange it, didn't I,
I had to reconstruct it, and bring it here, and lie to myself, and lie to you,

221

so that it could become something I could accept . . . and I felt so ashamed of myself . . . ashamed that I had to come here and lie to myself and to you . . . and I'm frightened . . . I had to work so hard to change it . . . it was such a feverish effort . . .

Co.: You just had to make it into something good. . . .

Cl.: I couldn't accept it the way it was . . . and yet, I did have to tell you— I just couldn't sit here and lie to you. . . .

And so these clients are growing and moving. For some, the growth and the movement is not too difficult, for they are young, and change is easier. For others, it is harder, but all are having an involvement with another human being in a therapeutic experience. Their movement is toward greater individual freedom and greater individual responsibility, and in becoming more aware of their own self they also become more aware of and more sensitive to their fellow humans. Only the strong and the secure can truly live with others in a condition of love and trust and respect.

THE ENDING

The ending of a series of counseling sessions should, of course, be only the beginning of a newer, brighter, freer life for the person who has been known as the client. This brighter life comes to be usually because the individual has become able to do what he felt he could not do before, and he has found that he does not have to do what he once felt he had to do. The two faces have come closer together, and living with self has become easier, more comfortable, more satisfying. This can occur, in a modest and undramatic fashion, when a child sees a counselor for only a single session, as well as at the end of a long series of painful and traumatic sessions.

The ending of a single session should pose no particular problem for the counselor, in that a time limit should be agreed upon and it should be held to, except in the most unusual circumstances. In a school, a counseling period usually fits in with a class period, and most students assume that a counseling session will last the same amount of time as a class session, although in some schools the two do not necessarily coincide. The inexperienced counselor may sometimes feel pressed by the client to continue for a longer period of time, but this is usually unwise, and it is beneficial neither for the client nor for the counselor. One indication of progress in counseling might be the assumption by the client of the responsibility for indicating that the time is up, rather than waiting for the counselor to take the initiative. Often, of course, a client might be emotionally involved and quite unaware of time; in such a situation the counselor, obviously, should not cut the person off right in the middle of an expression of feeling, but somewhere within the general time limit he should take the initiative in gently suggesting that the time is just about up.

In the ideal situation it is the client who determines, correctly, that he no longer has any need of the counselor's help, and that he can get along very well without him. This, however, does not always happen, and the "ending" may come in a variety of ways. Let us note a few of these.

1. In a school situation the counseling sessions usually end with the end of the school year. In many ways this is beneficial, in that the client knows in advance that, come May or June, he is going to have to go it alone. With some children, of course, who may be in more serious difficulties, referral would be a necessity if the counselor was not available during the summer months. Clients should know in advance if they have only a certain time available for counseling, and if a school counselor takes on a client for what would appear to be a series of counseling sessions during the month of May, he should point out that he will be available only until, say, the middle of June.

2. In most cases, when the client indicates his desire to terminate the counseling, the counselor will see no reason why he should not be acceptant of this desire. These clients in a high school, for example, would appear to know where they are going:

I really don't feel that it's necessary for me to come back. I feel that I'm able to . . . well . . . sort of . . . able to think for myself and decide just what I should and shouldn't do. . . .

Things have worked out. I went back to her and told her how I felt . . . I mean I let her know that I didn't like what was developing. After that talk things seemed to ease off . . . I sort of got it out of my system. I don't think it will be necessary for me to continue with counseling.

I've kind of tried out this new person that I've decided to become and it feels real good. I mean I think that there's definitely a sort of a change in me . . . I don't think I'll be seeing you for a while . . . I want to be on my own. . . .

Some counselors, after comments like these, would probably indicate their availability if and when they were needed. Others would feel that this determination should be made by the client without what might be considered as possible counselor encouragement to return for further counseling.

3. The counselor, however, may not always honestly feel that the client is wise in terminating. If the counselor is honest and genuine, he will relate these feelings to the client. He may feel that the client is terminating because of his distaste for the counselor, and suggest another counselor with whom the client might be able to relate more effectively. He may feel that the client is terminating because of his feeling of despair that nothing is happening, or possibly because of his feeling that too much is happening. In any case, it would seem that if the counselor is to be congruent, and genuine, then his positive regard for the client can include his expressing his feeling that the client is unwise to choose to terminate. The final choice, of course, would be left to the client, although even here there is potentially a sticky ethical problem. What if the client has disintegrated even more, and is presenting real evidence of almost totally disorganized, psychotic behavior—does the counselor still say to the client. "The choice is yours . . ."?

4. Some clients, of course, terminate without any previous notice or warning. They just don't come back. The counselor must be concerned with the part he had to play in this abrupt termination, and tapes of such final sessions can sometimes provide valuable leads as to why the client terminated. Some school counselors may have colleagues attempt to find out the "why" of the termination, since in such cases the client is usually still in school. Others would feel this unwise, and would not interfere with the client's right to terminate—abruptly or not.

5. Some counselors will take the initiative and pose the possibility of termination before it has been suggested by the client. Here again, if this is the honest feeling of the counselor, and if he is genuine, then it would seem that he should pass this feeling on to the client. Many counselors, of course, would say that they were simply reflecting or interpreting the feelings that the client was conveying to them. This would likely be the case, for example, with these counselors:

It seems that there's nothing more to talk about, eh . . . If you feel that there might be more to talk about, feel free to make an appointment.

It appears that you're now able to handle this problem. You're free to continue with counseling if you wish . . . or you can try to get along without it . . . the decision is up to you. . . .

We've been getting together now for a period of four months, and you feel that you've changed . . . you don't feel the need to be angry at the world any more . . . you're able to take things in stride. You can continue to come here if you want . . . the decision as to whether or not to continue with counseling is, as always, up to you.

Sometimes, too, the counselor may feel that he is being ineffective, that he and the client are simply going around in circles, and that nothing positive is happening. Again, if he does have this feeling, and if it appears to him that the client would receive more effective help from another counselor, then he should probably pass this feeling on the client. This may be even more of an ethical problem when this is a private situation, and the client is paying a fee. The client, of course, will not always agree with the counselor, and may indicate his feeling of satisfaction with what is happening, whether the counselor agrees with him or not. What then—does the counselor continue in a relationship that he feels is ineffective? And to what extent does this reflect on his own integrity, and on the value he places on his self?

6. Finally, realistically, it is likely that if the service was available, and if money was not a factor, there would be a large number of individuals who, periodically, off and on, would avail themselves of the services of a counselor as the pressures pushing in on them became too much to take alone. This is already happening to some degree, and as it becomes more culturally acceptable, and people can more easily avail themselves of such services without having the tab of "mentally sick" put on them, then there may be some decrease in the dreadful things that so many individuals must do to themselves, and, inevitably then, to others.

Here are a few comments that express the feelings of client John in his last session with the counselor:

Cl.: Boy, I've got that confidence in me. You can't beat it . . . and it's what I need. I've got the feeling that I'm going to amount to something because . . . I don't know . . . I figure that a lot of things that were bothersome to me before, I can handle now. I want to make out good in life, Mr. Del, and I figure I can. I really do . . . I don't know . . . I've got that ; . . somewhere, in my stomach some place, or in my chest some place . . . I've got that good feeling. The feeling that things are going to be okay for me if I use my head.

. . . .

Cl.: Well, now I'm steady about school. I mean I don't have my ups and downs. Everything can go along pretty good. Like I said, I don't love it, but it isn't like before. I used to hate it, and then I'd like it and then I'd hate it, and then again I'd like it. I mean I had crazy feelings—crazy ideas about school. I mean I didn't know why I was there, and what I was supposed to do. But now I know—now I know I'm here because I want to make something of myself.

. . . .

Cl.: Sometimes I get nervous about next year, but at other times I think of it as a challenge. I'd like to really see if what I've found out about myself is going to stick, or is it going to rub off in the first rainstorm. See, I don't know—I won't really know until next year, and the year after, and so on. Maybe I'll never know. Even if I did go to college, I'd probably never really know if I made it. I don't know. How does a person know when he's made it?

. . . .

Cl.: Maybe not . . . (long pause) . . . Well, I guess . . . (long pause) . . . I won't see you again, Mr. Del, for a long time . . . I'll see you to say "Hi" to, of course . . . but not like this . . . (long pause) . . . So long then, Mr. Del, and thanks, thanks for everything that you have done. . . .

Co.: So long, John.

And so John leaves Mr. Del. Mr. Del, being human, probably feels a bit sad, and a bit proud. For John's sake, he no doubt hopes that John will not have to see him again, and the final client comment, indicating counselor success, might well be, "Thank you—but I hope that I don't have to see you again."

John did become more capable of standing on his own feet; he did become more of a responsible individual, capable of standing up and answering for himself, and willing to do so. He was given no medicine, he was given no cure, but through a warm and human relationship with a skilled and educated person who respected him and understood him, he was able to marshal the strengths that he always had, and become a stronger and better person. This, then, is the experience known as counseling.

Chapter **10**

Operational Issues in Counseling

There are a number of operational issues in the process of counseling and psychotherapy, and some of them are of a "nuts-and-bolts" variety. As in most human issues, there are many human answers, and the divergence on many of these issues is no less today than it was several decades ago. The reactions that I present in this chapter are from my existential-humanistic point of view.

THE SEMANTIC PROBLEM

The various interpretations of words continue to cause differences among counselors. Many of these apparent differences are simply a lack of understanding of just exactly what one means when he uses a certain word or a descriptive phrase. Two words that still cause confusion are "counseling" and "psychotherapy," and neither really has any meaning until an individual counselor or therapist indicates what *he* means by each term. Thus we find individuals who call themselves psychotherapists doing what others would call counseling, and we find individuals who call themselves counselors doing what others would call psychotherapy. There are many differentiations between the two. One of the most common refers to counseling as dealing with a generally normal individual, and psychotherapy as dealing with an abnormal person; or some would say that counseling does not get to the same depth as psychotherapy; or some would say that counseling is concerned with the conscious, whereas psychotherapy deals with the unconscious materials. Bordin, for example,

227

states that the counseling relationship is characterized by less intensity of emotional expression, and relatively more emphasis on cognitive and rational factors than is the case in psychotherapy.[1] Mowrer refers to counseling as a process of giving help "to persons suffering from fully-conscious conflicts which are accompanied by so-called normal anxiety."[2]

Tyler saw the aim of therapy as some sort of personality change, while she felt that we should use "counseling" to refer to a helping process whose aim is not to change the person but to enable him to utilize the resources he now has for coping with life.[3] In a later revision of her book, however, she felt that effective counseling must include features of *choice* counseling, which she had viewed as counseling, and *adjustment* counseling, which she had viewed as therapy.[4] Which would seem to be another way of saying that counseling and psychotherapy are hard to distinguish from each other!

Buchheimer and Balogh see the approach in therapy as historic and symbolic, relying heavily on the reactivation and consideration of unconscious materials. The content of conversation is the consideration of past experiences and the reconstruction of that which has happened and has been repressed, thus causing distortions of the present. Through the counseling conversation, on the other hand, the individual will revise his distortions and thereby alter his behavior. The emphasis is on the present, and on verbal material that is within the individual's immediate awareness or that he can easily be made aware of.[5]

Byrne sees counseling and psychotherapy as having much in common, and he considers the major difference to be the degree to which psychotherapists uncover and work with hidden psychological dynamics because the individual seeking help reports a long-standing dissatisfaction with life, accompanied by long-standing ineffective or unwanted behaviors. He points out that the school counselor is not usually called upon to function as a psychotherapist, the reason lying in the relationship between function and clientele.[6]

1. Edward S. Bordin, *Psychological Counseling* (New York: Appleton-Century-Crofts, 1955), p. 15.
2. O. Hobart Mowrer, "Anxiety Theory as a Basis for Distinguishing Between Counseling and Psychotherapy," in Ralph F. Berdie (ed.), *Concepts of Programs of Counseling* (Minneapolis: University of Minnesota Press, 1951), p. 23.
3. Leona E. Tyler, *The Work of the Counselor* (New York: Appleton-Century-Crofts, 1961), p. 12.
4. Leona E. Tyler, *The Work of the Counselor* (New York: Appleton-Century-Crofts, 1969), p. 13.
5. Arnold Buchheimer and Sarah Carter Balogh, *The Counseling Relationship* (Chicago: Science Research Associates, 1961), p. x.
6. Richard Hill Byrne, *The School Counselor* (Boston: Houghton Mifflin, 1963), pp. 37–38.

Then, too, some medically oriented psychotherapists would tend to feel that the practice of psychotherapy is limited to the realm of those who possess a medical degree, while what the others do is counseling. However, there are many nonmedical psychotherapists who work in certain institutions with their medical colleagues; all do practically identically the same thing, and they call it psychotherapy.

While there may be a logical difference between intellectual guidance with a person whose stresses and strains do not control his actions and counseling with an individual whose actions are dominated by and subject to his emotional stresses, there is no such differentiation between counseling and psychotherapy. There is not always, for example, a clear and distinct line between the conscious and the subconscious. When a person is swimming, he is partly in the water and partly out, rarely completely submerged or completely out of the water. Most professional school counselors are well acquainted with students who are pushed by subconscious pressures as causes of their difficulties; and the purpose of the counseling is to help the student to work out these parts of his totality that are only dimly, if at all, understood and accepted. Sometimes, of course, the distinction is quite clear. Nevertheless, anyone who works with people who are under stress is going to have a difficult time cataloguing what he is doing as either counseling or psychotherapy on the basis of the conscious or the subconscious.

Similarly, with regard to the depth of the process, it is probably correct to say that, traditionally, most counselors in schools have not worked with people who are completely divorced from our reality, and might thus be called psychotic, but have worked rather with those who would possibly like to be divorced from our reality, but know they are not, and might thus be called neurotic. One of the obvious reasons is that most of the former individuals are to be found in hospitals or similar institutions, whereas, until recently, counselors were to be found in hospitals only as patients.

In the last decade, however, with the advent of a high level of preparation at the doctoral and post-doctoral levels for such professional workers as school counselors, counseling psychologists, rehabilitation counselors, and psychiatric nurses, it is obvious that people who may be called counselors are working with psychotic patients as are psychotherapists. On the other hand, a psychiatrist who has a private practice, or one who works in a university clinic or a counseling center, most likely spends the bulk of his time with individuals who are neurotic rather than psychotic; and thus he is, if we must have a difference, a counselor rather than a therapist.

Carl Rogers, who sees himself as a counselor working with clients, spent many years working with a schizophrenic population, while Albert Ellis, who sees himself as a therapist working with patients, spends most of his time with a neurotic population!

There are not only different levels of education for those who are involved in counseling and psychotherapy, there are different kinds of education as well. If we accept the definition of counseling given in this book, then it follows that those professional workers, whether called psychotherapists or counselors, are performing the same basic task, although they may be performing it in different ways because of their different educations and their different personalities. It might even be better to think in terms of psychotherapies, rather than psychotherapy. Then, possibly, psychotherapists who do different things would be more acceptable to each other, and would not threaten each other to the extent that they appear to today.

When one refers to the "practice of psychiatry," one usually means the practice of psychotherapy. Hence a psychiatrist might be described as a medical doctor who practices psychotherapy, while a psychologist is a Ph.D. who practices psychotherapy—though not all psychologists do. Psychoanalysis is generally considered by medical doctors to be a more intensive psychotherapy, although some differentiate between the two. Fromm-Reichmann commented years ago that there was no valid *intensive* psychotherapy other than that which is psychoanalytic or psychoanalytically oriented,[7] a statement that would obviously be challenged by many psychotherapists who, though working intensively with extremely disturbed individuals, do not think of themselves as psychoanalysts.

Indeed, the whole existential-humanist movement of the 1960's and the 1970's pointed the way to a more intensive involvement of humans with humans, but in a quite different direction than the traditional psychoanalysis.

Tyler's earlier reference to "no change" would seem to be rather pointless, since it would be impossible for one to utilize to a greater degree what he now has without undergoing any change! Nor can I see Buchheimer and Balogh's point of differentiation between the past and the present, since most individuals, when talking about themselves, mingle the past with the present. Even the schoolchild under modest stress will be likely periodically to bring in the past as he talks about the present.

It would seem to me that the competent, professionally educated school counselor, as he goes about his daily professional tasks, is going to become involved in practically all of the human relation-

7.   Frieda Fromm-Reichmann, *Principles of Intensive Psychotherapy* (Chicago: University of Chicago Press, 1950), p. x.

ships that have been described by various individuals as either counseling or psychotherapy—not in one day, or with one person, but
over a period of time, with many different children, many of whom
could not even be described as clients. He will work with some children almost entirely at a cognitive, rational level, and with others he
will spend much time in the area of feelings and emotions; with some
children he may provide simple answers, which will affect their fu-
tures but create no drastic change; some children will bring much
subconscious material to the surface, others practically none at all;
some children will spend much time on the past, which has taught
them to be as they are, and others will be concerned mostly with the
present. The counselor should be able to function effectively with
these children, and as long as he can, it matters little whether he
describes what he is doing as counseling or psychotherapy. If the
term "psychotherapy" is bothersome to certain school administrators or medical personnel, the counselor might just as well refer to
his function as counseling, and continue to do what he is doing anyway!

After all, the most "client-centered" of counselors is not going
to "reflect feelings" when the cheery new student asks if English 3
has as its teacher Mr. Brown or Mr. Smith. If the counselor knows,
he will likely say, "Mr. Brown." On the other hand, if a grim and
tense student says to the same counselor, "Well, I guess you should
know—which of these miserable courses in English has Smith as the
teacher," the counselor will most likely react to the feeling behind
the student's question, because obviously the student is not asking
an intellectual question. He is expressing a feeling. Similarly, the
counselor would feel that when a man quietly says, "I will kill myself
tonight," the counselor reaction will not be, "Oh, you mustn't do a
thing like that," because again the individual is expressing deep, intense feelings. Such a cliché as the one above would be a little better
than a rejection of the individual, who has possibly already been
rejected by all whom he has known.

It is surely idiotic for any counselor to defend any of his actions on the basis of his supposed methodology. One does not do
something because he is a this or a that, but rather because the
evidence has tended to indicate that this is the way that *he* can be
most helpful with the other person, and it matters little whether he is
functioning as a "vocational counselor," an "educational counselor,"
a "personal counselor," or a "psychotherapist."

After all, B. F. Skinner, *the* behaviorist of the century, received the "Humanist of the Year" award in 1972 from the Association of Humanistic Psychology, and Albert Ellis, *the* rational-emo-

tive therapist, is a member of the board of directors of the Association of Humanistic Psychology!

ECLECTICISM

Differences continue to exist among counselors as to the place of "eclecticism" in counseling, although, like other terms, much depends on just how one interprets it. A definition that Williamson gave over a quarter of a century ago would probably be as acceptable now as it was then:

> Counseling . . . may be thought of as embracing a wide variety of techniques, from which repertoire the effective counselor selects . . . those which are relevant and appropriate to the nature of the client's problem and to other features of the situation. . . . Each technique is applicable only to particular problems and particular students. . . . Rather, the counselor adapts his specific techniques to the individuality and problem pattern of the student, making the necessary modifications to produce the desired result for a particular student.[8]

McKinney described the eclectic counselor in this way:

> In view of the client's maturity and emotional balance he may be directive or non-directive. He may try to prevent certain conditions from arising, or he may correct an existing condition. He may put an emphasis on immediate relief or palliation, or direct his attention to a long term attempt at enabling the individual to achieve a reorganization of his personality. He may, on the other hand, see that the client requires treatment that is beyond his training and may seek consultation or make a referral to some specialist.[9]

Thorne has written a chapter that he entitles "Directive and Eclectic Personality Counseling," implying that there is an eclectic "method." But in the first paragraph of the chapter he writes, ". . . to make a definitive statement concerning the eclectic orientation that is basic for the proposed system of practice. . . ."[10]

8. E. G. Williamson, *Counseling Adolescents* (New York: McGraw-Hill, Inc., 1950), pp. 219–220.
9. Fred McKinney, *Counseling for Personal Adjustment* (Boston: Houghton Mifflin, 1958) p. 32.
10. Frederick Thorne, "Directive and Eclectic Personality Counseling," in James L. McCrary and Daniel E. Sheer (eds.), *Six Approaches to Psychotherapy* (New York: Dryden Press, 1955), p. 235.

Two decades later, Thorne is even more certain about the validity of his eclectic model. He writes:

The eclectic model is based logically upon thorough diagnosis. The whole concept of causation, or etiology, suggests that causes can be recognized and differentiated diagnostically. You must know what you are trying to cure before you can select the appropriate form of treatment.[11]

There is a vast difference, however, between an eclectic *orientation,* which should be part of the continuing education of every counselor and therapist, and an eclectic *method* of counseling.

Thus Marzolf states that

the eclectic in counseling is one who is willing to utilize any procedure which holds promise even though their theoretical bases differ markedly. . . . In contrast with the eclectic, the doctrinaire counselor resists all temptation to use any procedure, which, in his view at least, is incompatible with his theory. To do so would be intellectually disconcerting.[12]

One could certainly agree with Marzolf that any counselor who operated on the basis of allegiance to a theory, *per se*, would be worse than doctrinaire—he would be plain stupid. On the other hand, the consistency of a counselor may be the consistency of a basic personal approach to a human relationship.

If one thinks of the counseling process as consisting of a series of techniques, isolated from the personality of the counselor, to be used according to the client and the type of problem that he presents, then one can readily see how the counselor can be eclectic in his approach. He is eclectic in that he uses those techniques and methods that seem most appropriate for a certain client at a certain time. If, on the other hand, what are called methodologies are actually qualities of the individual counselor, it is difficult to see how the counselor could be eclectic. The counselor's sense of values, the counselor's deep feelings regarding the worth of the client, the counselor's feelings regarding his capacity and moral right to measure and evaluate, the counselor's feelings toward his basic function as a counselor—these are part of the counselor's self, and there must, surely, be a consistency of counselor self. The lack of support by some counselors for the practice of eclecticism in counseling arises basically because they equate it with counselor self-inconsistency.

11. Frederick C. Thorne, "Three Psychologists and How They Grew," *Psychology Today*, 6:58–63 (September, 1972).

12. Stanley S. Marzolf, *Psychological Diagnosis and Counseling in Schools* (New York: Holt, 1956), pp. 327–328.

233

This was probably part of the thinking of Rogers over two decades ago when he challenged the generally accepted concept of eclecticism:

These schools of thought will not be abolished by wishful thinking. The person who attempts to reconcile them by compromise will find himself left with a superficial eclecticism which does not increase objectivity, and leads nowhere. Truth is not arrived at by concessions from different schools of thought. [13]

If one is to think of eclecticism in terms of superficial techniques, then every counselor must, surely, be eclectic. If the counselor who asks a question sometimes instead of never asking a question, if the counselor who sometimes gives information instead of never giving information, if the counselor who sometimes gives direction instead of never giving direction is thereby eclectic, then it is difficult to see how any counselor could possibly avoid being eclectic.

Eclecticism in the professional educational and development of the counselor is essential, since without it the counselor can hardly arrive at any learned conclusions based on a great variety of evidence. Without such breadth we have the unhappy situation where Christians assume that religion means only Christianity, capitalists that democracy means only capitalism, Americans that good living means only America, and counselors that counseling means only Freudian, or client-centered, or psychoanalytic, or Adlerian. These are the individuals who, when they go to heaven, will have to live in restricted areas, surrounded by high walls, so that they may continue to live under the illusion that they are the only people there!

Although eclecticism may appeal to the student counselor as the democratic and broad-minded approach to counseling, if we are to speak of it as an actual method of counseling, then there are several serious questions as to its efficacy:

1. It carries with it the implication that counseling is a somewhat superficial bag-of-tricks technique. The counselor, as the technician who pulls out the appropriate treatment for the particular problem or individual, thus becomes one whose professional preparation should be a *training* rather than an *education*.

2. The view assumes too, generally without evidence, that there are certain techniques and procedures that for a certain individual in a certain situation are more effective and better than others. If anything, the evidence points the other way. There certainly is serious question whether or not a student counselor should learn

13. Carl R. Rogers, *Client-Centered Therapy* (Boston: Houghton Mifflin, 1951), p. 8.

that this particular technique is the right thing to do, under these circumstances, with this client. Because clients are not inanimate objects, or even organs, they have a habit of contradicting the counselor who has arrived at a set concept of just what to do at a certain time with a certain type of person.

3. It would not, surely, be doctrinaire to say that an individual must arrive at some degree of consistency with himself if he is to be honest and sincere, and thereby at least have some hope of being successful in working with other individuals. If the counselor, for example, cannot completely accept a client's attacks on the counselor's religion, then in the long run he might be better off to be honest with the client and admit that this does irritate him, rather than trying to pretend that he is acceptant and understanding about something to which he is actually reacting in an emotional manner. The client, too, is going to find it difficult to relate and get close to an individual who appears to fluctuate and change. Probably everyone can think of some people he has known who have posed a difficulty for him; although they have been nice and pleasant, he could never feel that this was the real person speaking. The real person was never revealed, most likely because the individual could not bear to reveal the real person to himself. Teachers, too, who know the frustration and difficulty children have with authoritarian parents, know the even more difficult time the children have if their parents lack even consistency in a vice. It is easier for a child to understand, and react to, and defend himself from a brutal father, than it is to react to a father who beats his child one day, then the next day cries and gives him a dollar to make up for his miserable behavior the day before.

Eclecticism, too, gives the counselor an easy avenue of escape at all times. It is much easier for the counselor to say to himself, "I am breaking this long silence because the client seems to be blocked, and I will use a new approach" than it is for him to say, "Why am I feeling pressured to break this client silence? What is it that makes me uneasy? Am I really acceptant of this client's right to be silent, or am I breaking the silence because it is beginning to threaten me?" It is easier for the counselor to say to himself, "I have answered the client's plea for support and help by telling him that he will be all right, because this is a technique that is sometimes useful" than it is for him to say, "I have answered the client's plea for help in this way because this sort of response reassures me, although it may be worse in the long run for the client." When the client says, "Okay, so maybe I am biased, maybe I am just white trash, but damn it, don't you think that evidence shows that Negroes in the South do know

235

less than the whites?" the counselor may find it easier to say to himself, "Well, the reason I agreed that there might be one or two studies that implied this was so because I felt that I needed to use a technique of agreement to give him some support" than to say, "The reason I made this statement was that I share his bias."

These examples could obviously be multiplied many times. If the counselor has arrived at some level of consistency of operation, then he must give himself a close scrutiny when he departs from it, and attempt to determine the why of his departure. When he has no consistency, there is little or no need for a check on himself, since he has accepted the concept that he does what he does for professional reasons only.

Thus in the long run, it would seem that the effective counselor is one who has worked out for himself, through the experience of experimentation, the means by which he can most effectively use himself in a human interaction known as counseling. His orientation has been eclectic, rather than parochial, and while his own life is in a constant state of movement and change, he has learned that there are certain modes of operation which are most effective for him, thus there is a degree of consistency in his operation as a counselor. While he is open to consider any means that will work with the client, he is aware that his own human limitations are such that he cannot be all things for all people. He is acceptant of the thought that there is no model, no method, no technique which will be consistently successful for him with any other human individual who may come to him as a client.

COUNSELOR DIRECTION AND COUNSELOR CONTROL

Traditionally, counselor direction and counselor control over the client was pretty much taken for granted, and both the medical model and the educational model generally reflected a "we know what's best for you philosophy." Both the student and the patient have generally been considered as individuals to whom something is done by somebody who knows more about it than they do.

Notes that were used some fifteen years ago in teaching residents and fellows in psychiatry in a Boston hospital are still probably fairly typical:

The course of the therapy, and the management, is directed and controlled by the doctor. The direction is determined by an appraisal of the patient's material, but once a working hypothesis in this respect is elaborated, the doctor follows this direction until the material is exhausted or until the doctor is blocked.[14]

In the same material, under the heading of suggested procedures for using minimal activity (sic), we note the following:

(1) Begin by a general question which cannot be answered by yes or no. Avoid leading questions. Avoid questions which suggest the answer. Use such questions as, "How are things going?" "How do you feel?" "What's been happening?" "What are you thinking about?" "What's going on in your head?"

(2) When the patient begins to talk, don't interrupt: allow him to go on. If he hesitates or stops talking, pause for a few seconds or longer and give him a chance to continue. If the silence continues, introduce another general, non-leading question as mentioned above.

(3) If the patient talks about topics which do not further your goal, allow him to continue for several minutes, while waiting for him to bring up the topic in which you are interested. If he persists in talking about irrelevant topics, show no interest in the material, take no leads, ask no questions. If necessary introduce another general question.

(4) As soon as the patient mentions a word or topic that you want to hear more about, hold him by one or more of the following devices in the order presented. Proceed to the use of more active techniques (d,e,f,g,h) if simpler techniques (a,b,c) do not succeed. You are trying to indicate "Go ahead, we're interested."

    (a) Non-verbal activity on the part of the doctor: look up, show interest by postural change, facial expression, nodding gestures. If a glance will do, say nothing.

    (b) Use sounds, conversational grunts, syllables, and ejaculations such as ah, uh uh, hmm, so, well, really, but, and. If a simple syllable will do, say no more. Reinforce the inflection with an encouraging look; let your voice carry along. Avoid an air of finality.

    (c) If the patient stops or heads away from the significant topic, repeat the patient's last word or phrase bearing on the topic. Say it with a rising inflection as though you were asking a question: "Upset?" "Blue?" "Your heart?"

14. Unpublished material.

(d) *If this fails, elaborate this last word or phrase with an incomplete statement: "you said . . ."; "you said you were . . ."; "you mentioned pain. . . ."*

(e) *If a patient persists in avoiding a topic, ask a* general *question about this topic which cannot be answered by a simple yes or no. If a general question suffices, do not make it specific. "What did you say about your headache?" "What do you mean?" "What did you mean by nervous?"*

(f) *In some cases, if these indirect procedures fail, you may have to resort to a direct question aimed at the pertinent topic, such as, "In what part of your head do you feel pain?" "What was the feeling in the dream?"*

(g) *If the patient shows overwhelming affect, you may drop the topic for the time being, and introduce another nonleading question as under (1) above, keeping alert for the charged topic later in the same interview or in a subsequent interview.*

These suggestions, it may be noted, are exactly the same sort of suggestions that would be given to the medical doctor who is being told how to treat a damaged kidney. There is no question here about who is in control, and any "nondirectiveness," as indicated above, is quite obviously a technique or method being deliberately used by the therapist to get the patient where he wants him to be. The patient here would appear to be very much the same patient who lies in the bed, passively waiting for the doctors to do with him what they will.

The typical psychiatric interview usually reinforces the patient's original feeling that the doctor is the one who is in control, and that he is the one who will determine what is to happen in the future.

In discussing such an interview, Fromm-Reichmann states:

The first interview should begin with the patient being asked about his complaints, and about the nature of his problems and his suffering, which made him or his relatives and friends decide to have the patient ask for the advice of a psychiatrist. Coupled with this, the acute distress which has precipitated the patient's decision to see a psychiatrist should be investigated. After that, the psychiatrist wishes to clarify, as early as possible in his contact with his prospective patient, whether the patient has come on his own volition, whether he has been ad-

vised to come by friends or relatives, or whether he has been
prodded into doing so against his own wishes.[15]

In most mental health clinics of which I am aware, the "intake interview" is regarded as somewhat of a sacred cow. Student interns are warned not to become involved in psychotherapy, but to follow a certain pattern in the interview. In some clinics, the patient must have three to six intake interviews before a staff decision is made as to what is to be done. This restriction may pose no problem for an analytically conditioned psychiatric intern, but it certainly does for an existential-humanist student counselor!

The following is fairly typical of the beginning of an intake psychiatric interview:

Interview 1

Co.: Will you sit there. What brings you here?

Cl.: Everything's wrong, I guess. Irritable, tense, depressed. Just, just everything and everybody gets on my nerves.

Co.: Yeah.

Cl.: I don't feel like talking right now.

Co.: You don't? Do you sometimes?

Cl.: That's the trouble. I get too wound up. If I get started, I'm all right.

Co.: Yeah? Well, perhaps you will.

Cl.: May I smoke?

Co.: Sure. What do you do?

Cl.: I'm a nurse, but my husband won't let me work.

Co.: How old are you?

Cl.: Thirty-one this December.

Co.: What do you mean, he won't let you work?

Cl.: Well, for instance I, ah, I'm supposed to do some relief duty two weeks, this month, next month, September, and he makes it so miserable for me that I'm in a constant stew. And he says that my place is home with the children. I agree, but I wa . . . I need a rest. I need to get away from them. I need to be with, oh with people. I can't stay closeted up in the house all the time.

Co.: How many kids are there?

Cl.: Two.

Co.: How old are they?[16]

15. Frieda Fromm-Reichmann, *op. cit.*, p. 45.

16. Taken from a record, *The Initial Interview in Psychiatry Practice*, Yale University, Dept. of Psychiatry (New York: International Universities Press, 1954).

The concept of doctor control over patient in the clinical situation differs very little from the concept of teacher control over student in the school situation. Just as the domination of the medical doctor over the patient had been pretty well accepted in psychotherapy, and still is, so the domination of the authority figure in the school, the teacher, and too often the counselor, over the child is taken for granted. The therapist domination and control in the preceding clinical example is no different from the counselor control in the following school example:

Co.: (pause) You've been working for your father for some time, is that right?

Cl.: Mm-huh.

Co.: How do you like working on the farm?

Cl.: Pretty well.

Co.: Do you . . . (pause) . . . Are you planning to work with your father this coming summer?

Cl.: Yes, if I don't continue school.

Co.: There is a possibility that you might stay in school this summer?

Cl.: Yes, sir. (pause)

Co.: Well, can you tell me a little bit more about your background? Tell me something about your home life.[17]

Another counselor, with Jane, a high school student (Cl) indicates much less direction and control:

Co.: You feel you'll take it to a point, and then. . . .

Cl.: Mm-hmm. Like those clothes. I know even Betty, my best girl friend now, says that, yeah, she's looking forward to college and the few weeks before, because her mother's going to want to go out and buy her clothes, too, and she would rather just skip it.

Co.: So your friend has the same problems about clothes, and her mother wanting to buy, as you do.

Cl.: Yeah, although she says that she likes her mother's taste, and she usually likes the things her mother gets her, but she doesn't like the bother of going out either. I don't like to buy a whole bunch of clothes at once because I—like when I bought this, I fell in love with it, and so I bought it, but I'd rather. . . . I like to buy underwear too. Why I don't know. Then there's no choice. You just buy some and wear it, but going out and looking for something when I have no idea what I want is too frustrating. I'd rather not do it. I don't like to be in crowds either, elbowing through Hudson's, anything like that.

17. Robert Callis, Paul C. Polmantier, and Edward C. Roeber, *A Casebook of Counseling* (New York: Appleton-Century-Crofts, 1955), p. 121, dialogue entries C17–C25.

Co.: You find it pretty uncomfortable, going through big crowds when there seems to be no point. You're not certain what you want. You'd rather wait when you have a specific object in mind, and then go and pick it out.

Cl.: I suppose quite a few people feel like that. I'm not alone.

Co.: You feel other people feel this way too.[18]

Cl.: Sure, some must. But then there's my mother. She feels that I've got to go out and get those clothes. I'll go with her.

Co.: You'll go to satisfy her . . .

One may contrast this last example with the domination and control expressed in these words:

> *In the course of rational psychotherapy, the patient is not merely shown that he has such irrational ideas as these, but the therapist persistently keeps attacking, undermining, and annihilating these idiocies. Even more to the point: the therapist teaches the patient how to observe, infer, and ferret out his own illogical thinking; how to trace this thinking back to its main ideological sources; and how to question, challenge, and uproot these asinine ideologies and to replace them with realistic, flexible, more effective beliefs.*
>
> *. . . the therapist often actively and unequivocally forces, persuades, cajoles, or practically pushes the patient into various kinds of actions which, in many instances, serve as the very best kind of counter-propagandizing influences.*[19]

And yet, the contrast is not as simple as it may seem. The brash, noisy counselor *may* basically be more acceptant and compassionate than the quiet, verbally "client-centered" individual. The student counselor can only answer this question by trying his utmost, possibly with some help, to reach some stage of self-actualization and genuineness so that he can accept himself, at whatever level he may be. He may then be able to evolve some methodology of counseling that will be best for him and best for those clients who relate with him, or he may, of course, also come to the conclusion that counseling is not for him. Certainly the student counselor should be wary of the counselor education program in which all the staff speak the same line—it is most unlikely that a number of genuine counselor educators who are free enough to be who they are will

18. William Evraiff, *Helping Counselors Grow Professionally* (Englewood Cliffs, N.J.: Prentice-Hall, 1963), pp. 117–118, dialogue entries C120–C128. © 1963. Reprinted by permission of Prentice-Hall, Inc., Englewood Cliffs, N.J.

19. Albert Ellis, "Rationalism and Its Therapeutic Implications," *Annals of Psychotherapy*, 1:55–64 (September, 1959).

all be the same, smiling the same smile, frowning at the same insult, but mostly beaming brotherhood at each other and at everyone else!

Corlis and Rabe answer their question, "Who is the boss?" by saying, "Nobody. Nevertheless, the problem raised by the question is not a straw man. Both patient and therapist will encounter their own problem of wanting to put down the other, or to raise him unnaturally." They also go on to say, "The therapeutic relationship is not an equal one in the sense of what each partner needs, but it is equal in the requirement that each must give all he can."[20] A criticism of Carkhuff and Berenson of client-centered counseling, namely, that "it has neglected the whole person of the therapist and the two way flow of communication,"[21] might be considered as a valid criticism of any counseling. While Blocher is talking about a teacher-learner model of counseling, he could be talking about any counseling when he describes the counselor as one who "can exercise responsibility in much of the counseling process while recognizing the individual's right to reach self-determined decisions or even to make no decision at all."[22]

Thus it would seem that there must be some degree of counselor direction, at least as long as the counselor is viewed as one who is involved in a human relationship with the client, and although the verbalizations of a counselor are to some degree reflections of his attitudes as a person, they themselves are less important than the attitude that causes the verbalizations—which may, after all, not always be what they seem. Some counselors believe deeply not only that the client can be, but that it is his right to be, the determiner of his future; that he, the counselor, is secondary in the counseling relationship; and that the direction should therefore come from the client, not the counselor. One might well debate the empirical reality of such a belief. Some will say that this is all right with neurotic individuals, but that it can hardly be correct with psychotic individuals who are completely divorced from reality.

But there are realities, rather than reality, and the reality of the schizophrenic patient is as "real" as the reality of the therapist who is working with him. It is the human involvement of the counselor that brings these realities closer together, and I cannot expect a client to touch my reality if I cannot touch his. One of the realities that I share with a person who is a client is that I may have a differ-

20. Rahe B. Corlis and Peter Rabe, *Psychotherapy from the Center* (Scranton, Pa.: International Textbook Co., 1969), pp. 48–49.

21. Robert R. Carkhuff and Bernard G. Berenson, *Beyond Counseling and Therapy* (New York: Holt, Rinehart and Winston, 1967), p. 68.

22. Donald H. Blocher, *Developmental Counseling* (New York: Ronald Press, 1966), p. 31.

ent kind of control and direction than he has, but it is a matter of *difference,* rather than *more or less.* The client has the power, and he can ultimately come to accept responsibility for the direction in which he will go, and thus move toward a higher level of individual freedom—and individual direction and control.

INTERPRETATION AND/OR REFLECTION OF FEELING

"Interpretation" and "reflection" are two words that have often been used to distinguish two different kinds of counseling, and yet it would appear that the difference is only one of degree. Before one can reflect a feeling, after all, he has to be interpretive about just what that feeling might be. He may be reflecting a feeling by saying "You are worried about this," but this is the counselor's interpretation. If, of course, the counselor did nothing but repeat words, which alas, is exactly the extent of what some counselors do, then he would not be interpretive. The reply "You are worried" to the statement "I am worried," is a repetition of words, and if this is the best the counselor can do, it is not likely that he is very effective.

McKinney thinks of interpretation as the assistance that the counselor gives to the client in seeing relationships between present behavior and underlying causes or motivations. He goes on:

It is well established that an effective counselor does not inter-pret behavior until the client is ready to grasp it and assimilate it effectively in living. Interpretation runs the gamut. The coun-selor may merely repeat in an integrated manner many of the statements the client has made during the interview so that he may see their implications; or he may point out underlying re-pressed motives. Probably the most effective kind of interpreta-tion consists of helping the client go just a little farther—just a little beyond where he was planning to stop.[23]

Buchheimer and Balogh, on the other hand, think of "surface" interpretation as a counseling lead, "depth" interpretation being that aspect of psychotherapy which seeks out the fundamental reasons for past and present behaviors.[24]

One might generally describe the reflection of feeling as the attempt by the counselor to understand from the client's point of view and to communicate that understanding to him. One might say

23. Fred McKinney, *op. cit.,* p. 277.
24. Buchheimer and Balogh, *op. cit.,* p. 54.

that there is less likelihood of counselor involvement in such a reflection than in an interpretation, and yet even here it is the counselor who is, in effect, saying, "This is the way I understand and feel you." Some would say that this differs little from skillful interpretation, since the effective counselor will never interpret too far ahead of the client. This is probably why, many years ago, Rogers had ceased talking about reflection and clarifying, and was saying instead:

[I]t is the counselor's function to assume, in so far as he is able, the internal frame of reference of the client, to perceive the world as the client sees it, to perceive the client himself as he is seen by himself, to lay aside all perceptions from the external frame of reference while doing so, and to communicate something of this empathic understanding to the client. [25]

Hora questions the value of interpretation for another reason:

That which is, speaks for itself. That which speaks for itself is understood. What is understood needs no interpretation. What is interpreted is seldom understood. [26]

Jung gives a word of warning to dream interpreters when he says, "Do anything you like, only don't try to understand." [27]

Fritz Perls did not see interpretation as having a place in his gestalt therapy, since he felt that it implied that the therapist knew more about the client than the client did about himself.

Even the interpretation of the analytical counselor, as he interprets the meaning of the transference relationship to the client, might be described as a reflection of subconscious feeling. This would also apply when he was interpreting to the client the possible meaning of various resistances that he might be expressing.

Thus probably all counselors, to some extent, reflect the feelings of the client—shallow and deep, conscious and subconscious, verbal and nonverbal—and what some call reflection, others will call interpretation. Far too many counselors, however, in the name of "client-centered," merely repeat over and over again what the client has said, until both become fearfully bored!

Some might say that Ellis (Co), for example, is reflecting feeling in the following example:

Cl.:   I don't know. I think it's natural being bothered by having people being disturbed and not understanding why they're disturbed. I mean, I can see

25.   Carl R. Rogers, *op. cit.,* p. 29.
26.   Thomas Hora, "Healing or Growth," *Annals of Psychotherapy,* 1:32 (Monograph 5, 1963).
27.   C. G. Jung, *Modern Man in Search of a Soul* (New York: Harcourt, Brace and World, 1933), p. 12.

why they might object, but I don't see why they don't want me to talk the whole thing out and find out why they're disturbed because I'm upset.

Co.: Well, if I'm hearing you correctly you're sort of saying that—ah—that you are not objecting to their getting upset, but you at least would like them to talk it out with you.[28]

While Rogers (Co) might appear to be "interpreting":

Co.: Yeah, yeah. But you felt he didn't quite understand you on that really.

Cl.: I thought that he felt I was being blunt, and that I just meant that I didn't want to talk to him any more.

Co.: And I, if I sense some of your feeling now, it is, uh, a little tenseness that, that maybe he didn't really get that, he felt you were shutting him off on something.

Cl.: Yes, that's what, and that isn't what I meant.[29]

But Rogers is *the* "client-centered" counselor, and Ellis is *the* "rational" psychotherapist!

Most beginning counselors who take some pride in their "analytic" or "diagnostic" title question or probe the client to death, while most beginning counselors who fly "client-centered" at their masthead "reflect" the client to distraction. Carl's counselor, for example, is reflecting feelings and statements:

Co.: You feel they happen more often than they should just to be nightmares.

Cl.: Yes. Seems like I never dream . . . (etc.).

Co.: You feel you're somewhere you really don't belong.

Cl.: Yes . . . (etc.).

Co.: No matter how you think about it or feel about it, or try and talk about it, it seems to still be there.

Cl.: Yes, it still . . . (etc.).

Co.: For a short period of time you feel that you are acceptable. People are not noticing you.

Cl.: Yes. I feel . . . (etc.).

Co.: So, even being accepted now and getting away from this feeling of being alone is a problem.[30]

Much of the superficial reflection is to ease the tension of the counselor, and there would be less direction if the counselor were

28. From the tape *Loretta,* American Academy of Psychotherapists.
29. *Ibid.*
30. William Evraiff, *op. cit.,* pp. 46–47, dialogue entries C80–C88. © 1963. Reprinted by permission of Prentice-Hall, Inc., Englewood Cliffs, N.J.

merely to keep quiet, or to make understanding sounds. Jane's counselor, for example, by his "reflection," may encourage her to keep
talking about what might be trivia:

Co.: You're worried about the cause of the drop.
Cl.: . . . . . .
Co.: You're wondering if you worry more about these things than other
people do.
Cl.: . . . . . .
Co.: You feel possibly if you stopped worrying about it they might
straighten themselves out.
Cl.: . . . . . .
Co.: You feel you should do things about this, do something for it instead
of worrying about it all the time.
Cl.: . . . . . .
Co.: You feel you should be working now.[31]

There is much more of an existential involvement with this
counselor:

Co.: You were starting to say I—I did something?
Cl.: I—sort of have a feeling that you forced some of it.
Co.: Oh. By what I did or by what I am as a person?
Cl.: By, in a sense . . . uh . . . you're telling me, "Listen, you're just going
around and about, now let's get to the point." And then I felt (pause)
this—if I went on going around, I'd never get to the point and I'd never get
well. Or—and that you would not continue therapy.
Co.: The fear of losing me?
Cl.: That—that was pretty strong.
Co.: But I never threatened you.
Cl.: No, I know. I don't know what it was. But I know I had that feeling.
Co.: Maybe you had another feeling too (pause), a feeling of a relationship
with me.
Cl.: Yes, I did—very strongly I remember until . . . uh . . . at one point
when—remember when I felt you were accusing me of terrible crimes and
. . .
Co.: Hm-mm.
Cl.: At this point . . . uh . . . it sort of went around and I (buzzer), you
became in a sense the opposite—an enemy, not as a friend.
Co.: At that time I was an enemy.
Cl.: Yes, I felt very strongly that you . . . now stop wandering around and
come to the point. (Laughs.)

31. *Ibid.*, p. 95, dialogue entries C164–C172.

Co.: Hm-m.

Cl.: And—(pause).

Co.: But you wanted to be a child then. (Pause.) Your psychosis represent-ed that, (pause). And remember I put it to you that you either take your psychosis or you take reality. It was up to you, remember?[32]

There is more of a combination of reflection of feeling and interpretation between these counselors and these junior high school clients:

Cl.: Dances, clothes, boys, parties . . . that's all they think of. . . . It's so stupid and foolish. . . . I'm glad I'm not like them.

Co.: I feel all these interests are ridiculous, but sometimes I feel, deep down, that I'd like to go to parties and dances and be popular like other girls. . . .

. . . .

Cl.: I love animals. . . . I want to get some kind of a job later on working with animals . . . particularly horses. . . .

Co.: Animals aren't like people . . . animals are friends—they're affection-ate . . . they'll return your love . . . they're loyal . . . I can trust them. . . .

These examples are pretty much out-and-out interpretation:

Cl.: I'm sort of cold toward him—it's hard to explain but . . . well, I sort of enjoy being distant . . . sort of testing him . . . trying to see just how much of my coldness he'll take.

Co.: The same sort of coldness that you told me exists between your father and mother.

. . . .

Cl.: I find myself sort of wanting to lose my books. . . . I doodle in book pages . . . blot out paragraphs . . . even destroy even numbered pages.

Co.: Maybe books represent infringements on your leisure time.

I would think that any counselor who sees himself as being involved with the client in a human relationship would have to be interpretive in order to share his feelings about himself and about the client with the client. Needless to say, this is much riskier for the counselor, and, possibly, for the client, than the rather safe reflection of feeling.

32. Arthur Burton, "Paradox and Choice in Schizophrenia," in Arthur Burton (ed.), *Case Studies in Counseling and Psychotherapy* (Englewood Cliffs, N.J.: Prentice-Hall, 1959), pp. 268–269. © 1959. Reprinted by permission of Prentice-Hall, Inc., Englewood Cliffs, N.J.

DIAGNOSIS

Diagnosis may be considered as the analysis of one's difficulties and the causes that have produced them. More clinically, it may be thought of as the determination of the nature, origin, and maintenance of ineffective abnormal modes of behavior. More simply, it might be considered as the development by the counselor of a deeper and more accurate understanding and appreciation of the client. Blocher sees diagnosis in counseling as

> the process through which the counselor comes to understand the client, the client's world, and the meaning that his interaction with that world has for him.[33]

Diagnosis of the more clinical sort has had a long and honorable medical history, and it is directly related to prognosis and treatment. Psychologists have generally accepted without question the need for diagnosis, and many counselors apparently operate on the assumption that effective counseling without diagnosis is impossible. Many student counselors tend to take diagnosis for granted without, possibly, asking enough questions as to just what diagnosis is, why it is needed, how accurate it may be, and what one does with a diagnosis once one has it. The diagnosis of some counselors assumes that the problems of the mind and the heart are the same as the problems of the physical body, even though it is rather difficult to see how those procedures that are successful in the treatment of a diseased kidney would be equally satisfactory in the treatment of fears developed in a child by insecure and frightened parents. Because the medical profession has generally taken for granted the concept that emotional disturbances are diseases, a person is frequently assumed to be a skilled practitioner in "mental health" if he possesses a medical degree, even though his psychological knowledge of personality disorders may be a good deal less than that of a student who has just been granted an undergraduate degree in psychology.

The diagnosis of a leg as inoperative because of a fracture of the tibia, caused by a sudden contact with a solid object, necessitating the setting and immobilization of the leg in a cast for several weeks, may not be as complicated as the diagnosis of a pain in the belly as an inflammation of the appendix, caused by unknown factors, necessitating immediate operative procedures for its removal; but neither of these can be compared with the complexity of the

33.   Donald H. Blocher, *op. cit.*, p. 130.

diagnosis of a relatively frequent psychological problem such as that of the very intelligent boy who consistently does very poor academic work, or that of the overly aggressive child who insists on pushing other children around.

It can be assumed that the purpose of diagnosis is to develop such a picture that intelligent action can be taken on the basis of it. The easier it is to arrive at the picture, the more likely it is to be accurate, and the action taken to be appropriate. Thus a broken leg may be such that the diagnosis is quite simple, or it may be a complicated break requiring an equally difficult diagnosis. But in any case, the problem, the injury, the ailment is something that, we might say, "is there." The task of the medical doctor is, nearly always, to do something about a difficulty that "is there." When the medical doctor gets into the treatment of certain physical diseases, however, a diagnosis of, say, cancer, does not do much good, because no one knows yet what causes cancer, and thus no one knows the treatment for it. In the majority of physiological ailments and organic ailments, however, the cause is known; and once this happens, a remedy is speedily found.

With emotional disturbances, however, knowing the cause is often a rather minor matter, and not too much can be done, just as the dentist cannot do much for the rotting and decaying teeth of his patient that he knows were caused by foolish diet when she was a child. He can, however, remove her teeth and put in a false set, not as good as the originals, but still not too bad. Like the dentist, I knew with a high degree of certainty the causes of the fears of one of my clients, and in time she knew the causes too, but this did not remove the fears. Probably the basic point here is that the dentist could remove the decayed teeth and put others in their place, just as the medical doctor could skillfully set the broken bone and initiate procedures to speed its healing; but in both cases the patient was outside of this activity. Others were doing something to parts of his body.

The existential-humanist counselor, however, is working with the client and with the perceptions the client has of himself and his life. The client may be very fearful, and the word "paranoid" on a diagnostic description does not make the client's fear any less real. He may come to feel eventually that many of his fears are groundless, and his new inner perceptions may then be closer to the outer perceptions of others about him. It will be *his* diagnosis, not one that we have imposed upon him.

Professional diagnosis by therapists is anything but consistent, and one may end up having as many ailments as he has diagnosticians. An interesting comment on the validity of diagnosis has been made by Wittenborn:

> If psychiatrists believe consistently that certain symptoms go together, the ratings which they make for their patients may reveal their belief concerning symptom-clustering. Accordingly, if syndromes are revealed among the symptoms, the possibility remains that the syndromes are more descriptive of consistencies which exist in the behavior of psychiatrists than they are descriptive of consistencies which exist in the behavior of patients.[34]

Some counselors, too, feel that in an understanding and acceptant atmosphere the client will come to see the "why" of his behavior, and any action that is taken will be *by him* on the basis of *his diagnosis* rather than that of the counselor. But, one might say, if the counselor is a student of psychology, he must have certain diagnostic understandings, and how can he avoid being diagnostic, at least in his own mind, even though he may not verbalize his conclusions to the client? There is little doubt that every effective counselor must see an enlarging picture of the client as the counseling proceeds, although this picture may be primarily one that is being developed by the client for himself and for the counselor.

On the other hand, while the goal is to help the client to develop an accurate picture of his life and living, it is obvious that the picture that he presents to himself, and to the counselor, may be totally inaccurate. As a matter of fact, this is why he is a candidate for counseling. As Corlis and Rabe put it:

> A diagnosis formulates how the patient is currently functioning. The diagnostic description contains his motivations and his customary patterns of responding.
>
> Whereas the descriptions come from the patient, the diagnosis comes obviously from the therapist. Frequently, the "presenting problem," the patient's complaint, is not the patient's real problem at all.[35]

Nonetheless, the only real "real problem" is the problem that is perceived by the client. A clinically accurate diagnosis makes little or no sense, counseling-wise, if it is not acceptable to the client. Probably the question for the counselor is: is the self-diagnosis of the client one that *he* has developed, with the counselor's help, or is it one that has been imposed upon him?

34. J. R. Wittenborn, "Symptom Patterns in a Group of Mental Hospital Patients," *Journal of Consulting Psychology,* 15:290–302 (August, 1951).
35. Rahe B. Corlis and Peter Rabe, *op. cit.,* p. 21.

Diagnosis, in a way, implies the possibility of "pigeonholing" the client as belonging to a certain category or a certain type; and the implication that follows is that for a certain type there is a certain treatment.

Categories are handy things to seize upon, and too frequently we see counselors who seem to operate on such concepts as: "John Smith—problem: lack of information"; "Mary Brown—problem: lack of assurance"; "Jim Bowie—problem: self-conflict." And indeed, the poor client is often categorized long before the counseling begins. The process of counselor direction has thus begun even before the client has had a chance to express himself to the counselor. On the other hand, some counselors would say that this does not necessarily apply, and that as long as the counselor is a professional and skilled therapist he will detect an incorrect or inappropriate diagnosis, and no harm will be done to the client. But counselors are human beings, and it would be a rare counselor indeed whose personal relationship with another individual would not be affected by the fact that he had already determined in his mind that there was a problem of a certain type that could best be treated in a certain manner. At best, it would seem that the open mind becomes somewhat clouded by prior diagnosis, and that a more appropriate procedure is to take the client where he is, as he is.

While Bijou was referring to behavioral counseling, he could have been talking about counseling generally when he stated that "diagnostic information would be sought only if it could be shown that such data would serve to advance some specific aspect of the counseling process."[36] Carkhuff and Berenson, however, are highly skeptical of diagnosis:

> . . . we have long felt that traditional diagnostic categories are not only often intellectually repugnant but usually meaningless for purposes of dictating differential treatment. Most frequently, the diagnostic constructs are not relevant to the lives, particularly the therapeutic lives of the clients.[37]

What happens, however, if a diagnosis is not established and the counselor starts off on the wrong foot? Knight expresses this danger when he says:

> This case clearly illustrates the importance of establishing a dynamic diagnosis before embarking on treatment. If diagnosis

36. Sidney W. Bijou, "Implications of Behavorial Science for Counseling and Guidance," in John D. Krumboltz (ed.), *Revolution in Counseling* (Boston: Houghton Mifflin, 1966), p. 45.
37. Robert R. Carkhuff and Bernard G. Berenson, *op. cit.,* p. 234.

251

*is bypassed, as in this case, much time may be lost and treat-
ment may not be used to best advantage. Fortunately for the
patient in this case, the supervisor's request to discontinue the
contact precipitated enough "distress" on the part of the patient that the therapist was encouraged to carry out more active diagnostic efforts. Had a dynamic diagnosis been sought
for earlier in the course of the contact with the therapist, more
time would have been available for a more thorough working
through of the patient's guilt, and for a more comprehensive
consolidation of therapeutic gains.*[38]

In the above example, however, the reason for the inappropriate therapy, if such was the case, seems to have been that the therapist *had* established a diagnosis that was incorrect or unacceptable
to the client.

In a way, the question of diagnosis brings up the earlier question of the role of the counselor as either a service individual or a
researcher. The latter is primarily a diagnostician. He tries to determine causes. He tries to answer the question "Why?" Although certainly no one would deny his crucial role in the study of the process
of counseling and psychotherapy, one may question the capacity of
the person who is primarily a diagnostician to relate in a meaningful
way with a client.

The "what" instead of the "why" is stressed by Glasser:

Our usual question is What? *What are you doing—not, why are
you doing it? Why implies that the reasons for the patient's
behavior make a difference in therapy, but they do not. The
patient will himself search for reasons; but until he has become
more responsible he will not be able to act differently, even
when he knows why.*[39]

Some counselors are not concerned with any previous diagnosis, and they will say, "I don't want any data on the client. We'll both
start together when he comes in to see me." While such an attitude
may seem farfetched and even shocking to some, I have been impressed by the number of counselors of varying hues who are advocates of diagnosis, but who disregard the diagnosis of others regarding a client, and operate on the basis of their own diagnosis after
they have seen him.

The individuality of counselors, and their disagreement even
among themselves with regard to professional questions, is shown in

---

38. Aldrich C. Knight, in Stanley W. Standal and Raymond Corsini, Jr., *Critical
     Incidents in Psychotherapy* (Englewood Cliffs, N.J.: Prentice-Hall, 1959), p. 148.
39. William Glasser, *Reality Therapy* (New York: Harper and Row, 1965), p. 32.

a most interesting fashion by the reactions of fifteen therapists to the question, "Do you make a diagnosis before therapy begins?" Reactions range all the way from Ackerman:

My answer to this question is emphatically in the affirmative. I consider it of the utmost importance to achieve a clear diagnostic definition of the patient's disorder before making any final commitment about accepting a patient for treatment. This does not mean, however, that the diagnostic study is pursued in any routine or ritualized manner. It is not a question and answer interview. The interview itself is a dynamic, openended process. Its flow is determined by the perception of significant cues as to foci of pathogenic conflict and anxiety. The early interview contact, while primarily diagnostic, is simultaneously oriented to the patient's therapeutic needs. Nevertheless, a final decision as to the acceptance of a particular patient for treatment rests on a clear picture of the patient's disorder. In order to apply therapy in a psychologically specific manner, one must know exactly what is wrong with the patient. The diagnostic study includes clinical psychiatric evaluation and, wherever other examinational procedures may be indicated, psychological studies, a home visit, a medical examination, and so forth.[40]

To Shlien:

No. Diagnostic techniques are not sufficiently valid, for one thing. Also, they do not help; if anything, they have an adverse influence on the relationship, since they tend to categorize the client in the counselor's eyes, and give the counselor an intimidating and unwarranted "expert" status (he should be an expert, in fact, but not on that basis), and in general focus attention on artificial and impersonal issues. Finally, there is no specific treatment to be applied, so of what use would specific diagnosis be if it were accomplished? Psychotherapy is not medicine. Human misery is not an organic disease.

To clarify, diagnosis as discussed here does not mean the judgment exercised by the counselor at almost every step. Neither is it prognosis, which assesses the constructive resources and estimates the probability of achieving health. Diagnosis is the classic psychiatric classification and description which is static, and focused wholly on pathology. Therapy, in contradistinction, has a fluid tone, and anticipates change. It will en-

40. Nathan W. Ackerman, in Arthur Burton, *op. cit.*, p. 70. © 1959. Reprinted by permission of Prentice-Hall, Inc., Englewood Cliffs, N.J.

counter the pathology ("what is wrong") but can rely only on "what is right" with the organism.

We do indeed use measures of change in therapy, but these are for research to discover the facts about change in groups of clients, and these measures are not yet so keen as to be satisfactory for that purpose, much less for individual diagnosis.[41]

Some of the more analytically oriented counselors feel that diagnosis is essential, and that our current major problem is the inaccuracy of diagnosis. They would probably agree with Mahan when he says:

But the most striking result is the confirmation once again of the difficulty of predicting overt behavior from psychological test data. Prediction unfortunately does not follow directly from diagnosis; the "over-determination" of human behavior makes extremely hazardous the effort to isolate variables when it is the interaction of variables that is paramount. Perhaps the time has come when the training programs in school psychological services must integrate into their emphasis on individual understanding the psychological study of social situations, roles, institutional pressures, and . . . "treatments."[42]

The answer to more accurate and empirical diagnosis, of course, is the replacement of the human being by the machine, and if diagnosis is seen as the primary function of the counselor, there would seem to be no good reason why he should not also be replaced by the machine. Meehl and Dahlstrom describe the problem of using the "too human" clinician in diagnosis:

While it would not be too surprising to find that the "clinical eye" has trained itself to recognize configurations not readily identified by conventional linear methods of statistical analysis, it might be presumed that the clinician's subjective judgment, however experienced, assigns less than optimal weights. In addition to this systematic bias, the human judge throws in some more or less random error variance due to his unreliability.[43]

41. John M. Shlien, "Time-Limited, Client-Centered Psychotherapy: Two Cases," in Arthur Burton, *op. cit.*, p. 349. © 1959. Reprinted by permission of Prentice-Hall, Inc., Englewood Cliffs, N.J.
42. Thomas W. Mahan, Jr., "Diagnostic Consistency and Prediction: A Note on Graduate Student Skills," *Personnel and Guidance Journal*, 42:364–367 (December, 1963).
43. P. E. Meehl and W. G. Dahlstrom, "Objective Configural Rules for Discriminating Psychotic from Neurotic MMPI Profiles," *Journal of Consulting Psychology*, 24:375–387 (October, 1960).

Thorne shares these doubts about the accuracy of clinical diagnosis, although he is not quite so eager to replace the human by the machine:

Two decades of research on clinical judgement show that most classical diagnostic methods are either invalid or irrelevant. There is increasing evidence that the majority of the best-trained clinicians cannot make valid judgements or predictions. We must assume then, that something must have been grossly wrong with their training.[44]

I would feel that diagnosis in counseling is inappropriate for two very basic reasons. In the first place, there is very little agreement among diagnosticians as to the accuracy of their diagnosis, so it would seem reasonable to assume that the client is safer without it. Much more basic, however, is the fact that diagnosis misses entirely the reality of the inner person. It is the measure of me from the outside in, it is a measure of me by others, and it ignores my subjective being, which is the being that I know, and with which I live. Rather than developing an ego-satisfying diagnostic picture of the client, the counselor should strive to share the client's perceptions of himself, and to help him, possibly, to modify and change those perceptions.

TESTING AND COUNSELING

Testing is one of the major methods of developing a diagnostic picture of the client, and thus the question of the place of testing in counseling is very much linked to the place of diagnosis in counseling.

Although not all counselors would agree as to the place, if any, of testing in counseling, the majority who do see testing as a part of counseling stress that the information that is garnered as a result of testing must be for the use of the client himself, not for the use of the counselor. In other words, the information derived from testing is for the client, and the determination as to what to do about it is the responsibility of the client. Tyler comments that tests are used in counseling to enable the client to find out some things about himself that could not be discovered as conveniently in other ways.[45]

44. Frederick C. Thorne, "Three Psychologists and How They Grew," *op. cit.,* pp. 58–63.
45. Leona Tyler, *op. cit.,* p. 89.

Most counselors operate on the assumption that the more a client *knows* about himself the better he *understands* himself, and knowing is usually viewed in a cognitive sense. Byrne would reflect the feeling of many counselors when he says that

> the success of counseling depends partly on increasing the student's understanding of himself. In many instances growth of understanding does not require reference to cumulative record data but can be attained solely through interview processes. Usually, however, reference to appraisal data, including those obtained by testing, is fruitful.[46]

However, the extent to which I can change when I see or hear something that clashes with my concept of me must surely be related to my level of self-actualization, to the degree to which I have become a free individual. Thus it would seem reasonable to assume that only those rather solid students with a high level of self-understanding could internalize and make use of critical information about themselves.

Also questionable, of course, is the assumption that the more a counselor knows about the client, the more effective he can be with him. Berdie, Layton, Swanson, and Hagenah appear to agree with this statement when they say that "no experimental evidence at present justifies the assumption that *effective counseling depends on the counselor's knowledge about his counselee.*"[47] Yet they operate on the assumption that "*the more information we have about students, the better we can work with them.*"[48] And again, "Our thesis has been that test scores and other counseling information are used to help the counselor and the counselee to originate and study hypotheses concerning the counselee's future behavior."[49]

The most obvious reason why a counselor would use tests would be, as indicated, to gather more information about a client, information that he might feel that he could not obtain as accurately and as quickly in any other way. When counselors of various orientations discuss clients or patients—frequently called, not without some significance, "cases"—they normally have the results of test data, and the psychologist is often considered to be the fellow who provides the counselor with this information. The counselor who feels that he needs this information must need it either to pass on the client or to help him in his work with the client. In any case, this is a

46. Richard Hill Byrne, *op. cit.*, p. 29.
47. Ralph F. Berdie, Wilbur L. Layton, Edward O. Swanson, and Theda Hagenah, *Testing in Guidance and Counseling* (New York: McGraw-Hill, 1963), p. 121.
48. *Ibid.*, p. 11.
49. *Ibid.*, p. 133.

counselor-directed procedure, in which there is no doubt that the counselor has decided that he needs to know more about the client; he determines what clients will be tested, when they will be tested, and how they will be tested.

It has already been pointed out that many counselors who see diagnosis as an integral part of the counseling process have little use for anyone else's diagnosis. Thus, even if exhaustive test data are provided by some hardworking psychologists, as often as not these data are either politely ignored or thrown out the window by the current counselor. Even diagnostically oriented counselors often tend to put little weight on the results of measurement devices; they are more likely to operate with a client on the basis of their own evaluation of him, with, possibly, suggestions from several of their colleagues. A "psychiatric examination" is more often than not the pooled judgment of several therapists, or sometimes even the judgment of one therapist after a brief interview with the patient. A psychological examination usually refers to the use of standardized instruments of measurement. Whether the more subjective personal interview is any better or any worse than the standardized tests is open to debate, although some counselors would consider both of them unreliable and invalid.

The counselor may find no particular problem on this issue. He has no need for test data, if *he* is not going to *do* something for somebody, but rather help someone to make some decisions for himself, and thus to do something for himself. He does not have to know, from test data, whether a client is an underachiever or an overachiever. The client who has a problem related to academic achievement will, generally fairly soon in the counseling process, present both to the counselor and to himself his picture of a person who is doing more or less than he probably could do. Although the one who is doing more might be more of a problem for himself, the academic society generally considers only the one who is doing less to be a problem. In most schools today, the guidance department will have provided the child, fairly early in his school career, with some information as to where he stands with regard to achievement tests or measures of general aptitude and intelligence. The counselor may feel that he had no particular need for this information, and that the client would make use of it if and when he wanted to.

One might say, "Well and good, but what happens if a client describes himself as an intelligent student who is doing poorly, whereas he is actually achieving at his level of capacity?" Actually, an IQ of 150 means nothing to a person who has come to see himself as a very dull person, with a low intellectual level. Nor does a low IQ mean anything to a person who has learned that he must be an intelligent person. The first individual, from an operational and a realistic point of view, has a low level of intelligence, and the second person has a high level of intelligence. The counselor does not have to know, and does not particularly want to know, before he sees the client, that there is an inconsistency between what some evidence says that the client possesses in the way of capacity and what he sees himself as possessing. If the counseling develops as it can, both the counselor and the client will come to feel "Why must I push myself to do what I know I can't do?" or "Why do I have to convince myself that I can't do anything, while I really know that I can do a good deal more than I have been doing?"

If the counselor operates at the level of the client, and the first individual mentioned above is, for the time, a person of low intellect because *this is what he feels himself to be;* and the second person is a person of high intellect because this is what he feels himself to be. This situation is no different from that of the client who is helped by most teachers, but feels that all teachers are picking on him, or the client who insists that the principal is out to get him, although the principal is sincerely concerned with trying to help him. Most people, however, when the threats and the fears and the pressures are no longer present, will tend to come to a better balance between what they have and what they want. The student with high intelligence may come to have less need not to do well academically, and thus will almost automatically do better. The student with low intelligence will become more secure with himself and with what he has, and will have less need to convince himself that he can do more than he actually can. The student with musical talent will feel the desire to develop and make use of his aptitude when he no longer has to show someone that he cannot do anything that that person wants. The boy who has no liking for athletics will no longer bloody himself in athletic competition, since he will be secure enough to accept the loss of the affection of a neurotic father that is related solely to athletic achievement.

It is true, of course, that the school counselor is concerned with many activities other than counseling. He may be one who makes use of test data for placement and selection, but he should not feel any particular personal need for test data on those students who come to him as clients. One might assume, too, that the professional education of the counselor is such that he knows enough about human beings and human behavior not to need test data to give him a fairly accurate picture of this person who is called the client.

One may then ask, does this fellow who calls himself a counselor, then, ever make use of tests? *Some* counselors would answer, "Yes, if the client wants them," although we might at least wonder here about the extent to which counselor imposition increases as he becomes more involved in the use of tests. It would probably be fair to say that, in most schools and with most counselors, the client has little or no choice in the matter of "test or no," and that the meaning of the test data is the counselor's version, presented to the client.

Patterson, however, feels that as long as the client indicates a desire or need for the kind of information that tests can provide, then tests can be a legitimate part of counseling.[50] But even if the counselor did present test data to the client simply as information, with no personal involvement, and even if the client was the one who determined what tests he would take, it is still the counselor who has decided what tests are available, and thereby has been evaluative, since we can assume that there is no school where the client simply puts his hand in a test grab bag containing all tests, and pulls out what he wants; and since he doesn't know much about tests, it would be rather pointless saying, "What would you like to take? You make the decision."

Again, however, we must distinguish between the perfectly capable and rational student who wants further information about himself in the way of test data, so that he can compare himself with others as to intelligence and interests and aptitudes, and is thus in need of *guidance,* and the student under stress and strain, who sees tests as the answer to his problems. Even in these days, however, when testing, if not counseling, has become socially acceptable, the odds are that most individuals who seek testing are really in need of counseling although they seek testing to supply answers to their problems, tests supply only information, and few individuals under strain have their problems dissolved by the presentation of information, valid or otherwise. Thus when the client says, "Do you think that some testing might do me good?" a reply that I would think would be appropriate would be, "Well . . . I don't know. . . . Do you think that the answers that tests will give you will be better than the answers that you can give to yourself?"

The counseling session might develop into a situation where a good deal of information with regard to test data would be supplied by the counselor to the client. In more cases than not, however, the original request for testing need not actually develop into testing unless the counselor is so unskilled as to miss the feelings being expressed, and blunders ahead with a voluminous discussion of tests and testing without ever giving the client a chance to get closer to what he was trying to say when he tentatively asked the question

50. C. H. Patterson, *An Introduction to Counseling in the School* (New York: Harper and Row, 1971), p. 145.

about testing. Even when the client comes in for the sole purpose of testing, as often occurs in a vocational guidance center, more often than not the client is in need of counseling—possibly vocationally oriented, but still counseling, rather than vocational testing. The client who, after a number of counseling sessions, rather consistently raises the question of testing, may feel secure enough so that he can go to the point of taking a look at some test data; or, of course, he could, becoming more threatened, be looking for an easier way out. The good counselor, however, should be able to help the client to see just why he wants test information. When the client can see this, he may have no further need for testing; or, on the other hand, he may be even more certain, but for possibly different reasons, that it would be good for him to take a battery of tests.

If the latter situation did develop, I could not be involved, not so much because I would be inadequate (which would be true), but because I would feel that I was doing something that would remove the client even further from himself. (It probably would be correct to say that in the schools and clinics of America this definitely represents a minority point of view!)

A majority point of view would likely be represented by Dinkmeyer and Caldwell, who say, "Certainly the counselor, as a trained resource person in both formal and informal testing, should be deeply involved at all phases of the testing program,"[51] and Shertzer and Stone, "When well versed in test theory and practice, the counselor can use test scores as significant contributions to the clinical aspects of his work,"[52] and Bernard and Fullmer, "Let the student take tests which might indicate inclinations, but interpret them as being guides and suggestions."[53]

All of these, to me, avoid or ignore the reality of the inner self of the person, and they give a measure which is not a measure. Boy and Pine reflect this feeling when they say:

> Much counseling practice operates on the principle of historic and external causation. The use of tests in the counseling process is a reflection of this principle. Testing is an evaluative procedure in which the client's behavior is sampled and measured against an external criterion.[54]

51. Don C. Dinkmeyer and Charles E. Caldwell, *Developmental Counseling and Guidance* (New York: McGraw-Hill, 1970), p. 320.
52. Bruce Shertzer and Shelley C. Stone, *Fundamentals of Guidance* (Boston: Houghton Mifflin, 1971), p. 235.
53. Harold W. Bernard and Daniel W. Fullmer, *Principles of Guidance: A Basic Text* (Scranton, Pa.: International Textbook Co., 1969), p. 277.
54. Angelo V. Boy and Gerald J. Pine, *The Counselor in the Schools: A Reconceptualization* (Boston: Houghton Mifflin, 1968), p. 246.

Thus if one sees the other person, in the traditional scientific pattern, as being what one is measured to be by outside and external criteria, then testing—and diagnosis—should be an integral part of the counseling process. If, on the other hand, one sees the basic reality of the human as being from within, then testing and diagnosis will tend to remove the person even further from the reality of who he is.

ADVICE AND INFORMATION

The school has been, and still is, an institution which might be accurately described as a place where students are given information and are advised as to what to do with it. Since school counselors are direct descendants from schoolteachers, it is not surprising that many see their function as being much like that of teachers, and they consider advice and information as their basic tools.

As ideas about the role and function of the counselor change, so will perceptions regarding the place of advice and information, but change is slow. Again, the school is still a place where information is given to a student, rather than a place where information is developed and sought out by the student to fit his own particular person. Advice about advice given years ago by Williamson would probably be as acceptable to most school counselors now as it was then. It would also likely be acceptable to many behavior therapists, reality therapists, and rational-emotive therapists. In fact, it sounds just like Albert Ellis:

> . . . *the counselor is ready to advise* with *the student as to a program of action consistent with, and growing out of, the diagnosis. For convenience, we may summarize methods of advising under the headings,* direct, persuasive, *and* explanatory.[55]

Even here, however, it should be remembered that many counselors, when talking about the place of advice, are thinking in terms of teaching rather than counseling. There would obviously be much more of an argument for the offering of advice to a rational individual under no stress or strain, than for giving advice to a highly disturbed individual who might clutch it as a complete answer to his difficulties, or reject it and the counselor completely. As in so many other issues in counseling, the place of advice and information is

55. Williamson, *op. cit.*, p. 233.

directly related to the person of the counselor, and his views about people and their potential. The psychiatric and psychological literature, in clinics and in schools, has generally accepted the use of advice and information by the counselor or therapist as part of his function. I would think that these comments would be as descriptive of practicing counselors and therapists now as they were when they were written. Consider Sullivan, for example:

> *Thus the advice comes in at the very end to round out the obvious. As a psychiatrist, you see, I sometimes have to round out the obvious, because there are some people, notoriously obsessionals, who are very unwilling indeed to draw a conclusion—and therefore the psychiatrist gives them the conclusion. Actually, the "advice" is for the most part an overwhelming display of the factors relevant to the problem plus a clear statement by the psychiatrist of what he firmly believes can be done about them.*[56]

Another psychiatrist, Colby, comments as follows on this issue:

> *One type of interposition common in the beginning, as well as at other stages of the therapy, consists of advice. At times the therapist must offer practical suggestions to the patient whose reality judgment is so impaired as to jeopardize his best interests. For example, a patient whose concept of his body is distorted may be advised not to undergo the plastic surgery he has planned. Or it may be suggested that a patient change his living quarters where he is under the constant unnerving pressure of homosexual feeling toward a roommate. As with all advice-giving on the part of the therapist, it should be done cautiously, and in small doses. The therapist must be prepared for the prospect that often his advice will not be taken, or, even worse, that it will be followed but have bad results.*[57]

Hadley, too, accepts the use of advice as legitimate, but suggests caution:

> *Suggestion and the giving of direct advice are techniques similar to reassurance and should be used with the greatest of caution. In nearly all counseling relationships the counselor is a figure of authority to his client. Consequently, even offhand suggestions of alternative behavior patterns or remarks not in-*

56. Harry S. Sullivan, *The Psychiatric Interview* (New York: Norton, 1954), p. 213.
57. Kenneth Mark Colby, *A Primer for Psychotherapists* (New York: Ronald Press, 1951), p. 150.

tended as suggestions may do great harm to the client if they are not carefully thought out.[58]

Marzolf also suggests the use of advice, with caution, although he does not actually use the term:

At certain times and under certain circumstances, suggestions may be made to the client without arousing resistance, a possible result of the counselor's intervention in the thinking of the client. A young client may not consider a particular course of action merely because he has never known about it or thought about it. One may also suggest sources of information, ways of approach to teachers about situations that have confused the client, courses of study to consider, occupations to investigate, or ways to improve social effectiveness. Such suggestions should not, however, be made so freely so as to deprive the youth of all opportunity to do his own problem-solving and thus make him dependent.[59]

However, I would feel that the more a client asks for advice, the less likely it is that advice will be of any benefit to him. The measure of the stability of an individual is the extent to which he is free to reject, or accept advice, without rancor or hostility or tension.

Ingham and Love express a somewhat similar point of view on the question of advice:

. . . or he could seek an answer from the counselor about whether to marry, get a divorce, or have children; about extramarital sex experience, educational or vocational choices, or the continuation of psychotherapy. Almost any important decision that a person must make can be brought to the therapist's office. The therapist should not feel that he is in a position to know what the other should do, let alone decide for him. . . . Furthermore, even if he were right (as of course he often would be), it would ordinarily be undesirable for him to express his opinion so that it could be received by the patient as advice.[60]

Advice and information are not, of course, the same thing. The latter is factual, objective and pragmatic. The amount of information we need in order to survive in the modern world increases at an alarming rate, so the debate is not over "Do we need information?"

58. John M. Hadley, *Clinical and Counseling Psychology* (New York: Alfred A. Knopf, 1958), pp. 156–157.
59. Stanley S. Marzolf, *op. cit.*, p. 552.
60. Harrington V. Ingham and Leonore R. Love, *The Process of Psychotherapy* (New York: McGraw-Hill, 1954), p. 22.

but rather "Is it the *primary* business of the counselor to provide information?"

The general acceptance of the gathering and dissemination of information as a basic function of the counselor is seen in the following comments. Downing asserts that "the counselor is responsible for the conduct of the information service,"[61] while Kowitz and Kowitz state: "The value of records is such that an effective guidance operation cannot eschew them because of some operational problems."[62] The attitude of Shertzer and Stone is clear when they say, "During interviews with students, counselors often need to give information about occupations, educational opportunities, and personal-social relationships, since such information may be vital to self-exploration."[63]

Information is viewed as essential in the counseling process by Delaney and Eisenberg:

In this process, information and information systems may be seen as helping the client perform four vital functions: identifying available alternatives; generating criteria to evaluate; anticipating potential consequences of implementing each alternative; and assessing the likelihood that each alternative can be effectively implemented.[64]

Dinkmeyer and Caldwell see the gathering of information from a variety of sources as a basic counselor function,[65] while Blocher, Dustin, and Dugan view the information system as being the prime concern of the counselor.[66] They describe it as "the guidance subsystem that is responsible for generating, coding, storing, retrieving and disseminating information relevant to planning."

Some writers are more wary about the use of information by counselors. While Combs, Avila, and Purkey, in discussing the helping process, say that "the process requires helping clients to obtain whatever information is needed with the greatest possible dispatch," they also add: "It is not enough that information should seem important to the receiver; it must also be related to his current problems or

61. Lester N. Downing, *Guidance and Counseling Services: An Introduction* (New York: McGraw-Hill, 1968), p. 194.
62. Gerald T. Kowitz and Norma G. Kowitz, *An Introduction to School Guidance* (New York: Holt, Rinehart and Winston, 1971), p. 104.
63. Shertzer and Stone, *op. cit.,* p. 323.
64. Daniel J. Delaney and Sheldon Eisenberg, *The Counseling Process* (Chicago: Rand McNally, 1973), p. 154.
65. Don C. Dinkmeyer and Charles E. Caldwell, *op. cit.,* pp. 202–206.
66. Donald H. Blocher, E. Richard Dustin, and Willis E. Dugan, *Guidance Systems: An Introduction to Student Personnel Work* (New York: Ronald Press, 1971), p. 181.

interests if it is to be truly effective" and warn: "Whether information can be truly communicated will be dependent on the readiness of the receiver to absorb it."[67] Lifton, too, limits the use of information by the counselor when he says:

> Information, as contrasted from advice, then, is provided only when the people seeking a solution which clarifies their problem see need for knowing alternative ways to reach their goal and are willing to accept responsibility both for implementing their decisions and for accepting the fruits of their action.[68]

Boy and Pine are more than skeptical about the place of information anywhere in counseling:

> Unfortunately, school counseling today all too often revolves around the dispensing of information and advising, not because anyone is able to justify these functions, but because they are the base of the operational pattern of the typical secondary school. Dispensing information and advising are what teachers and administrators have historically done in the name of education, and such activities are considered to be the functional core of the counselor's role.[69]

Another issue, which is definitely ethical in nature, is the question of the dissemination of information gathered about the client by the counselor to people other than counselors, and the use of this information by others in ways which may be damaging and hurtful to the client. The question here is really twofold: there is the question of whether or not the counselor should accept the gathering of information about the client and its transmission to other agencies and individuals as part of his professional function, and there is also the question of the extent to which this is a breach of the ethical obligation of the counselor to retain as confidential much of the personal information which he has about the client. This ethical issue will be examined in the next chapter.

"Relevant" information may also be of no help. When a high school student who has been driven by compulsive parents to excel academically is provided with information that indicates that his chances of getting into a decent college are most remote, it is unlikely that he will say, "Thank you," and relax. Information may not

67. Arthur W. Combs, Donald L. Avila, and William W. Purkey, *Helping Relationships: Basic Concepts for the Helping Professions* (Boston: Allyn and Bacon, 1971), pp. 255–259.
68. Walter M. Lifton, *Groups: Facilitating Individual Growth and Societal Change* (New York: Wiley, 1972), p. 70.
69. Angelo V. Boy and Gerald J. Pine, *op. cit.*, p. 166.

have quite the personal sting of advice, but when it clashes with one's concept of who he is, its immediate effect is not likely to be very positive.

Information may be traumatic (What is my IQ?) or it may be of no particular relevance (Do you like hockey?) or it may be supportive (Do you have many clients like me?); but in any case it is of little help to the client in his growth toward a better understanding about himself. Several of my psychiatric colleagues feel the same way about the M.D. therapist's functioning as a medical doctor rather than a therapist, and giving medical information or advice to the patient. The medical doctor does certain things for the patient that the therapist does not do, and he gives certain things to the patient that the therapist does not give. It is difficult to be two people whose functions contradict each other.

Many of the clients who come in to see the school counselor, of course, are going to be quite capable of using relevant information, *and if they want it, and if the counselor has it,* there would seem to be little reason for withholding it. Even though in the actual counseling relationship information will play a very minor role, the school counselor will periodically be called upon to supply information. There would seem to be no reason why he could not do so and at the same time maintain his counseling relationship with the client. Generally speaking, however, he should be seen not as the giver of information, but rather as the individual who will help a person to get to the point where he can make sensible use of sensible information. In any case, in the very near future it is likely that the information-giving function of the counselor will be taken over by the machine, so that the counselor can become involved in his professional function—counseling. The client will be helped to be the active generator and procurer of information rather than the passive recipient of it.

QUESTIONS

Questioning is a routine method of getting information, and many counselors unfortunately see counseling as either asking questions of the client or answering questions from the client. If the counselor asks questions, we can assume that he must have some idea as to how he is going to use the answers to the questions. Sometimes, however, it is difficult for me to understand just why certain questions are being asked. In the following clinical situation, for example, what will the therapist do with the information that he gets? (D-therapist and P-patient)

D.: Tell me how you are feeling and when it started, can you?

P.: I think so. I feel, I don't know, I feel at ease with certain people and with others I don't feel at ease. Like I'd say it started when my father got sick. I . . . I sort of took it on myself. I thought maybe it was my fault when my father got sick. I know that things have not been going too smoothly at home. I was out of work all summer, and there were many arguments, so when my father got sick I thought maybe it was my fault, but that feeling went away, of course. But my nerves haven't been the same since that.

D.: Since he got sick?

P.: That's right—I just seem to be ill at ease—now I mean I am talking to you—I feel natural now. With certain people I do, but at home I don't. I don't understand it.

D.: You spoke before about feeling disappointed.

P.: I have a depressed feeling. I—it's so hard to explain—I feel like I am waiting for something to happen, and it's never going to happen—and I feel like I gotta run away and I go out of the house and—well, I want to go right back home again. I know there's nothing out of the house. I don't have too many friends. I was going with a buddy but he's down south now and I have a feeling—and I have a lonesome feeling, to tell you the truth. (Sighs.) I don't know—I don't know what I'm looking for—forward to something that's not going to happen.

D.: Is it dreadful do you think, what might happen, or is it pleasant?

P.: Well, that's just it, I don't know. (Pause.) I've been going out very seldom now. I stay around the house all the time—I'm working in the store all the time, and well, I go to the movies, and that's all. We close now Thursday night and Sunday night, but I go to the movies or I go to a friend's house or relatives. But Saturday night was the first time for a long time that I went out since my father's been sick. That happened so suddenly. On a couple minutes' notice I went out. But when I got up Sunday morning I felt all right until I started to get a depressed feeling. I couldn't understand what it was, and I thought maybe I was sick or something—because I have had pains in my stomach all the time and my mother kept saying, "Why don't you go to the doctor," and I thought maybe I'll put it off until tomorrow and it will go away.

D.: Do you have any idea what you might be depressed about?

P.: I dunno. I thought it might be that I'm lonesome. You know, I feel like I'm alone. Even when I'm with a lot of people I feel like I'm alone.

D.: Hasn't it always been that way?[70]

70. Ruben R. Pottash, "A Psychotherapeutic Interview with an Adolescent," in Benjamin Harries Balster (ed.), *Psychotherapy of the Adolescent* (New York: International Universities Press, 1957), pp. 160–164.

It is even more puzzling to try to figure out just what use this school counselor is going to make of the information he receives:

Co.: Can you tell me a little more about how you seem to be held back?

Cl.: Well, mathematics mostly.

Co.: Mm-huh. How does that affect you?

Cl.: Well, I haven't done very good on the tests in taking them.

Co.: Mm-huh (pause). Could you tell me a little bit about your background, where you are from, what you plan to do, and so forth?

Cl.: Well, I'm from (name of town).

Co.: Yes.

Cl.: Have you ever been there?

Co.: No, but I know where it is.

Cl.: I'm in pre-vet school. I'd like to take up veterinary medicine if I can make the grade.

Co.: Mm-huh.

Cl.: That's my only trouble.

Co.: When did you decide on veterinary medicine?

Cl.: Well, I've been kind of interested for some time. I live on a farm and I work with a lot of livestock.

Co.: Do you know any veterinarians?

Cl.: Well, yes, our local veterinarian.

Co.: Mm-huh. And you'd like to be doing the work he seems to be doing at the present time?

Cl.: Yes.

Co.: You haven't worked with him, though, while he is working with animals, or anything like that?

Cl.: Well, yes, I've worked some.

Co.: Have you?

Cl.: Mm-huh.

Co.: What made you choose veterinary medicine as the field you wanted to go into?

Cl.: Well——

Co.: (Counselor interrupts) Was it any one person or just working on the farm?[71]

Generally, I can see little point in asking questions of this nature of a client, since I do not see myself as directing him to where I want him to go, but rather helping him to look at where he is and where he wants to go. I try to help him to expand his horizon rather

71. Robert Callis, Paul C. Polmantier, and Edward C. Roeber, *op. cit.*, pp. 105–106, dialogue entries C1–C13.

than imposing mine on him. In this process, however, the client will very often ask questions of me. Let us look at some of the questions about questions.

1. There are questions that are obviously expressions of feeling rather than questions per se. When a client exclaims, "How do you expect me to go on living with her?" or "What am I supposed to do when she tells me I'm a bum—just sit there and take it?" or "Who is to blame anyway—me or my husband?" or "How can you or anyone else expect me to take that job?" and so on, these are not really questions, although some student counselors might actually react to them as if they were questions demanding intellectual answers. I would feel that a proper reaction to the above statements would be either some understanding nod, or "Uh-huh," or "Hmmmm . . .," or a reflection of feeling such as "It's pretty hard to see just how you could do that," or "That's asking quite a bit," or, "Is it one, or the other, or maybe both of you?" or "It's pretty unreasonable for anyone to expect such a thing of you," and so on. The counselor who is alert to, and reacting to, the expressed feelings of the client will not make the mistake of thinking that every statement that sounds as if it had a question mark after it must have an answer by the counselor.

Sometimes such a question may be a desperate request for reassurance. The counselor may feel more impelled to answer such questions as "Surely *you* don't expect me to go ahead and do that, do you?" or "Can't anyone help me in this—must I *always* be alone?" But here again it is the feeling to which the counselor should react. The tone should be gentle and understanding, but it would seem better that the words be, possibly, "Surely there is *someone* who does not feel that you have to do this" or, "Isn't there ever *anyone* who seems to be with you?" Note here too that while the counselor may feel compelled to say, "I don't feel that way," or, "But I am with you," the real deep feeling on the part of the client that *this is actually so* will come only when he can say, maybe just to himself, maybe to the counselor too, "But there is someone—*you* don't expect me to do that," or "Why . . . I'm not alone, I'm not alone . . . there *is* someone."

A somewhat similar sort of question may be asked when the client feels threatened by what he thinks might be a negative reaction of the counselor to something that he has said. Thus if the client, who has been talking about the stupidity of all of the people who vote the Democratic ticket, suddenly pauses and says, "By the way, are you a Democrat?" It is fairly clear that he has said to himself, "What if this guy is a Democrat?" Or it could be that this is his way of expressing his contempt for the counselor, assuming that the counselor is a Democrat. If the answer is no, the counselor might be tempted to take the easier and safer road and say no. If the answer is yes, however, he might feel that he has only a choice of lying, of telling the tension-evoking truth, or of trying to avoid answering the question either by asking some other question, or by detouring around it.

Again here, either a yes or no answer, true or false, counselor comfort or no counselor comfort, is not really reacting to what the client is saying. A fairly safe rule of thumb in this matter is "Don't tell lies"; so we could dispense with the lie, if not for moral reasons, then for the empirical reason that when a counselor lies, it will eventually, and probably fairly soon, catch up with him. An honest reaction to the statement might be: "You mean that after all that you've said about the Democrats, you're a bit concerned about what I am." This might very well get a reaction of, "Well, yes, what are you?" At this point the best reaction might be a simple, truthful answer, something to the effect, "Well, actually, in trying to figure out some of your difficulties here what I am really doesn't make any difference, does it?" Actually, clients rarely press for an answer, but if they do, it would seem rather pointless to endlessly go around in a circle, all in the name of "reflection of feeling."

2. A question that relates to the personal involvement of the counselor, however, may be a somewhat more complicated matter. The client is conceivably after more than just an answer when he asks, "By the way, are you married?" or "How do you get along with children?" or "Did you ever fail any subjects when you were in college?" or "Did you ever get fired?" or "Do you believe in going to church?" and so on. Unlike the previous type of question, these questions are probably asked by the client as questions to which he wants answers, possibly for reassurance, possibly to help him feel superior to the counselor, possibly to help him feel closer to the counselor. When a woman client who is having trouble with her children asks the counselor, "Are you married?" a very likely next question is "Do you have any children?" to be followed by "How do you get along so well with them?" The development of such inquiries brings into question the effectiveness of the counselor; has he in some way given the client the feeling that he is a friendly confidante rather than a warm and professionally competent counselor?

Whatever the reason for questions of this nature, the counselor may find "reflection of feeling" on such occasions not easy, for the very obvious reason that there is little or nothing in the way of feeling to reflect. Many counselors feel that a brief, noncommittal, nonencouraging answer is as good a response, generally, as any; and if the question is pushed, then there is more in the way of feeling to which the counselor can react. "You really want an answer to a question like that . . .," and so on. There would be a difference of opinion on counselor reactions to this sort of question, although there would be general agreement that the counseling session is not a question-and-answer period, regardless of who is doing the questioning and who is doing the answering. The student counselor may sometimes find himself bogged down in this sort of situation, waking up suddenly to the fact that he has become an answer man, with the questions more and more personal and his involvement deeper all the time. Even at this point, however, it is better to extricate oneself, even if it means threat to the client and possible disruption of the counseling, since what is happening is not likely to be good for either the counselor or the client. It may be, sometimes, that the best counselor reaction to the probing and pressing question by the client, "Come on now, tell me, how do you get along with your wife?" would be: "Well, an answer to that question, you know, really wouldn't be of any help to you or to me . . . but it's sort of interesting why you keep pressing me with that question."

3. Another form of question is the one that seeks an interpretation of the client's actions or thoughts or dreams. For example, a client may talk for some time, without any indication of undue stress or strain, about the difficulty of making choices, and then, in a conversational tone, ask, "What does that mean, anyway? Do you know any of the possible reasons why I just seem always to shy away from making any decisions?" Or he might say, "And then one of those dreams that I always have, and have had for years, is that I'm standing on a block of ice that gets smaller and smaller and eventually disappears, and I fall into the water. What does that mean, anyway?"

Again here, there is little in the way of feeling to which the counselor may react; this is a straight question, asked as a question. There may, of course, as with other questions, be many ulterior or subconscious motives, but overtly at least these questions are asked as questions. Whether the counselor does or does not know what the behavior or the dream might mean, he should be wary about passing on to the client his version of its meaning. An intellectual presentation may not mean any more than the intellectual presentation of an intelligence test score of an IQ of 115 to a person who considers himself stupid. A person *must be* as he sees himself, and will change only when he can accept change, not when evidence indicating that he is different is presented to him.

Usually the counselor would react to this sort of question. He might say, "Well . . . I gather it's pretty hard for you to see any meaning to this sort of behavior"; or possibly "It's pretty important for you to find some reason behind this behavior of yours." Some might press the client with "Well, hard to say . . . what do you think it might mean for you?" There might thus be a variety of *reactions* to the question, but most counselors would agree that the counselor would not, at least immediately, answer it. On the other hand, a counselor who was competent in the matter of dream interpretation, might feel that at a certain point, he would present his interpretation of the dream to the client.

4. Then, of course, there are noncommittal questions, in relation to which the most logical procedure is to answer them simply and briefly. A client, finding it difficult to start talking, might say, "This is certainly a cold spell that we are having, isn't it?" Although some counselors might feel that the client's uneasiness should be reflected, this would seem a somewhat cold manner in which to initiate a relationship. Why not just give a pleasant "Yes, it really is cold weather that we have been having," and the odds are that the client will be reassured that the counselor is human and will continue in a different vein. The counselor should be consistent, and he will almost certainly be different from what the client expects, but he need not be so different as to appear abnormal. Such a result sometimes comes about when the student counselor, trying to be "client-centered," refuses to react to any question, and the client, reasonably enough, feels that the counselor is a very queer fellow indeed! The client would be equally disturbed by a student counselor who, impressed with his analytic skills, attempted to interpret the psychosexual meaning of the above question!

It would seem to me that a good rule of thumb is to react to the feeling expressed in the question rather than to the content of the question. If one does react to the content of the question it should be brief, and it should not encourage added questioning of the counselor by the client. Needless to say, however, the counselor's reaction to a client question should not make the client feel rejected or out of place. Individual freedom means the right of the client to ask anything he wants to ask!

SILENCES

Client silences often cause some strain for the student counselor. Many student counselors complain, in fact, that most typescripts and tapes always seem to record clients who are very willing to talk, and all the counselor has to do is grunt every now and then, or decide when or where he should interrupt the client. There are several points that might be noted on this question.

1. The beginning counselor will likely find that client silence poses a threat to him. As the silence lengthens, the pressure on him to do something about it builds up—usually not for the welfare of the client, but rather to ease his own tension. Thus, logically, we might say that the counselor should aim for a degree of personal security such that whatever action he takes on the matter of client silence will be taken solely for professional reasons. Since most would agree that counselor comfort is important, and that there should be honesty in the client-counselor relationship, it is an interesting question whether or not the counselor who feels this uneasiness should be honest and indicate this feeling to the client. Most counselors would say no to this, but some, possibly an increasing number, would say yes.

2. Silences, as much as words, are indicative of feelings. The counselor who reacts basically to client feelings might use such comments as "It's pretty difficult to get started talking . . ." or "This is a real tough thing to talk about . . . it would seem easier maybe just to let it lie" or "It's a real nice feeling . . .," and so on. The counselor here must be almost intuitive as to what the client is feeling; while his words will sometimes be a fairly obvious reflection of feeling, it may sometimes be that if the counselor is to speak at all, it will be in the form of an interpretation.

Some counselors feel that there should be a reaction from the counselor if the silence appears to become threatening to the client, and thus the counselor might, under certain circumstances, take over the direction of the session. Very often, when a good relationship has been established, the client will indicate that there is no need for counselor verbalization. I once interrupted a long client silence, and was gently chided by the client. She was doing quite all right, and didn't need my talk!

3. Silence can also be therapeutic, and probably this is one of the attractions of a church. It is one of the few places where one can go and meditate quietly, without any interruptions. The counselor's office is another place where the same thing can take place. The client may be having a real therapeutic experience when he is silent, just as much, if not more, than when he is talking. Most counselors have had the experience of sharing a warm and unique silence with a client, where both client and counselor could almost feel the growth that was taking place.

Counselors who feel that they just must talk, and who feel silence difficult, might ponder over the results of a study reported by Cook. He found that the lack of silence (at least 97 percent speech in a number of two-minute segments) characterized the unsuccessful

273

counseling sessions, whereas the lesser percentage of speech tended to characterize the more successful counseling sessions.[72]

MISCELLANEOUS ISSUES

Another reaction that may cause some counselor concern is an unexpected statement by the client, although this should occasion no despair on the part of the student counselor as long as it does not result in his anxiety. It is one thing to be surprised; it is quite another to be frightened. A beginning interview may be progressing in a conversational way when suddenly the client says, quietly, "Did you know that I was a Lesbian?" or "By the way, I slept with the dean over the weekend," or "Are you nervous? . . . You look that way," and so on. As long as the counselor is a secure and acceptant individual, he does not have to worry about the long-range negative effect of his momentary loss of aplomb. Probably every counselor has his list of "bloopers," where he made statements that are obviously ridiculous to even the greenest of student counselors. I have recorded one example where the client says, "Say, you look sort of puzzled . . .," and the reply that comes back is, "Who . . . me . . . no." The client's logical reaction to this was a laugh, but the relationship at least appeared to be good, and a few minutes after this exchange the client was deeply involved in his problem. In a discussion of this example, it was suggested that *if* the counselor really was puzzled, a more appropriate answer would simply have been, "Well . . . yes . . . I am sort of puzzled." In this case, however, the reaction would not have been an honest one, since the counselor, at least during the interchange, was not aware of being puzzled; he was just surprised—and of course a counselor should *never* be surprised!

Unexpected and violent oaths, unusual or bizarre statements may, for a while, pose problems for the student counselor, but in the long run they will not be a serious issue as long as he is not actually threatened by them. If, however, he is, and if such statements are taken as a challenge, to be reacted to as a challenge, or as the sort of thing about which people simply do not talk, then the counselor is in need of some assistance to solve his own problems. Such situations as these will become counseling problems only if they represent a personal problem for the counselor.

A question that is raised by some students is "Where do you sit and do you look at the client all the time?" It would be safe to say

72.   John J. Cook, "Silence in Psychotherapy," *Journal of Counseling Psychology,* 11:42–46 (Spring, 1964).

that the counselor does not sit with a desk between himself and the client; a general position is one where both client and counselor can look at each other if they want to, or look away from each other without any awkwardness. A counselor has to use his own judgment as to just how consistently he looks at his client; obviously, too, this will vary with clients, and vary with the individual feelings of any one client. A counselor should be able to look steadily at the client if need be, but he should be sensitive enough not to give the impression of staring at him. The counselor's "looking at the client" should be governed by good sense and good taste.

The highly colored, risqué, or just plain dirty joke may also pose an early problem for the counselor—again possibly a means of testing the counselor, or it may be just a part of the normal expression of the client. If the counselor has led such a sheltered life that he cannot understand the joke, then he will have his problems, although he might not be quite so badly off as the counselor who understands the joke, but is horrified that a child could come forth with such a statement. We can assume both that these individuals need some assistance if they are to become effective counselors, and that their relationship with the client is likely to be somewhat strained. The more mature counselor, on the other hand, can be acceptant of the client's feeling of humor in what he has said, and be neither frigid nor boisterous in his reaction. Nevertheless, some "jokes," such as those of an "anti" nature, may prove a problem for the student counselor, inasmuch as the client will be alert to detect any indication of approval or condemnation on the part of the counselor.

The complete lack of choice possible to some clients may also pose a problem. This is most obvious in the school situation, where, even though the client may be raging at the mean and miserable behavior of a teacher, he has no choice about leaving the teacher. He has to stay in school, and, more often than not, he has to go back to the same teacher. Such a lack of choice is a basic cause of many of the problems that are presented to the school counselor, and very often the fact is that the child must endure, for another year or two, an unrealistic curriculum, and quite possibly equally unrealistic and unsympathetic teachers. This is enough to test the mettle of a mature adult, and we can assume that an immature but nevertheless basically sound child is going to need some help to come through the experience a strong and stable individual.

Because youth must have practice in making its own decisions, many children would find school a better place if they were able to make the choice to withdraw from it, as they can from college, for a year or so. Their decision might be a poor one, for an unhappy school experience is not always because of a poor curriculum and poor teachers. Nevertheless, the adolescent grows up in a more realistic environment when he knows that he *can* make a choice, and that when he has made it, *he* will be held responsible for it. In our present culture, unfortunately, it almost seems that we are moving to a situation where the age of self-determination may never be reached. We may yet get to the point where, when mother has at last been removed from the picture, after the individual has been "educated" for many, many years, has been married, and has become a father, the state will take over. Then the individual may live in a happy state of irresponsibility for the rest of his days, letting someone else make his decisions for him, and thus never having to blame himself for anything that might go wrong. This state of total determinism never can, of course, be reached, and the counselor can help the child to develop the capacity for independent action, even though he may, for the moment, necessarily live in dependency. When the time comes, the child will then be capable of becoming a truly independent individual, standing on his own feet, and making his own way, and will have no need for counselors.

Chapter 11

Theoretical Issues: Ethical

The counselor, like anyone else involved in a close and intimate human relationship, will periodically find himself face to face with ethical issues. And more often than not, the dilemma will be that there will be no easy answer, one way or the other. The counselor will find himself a part of what could be life-and-death decisions, and as long as he is involved, as indeed he must be if he is to be a counselor, then the problems he faces are obviously ethical in nature. The crucial ethical issue is the existence of a human being as a free individual and as a contributing member of the society of which he is a part.

And it is this issue, beginning in the decade of the 1960's, and continuing into the 1970's, that has challenged, and is challenging, the very existence of many of the professional "helping" organizations. The lack of involvement of professional "helping" organizations in human and social issues became dramatically evident in the 1960's, and the continuing growth of new and splinter groups in the 1970's is evidence of current dissatisfaction with the traditional practices of such organizations. New divisions in both the American Personnel and Guidance Association and the American Psychological Association stress human and social concerns. New organizations such as the American Academy of Psychotherapists and the Association of Humanistic Psychology are protests against the traditional direction of psychological and medical organizations.

Both the APA and the APGA have, for a number of years, had committees which deal with issues of an ethical nature, although many members would feel they are not concerned enough with issues of a broader human and social nature. The American Psychological Association's Committee on Scientific and Professional Ethics and Conduct and the American Personnel and Guidance Association's Committee on Ethics have a double function in that they are supposed to protect the counselor from the public (the counselor has no protection in the matter of legal suit) and the public from unethical counselors.

The American Psychological Association published a booklet entitled "Ethical Standards of Psychologists" in January, 1963. This has been amended and reprinted in September, 1965, and December, 1972. In addition, the American Psychological Association, in an attempt to promulgate a set of national standards for providers of psychological services, created, in March, 1970, its Task Force on Standards for Service Facilities. This task force published a set of standards in February, 1974. Also available from the Association are "Ethical Principles in the Conduct of Research with Human Participants" and "Standards for Educational and Psychological Tests." In the summer of 1974 a committee of the American Personnel and Guidance Association was revising and updating its code of ethics to meet the changing value systems.

All of these committees have a remedial and helpful function and there are counselors and psychologists today who think of them as professional groups that gave them much assistance during a difficult time.

In 1960 the American Personnel and Guidance Association took its first legal step in defending one of its members. A previous circuit court decision, described below, had been appealed to the state supreme court:

The Circuit Court of Dunn County (Wis.) recently ruled that a guidance counselor had no legal responsibility for the suicide of a counselee student.

Claiming their daughter was emotionally disturbed, the parents of the student in question charged the guidance counselor with negligence in three counts: failure to notify the parents of her condition; failure to secure psychiatric treatment for her; and failure to provide proper guidance.

The court stated in effect, that the counselor was a teacher, not a medical expert. To expect him to recognize the student's condition without benefit of necessary training and experience "would require a duty beyond reason," the court stated.[1]

The association then filed with the supreme court a brief that presented a significant argument that had not been raised before,

<hr>

1. *College and University Bulletin,* XII:3 (October 15, 1959) (Washington, D.C.: Association for Higher Education, National Education Association).

namely, that a counselor cannot be held liable for an event that occurs weeks after counseling, and particularly when a medical question is involved. The result was that the original decision of the circuit court was upheld, and the association had functioned effectively in protecting the rights of one of its members.

It is extremely difficult, however, to protect the unwary public from the various quacks who call themselves counselors and psychologists—both of these being omnibus terms that can mean almost anything. Such individuals find that the title "Doctor" gives them added authority and more business and that though it can be a title easy to acquire, few clients will ask, "What is your doctorate and where did you get it?" As has already been mentioned, there are numerous institutions where one may receive a doctor's degree in wondrous and various fields by going through the motions of taking an extension course and paying a rather substantial sum. To the shame of the professions of education, psychology, and counseling, there are individuals possessing high positions who proudly parade such "degrees."

Unhappily, however, the evidence on the effectiveness of counseling and psychotherapy would tend to indicate that the possession of a more "legitimate" degree is no guarantee of success. In fact, many leaders in our field feel that graduate programs in counseling and psychology tend to dehumanize a person and make him less effective in a human relationship. I would agree with this rather gloomy assessment. We also know, of course, of the astonishing success rate of many "lay therapists" when contrasted with professional therapists. All of this makes it clear that the effectiveness of our professional organizations in doing what they claim they do is a major ethical issue.

Any counselor who has worked on a committee concerned with problems of ethical behavior soon realizes that it is a very "sticky" area where, far more often than not, there is no clear-cut indication, with no doubts whatsoever as to whether the behavior of a counselor in question was unethical or not. Any committee making a decision on the ethical behavior of a counselor must at all times be keenly aware of the ethical soundness of its own position.

Over two decades ago, the Americam Psychological Association attempted to answer this question by posing a whole series of questions and situations, and then giving the reactions of the committee to them.[2] Not all members of the American Psychological Association, however, agree with all of the answers as given by the

2. *Ethical Standards of Psychologists* (Washington, D.C.: Committee on Ethical Standards for Psychologists, American Psychological Association, 1953).

committee. Every counselor, sooner or later, must face some of these ethical issues as personal problems, which must be answered personally.

In discussing unethical practices, Schwebel makes three "assumptions":

1. *Self-interest causes both unethical behavior and unethical practice. The personal profit motive may be a cause, the need for self-enhancement may be a cause, and the need to maintain security and status may be a cause.*
2. *Unsound judgment due to inadequate training and/or unsupervised experience, or due to ineffective selection, causes unethical practice; but since self-interest is not a primary factor, the behavior of the psychologist is not unethical. Unsound judgment may be shown in maintaining confidences in staff relations or in maintaining confidences about antisocial behavior.*
3. *Ignorance causes unethical practice. Here too, since self-interest is not a primary factor, the behavior of the psychologist is not unethical. Ignorance of technical information may be a cause, or ignorance on the part of the counselor of his own values, especially those that are incompatible with respect for the integrity of the individual, may be a cause.*[3]

Some readers would probably question Schwebel's statement that incorrect behavior caused by ignorance is not unethical; or some might say that while it might not be unethical of the individual, it is unethical for the employer to hire such a person without checking on his credentials; and it is unethical of the graduating institution to graduate a person who is so ignorant. It would seem that somewhere along the line, when injury is done to a patient or a client in a supposed professional relationship, then somebody, somewhere, has committed an unethical act.

STATE CERTIFICATION AND PROFESSIONAL ACCREDITATION[4]

The legal determination of what is required to educate a counselor continues to be controlled by state departments of education, and

3. Milton Schwebel, "Why Unethical Practice," *Journal of Counseling Psychology,* 2:122–128 (Summer, 1955).
4. *See* Dugald S. Arbuckle, "Current Issues in Counselor Education," *Counselor Education and Supervision,* 7:244–252 (Spring, 1968). Copyright 1968 by the American Personnel and Guidance Association.

thus in the United States there continue to be fifty versions of what is necessary to educate an individual so that he might be "certified" to be a counselor. It is obvious that one may question the professional status of any occupation when the criteria for certification vary drastically from state to state, and when the determination of professional adequacy is made by state department of education officials, some of whom would have little professional standing in the very field whose workers they certify! Equally distressing, of course, is the fact that certification is generally, not by graduation from an accredited program, but rather by an official determination, usually person by person, as to whether the applicant has satisfied the official's interpretation of state requirements for certification. While the official requirements change with painful slowness, interpretations of these requirements vary as the personnel vary, and when personnel turnover is high, so is the level of confusion. In the state of Massachusetts, for example, despite the efforts of professional individuals and organizations, and some legislators, requirements put into effect in the year 1956 remained unchanged until 1975. The change, basically, was from requirements of four courses (not including clinical practice) and a teaching certificate to a requirement of a master's degree, including clinical practice. Even a conservative individual would hardly describe this as a radical change!

Thus on the basis of state certification, the position of the school counselor is not a definable position, at least on the national level, and the student who sees counseling in the schools as his future occupation will immediately note a wide divergence as to the criteria for the professional education of the counselor.

Dissatisfaction with this individual, state-by-state pattern of counselor certification was evident well over a decade ago, and various members of the American Personnel and Guidance Association began to press for professional approval or even accreditation of programs of counselor education by the appropriate professional body. A major step came in 1962, with the publication by the American Personnel and Guidance Association of six position papers on standards which should be developed for the selection and professional preparation of secondary school counselors.[5] In the same publication it was indicated that a revised statement would be published by January, 1964, thus "allowing time for further consideration before action is taken by the 1964 Senate."[6] A revised set of standards was voted upon and accepted by the Association for Counselor Edu-

5. *Counselor Education: A Progress Report on Standards* (Washington, D.C.: American Personnel and Guidance Association, 1962).

6. "Standards for Counselor Education in the Preparation of Secondary School Counselors," *Personnel and Guidance Journal*, 42:535–543 (January, 1964).

cation and Supervisions at its 1967 convention in Dallas. A "revised revised" set of standards was approved by the membership in 1974.

These organizational activities of the 1960's have continued into the 1970's, but it is extremely doubtful if they have had much impact on the level of humanness and professional competence of the person known as a counselor. "Standards" might always be somewhat suspect, since they are based on opinion, rather than the evidence of empirical research. The general way to develop a "standard" is to have scores of committees contribute opinions, and the majority opinion has eventually appeared as a "standard." This might be considered as the democratic approach to research, and it is somewhat akin to having the teacher determine the "right" answer by having the students vote on what they consider to be the "right" one. The "opinion" procedure would be questionable even though it were the opinion of those individuals in the country who have shown over the years that they have a high level of understanding in the field of counseling and counselor education. This, however, has been anything but the case, so that the second major flaw is that the opinions are not even valid as expert opinion. The U.S. Office of Education lists hundreds of institutions as having programs of counselor education, and this is to be expected, since the way one gets listed is to say that one has a program of counselor education! Nor does one have to have too much involvement in counseling and counselor education in order to become a member of the Association for Counselor Education and Supervision. Thus an opinion from one who has little or no involvement in counseling and counselor education becomes just as valid in determining a "standard" as does the opinion of one who has spent his life in the field.

Thus the standards, whatever they might be, might be questioned from a research point of view, and a perusal of them tends to buttress the fact that they represent opinion rather than evidence. It is not so much that there is anything questionable about the standards as such, but it is rather that the standards do not get at what would appear to be the crucial elements of a counselor education program. Thus it could well be that two programs could be rated as acceptable on the basis of the standards, but one would prove to be quite ineffective, the other quite effective. Much stress is placed on the cognitive aspects of the program, and much of it reads somewhat like a program for the education of chemists. The standard referring to self-understanding and self-evaluation of the student counselor is dealt with rather casually, the statement being that "opportunities ... are provided." More important would be the extent to which the opportunities were used, and what was the result of their use. After all, the provision of a gymnasium in a school is not necessarily any indication of top physical condition among the students! The practicum experience, of necessity, is described in a cognitive sense, and a top-ranked practicum, according to the standards, could very easily prove to be totally meaningless to a group of students. In a similar manner, the qualifications of the "well-qualified" staff are described in the usual terms of degrees and experience.

Thus, on the whole, the certification of professional competence of counselors, at both the state and the professional level, leaves much to be desired. Currently, counselors can be "certified" by the state, and blessed by their professional organization, and still be highly incompetent in the matter of professional skills and knowledge and understanding. Even worse, however, is the fact that the dedication of many to the cause of human and social welfare may be questioned, and the humanness of their person may even be doubted! The education of the counselor will be looked at in more detail in the next section.

THE INVOLVEMENT OF THE FEDERAL GOVERNMENT

Federal involvement in public education has, of course, been an issue for many decades, but it was only in the 1960's that it became an issue for counselor education. No matter what one may say, federal money *does* represent some degree of federal control, and with the passage of the National Defense Education Act in 1958, counselor education became involved in the ethical issue of federal money and federal control. In the ten years that followed, tens of millions of dollars were expended on NDEA Guidance Institutes and NDEA Fellowships, and the writing of proposals became a required skill of at least one member of every department of counselor education! There is little question that this vast expenditure of public funds increased the number of counselors in schools, but whether it increased the quality of counselors, and the quality of the education in the schools where they worked, is another question.

As the expenditure of funds increased, so did the level of bureaucratic control, and the so-called quality of a program became increasingly dependent on the whims of a few federal officials, most of whom had little experience or knowledge of counseling and counseling programs. Indicative of this was the fact that the professional qualification of the head of the Division of Educational Personnel Training was a Ph.D. in mathematics!

With the change of administration in 1968 the money spigot was turned off, and by the mid-1970's the flow of money was reduced to a trickle. This too, no doubt, will change, but it is unlikely that the easy money of 1958 to 1968 will be repeated in the forseeable future. In looking back, it would probably be quite safe to say that the proposals for counselor education that had been funded by the U.S. office hardly satisfied a criterion of counselor education effectiveness based on empirical evidence. In a survey of nine of the full year proposals that were funded for the year 1967–68, one may note many similarities. In all, the objectives were broad and human and highly desirable and bookish, but there is serious question as to the extent to which the program was built around the objectives, as contrasted with the objectives being fitted to the program. The programs that were offered were primarily cognitive in nature, with the stress on knowledge and knowing. The offering was overwhelmingly via courses, for which semester hours of credit were offered, and in which, we can assume, the student had the usual experience of being evaluated and judged on the basis of someone else's version of what he knew. The major stress was on the development of knowledge in the broad area of the social sciences, it was to a lesser degree on knowledge about the client, and it was to a still lesser degree on knowledge about the counselor. In only two institutes was there a planned no-credit experience of self-understanding and self-appraisal. There was minimal evidence of any belief in the concept that the major resource that the counselor brings to counseling is himself, at least in the sense that minimal stress was placed on the self-development and self-understanding of the counselor. The most important ingredient in any program—the staff—remained generally little more than unknown names to the evaluators. We knew little more than that most of the staff had doctoral degrees and a few years of experience in counseling or teaching, which may mean much, or little. Thus, the U.S. Office, in a way, played a game of blindman's buff with the professional education of schools' counselors, as well as with the American taxpayer's dollar. Many of the proposals which were funded might have provided an effective experience in counselor education, but the odds are that many which were not funded might have provided an even more effective experience. On the whole, the proposals which were funded did not appear to be too different from, or any more effective than, most standard counselor education programs in many institutions around the country.

It is of interest, and some concern, to note the recommendations that were made by the Special Subcommittee on Education of the House of Representatives after its investigation of the Division of Educational Personnel Training. The recommendations, three in number, said little or nothing, and no statement was made regarding the control and direction of counselor education programs by the Division of Educational Personnel Training. From this we may reasonably enough assume that the committee approved of the degree of control and direction of a professional program by the federal government.

The American Personnel and Guidance Association, too, would appear to have been more concerned with the lack of federal funding (in the quotation below, called "diminishing interest") than with the manner in which federal funds were used. An official publication of the association, for example, stated:

> *The American Personnel and Guidance Association and its members have viewed with alarm the diminishing interest, organization and effort of the Office of Education in providing services, information and technical staff for the guidance profession. . . . The Farwell task force is designed to initiate a remedy for the general lack of leadership exerted by the Office of Education.*[7]

It might be that if the American Personnel and Guidance Association had shown better leadership on questions dealing with the use of federal funds, they would have a better argument for increases now in federal funding. The current political activities of APGA, however, would tend to imply that the organization still believes that increases in federal funds automatically mean increased quality of counselors and counselor education. The fallacy of this assumption has surely been proved in the 1960's, and organizational involvement in answering the question "What is a quality program?" should precede political action for more money.

THE QUESTION OF CHANGE[8]

There would be little argument that the major function of the counselor is to help the client to change in some way. The change may, of course, be very minor, but the very fact that the client comes to the counselor means that he is saying, "I want to know something, or do something, or in some way have something happen to me so that I will be not quite the way I am now." It may be a student simply asking about information on several colleges or it may be an individ-

---

7. *Guidepost* (Washington, D.C.: American Personnel and Guidance Association), 11:2-3 (February, 1969).
8. See Dugald S. Arbuckle, "Values, Ethics and Religion in Counseling," *National Catholic Guidance Conference Journal*, 13:5-17 (Fall, 1968).

ual caught on drugs, seeing nothing ahead but the choice of slow destruction by drugs or more immediate death by suicide. In both cases, the counselor would be involved with the client in the process of change—and both would pose an ethical dilemma, a very minor one in the first case, a major one in the second case. What are some of the facts of this dilemma of change?

1. Tremendous as our powers of change may be today, those who are involved in operant conditioning assure us that they are nothing compared with what lies just around the corner. Some see the counselor of the future as a behavioral engineer, and a rather routine problem brought to the counselor might be the predetermination of the sex of a planned child. Somewhat more complicated, but quite within the realm of the reality of the not too distant future, would be the request for counseling in the determination of whether or not a planned child will be a genius or a person of low-level intelligence or, possibly, one who will be able to withstand unusual environmental stresses and strains. At such a stage, of course, sexual involvement for the purpose of reproduction would be distinctly old-fashioned, and too risky, since one would not know in advance what kind of child was going to be born. Even now scientists can put together a simple form of deoxyribonucleic acid (DNA), the bodily form of every organism on earth, with full biological power. The goal ahead is to rewrite the genetic code, and thus redesign the bodily form of organisms. Man might then take direct command of the evolution of his own body, right from the very creation of life itself.

Thus the power of the control and direction and manipulation of one human by another is, without doubt, going to increase tremendously in the very near future, and Vance puts it modestly when she says, "Certainly man's understanding of technique in the behavioral sciences far surpasses his understanding and commitment to certain goals."[9] If this poses somewhat of an ethical dilemma now, it will soon pose the question of the very survival of the human race, as individual human beings, with individual rights and individual integrity. Even today we all know some "counselors" who are so fascinated by the technology that their mode of operation differs very little from that of the experimental psychologist in his rat laboratory. The person of the creature being experimented with is of no particular concern; the fascination of the counselor lies in his ability to change and modify the "other" almost as he wishes. Tillich was certainly correct, at least for some counselors, when he said that "technique has become not merely a means to an end, but an end in itself."[10]

9. Barbara Vance, "The Counselor—An Agent of What Change," *Personnel and Guidance Journal*, 45:1012–1016 (June, 1967).
10. Paul Tillich, report of a speech given at M.I.T., in *Time*, April 21, 1961, p. 57.

May felt this pressure when, in talking about existentialism, he said that "it seemed to many observers to be ineffectual against the onmoving lava of conformism, collectivism, and the robot man."[11] But he also voiced the feeling and the faith of the existentialist, as well as those who would distinguish individual man from a random collection of behaviors, when he added, "No matter how great the forces victimizing the human being, man has the capacity to know that he is being victimized, and thus to influence in some way how he will relate to his fate. There is never lost that kernel of the power to take some stand, to make some decision, no matter how minute." But the hard fact of life, neither moral nor immoral, is that the power to change grows daily. This reality must be faced by the counselor, and he must raise for himself the question of where he stands, today and tomorrow, rather than looking wistfully backward at a yesterday that is gone.

2. As the power to change grows, the more serious becomes the simple question, "Who determines who will be changed, and what will be the direction of the change, for what purpose?" Our Western civilization has been generally based on the supremacy of man over the state, and this shows in the political concept that the government is our voice, not our master, and when it no longer is our voice, then we change it. While most Americans would still hold to this concept in theory, its practice has often been, at best, rather halfhearted. Counselors, as any student could tell, show a wide variance in their practice of the concept of "individual rights," especially the rights of the young as contrasted with the old. Van Kaam, for example, is very much on the side of the individual when he says that

> when I am acting as an authentic counselor I want the unique personality, the freedom, the spontaneous initiative of my counselee; I want him to grow in his own independent being. . . . Therapeutic care does not want to force, to push, to impose, to seduce. What is more, as soon as the counselor tries to overpower the counselee, if only by suggestion, his activity is no longer therapeutic care.[12]

Williamson, however, shows some doubts about the capacities of the individual when he says, ". . . does he have the right to become less than he could become . . . unfortunately . . . many of us are inclined to let the individual make his own choice in a simplistic

11. Rollo May, *Existential Psychology* (New York: Random House, 1961), pp. 41–42.
12. Adrian van Kaam, "An Existential View of Psychotherapy," in Dugald S. Arbuckle (ed.), *Counseling and Psychotherapy: An Overview* (New York: McGraw-Hill, 1967), p. 36.

misunderstanding of freedom within democracy."[13] Moser seems to place a somewhat questionable capacity on the shoulders of the clergyman, while giving no credit to the client, when he says, "Since God is able to direct the clergyman in other areas, the same power will abide in advice giving."[14] This attitude is apparently ecumenical, since Saalfield, a priest, reflects somewhat similar feelings when he says, "The Catholic counselor should ask the pupil 'How often do you go to Mass and confession?' Catholic counselors must create right attitudes."[15] Many students in schools and colleges will attest to the wide divergence between the supposed acceptance of the theory of individual rights, and the actual practice of this belief. It is unfortunate that counselors are among those who show a high level of distrust of the capacity of the young, or for that matter, of anyone other than themselves, to determine the direction that one might go.

The feeling that "I know better than you what is the best direction for you" is all too common when the young are with the old, when parents are with their children, when teachers are with students, and even, alas, when counselors are with clients. Shoben points to the major flaw in this attitude when he says that "it is equally a mistake to assume that predictive success or the power of behavioral control somehow reveals the normative ends toward which conduct may properly be directed."[16] Van Kaam is speaking to the same issue, when in talking about the teacher, he says that "he should create the ideal conditions in which the child himself can awaken to these values; and the most ideal condition for this awakening of a spontaneous insight and estimation is not to force such ideals upon him. In that case we prepare him only for hypocrisy or an uncreative mechanized life or even neurosis."[17]

But man in a sense is conditioned not to believe in himself, he is conditioned away from himself. He learns all too frequently, from his parents, his teachers, his clergymen, how not to become the authentic person, how never to experience the ecstatic thrill that comes only to those who are free—free to live and free to die, but never to be chained. The respect that one has for his freedom and his

13. E. G. Williamson, "Youth's Dilemma: To Be or to Become," *Personnel and Guidance Journal*, 46:173–177 (October, 1967).

14. Leslie E. Moser, *Counseling: A Modern Emphasis in Religion* (Englewood Cliffs, N.J.: Prentice-Hall, 1962), p. 116.

15. L. J. Saalfield, *Guidance and Counseling in Catholic Schools* (Chicago: Loyola University, 1958), p. 80.

16. Edward J. Shoben, "Personal Worth in Education and Counseling" in John D. Krumboltz (ed.), *Revolution in Counseling* (Boston: Houghton Mifflin, 1966), p. 63.

17. Adrian van Kaam, *The Art of Existential Counseling* (Wilkes-Barre, Pa.: Dimension Books, 1966), p. 70.

rights is usually reflected in the respect that he shows for the rights and the freedoms of others. The autocrat is always the slave, since his continuing lack of trust in others is merely a reflection of his lack of trust in self.

The counselor too, of course, is a conditioned product of his society, but the counselor should be different. He should be the one who has somehow intervened, with help or on his own, and cut into the bland and painless process that is manipulating and modifying and molding him into a faceless image. He is the one who somewhere has said, "Wait. What is this? Must I do this? Must I become this person? Why?" He has assumed control of his own destiny, and he has accepted responsibility for the direction he might go. He is a free man, and he expects neither a kindly God nor a kindly nature to lead him by the hand, and accept responsibility for his life and living. Nor is he fearful of what a vengeful God or a vengeful nature might do to him. He can accept the risks of living the free life of the free man.

As a free person, the counselor cannot ignore the causes of human misery that may lie all around him. The counselor in an inhuman school does little to help when, by his human actions, he helps to perpetuate the system that is in the process of destroying the children. The counselor, as a professionally competent and responsible human being, cannot remain in an office, helping a few children, while that which creates the human problems goes on unabated. The counselor cannot accept as "reality" the fact that a woman who must farm out her seven children will continue to have more; the fact that girls in their early teens become mothers because religious sensitivity might be offended if one talked about contraception; the fact that both the curriculum and the staff show a distinct prejudice toward minority groups and women; the fact that a school committee consists of a group of unprincipled political hacks; the fact that some teachers are simply incompetent and care nothing about the welfare of children; the fact that some parents are capable only of breeding, not of parenthood; the fact that the school does not serve the needs of the children in the community; the fact that the school is an oppressive arm of an oppressive system. In many schools and many communities these facts are reality, but the responsible counselor does not accept them as some inevitable unchanging fact. It is both the professional and human responsibility of the counselor to become a factor in changing these causes of human distress. The school counselor *is not* the arm of the system, but rather the voice of children, many of whom are being destroyed in the name of education.

289

COUNSELING WITH MEMBERS OF MINORITY GROUPS[18]

The term "minority groups" has almost ceased to have any meaning, since it can mean anything anyone wants it to mean. Even people who represent a majority of the human population, namely, women, are often referred to as oppressed members of a minority group! In many ways, a rational discussion of these words has almost become taboo, and it is astonishing how some people tread as delicately in this area as if they were walking on eggshells!

Being a member of a minority group does not necessarily mean that one must thereby feel inferior to members of the majority group. Certainly the European colonizers who overran most of the world in the past few centuries were members of a minority among those they conquered—in race, religion and nationality. But they did not feel inferior. Indeed, they felt very superior, and the vast majority of the people were relegated, until very recently, to an almost subhuman status. True, the Europeans had the power, but even when they were captured and killed, they had no doubt in their minds that they were being killed by savages who were their inferiors. The point here, of course, is that it is a state of mind that relates "minority" to "inferiority." Rationally, it would seem that one should be more likely to have twinges of superiority instead of inferiority if a person has done rather well in a culture in which he is a member of a minority group. "Black is beautiful" does indeed make good sense as long as it means that "I, who happen to be black because my parents were black, am beautiful." It makes no sense at all, however, if what it means is that "I am beautiful *because* I am black." Beauty is an inner product of the individual; the color of one's skin is not. A black person or a white person *can* be beautiful; a man or a woman *can* be beautiful; one who is young or one who is old *can* be beautiful; a Russian or an Italian or a Ghandian or an American *can* be beautiful; a Chicano or an Indian or an Anglo *can* be beautiful. But none of these people are beautiful simply because they can be described by any of these terms.

Another difficulty that we have is a semantic one. The word "disadvantaged," for example, has usually been considered to be almost synonymous with "minority," and it has become a cultural assumption that the "disadvantaged minority" are "inferior." It would not, I think, be too harsh to say that many teachers and many counselors unfortunately accept this totally inaccurate assumption. A term that has appeared fairly recently in the literatue is "culturally

18. Dugald S. Arbuckle, "Counseling with Members of Minority Groups," *Counseling and Values*, 16:239–247 (Summer, 1972). Copyright 1972 by the American Personnel and Guidance Association.

distinct," and, in some ways, this is more accurate, since an individual member of a minority group may be more distinct than disadvantaged. Senator Brooke is distinct, as the only senator with a black skin, but he is certainly less disadvantaged than most white men. Mrs. Harris, the wife of Senator Harris, is distinct with her Indian heritage, but she, too, is less disadvantaged than most American women.

In a civilized society, there should be no disadvantage to being a member of a minority group, but unfortunately our current level of human development is such that we have not yet achieved this goal. There is probably no more crucial task for the school counselor than to help those young people who happen to be members of minority groups to come to *believe,* in their guts, as well as understand in their heads, that the fact that they have to overcome certain real obstacles is in no way related to personal inferiority. The most dreadful part of bigotry is not the actual practice of it, but the fact that the victim comes eventually to believe that he actually is what the bigoted ones say he is. When a person can, with some degree of accuracy, say to himself that the extent to which he is disadvantaged derives from the culture that surrounds him rather than from his own personal inadequacy, then his perspective of himself will be much different. He may then come to feel less pressed to do what the majority culture implies he should do and be the way it implies he should be. And for this expression of individuality, of course, he will be willing to pay a price.

There is nothing negative, per se, about being different from most of those around me, unless, of course, the difference causes real and immediate difficulties. If my intellect is at the moron state, or if I have a physical disability that means that I cannot run, then I do have real immediate problems. In the vast majority of cases, however, the difference becomes a problem because we are conditioned to believe that it has negative connotations. There are many agents of this conditioning, and certainly the school is one of them. The individuals who are part of this conditioning are usually either members of the majority group who have accepted the assumption of the inferiority of anyone who belongs to the minority group, or members of the minority group who have accepted the assumption of their own inferiority. In both cases, the young people who are being conditioned come out of their school experience with a worse perception of their self than when they entered it.

Desegregation of bodies in schools does little if nothing happens to the minds and the hearts of the individuals who work with the children, and the frustrating reality is that the minds and hearts of people do not change quickly. Possibly minds change faster than hearts, and quite frequently members of majority groups will vote for legislation which they actually disapprove of and will then try, subtly or openly, to subvert the very legislation for which they voted. There is probably no better indication of a healthy and civilized society than one in which there is no difference between the rights and privileges of *all* people, regardless of whether they represent the minority or the majority. But unfortunately, many human beings are too weak to accept a concept of human equality, and they find an unhappy kind of comfort in feeling either superior or inferior to some other group of fellow humans. Most organized religions tend to preach that "we are all God's children" out of one side of their mouths, but at the same time they make it fairly clear that *we* are the special ones, a cut above our brothers and sisters! This has been, over the centuries, one of the most attractive features of organized religion, and in a way it has been a dreadful indication of the power of indoctrination over the mind. One might easily come to despair about the importance of reason when a few million Americans, representing a fundamentalist religious group, can actually believe, without any shadow of a doubt, that they, and they alone, will eventually arrive at the promised land. They will probably need counseling assistance when they discover, if they get to where they expect to get to, that others, not of the true faith, are already there!

Let me now discuss what I would consider to be some of the issues related to the counselor and his *professional* involvement with individuals who are members of minority groups.

1. It is clear, of course, that the counselor, as a member of the human species, carries with him into the counseling relationship his own values, and a major factor affecting one's values is whether or not, over the years, one has been a member of a majority or a minority group. It should be stressed, however, that it is only one of many factors, and one cannot say that *all* black clients will react in one way and *all* white clients in another way. Nor can one say that all poor black Catholic female clients will react in one way and all poor white Catholic female clients will react in another way. On the other hand, the greater the differences resulting from the variables, the more likely it is that the clients and counselors will carry with them different values. It would be fair assumption that the values of a poor black Catholic female are somewhat different than those of a rich white Jewish male! It is also reasonable to assume that a counselor education program should be very much interested in these differences in values, since one of these people may be a counselor and the other may be a client. There is general agreement that the person of the counselor is of crucial importance in the counseling relationship, and if the values of the counselor, rather than enhancing the counsel-

ing relationship, affect it in a negative way, then they should be questioned. Thus, the question is not so much whether the counselor is black or white, Chicano or Indian, poor or rich, male or female, Jew or Christian, but rather what are the values this person has learned as a member of any of these groups. If the white person has learned that black people should be treated as unworthy, and if the black person has learned that the white person is to be despised; if the Jew has learned that the Christian is dull and lazy and not trustworthy and if the Christian has learned that the Jew is an aggressive money-grabber; if the female has learned that men are chauvinists who should be castrated, and if the male has learned that the female is a good body without a head; if the well-off person has learned that the poor are poor because they are lazy, shiftless bums, and if the poor person has learned that the only reason he is poor is because of the oppression of the cruel rich person—then, indeed, the counselor education program has a job to do!

I have painted a somewhat dismal picture here, and, hopefully, most students in counselor education could hardly be described as above. Nonetheless, counselors do carry their values into the counseling relationship, and there *are* values which may well make the counselor a dangerous, rather than an ineffective, person. If the behavior and attitudes of a student counselor clearly imply rejection of others, or of self, or the assumption of inferiority or superiority of others, or of self, because of race or sex or religion or age, then the student counselor must be helped to overcome this personal handicap. We should face the fact that he or she should probably be removed from the program if nothing can be done about this behavior and attitude. This may seem harsh, but the hard fact is that student counselors are admitted to and graduated from most programs on the basis of evidence of intellectual capacity. Very few student counselors are removed from programs because their values are such that they should not be involved in a counseling relationship with another person. And it is begging the issue to say that this is a very delicate matter. It *is* a very delicate matter, but the counseling relationship is a very delicate matter too, and the future of another human being may be directly related to the values of the person known as the counselor. The staff and the students of Counselor Education Departments must accept this evaluative responsibility, and it is not enough to graduate as counselors individuals about whom we can say no more than that they are intellectually competent.

2. Any person who is a member of a minority group in a one-man-one-vote culture has had, and will likely continue to have, for the forseeable future, special kinds of problems which are not those of the members of the majority group. This would not apply, of

course, in an autocracy in which the power was in the hands of members of the minority. For many centuries white people had almost total power in many parts of the world in which they represented a very small minority of the total population. But in those societies in which there is some degree of individual freedom, the members of the majority usually expect the members of the minority to do things the majority way. In fact, many Americans define "democracy" as the rule of the majority over the minority. The 203 million people who live in America are not likely to adopt the ways of the some 22 million black Americans, or 5 million Chicanos or 1½ million Puerto Ricans, or fewer than 1 million Indians.

I would think a more humane definition of "democracy" would be the protection of the individual rights of the minority, which does not have the power, by the majority, which does have the power. I suppose the more civilized a society, the more likely it is that this latter situation would prevail, but human prejudice is a human rather than an American invention. The Asian minority in Kenya, the Biafran minority in Nigeria, the Bengalese minority in Pakistan, the Catholic minority in Northern Ireland, the Protestant minority in Spain, the Chicano minority in the United States—these are but a few of the hundreds and thousands of minority groups around the world who suffer, in various ways, because they have committed the sin of being minority groups.

Members of a minority group are often put in a cruel dilemma in that the more they stress their differences, which they must do in order to survive as a minority group, the more likely it is that they will be ostracized or penalized by the members of a majority group. It is difficult in any society to become accepted by members of a majority group if one insists on retaining patterns of behavior and living which make one obviously different from the majority. Many people still see "difference" as threatening. There is no better example of this than the astonishing degree of resentment and anger that many adults feel toward long-haired youths, even though many of these adults are Christians whose Saviour not only was a long-haired youth, but also wore sandals and a robe and apparently spent a lot of time meditating in the countryside instead of working hard helping his father!

The stress on differences, of course, is for many people the very essence of self-identification. True, it is a neurotic pattern, and it is a weak individual who sees himself as being somebody only because he is a he instead of a she, white instead of black, Catholic instead of Jew, American instead of Italian. All of these, after all, were his before he was born, and the healthy personality is one who takes pride in self in the answer to the question, "Who am I, in the sense of what I have done with my life and my living?" The other characteristics are simply accidents of birth. Nonetheless, this is the way many people are, and often it is more important for the member of a minority group to feel that "I am different" than it is for the member of the majority group to feel that he is different.

The counselor is faced with a real problem on this issue. Should he help the young member of a minority group to have pride in his identity, and become acceptant of the likelihood of varying degrees of rejection and outright hostility from members of the majority group? Or should he help him to minimize the importance of many of the things which make him "different," and thus increase the likelihood of his becoming accepted by members of the majority group but rejected by members of his own minority group, many of whom will see him as a renegade who has deserted his own people. A counselor who is a member of the minority group, at least by the standard means of identification, may sometimes have an even greater problem of identification, than a counselor who is not a member of a minority group. I know two women who are in my professional field—they are young, they are beautiful, they have doctoral degrees, they are professors, they wear good clothes, they live in expensive apartments—and one is black, the other white. The black woman has no more desire to live in a slum in a city than has the white woman to live in a shack in Appalachia. Yet the black woman is sometimes considered to be a traitor to her race for no reason other than the fact that she lives a rather comfortable life much like that of her white colleague. Hopefully, we may someday achieve a society in which these two women would be looked at by other people, black and white, for who they are and what they have done, and color of skin would be an interesting but otherwise unimportant fact of life.

But this is not yet, and it would seem that the first thing a counselor must do is help the young person to accept the reality that he is a member of a minority group, he is going to stay a member of a minority group, and that pride in self need have nothing to do with being a member of a minority or a majority group. In the long run, he can work to reduce the prejudice that is directed toward him by others, but the far more important thing is that *he* becomes the one who determines what that behavior means *for him*. He may then still be persecuted, but he will never become the victim of the persecution. He may choose to live a more segregated life, and thus live in a mini-culture in which he is not a minority member, and accept the restrictions of such a kind of life. Or he may choose to become a member of the larger culture in which he will continue to represent a minority and face different kinds of restrictions, even though the life he lives will be very much the same as that of his fellows who are members of the majority. Unfortunately, in too many schools in this country, counselors as well as teachers perpetrate the cruel myth that minority and inferiority are synonymous, and there is nothing much the person can do about it, or the equally cruel hoax that being a member of a minority group really doesn't make any difference, and hard work will produce the same results as it will for those children who are members of the majority group.

The counselor may also help the child in becoming more acceptant of the reality that the more an individual stresses his differences from the mainstream of the culture, the more likely it is that he will be rebuffed and rejected by that culture. The black American who insists on being called by an Arabic name and referred to as an Afro-American; the Orthodox Jew who holds rigidly to his dietary code; the Chicano who speaks Spanish on the job where nearly everyone else speaks English; the Indian who arrives late for work because, he says, it is part of his way of life—for all of these acts of accentuating of differences, the individual must be prepared to pay a price. The child should be helped to understand the differences between what is and what should be. While he may work to change the world that is, that, for the time, is the world in which he, and all the rest of us, live. One can either accentuate or deemphasize one's differences and still retain one's identity, but the results of either choice must be clearly understood. It is possible to adjust to the demands of the majority culture without either submitting to them or being destroyed by them.

3. It is crucial, of course, that the counselor, whether he be a member of a minority or a majority group, has achieved a level of self-identity and self-actualization such that he is totally understanding and acceptant of differences in human beings. Indeed, we can hardly believe in individual freedom and talk about the sameness of people at the same time. It is the differences in human beings that make them unique, and these should be valued and respected. Thus the counselor may work in a school where the examples of the differences mentioned above will produce difficulties for the children both in the school and in the community. Over the long run he will work to change these attitudes in the school and the community, but his more immediate counseling function will be to help the child to adjust to the reality of these attitudes, to understand them for what they are, and to develop a positive self-image in spite of them.

The counselor will also be understanding of the irrationality and the hostility that sometimes accompany the expression of differences by members of minority groups. Examples of this irrationality that appear in the literature might be seen in Gardner saying, "A necessary (and possibly sufficient) characteristic of the ideal counselor is to be a feminist,"[19] or Ream saying that "once it was the old who had the wisdom; now it is the young,"[20] or Smith saying that "blackness is a dignity."[21] In a cognitive sense, such statements might be questioned, but in an affective sense they are expressions of the feelings and the values of the person, and the counselor, surely, should be capable of accepting them as such. So too, when the Chicano youth says, "I choose to call myself 'Juan'—want to make something of it?" the counselor should be comfortable enough so that it soon becomes quite clear that he sees no reason whatsoever for making something of it. Nor is he too concerned about the degree of rationality of the statement, in that it was most likely Juan's parents who choose to call him Juan rather than Juan himself!

Understanding is a two-way street, and one of the functions of the counselor is to help the youthful member of a minority group to realize that members of majority groups are individuals too, and minority group members should be as acceptant of the differences of majority group members as they expect them to be of their differences. Often, the valid answer to the question, by a member of a minority group, "Why did you say that?" is not "Because I am a racist" but rather "I didn't know." And there is a big difference. Many white Americans, for example, are never quite sure whether a black American prefers to be referred to as a negro, black, or Afro-American, since each description is preferred by certain black Americans who often become angered, and use the word "racist," when another word is used. Aragon and Ulibarri refer to the Chicano community applauding the appointment by Jack Kennedy of his brother as chief legal adviser, while the WASP community was shocked and dismayed, and they say, "Learn, amigo, learn."[22] Indeed, amigo should learn this cultural attitude of the Chicanos. But the 5 million Chicanos should also learn to be acceptant of the attitudes of the some 198 million non-Chicanos on this issue.

So, too, when Palomares indicates with deep feeling that he is a Chicano, *not* a Spanish-American,[23] he should keep in mind the fact that he may be speaking to an Anglo who has just been called a

19. Joann Gardner, "Sexist Counseling Must Stop," *Personnel and Guidance Journal*, 49:705–714 (May, 1971).
20. Charles Ream, "Youth Culture: Humanity's Last Chance," *Personnel and Guidance Journal*, 49:699–704 (May, 1971).
21. Paul M. Smith, "Black Activity for Liberation Not Guidance," *Personnel and Guidance Journal* 49:721–726 (May, 1971).
22. John A. Aragon and Sabias R. Ulibarri, "Learn, Amigo, Learn," *Personnel and Guidance Journal*, 50:87–89 (October, 1971).
23. Uvaldo H. Palomares, "Nuestros Sentimientos Son Iguales, la Diferencia es en la Experiencia," *Personnel and Guidance Journal*, 49:721–726 (October, 1971).

racist because he did not refer to an American with a black skin as an Afro-American! The very deep feelings that Palomares indicates he has about his *chicanismo* are not necessarily the feelings of all five million Chicanos, and any counselor who would assume this is illustrating the worst kind of ignorance. The middle-class black American who lives in suburbia is as resistant to low-income housing that will bring in poor, mostly black families as are his white fellow suburbanites. A human being cannot be defined by the name of the culture of which he is a part.

4. A multiplicity of cultures make up America, and it is naive to assume that every American is going to have a deep understanding and appreciation of all of these cultures. The counselor, however, is a professional, and part of his professional qualifications should be a broad understanding of the major cultures that make up America, and a very deep understanding and appreciation of that particular culture which may be predominant where he lives and works. The Chicano who works as a counselor in a certain part of Boston should make it his business to understand the black community, the Anglo who works in a certain community in California should know the Chicanos, and the black American who works in Arizona should be aware that there is an Indian culture which differs from his.

Even here, however, a cognitive understanding of a culture is difficult enough, and a cognitive understanding of the meaning of that culture to a particular human being who happens to be a member of it is still more difficult. But the crucial factor, really, is the affective understanding and acceptance, by the counselor, of the different values and ways of life and living that are held by the client. Clients are quick to forgive ignorance—if it is not overdone—when they know that the heart of the counselor is in the right place. When I read the literature, and hear the voices of children and youth who are members of minority groups talking about counselors, all they appear to be asking is that people who are called counselors finally start functioning as professional counselors. They are saying, "Listen to us—understand us—respect us—do not try to change us to your ways, but help us to develop our own ways—help us to have pride in self—be someone who appreciates differences in people rather than being frightened by them—if you do not know certain things about us, tell us, and we will help you learn—be warm, be human, be our brother or our sister—let us decide what is important in our lives, and help us to achieve these important things, but do not tell us—you accept our values, and we may become more open to yours—love us, and feel in your heart that each one of us, just as we are, is a very important person—be a real counselor."

And the fact that tens of thousands of children and youth

must speak in this way, as if they were asking for some special favor, is an indictment of counselors and counseling. It very strongly implies that there are many men and women who are counselors who are not fit to be counselors. All that is being asked is that we be knowledgeable, understanding, and compassionate human beings. If most of us who are counselors cannot be like this, then the demise of the counseling profession is overdue.

CONFIDENTIALITY[24]

Many counselors would agree that the confidentiality of the counseling relationship is the crucial factor without which counseling would be impossible. There are a number of areas in which this confidentiality becomes an issue:

1. Information about the client, and the use of it, is probably the major area where the confidentiality of the counselor is challenged. While counselors might differ with each other about the kind of information which they might need, and the use to which they would put this information, most would likely agree that as long as this is within the context of the counseling relationship, the only purpose of the information is to help the client in his growth and his development and his actualization. If some of this information goes beyond the limits of the counseling relationships, however, it may obviously be quite damaging, and I have the uneasy feeling that a good deal of information that has been gathered as a part of the counseling relationship is transmitted to admissions or employment officers, who then use it as the reason for their rejection of the student. A counselor might talk to a hospital psychiatrist about the latent homosexuality of one of his high school clients, and certainly no harm or damage would be done to the client, but the same information transmitted to an employment or admissions officer might well blight the student for the rest of his life. A counselor might talk to a doctor about his quandary in trying to help a student who has been using marijuana, but the results would be quite different if he passed this information on to an employment or admissions officer. A counselor might be helping a client to struggle through his concern over a continued record of cheating over a period of time, but this same information conveyed to an employment or admissions officer, as part of the student's school record, would be disastrous.

24. Dugald S. Arbuckle, "Counselors, Admission Officers, and Information," *School Counselor,* 3:164–170 (January, 1969). Copyright 1969 by the American Personnel and Guidance Association.

Thus, it would appear to me that there is a very real question concerning the extent to which school counselors are guilty of an immoral and unethical breach of confidentiality in the transmission of information about students who have been clients, to employment and admissions officers.

The hub of the question, of course, is what information is considered to be "confidential," and just what is meant by the term "confidential." Heayn and Jacobs refer to four levels of openness, with Level 1 being the most open and Level 4 being the most confidential. In Level 3 they include such "matters of judgment" as student descriptions, staff recommendations, psychological reports, psychiatric evaluations, social service reports, medical information, legal information, and agency reports.[25] If to this latter level we were to add the counselor's own reports (if the counselor believed in the writing of such reports), then could we not say that this information, which was for the professional use of the counselor, came under the description of "highly confidential"? As such, it would not be available to employment or admissions officers, only to those who might be regarded as the counselor's professional colleagues, involved in the counseling process. Even here, of course, there would be safeguards and restrictions, and certainly information given to the counselor directly by the client should be revealed to another professional colleague only with the knowledge and approval of the client.

The information that would be given to employment and admissions officers might be somewhat like that in Level 3 above, but this would be between the school administration and the teachers, and those seeking the information. This would be considered to be an administrative function, and teachers and administrators are not being incongruent in accepting a function which is evaluative and judgmental of students, since this is part of their professional task. Even here, of course, one might hope that descriptions of students would be objective rather than subjective, but the collection and distribution of such information would be the business of the school administration. One of the sources of information about the student would likely be the teacher, who should surely be capable of writing student descriptions if such are necessary. The counselor simply would not be considered to be one from whom the administration could get information about the personality characteristics of the student, to be passed on to others.

Many school counselors spend much of their time accumulating information, some of it personal, some of it gathered during

---

25. Maurice H. Heayn and Howard L. Jacobs, "Safeguarding Student Records," *Personnel and Guidance Journal,* 46:63–67 (September, 1967).

counseling sessions, some of it very judgmental. This information is passed on to employment and admissions officers, and my impression is that the majority of counselors who are doing this are doing so quite willingly, and do not feel under any particular duress. There are exceptions to this, of course, one such being a group of eight counselors (Craig, Cravens, Handly, McCormick, Pounds, Schere, Wells and Winans in Kirkwood High School, in Kirkwood, Missouri). They stated: "Undue expectations are being placed on secondary guidance counselors in the college admission process. We wish to reflect our serious doubts upon the type of information requested by numerous colleges and universities in their recommendation forms." They went on to say: "Professional counselors are placed in an unethical position when required to officially recommend that a specific student and a specific college are compatible."[26]

Unfortunately, seven years later, in the summer of 1974, their problem still existed. These counselors had received little support from their colleagues in neighboring schools, many of whom were apparently quite happy to participate in this kind of activity. Nor did they receive much in the way of support from local and state professional organizations.

Such comments about students, which might be considered to be highly questionable coming from any source, are still being supplied by counselors to employment and admissions officers. I saw one counselor's report, which is available for admissions officers, which describes a girl as being "very much of the hippie type." In another school, another counselor's report, in describing a boy, uses the word "very effeminate" several times. These descriptions, as is often the case, may describe the writer of the report better than they do the person who is supposedly being described, but it is surely obvious that such comments will hardly be helpful to the student when he is applying for a job or trying to get into a college. We may note that APGA stresses that the "major responsibility (of the counselor) is to assist individuals through the counseling relationship" and that "he works with other individuals in the employment environment . . . *for the benefit* of the counselee." Also, they state that "he should not be expected to perform tasks inconsistent with his professional role as a counselor." ASCA stresses that the counselor should "assist *each* pupil," as his major function, but also, it adds, "assist parents" and "assist other members of the staff." When anyone in the school makes a statement which may be prejudicial to the future of a student, then there should at least be no question about

26. Craig, et al., "Reader Reflections," *School Counselor,* 15:148–150 (November, 1967).

its accuracy and its objectivity, but it is surely not within the realm of the professional function of the counselor to make such a statement.

Entirely apart from the ethical aspects of such statements, the counselor leaves himself legally vulnerable. A 1968 court case involving Bates College in Maine, for example, ruled that a counselor's recommendations and other school records are not privileged information. The case involved the parents of an applicant from Connecticut who wished to see a copy of the transcript of the applicant's high school record which they thought contained some misinformation as well as some derogatory remarks by a counselor. Bates College refused to reveal this information and subsequently their records were subpoenaed. After a number of hearings with the State of Maine Superior Justice, the judge ruled against Bates College on the grounds that the transcript, recommendations, etc., were not privileged information.

The following principles of operation, on this question of the using of information, would appear to be feasible, and they should present no insurmountable obstacles.

(a) The school should accept the responsibility for maintaining a close relationship with admissions and employment officers, and it should contribute *certain* information to these individuals. This should be the semipublic kind of information that is to be found in school records regarding the student's academic ability, his intellectual capacities, and the more subjective reaction of teachers or administrators who may be familiar with him. The primary purpose of the university is the intellectual development of the student, and it is highly questionable to refuse a student admission because of some real or fancied moral lack, or to say that one must have a certain level of emotional stability before one is admitted.

(b) The gathering of this information should be a school administrative responsibility—grades, intellectual and academic test scores, and teacher's or administrator's recommendations. Such information would logically be collected by a vice-principal or by a placement officer, if such a position existed. Counselors might periodically use such information to help students, but any contacts from colleges and universities would be with the school administration, not with individual school counselors. Students should clearly understand just what information is available to potential employers, college admissions officers, and others who might have a legitimate use for it.

(c) The personal information the counselor receives from clients, as a part of the counseling relationship, *must* be kept confidential. If it isn't, he won't receive very much, and if any counselor in almost any high school is not intimately acquainted with various activities that are going on, it is likely to be so not because little is happening, but because the students feel that the counselor can't be trusted with certain information. Students who are in schools where the counselor is the major determiner of whether or not they get into a college or get a job have made it clear to me that the information they give to the counselor is carefully guarded, and sometimes downright false.

Nor can a counselor ethically say, "Well, I give good information about students but I never give bad information," since if he does give information he accepts an ethical responsibility for the validity of the information he conveys. He either gives no information about the individual client, or he gives out information which may be either helpful or damaging to the client. If a school guidance director asked my opinion about one of the counselor-education graduates, I would give my honest opinion, because this is the kind of relationship I have accepted with the student and he knows it and I know it. He knows, as well as I, that I have an ethical responsibility in my relationship with the employer, as I would with an admissions officer in a graduate school. With a person whom I have had as a client, however, I have no information to convey, because I do not see this as my accepted professional responsibility.

This does not mean, of course, that the counselor goes around with sealed lips, totally alienating everyone; nor does it mean that the counselor should not sometimes take overt action to do something about that which is causing stress and trouble for students. A counselor can do something about an impossible curriculum or an impossible teacher without revealing individual confidences, just as he can do something about student behavior which is damaging to certain students. He *is* a part of the school system, but he *is not* an administrator or a teacher, with the authority and the particular responsibilities of the administrator and the teacher.

(d) The counselor will likely have his own personal records, hopefully kept to a minimum, and the information here should be confidential in fact as well as in theory. The purpose of this information is very simple—it is to help the counselor to be more effective in his relationships with his client, and the client should surely have the right to feel secure in his knowledge that this is as far as this information goes. Such information should periodically be destroyed, and a good rule of thumb for any counselor is that if one has information that might in the future be damaging to a client, then get rid of it.

2. The question of confidentiality has become more of an issue in recent years with the vastly increased use of audio and video tapes in counselor education. While it is generally agreed that a

303

counselor should not record, or make use of a one-way mirror or a closed-circuit television camera without the approval of the client, Marcuse, some years ago, presented an interesting defense for the use of covert recording:

> *The whole purpose in covert recording, if such be indicated as required by the data, is to enable one to obtain more information, to facilitate rapport, and in the long run (it is hoped) to be of benefit to the individual therapeutically. . . .*
>
> *To reiterate, concentrated sulphuric acid, a scalpel, or morphine may certainly be misused, but this does not constitute an argument against their legitimate use. . . .*
>
> *Whether research is concerned with the nature of the behavior involved in jury decisions or how best to aid a patient requesting therapy, the best method for eliciting such data should be used. Doing this is both proper and needed. Covert recording can respect the patient's confidence and can be constructive.*[27]

It is true, of course, that counselors generally would consider it quite ethical to make covert recordings of children or of psychotic patients. When this is the case, one might well ask how the counselor determines whether or not the individual is old enough not to be a child, or stable enough not to be psychotic, so that he will know when to record covertly! Covert recording carries with it a good deal in the way of invasion of the privacy and rights of the individual, and it would seem that the counselor should not record unless the client gives his approval. It is true, of course, that this means that the counselor will sometimes be unable to record sessions that would have been worthwhile for the education of student counselors, for the education of the counselor himself, and for a greater understanding of the client.

Many mental health clinics still react to taping as if it were some revolutionary new technique, and for some strange reason many senior psychiatrists and psychologists who supervise other students are very shy about allowing students to hear any of their tapes. In many cases, of course, this is no problem, since there are no tapes. In fact, it would appear to me that there still are many psychotherapists who have not yet heard the sound of their own voices, let alone seen what they look like! In many communities, of course, taping is a sensitive issue, but I have a distinct impression that more often than not, counselors are more disturbed by taping than are either clients or members of the community.

27. F. L. Marcuse, in "Comment," *American Psychologist*, 12:278–279 (May, 1957).

If one is to have a recording of a beginning session, however, it must be covert in that the recorder is on when the client comes in. The counselor should, of course, immediately ask permission of the client, and then, even if he is turned down, he at least has a recording of his being turned down! Many counselors question the wisdom of recording a first session, since the client is under stress anyway, and having to begin the conversation by requesting permission to record is possibly not the best way to establish a feeling of rapport.

Some counselors feel that since one never knows which sessions will be particularly good ones for the purposes of research and teaching it is best to record all sessions, even though most of them will be erased. It sometimes happens, too, that in a certain session the counselor is faced with an unusual situation, or some challenging and threatening incident; and it is obviously beneficial if he has the session on tape so that he can study his own reactions.

3. A related question is the extent to which audio and video material and other data on clients should be used for teaching and learning. Most counselors would probably agree that one never uses such material unless it is with a professional group for professional purposes. Most would also agree that when audio and video tapes are used they are always edited, since not only the identity of the client is usually revealed in a counseling session, but a good deal of confidential information about other individuals as well. Most would agree, too, that a tape should not be used if the client has explicitly stated that it is not to be listened to by any person other than the counselor. On the other hand, most counselor educators probably have tapes whose use has been accepted by the client because of his trust in the counselor, but which the counselor will not use because of the possibility of identification. In the long run, the counselor must use his own professional understanding, and his sense of decency, being always aware that the client may have given his consent only because he felt a debt of gratitude to the counselor, and that one is never quite sure how professional all members of a professional group may be.

There would seem to be little question that movies and videotapes of actual counseling sessions should be used only with the consent of the client, and that they should be shown only to those individuals whose professional status is assured. This would raise some question as to whether such movies should be shown to large classes of students taking courses in counseling. Tapes and movies of counseling sessions are for the professional improvement of counselors and student counselors, not for recreation and amusement. Respect for the individual implies respect for the confidentiality of what goes on, an attitude required of every member of a group just as much as it is of the individual counselor.

4. Much the same thing applies in any staff discussion of a "case" in which various records are usually referred to. The counselor discussing the client should be very careful that he does not needlessly disclose material that is confidential, although some people would say that this is greatly affected by the personnel at the staff meeting. If, for example, it happens to be a meeting of the counseling staff with certain deans, teachers, and others to discuss the problems of a certain student, it is likely that what the counseling staff will say will be a good deal more restricted than if the people at the meeting were fewer in number and limited to the counseling staff. Names of individuals other than the client should be brought in only when necessary for an intelligent discussion of the problem, and they should certainly never be brought in for "thrill" or to show off. Respect for the client should also include respect for the individuals who are involved with the client. A counselor once, in a staff meeting, elicited comment by disclosing that one of the girls involved with his client was the daughter of the principal—a disclosure showing respect for neither the principal nor his daughter, since there was no need whatsoever for their being identified.

Sometimes, too, the client or patient being discussed will be present and will be questioned by different members of the staff. I can understand this, but I question the ethics of having a larger group of spectators surrounding the smaller group of staff and patient to observe what is going on. I have been present at such meetings, and too frequently the reaction of some members of the audience shows a high level of lack of sensitivity and total disregard for the client. They react as if they were in a movie. This, to me, is unethical behavior.

At the university level, the presence at staff meetings of graduate assistants and fellows may also raise a problem, in that the client being discussed may well be a colleague of one of the individuals present. When this happens, it is probably just as well that the graduate student affected should leave the discussion, since he is put in an embarrassing, if not unethical, position. Another problem occurs when graduate students have access to records that are of a confidential, or at least a semiconfidential, nature. Such a student always occupies an "in-between" status; the students see him as partially a staff member, whereas the staff people see him as primarily a student, and the poor fellow has to function as both! As much as possible, there should be a clarification of his status—to himself, to the staff, and to the students, but the problem will always remain to some extent.

OTHER ETHICAL ISSUES

Another ethical question concerns the extent to which the counselor should let the counselee know about any overt action that he might take on behalf of the client, if, indeed, he should take any at all without the suggestion, and certainly the agreement, of the client. Should the counselor take steps to change what he knows to be a very negative home situation when he feels that he has a good chance of being successful, even though he also knows that the client would probably not want him to take any action at all? Should the school counselor talk to a teacher who, because of his lack of understanding of the true situation in which a boy is involved, is making things difficult for him, even though the boy is afraid that he will get into trouble if the counselor talks to the teacher? Should the counselor intervene with school authorities when he knows, from counseling sessions with another student, that a boy is being punished for deeds that were actually committed by someone else? Should a counselor talk with children who are showing a lack of understanding and acceptance of another child because of their possible misconceptions about her?

A somewhat similar problem often occurs when the counselor works in a health service, a psychiatric clinic, or any other hospital setting. There the clients, or patients, will with increasing frequency ask for various kinds of medication to make them sleep, to keep them awake, to steady their nerves, to reduce their tension, and so on. Whether the counselor is a medical therapist or a nonmedical therapist should have no effect on the procedure in a case such as this, but some counselors do not want to appear as the doer or giver of things, and the client would be referred to medical personnel, who would make the decision whether or not the individual should have medication. In some cases there might be consultation between the medical doctor and the counselor, but it would be the medical doctor, not the counselor, who made the decision, even if the counselor was also a medical doctor. The basic reason is not the somewhat outdated fact that only the medical doctor has the legal authority to prescribe such medication—since many psychologists and other nonmedical therapists have equal knowledge of such medication and its effects—but simply the fact that the act of prescribing the medication puts the counselor in a position of authority and decision.

Indeed, the use of drugs in mental health clinics, in psychiatric hospitals, and, increasingly, in schools, is a major ethical issue. Drugs have a place, but the overwhelming reason for their use in clinics would appear to be not to cure or change, but rather to repress behavior that is causing problems for others. Similarly, in

307

schools, there has been an alarming increase in the use of drugs with overt acting-out children to calm them and make them more manageable without, of course, doing anything about the causes of the acting-out. This is another of those realities that cannot be ignored, and the counselor must take a position on it.

Referral may also become a problem of an ethical nature. When the client wishes to be referred elsewhere, normally it raises no problem—unless, of course, the client wishes to be referred to someone who is known professionally as an unethical individual, and this would not often happen. It may happen, however, that the counselor decides that he cannot ethically continue a relationship because of his feeling of lack of capacity to work with the client, but the client refuses to be referred, insists that he is quite satisfied with the present situation, and will cease to have any counseling if the counselor refers him. Another such situation occurs when the counselor with a private practice is being paid for sessions that he feels are doing nothing for the client, and he has the choice of continuing with the client, who will not accept referral, or terminating a client who does not wish to be terminated. Still another problem comes when it is obvious that an individual should be referred, but there is nowhere to refer—although the counselor would feel that it is very rarely that understanding and acceptance are not of some help to any individual. The reverse side of this coin, and one that frequently occurs in schools, is when a person who calls himself a counselor feels that he must refer practically every potential client who reveals anything in the way of a personal problem. When this is the case, surely the individual should be called a referral technician rather than a professional counselor!

The part-time counselor will soon find that the fact that he has several jobs will raise some special ethical problems for him. If he is a teacher and counselor, for example, he will find conflict between his allegiance to a group of children as a teacher and his allegiance to an individual child as a counselor. He may find that, as a teacher, he is expected to be freer with information about a child than he feels, as a counselor, he should be. He may find that parents regard him as a teacher, and he cannot, in effect, say to parents as well as to teachers and school administrators, "But you cannot expect me to do that because I am a counselor," since they will immediately reply, "But you are also a teacher, are you not?" Although this conflict of allegiance raises many difficulties for the teacher-counselor, most of them can be reduced if the teacher feels that he can function better as a teacher if he operates nearly all the time as a counselor.

These difficulties are well-nigh insurmountable, however, for the individual who is a principal. A surprising number of schools still refer blithely to the fact that their counseling is done by their principal, but this surely shows a lack of understanding of counseling and the functions of the counselor. As a principal, one owes allegiance to the teachers, and to a lesser degree to the community; and one cannot function ethically as a counselor if his primary concern is any other than the individual child. Thus, any counselor going into a new position, particularly in a school situation, should know in advance just what is expected of him, or he may find himself saddled with tasks that make his title of counselor nothing but a mockery, and he might well be accused of unethical behavior, or ignorance, or both, if he accepts such conflicting tasks. A school system needs superintendents, and principals, and teachers, and they may be fine and honorable individuals; but they do not, and they cannot, function effectively as counselors.

As the counselor becomes more involved, in a preventive sense, with the causes of human distress, this relationship with other members of the school staff may become a problem, since some of them may be the causes of some of the problems that children may be having. How does a counselor behave as a member of a "team" that has among its members an autocratic principal and a teacher whose racial prejudice is blatantly obvious? What does the counselor do as a member of a community "team" that has as one of its members a clergyman who feels that the use of contraceptives is the work of the devil? The counselor, very often, is a careful subversive or a discreet radical, but he cannot always remain on the balance beam. Sometimes, there is no "good" choice—only the better choice.

Another question deals with whether or not the counselor can excuse unprofessional behavior because of ignorance. His behavior might be excused by others, but the question here is whether or not the counselor can look himself in the eye and say, "There was nothing unethical about that; I was just stupid." It surely seems within the realm of ethical behavior to say that any individual is being unethical if he attempts professional tasks that he is incapable of performing because of his lack of skill and knowledge. Certainly a counselor's fellows should not condemn, but rather try to help; yet each individual counselor may wonder if he is functioning in an ethical manner when he becomes involved in a close and possibly crucial human relationship with another person, and at the same time knows that he does not know what he is doing. Any counselor, of course, no matter what his experience, is going to face situations that he cannot understand, and at times be faced with questions for which he has no answer, but this is part of his professional work, rather than an involvement in a situation about which he knows nothing.

A final ethical question concerns the inconsistency of counselors rather than their ignorance. This is a particularly pertinent problem during the education of the counselor, and too frequently the assessed "effectiveness" of the student counselor would appear to depend more than anything else on just whom he happens to have as a supervisor. In Evraiff's book,[28] for example, the following comments were made by the various reviewers regarding the effectiveness of several student counselors:

The counselor of Carl, for example, had the following said about him:

From Arbuckle: *You start off very dominant, but appear to become more acceptant of the client, who seems to make real progress. You tend to be too concerned with techniques and methodology.*

From Stefflre: *Your third interview was good, but the last was not very good. You were not "close" to the client.*

From Roeber: *By interview three you were doing pretty well, but you withdrew too much in the last interview—you became a silent partner. You follow the words, but not the melody.*

From Dugan and Blocher: *You made excellent use of techniques, and created a warm, positive relationship. In the last interview Carl was able to talk more positively about himself. You need to accept more responsibility.*

Jack's counselor might have heard the following:

From Arbuckle: *You have difficulty accepting Jack, and insist on dominating and controlling him. You tend to be too technique-centered. You are not too aware of "self" as yet, but you show high promise of self-understanding.*

From Stefflre: *You follow the "party-line," but you are on your way to becoming a competent counselor—and a free person.*

From Roeber: *You are too "methodology"-centered. You did not establish too much in the way of a positive relationship with Jack.*

From Dugan and Blocher: *You were too "technique"-centered. There appeared to be little or no communication with Jack. You appear to have no goals.*

28. William Evraiff, *Helping Counselors Grow Professionally* (Englewood Cliffs, N.J.: Prentice-Hall, 1963), pp. 366–367. © 1963. Reprinted by permission of Prentice-Hall, Inc., Englewood Cliffs, N.J.

Jane's counselor might hear:

From Arbuckle: *You understand intellectually, but did not appear to get close, and to empathize with Jane. You stressed the intellectual content rather than the feelings, which were more apparent on the tape than in the typescript.*

From Stefflre: *You did little more than respond with statement of content. You were skilled in omission, and you appeared to avoid areas where you felt uncomfortable. I have respect for your analytic ability.*

From Roeber: *You appeared to be dedicated to a client-centered methodology. You have more than the ordinary talent for counseling.*

This suggests that supervisors of student counselors should be very wary of the validity of their own assessments, and it also raises a question as to the extent to which supervisors are dedicated to helping the student counselor grow toward effectiveness in his own way rather than simply becoming a pale carbon copy of the supervisor in order to receive a positive assessment. Some student counselors may never be able to determine just how effective they can be because their supervisors will never give them a chance to operate as they really are. While it may be expensive, it would seem highly desirable from an ethical point of view for every student counselor to be evaluated by several supervisors so that there might be more chance that their personal bias could be canceled out.

EXAMPLES OF ETHICAL PROBLEMS

One of the marks of a professional counselor is the way he measures up to various ethical issues that press in upon him. Many of these issues represent, basically, assaults upon the integrity of the counselor. One school counselor, for example, has mentioned the following as examples of ethical issues that involve him:

The pressure brought on by the insecure and autocratic administrator who wants the counselor to reveal confidences.

The problem of being aware of environmental imperfections yet not being able to do anything about them because action would demand the revelation of client confidences.

The prostitution of the counselor's professional role.

The pressure brought by various people not to involve myself in therapeutic counseling.

311

The self-protecting reactions of decision-making groups only willing to see one side of the coin.

The protection that tenure laws afford the incompetent teacher.

The badgering of youngsters as part of the educational process.

The badgering of teachers as part of the educational process.

The badgering of offspring as an aspect of parenthood.

Another school counselor has experienced the following ethical problems:

Pressures on the counselor to reveal confidences given in the counseling relationship.

Parental perception of the counselor as an investigator and enforcer.

Parental expectation that the counselor will manipulate teachers for the benefit of the client.

Pressures that the counselor should act as a teacher—i.e., "the counselor should not listen to kids—he should explain and discipline."

Adult pressures and expectations for the counselor to act as an intermediary on their behalf—as an instrument by which some would like to control youngsters and make them conform.

The pressure exerted subtly and overtly on the counselor to help the client to adjust, but not necessarily to grow if growth and development are not in harmony with adult standards and goals.

Wrenn presents a few examples of ethical questions:

(a) How can consultation be had with another person about the student without violating the student's confidences? (b) What is ethical for the counselor when the student, within the counseling relationship, relates wrong-doing or crime? (c) When fellow counselors, teachers, or administrators inquire about a counselee, how does the counselor keep their good-will while maintaining the integrity of his relationship with the student? (d) What does the counselor do when the problem is over his head but there is no referral agency available, or the student will not accept referral?[29]

Here are some examples of ethical issues faced by different counselors:

29. C. Gilbert Wrenn, "Status and Role of the School Counselor," *Personnel and Guidance Journal*, 36:175–183 (November, 1957).

Example 1

John Rose saw the counselor at the beginning of his senior year in high school. He impressed his counselor as a sincere, highly motivated young man, who found in these interviews an opportunity to express himself at least partially. The counseling sessions, however, also revealed a tendency to unrealistic thinking, a strong undercurrent of anxiety, and at times some degree of confusion.

While part of John's problems were immediately connected with school, his deepest concerns were inevitably related to his home situation and background. During his childhood, from the age of about five or seven to his early teens, he had been forced to live apart from his parents as simply another member of the large family of one of his uncles, who resided in Texas. Both parents had come from lower socioeconomic groups and had received but a limited education. The father, a carpenter by training, had worked in mines and factories, but now made little effort to find employment, leaning on the bottle for his chief support. The mother, although still employed, had also fallen into the habit of excessive drinking. Life within the home was one of frequent arguments, discord, and nagging, with very little understanding. Basically, within his family either in the past or the present, John had found little attention, affection, or self-expression.

In the spring of his senior year, John was booked by the police on the charge of exhibitionism in the Townsville Public Library. Released with a warning, he reported his difficulty to the guidance office at school. Referred to the school psychologist, John's problem was diagnosed as requiring long-term treatment. Since the facilities for such treatment were not available at the time within the school structure, he was given a second referral to the hospital clinic and advised to leave school until such time as he might wish to return and at the same time could be psychiatrically cleared for further study.

In the period of a little over a year since John left school, he has returned several times for talks with his counselor, including one visit to his counselor's home. These sessions have had two main purposes from John's point of view: (1) to enable him to release some of his feelings and obtain some approval for his various efforts at obtaining personal and social adjustment; and (2) to obtain guidance and approval in his search for vocational adjustment.

During interviews John has readily admitted the fact that he has not been wholly successful in combating the need to exhibit himself, and a number of isolated instances have occurred since his leaving school. However, he was making serious efforts to fight the

313

need, and with some degree of success. Unfortunately, the clinic had found it impossible to admit him immediately because of caseload. His counselor urged him to keep applying for early admission but, after a year of delay on the part of the clinic, encouraged him to seek admission at another clinic. At this time, it would appear that the clinic at another hospital will be able to give him treatment.

Following his departure from school, he took and held a factory job that offered some security but none-too-high pay and little opportunity for advancement. He is strongly motivated to rise above his present socioeconomic level, but is restricted by his lack of higher education or specialized training.

(1) An additional element of his predicament is represented, however, by the usual necessity of completing the personal history data found on most application forms for any higher-level or more interesting occupational outlet. Recently he was seeking a bank job in which he was highly interested. The application form called for previous education, reasons for leaving school, and any police history. He left the form incomplete and came to see his counselor for advice. "Almost any job I really want asks these questions. I'm almost sure to be stymied in getting ahead if I tell the truth. If I don't get a better job, I'm going to be just so much more unhappy . . . and if I'm always under this pressure, I'm going to find it all the harder to keep out of trouble. What should I do?" What should the counselor advise John? To tell the whole truth? Avoid jobs with such searching questionnaires? Conceal his personal history?

(2) Recently, his counselor was contacted by a representative of an agency to obtain information relative to his clearance for employment. What information if any should be released by his counselor? Should he urge the boy not to use his name as a reference? Should he inform the boy in advance as to what he would feel obligated to disclose if used as a reference? These are the specific questions asked by the representative of the agency:

1. Would you recommend John for employment?
2. Do you consider him to be a stable, well-adjusted individual?
3. Do you think that he will get along well with fellow employees?

Example 2

Bill Din is a college freshman. He seemed to have no really valid motivation for attending college other than his father's desire to have him in college. His academic record for the first semester was poor and he was placed on probation, although all objective evidence seems to indicate that he is a student of superior ability. In working with the student to try to develop some worthwhile motivation, the counselor became involved with a friend of the father.

In time, this friend informed the counselor that the boy's mother is dead, and the father is serving a jail sentence as the consequence of some "sharp" business dealings. Thus the boy has no parental guidance or direction and is left almost entirely to his own devices, being alone at home with a housekeeper while his father is imprisoned. He is well-to-do, has a new Cadillac convertible car of his own, and spends all of his time "living a gay life."

One of Bill's instructors comes to the counselor to get some information regarding Bill. He has discovered that Bill has superior ability, which is evident on the few occasions when he does some academic work. But he wonders about the boy's family situation. Why does he seem to be so poorly motivated? Under these circumstances, and with the knowledge that the counselor possesses, how much or how little should he pass on to the faculty member?

Example 3

Mary San is a college sophomore. She is friendly and pleasant in all relationships with other students and faculty. Prior to entering college, she was in Europe for three years working as a secretary. During this period of her life, she developed a keen interest in international affairs. Apparently her group there spent considerable time in the discussion of the world situation and in deciding what should be done to insure the future peace of the world. As a result, she returned to the United States critical of the way our government was handling foreign affairs and with a general feeling that the solution might be a drastic shift in social and political organization.

Although Mary came from a substantial, conservative Midwestern home background, she has always had some tendency toward inward revolt against the conservative point of view. It was interpreted by her family, however, as the "enthusiasm of youth," and since it reached only minor proportions, such as occasional family arguments, the family thought little about it. Later they became quite distressed by her activities. The time spent in Europe seemed to intensify these feelings. After returning, she worked for about a year in a textile factory before entering college. Here she became very much interested in union activities, and the excitement involved in those activities seemed to stimulate her further. She came to a conclusion that labor work would be her chosen vocational field, a decision that led to her desire for further education.

While a student, she has continued her contact with the union movement. By a fellow student with somewhat similar inclinations, she was introduced to a local "progressive" group with members from local colleges. This organization is very active and probably provides further fortification of her "liberal" or extremist tendencies.

Mary is very active in extracurricular affairs, her interests centering mainly in student government and the school newspaper. She is also active in the political organization called Americans for Democratic Action.

About three weeks ago, an FBI agent called in the course of a routine loyalty check on this girl, who is being considered for a position of trust in the government. Since much of the preceding information had been obtained from the counselee and her parents through interviews, what is the counselor's position? What information should be given to the FBI agent?

Example 4

Horace Pen established himself early in college as an unusual student. He was very able, very personable, and impressed one immediately as possessing qualities of leadership. He had served a two-year hitch in the Air Force before coming to college.

When class elections were held shortly before Christmas recess, he was elected freshman president. He quickly demonstrated his abilities both as class president and also as representative of the Student-Faculty Assembly.

A review of his two-year record—or rather of his record up to about Easter of his sophomore year—indicated the extent to which he had won not only student but faculty attention. At about Eastertime, one of the departmental chairmen requested that Horace be given a work scholarship and be assigned to him. The request was carried out, and Horace began his duties. Later, by sheer accident, an instructor noticed that a boy who had not turned in a major assignment had suddenly acquired an A grade for it. A check of records indicated that not only had this change been made but that at least two others had occurred. It soon became evident that the records had been left briefly where they were available to Horace and to no other student. When Horace was interrogated about the situation, he admitted that he had made the changes.

In due course, the case came before the school department heads. They were reluctant to give the boy a dishonorable dismissal because of his previous record, even though it was felt that such action was indicated. Horace was finally permitted to withdraw with the understanding that application for readmission at a future date would be denied.

About a year later, Horace applied for admission to a Midwestern university and his counselor received a letter requesting information about his withdrawal.

(1) What is the counselor's ethical obligation in such a situation?

(2) Does the fact that a complete statement of the case would likely lead to rejection have any bearing on it?

Example 5

Henry Dot has completed his sophomore year at college. The victim of a broken home in his early youth, he was raised by three uncles who did what they could for him. However, he was forced to shift for himself and worked at odd jobs from a very early age. He was graduated from high school at the age of nineteen, having missed a full year of schooling because of ill health. He served two years in the Navy following high school and became interested in teaching.

Following his military service, he did various jobs and became manager of two stores. But he wanted to get a college education and train to be a school teacher. As a college student, he maintained a satisfactory record and impressed the faculty as a very conscientious, sincere, and intellectually curious young man. On his own, he visited the counseling center and requested assistance for some problems of personal adjustment. The school psychiatrist, feeling that he was a rather disturbed young man, suggested psychotherapy, which Henry has been receiving regularly at the VA Mental Hygiene Clinic. His irregular home background has probably contributed to his problems of personal adjustment, and originally there seemed to be a question of needing some help in making a more satisfactory heterosexual adjustment. Henry's counselor has worked closely with him. The psychiatrist at the Mental Hygiene Clinic feels that he has made considerable progress and now has rather good insight regarding his problems of adjustment. Some additional therapy is indicated at this time.

Henry has applied for admission as a junior to several teachers' colleges. The counselor's problem is: (1) Should he recommend such an individual for teacher training? (2) If so, how much of this information should be passed on to the other institution or school?

Test scores indicate that he is a young man of superior ability. His interest in teaching seems to be strong and genuine. He has had valuable related work experience. But what of his own emotional adjustment at this stage? Also, is the counselor violating the student's confidence if he passes on any of this information?

Example 6

Sally Rin was probably one of the most able students in the college that she attended. All scores on the Ohio State Psychological Examination would place her at, or above, the 95th percentile, liberal arts college freshman norms. She was also one of the most confused and distressed young women ever to come to this counselor's attention.

Her family background was substantial. Her father was a medical doctor. Her mother had graduated from a well-known Southern women's college. A brother was preparing for the priesthood in the Roman Catholic Church.

Sally had been sent to school in Italy for two years. While in Rome, she had observed certain things, of which her interpretations had a profound effect upon her. This was evident in her cynical attitude toward life, toward people and religion, and toward the Roman Catholic Church in particular. Her attitude was very distressing to the family.

In discussions with her counselor, the reasons back of this attitude became evident. While in Rome, Sally had seen children starving almost outside the Vatican walls, while inside everything seemed to go on as usual. As she put it, "I could not understand how the Church could stand for Christian principles and do nothing about these poor impoverished people. I can never again swallow the stuff they put out." It was evident that a terrific conflict had been set up in this counselee's mind. Now she was disturbed by the effect that her attitudes had upon her family. Also the loss of her religious faith had taken away from her the very basis of her former stability, and she realized it. She said that sometimes the only solution seemed to be suicide.

Her parents had suggested that she take her problem to the local priest. This she refused to do, saying "What could he do except urge me to return to the Church? I would rather talk with a Protestant minister, even though I don't think that he could help me."

What should the counselor do in helping the student to solve this difficult reorientation? With whom should the case be discussed?

The following are hypothetical counseling situations involving a conflict of responsibility:

Ethical Situation 1

On the day set for final examinations for senior english, Mrs. Weber discovers that some exam sheets are missing from her filing cabinet. She informs the students that their test will have to be postponed until the next morning, graduation day, since she will have to construct a new test. During a counseling conference on the same day, Gary tells the counselor that he had access to the stolen test and knows who took it. Finally he admits it is his friend Bob who was the guilty party. Gary and Bob are college-bound seniors who might not be allowed to graduate if the counselor were to report this. After talking with the counselor, the boys suggested that they would give back the tests if he, the counselor, would return them to the teacher without indicating who had stolen the test sheets. What should the counselor do?

Ethical Situation 2

Jean has come to the counselor for several sessions during the past two months, but it is only at the one yesterday that he learns that she is pregnant. She tells him that she has told only one other person, her best friend, who helped to arrange for an abortion. Jean is planning to go to a nearby city the next day, Saturday, for the abortion. Her parents have been told that she is staying for the weekend with a friend, whom they know well. Jean is obviously upset by the prospect of the abortion, but tells the counselor that she "would rather die" than tell her parents. Jean also refuses to name the father of her expected baby. The counselor urges her to confide in her parents, and when Jean continually refuses, he is puzzled. Should he inform the parents? Or what?

Ethical Situation 3

Ken D., a high school senior, revealed during a counseling relationship that he had engaged in homosexual activities for about a year. He had become increasingly worried that he would be "found out" and this anxiety caused a drop in his school achievement, which was the "reason" he came to see the counselor. He also expressed hope that he might learn to prefer heterosexual relationships, although he had been repeatedly disappointed and continued to be attracted to males. The counselor, who was rather inexperienced, had not encountered such a problem before and did not know whether to refer Ken to a psychiatrist or try to counsel him. He chose the latter alternative, although felt later that he hadn't helped Ken at all. Two years following Ken's graduation from high school, the counselor received a recommendation form from a prospective employer. Ken had applied for a job as a counselor in a boys' summer camp. Should the counselor mention his knowledge of Ken's homosexual tendencies?

Ethical Situation 4

Helen has come to see the counselor at the recommendation of a teacher who is concerned about Helen's failure to keep up in her schoolwork. Usually she is a B student, but for the last three months, she hasn't maintained a C average. Helen is quite negative for the first two counseling sessions. At the third session, however, she tells the counselor that she has been associating with a group of older teenagers who have been taking LSD. The police have been aware of this group for several months but haven't been able to find out who the "ticket agent," or source of the LSD is. Helen eventually tells the counselor the names of all the members of the group, after she feels she can trust him. One day the principal approaches the counselor. He tells him that the police have asked the principal if he has any clues as to possible leads in the case. Should the counselor tell the principal anything?

Ethical Situation 5

An unmarried male counselor, the only counselor in a small school, has been counseling a high school girl who is known by many students and teachers to be sexually promiscuous. The counseling has been somewhat successful, but also of longer duration than usual. A few of the teachers and some of the students have been speculating as to the true nature of the counseling attention. The parents have called the principal to ask him if there is any truth to the gossip that the counselor is behaving "immorally." Rumors have become strong enough to cause the principal to pressure the counselor to cease counseling this particular girl. The counselor feels, however, that to terminate counseling at this point would destroy all the good that has been accomplished. Also, there are no alternate counseling opportunities immediately available for her. He feels a strong professional obligation to the girl, but also to his school. How can he best proceed under these circumstances?

Ethical Situation 6

Mr. Williams, the history teacher, knows much about history but little about teenagers. He displays his ignorance frequently in class, in teachers' meetings, and socially. Many of the students dislike him or feel sorry for him, but few have any respect for him. Recently, he has had a rash of flat tires, garbage deposited on his porch, and broken windows. The counselor learns during his meeting with Tom, a rowdy freshman, that Tom's gang has been responsible for Mr. Williams' calamities. Tom defends his actions, saying that no one likes Mr. Williams and everyone wants him to quit teaching. Tom indicates that the incidences of disturbance will continue. The counselor has a close relationship with Tom and does not want to break his confidence. However, he is also concerned about Mr. Williams. What should he do?

Ethical Situation 7

Mr. X, an elementary school counselor, has talked several times with Mary, a fourth grade student who is quite unhappy and has low school achievement. Mary discloses to the counselor that her father is gone much of the time, and when home, is usually drunk. He beats both Mary and her mother occasionally. From others of Mary's comments, the counselor concludes that Mary's mother is of questionable character, too, and has several men friends. One day a representative of the State Department of Children and Family Services comes to Mr. X, asking for information about Mary. He says that neighbors have called the department with complaints that Mary is severely neglected, often left alone all night. They contend she is improperly fed and clothed. The counselor is asked to disclose information gained in counseling so that it may be used as evidence to remove Mary from her home environment. What should the counselor do?

Ethical Situation 8

During a counseling relationship with David, the counselor administered the Mooney Problem Check List and the MMPI. David had indicated that he was worried about his mental health and sometimes
thought he was "going crazy." Some months later, the principal
asked the counselor for all of David's records, since David was transferring to another school. The principal also said David was transferring because of recurrent problems with other children and teachers.
Should the counselor include the MMPI and Mooney Check List information?

Chapter 12

Theoretical Issues: Professional

There are a number of "theoretical" issues that, in a sense, become practical for the counselor because of the very nature of his work. For the existential-humanist counselor particularly, an increasingly important issue has to do with the whole question of reality and realities. Such counselors are not satisfied with the traditional scientific version of reality as that of which my immediate senses are aware. They see realities that may well go beyond the senses.

REALITY

Huxley talks about the "other" reality when he says:

> But for those who theoretically believe what they know in practice to be true—namely, that there is an inside to experience as well as an outside, the problems posed are real problems, all the more grave for being, some completely insoluble, some soluble only in exceptional circumstances, and by methods not available to everyone.[1]

Murphy too, stresses this other reality that science and counseling usually miss:

> The inner world has become just as real as the outer world; hardly anyone in an odd corner dares anymore to refer to the

---

1. Aldous Huxley, *The Doors of Perception and Heaven and Hell* (New York: Harper and Row, 1963), p. 14.

world of fantasy as "unreal." It may be called a different kind
of reality, but even this does not seem coercive or constraining
upon us.[2]

It is the search, and the action and the motion that are real,
rather than some preconceived "reality" that one must seek out. It is
likely that Fromm means this when he says, "All that the human
race has achieved, spiritually and materially, it owes to the destroy-
ers of illusions and to the seekers of reality."[3] One might reword this
slightly, and say that our debt is to those who create the new realities and are unwilling to accept the old as fixed and rigid and immu-
table. Sartre is looking at the same question when he comments:

There is no reality except in action . . . man is nothing else than
his plan; he exists only to the extent that he fulfills himself; he
is therefore nothing else than the ensemble of his acts, nothing
else than his life.[4]

When May says, "There is no such thing as truth or reality for
a living human being except as he participates in it, is conscious of it,
has some relationship to it,"[5] he is expressing the phenomenological
concept that reality lies in the individual's experience of the event
rather than in the isolated event. One might also say that there is,
really, no "event" without the human individual. Hatreds and bogey
men and chairs exist only as they appear to the individual as they
become a part of his experiencing, his living. Thus, we may say that
there *is* a world of reality; but, on the other hand, it cannot be reality
apart from the people who are the basic part of it. This is a problem
faced by all student counselors, and even many of the more sophisticated and experienced counselors and therapists still appear to feel
strongly that "reality," for them, must somehow also be reality for
their client. Rather than accepting him, and thus his reality, and living through it and experiencing it with him, they sit on the outside,
subtly or directly imposing their concepts upon him. They thus impede and make more difficult his growth toward greater freedom
and self-actualization. It is difficult to modify or change one's reality
if one is never allowed to experience deeply just what that reality
might be. The insightful counselor, however, sooner or later be-

2. Gardner Murphy, *Freeing Intelligence Through Teaching* (New York: Harper and
   Row, 1961), p. 38.
3. Erich Fromm, *Beyond the Chains of Illusion* (New York: Pocket Books, 1962), p.
   173.
4. Jean-Paul Sartre, *Existentialism and Human Emotions* (New York: Wisdom Library, 1957), p. 32.
5. Rollo May, *Existential Psychology (New York: Random House, 1961), pp. 17–18.*

comes involved in asking just what reality is, anyway, or whether there is any such thing as an absolute reality. Is reality what we see, and is a wooden table therefore a hard solid piece of matter, rather than consisting of billions of atoms in wild motion, which is the way a table may be seen by a physicist? Is the "color" that a color-blind person sees not real, and the real color that which is seen by people who are not color-blind? Is the avid skier being unrealistic when he glories in the wonderful two feet of snow that has just fallen, while all his non-skiing friends groan about the miserable weather? Are the psychosomatic headaches real, or can we say to a person who moans with the pain of such a headache, "It isn't really a real headache, so you don't really feel anything"? Can we say that the handsome woman with beautiful hair, who says, "I'm a mess, and my hair is just like a mop!" is divorced from reality?

This ability to live another's reality with him might be considered as a description of empathy. This also means that the counselor is one who can live certainly in a world of uncertainty, one who accepts the probability in living with security. All too frequently in counseling, it really is "cases" that we are discussing, and with which we are working, whether we are in a staff conference "case" discussion, or involved in an actual counseling session. We operate with events and problems, and questions and supposed meanings, and the real-life experiencing person, either represented (and nothing more) on a piece of paper, or the flesh-and-blood person in front of us, is ignored and unseen, and we give him little help in the struggle to see who he is, because it is not "him" with whom we are relating.

In a different way, Barry and Wolf are saying much the same thing when they discuss the myths of the vocational counselor:

The word realism is essentially a mask for value judgments about the practicality and practicability of an idea, a feeling, a plan. . . . Realism is a judgment dependent upon time and the point of view of the person making it.[6]

It is likely that thousands of students throughout the United States have sat in classrooms and offices, today, listening to their teacher or their counselor as he said, among other things, "Now, Joe, let's be realistic about this. . . . " The counselor is indeed making a value judgment, and even worse, he is imposing an absolute reality (his) upon his unfortunate victim.

The more the counselor looks at the question of reality, which

6. Ruth Barry and Beverly Wolf, *An Epitaph for Vocational Guidance* (New York: Teachers College, Columbia University, 1962), pp. 90–91.

in a way is like the cultural version of truth, the more likely he is to conclude, at least temporarily, that there are two broad sets of realities. There is the reality of the group, and there is the reality of the individual. The simple but questionable way in which many people have solved this dilemma is to conclude that reality must be whatever the majority says it is; according to this view, the more the individual moves away from the concept of the group, the more odd or queer or the crazier he is. This concept might lead to only minor difficulty if one could live in a completely homogeneous society and never leave it, or never become aware that this is only one of many societies, each one having its own set of realities. The scientist may feel that he can easily avoid this difficulty by equating reality with truth. What has been proven empirically to be true is real, and, for the rest, we don't know whether it is real or not. But the "rest" is what daily surrounds almost everyone, and even scientists will haggle over their pitifully small set of "truths." The clergyman may equate reality with "God's truth," but if he is an intelligent clergyman he will have to admit that there are almost as many "God's truths" as there are religious denominations, or even more. As Chenault puts it:

> Consensus is not a valid criterion of truth. It ignores the very personal nature of philosophy and the freedom and right to base professional practice upon it.[7]

For the counselor, at least, it might be best to consider the concept that while there may be a broad set of realities accepted by most of those with whom we live, each individual operates on a set of personal realities. What is real to the client, but not real to the counselor, is nevertheless, as far as the counselor is concerned, *real*. The counselor relates with his client's reality, not his own. This personal reality applies to everyone—the stable, the normally neurotic, and the psychotic; and at least the first two of this trio should be able to see it in operation with themselves, if they look carefully at any time. Unhappiness because one cannot afford two cars is just as real as a people's democracy where no one has the right to vote; fear of a dark room is just as real as a state of freedom where one does what the autocratic ruler says he must do; tension over skin blemishes that no one can see is just as real as a system of student government where the faculty determines what the students can do; student despair because of getting a B now and then instead of all A's is just as real as the inferiority feelings of some individual because of his ra-

---

7. Joann Chenault, "Professional Standards and Philosophical Freedom: A Peaceful Coexistence," *Counselor Education and Supervision*, 3:8–12 (Fall, 1963).

cial background. All of these things are real to some, unreal to others, but it is the function of the counselor to work with the reality of the client, and, possibly, to help him to come ultimately to a different concept of reality.

It is also real, however, to say that no one individual lives his life alone. While one may stress the need for the individual to be satisfied with his self, to feel that "I am doing my thing," this cannot be considered without taking into account the effect this may have on others. The way the person perceives the world around him is real, but the actuality of that world is also real. Glasser feels that a common characteristic of all patients is that they deny the reality of the world around them. He goes on to say, "Therapy will be successful when they (patients) are able to give up denying the world and recognize that reality not only exists but they must fulfill their needs within its framework."[8]

Thus while the counselor is acceptant of, and works with the reality of the client, he is not unaware of the reality of the world that surrounds the client. It is unlikely that any counselor would say that he would be happy to see the client live on in the reality of his world in which he cannot eat because he feels that various members of his family are trying to poison him. Thus in this situation the counselor can be acceptant of the reality of the client, but at the same time would try to help the client to change that perception so that his reality would mesh with that of the outer world, and he could come to see that members of his family were not trying to poison him. The stress in society today is due not only to the imposition of society on the individual, but also to the insistence of the individual that his rights must take precedence, regardless of the price that others may pay. A society of free men, however, does not consist of those who impose on others.

School counselors sometimes find it particularly difficult to move beyond their own cultural concept of reality, and they tend, too, to associate reality with things that can be seen or touched or smelled or heard. It takes time and experience before they can go beyond their primary senses and be able to accept the concept that goblins really are in that room because a child believes they are; that big blemishes really are on the adolescent girl's face because she believes they are there; that a man really is poor, although his bank balance is over $100,000; that the student with one B and all the rest A's really is doing miserable work.

The effective counselor is one who accepts a world of realities, especially the inner reality of a client, which may not always mesh

8.   William Glasser, *Reality Therapy* (New York: Harper and Row, 1965), p. 6.

with the outside reality. The inner life of the client is very real, even though we may not understand it. Trying to "understand," at least in an intellectual sense, may impede the expansion of one's consciousness, and for the existential-humanist counselor this expanded consciousness is very real.

THE COUNSELOR AND THE EXPANDED CONSCIOUSNESS

I sometimes wonder if homo sapiens, in his earlier stage of development, say one million years ago, was possibly closer to who he really was because his cerebral capacities were not as well developed as they are today. Increasingly, it would seem to me, our ability to think gets in the way of our ability to live our life in the fullest sense, a life which is well beyond what our intellect can interpret to us. In academic and educated circles, however, anything that is considered to be nonintellectual is highly suspect. Thus, much of our behavior that is, actually, quite irrational and anti-intellectual must be defended as being rational and intellectual. The highest goal in life, it would appear from what most counselors and therapists and educated people in general say, is to learn how to function as a totally rational being. I would think, and, even more, feel, that such a life would be empty of much of what is within our grasp to experience, and that a person living such a life is deprived, devoid of the inner part that is the flesh on the bones of the intellect. It is not at all a question of mind over matter, or even mind and matter, but rather our developing the inner freedom to allow ourselves to experience altered states of consciousness, to flow free, to go with the river, to be who we can be.

I can see several issues which are particularly pertinent to this notion of expanding and going beyond one's consciousness:

1. We cannot "know" that which is beyond knowing, and any human experiencing is a good deal more than knowing *about*. In a knowledgeable and diagnostic sense, many counselors are quite capable in their relationships with a client. They may, however, be quite ineffective in terms of a meaningful human relationship with a client because they are incapable of feeling with him, going where he goes, beyond the realm of the intellect. Some counselors are comfortable when talking about problems, but are decidedly uncomfortable if any attempt is made to get them involved in a feeling sense with the human being who has a human problem. Confrontation is often more bothersome to the counselor than it is to the client.

Thus the counselor who has never been stoned on marijuana may hear the client verbalizing his feelings while stoned, but he can never understand the total communication because he has never experienced what is being communicated. The client cannot fully share his experience with the counselor, no matter how earnest and caring the counselor might be. On the other hand, if the counselor is an individual who has been high or stoned in a natural sense, if he is quite aware, in an experiential way, of the wildness and ecstasy of feelings that are available to him without drugs, then he can come very close to the client who has used artificial means to obtain a high. Obviously, more often than not, the counselor cannot have had the particular experience which produces a particular feeling. The male counselor will never experience giving birth to a child, and no counselor will have had the experience of dying.

But the counselor, if he is to be able to share closely with the client, must have lived with more than just his intellect. As Adler put it some years ago, "The best knower of the human soul will be the one who has lived through passions himself."[9] Even Freud hardly sounded scientific and objective when, as we have earlier stated, he said:

Cases which are thus destined at the start to scientific purposes and treated accordingly suffer in consequence; while the most successful cases are those in which one proceeds, as it were, aimlessly, and allows oneself to be overtaken by any surprises, always presenting to them an open mind, free from any expectations.[10]

All too frequently, unfortunately, the training and education of counselors stresses intellectual prowess and ignores almost totally the experiential capacities. Counselors and therapists often know only about the expanded consciousness in an intellectual sense, rather than as a direct experience. I would agree with Weil when he comments that

psychiatrists should listen to what their patients say about drug experiences; patients often know more about the workings of the conscious mind from direct experiences than doctors do from their intellects.[11]

2. We have been so conditioned to distrust any altered state of consciousness that we must use various external measures to ex-

9. Alfred Adler, *Understanding Human Nature* (Greenwich, Conn.: Fawcett Publications, 1927), p. 22.
10. Sigmund Freud, "Recommendations for Physicians on the Psychoanalytic Method of Treatment," *Collected Papers, 11* (London: Hogarth Press, 1925), pp. 326–327.
11. Andrew Weil, "The Natural Mind," *Psychology Today,* 6:51–59 (October, 1972).

plain why we can do what we could actually do without these external measures. This is likely the major reason we have doctors, therapists, medicine men, gods, and other "beyond-me" means of doing things for us. Members of helping professions usually "help" us to remove blocks to our growth and movement that have actually been established by us. It is our faith in the healer that provides us with the necessary motivation that in turn enables us to get "well." Professional helpers are testimony to the astonishing degree to which we are conditioned to believe that we cannot do alone what we actually can do.

Most religions condition the faithful to believe that magical powers reside in some supreme supernatural being, and this belief is reinforced by the periodic occurrence of miracles. Often, there is no doubt that what happens is indeed a "miracle," but God is given credit for doing something about the individual's human condition. If the person believed in himself and his capacities as much as he believed in the power of God, then almost certainly the same positive results would take place. The only difference would be that the individual would be somewhat more accurate with regard to who was being credited with bringing about the miracle. This would likely increase his own self-esteem, since it is nice to believe that God may help me, but even nicer to believe that I can help me.

Christian Scientists put their faith in God rather than in medical doctors, and their "get-better" record stands up very well when measured against the standard medical treatment for much of our so-called medical ills. As a child, I can remember having absolute faith in the wisdom of my mother. For almost any ailment or bruise she had a standard remedy. It was: "Have a glass of water, son, go to bed and have a good sleep, and you will be fine in the morning." Almost invariably, I was, and my mother's treatment was just as effective as the treatment by means of the medical aids that stock the average medicine cabinet today, as well as being economically and psychologically more sound. True, I was putting faith in the infallibility of my mother rather than in my own self, but I was a bit closer to me than I would have been by putting my faith in God or pills!

Hall is saying much the same thing in reference to our entire society when he states:

Man is now in the position of creating the total world in which he lives. . . . In creating this world he is actually determining what kind of an organism he will be.[12]

12. Edward T. Hall, *The Hidden Experience* (New York: Doubleday, 1969), pp. 65–66.

One of the sad, although understandable, themes that runs through much of the literature on prejudice is "I cannot be free until I make them let me be free." The fact of external prejudice is very real, but if my feelings of worth are dependent on the other's smiling upon me, or my taking over his power so that I can do to him what he did to me, then indeed I will never find that for which I search. If I am fortunate, I may, like George Bernard Shaw's black girl in search of God,[13] find that that for which I search resides within me.

This self-abasement is evident in much of the "liberation" literature on sex and race. Kasten, in saying: "To the radical therapist who is concerned that the existence of oppressive institutions precludes happiness, even for the most well adjusted,"[14] is accepting the total inability of the individual to do anything about his human state until the institution changes. The black person, or the female, does not become someone by a change in legal restrictions, or by the gracious smile of the white person or the male. It is a person's pride in his own ability to stand on his feet, his satisfaction with self, that creates the changes in people and institutions. The reason prejudice remains so rooted today is because we continue to fantasize that if and when someone removes restrictions, we will automatically achieve a state of individual freedom. Freedom will never come to those who wait for it to be granted, or to those who feel that all that is required is the destruction of the immediate oppressor. In many countries today, black oppressors have taken the place of their white predecessors, and in some places in the United States female oppressors have replaced males. Unfortunately, however, oppression remains.

The stress is always on the external. The song "Young, Gifted and Black" is an understandable attempt to help a young black person to have pride in self. But the young black person, like the old white person, can also feel that we all were young once, and that we all become old, and that we are born black or white or brown. We have nothing to do with any of that. I can, however, be beautiful, not because I am black or white, or young or old, but rather because I have made myself into a beautiful human being. *I* am the one who has made *me* beautiful. This is my existential freedom.

This external stress is seen in another way in a "letter to the editor" by Pedro in which she reacts critically to a paper that I had published. She protests my use of the word "humanist" and would prefer "feminist," defined as a person who seeks social and political

13. George Bernard Shaw, *The Adventures of the Black Girl in Her Search for God* (London: Capricorn Books, 1971).
14. Katherine Kasten, "Toward a Psychology of Being: A Masculine Mystique," *Journal of Humanistic Psychology*, 12:23–24 (Fall, 1972).

rights for women.[15] But the word "feminist" maintains the very differentiation to which she is opposed. A humanist is concerned, in a gestalt sense, about *human* injustice and prejudice, a learned ailment to which we are all vulnerable. One should not limit one's search for justice to any particular segment of the human race or, inevitably, there will be justice for none.

Recently, I read a series of comments by women in an Association for Humanistic Psychology *Newsletter*.[16] They read somewhat like testimonials offered at an Alcoholics Anonymous or a Christian Science meeting. I was struck by the fact that the speakers were talking about what *they* did for themselves and to themselves. They were not talking about what someone else did for them, or about something they took which gave them the strength of ten. Rather, they were talking about capacities they had had for a long time, and about actions they took that they could have taken earlier. They were different people, and, from the comments, quite obviously freer and happier and better people, because they finally began to stir and to become the persons they could be. Each moved closer to her own being, rather than vainly striving to be a stranger shaped by someone else.

Krishnamurti is an example of an Eastern philosopher who sees the only solution to human problems as lying within oneself.[17] He feels that society, or any human organization, cannot provide my answers for me. Only within myself can I find the life that is best for me.

For the young in the last decade drugs have provided the external rationale for achieving a high, getting into a world beyond the everyday consciousness, the moving into a stoned land where life is different, the tripping beyond our current conscious restrictions. But they do not really remove themselves from one world and go into another. They use the rationale of the drug to open a door and pass into another room in their own house, but this they always had the potential to do. Innumerable studies show that even experienced marijuana smokers get the same effects when they smoke placebo, as long as they firmly believe that they are smoking good marijuana. I can remember four young marijuana smokers, two of whom were drug virgins who had been convinced that they should try it even though they were terrified of what might happen. They had, of course, a very bad time, while the two experienced smokers had, as

---

15. Joan Daniels Pedro, "Feedback," *Personnel and Guidance Journal*, 51:166–167 (November, 1972).

16. *Newsletter*, Association for Humanistic Psychology, November, 1972.

17. J. Krishnamurti, *The First and Last Freedom* (London: Victor Gollancz, 1969).

they expected, a very pleasant time. It is true that drug use does have physiological effects, but it is humanly impossible to have a circumstance where the psychological can be totally divorced from the physiological.

Most reformed drug addicts, who frequently become members of drug panels, are reflecting their whole life-style when they talk about drugs rather than merely the effects of drugs upon them. It might be that drug panels or committees should have as members more stable individuals who are still taking drugs, but with care and discretion. It is likely that most members of drug panels would say that they consume alcohol (a drug) with care and discretion.

An interesting commentary on the state of our human development is the fact that while faith in some supreme being is suspect enough in the fraternity of the educated, faith in oneself would appear to be downright heresy! Probably the greatest disservice that Skinner has done to his fellow humans is to reinforce the feeling of individual helplessness, to make easier the acceptance of a philosophy of self-irresponsibility. It is a world in which all of our woes and joys are of others, never of ourselves. Skinner's society is the ultimate serfdom, and happiness, like everything else, comes from the outside, from "them," if, of course, they wish to grant us happiness.[18]

But this need not happen. It is not inevitable. It will happen only if an individual human being allows it to happen. As Ellul puts it:

> . . . if many—if each one of us—abdicates his responsibilities with regard to values; if each of us limits himself to leading a trivial existence in a technological civilization, with greater adaptation and increasing success as his sole objectives; if we do not even consider the possibility of making a stand against these determinants, then everything will happen to us as I have described it, and the determinants will be transformed into inevitabilities.[19]

It is interesting to note that these words, written over twenty years ago in France, make good sense to many people today. Hall asked a well-known psychologist if he felt like a puppet. He answered:

> Well, I've quit smoking, and people complain that I feel too powerful. I don't, but I certainly don't feel a lack of power. I

18. B. F. Skinner, *Beyond Freedom and Dignity* (New York: Alfred A. Knopf, 1971).

19. Jacques Ellul, *The Technological Society* (New York: Alfred A. Knopf, 1970), p. xxix.

have been fairly successful in doing what I want to do. I should suppose that I have persuaded a lot of people of a lot of things, but I must confess that I am concerned that I have not been more persuasive.[20]

On being asked if he felt he could influence his own environment he answered:

I certainly do. I do all the time, as my environment influences me. I am the person I'm most concerned with controlling.[21]

This psychologist would appear to be very much like the sort of person described by Ellul. It is of some interest to note that his name is B. F. Skinner!

Ellis is an example of one who worships at the shrine of the intellect. In discussing transpersonal psychology, he says that

any meaningful concept of God involves the undefinable and supernatural, hence it is not really within the realm of scientific or clinical discourse. Moreover, a faith-impelled believer in God or any kind of magic to some degree breaks with reality and worships at some supernatural shrine; consequently, he cannot possibly have maximum autonomy and self realization.[22]

But faith in God, or faith in one's intellect, or faith in one's total self are all *faith*. The crucial difference is that if my faith is in my own ability to go beyond limitations set by others, or by my own intellect, then I am indeed closer to being a responsible free human being.

3. This faith in the external, the out-of-me, has another unfortunate by-product, namely, the treatment of the symptom rather than that which creates the symptom. This adds to the fantasy that most of our human ailments are diseases that can be cured. A good example of how lay magazines support this inaccurate assumption is *Newsweek* magainze, January 8, 1973, in which the lead article was "Depression." The gist of the article was that depression is a disease, like mumps, and psychiatrists and laboratory researchers are on the road to finding a cure by discovering various and sundry new kinds of drugs and other external treatments. There was practically nothing to suggest that depression might be an individually created state

20. Elizabeth Hall, "Will Success Spoil B. F. Skinner?" *Psychology Today*, 6:65–72 (November, 1972).
21. *Ibid.*
22. Albert Ellis, "What Does Transpersonal Psychology Have to Offer the Art and Science of Psychotherapy?" *Voices*, 8:10–20 (Fall, 1972).

of consciousness which could, in turn, produce chemical reactions in the body.

Our natural reaction to the human problem of racial and sexual prejudice illustrates this stress on symptoms. Instead of investigating the causes, we try to stamp out the acts. The result often is that prejudice on both sides is reinforced. It would be fair to say, surely, that one of the reasons for white prejudice against black people is ignorance and fear. But instead of trying to help white people understand their usually groundless fears, and then do something about them, they may be taught more "appropriate" language. This does nothing about the attitudes which have created the inappropriate language. The continuing prejudice simply takes on different forms, because the humans who practice prejudice have not been helped to change the attitudes which create it.

We also try to remedy the "drug problem" by attacking the symptoms, namely the taking of drugs, and ignoring the causes. This does absolutely nothing about the very real basic human problem that is illustrated by the excessive use of drugs, or about the conditions that help to create it. Drugs are the product of a human condition, not the cause of it. It is likely that the young men in the Army who use drugs, like college students, (who, unlike soldiers, are pretty much unmolested), could give a much more accurate picture of the "drug problem" and what should be done about it than all the various investigating committees and groups who come forth with endless and futile reports.

4. Another aspect of the expanded, more highly developed state of consciousness is that it takes us beyond the need for an either/or world, a world which is a creation of those individuals who have been unable to develop and actualize their self beyond the point of needing external and false security. In the either/or world I am strong because someone else is weak, I am capable because I know someone who is less capable than I, I am beautiful because there are other people who are not beautiful. All of this, of course, represents the needs of a human who has not yet become capable of accepting the inner reality of his own strength, his capabilities, his beauty. He cannot see the goodness and virtue in himself, but has to depend on the assumed lack of it in someone else to buttress his feelings about himself.

Counseling and psychotherapy have encouraged this either/or illusion with their division of the population into "normal" and "abnormal," "sane" and "crazy," "sick" and "well." Much professional time is spent in a useless diagnostic merry-go-round of putting people into pigeonholes. Medical and psychological diagnostic categories are cultural inventions to describe people who, in one way or the other, do not fit the cultural norm. The categories are actually quite limited as well as being invalid, and once someone comes in for "help" he *must* be put in one of the few categories available. It is as if in physical medicine we had discovered six diseases, and from this time on anyone who is described as sick must be put in one of the six.

A perfect example of this quite irrational categorization is seen in a report by Rosenham, a professor of psychology and law. He and eleven others, including three other psychologists, a pediatrician, a psychiatrist, a painter, and a housewife, all quite "sane," had themselves committed to mental institutions. Once committed, they described their life history as it actually was, and behaved as they did in their normal life. However, the only people who perceived the pseudo-patients as normal were other patients. The staff continued to insist that they were schizophrenic or manic-depressive. It took up to fifty-two days to get out of the hospital. Three "walked out," and the other nine were discharged with the diagnosis "schizophrenic in remission."[23]

Laing is one who has spoken out against the medical categories of the day which supposedly distinguish the normal from the abnormal. He suggests that "insane" people are reacting in a totally rational way to an insane and irrational society.[24] This is likely the reason why he himself is considered by some of his fellow psychiatrists to be a bit queer, if not downright abnormal! Ellul is another who feels that in a rational and technological society human spontaneity has no expression except madness.[25]

Castaneda too, takes us into a world of experiencing, where our unreal becomes real, where what we would consider madness becomes reasonable and acceptable.[26] It is a world far removed from that of the "rational" man.

It is tragic, too, that in the struggle for human liberty and justice, the either/or concept is automatically accepted. It is a sad sort of "Either you are somebody, or I am somebody, but we can't both be somebody." Kasten is quite correct when she states that there is no way a woman can be "feminine" and a man "masculine," and also be fully "human." She then falls into the either/or trap by

23. D. L. Rosenham, "On Being Sane in Insane Places," *Science* 179:250–258 (January, 1972).

24. R. D. Laing, *The Politics of Experience* (New York: Ballantine Books, 1967).

25. Jacques Ellul, op. cit., p. 73.

26. Carlos Castaneda, *The Teachings of Don Juan: A Yaqui Way of Knowledge* (New York: Simon and Schuster, 1969) and *A Separate Reality: Further Conversations with Don Juan* (New York: Simon and Schuster, 1971) and *Journey to Ixtlan: The Lessons of Don Juan* (New York: Simon and Schuster, 1972).

talking with approval about the existence of, and need for, the Association of Women in Psychology, "feminine" therapists, and "feminist" psychotherapy.[27] We see this same parochial and separationist attitude in the Association of Black Psychologists and in the Catholic Psychological Association. We have a long way to come on the road to human development when even at the professional level we must have such a totally artificial separation of one human from another.

At a higher level of consciousness, life is accepted and acceptable as a constantly changing panorama. It is motion, and when change ceases, so does life. Such a view of life accepts the reality of ambivalence, and the fact that there are many answers to one question, many ways to do the "right" things, presents no threat. How crucial, and how difficult it is, to develop ourselves to the point of easy acceptance of this reality of the ambivalence of life. With this acceptance I am actually capable of including others in my life. I have no need to exclude them. I can truly say, "Come in—as you are—be with me. Since I am the measure of me, you are no threat to me."

This is not what our schools teach our children. In common with other social organizations the school conditions children into the acceptance of the either/or. One has to win or lose, pass or fail, be a good or bad student, be popular or unpopular. Achievement is always measured in terms of comparison with others, rather than with one's own needs and satisfactions. Every child has to know thus and so within a certain period of time, or he does not know it at all. All of this, of course, totally ignores the reality of the individual differences of each child.

A gloomy picture of what might lie ahead, in this objective, rational world of the future is painted by Ellul:

> With the final integration of the instinctive and the spiritual by means of these human techniques, the edifice of the technical society will be completed. It will not be a universal concentration camp, for it will be guilty of no atrocity. It will not seem insane, for everything will be ordered, and the strains of human passion will be lost amid the chromium gleam. We shall have nothing more to lose and nothing to win. Our deepest instincts and our most secret passions will be analyzed, published and exploited. We shall be rewarded with everything our hearts ever desired. And the supreme luxury of the society of technical necessity will be to grant the bonus of useless revolt and of an acquiescent smile.[28]

27. Katherine Kasten, op. cit.
28. Jacques Ellul, op. cit., p. 426.

Oates, however, is more optimistic, and she feels that we may have actually turned the corner. She says:

We have come to the end of, we are satiated with, the "objective," valueless philosophies that have always worked to preserve a status quo, however archaic. We are tired of the old dichotomies: Sane/Insane; Black/White; Man/Nature; Victor/ Vanquished, and above all, the Cartesian dualism—I/It. Although once absolutely necessary to get us through the exploratory, analytical phase of our development as human beings, they are no longer useful or pragmatic. They are no longer true. [29]

Her optimism may be premature, but there is no question that if we are to expand our state of living, if we are to go beyond the narrow restrictions of the intellect, then we must be able to leave behind, as a no longer needed form of security, this either/or state of mind.

The lessening of this need for dichotomy also means that feelings and intuition are acceptable as conditions that go along with rather than replace reason and intellect. Mystics and men of God have always been acceptable in our culture even though they talked about the "beyond," seeing and touching God, and having visions. It is somewhat ironic that seeing a vision of the Virgin Mary might result in sainthood, whereas if one conversed with ghosts the likely result would be incarceration as an insane individual. Thus we have actually accepted the idea of an expanded consciousness, but in a very restricted manner. Increasingly, however, men and women of high professional stature, people who are hard to categorize as insane or crazy, are going beyond the realm of the intellect. It may well be that soon the inner subjective world, which we can experience but never specifically know, will become accepted for the reality that it is.

COGNITION, KNOWLEDGE, UNDERSTANDING, INSIGHT

The counselor who stresses the reality of an inner world, and a world beyond our consciousness, does not accept the world we intellectually know and understand as the sum total of our being. We talk about counseling as a process, a relationship, an experiencing, but at

29. Joyce Carol Oates, "New Heaven and Earth," *Saturday Review*, 55:51–55 (November, 1972).

the same time many counselors would appear to feel that clients and counselors can, somehow, come to *know* their way out of their difficulties. Certainly no one would deny the relationship between freedom and knowledge, but one can know without being wise enough to be free. As Whitehead comments:

> *You cannot be wise without some basis of knowledge; but you may easily acquire knowledge and remain bare of wisdom. Now wisdom is the way in which knowledge is held.* [30]

And again:

> *In a sense, knowledge shrinks as wisdom grows; for details are swallowed up in principles.* [31]

Much earlier, Cowper contributed a related thought:

> *Knowledge is proud that he has learned so much, Wisdom is humble that he knows no more.* [32]

The behavioral science concept of man has also tended to delude many counselors into the belief that by knowing about man they could also know man. One may learn about man by examining him, by studying him and analyzing him, but one may still be a long way from knowing the real man. Only by an experiencing and living-with can the counselor come to know the real person-in-being, the existential man.

Counselors have generally accepted the concept that the more we know about the client, the better our chance of being effective with him. We might wonder, however, whether the material we use to get to "know" the client may possibly move us away from him, and help us to develop a highly distorted and biased picture. Each time a piece of information about one human being passes through another human being it comes out a little less like the original. Often, for example, we may have several reports from the teachers of a child, but we have no reports on the teachers or the circumstances under which the reports were made. Even when we have what might be called standardized test data we should keep in mind the fact that the people who administer the tests, and those who interpret the test data, are not standardized!

We might hypothesize, at least, that the client with whom we

30. Alfred North Whitehead, *The Aims of Education and Other Essays* (New York: New American Library, 1960), p. 41.
31. *Ibid.*, p. 48.
32. James Robert Boyd (ed.), *The Task, Table Talk and Other Poems of William Cowper*, Book VI, *Winter Walk at Noon* (New York: A. S. Barnes and Co., 1853), p. 297.

are working is the person who is now in the office with us, and this person may or may not bear much resemblance to the person as categorized in an information folder. We may also wonder about the relative importance of the degree to which the person present apparently differs from the test data person. In speaking to a group of psychoanalysts, Hartmann was expressing the same general feeling when he said, "Despite what the great Plato thought about it, we do not believe in a simple correlation between the steps toward insight and the steps to moral improvement."[33]

This skepticism about the extent to which knowledge helps us to actually know a person is also indicated by Walsh when he says, "I am not at all certain that the help that they receive is a direct result of our sophisticated knowledge of the mind, unless in the process of accumulating that knowledge we have also gained wisdom and compassion for and about people."[34] We may thus question the extent to which human understanding, and thus human communication, is dependent on the possession of didactic information, often of a highly questionable nature from equally questionable sources, and raise at least the possibility that this may pose a real hindrance to the development of a deep and basic understanding between two people.

The concept of the relationship between knowing and insight is a product of both our formal educational system and psychoanalytic therapy. In the more traditional psychoanalysis the therapist imparted insight so that the patient could understand his unconscious mind and unconscious motivations, and the imparting of knowledge to the student by the teacher has been viewed as the primary function of the school.

The "knowing about" is found in both the school curricular experience and in counseling, and in schools we usually see what we might call either an "information" counselor, or a "diagnostic" counselor. These counselors are both concerned primarily with the transmission of information *to* the client, although the typical information counselor would probably be transmitting educational and occupational information, while the diagnostic counselor would be more likely to be transmitting an interpretation of personal test data about the client. Thus the first counselor would likely find communication most difficult, since often he is transmitting, at best, information that *he* thinks the client wants and needs. The diagnostic counselor, on the other hand, is at least transmitting information *about* the client,

33. Heinz Hartmann, *Psychoanalysis and Moral Values* (New York: International Universities Press, 1960), p. 91.
34. Richard P. Walsh, "Comment," *American Psychologist*, 16:712–713 (November, 1961).

but it is still *from* the counselor *to* the client. Often too, of course, not only is the information dubious and questionable, but the client is a rather passive or even unwilling recipient of the information. Frequently, the basic purpose of this transmission of information is the manipulation and direction of the client so that he may become more "adjusted," more able to fit easily and comfortably into the status quo, and a less curious, questioning, rebellious member of his society. These counselors see the gathering and interpretation of knowledge, and its transmission to the client, as their basic function.

The counselor who is concerned with a basic human relationship, on the other hand, is one who thinks in terms of "the client to me," as well as "me to the client." Thus his verbal communication is based on the client as he presents himself, rather than on the client as he is presented by others and by test data. He has no preconceived information to give to the client, unless it is information that the client desires, information that will be helpful in the process of communication. Since most communication, however, is not really very deep if it is at an information level, it is not too often that information, per se, enters into the relationship between this counselor and the client. The bare-bones statistic of an IQ of 91 for a college freshman, who is being driven to desperation by the difficulty of his courses and the pressure of his professors and his family, is of no importance whatsoever to the counselor who sees himself involved in a warm and human relationship with another person, and in attempting to communicate nonverbally to that person his depth of understanding and acceptance.

If we are to think of man as a determined set of behaviors, then we could agree that ultimately every facet of man will be put under a microscope and examined, and prediction and control of the human race will become a part of an exact and empirical science. We might, on the other hand, hypothesize that one of the reasons why both psychology and medicine have never really got close to man, the total living being, is that they have fallen into the trap of empiricism. To medicine, man is a disease; to psychologists, he is a problem; to psychiatrists, he is a disease-problem; and to counselors, too frequently, he appears to be a profile of the results of various tests and examinations. Science has generally accepted the words "cognitive" and "meaningful" as somewhat synonymous. At least I think that science would probably say that the less cognitive a picture of man is, the less meaningful it is. My own perception would be that man—not man's behavior, since you cannot cut one off from the other, but man, the total existential being, if you will—is not really subject to empirical examination, and that both a human experience and a human being could mean very little in a cognitive sense, and yet at the same time could be overwhelmingly meaningful.

The empiricist would likely put knowing—cognition—above feeling, but we can know in an empirically cognitive sense without understanding in a feeling sense, and we can understand a fellow human without "knowing about" him, although we might consider "knowing about" to be more cognitive than "knowing."

It may also be that some counselors know much about the client, but have confused this knowing with self-understanding on the part of the client. They may then add to this confusion by "giving" the client more supposed knowledge, from some outer source, about himself. Roessler comments on this point:

> But the term "cognitive," for me, denotes too much intellectual emphasis in the psychotherapeutic process . . . the process of change . . . is really more a function of experiencing oneself in totality.[35]

As does Hora:

> But if cognition, which is another word for understanding . . . if understanding, clarification, elucidation, seeing the light, seeing what one really is, if this is the focus of psychotherapy, then one would be careful not to say more, not to talk too much because it might hamper understanding . . . . So then, not the explicit, but the implicit will have the therapeutic value, and so there will be less and less talk.[36]

Jung would appear to have been thinking in a somewhat similar manner when he said:

> We appeal only to the patient's brain if we try to inculcate a truth; but if we help him to grow up to this truth in the course of his own development, we have reached his heart, and this appeal goes deeper and acts with greater force.[37]

As does Gendlin:

> Now that psychotherapy is widely thought to involve a concrete feeling process, we are less specific about the (still vital) role of cognitive symbols and exploration . . . . Apparently, any good

35. Robert L. Roessler, "Psychotherapy: Healing or Growth," *Annals of Psychotherapy,* 4:10 (1963).

36. Thomas Hora, in *Annals of Psychotherapy,* 4:10 (1963), p. 33.

37. C. G. Jung, *Modern Man in Search of a Soul* (New York: Harcourt, Brace and World, 1933), p. 9.

vocabulary can be used as a symbolic tool for "working through" and interacting.[38]

There are some counselors and some counselor educators who might say that the above words do not apply to them because they are not involved in this "personal counseling or therapy sort of business," but rather in the "talking to, telling, information business." I would think that any form of human communication between the counselor and the client is personal, and the above words apply just as much when the client is a child who comes in to talk easily with the counselor about his job plans for the next year, as they do when the client is a child driven to desperation by his neurotic parents. They may apply even more in the former case, because it is in this talking relationship that the counselor may be most easily lulled into the false security of verbiage, just as the teacher who drones on endlessly assumes that the children *must* be learning something.

All of this, too, raises serious questions about the place of insight in the counseling process. Insight has generally been equated with self-understanding. The person who is insightful knows where he stands; he knows what he has and what he does not have. Insight usually implies, too, that not only does the individual know his assets and liabilities, but he operates with some reference to them. Thus an individual who knows that he has a low intellectual capacity but deliberately takes on a job that requires high intellectual capacity might be considered as having little insight. He knows his limitations, but he ignores them. Interestingly enough, however, despite the general acceptance of this point, it is contradicted by many school counselors who seem to feel that all that is needed for improvement is the first part of this insight—the knowing. Thus, more often than not, the use of test data in schools seems to assume that all the counselor has to do is test the students and tell them what they have and what they do not have, and everyone will live happily ever after. Certainly for the counselor, insightfulness, if it is to be considered at all, must include the assimilation and internalization of knowledge, so that it becomes a part of the total operational individual rather than an intellectual appendage. Each of us gradually develops a basic operational self-concept, and it is difficult to see how one can expect a person blithely and easily to accept a piece of information that means that this self-concept has to be altered drastically.

It should be noted, too, that an individual may wish, desperately, to change certain attitudes and feelings whose causes and de-

38. Eugene T. Gendlin, "Subverbal Communication and Therapist Expressivity: Trends in Client-Centered Therapy with Schizophrenics," *Journal of Existential Psychiatry*, 4:105 (Fall, 1963).

velopment he has come, possibly through counseling, to understand very well. Thus the client may say, "I know all these feelings that I have are just superstitions, and that they are not really religion at all, and I know why I have believed them. But why must I still go on believing them when I don't want to and when I know they are silly?" The client must go on believing them because he still needs to go on believing them, and he will continue to do so until his self is altered.

The place of insight in the therapeutic process has tended to be downgraded in recent years. Glasser, for example, in discussing Reality Therapy, says, "we emphasize behavior; we do not depend upon insight to change attitudes because in many cases it never will."[39] Wolpe and Lazarus, in indicating how behavior therapy differs from psychoanalytic therapy, say "Behavior therapists, by contrast, regard rational corrections as, in most instances merely a background to the specific reconditioning of reactions that usually belong to the autonomic nervous system."[40] Holland simply says, "We can therefore regard insight as potentially useful, but as neither sufficient nor necessary to modifications of the patient's behavior in a psychotherapeutic situation."[41]

Counselors who see the human relationship as the crucial factor in counseling, tend to think in terms of experiencing rather than the gaining of intellectual insight. Beier comments that "We speak specifically of 'experiencing' rather than of 'having insight,' because these two objectives can be most successfully realized when the patient is alerted to his own immediate behavior as it occurs . . . and not when it is discussed with him in the abstract."[42] Corlis and Rabe, in discussing a counseling session, say, "To repeat, the patient's experiencing is needed, not the explaining."[43] Carkhuff and Berenson, who view confrontation as the critical element in counseling, see insight as being of negative importance rather than of no importance:

> At best, insight inundates affect with ideas and drowns it in a whirlpool of words. At worst, the person is left with the feeling of being splintered into a thousand pieces, in contact with the

39. Glasser, op. cit., p. 51.
40. Joseph Wolpe and Arnold A. Lazarus, Behavior Therapy Techniques (New York: Pergamon Press, 1966), p. 131.
41. Glen A. Holland, Fundamentals of Psychotherapy (New York: Holt, Rinehart and Winston, 1965), p. 38.
42. Ernst G. Beier, The Silent Language of Psychotherapy (Chicago: Aldine Publishing Co., 1966), p. 54.
43. Rahe Corlis and Peter Rabe, Psychotherapy from the Center (Scranton, Penn.: International Textbook Co., 1969), p. 74.

fact that he has no identity of his own, only fitting in relation to specific people and situations.

. . . Thus, the alienated person who seeks only insights slowly decays while having the illusion of making progress.[44]

The counselor is little concerned with insight as interpreted in terms of intellectual understanding. He is concerned if it is to be related with process, if it is to be an experiencing, a living, a being again with real and deep feelings. Thus the insightfulness of the client may include the experiencing again of the dreadful feeling of aloneness, but an aloneness that after a while is not the same, because there is someone this time who cares, someone who is concerned. Maybe it could be thought of in terms of a noun or a verb. If a noun, it doesn't matter too much; if a verb, it matters very much. If the client is now a person who no longer feels alone in a strange world, then insight, in terms of the traditional concept of understanding, is more than likely a by-product. In fact, the client might well say, "Of course, I know now that I'm not alone, but then I always did *know* that I was not alone, only I didn't believe it before." He knew intellectually, but he didn't believe what he knew. Now he believes, and we might say that it does not matter too much whether he knows or not.

This client, for example, did not have any clear knowledge about just what had happened when he said:

The degree of trust I have in myself has a close relationship to how well I know myself . . . . I've learned something—about myself—in a tentative sort of way—that I didn't know even a few weeks ago—(pause)—maybe I'll talk about that . . . .

In the book by Burton that has already been referred to several times, there is a series of questions at the end of each of the fifteen case studies.[45] One of these questions is "Do you feel that this case developed significant insight? If not, can improvement be maintained?" It is of interest to note that twelve of the fifteen answers said, in varying ways, "Yes" or "No." One gave a reaction that was somewhat similar to that which has been presented in this book. The other two were as follows:

If by insight is meant conscious insight, then the answer is "no." If by insight is meant unconscious, then the answer is "yes." In either case, the patient has maintained her improve-

44. Robert R. Carkhuff and Bernard G. Berenson, *Beyond Counseling and Therapy* (New York: Holt, Rinehart and Winston, 1967), p. 177.

45. Arthur Burton (ed.), *Case Studies in Counseling and Psychotherapy* (Englewood Cliffs, N.J.: Prentice-Hall, 1959).

ment for a period of five years. (Conscious insight has the quality of intricate fact-finding or even of simple memory of related details. Through hindsight, the patient forms such details into a significant gestalt. Unconscious insight has a quality of experiencing in the present a previously not accepted capacity. The patient may never become aware of what has occurred in him to change his behavior.)[46]

Intellectual insight is no longer a sine qua non *of improvement in psychotherapy. It may be epiphenomenal but not necessarily causal. While we know very little about emotional insight, some such experience may take place. However, this is a function of the Begegnung and the change in the vector forces which come about through it. Such process is largely symbolic. (I have since regretted formulating this question for the Addendum except that heuristically it does reveal the present state of insight in modern-day psychotherapy.)*[47]

Insight, then, would appear to be an understanding that one may gain about himself, but it is a product of experiencing more than knowing. The counselor is an individual who should have achieved a high level of self-understanding, and the evidence would tend to indicate that sensitivity to others is a function of insight into oneself.[48] Nor is this self-understanding or insight something that one acquires from someone else. As Dreikurs says, "The therapist gave her strength, but no insight or reorientation."[49]

Insight is a sort of an end product. It is a deep and meaningful understanding, by me, about me, and about others. These comments, from junior high school clients, are insightful, but their cognitive respectability is of little importance compared with the fact that they are understandings arrived at by the children as a result of their human relationship with an insightful counselor:

The more pressure a teacher puts on a kid the greater the chance that the kid will resent whatever it is that the teacher is trying to do. A kid will do anything for a teacher who respects him.

46. *Ibid.,* p. 256. © 1959. Reprinted by permission of Prentice-Hall, Inc., Englewood Cliffs, N.J.
47. *Ibid.,* p. 280.
48. See William J. Mueller, "The Influence of Self Insight on Social Perception Scores," *Journal of Counseling Psychology,* 10:185–191 (Summer, 1963).
49. Rudolph Dreikurs, in Stanley W. Standal and Raymond J. Corsini, *Critical Incidents in Psychotherapy* (Englewood Cliffs, N.J.: Prentice-Hall, 1959), p. 70.

When are people going to start putting some of the blame on the school when a kid quits? He could be quitting because he's bored right out of his skin by subjects that have been forced on him, and have no use in his life.

You learn more when you do something in class . . . when you're involved . . . when you're participating instead of watching and listening . . . like when you're in science and you do the experiments. . . . I really learn something.

It's too bad the world isn't the kind of place a kid could get into trouble without getting into trouble—you know what I mean? Everybody gets so hot and bothered about delinquents and stuff like that, but if kids could have a chance to have some fun and excitement, and could do things with a little kick in them, they'd be all right. But all the adults want you to play the game with their rules. . . . The only trouble is they forget we're not adults. It's a lot more fun for us to break rules than to keep them.

EMPATHY AND CONGRUENCE

An empathic relationship is achieved when the counselor is able to work within the client's frame of reference, within the client's reality, responding with sensitivity to both the superficial and the deeper feelings of the client, some conscious, some unconscious. The counselor must also be able to communicate to the client his awareness of the client and his awareness of himself, and to do this he must be a genuine and congruent individual. The self that is communicated to the client must be genuine and human, and the counselor who can only repeat words or mumble, or ask clinically correct questions like a machine, or set up appropriate experiences for the client like an engineer—such a counselor is obviously going to have a difficult time establishing an empathic relationship with a client. Carkhuff and Berenson put it succinctly and well when they say, "If there can be no authenticity in therapy, then there can be no authenticity in life."[50] Corlis and Rabe are equally expressive when they say, "He gave the shirt off his back and has not been heard of since. So much for the Good Samaritan."[51]

Probably all counselors would agree that there is both a cognitive and an affective component in the achievement of an empathic

50. Carkhuff and Berenson, *op. cit.*, p. 29.
51. Corlis and Rabe, *op. cit.*, p. 37.

relationship with another human being, but some would obviously stress one a good deal more than the other. It is interesting to note that Wolpe, who sees himself as a "behavioral scientist," chides some of his fellows, who, "espousing notions of rigid behavioral engineering imagine that one can do without such personal influencing processes."[52]

In describing the client, Buchheimer and Balogh say:

> *The way he constructs his reality and the percepts he has of himself determine the way he addresses himself to his life's tasks and the goals he formulates for his life's work. It is important therefore, that the counselor allow the person with whom he is to work freedom in self-expression as well as expression of self in relation to problems and goals.*[53]

It is in the empathic climate that this expression of self can develop, and it is through this self-expression that one gradually comes, possibly, to perceive himself in a different manner. Man has many faces, but there is one face, for each of us, that is more basic, more real, and the client comes to sense this face when he is able to accept the current face. He can say, as has been said to me, "You know, when I actually could accept me as I was, then, right at that moment, me wasn't the same any more." As Hora puts it:

> *. . . if a human being attains the level of integration where he really can be what he really is, then every moment and every manifestation of his life will be a creative one.*[54]

And to be what one is, one must be a congruent, genuine, self-actualized individual. One must be able to be easily honest with oneself, and I would agree with Rosenfels that "wisdom is the product of an unfailing honesty."[55]

The congruent individual, too, is one who can perceive accurately, and Lesser has reported on an interesting study, which indicated that mere feelings, by the counselor, or similarity with the client, were not conducive to counseling progress and empathic understanding. More basic was the correct perception, by the counselor, of similarity, or lack of it.[56] In a somewhat related fashion,

52. Wolpe and Lazarus, *op. cit.*, p. 29.
53. Arnold Bucheimer and Sarah Carter Balogh, *The Counseling Relationship* (Chicago: Science Research Associates, 1961), p. 3.
54. Hora, *op. cit.*, p. 51.
55. Paul Rosenfels, *Psychoanalysis and Civilization* (New York: Libra Publishers, 1962), p. 83.
56. William M. Lesser, "The Relationship Between Counseling Progress and Empathic Understanding," Journal of Counseling Psychology, 8:330–336 (Winter, 1961).

Buchheimer has pointed out that in an empathic relationship cognitive perception of the other person becomes the capacity to perceive the counselee's frame of reference.[57]

Thus this honesty with self, this genuineness, this self-congruence on the part of the counselor, would appear to be the crucial factor in the development of an empathic relationship in which the client also might move toward actualization and freedom. This means, too, that the counselor must be free to feel his feelings during the counseling relationship, rather than bottling them up or presenting both to himself and to the client a blank face and pretending that he has no feelings. Since the counselor is a self-actualized individual, these feelings will be directed at himself, rather than at the client. This point is illustrated by Roessler, when, in discussing another therapist's description of his feelings during a counseling session, he comments that

> we could have been annoyed, irritated, and expressed this . . . the same consequences, so long as it wasn't "Damn you for behaving this way," and instead, "I'm annoyed, I'm frustrated. Something's wrong, and something needs to be done."[58]

This also stresses, obviously, the crucial necessity of counselor education centering on the deep and meaningful understanding *of the counselor* by the counselor, rather than on a superficial cognitive understanding of the client.

TRANSFERENCE AND COUNTERTRANSFERENCE

The phenomena of transference and countertransference have been, and still are, an important part of psychiatric literature, although little reference is usually made to them in counseling literature. If counselors however, see counseling as an intimate human involvement with another person or persons, then they should have some awareness of these phenomena so that they might be more aware of their potential occurrence, and be able to differentiate them from a more psuedo sort of transference that probably occurs with all counselors. Most analytically oriented counselors would tend generally to

57. Arnold Buchheimer, "The Development of Ideas about Empathy," *Journal of Counseling Psychology*, 10:61–70 (Spring, 1963).

58. Roessler, *op. cit.*, p. 27.

be acceptant of the following somewhat traditional descriptions of transference. First we may note Alexander:

> *The principal therapeutic tool is the transference, in which the patient relives, in relation to the therapist his earlier interpersonal conflicts. Regression to the dependent attitudes of infancy and childhood is a constant feature of the transference, and, in the majority of cases, the central one. This regression in itself has a supportive effect. It allows the patient to postpone his own decisions and to reduce the responsibilities of adult existence by retiring into a dependent attitude toward the therapist which resembles the child's attitude in the child-parent relationship.*[59]

Then Hendrick:

> *For when a patient recounts free associations, he soon speaks of events or phantasies of vital interest to himself, and when these are told, the listener is gradually invested with some of the emotion which accompanies them. The patient gradually begins to feel that the sympathetic listener is loved or hated, a friend or an enemy, one who is nice to him or one who frustrates his needs and punishes him. The feelings toward the listener become more and more like those felt toward the specific people the patient is talking about, or, more exactly, those his unconscious "is talking about." This special case of object-displacement during psychoanalysis is called transference.*[60]

And finally, Horney:

> *Freud observed that in the analytical situation the patient not only talks about his present and past troubles, but also shows emotional reactions to the analyst. These reactions are frequently irrational in character. A patient may forget entirely his purpose in coming to analysis and may find nothing important except being loved or appreciated by the analyst. He may develop altogether disproportionate fears about jeopardizing his relationship to the analyst. He may transform the situation, which in actuality is one in which the analyst helps the patient to straighten out his problems, into one of passionate struggle for the upper hand. For instance, instead of feeling relieved by some clarification of his problems, a patient may see only one*

59. Franz Alexander, *Psychoanalysis and Psychotherapy* (New York: Norton, 1956), p. 154.
60. Ives Hendrick, *Facts and Theories of Psychoanalysis* (New York: Alfred A. Knopf, 1958), p. 193.

fact, that the analyst has recognized something that he was unaware of, and he may react with violent anger. A patient may, contrary to his own interest, secretly pursue the purpose of defeating the analyst's endeavors.[61]

The general concept held by both the medical doctor psychotherapist and the counseling psychologist is that this transference relationship takes place in psychotherapy, and that it is the working out, the explaining of these transferred feelings, including resistances and hostility, that helps the client to move ahead. It is important for the student counselor to note that when such a transference relationship does develop, it is not a case of superficial feeling, or of dislike on the part of the client for the therapist because he is like someone the client used to know. It is, rather, an infusion of feelings into the therapist, so that the therapist *is* the hated and autocratic father of twenty years ago, and the resistances that develop are as "real" as they can be. It is not that the client thinks he can now see how hostile and submissive he felt toward his father—he *is* hostile and submissive, and the therapist *is* his father. It is the gradual understanding of the why and the what and the how of this phenomenon that helps the client to greater growth. As Mowrer says:

Rather does the therapist help the patient to see what he is trying to accomplish by means of his "transference" behavior which is now just as real and just as meaningful as it originally was—and to understand the circumstances in which this type of behavior originated and why it was not earlier resolved.[62]

Thus the client comes to feel as he once felt, but there is a difference. Although he is feeling as he did before toward a superior figure, this authority figure is now one who will be acceptant of his negative feelings, and will help him to understand them rather than reject him and strengthen his basic negative feelings.

Such authority and superiority of the "doctor" or the therapist are stressed again and again in psychoanalytic literature. This reaction is easy to understand, particularly with the medical doctor therapist. Here is a person who has had a background of education and training and work where without a doubt in the vast majority of the cases he does have the answers as to what to do about the ailments of a patient—a patient who, most often, does not know what is wrong with him, and does not know what to do about it. The

61. Karen Horney, *New Ways in Psychoanalysis* (New York: Norton, 1939), pp. 154–155.
62. O. Hobart Mowrer (ed.), *Psychotherapy: Theory and Research* (New York: Ronald Press, 1953), p. 567.

doctor is in authority, and he *is* the superior figure. Nor does working in a hospital tend to diminish the feeling. There the therapist is in
an environment where the patients are very often psychotic, or are
assumed to be psychotic, and in the staff relationship the therapist
finds himself at the top of the hierarchical ladder. Although there
may be frequent reference to teamwork, it is usually quite evident
who is the top sergeant of the team! Thus the phenomenon of transference is very definitely related to the authority and superiority of
the therapist. If the therapist did not have such authority and superiority in the eyes of both himself and his client, then we might raise
the question of whether or not transference would take place. On
this point Rogers writes:

> For the analyst this means that he interprets such attitudes,
> and perhaps through these evaluations establishes the charac-
> teristic transference relationship. For the client-centered thera-
> pist this means that he attempts to understand and accept such
> attitudes, which then tend to become accepted by the client as
> being his own perception of the situation, inappropriately
> held. [63]

Corlis and Rabe are even more skeptical about the traditional
ideas toward transference. They say:

> What is transferred to the therapist are the patient's attitudes.
> If a transference relationship is to result, the therapist must
> then fall into the role which the patient "transfers" upon him.
> Traditionally, this distortion imposed upon the relationship is
> encouraged. In our technique we do not encourage it. [64]

Thus, the client may have the feelings that are possible of
transference in the transference relationship, but they are not transferred to the counselor if the counselor has become to the client the
sort of person that the counselor can be. It is on this point, indeed,
that some counselors present a most valid and reasonable criticism:
Can the counselor really be this sort of person, both to himself and to
the client? The counselor, after all, does know more than the client
about the psychology of personality disturbances. He is very frequently, in the hierarchy of values, someone who is considered to be
more important than the client; and he is the one to whom the client
goes to find answers, or at least to go through some experience that
will make him a better adjusted person. How, then, can the coun-

63. Carl R. Rogers, *Client-Centered Therapy* (Boston: Houghton Mifflin, 1951), p.
    218.
64. Corlis and Rabe, *op. cit.*, p. 95.

selor avoid being superior and authoritative, both in his own eyes and in those of the client?

This is a question that no counselor can answer in an absolute fashion. Certainly, more in the way of knowledge and emotional stability on the part of one individual does not mean actual or felt superiority to someone else. A counselor may feel very deeply the worth and dignity of his client. He respects him as a fellow man—not as a client, not as a disturbed person, not as a selfish creature—simply as a fellow human being. How well and how honestly does he do this? Each counselor must try to answer that for himself.

If, in either group or individual therapy, the counselor is to become completely accepted by the other members of the group (one or more), as a member of the group, it would seem that he must lose his identity as the "leader." As long as he is the leader, in the mind and in the feelings of the client or the other members of the group, he cannot be a member of the group; he remains an outsider. As an outsider he is suspect, and he is, needless to say, one on whom it would be very easy to transfer feelings. In a normal group session, for instance, a leader statement such as "What one of you said there a few minutes ago made me feel sort of mad" would cause the defensive flags of most of the members of the group to rise. This would happen because the leader is still the leader. He is the *outside* critic.

But in some group sessions, and in some counseling sessions, the situation changes. The leader gradually disappears as the leader, and becomes rather a member of a group (of two or more) going through an exciting experience. The counselor may feel that while the counselor is the sort of person who is not very often threatened or disturbed, he is, nevertheless, a human being. If, at a certain point, as he is immersed with the client in the client's expression of feelings, he realizes, "This sort of worries me," then it may be better that, remaining at all times honest, he express his feeling to the client. If the counseling relationship has developed as it *can* develop, the client will not be threatened by such an expression of feeling on the part of this other person (not the boss, or the authority, or the head man) who is going through this experience with him. On the other hand, we can assume that if the counselor, in order to maintain his integrity and honesty, must be continually telling the client that he is worried or concerned by something in the discussion, then this person should be the client rather than the counselor!

It is likely, too, that there is a wide variance on the part of counselors in their ideas of just what constitutes transference. Might one not be liked or disliked by a client in a purely personal manner? Since counselors, after all, have had people fall in love with them (and vice versa) in a noncounseling relationship, we could probably assume that some clients might fall in love, or some reasonable fac-simile thereof, with a counselor in his office as well as outside his office. On this question one therapist writes:

> *Much of what is cavalierly called "transference" by many therapists, and dogmatically interpreted to their patients as such seems actually to be the patient's becoming attached to the therapist on a fairly clear-cut reality basis. The therapist is, after all, usually quite intelligent; a sympathetic listener; fairly cultured; of good socioeconomic standing; and seemingly of a suitable age to many of his female patients. . . . This is not to gainsay the fact that in many instances patients fall in love with their therapists because the latter unconsciously represent father-figures, authority-symbols, and so forth. . . . But to insist that classic transference exists where it patently does not leads to other difficulties, including the avoidance of some of the pa-tient's basic desires and the forcing on her of a false interpreta-tion.*[65]

These client comments, for example, were made to counselors:

> *Client 1: People don't really care about people . . . you don't really care what happens to me . . . you're getting paid to sit and listen to me but you don't really give a damn whether I sink or swim.*
>
> *Client 2: And then he stood there yelling at me to straighten out the wheels on the car. I clenched my fist and put it up to his face (does this to counselor) . . . and then I yelled back . . . (yells at counselor) . . . yell at me again and I'll break your neck."*
>
> *Client 3: And for that brief vacation she really filled a void in my life. . . . We talked for hours and it really made me feel as if someone cared . . . like . . . like now I know . . . I have a feeling that you care for me . . . because . . . well . . . you've given me the . . . I mean . . . a chance to talk . . . a chance not to be lonely.*
>
> *Client 4: And I guess maybe I love you. . . . That's all right, isn't it. . . .*
>
> *Client 5: All I ask is not to be interrupted when I'm saying something. . . . If there's anything I despise it's being cut off in the middle of a sentence. . . . She always did that to me and now when you do it . . . well, just don't. . . . I won't be able to talk to you if you do.*
>
> *Client 6: There are just the two of you—and I love you both, but in a different way.*

65. Anonymous author, in Standal and Corsini, *op. cit.*, pp.90–91.

Client 7: *Yeh . . . I could always make him anxious . . . and right now you're anxious, aren't you?*

These are certainly examples of highly personal expressions of feeling by the client toward the counselor, but the counselor would not appear in these examples to be anyone other than himself. In a way, the client feelings may be being transferred to him from someone else, but in the mind of the client he still retains his identity as the counselor, rather than becoming some earlier authority figure.

These examples could be described as transference if we use the description given by Bellak and Small who say, "In the present discussion, transference is used broadly as comprising all the non-rational sentiments of the patient toward the therapist including hopes, fears, likes, and dislikes."[66]

Although Bordin agrees with the concept that the therapeutic process is possible without the development of the transference relationship, his reasoning that this is because of the lack of depth of counseling is to be questioned:

Because the counselor deals with relatively well-integrated individuals who are reasonably free of intense conflicts, his clients are not likely to exhibit many transference phenomena and will not readily develop intensive transference relationships unless subjected to quite ambiguous relationships over a relatively long period of time. Since most clients will not come with a profound therapeutic orientation, deep transference can take place in only a minority of instances.[67]

Historically, the attention of therapists has been directed toward the behavior of their clients; thus it might be assumed that attention would be directed at the transference of the client's feelings toward the counselor rather than at the transference of the counselor's feelings toward the client. This phenomenon of countertransference has been defined, like transference, as ranging all the way from an omnibus inclusion of all of the feelings of the counselor toward the client to the more subconscious and suppressed feelings of the counselor that may be brought out by the transference of feelings from the client.

Generally, however, as in transference, there is a differentiation between a surface relationship—such as a Baptist counselor's possible feeling of irritation toward a client who continually utters anti-Baptist statements—and the possible development of subtle but

66. Leopold Bellak and Leonard Small, *Emerging Psychotherapy and Brief Psychotherapy* (New York: Grune and Stratton, 1965), p. 40.
67. Edward S. Bordin, *Psychological Counseling* (New York: Appleton-Century-Crofts, 1955), p. 150.

deep feelings of paternalism toward a younger male client who iden-
tifies with the counselor as an autocratic father figure.

These counselors, for example, have become personally involved, and their expressions are indications of their own concern
about themselves, rather than about the client. Again, these are
hardly examples of countertransference in the classic sense, although the counselor is transferring some of his personal feelings
over to the client.

Counselor 1: *I can't, Martha, I can't—you must do it.*

Counselor 2: *Don't you realize that I really do care what happens to my clients. I care what happens to you—I always have.*

Counselor 3: *Anxious . . . who . . .? . . . me?*

Counselor 4: *Well, I wouldn't say that to him. . . . You've
always been sort of meek and mild and if you ever said anything like that . . . well, he might think that I encouraged you to
say it . . . that I sort of encouraged you to rebel. Saying that
would only lead to more trouble for you.*

Counselor 5: *It would be nice if you mentioned to your
mother how much I've been able to help you in counseling.*

Counselor 6: *Your search for justice may not bear fruit . . .
trying to find a universal kind of justice could make a person
bitter because maybe it doesn't exist.*

Most counselors could probably understand, and possibly see
in themselves the sort of feelings described as countertransference
by Hafner:

> *In this phase of treatment my counter-transference for the first
> time became a serious problem. After several apparently fruit-
> less hours, I felt considerable unrest creeping up in me, since I
> was increasingly groping in the dark in front of my silent pa-
> tient. I felt pressed to do some active analyzing, but I had to
> concede to myself that in this situation activity on my part
> might well have endangered everything that had been achieved
> so far. Gradually, I felt a certain resignation. I feared my treat-
> ment could fail after all. Thus I recognized aggressive impulses
> within myself coming up against Gisels as I anticipated the
> frustration of my own wish for a successful completion of her
> treatment. I experienced these hours that apparently had
> passed uselessly as a waste of time.*
>
> *Under these circumstances I found it difficult to carry
> through the treatment with a persistently friendly attitude. But
> it seems, after all, that I succeeded in it. . . .* [68]

68.   Heinz Hafner, "A Case of Pseudo-Neurotic Schizophrenia," in Burton, *op. cit.*, p.
      302.

Although the therapist here did not verbalize to the patient his feelings about her, the fact that he can write easily about them, the fact that he could consciously be aware of them and acceptant of them, might, in a way, be a reflection of his own honesty and security; and it was to this that his patient was reacting, so that she could feel, correctly, that he was basically being kind and understanding toward her. I would tend to think of this as a human experience. If that is what is meant by countertransference, then it would be difficult to see how any counselor could avoid being involved periodically in such an experience.

PART FOUR

The Counselor

Chapter 13

The Counselor as a Person

Every individual human is affected by, and a part of, the world that surrounds him. The counselor, particularly the school counselor, lives, professionally, in the world of the young, and I fear that the gap between the counselor and his younger clientele is increasing rather than decreasing. The counselor tends to be a "Learn from— what others passed on to you from yesterday, and be happy in spending today preparing for tomorrow" sort of person, while the young client cries out, "Relevancy—to me—now—today." What is this world, which the counselor must understand and be able to be a part of, if he is to be successful?

THE WORLD OF THE COUNSELOR[1]

The mad, lemming-like rush for higher education which marked the 1960's has abated somewhat in the 1970's. However, in order to be culturally virtuous and legitimate one must still start his formal education at the tender age of three or four and continue it well on into what used to be known as the stage of adulthood, the early twenties.

While some would say that the phenomenon known as "adolescence" goes back to the Industrial Revolution most American adults would only have to trace their ancestry back two or three generations to lose any trace of adolescence. A century ago, the adolescence of most young people was, at best, brief, and adulthood

---

1. Dugald S. Arbuckle, "The Counselor: Relevant or Irrelevant?" *High School Journal*, 54:265–275 (January, 1971).

came early. The young girl was usually a mother before she was out of her teens, and the young man was earning his way, either supporting his own young family or helping to support the family of his parents, before he was out of his teens. Higher education was reserved for the elite, and possibly effete, few.

Thus the period of time that must pass before an individual can become accepted as a contributing member of the adult society becomes steadily greater, and as does the frustration of the young individual who may see himself as being kept indefinitely in a stage of dependent childhood. Keniston has recently commented that "we have a large group of people who are psychological adults and sociological adolescents,"[2] and in another publication, he suggests a new post-adolescent stage, the stage of youth.[3] But regardless of what one might call this delayed period of non-adulthood, it is marked by dependency on others, and, in a sense, a degree of irresponsibility. There are different thoughts as to the effect that this has on the young. Bettelheim, for example, states that he is "convinced that keeping our young people in a state of limbo for so many years must have deleterious effects" and goes on to say: "At the prime of their lives students are getting a four-year paid vacation. They realize this and are ashamed of it."[4] Blaine, too, feels that "many college age men and women feel guilty about being given so much without having earned it," and that as a result, "they cast about for risks to take in order to test their capacities as well as their courage."[5]

These comments, however, reflect the feeling of adult scholars of another generation, and one may wonder if they are reflecting how *they* would feel in similar circumstances, rather than giving an accurate picture of the feelings of the young. One might theorize that if a twenty-four-year-old individual has grown up in a culture in which it is assumed that someone else pays your bills until you are twenty-five years of age, he will feel no more guilt than would the seventeen-year-old who grows up in a culture in which it is assumed you are looked after until you are eighteen years of age. Carey, in fact, feels that one of the current trends is away from the traditional view that the young have never "had it so good."[6] He also points out

2. Mary A. Hall, "A Conversation with Kenneth Keniston," *Psychology Today,* 2:16–23 (November, 1969).
3. Kenneth Keniston, *Young Radicals* (New York: Harcourt, Brace and World, 1968).
4. Mary A. Hall, "A Conversation with Bruno Bettelheim," *Psychology Today,* 2:20–24 (May, 1969).
5. Graham B. Blaine, Jr., "What's Behind the Youth Rebellion?" *Boston Sunday Herald Traveler,* Nov. 16, 1969, pp. 22–27.
6. Richard W. Carey, "Student Protest and the Counselor," *Personnel and Guidance Journal,* 48:185–191 (November, 1969).

four other trends, namely, away from the traditional view that it is the individual's responsibility to make the education offered him relevant, or he is at fault; away from the traditional view that a rule is a rule, and right or wrong, it must be obeyed; away from the traditional view that school rules were made for the purpose of insuring essential controls or for making a better educational environment; and away from the traditional view that we have adequate processes available to bring about needed changes in laws and institutions.[7] In my experience the affluence of the young would appear to be generally taken for granted, but what does cause soul-searching is the lack of involvement and the inability to do something, personally, about what they see as the many evils of the society in which they live.

And the years of experience in an educational system which generally operates on the assumption, even at the university level, that students are still basically irresponsible children, leaves its mark. The very fact that the majority of students still put up with the "*loco parentis*" attitude, in which the university assumes the role of the benign and caring parent, indicates the degree to which they accept the concept of their own irresponsibility. It is sad indeed when an eighteen-year-old girl indicates that she still needs a secluded dorm and the watchful eye of a proctor to keep her from becoming a sex-mad drug addict. Somewhere along the line, her educational experience must have been deficient if at the age of eighteen, her personal behavior is still primarily determined by the rules, regulation, and authority of others. This shows, too, in the inability of many students to go beyond the point of criticizing what is wrong. When an instructor or administrator agrees with such criticism, and then asks for well-thought-out suggestions as to what might be done, the number of volunteers drops off sharply. Riesman, feels that "even where students have obtained the power to control their own lives and their own education, they find it difficult to create the structures that would sustain an ongoing cooperative and an ongoing self-directed educational process."[8] Hadden, in a somewhat similar vein, states that "for all their abstract realism, students lack a realistic sense of what their ideals imply in terms of social and public action. . . . The critical question is whether their social idealism . . . will be moulded into a commitment to transform society toward their goals. Or will it become the hypocrisy of the present generation raised to a higher level of rhetoric?"[9]

7. *Ibid.*
8. George T. Harris, "The Young Are Captives of Each Other," *Psychology Today*, 3:28–32 (October, 1969).
9. Jeffrey K. Hadden, "The Private Generation," *Psychology Today*, 3:32–35 (October, 1969).

363

But one can only learn responsible action by the acceptance of responsibility, and the acceptance of responsibility means that one will likely fail more often than one will succeed. In the long run the counselor is not helping the client in his struggle toward freedom by accepting responsibility that is rightfully and morally that of the client, not the counselor. If the school as an institution insists on teaching irresponsibility to the young, the counselor should stoutly resist and insist on the intellectual and moral right of the young to learn their own way, not simply to ape that of the generation that has preceded them.

Adult counselors usually represent a generation that assumes that the ability to postpone immediate gratification for the furtherance of goals that lie ahead is a sign of maturity. Indeed, this was Freud's definition of maturity, and he saw children as those who lived by the pleasure principle and demanded gratification now. On this basis many adults today view the aging young as children, and they refer to them as the "instant sex, instant pot, instant everything" generation. Ayn Rand, in a Boston lecture, commented rather scathingly: "The philosophy, if you can call it that, of Woodstock was 'now, now, love, love, love, now,' and these are the same people who had absolutely no regard for the property of residents of Bethel, New York. Who paid for this love? Apparently the unloved people did."[10] The philosophy that supports the concept that youth is the time to prepare for the future takes for granted, however, that there will be a future, and that that future will not be too drastically different from the present. Thus the young are supposed to prepare generally, for they *know* will happen in the future.

Today, however, many of the young, fat and affluent, stuffed with the material goodies that have been provided for them by others, are not particularly enamored of a future society based on the present. In an ironic sense, it is the very success of modern technology that has made possible the current dissatisfaction with a technological society. We, old and young, now live in a society of rapid change, with the ever-present threat of instant annihilation hanging over our heads, and the reality is that today cannot be viewed as the measure for tomorrow. As Friedenberg stated, "It is becoming increasingly unrealistic for the school to demand or promise *anything* in the way of long range career expectations."[11] In a more specific sense Marr indicated: "For certain occupations . . . such as occupations in the social sciences, the future entrants seem to continue without a firm or final specification until they come to an age when

10. Ayn Rand, as quoted in the *Quincy Patriot Ledger*, Nov. 10, 1969, p. 42.
11. Edgar Z. Friedenberg, *Coming of Age in America* (New York: Random House, 1963), p. 173.

changes in interests, values and personality factors, increase their inclination for these fields."[12] It is likely that, for at least the immediate future, this uncertainty will continue to expand, and counselors who view their major function as the assistance of rather compliant youngsters to happily prepare for a tomorrow will face increasing frustration and a widening communication gap.

But the school, and the vast majority of both teachers and counselors in it, continues to reflect a pattern of life and values which makes increasingly less sense to an increasingly large number of students. The adult may say that it is impossible to have a life in which everything that one does is relevant and meaningful now, and that one must spend some of the present doing what may not appear to be too relevant, or to bring much pleasure, if there is ever to be a future. The young, however, will say that while this may be so, there is a great deal of their current life which is irrelevant, and they are not satisfied to continue in this way. And who could deny that much of what goes on in the school is, for an increasing number of youth, totally irrelevant? It is no accident that the youth who are most critical of their educational experiences tend to be the most creative and capable, and they would appear to voice the feelings of many of their less verbal fellows. Underground newspapers in high schools, for example, while they are often condemned by both parents and teachers, represent a far higher level of creativity and literary excellence than does the deadly dull school paper.

The failure of the school, generally, in the matter of the education of the young for the acceptance of a responsible human sexuality may be traced to an adherence to the "Don't do anything new but prepare for tomorrow" philosophy, which generally led to irresponsible sexual behavior, since self-responsibility was never stressed. Today we see much the same pattern in the matter of drug abuse, and the young are exhorted: "Don't do it," much as they have been with regard to sexual behavior. The attitude is generally repressive and punitive, there is minimal acceptance of the young, and all drugs appear to be considered to be equally bad. This would appear to be the attitude of counselors, as well as teachers and administrators, and most articles on counselors and drugs have nothing whatsoever to say about the counseling, if any is needed, of youth who may be involved in the use of various kinds of drugs. In a fairly typical paper, for example, Hatt says:

The counselor has the responsibility of informing himself, faculty members, parents and students about the dangers inherent

12. Evelyn Marr, "Vocational Maturity and Specifications of a Preference," *Vocational Guidance Quarterly,* 18:45–48 (September, 1969).

in the use of drugs. . . . one of his major concerns will be to develop a dialogue with users and potential users so that they will have an opportunity not to withdraw from the mainstream of school and community life into their subculture. [13]

Many students, however, would feel that a "user" of marijuana is not necessarily one who has withdrawn from the mainstream of society, and the crucial question for counselors should not be how to get people back into the mainstream of the school, but rather what is wrong with the mainstream of our school that makes so many of the best young minds want to withdraw from it. The assumption of the superiority of the current school culture is hardly the best way to encourage a dialogue with those who have rejected it as inadequate. And it is this assumption of the superiority of the adult pattern of life and living, and a resentment of any questioning of it, that makes a significant proportion of the young apathetic, a somewhat smaller number cynical and skeptical, and a still smaller number violent and destructive. There is an alienation, and this produces not only a here-and-now philosophy, but also a "Let's feel more and think less" way of living.

The acceptance of the existential concept of stressing today rather than yesterday or tomorrow is obviously related to the development of an openness and acceptance of feelings rather than, in the name of reason, a repression of them. Flacks feels that "the central conflict between dominant and humanistic cultures is the opposition between self-control and self-expression." [14] To many students, the counselor represents the self-control philosophy of the school, whereas he sees a meaningful life as one in which there is a high level of self-expression, and thus a higher level of personal honesty. In many ways the school would appear to have become the enemy of self-expression, and it is ironic that high academic achievement, which is often considered to be the major reason for the existence of the school, bears no relationship to real-life measures of creativity and achievement. Thus the school, in a sense, is engaged in a gigantic social hoax, willingly abetted by school counselors, and the only ones who resent and resist this suppression of self are an increasing number of youth who are generally considered to be rather queer and definitely not the all-American type.

In many ways the struggle of youth against the school is very much the same as the struggle in which professional therapists are involved with their clients. As we have seen, Carkhuff and Berenson

13. Irving Hatt, "The School Counselor and Drugs," *School Counselor*, 17:14–17 (September, 1969).
14. Richard Flacks, "Student Activists: Result, Not Revolt," *Psychology Today*, 1:18–25 (October, 1967).

stress the need for authenticity when they say, "If there can be no authenticity in therapy, then there can be no authenticity in life,"[15] and Corlis and Rabe invoke the human need to experience and feel when they say, "To repeat, the patient's experiencing is needed, not the explaining."[16] In viewing his function as a psychotherapist, Jourard says:

> My criterion of success in this quest is not solely whether my behavior appears "normal" to others; but rather, my experiences of feeling free, responsible, potent, and alive. The criterion of success has shifted from exclusive attention to behavior to the person's experience.
>
> I have been far too long aware that in appearing normal to others, I felt benumbed and dead within, a habit-ridden plaything of social pressures and expectation. And I have known too many people—fellow seekers (I used to call them patients)—who were exemplary in their conduct, but dead or desperate on the inside.[17]

Thus the very chains from which the therapist hopes to free the client are the ones that society has wrapped around him, and probably the most potent agent of society in this process of capturing the soul and the spirit is the school. It would surely not be unfair to say that teachers and counselors are much alike in that *most* of them aid society in this process of enslavement, rather than trying to help the individual to extricate himself so that he can once again breathe, so that he can roam free, so that he can truly say, "*I* must be the one to answer for myself."

Thus the cry of youth to experience and to feel is a cry that is heard by the out-of-school therapists, but not very often by the school counselor. This inability of the school to listen has, without doubt, pushed some students to the point where they are apparently willing to throw out the baby in order to get rid of the bath water. And it is unfortunate when supposedly educated youth get to the point of cynicism and desperation such that all thinking and any sort of "Let us try to reason this out together" becomes suspect. May expresses his concern about this attitude when he says:

> They seek honesty, openness, a genuineness of personal relationship; they are out to find a genuine feeling, a touch, a look

---

15. Robert H. Carkhuff and Bernard G. Berenson, *Beyond Counseling and Therapy* (New York: Holt, Rinehart and Winston, 1967), p. 29.

16. Rahe B. Corlis and Peter Rabe, *Psychotherapy from the Center* (Scranton, Pa.: International Textbook Co., 1969), p. 74.

17. Sidney M. Jourard, "The Therapist as a Guru," *Voices* 5:49–51 (Summer/Fall 1969).

in the eyes, a sharing of fantasy. The criterion becomes the intrinsic meaning, and is judged by one's authenticity, doing one's own thing, and giving in the sense of making one's self available for the other. . . .The error in this new morality is the lack of content for these values. The content seems present, but it turns out to be based on whim and temporary emotion.
    Where is the permanence?[18]

This concern is warranted, and yet one must wonder if the young people described are less free, and thus less capable of contributing to society, than are their culturally more "normal" counselors and teachers. These are the people, after all, who supposedly provide the young with experiences that help them to become responsible members of their society.

THE COUNSELOR AS A PERSON

The counselor, not unlike other humans, cannot ever be, nor indeed ever should be, what he supposedly could be! With the counselor, however, there is great discrepancy between versions of who he *is*, let alone should be. This is to be expected, since humanity, and life and living, is not viewed in the same manner by those who hold to an existential-humanist viewpoint, as contrasted with the views of the behaviorial scientist. This book, obviously, is written with the former point of view.
    Ruskin, in discussing great men, could well have been talking about the counselor or psychotherapist when he said, "that the first great test of a truly great man is his humility. I do not mean, by humility, doubt of his own power, or hesitation in speaking his own opinions; but a right understanding of the relation between what *he* can do and say, and the rest of the world's sayings and doings."[19]
    If counseling becomes identified as a distinct and unique professional occupation, then it is likely that the counselor will also be identified as a unique and professional individual. Currently, however, we still have numerous definitions, concepts and ideas about counseling and counselors, and it would probably be more valid to talk about the personalities of counselors rather than the personality of the counselor. However, because of an optimistic nature, I retain the heading that is used above.

18.   Rollo May, "Love and Will" *Psychology Today,* 3:317–364 (August, 1969).
19.   A. H. R. Ball (ed.), *Ruskin as Literary Critic* (Cambridge: Cambridge University Press, 1928), pp. 248–249.

The major sources of information about the person of the counselor are the ideas and opinions of the theorists and practitioners, and various studies which tend to imply that the person known as the counselor does have certain characteristics which differentiate him from the general population. Over twenty-five years ago, for example, the National Vocational Guidance Association issued a publication on counselor preparation that referred to the general characteristics of counselors as being a deep interest in people, patience, sensitivity to the attitudes and reactions of others, emotional stability and objectivity, a capacity for being trusted by others, and respect for the facts.[20]

Hamrin and Paulson reported a study in which counselors themselves listed the traits necessary for counseling, in order of frequency, as understanding, sympathetic attitude, friendliness, sense of humor, stability, patience, objectivity, sincerity, tact, fairness, tolerance, neatness, calmness, broadmindedness, kindliness, pleasantness, social intelligence, and poise.[21] This study would have been more interesting if there could have been some indication of the extent to which clients felt that these counselors possessed the traits that they themselves said were essential for good counseling.

Rogers has stated that the counselor should (1) be sensitive to human relationships; (2) have an objective attitude and an emotionally detached attitude—in short, a capacity for sympathy that is not overdone; (3) have respect for the individual and an ability and willingness to accept the child as he is, giving him freedom to work out his own solutions; (4) understand himself, and his emotional limitations and shortcomings; (5) know human behavior.[22]

An earlier summation of the evidence and research on the question of who counselors are and what they should be is to be found in the classic volume by Jones,[23] and a summation by Cottle.[24]

Weitz has pointed out three traits that he considers essential for counseling effectiveness: security, a sense of self-acceptance; sensitivity, the capacity of generalizing one's own feelings of self-acceptance to the acceptance of other people; and objectivity, the capacity to distinguish between objective and symbolic behavior, and yet understand the intimate relationship between the two.[25]

20. National Vocational Guidance Association, *Counselor Preparation* (Washington, D.C., 1949).
21. S. A. Hamrin and B. B. Paulson, *Counseling Adolescents* (Chicago: Science Research Associates, 1950).
22. Carl R. Rogers, *Counseling and Psychotherapy* (Boston: Houghton Mifflin, 1942).
23. A. J. Jones, *Principles of Guidance* (New York: McGraw-Hill, 1951), pp. 542–583.
24. William C. Cottle, "Personal Characteristics of Counselors: I," *Personnel and Guidance Journal*, 31:445–450 (April, 1953).
25. Henry Weitz, "Counseling as a Function of the Counselor's Personality," *Personnel and Guidance Journal*, 35:276–280 (January, 1957).

In the last few years, what would at least appear to be an interesting change has occurred in the various "should be" articles that are written about counselors. Older articles by counselors and counselor educators, such as some of those just mentioned, tended to refer to broad and general characteristics of what might be generally described as "good" people. Those referring to more specific aspects of human behavior tended to be written by psychologists or therapists. Today, however, this stress on the more psychological aspects of the human being of the counselor is to be found in almost all of the literature. Emphasis is placed on the counselor's ability to look at, and to understand, and accept, *his* self, as well as the self of the other person.

For example, some years ago Hobbs was less representative than now, when he stated:

> The life style of the counselor is perhaps as important as his competencies, and whereas one would expect a multiplicity of life styles among counselors, there are two ingredients which I would hope our training programs would uniformly foster. One of these we might call a sense of time or dimensionality; the other is creativity, and the two may turn out to be different faces of the same coin.[26]

So was Wyatt, when he was warning about the temptations encountered by the therapist:

> (a) The gratification of his instinctual needs in the disguise of therapeutic activity which is likely to follow along the repetition of certain subjective patterns of his own development; (b) indulgence in the narcissism which the therapeutic situation amply occasions.[27]

More representative are Stone and Shertzer, when they say:

> The true professional knows not only who he should be but also what he is. . . . All too many counselors invest their energy in arguing what they should be without stopping to look at what they are both personally and professionally. . . . The counselor who waits upon an externally supplied solution to his questions "Who am I?" and "What do I do?" does a disservice to himself and to the profession.[28]

26. Nicholas Hobbs, "The Compleat Counselor," *Personnel and Guidance Journal,* 36:594–602 (May, 1958).
27. Frederick Wyatt, "The Self-Experience of the Psychotherapist," *Journal of Consulting Psychology,* 12:83–87 (February, 1948).
28. Shelley C. Stone and Bruce Shertzer, "The Militant Counselor," *Personnel and Guidance Journal,* 42:342–347 (December, 1963).

And Appell, when he comments:

> The most significant resource a counselor brings to a helping
> relationship is himself. It is difficult to understand how a coun-
> selor unaware of his own emotional needs, of his expectations
> of himself as well as others, of his rights and privileges in rela-
> tionships, can be sensitive enough to such factors in his coun-
> selee. More than that, it would seem that he needs to experi-
> ence himself as a person of worth and of individuality before
> he can afford another such privileges. Indeed, in a most pro-
> found sense, the greater his congruence, the freer he can be in
> assisting others to actualize themselves.[29]

Boy and Pine describe the counselor's personal problems as
discovering his professional identity, freeing himself of himself, developing a humanistic attitude, being professionally secure, counselor anxieties, transference and countertransference.[30] They comment that "the school counselor must be sensitive to his own desires
to 'wrap up a case' and to how much such an attitude can influence
him to prod the client instead of allowing him to proceed at his own
rate in solving a problem."[31]

Williamson, while talking in a rather odd way about the counselor as technique, indicates that the counselor's philosophy of human development should show through his behavior, that his efforts
at relating effectively with the student must issue from his own acceptance of himself as he is, and his behavior should be such as to be
identified as the carrying on of his own "independent intellectual
life," both in his own technical field and in the broad literature of
human cultures.[32]

Van Kaam, in describing the ideal therapist, sees the crucial
human characteristics as flexibility, acceptance, gentleness, and sincerity.[33] Boy and Pine see the role of the counselor as being basically
an extension of his essence as a person, and they describe such roles
as the concessionary counselor (who defines his function in terms of
what is best for him); the mechanistic counselor (who is frequently a
former teacher who is conditioned to answering questions); the guidance counselor (in which two distinctly separate processes are con-

---

29. Morey L. Appell, "Self-Understanding for the Guidance Counselor," *Personnel
    and Guidance Journal,* 42:143–148 (October, 1963).
30. Angelo V. Boy and Gerald J. Pine, *Client-Centered Counseling in the Secondary
    School* (Boston: Houghton Mifflin, 1963), pp. 188–202.
31. *Ibid,* p. 189.
32. E. G. Williamson, "The Counselor as Technique," *Personnel and Guidance Jour-
    nal,* 41:108–111 (October, 1962).
33. Adrian van Kaam, *The Art of Existential Counseling* (Wilkes-Barre, Pa.: Dimen-
    sion Books, 1966), pp. 140–149.

fused); the vocational counselor (where traditionally one attempted to match the man to the job).[34]

Nor are such statements limited to individuals. In a joint report by the New York State Counselors Association and the New York State Association of Deans and Guidance Personnel, essential personal competencies of the counselor are described as:

> ... a knowledge of self: needs, values, strengths, and weaknesses. ... an understanding and acceptance of individual differences: intellectual, personal, physical, cultural, and socioeconomic. ... the capacity to relate to and work with others. ... skill in communicating with others. ... the ability to recognize a need for continual personal and professional development.[35]

The report of the Committee on Professional Preparation and Standards of the American Personnel and Guidance Association, accepted at the annual convention in San Francisco in March, 1964, described as basic qualities of the effective counselor a belief in each individual, a commitment to individual human values, alertness to the world, open-mindedness, understanding of self, and professional commitment. A statement of policy for secondary school counselors was accepted by the American School Counselors Association at the same convention. It described the counselor as follows:

> The counselor is dedicated to the idea that most pupils will enhance and enrich their personal development and self-fulfillment by means of making more intelligent decisions if given the opportunity to experience an accepting, non-evaluating relationship in which one is helped to better understand himself, the environment he perceives, and the relationship between these. Counseling is essentially such a relationship. The school counselor views himself as the person on the school staff with the professional competencies, behavioral science understandings, philosophical orientation, and position within the school necessary to provide such help to pupils.

These, then, are thoughts and ideas, by individuals and organizations, as to who the counselor should be, and they are important in

34. Angelo V. Boy and Gerald J. Pine, *The Counselor in the Schools* (Boston: Houghton Mifflin, 1968), pp. 44–56.
35. *An Exploration of the Role and Preparation of the Counselor in the Secondary School.* A Report of the Professional Advancement Committee of the New York State Counselors Association and the Professional Development and Research Committee of the New York State Association of Deans and Guidance Personnel, 1963.

that they will play a major role in the development of the counselor of tomorrow. Is this the way, however, that the counselor is today? Let us look at some of the evidence that describes the counselor as he is today. There is, obviously, no such thing as "a counselor"—he comes in many sizes and shapes. There are, however, certain similarities among professional counselors, and there are certain differences that may be caused by their orientation, their background, where they were educated, and the sort of education they experienced. I made a study of certain differences between student counselors who were chosen by their fellows as potential counselors and those who were rejected by their fellows. Those who were chosen by their fellows as individuals they would like to have as counselors showed a higher degree of confidence (as measured by the Heston Personality Inventory) than those who chose them. They were more normal in that they scored lower on the Hypochondriasis, Depression, Paranoia, Hysteria, Schizophrenia, Social I.E., and Psychasthenia scales (as measured by the Minnesota Multiphasic Personality Inventory). They showed a higher degree of interest in such areas as social service, persuasive, literary, and scientific activities (as measured by the Kuder Preference Record). On the other hand, those students who were rejected by their fellows as potential counselors indicated less in the way of home satisfaction than those who chose them. They were more abnormal in that they scored higher on the Hypochondriasis, Paranoia, Hysteria, Schizophrenia, Psychopathic Deviate and Hypomania scales. There were no significant differences in interest areas.[36]

Several years later, in a somewhat similar study, forty participants in an NDEA Guidance Institute judged each other as potential counselors. The nine "most-chosen" participants were compared on a number of variables with the nine "least-chosen." Most-chosen participants had a higher academic performance, somewhat more appropriate Strong scores, and less dogmatism as indicated on the Rokeach scale.[37]

In another study using an NDEA Institute population, the criterion for "good" or "bad" counselor was supplied by the staff ranking the student counselors in the order in which they would hire them as counselors. Using this criterion, the perceptual organization of effective counselors was significantly different from that of less effective counselors. The more effective counselors tended to per-

36. Dugald S. Arbuckle, "Client Perception of Counselor Personality," *Journal of Counseling Psychology*, 3:93–96 (Summer, 1956).
37. Buford Stefflre, Paul King, and Fred Leafgren, "Characteristics of Counselors Judged Effective by Their Peers," *Journal of Counseling Psychology*, 9:335–340 (Winter, 1962).

ceive from an internal rather than external frame of reference; they perceived in terms of people rather than things; they perceived people as able rather than unable, dependable rather than undependable, friendly rather than unfriendly, worthy rather than unworthy, identified rather than unidentified; they perceived their self as enough rather than not enough, revealing rather than not revealing; they perceived their purpose as freeing rather than controlling, altruistic rather than narcissistic, in larger rather than smaller meanings.[38]

Using an audio scale, O'Hern and I found that student counselors in seven summer NDEA Guidance Institutes who were considered to be most sensitive as counselors were significantly younger, they had attained a lower educational degree, and they had been employed fewer years than those who were considered to be least sensitive.[39] These results raise some questions about certain assumptions having to do with counselor effectiveness! In an earlier study by Abeles, somewhat related results were found when it was determined that the differences between student counselors rated by supervisors as more or less promising were in values and interests rather than in ability and general adjustment.[40]

Truax, Carkhuff, and Douds appear to be satisfied that enough evidence has been produced to indicate that the three therapist characteristics that determine the depth of self-exploration on the part of the client are therapist empathic understanding, therapist nonpossessive warmth, and therapist self-congruence or transparency.[41]

Comrey described some of the differences among samplings of American Psychological Association members with different professional interest areas. Those with interests in counseling and guidance thought that more psychologists lived up to their standards of what a psychologist should be than not; they judged religion to be more of a positive force in their lives than the others; they liked group projects; they liked administrative work in psychology; they liked psychotherapy; they liked teaching; they wanted to spend more time with their families; they wanted to do something for society; they wanted to help people who needed help; they were less productive of research articles than other groups; they had spent less of

38. Arthur W. Combs and Daniel W. Soper, "The Perceptual Organization of Effective Counselors," *Journal of Counseling Psychology*, 10:222–226 (Fall, 1963).

39. Jane S. O'Hern and Dugald S. Arbuckle, "Sensitivity: A Measurable Concept?" *Personnel and Guidance Journal*, 42:572–576 (February, 1964).

40. N. Abeles, *A Study of the Characteristics of Counselor Trainees* (doctoral dissertation, University of Texas, 1958).

41. Charles B. Truax, Robert R. Carkhuff, and John Douds, "Toward an Integration of the Didactic and Experiential Approaches to Training in Counseling and Psychotherapy," *Journal of Counseling Psychology*, 11:240–247 (Fall, 1964).

374

their time in positions where they had to do research; they believed that most institutions placed too much emphasis on research; they believed that less emphasis should be placed on research in training clinical psychologists; they were less interested in doing research; they attended either few or many professional meetings; they neither liked nor disliked competitive situations; they devoted either few or many weeks to vacation from professional work; they were less interested in sex; they liked a job where forty hours per week were devoted to teaching and preparation; they liked a well-paid teaching position in a small college.

On the other hand, predominant among those with interests in psychotherapy were some of the following attitudes: they allowed the expressed interests of graduate students to determine the content of a graduate course; they liked the idea of doing counseling and guidance; they wanted to help people who needed help; they had less resentment than others of a colleague who was a homosexual or an adulterer; they spent neither very little nor an excessive number of evening hours on professional work; they neither strongly liked nor disliked competitive situations; they expected to reach a higher income; they found it less unpleasant than many to be alone; they believed that life in our society is too competitive; they found mathematics distasteful; they were most interested in having quite a lot of money; research was not their forte.[42]

In an interesting article on neurotic interactions between counselors and clients, Lawton refers to some of the therapist's insecurities as being expressed in the following ways. The therapist tends to dominate the patient because of his fear that he will lose control of the relationship; he competes with other significant authority figures in the life of the patient; he showers the patient with excessive love and attention, going to extreme lengths to prevent marriage failure (his attitude seems to be "This marriage must succeed"); he functions as the child of the patient, misses him when he is away, and welcomes him back with a sigh of relief and pleasure; he indicates a sort of Pygmalion complex, in the sense that he needs to make the patient like the therapist; he resents the patient's demands; fearing the patient's hostility, he tries to appease him; he is unable to stand the patient's tension and anxiety. On this latter point, Lawton points out, this sort of anxiety is likely to result in glittering pseudo-optimism: "Don't worry; everything will be all right!"[43]

42. Andrew L. Comrey, "Publication Rate and Interest in Certain Psychologists," *American Psychologist*, 11:314–322 (July, 1956).
43. George Lawton, "Symposium on Neurotic Interaction in Marriage Counseling," *Journal of Counseling Psychology*, 5:28–33 (Spring, 1958).

In the same paper Lawton points to the seductive role of the more immature therapists. Verbal wooing may take the form of calling the patient by his first name too soon or without ascertaining the patient's wishes; of using affectionate or meaningful intonation of words; engaging in long, cozy telephone conversations; talking, explaining, interpreting excessively; asking for deep material too soon or too obviously. Nonverbal seduction of the patient may take such means as visiting the patient's home at the request of the patient whenever the latter undergoes an emotional emergency connected with transference; giving affectionate or meaningful glances; putting an affectionate hand on the patient's shoulder or giving a parental pat; allowing the patient to telephone regularly after hours or to see the therapist at times not ordinarily office hours; charging the patient a fee which the patient feels is lower than called for in a particular situation and letting the patient know that this is done because the therapist likes him; regularly overrunning the usual and conventional time limits for sessions.

In another paper from the same symposium, Harper lists still other neurotic interactions among counselors as being the pose of objectivity, the overemphasis on likability, and the effort on the part of the counselor to show that he is a good fellow, just like everyone else.[44]

A study by Fiedler indicated that there was less in the way of differences among expert counselors of supposedly different orientations than there was among inexperienced counselors of supposedly similar orientations. The expert counselors were close together in their ability to understand the client's meanings and feelings; their sensitivity to the client's attitudes; their warm interest in the client without emotional involvement.[45]

On the other hand, there would seem to be no doubt that counselors do use different techniques and methods. Strupp, for example, made a study of Rogerian and psychoanalytically oriented psychotherapists, and while the differences tended to diminish among the more experienced as compared with the less experienced, there were, nevertheless, significant differences. For example, with the Rogerian psychotherapists, 75.5 percent of the responses were of a restating, clarifying, reflecting type, whereas only 14.2 percent of the psychoanalytically oriented psychotherapists used this type of re-

44. Robert A. Harper, "Symposium on Neurotic Interaction in Marriage Counseling," *Journal of Counseling Psychology*, 5:33–38 (Spring, 1958).

45. Fred Fiedler, "Quantitative Studies on the Role of Therapists' Feelings Toward Their Patients," in O. Hobart Mowrer (ed.), *Psychotherapy: Theory and Research* (New York: Ronald Press, 1953), p. 296.

sponse; 9.8 percent of the responses of Rogerians were of an exploring nature, asking for clarification, or expressing feeling, while 35.6
percent of the responses of non-Rogerians were of this type.[46]

In a later study, Strupp gave evidence of differences in the
attitudes of psychoanalytic and client-centered counselors, as indicated by their reactions to the showing of a sound film of a first
interview. The client-centered counselors judged the prognosis with
therapy to be more favorable than the members of the psychoanalytic group; a larger proportion of the Rogerian counselors than of
the others professed a positive attitude toward the client; Rogerians
either declined to specify attitudes and behaviors that the therapist
should encourage in therapy with his patient or stressed the expression of feelings, while the others stressed such things as a sense of
responsibility, increased socialization, and relating feelings and
symptoms to interpersonal situations. Conversely, psychoanalytic
therapists were more likely to discourage attitudes and behaviors
such as intellectualization, obsessive ruminations, self-pity, self-de-
preciation, helplessness, refusal to accept responsibility, demanding
attitudes, and acting out; Rogerians tended to say they would discourage nothing or leave it to the patient. No member of the Rogerian group advocated strictness by the therapist, as contrasted with
more than one-third of the members of the psychoanalytic group,
who considered strictness therapeutically desirable. Rogerians commented on the patient's feelings and attitudes, but in contrast to the
others, paid less attention to such clues as gestures, bodily movements, manner of speaking, the patient's past and present interpersonal relations with his mother, wife, brother, or father. In handling
the transference problem, Rogerians recommended understanding,
clarification, and reflection; analytically oriented therapists preferred an interpretive approach. Rogerians were more definite in
their assertion that they would have conducted the interview in a
different manner. They dissociated themselves from the therapist's
approach, tending to evaluate his performance as inadequate; the
analytic therapists considered his performance reasonably adequate.
Over 75 percent of the Rogerians said that they would have spent
somewhat less or considerably less time in obtaining data on the
patient's life history than did the film therapist; almost one-half of
the analytic group said that they would have devoted somewhat
more or considerably more time. The majority of the Rogerian therapists described their attitude toward the therapist in the film as

46. Hans H. Strupp, "An Objective Comparison of Rogerian and Psychoanalytic
     Techniques," *Journal of Consulting Psychology*, 9:1–7 (February, 1955).

negative, whereas most analytically oriented therapists professed a positive or neutral attitude.[47]

Another interesting picture of counseling methodology was obtained in a study by Wicas and me that tended, among other things, to indicate that there was as much disagreement among counselors who received their training for the doctorate in the same institution as there was among those who received their doctorates in different institutions. Thus, among the members of the jury that was used in the study, the four experts who had the greatest number of "client-centered" responses had received their doctorates at, respectively, the University of Chicago, Columbia University, the University of Minnesota, and Harvard University. There was no significant difference in the degree of "client-centeredness" or the responses of four members of the jury who received their training at Columbia, as compared with the four members who received theirs at Chicago.[48]

The possession of a medical degree has historically come to be generally accepted as a requirement for competence in the matter of therapy of any kind, including psychotherapy and counseling. There is little or no actual relationship between the possession of such a degree and competence in psychotherapy, and medical doctors are the first to agree that their background gives them little in the way of understanding or skill when dealing with matters that are psychological. Many psychiatrists would agree with Colby, who tends to feel that his medical background was a hindrance rather than a help in his development into a capable psychotherapist.

> *Outstanding among educationally induced handicaps are detachment and dehumanization achieved in medical school. One tends to become interested almost entirely in diseases per se rather than in the people who have diseases. A once-active imagination may become stunted in the name of false scientific objectivity. The traditional medical single cause-and-effect concept of disease narrows the observation and sympathetic understanding of inter-human processes. . . . In the matters of treatment also, medical attention directs the axis of the student's interest toward mechanisms that can be seen and touched.*[49]

47. Hans H. Strupp, "An Objective Comparison of Rogerian and Psychoanalytic Therapists in an Initial Interview," *Journal of Consulting Psychology*, 22:265–274 (August, 1958).
48. Dugald S. Arbuckle and Edward Wicas, "The Development of an Instrument for the Measurement of Counseling Perceptions," *Journal of Counseling Psychology*, 4:304–312 (Winter, 1957).
49. Kenneth M. Colby, *A Primer for Psychotherapists* (New York: Ronald Press, 1951), pp. 20–21.

Freud, as the first outstanding "psychotherapist," stressed the fact that the possession of a medical degree had little or nothing to do with effectiveness as a psychotherapist. Freud's medical colleagues, however, paid no attention to this feeling, and medicine took over the responsibility for the study of human personality, conscious and unconscious. We are still caught in the confusion of talking about "mental health," and "mental illness," when we are discussing problems and tensions and disturbances that are primarily the result of the psychological process of learning rather than the physiological process of being born.

Mowrer has this to say on the subject:

We psychologists do not, I believe, object in principle to the type of authority which psychiatrists wish to exercise, or to our being subject to other medical controls, if they were truly functional. But authority and power ought to go with demonstrated competence, which medicine clearly has in the physical realm but, equally clearly, does not have in "psychiatry." Despite some pretentious affirmations to the contrary, the fact is that psychoanalysis, on which modern "dynamic" psychiatry is largely based, is in a state of virtual collapse and imminent demise. And the tranquilizers and other forms of so-called chemotherapy are admittedly only ameliorative, not basically curative. So now, to the extent that we have accepted the "illness" postulate and thus been lulled under the penumbra of medicine, we are in the ungraceful maneuver of "getting-out."[50]

Since the possession of a medical degree is assumed by some to be an absolute prerequisite to the practice of psychotherapy, a book that takes a look at the applicants to medical schools is of much interest.[51] Kelly, discussing the results of an intensive testing and evaluation of one graduating class from one medical school, makes the following comments:

Essentially, our medical students are persons who, if they were not becoming physicians, would be planning to become manufacturers, big businessmen, production managers, engineers; they are not the kind of people who would become teachers, ministers, social workers, i.e., professional persons interested in doing something for the good of mankind. As a group, the

50. O. Hobart Mowrer, "'Sin,' the Lesser of Two Evils," *American Psychologist,* 15:301–304 (May, 1960).
51. Helen Hofer Gee and John T. Cowles (eds.), *The Appraisal of Applicants to Medical Schools* (Evanston: Association of American Medical Colleges, 1957).

*medical students reveal remarkably little interest in the wel-
fare of human beings. . . . All of the evidence available to us
leads to the conclusion that the typical young physician has
little interest in cultural aspects of the society in which he lives,
has very little sensitivity to or feeling for the needs of the community, and is generally not inclined to participate in community activities unless these contribute to his income. I am not
saying this is true of all physicians; I am saying this is true of
the model young man going into one medical school.*[52]

In this same report, too, Handler, discussing the results of psychiatric interviews with three classes of freshmen medical students,
comments as follows.

*Our impression was that the majority of the students we saw
were quite conformist, emotionally constricted young men and
women, given to internalizing their hostility either with depres-
sive or compulsive traits for the most part, or sometimes with
somatic manifestations. We felt that there was a high premium
put on this in pre-medical competition, and, provided that it
was not too extreme, we thought of this matter of conformity
and constriction as actually one of the criteria of success both
in premedical work and in getting through medical school.*[53]

On the basis of a more comprehensive study of data obtained
from nearly 2,500 first-year medical students in twenty-eight medical schools, Gee describes the "average" entering medical student as
a man who values the pursuit of scientific truth above all. He values
prestige and power next to theoretical values, but holds these values
no higher than does the average college student. He is considerably
less interested in economic and material gain than is the average
college student, and somewhat more interested in the cultural aspects of community life. He is strongly motivated by needs to
achieve and to work hard and persistently toward achievement of
his goals. He is not prone to be motivated through altruistic love of
his fellow man, it is true, but he is likely to want to understand why
that fellow man behaves as he does, and is likely to be motivated by
a desire to help him when he is in trouble and to treat him with
sympathy and kindness. His interests cannot be characterized as
being very much like those of social workers; they are more like
those of physicians, osteopaths, and public administrators. But he is
more likely to have the interests of a teacher or social worker or of

52. *Ibid.*, pp. 195–196.
53. *Ibid.*, p. 68.

an author-journalist than he is to have the interest of a businessman or farmer.[54]

These various statements may be somewhat contradictory, but they are probably representative. They tend to raise at least some doubt as to the validity of the concept that the possession of a medical degree is a prerequisite for the practice of psychotherapy.

There is also evidence of a difference between psychiatric and psychological opinion regarding personality disturbances. Glosser contacted 90 psychiatrists and 60 psychologists, and had a 56 percent return from the psychiatrists and a 61 percent return from the psychologists. Glosser's questionnaire consisted of 100 statements of opinion regarding psychological disturbances. On 81 percent of the items there was a virtual unanimity of opinion. On 63 of the 100 items, however, a higher percentage of psychologists than psychiatrists selected the "?" response indicating some doubt or skepticism of the validity of either a "yes" or "no" response. The psychiatrists leaned more strongly toward psychogenic than physiogenic concepts, generally opposing physiological, biological, and biochemical accounts of mental and personality disturbances. They expressed a favorable attitude toward the psychodynamics of Freudian and psychoanalytic theory. The psychologists were somewhat more inclined to accept the existence of underlying physiological disturbances in mental disorders. They were more inclined to oppose certain Freudian and psychodynamic concepts. They were somewhat more inclined to accept hereditary influences in the susceptibility of the individual to certain mental and personality disorders, and more strongly opposed to the view that therapy cannot exist without direction. On this latter item, the reaction to the statement "Therapy cannot exist without direction; therefore, the nondirective method is not really therapy" for the psychiatrists was 32 percent "yes," and 44 percent "no," whereas the reaction of the psychologists was 8.3 percent "yes," and 70 percent "no."[55] This is probably suprising to many psychiatrists and psychologists!

Wicas and Mahan found that counselors who were rated high by their peers and supervisors achieved a pattern of scores that indicated that they were anxious, sensitive to the expectations of others and society, patient and nonaggressive in interpersonal relationships, and concerned about social progress, but always with appropriate self-control. On the other hand, the evidence also indicated the lack of high scores on measures of originality and venturousness; the rejection of contemplation and receptivity to inner experience;

54. Personal communication from Dr. Gee to the author.
55. Harry J. Glosser, "Psychiatric Versus Psychological Opinion Regarding Personality Disturbances," *American Psychologist*, 13:477–481 (August, 1958).

the danger that these counselors will not persist in the face of opposition; the highly conservative nature of their orientation to social problems.[56]

Demos and Zuwaylif, in a study whose interpretations were later to be questioned, found that the Allport-Vernon-Lindzey Study of Values and the Kuder Preference Record did not discriminate between the most effective and the least effective counselors. On the Edwards Personal Preference Schedule, on the other hand, the most effective counselors indicated significantly more nuturance and affiliation, while the least effective counselors exhibited more autonomy, abasement and aggression.[57]

It has been hypothesized that effective male counselors need to deviate from normal male norms in the direction of femininity, whereas effective female counselors need not deviate from the norms for women. In an interesting study on this subject, however, McLain found that while male counselors did deviate significantly from the norms for men in general on three of six scales selected to measure femininity, the women counselors also scored significantly in the direction of masculinity on three factors![58] This tends to imply that in this particular study population, the male counselors possessed some of the feminine traits considered necessary for effective counseling, whereas the female counselors possessed certain male traits that are not considered to be necessary for effective counseling.

But we live in fast-changing times. And it may be that in the decade of the 1970's we will be so busy trying to adjust to the revolution of the 1960's that we will be unaware that new times are upon us, and the 1970's are quite distinct from the 1960's! We seem always to be a decade, if not a generation, behind. It is likely that a comment made by Shertzer and Stone, applicable to the 1970's, will be just as applicable to the 1980's:

> An overriding conclusion to be drawn from a review of the literature pertaining to interests and personality characteristics and counseling effectiveness is that the findings so far have been inconclusive and often conflicting and that additional research is needed.[59]

56. Edward A. Wicas and Thomas W. Mahan, "Characteristics of Counselors Rated Effective by Supervisors and Peers," *Counselor Education and Supervision,* 6:50–56 (Fall, 1966).
57. George D. Demos and Fadil H. Zuwaylif, "Characteristics of Effective Counselors," *Counselor Education and Supervision,* 5:163–165 (Spring, 1966).
58. Edwin W. McLain, "Is the Counselor a Woman?" *Personnel and Guidance Journal,* 46:444–448 (January, 1968).
59. Bruce Shertzer and Shelley C. Stone, *Fundamentals of Guidance* (Boston: Houghton Mifflin, 1971), p. 158.

PERCEPTIONS OF COUNSELORS[60]

There continue to be great discrepancies between the way in which counselors perceive themselves, and the way in which they are perceived by others. Counselors' perceptions of themselves have probably changed less than the perceptions of others about them. At the more cognitive level, a recent study by Ginzberg attacks counselors for not doing what Ginzberg feels they should be doing, and states flatly that their impact has been minimal.[61] At the other end of the continuum, a number of voices, filled with heat and passion, have accused the counselor, as a member of an oppressive society, of being effective only in a negative sense. One might almost come to the depressing conclusion that all male counselors are oppressors of women, all white counselors are oppressive of black people, all heterosexual counselors are the oppressors of homosexual individuals, and all adult counselors are the oppressors of the young!

In any occupation the personality of the worker is related to his effectiveness on the job, but nowhere is this more crucial than in those occupations which stress the human relationships between people. There is a direct relationship between the person of the counselor and his effectiveness in that particular kind of human relationship known as counseling. Here, too, we may note that sometimes in the literature there is a tendency to create a "should-be" counselor who will forever remain a figment of one's imagination, since he is a totally nonhuman creature, devoid of any human vices, but possessing all the wisdom and compassion to be found over the eons of the existence of the human race!

No matter how irrational and unrealistic the "should-be" voices may be, however, it is important to listen carefully and to hear them, because more than anything else, they represent an increasing dissatisfaction with what is. And if any society is to remain viable, and to survive and move ahead rather than regress, it must pay attention to its critics. For most humans, violent revolution is an answer only when they have nothing to lose. It is neither an adequate nor a rational answer when they have much to lose and little to gain.

Many of the more activist and critical voices are themselves representative of the characteristics that they decry in the counselor. All too often, when the counselor is accused of being a sexist and/or

60. Dugald S. Arbuckle, "The Counselor: Who? What?" *Personnel and Guidance Journal*, 50:785–791 (June, 1972). Copyright 1972 by the American Personnel and Guidance Association.

61. Eli Ginzberg, *Career Guidance: Who Needs It, Who Provides It, Who Can Improve It* (New York: McGraw-Hill, 1971).

383

a racist and/or an "age-ist" and/or an elitist (which he sometimes may well be) the only rationale the critic can find is the sex or the race or the age of the accused individuals. Surely there is not greater example of the irrationality of prejudice and bias than to make a blanket condemnation of an *individual* human being because of race or sex or age. One should not be bound by one's heritage, good or evil, and we cannot prove ourselves by our ancestors. Malcolm X and the men who killed him were all black people, but they were quite different kinds of human beings; Betty Friedan and Mrs. Richard Nixon are both women, but they too, are somewhat different; and certainly the late Fritz Perls and Nathan Pusey, the retired president of Harvard University, could be called "older" men, but there was much they did not have in common! The automatic assumption of certain kinds of behavior on the basis of inherited characteristics surely can be refuted by the evidence of the primary impact upon us of the moment-by-moment human experiences. One does not have to swear an oath on a Skinnerian bible to be open to the reality of this evidence.

The battle against the very real injustice suffered by women, and the attempt to modify the dominant place held by men over the ages, is hardly helped by solemn and pontifical statements such as those by Gardner: "A necessary (and possibly sufficient) characteristic of the ideal counselor is to be a feminist" and "today, it is probably not a serious misrepresentation to say that all counselors are sexist," and still again, "women as people do not exist anywhere but in the as yet unrealized dreams of feminists."[62] These comments should be balanced against those such as Barwick's when, in talking about some women, she says that "such women have a level of hostility against society and I think against Men and specifically against sex of a degree not shared by the majority of women."[63] We might, too, note Gorer's description of peaceful societies, that "they all manifest enormous gusto for concrete physical pleasure—eating, drinking, sex, laughter, and . . . they all make very little distinction between the ideal characteristics of men and women, particularly that they have no ideal of brave, aggressive masculinity."[64] The goal of the counselor, regarding the item of sex, should be to move toward being neither a feminist nor a masculinist but rather a humanist, who can experience compassion and love for all people, while accepting the reality that at certain times a man will behave in a

62. Joann Gardner, "Sexist Counseling Must Stop," *Personnel and Guidance Journal*, 49:705–714 (May, 1971).

63. Eric Staff, "An Interview With Judith Barwick," *Capsule*, 4:3–9 (Spring, 1971).

64. G. Gorer, "Man Has No 'Killer' Instinct," *New York Times Magazine*, Nov. 27, 1966.

different way toward a woman because she *is* a woman, and a woman will behave in a different way toward a man because he is a man. For the sake of the maintenance of the human species, let us hope that this difference continues to exist!

Another oft-heard charge against the current counselor is that he is an elitist, and that in the new society there will be no room for such creatures. For example, "Collective" says that "these (racist and sexual chauvinist attitudes) and elitism and competitive leadership must be worked out." Later in the same paper they state that "the counselor realizes that the changes we are talking about go hand in hand with changes in life style if society is really to meet the needs of its people."[65] The contradiction here, of course, is that "Collective" obviously feels that its members are of the elite, even if they don't like to admit it, since they assume that they know what is good for "the people." The same elitism is to be noted in all of Gardner's comments quoted above, and in a comment by Ream, who says that "our first task must be to admit . . . we don't know what's happening."[66] Ream obviously does not believe this about himself, since he proceeds to tell all his readers what they should do about their unfortunate situation!

The refusal to accept one's elitism, or at least one's feeling of elitism, probably produces a more arrogant type of individual, and hopefully the new counselor will be more honest about his elitism. It is likely that most of us in the helping professions see ourselves in some way as being "elite." The counselor, after all, has accepted a position that assumes his capacity to help the person who comes to him for assistance. This, surely, is a form of elitism, however, but it need not include a desire to control or change the client to the counselor's image. Many of those who criticize elitism, however, by their very words, make it very clear that they would fit comfortably into Skinner's group of controllers of society. As we have seen, Skinner says that "we must delegate control of the population as a whole to specialists—to police, priests, teachers, therapists and so on, with their specialized reinforcers and codified contingencies."[67] Among Skinner's many virtues is that of honesty. He agrees he is one of the elite, and who, by the way, could argue with him on that!

Another curse of the counselor of today appears to be his age, and the onset of senility and idiocy would almost appear, according

65. Collective, "Vocations for Social Change," *Personnel and Guidance Journal*, 49:740–745 (May, 1971).
66. Charles Ream, "Youth Culture: Humanity's Last Chance," *Personnel and Guidance Journal*, 49:699–704 (May, 1971).
67. B. F. Skinner, "Beyond Freedom and Dignity," *Psychology Today*, 5:37–80 (August, 1971).

to some of the literature, to take place at about the age of thirty-one. This leaves those of us who have long since passed this age in a very precarious position, with our only solace being the thought that maybe somehow we have managed to outwit the years! Ream, for example, tells us that "once it was the old who had the wisdom; now it is the young."[68] He also tells us that our youth are an oppressed colony, although one may wonder how the young, who are so wise, have allowed the ignorant old to oppress them! Part of the problem here, of course, is the fact that the young live in a society which prolongs the stage of social adolescence well into their twenties, and they are probably less oppressed by the older society than they are captured by it. This stretched-out period of dependence tends to create a fantasy about individual responsibility. A little poem by Brandon Leavitt, for example, sadly says that "you can do anything you want, you can write anything you want, you can do anything you want to do—that's what they told me," and then goes on to indicate how it didn't work out that way, and the young author is told, "Don't do it here."[69] If some older man were to say this to a younger boy, his irresponsibility would be slightly greater than the gullibility of the young person for believing him. There can be no individual freedom in a society in which anyone can do anything he wishes to do. Only when one can accept responsibility for the impact on others of everything about his life and living can he make any claim to having got even faintly close to the achievement of individual freedom.

Silber probably reflects an adult point of view, but more important, he has the weight of evidence on his side, when he says that "only after living through a carefully selected series of developmental stages do human beings acquire depth, range, strength, and flexibility as persons."[70] And the evidence also indicates that the normal developmental tasks cannot be made up with expectations of similar results. What might be a normal developmental task for a teenaged girl will have disastrous results if it is to be first experienced by a fifty-year-old woman. Skinner is even more skeptical about the ability of the young, as well as the old, to design their own lives, since he feels that "the problem is not to design a world that will be liked by people as they now are, but to design one that will be liked by those who live in it. . . . a world that would be liked by contemporary people would perpetuate the status quo."[71] While many an individ-

68. Charles Ream, *op. cit.*

69. Brandon Leavitt, "Just Do Not Do It Here," *Personnel and Guidance Journal,* 49:704 (May, 1971).

70. John R. Silber, "The Pollution of Time," *Center Magazine,* 4:2–9 (September/October, 1971).

71. B. F. Skinner, *op. cit.*

ual who may happen to be young will be wise beyond his years, wisdom is generally a product of much experience in life and living.

Then, too, there is the matter of race. Some Americans, black and white, feel that only black people can get close to and understand black people, and they would appear to advocate a segregated existence. Smith, for example, makes a typical sweeping generalization when he says that "the white man does not give a damn about black people," that "blackness is a dignity that belongs to no other group in the United States," and, again, that "we are somebody."[72] Gunnings expresses similar feelings when he says that "if a professor is of a different racial or cultural background, he cannot interpret data and make inferences from a black perspective. Black students need to receive guidance and instruction from black teachers who live and understand blackness."[73] This attitude, while understandable, is pessimistic, since it tends to imply that change in human attitudes and values is impossible. If the white student counselor who has certain racist attitudes is doomed to maintain them for life, how can the black counselor hope to help the black client who has deep feelings of inferiority and worthlessness? This does not, of course, deny the evidence suggesting the *current* lack of rapport between black and white people in a helping relationship.[74]

Other counselors and psychologists tend to stress the cultural rather than the racial factor as being crucial. Bell, for example, points out that the black psychologist "frequently deludes himself into thinking that he can automatically make the transition from the academic to the black community."[75] Proctor comments that "black students do not need weak, inept black hirelings, whose only qualification is their blackness, to help them,"[76] and Vontress expresses a somewhat similar feeling when he says that "achieving such an understanding may in some ways be more difficult for black counselors than for their white counterparts. As members of the black bourgeoisie, black counselors have a problem of authenticating themselves."[77]

72. Paul M. Smith, Jr., "Black Activity for Liberation, Not Guidance," *Personnel and Guidance Journal*, 49:721–726 (May, 1971).

73. Thomas S. Gunnings, "Preparing the New Counselor, *Counseling Psychologist*, 2:100–101 (1971).

74. George P. Banks, "The Effects of Race on One-to-One Helping Interviews," *Social Service Review*, 45:137–146 (June, 1971).

75. Robert L. Bell, Jr., "The Culturally Deprived Psychologist," *Counseling Psychologist*, 2:104–107 (1971).

76. Samuel A. Proctor, "Reversing the Spiral Toward Futility," *Personnel and Guidance Journal*, 48:707–712 (May, 1970).

77. Clemment E. Vontress, "Counseling Blacks," *Personnel and Guidance Journal*, 48:713–719 (May, 1970).

The counselor is neither blessed nor cursed by being, by the accident of birth, either black or white. The manner in which a white or black counselor has developed racist attitudes is no different from the manner in which a black child in a city ghetto and a white child in a long-dead mining town have developed attitudes of defeatism and hopelessness. None were born the way they are, but they learned to be the way they are. Surely no one can claim to be a counselor unless he has a very strong belief that they can also learn to have a self-identity, to have pride in self, to be somebody instead of nobody. Russell stresses humanness over race when he says that "there is no special mystique involved in relating to the black student; hence the counselor need not assume any kind of unusual posture or resort to tactics, techniques or approaches he would not use with other students."[78]

This humanness and understanding and acceptance of one's fellows cannot be taken for granted, and it should be the central core of any program of counselor education. Stranges and Riccio refer to the "serious need for counselors to have specific training emphasizing the characteristics and needs of the cultural groups to be served."[79] Charnofsky, in discussing the movement of black people toward self-awareness and pride, says that it is "the counselor's task to make himself be in such a way that he understands the nature of the movement, the depth of the resistance to it, the general tone of exclusivity of America's larger culture, and the need for true empathic and human support."[80] Aspy is describing this sort of person when he states that "the hope for constructive human relationships in our society lies in producing people who can tell it like it is in a caring way to people they really understand. These are 'whole' men who have courage, sensitivity and love."[81]

Some years ago Rogers postulated a few questions that he, as a counselor, would ask of himself. It may be noted that he stresses the existential-humanistic "What kind of human being am I?" rather than "What do I know?" or "What skills do I possess?":

1. *Can I be in some way which will be perceived by the other person as trustworthy, as dependable or consistent in some deep sense. . .?*

78. R. D. Russell, "Black Perceptions of Guidance," *Personnel and Guidance Journal*, 48:721–728 (May, 1970).
79. Richard J. Stranges and Anthony C. Riccio, "Counselor Preferences for Counselors: Some Implications for Counselor Education," *Counselor Education and Supervision*, 10:39–46 (Fall, 1970).
80. Stanley Charnofsky, "Counseling for Power," *Personnel and Guidance Journal*, 49:350–357 (January, 1971).
81. David N. Aspy, "Empathy—Congruence—Caring Are Not Singular," *Personnel and Guidance Journal*, 48:637–640 (April, 1970).

2. Can I be expressive enough as a person that what I am will be communicated unambiguously. . .?

3. Can I let myself experience positive attitudes toward this other person—attitudes of warmth, caring, liking, interest, respect . . .?

4. Can I be strong enough as a person to be separate from the other? Can I be a sturdy respecter of my own feelings, my own needs, as well as his? Can I own and, if need be, express my own feelings as something belonging to me and separate from his feelings? Am I strong enough in my own separateness that I will not be downcast by his depression, frightened by his fear, nor engulfed by his dependency?

5. Am I secure enough within myself to permit his separateness? Can I permit him to be what he is—honest or deceitful, infantile or adult, despairing or overconfident? Can I give him the freedom to be . . .?

6. Can I let myself enter fully into the world of his feelings and personal meanings and see these as he does? Can I step into his private world so completely that I lose all desire to evaluate or judge it . . .?

7. Can I receive him as he is? Can I communicate this attitude? Or can I receive him only conditionally, accepting some aspects of his feelings and silently or openly disapproving of other aspects . . .?

8. Can I act with sufficient sensitivity in the relationship that my behavior will not be perceived as a threat . . .?

9. Can I free him from the threat of external evaluation . . .?

10. Can I meet this other individual who is in the process of becoming, or will I be bound by his past and by my past . . .?[82]

Two counselors, wondering about why they happen to be counselors, are, in a way, answering for themselves some of these questions. One of them says:

> The essence of democratic life is a person's individuality. In our society the individual can easily become the victim of the group. The individual finds it difficult to be himself, to be the master of his fate, because of the pressures of conformity that the group imposes upon him. The individual can become swallowed by the group. A person's individuality is consumed because of the neurotic need of the group for conformity. The

82. Carl R. Rogers, "The Characteristics of a Helping Relationship," *Personnel and Guidance Journal*, 37:6–18 (September, 1958).

*individuality of the free thinker is the cornerstone of our demo-
cratic life. In a totalitarian state there is no room for individuality. In a democratic state the individual must be preserved.
It is from the free thinking of an individual that a democracy
thrives. I guess I'm a counselor because of a caring for the individual and the things that his free spirit can contribute to mankind. I desire to see the individual function freely so that whatever he contributes to civilization will be a maximal
contribution, an unrestricted contribution. Enlightened ideas
that improve civilization come from men who are free enough
to think and to create. I am a counselor because I think I can
help men to be free. I am a counselor because I believe in democracy, and without the free-thinking individual who is master of himself there is no democracy. I feel that as a counselor I
can help man to be free, and thus preserve democracy.*

The other counselor, half a continent away, comments:

*I see my function as a counselor as providing a growth-produc-
ing and non-threatening environment for the client. I see my
function as establishing a relationship in which I can communicate understanding and acceptance. I am committed to the
idea that nothing is more important to the individual than self-
understanding. I can imagine no more worthwhile goals than to
help my client and myself to achieve self-understanding.*

Counselors, like other humans, are usually measured in somewhat subjective terms. Johnson, Shertzer, Linden and Stone, for example, found that counselees, peers and supervisors reacted favor-
ably to male counselors who were affable, friendly, likable,
accepting, capable and satisfied, and to females who were outgoing,
confident, efficient and assertive.[83]

In the long run, of course, it is the concept that the client has
of the counselor that will determine the effectiveness of the counseling relationship. And the perceptions of counselors as to who they
are are not always the same as the perceptions of clients. A study by
Strowig and Sheets, for example, indicated that students perceived
counselors as counselors more negatively than as deans.[84] This at
least implies that students do not see the functions of counselors as
they are perceived by counselors. In a study involving counselors

83. Dorothy Johnson, Bruce Shertzer, James E. Linden, and Shelley C. Stone, "The
    Relationship of Counselor Candidate Characteristics and Counseling Effective-
    ness," *Counselor Education and Supervision*, 6:297–304 (Summer, 1967).
84. R. Wray Strowig and Stanley E. Sheets, "Student Perception of Counselor Role,"
    Personnel and Guidance Journal, 45:926–931 (May, 1967).

and Upward Bound students, Grande found that, to a greater extent than the Upward Bound students, counselors regarded the guidance program as an important element in the total value of the school; they believed that removal of the program would leave a serious void in the school program, and that the guidance services needed to be expanded. On the other hand, to a greater degree than the counselors, the students felt that the guidance program was not essential, although it did have something to offer, that specialized guidance personnel were outsiders, and that the guidance program confused students and made them begin to doubt their individual judgments.[85]

Here are some of the more positive perceptions of junior high school boys and girls about the counselor they have experienced:

"He's me . . . in some strange and mysterious way he's felt exactly the way I've felt about things."

"That's not complicated—he's simply someone to whom I can talk easily and honestly. He's someone I don't have to put on a front with."

"He's someone who really cares about me and what happens to me."

"He's a person who has the time to help me in dealing with my parents."

"He's not easily shocked—no matter what I tell him."

"I suppose—well—he's someone I can trust. He isn't always judging me—he's letting me judge myself."

"He's someone to whom I can turn when things pile up . . . someone who helps me deal with this business of living."

"He's someone who doesn't get mad when I tell him about my foolish plans for the future."

"He's someone who doesn't get bugged when he hears about kids and what they're like."

"He's someone who makes school tolerable . . . if I couldn't get together with him I'd have quit school a long time ago."

"I'm making my own decisions for the first time . . . whatever he did helped me to do this."

Students, in evaluating a counseling program, described counselors in this way:

"I thought that my counselor really took an interest in me and my problems."

"I like to have a counselor because it gives me a chance to say things."

85. Peter P. Grande, "Attitudes of Counselors and Disadvantaged Students," *Personnel and Guidance Journal,* 46:889–892 (May, 1968).

". . . I can talk on just about anything that is on my mind."
"They let you get things off your mind that you couldn't tell to anyone else."
". . . the counselor listens to me and my ideas and doesn't give out wisecracks like my teachers."
"The counselors are very understanding."
"He always listened to what I had to say first."[86]

Not all student clients, however, see the school counselor in such a positive light. Here are a few comments from students who have experienced counseling:

"I wouldn't go to the counselor because he is so dense."
"Counselors have no wisdom. . . ."
"He is just like my father. . . ."
"He stands up for the teachers and protects them. . . ."
"Counselors tell the teachers what we say. . . ."
"They just sit around and get paid for nothing. . . ."
"I don't want to bother him . . . he probably has problems of his own. . . ."

THE VALUES OF THE COUNSELOR

Needless to say, the perceptions that others have of counselors are reflections of *their* values, while the perception the counselor has of himself is a reflection of his values. I would assume that there would be certain values which would be a part of an effective counselor, while others would reflect an ineffective counselor.

Counselors with different values apparently differ in what they do well and what they do poorly, as one would expect. In a study by Watley, for example, counselors with a trait-and-factor orientation differed significantly from those with a client-centered orientation in their ability to predict freshmen grades and persistence and success in an educational major.[87] Thus if the ability to predict is considered to be an important characteristic of the counselor, it would appear that counselors whose values reflected a trait-and-factor orientation would be a better bet than those whose values reflected a client-centered orientation. A study by Barre, on the other hand, tended to indicate that both clients and counselors agreed that

86. Angelo V. Boy and Gerald J. Pine, *The Counselor in the Schools* (Boston: Houghton Mifflin, 1968), p. 305.
87. Donivan J. Watley, "Counseling Philosophy and Counseling Predictive Skill," *Journal of Counseling Psychology,* 14:158–164 (March, 1967).

counselors who showed high achievement needs, high original thinking, high vigor and low order needs are rated as being more helpful,
facilitating a closer relationship, and showing empathy for their clients.[88] Thus if a close empathic counselor-client relationship was
considered to be critical, then counselors of this kind would be a
better bet. In a study of general counseling effectiveness, Whitely,
Sprinthall, Mosher, and Donaghy found a high relationship between
the effective counselor and cognitive flexibility, which refers to dimensions of open-mindedness, adaptability, and a resistance to premature closure in perception and cognition.[89] In this study at least,
the counselor who had a higher level of individual freedom, and was
less a conditioned product of his culture, would appear to be more
effective.

Few would disagree with Robb that "the search for truth must
be undergirded by a personal sense of intellectual honesty and openness. If these qualities of mind are not present, the possibility for
self-delusion threatens our honest pursuit of the truth."[90]

Thus it would seem that one might at least theorize that if we
hold to the importance of individual freedom, and if we believe in a
society in which the dignity and the rights of individual man are the
primary reason for the existence of the state, then the values of the
counselor might at least be characterized by the following:

1. An openness and a flexibility, which means that the counselor is not the slave of any dogma, religious or secular, professional
or personal. The belief of a person is a part of his experiencing and
living, and his beliefs and values are open to change as circumstances and people change. The counselor does not believe because
he has to, and he accepts personal responsibility for his beliefs. All
his beliefs are thus laced with rationality, and he does not continue
to believe what has intellectually been shown to be false.

2. The counselor accepts a belief as an area in which we may
not know, in an empirical sense, and thus it is irrational to argue that
one person's belief is right and that of another is wrong. In a religious sense this would mean that one could be devout and still accept the possibility of error, and this, in turn, would of course mean

88. Carole E. Barre, "Relationship of Counselor Personality and Counselor-Client
    Similarity to Selected Counseling Success Criteria," *Journal of Counseling Psy-
    chology*, 14:419–425 (September, 1967).

89. John W. Whitely, Norman A. Sprinthall, Ralph L. Mosher, and Rolla T. Donaghy,
    "Selection and Evaluation of Counselor Effectiveness," *Journal of Counseling
    Psychology*,14:226–234 (May, 1967).

90. J. Wesley Robb, "Self Discovery and the Role of the Counselor," *Personnel and
    Guidance Journal*, 45:1008–1011 (June, 1967).

that religion would be an area of uncertainty rather than an area of certainty. "I believe" would never be confused with "I know," and there would be little point in closing one's mind to a colleague, or killing one's fellowman because of a differing belief, since one would accept the possibility that the colleague or the fellowman might be right.

Since belief is a matter of faith, it would seem logical to suggest that the counselor, at least, should believe positively. Why not hold to the belief that man *can* grow and develop and that he has within him the seeds of self-actualization, rather than holding to the belief that man is vicious and evil and must spend his life battling the evil forces that reside within him? A belief is not factual, but it is a fact that one believes. When one views the other person and feels "You *can* do it, you *can* stand up straight and tall, you *can* experience freedom," then what happens in the human relationship *is quite different* than when one views the other person as evil and hopeless and condemned. This latter statement is a statement of fact, not of belief!

3. The counselor will personally exemplify a high level of personal freedom and self-actualization, and he will thus have no need to impose on others. He may serve as a model, not to be imitated and followed, but rather a model from which the other person can draw strength and gradually develop his own concept of self, his own person, and thus become capable of experiencing a high level of personal freedom.

The possession and awareness of values by the counselor need not imply the need to impose these values on others. On the other hand, it is likely that every counselor would feel there are certain aspects of what might be called a value system that would bring disaster upon the client, and he could not be acceptant of them as a satisfactory way of life. A client might feel that heroin was a part of his way of life, and was good for him, but surely few counselors would agree. Most counselors, however, tend to be too imposing rather than too acceptant of the values of others. Vance, for example, states that

> unless the counselor is aware of his own values and the ethics of his own profession, it is likely that he could accept any behavioral goal as stated by the client . . . [and] unless the counselor is aware of what he believes should constitute desirable and undesirable behavior, both for himself and for his client.[91]

91. Barbara Vance, "The Counselor—An Agent of What Change?" *Personnel and Guidance Journal*, 45:1012–1016 (June, 1967).

And Sanborn says:

We operate in schools, and schools are developmental institutions. . . . What, in terms of behavioral characteristics of students who go through your school, do you look for in order to determine whether you earn your salary or not?[92]

It is important, however, that what the counselor considers to be "good" behavior for himself is not imposed on others as good behavior for them, and the counselor should be acceptant of the reality that what the school considers to be "desirable" behavior for children may not be desirable behavior for the positive development of one single unique human being.

The counselor, then, should be one whose values are marked by a strong faith in people, a belief that people *can* grow and develop, that they can stand tall, and have pride in self. To become this sort of person, the counselor must be a knowledgeable person, but far more important, this knowledge must have helped him move along the road to wisdom, which includes compassion and love and understanding, ingredients that are often missing from knowledge. To me this is an existential-humanistic conception that stresses self-actualization, but I would think of it as a philosophy of human beings rather than a theory or methodology. Counselors could use various methodologies and techniques and still be aptly described as existential-humanistic, depending on how they answered the question, "*Why* are you doing what you are doing?"

92. Marshal P. Sanborn, "Following My Nose Toward a Concept of a Creative Counselor," *School Counselor*, 14:68–73 (November, 1966).

Chapter *14*

Functions of the Counselor

For those of us who have been involved in the field of counseling for some time, the 1960's stand out as the decade of the counselor. At both a government and a professional level there was great activity, sometimes even frenzied, greater than any previous decade, and, very likely, greater than in any decade to come. The National Defense Education Act of 1958 became functional in the 1960's, and it was followed in 1968 by the Education Professions Development Act. Gilbert Wrenn's 1962 book, *The Counselor in a Changing World*, had a major impact. Various statements on the education and functions of the counselor came forth from the American Personnel and Guidance Association and various divisions of the association in 1964, 1966, and 1967.

In the 1970's federal funds for counseling and the education of counselors have not totally disappeared, but there is nothing to approach the heady days of the NDEA! Regardless of changes in administration, it is likely that far more valid evidence of effectiveness is going to be expected before federal funding is even considered. Professional organizations continue to increase in size and proliferate in numbers, but the activity and the motion is not the same as in the 1960's. Gilbert Wrenn's 1973 book, *The World of the Contemporary Counselor*, is as excellent as the earlier one, but its impact is not the same.

It is interesting to note how human events must overtake us before we become aware of them, even though we *know* about them long before. Even now, books still talk about the continuing dizzying increase in the numbers of counselors, even though we know that all school personnel greatly outnumber the number of positions that are

396

available for them. There will always be room, of course, for really good school counselors, but the hard reality is that there are more counselors than there are counseling positions, and this trend will not likely change sharply through the 1970's. The continuing decrease in the rate of increase of population has been evident in the statistics since the late 1960's, but in 1973 school personnel suddenly realized that the problem with school plants was not how to build more elementary schools, but rather how to go about closing an elementary school that is no longer needed. This trend, too, will likely continue through the 1970's.

The 1970's are simply quite different from the 1960's and counselors working with children or adults will not be effective if they do not realize this fact of life. It may be that John Kennedy and Camelot represented the hope and the optimism and the involvement of the 1960's, whereas Richard Nixon and Watergate represent the pessimism and the sullen passivity of the 1970's. By the time these words are read, of course, they may be totally outdated!

One thing at least has remained consistent, and that is the continuing debate and confusion regarding the functions of the counselor. "What does the counselor do?" is as much a topic of conversation at professional conventions now as it was in 1950, let alone 1960! In this chapter I would like to look at the professional and psychological perceptions of counselor functions, then at the confusion and debate over counselor functions, and finally make a few suggestions as to what we might do about it.

PSYCHOLOGICAL AND PROFESSIONAL PERCEPTIONS OF THE FUNCTIONS OF THE COUNSELOR[1]

Most counselors would probably agree that what the counselor does is psychological in nature, even though some may see him as being very much akin to a teacher. Generally, we talk in a broad sense of the counselor being one who understands children and their behavior and who is able to help them to become more effective individuals who can make more sense out of their educational experience and their day-to-day living. Later, they will be able to make educational, vocational, and personal choices which will be best for them. Certainly all would agree that this process of learning is psychological in nature. It may be Super saying, "Students should be helped to

1. Dugald S. Arbuckle, "The School Counselor: Educator, Psychologist or What?" *School Counselor*, 14:132–138 (January, 1967). Copyright 1967 by the American Personnel and Guidance Association.

understand their own needs and the available resources in these terms, and to see how these resources may be used to meet their peculiar needs,"[2] or Gaither, Hackman, and Hay saying of vocational counseling that "it . . . starts with the individual's perception of himself (realistic or not), and in succeeding interviews the counselee learns more about the world of work and how various fields of work can meet his needs,"[3] or Mathewson pointing out that "information may be *disseminated* but it is not necessarily *assimilated* effectively by the individual or his parents and applied wisely to his individual case. For that to happen an individual needs to have a pretty good understanding of himself as well as a motivation toward a continuing process of connecting up a maturing self-definition with social requirements and opportunities."[4] They are all, surely, describing a process which is basically psychological in nature, even though it is being performed in an educational setting.

There are, however, other specialized personnel in the schools whose functions are also psychological in nature, and there is a remarkable similarity when one examines the functions of school social workers, psychologists, and counselors.[5] Here, for example, are a few descriptions of functions, with a few key words removed:

No. 1: *. . . will perform a counseling function with pupils as well as parents and teachers . . . will perform a consultative function with parents and with other school and community personnel . . . will perform a coordinating function in integrating the resources of the school and community . . .*[6]

No. 2: *Assists each pupil to meet the needs and understand himself in relation to the social and psychological world in which he lives. . . .Assist each pupil to meet the need to develop personal decision making competency. . . . Assist all members of the staff to understand the importance of the individual pupil. . . . Determine the influence of the school program on pupil educational and psycho-social development. . . . Inform other staff*

2. Donald E. Super, "Goal Specificity in the Vocational Counseling of Future College Students," *Personnel and Guidance Journal,* 43:127–134 (October, 1964).

3. James W. Gaither, Roy B. Hackman, and John E. Hay, "Vocational Guidance: On the Beach," *Vocational Guidance Quarterly,* 11:75–79 (Winter, 1963).

4. Robert H. Mathewson, "Manpower or Persons: A Critical Issue," *Personnel and Guidance Journal,* 43:338–342 (December, 1964).

5. *See* Dugald S. Arbuckle, "Counselor, Social Worker, Psychologist: Let's Ecumenicalize," *Personnel and Guidance Journal,* 45:532–538 (February, 1967).

6. "Preliminary Statement: Joint ACES-ASCA Committee on the Elementary School Counselor," *Personnel and Guidance Journal,* 44:659–661 (February, 1966).

members of significant changes in the school and non-school environments which have implications. . . . Assist parents to understand the developmental progress of their child, his needs, and environmental opportunities . . . interpret to the community . . . promote in the community nonschool opportunities . . . use community resources.[7]

No. 3: *. . . understanding and providing help, within the program of the school, for children who are having difficulties in using the resources of the school effectively . . . an approach . . . based on his understanding of human behavior, his skill in relationship and interviewing, and his ability to use school and community resources.*[8]

No. 4: *. . . in all areas of personal and social maladjustment, as well as academic difficulties, physical deficiencies, and confusion regarding educational and vocational choices.*[9]

No. 5: *. . . psychological counseling and guidance with such specific activities as individual child guidance, individual parent counseling, student counseling groups, and parent discussion groups; consultation, with such activities as consulting with individual teachers, teacher discussion groups, research and educational development, and referral and community services; individual and psychological evaluation, including such activities as case study, examination, diagnoses, recommending, reporting, and follow-up procedures.*[10]

No. 6: *. . . educational diagnosis, educational remediation, personality diagnosis, and personality remediation.*[11]

It might be difficult for an outsider to believe that these examples refer to what are considered to be "unique" functions of three different groups of professional workers. Even those who read these words may have some immediate difficulty in realizing that the first example describes the functions of the elementary school counselor,

7. "Tentative Statement of Policy for Secondary School Counselors," *Personnel and Guidance Journal*, 42:195–196 (October, 1963).

8. J. C. Nebo (ed.), *Administration of School Social Work* (New York· National Association of Social Workers, 1960), p. 17.

9. Jean R. Pearman and A. H. Burrows, *Social Services in the School* (Washington, D.C.: Public Affairs Press, 1955), p. 4.

10. Robert E. Valett, *The Practice of School Psychology* (New York: Wiley, 1963), pp. 7–8.

11. May Alice White and Myron U. Harris, *The School Psychologist* (New York: Harper, 1961), pp. 5–6.

the second those of the secondary school counselor. Examples three and four describe the functions of the school social worker, and the last two examples describe the functions of the school psychologist.

It is obvious from these definitions, which I think are fairly representative, and are at least "semiofficial," that all three groups view themselves as working in the same milieu, namely the school and its immediate environment, and with the same basic population: the children and those who most immediately affect them—teachers, parents, and the community. To varying degrees, all three see their functions as involvement in counseling, appraisal and consultation, with children, teachers, parents, and other school personnel, and various members of the community.

The psychiatric profession has generally shown little understanding of the school, and particularly of the functions of the school counselor, and one is almost tempted to say, after perusing the psychological literature, that the psychological version of the school counselor is that he is "the little man who isn't there."[12] In the 1967 and 1968 issues of the *Journal of Counseling Psychology*, for example, the articles which are centered around "counselors" refer almost without exception to either graduate students or college or university counselors.[13] The term "school counselor" is practically nonexistent in this particular sampling of the literature, as is the term "mental health." The same pattern holds in the 1973 issues of the same journal.

In perusing the 1967 and 1968 pages of the *American Psychologist*, I find six issues that discuss mental health and disturbed children and schools. Again, however, the school counselor is noticeable by his almost total absence. Mariner, for example, in examining professional education in the mental health field, describes the four professional groups which he sees as providing most of the professional psychotherapeutic help in this country and then goes on to say, "There are, of course, others who supply such help—some clergymen, nurses, and even aides in certain psychiatric hospitals."[14] The school as an institution and the school counselor as a person are viewed as having nothing to do with the provision of therapeutic help for children. Brown and Long, in a paper on psychology and community mental health, totally ignore the existence of the school

12. *See* Dugald S. Arbuckle, "The School Counselor as a Therapist" (unpublished paper).
13. Such as Andrew Thompson and Robert Zimmerman, "Goals of Counseling: Whose? When?" *Journal of Counseling Psychology*, 16:121–125 (March, 1969).
14. Allen S. Mariner, "A Critical Look at Professional Education in the Mental Health Field," *American Psychologist*, 22:271–281 (April, 1967).

and the school counselor.[15] The staff people mentioned are psychiatrists, psychologists, and social workers, and there is not the slightest implication that the school might possibly have some concern with the psychological health of children. The term "school counselor" is even less visible in the 1973 issues of the *American Psychologist.*

Hobbs, in discussing a school for emotionally disturbed children, referred in 1966 to a "training program to prepare a new kind of mental health worker, called a teacher-counselor,"[16] apparently unaware of the fact that a somewhat similar person, needed for all schools, was the basis for a book, *Teacher Counseling,*[17] published in 1950. While he does mention the place of the liaison teacher in helping to maintain communication between the regular classroom and the special school, there is no reference to the school counselor. It seems strange that "teacher" should somehow be more involved in the therapeutic function in the school than "counselor"! Implicit here, too, is the idea that "emotionally disturbed children" are a special breed of children who do not belong in the regular school, and that school staff should not be expected to be able to work with such children.

Hersch, in referring to a "revolution" in mental health, describes the revolution as an overthrow of the status quo and the centering of attention on the community and the population rather than the individual.[18] Nowhere is the school or the counselor mentioned as having anything to do with this revolution. A paper by Bardon probably sums up the attitudes expressed in these various psychological journals. He refers to an array of pupil personnel service workers who will perform the functions now carried out by the school psychologist, but not by the *new* school psychologist as he envisages him. Among these workers "will be psychodiagnosticians, test technicians, child development specialists, home and school counselors, elementary guidance workers." These workers he views as "technicians," trained at the bachelor's, one-year and two-year graduate level, and they will be thought of as "educational specialists," not directly involved with psychology per se.[19]

15. Bertram S. Brown and Eugene S. Long, "Psychology and Community Mental Health: The Medical Muddle," *American Psychologist,* 23:335–341 (May, 1968).

16. Nicholas Hobbs, "Helping Disturbed Children: Psychological and Ecological Strategies," *American Psychologist,* 21:1105–1115 (November, 1966).

17. Dugald S. Arbuckle, *Teacher Counseling* (Cambridge, Mass.: Addison-Wesley, 1950).

18. Charles Hersch, "The Discontent Explosion in Mental Health," *American Psychologist,* 23:497–506 (July, 1968).

19. Jack I. Bardon, "School Psychology and School Psychologists: An Approach to an Old Problem," *American Psychologist,* 23:187–194 (March, 1968).

These attitudes are generally reflective of the psychological literature and of psychologists, and they are, possibly, one of the major reasons for the crawling pace of what we know as mental health. The school is apparently seen as a place where children are forced to go to be taught something which in some dim future will be of value to them. School counselors would appear to be viewed as a part of this teaching team, not unlike the teachers, and neither would appear to have any major interest or concern or involvement in the therapeutic growth of the child. But surely the school is overwhelmingly the obvious, the only, place where prevention can really have meaning. Until the concept of the therapeutic classroom becomes an accepted and integral part of the daily education of every child, we will continue to have clinics and hospitals making their possibly gallant, but futile, gestures, in attempting to stop the flood of disturbed children who will increasingly pour down upon them, and may eventually overwhelm all of us. But the psychologists generally, continue to have their experimental classes, and do their bits and pieces of research, and the impact on what happens in the classroom, day by day, is infinitesimally small. If we are really seriously interested in the development of the psychologically healthy mind and body, rather than in the cure of diseases, then that institution which is supposed to be totally dedicated to human growth and development, namely, the school, is the major social institution where this can take place.

But the rash of books in the 1960's and the 1970's on how schools should be, on what is wrong with schools, and what is necessary if real learning is ever to take place, and the development of "free" schools and "new" schools, would appear to have had minimal effect on education in America. The changes that have taken place in the public and private schools of America in the last few decades have been mostly superficial, and the basic school—its purpose and its operation—have changed very little.

The discrepancy between what children need in the way of an educational diet, in order to become effective human beings, and what they get, is especially obvious in the city schools of America. Here we have schools functioning in what would seem, sometimes, to be a total unawareness of the children and the culture of which they are a part. Allied with them are so-called mental health institutions that would likely have been ineffective in Freud's Vienna at the turn of the century, let alone the inner city of Chicago or New York or Boston or Cleveland in 1975!

The various policy statements of professional organizations regarding counselor functions read well, but the extent to which they are implemented in schools might be questioned. In 1964 two policy statements appeared, and they pretty well represent the professional attitude today. The American School Counselors Association, for example, described the major professional responsibilities of the school counselor as the following:

1. *Assist each pupil to meet the need to understand himself in relation to the social and psychological world in which he lives. This implies helping each pupil to understand his aptitudes, interests, attitudes, abilities, opportunities for self-fulfillment, and the interrelationships among these.*

2. *Assist each pupil to meet the need of accepting (defined as being able to behave consistent with) his aptitudes, interests, attitudes, abilities and opportunities for self-fulfillment.*

3. *Assist each pupil to meet the need to develop personal decision-making competency. Included is the responsibility of assuring that the pupil's opportunities for self-understanding and self-fulfillment are not restricted by the group consideration and processes inherent in schools.*

4. *Assist all members of the individual staff to understand the importance of the individual pupil and to provide information, material and consultative assistance aimed at supporting their efforts to understand pupils.*

5. *Determine the influence of the school program on pupil educational and psycho-social development, and to convey such information to other staff members.*

6. *Inform other staff members of significant changes in the school and nonschool environments which have implications for instruction, the psycho-social well-being of pupils, and to participate in related program development.*

7. *Assist parents to understand the developmental progress of their child, his needs, and environmental opportunities, for purposes of increasing their ability to contribute to their child's development.*

8. *Interpret to the community the importance of consideration for the individual and the contribution of the school counseling program to that end.*

9. *Promote in the community nonschool opportunities necessary for pupil development.*

10. *Use and/or promote community resources designed to meet unusual or extreme needs of pupils which are beyond the responsibility of the school.*

The report accepted by the American Personnel and Guidance

Association at its annual convention in 1964 described the role of counselors as follows:

1. *The major responsibility of the counselor is to assist an individual through the counseling relationship to utilize his own resources and his environmental opportunities in the process of self-understanding, planning, decision-making and coping with problems relative to his developmental needs and to his vocational and educational activities.*

2. *The counselor also engages in related activities. For example, he makes effective use of the services of other professional personnel through referrals and consultation. He works with other persons in his employment environment in a manner which facilitates the achievement of desirable objectives for the benefit of the counselee. He may perform additional services for which he has the necessary preparation and the nature of which is such that they are logically his professional responsibility within the setting in which he works. However, he should not be expected to perform tasks which are inconsistent with his professional role as a counselor, or which are inappropriate for the social institution for which he works.*

3. *In all of his professional activities, the counselor maintains a high level of ethical practice in accordance with the Code of Ethics of the American Personnel and Guidance Association.*

4. *The counselor expects that in the employment setting in which he works conditions will be maintained which will enable him to work in a professional manner. These conditions include freedom to exercise his skills on a professional level, time to perform the counseling function, and adequate facilities.*

A joint ACES-ASCA committee, in 1966, described the major functions of the elementary school counselor as counseling with pupils as well as with parents and teachers; consulting with parents and other school and community personnel; coordinating and integrating the resources of the school and the community.

The increasing stress in the 1970's has been to get the counselor out of the office, working with individual clients, into a greater involvement with groups of students, teachers, parents, and other members of the community. The code of ethics adopted by the American School Counselors Association in October, 1972, for example, stresses the responsibilities of counselors to pupils, to parents, to faculty administration and colleagues, to the school and the community, to self, and to the profession. This is laudable, and necessary, but care must be taken that the counselor does not become so fragmented that it is impossible to describe any professional function as *primarily* that of the counselor.

The professional stamp of approval must be on counselor education programs just as it is on counselors. This approval of counselors should come from the institution rather than from the state department of education or, rather, the approval of the state department should come through the institution. Once a counselor education program has been approved by the professional organization as first rate, a graduate of that program should meet state certification requirements anywhere in the country. There should be no need to have state department detectives checking to see if he has had this course, this course, and this course—never, of course, asking where and from whom he took the courses! This also means that institutions will have to be named, identified, and periodically checked to determine the caliber of their programs. One does not become a medical doctor, a dentist, a lawyer, or an architect by attending a few classes at almost any institution in the United States. There are certain institutions that have professionally acceptable medical schools and law schools and schools of engineering, and so there must soon be certain institutions which will be identified as having professionally acceptable programs of counselor education.

Once the school counselor becomes a graduate of one of the relatively few professionally acceptable counselor education programs, then we may see a rapid reduction in both the "part-timeness" of his education and the "part-timeness" of his function. There may even, for a time, be a reduction in the number of people who are entitled to the name "school counselor." This is not all bad, since the major problem in school counseling today is not lack of quantity, but lack of quality. Ideally, we must try to increase the number of qualified school counselors, but it is better to have fewer qualified counselors than to have more unqualified counselors, and thus live under the illusion that numbers of bodies will satisfy our problem.

AREAS OF DEBATE OVER COUNSELOR FUNCTIONS[20]

The counselor is still bedeviled by a lack of professional identity, and both within and without the school milieu the comment "I am a

20. See Dugald S. Arbuckle, "Does the School Really Need Counselors?" *School Counselor*, 17:325–331 (May, 1970) and Dugald S. Arbuckle, "The Conflicting Functions of the School Counselor," *Counselor Education and Supervision*, 1:54–59 (Winter, 1961). Copyright 1970, 1961 by the American Personnel and Guidance Association.

counselor" carries with it no consistent meaning. There are a number of areas of debate over this question of function:

1. After several decades, the gap between what the school counselor actually does and what the professional programs of counselor education supposedly prepare him to do, is, with few exceptions, just as wide as ever. There are, basically, two points of view. One sees the counselor as one who is not too different, either in training or attitude, from the teacher and administrator, and whose functions are varied and geared to the needs of the school, as perceived by the administrators and teachers, but not necessarily by the children, the parents, the community—or by empirical evidence.

The other point of view sees the counselor as having a discrete and definable function, quite different from that of teachers and administrators, and therefore requiring a different kind of person with a different kind of professional education. Such an individual's functions would be determined primarily by what evidence says about the needs of the children and adults in the school and in the community, and they would be functions that are not being performed by other school personnel. Currently, it would appear that the latter represents a minority point of view, although I may be being unduly pessimistic!

The first point of view was generally acceptable until fairly recently. In a study conducted in the 1920's, for example, Edgerton found that counselors felt that their functions consisted of (1) interviewing students; (2) teaching classes in occupations; (3) finding jobs for students and following them up; (4) administering tests; (5) doing research in the study of occupations.[21]

At that time, as would be expected, the counselor's concept of his role was almost entirely vocational. Some years later, Cox undertook an investigation of a group of counselors in secondary schools throughout the country. She found that their functions, in order of frequency, were (1) work with parents; (2) educational-vocational-emotional guidance of pupils; (3) supervision of tests, both giving tests and interpreting test results; (4) cooperation with law enforcement agencies; (5) consultation with employers; (6) discipline; (7) placement; (8) coordinating the guidance program of the school; (9) home-room supervision; (10) cooperation with community guidance agencies; (11) teaching; (12) chaperoning parties and social needs; (13) follow-up of pupils who had left school.[22]

This study tended to point up the increasing and conflicting functions that were supposedly performed by the counselor. About

21. A. H. Edgerton, *Vocational Guidance and Counseling* (New York: Macmillan, 1926).
22. Rachel D. Cox, *Counselors and Their Work* (Harrisburg: Archives Press, 1945).

the same time, Wright, in a report of an analysis by Minneapolis counselors of their function, indicated that the secondary school counselors felt that their job consisted of (1) checking credits for graduation and college entrance; (2) advising those students entering and those in military service; (3) interviewing and counseling failing students; (4) handling employment; (5) arranging group conferences; (6) writing letters of reference for pupils who were in school or who had left school; (7) conferring with students planning to withdraw from school; (8) doing clerical work; (9) conferring with teachers about pupils' problems.[23]

Another study of high schools in the state of Washington indicated that counselors were expected to orient eighth-graders; provide occupational information about colleges; provide a testing program for the four years, and assume the responsibility for recording the data; provide for social development; make adequate provision for exceptional students; arrange adequate occupational placement; do follow-up studies; evaluate the program for future improvement; and organize their time so as to be able to do individual counseling.[24]

The more recent literature tends to reflect the debate between both points of view. Patterson, for example, states:

As a professional person, the counselor is, or should be, able to have some influence in determining the nature of his job. He must not allow his duties to be dictated by others aware of the needs children have for class personal relationships.[25]

Gelatt, a director of guidance, in reacting to this paper, says that "guidance, or counseling, or pupil personnel or whatever it is called in the schools, is there for the purpose of helping the schools achieve their objectives."[26] While Gelatt does add that if the counselor doesn't like the school's objectives he should do something to change them, the change will be minimal if one is committed to achieving objectives with which he does not agree.

Boy and Pine feel that school counselors and other members of the pupil personnel services team "make their most significant contributions through cooperative and collaborative processes, and not by skewing and distorting one another's roles so that they lose

23. Barbara H. Wright, "Minneapolis School Counselors Analyze Their Jobs," *Occupations,* 24:214–219 (Janury, 1946).

24. Werner C. Dieckmann, "What Kind of Guidance and Counseling Programs in the Small School," *Bulletin of the National Association of Secondary School Principals,* 37:233–235 (November, 1952).

25. C. H. Patterson, "The Counselor in the Elementary School," *Personnel and Guidance Journal,* 47:979–986 (June, 1969).

26. H. B. Gelatt, "Ridiculous," *Personnel and Guidance Journal,* 47:987 (June, 1969).

407

their unique qualities of effectiveness."[27] In a reaction to this, Dustin says that "any proposed 'solution' to the question of counselor role must be practical and meet the needs of the current school setting."[28]

The effective counselor, as described by Carkhuff and Berenson, is "a person who can understand his (or her) internal and external and physical, emotional, and intellectual worlds with sensitivity and can act upon these worlds with responsibility," and can thus "enable others to understand their worlds with sensitivity and act upon them with responsibility."[29]

Such a counselor does not fit the description of Siegel, a guidance counselor, when she makes the astonishing comment that "counselors serve schools. They must perform as the school dictates."[30] Nor would Money, another school counselor, likely agree with Siegel; she urges: ". . . let us bid farewell to Guidance, the nation's Pandora's box, and make a school counseling a skilled, devoted and worthwhile service."[31]

In describing his version of school counseling, Darter, a school counselor, says that it "respects the personal autonomy of the counselee, and it reflects the counselor's faith in the counselee's ability to learn and to solve his own problems."[32] This obviously differs from the concept of Ricker, a director of guidance, who states that "regardless of what is done on the college campus, the counselor 'on the firing line' is going to be concerned with problems that must be resolved in a classroom setting."[33]

2. Many educators, and many individuals who are called counselors but see themselves primarily as educators, are unwilling, or unable, to entertain the thought of any differences in professional functions between counselors and teachers and school administrators. This is partially due, of course, to the curse of the teacher heritage of the counselor. It is interesting to note that school personnel

27. Angelo V. Boy and Gerald J. Pine, "A Sociological View of the Counselor Role," *Personnel and Guidance Journal,* 47:736–740. (April, 1969).

28. Richard Dustin, "Let's Not Wait," *Personnel and Guidance Journal,* 48:85–86 (October, 1969).

29. Robert R. Carkhuff and Bernard Berenson, "The Counselor Is a Man and a Woman," *Personnel and Guidance Journal,* 48:24–28 (September, 1969).

30. Betty Siegel, "Evaluating a Guidance Counselor," *School Counselor,* 16:309–311 (March, 1969).

31. Dolores Money, "Eliminate Guidance in the Public School," *School Counselor* 16:303–304 (March, 1969).

32. Richard Darter, "Is It Time to Review the Goals of Counseling?" *School Counselor,* 16:229–232 (January, 1969).

33. George A. Ricker, "Must Counselors Have Taught?" *School Counselor,* 17:40–46 (September, 1969).

are not threatened or angered when one points out that such people as the nurse, the social worker, and the psychiatrist have different functions from those of the teacher and the administrator. Nor is there ever any assumption that because they do have different professional identities it is impossible for them to work with other school personnel. Yet somehow it is different with the counselor, and many school personnel, including counselors, apparently feel that counselors must be professionally indistinguishable from teachers and administrators if they are ever going to be able to work together.

There are many tasks that must be carried out to continue the necessary functions of the school, and while all of these tasks may be defended as being needed to achieve the broad and immediate goals of the school, they are tasks that cannot be done by one person, even assuming that he had the time. This is so because of his inadequate knowledge and education, because of his lack of skills, because of his personality structure, and because certain functions clash with other functions. Thus, a perfectly good mathematics teacher might be a very poor English teacher because he doesn't know English, and isn't interested in it; a perfectly good English teacher may be a poor physical education teacher because he lacks the physical coordination necessary for this task; a principal may be effective because he is the sort of person who likes organizing and administering and directing and controlling. All of these people *may* become good school counselors if they have, or if they develop, an understanding of people and human behavior, if they are deeply but not too neurotically interested in working with individuals as individuals, and if they master the knowledge and the skills that are part of the repertoire of the school counselor. They *may*, it should be noted, become effective school counselors, but they cannot do so while they still retain their previous occupational functions, since effectiveness as a teacher or a principal may often be equated with ineffectiveness as a counselor.

Papers or articles or talks that suggest the possibility of the school counselor being involved in a therapeutic sense usually produce a sharp and sometimes quite violent reaction. Krueger, for example, warns school counselors about the grave effects of taking seriously such terms as "relationship" and "acceptance."[34] Venn, in describing the training of the counselor, says that he must have "courses in school administration, curriculum development, and school guidance itself. He must be a teacher on assignment, like a school administrator, not a specialist from another profession work-

34. Albert H. Krueger, "Letters and Comments," *Personnel and Guidance Journal*, 45:1033–1044 (June, 1967).

ing in the school."[35] Sexton says that "the less we emphasize the psychological, the psychiatric, and anything therapeutic, the better the feeling the students will have toward counseling."[36] O'Hara turns the counselor into a teacher when he presumes enough openness in the client to accept information-giving as the role of the counselor.[37] When I suggested in a paper that counselors, psychologists, and social workers might get together and be given the more generic name "school counseling psychologist,"[38] I was put in my place with a "riposte" by Paulson, which ended with the statement, "School counselors and school social workers are justly proud of their own names."[39] Brammer, who had the temerity to write a paper entitled "The Counselor Is a Psychologist,"[40] was dismissed with such statements as, "Pathetically, the few statements in this presentation that can be deemed valid by an objective observer of counselors' work . . ." and "Brammer's proposal to discard the guidance model for counselor education is, then, alarmingly absurd."[41]

Collins, who is a dean of instruction, says that "junior college counselors are not psychiatrists, not clinical counselors, nor depth psychiatrists, and those who overtly or covertly hold to such pretensions should be disabused of them."[42] Payne, a past president of the American Association of School Administrators, comments that a number of his faculty "do not believe that a counselor can help them in their understanding of a pupil in a class situation unless the counselor has actually had classroom experience" and that "in the normal working day of a school counselor he is usually expected to perform both services (counseling and disciplining)."[43]

Hoyt, a past president of the American Personnel and Guid-

35. Kenneth Venn, "Letters and Comments," *Personnel and Guidance Journal,* 46:73 (September, 1967).

36. John M. Sexton, "A Reaction to the ASCA Statement of Policy for Secondary School Counselors," *School Counselor,* 12:132–135 (March, 1965).

37. Robert P. O'Hara, "Counseling and Vocational Psychology," in Dugald S. Arbuckle (ed.), *Counseling and Psychotherapy: An Overview* (New York: McGraw-Hill, 1967). p. 113.

38. Dugald S. Arbuckle, "Counselor, Social Worker, Psychologist: Let's Ecumenicalize," *op. cit.*

39. Blanche B. Paulson, "Riposte," *Personnel and Guidance Journal,* 45:539–540 (February, 1967).

40. Lawrence M. Brammer, "The Counselor Is a Psychologist," *Personnel and Guidance Journal,* 47:4–9 (September, 1968).

41. Joseph L. Felix, "Who Decided That?" *Personnel and Guidance Journal,* 47:9–11 (September, 1968).

42. Charles C. Collins, "Junior College Counseling: A Critical View," *Personnel and Guidance Journal,* 43:546–550 (February, 1965).

43. J. Win Payne, "Impact of the ASCA Statement of Counselor Role," *The School Counselor,* 12:136–139 (March, 1965).

ance Association, is apparently acceptant of such ideas, when in referring to the counselor's functions, he says that the counselor "regards the principal as his administrative superior and as the one person responsible for the direction of the guidance program."[44]

If the counselor is seen, and if he sees himself, as having functions which are no different from those of teachers and administrators, then there is little doubt that he will be seen by great numbers of students as being more concerned with the maintenance of the school as an establishment than with the helping of the student as a unique human being. Van Riper, in reporting on a study, comments that it "appears that the work of the counselor does not provide him with a role which is easily distinguished from that of the teacher or principal and, consequently, prevents the counselor from attaining a separate identity."[45]

In a book review, Aubrey takes me to task and perceives me as suggesting that the counselor is "posing as a knight in shining armor while 'rescuing' the subjected individual from coercive teaching, an unfeeling administration and a dull uninteresting curriculum."[46] But is this not the professional responsibility of the counselor, even though he may not be a knight in shining armor? Surely none would deny that there are, throughout the United States, tens of thousands of coercive teachers, that there are scores of administrations that are cold and unfeeling, and that a significant proportion of the school curriculum is dull and deadly and oppressive and irrelevant. This does not mean that teachers and administrators should not be concerned with these problems, or that many of them are not very much concerned about them. But it is the *professional responsibility* of the school counselor to do something about those school conditions which are harming students, and surely anyone involved in schools would have to be blind to be unaware of the fact that tens of thousands of young people are being affected in a negative way by their school experiences. Goldman puts it well when he says that "if they do nothing else, counselors should listen to students, and sound an alarm to let the faculty know when school is irrelevant or inappropriate or unnecessarily dull. Of all the people in a school or college, counselors should be the first ones to recognize insults to motivation."[47]

44. Kenneth B. Hoyt, "Guidance: A Constellation of Services," *Personnel and Guidance Journal,* 40:695–699 (April, 1962).
45. B. W. Van Riper, "Student Perception: The Counselor Is What He Does," *School Counselor,* 19:53–56 (September, 1971).
46. Roger F. Aubrey, "Book Reviews," *Personnel and Guidance Journal,* 69:867–898 (June, 1971).
47. Leo Goldman, "An Award for Low Correlations," *Personnel and Guidance Journal,* 49:610 (April, 1970).

School administrators, even more than schoolteachers, would appear to have difficulty in accepting the idea that counselors might have professional functions quite different from those of teachers.[48] We could probably assume, for example, that school administrators would not accept the following statement by Weitz: "It is interesting to note that the typical administrator not only cannot provide the kinds of guidance described here, but he also cannot separate the guidance and instructional functions in general administrative practice."[49] Nor would some accept the line separating the two as spelled out by Mathewson:

> *The crucial line separating the educational counselor from the administrative officer, the admissions officer, or the industrial personnel officer is that the counselor is primarily concerned with personal and not institutional or social needs, and is engaged in educative and interpretive functions, not selective, placement or recruitment functions.*[50]

Are counselors and administrators different persons, then, with different kinds of values? Does the difference in attitude arise because they are different as people, rather than because they represent a different occupational group? There is at least some evidence to suggest that this might be so. Chenault and Seegars, for example, concluded after a study that counselors and principals were both essentially dominant persons, with principals leaning toward the tolerant side. Principals would have liked their counselors to be firmer and more aggressive.[51] Another study indicated that, on the matter of values, counselors and administrators both ranked high on self-realization and altruism, and low on money and security, although administrators did rank higher than counselors on money. The most significant difference was the high evaluation placed on control by the administrators.[52] Still another study, comparing the attitudes of counselors with women deans', indicated that deans were more authoritarian, more persuasive, less sympathetic and less understand-

48. See Dugald S. Arbuckle, "A Question of Counselor Function and Responsibility," *Personnel and Guidance Journal*, 47:341–346 (December, 1968).

49. Henry Weitz, *Behavior Change Through Guidance* (New York: Wiley, 1964), p. 64.

50. Robert W. Mathewson, "Manpower or Persons: A Critical Issue," *Personnel and Guidance Journal*, 43:338–342 (December, 1964).

51. Joann Chenault and James E. Seegars, Jr., "The Interpersonal Diagnosis of Principals and Counselors," *Personnel and Guidance Journal*, 41:118–122 (October, 1962).

52. Buford Stefflre and Fred Lergren, "Value Differences Between Counselors and Administrators," *Vocational Guidance Quarterly*, 10:226–228 (Summer, 1962).

ing than college counselors.[53] In a study of needs, Kemp concludes that the counselor, more than the principal, satisfies his need to understand how others feel about problems, to put oneself in the other's place, to form new friendships, to share with friends, and to say things so that he might discover the effect they will have on others. The principal, more than the counselor, satisfies his need to be successful, to solve difficult problems, to be recognized as an authority, to complete the undertaking, to persist with the problem although no progress is apparent, to do what is expected, to conform to custom, to tell others they have done well, to follow a plan, to organize details and have things run smoothly.[54]

Knock and Cody, in a study of counselor candidates, teachers, and administrators, found that persons preparing for careers as school counselors appeared to be more student-centered than currently employed school teachers and administrators.[55] Fotiu found that principals tended to be more satisfied than counselors about the current role of secondary school counselors.[56] One of the results of a study by Sweeney was the indication that principals see the counselor as a quasi-administrator, and they prefer more administrative-type leadership among counselors.[57]

Thus it would seem that, in general, the counselor and the administrator are two different kinds of people, and the professional responsibilities they accept are a reflection of this difference. Let us note what school administrators appear to be saying about counselors and their functions:

a. There is a degree of suspicion, particularly among school administrators and some teachers, of things psychological and therapeutic. This very attitude might at least be one of the reasons why, for some children at least, the learning that takes place in school is minimal. While counselors might disagree on methodological procedures, there would be little argument about their therapeutic role, even if this may mean nothing more than providing a therapeutic

53. Mary Elizabeth Reeves and Dugald S. Arbuckle, "The Counseling Attitudes of Deans of Women," *Personnel and Guidance Journal,* 41:438–445 (January, 1963).

54. C. Gratton Kemp, "Counseling and Need Structure of High School Principals and of Counselors," *Journal of Counseling Psychology,* 9:326–328 (Winter, 1962).

55. Garry H. Knock and John J. Cody, "Student-Centeredness: A Comparison of Counselor Candidates, Teachers and Administrators," *Counselor Education and Supervision,* 6:114–119 (Winter, 1967).

56. Peter G. Fotiu, "Do Counselors and Principals Agree?" *School Counselor,* 14:298–303 (May, 1967).

57. Thomas J. Sweeney, "The School Counselor as Perceived by School Counselors and Their Principals," *Personnel and Guidance Journal,* 44:844–849 (April, 1966).

milieu in which the student may be helped to learn and to grow. Some counselors may be more information-centered than others, but in their helping and caring relationship with students, all have a therapeutic involvement. Indeed, many teachers would be the first to say that if one is to be really involved with a student in the learning process, a therapeutic atmosphere is an absolute requisite. Most counselors, too, would see themselves as psychologists, at least in a generic sense, whether or not they might carry such a title. After all, they are concerned with people, and their behavior, and the learning process. This, surely, is in the realm of psychology. The term psychiatric is often used with the other two, and this probably brings visions of a couch and a man with a beard and an Austrian accent! Actually, whether one uses the term psychological or psychiatric, it would seem that an understanding of some of the abnormalities of human behavior, and at least some degree of skill in counseling and diagnosis, would be minimal requisites for anyone who calls himself a school counselor.

b. The administrator often sees no apparent clash between differing functions and responsibilities. This is most often noted in the assumption that the disciplinary, the evaluative, and the authority roles of the teacher and the administrator in no way interfere with the functions and the responsibilities of the counselor. Many children, of course, are secure and solid enough so that evaluation and disciplinary action will have little effect on them. The rub, however, is that the children and adults who are like this are the ones whose evaluations are usually quite positive, and who are very seldom the recipients of disciplinary action. The individuals who are least equipped to take the blows and the discipline are the ones who most often receive them. All too frequently in schools the smiles, the approving nods, and the "That's good" go to those who least need them. In universities, administrative deans still insist on talking about "educational" value and use phrases like "We're really trying to help the student" at hearings of various disciplinary boards at which punishment is being meted out. Surely this is, psychologically, plain nonsense. The administrator who, while disciplining the individual, is at the same time encouraging him to feel free to express his feelings might be accused of at least some degree of schizophrenia!

It would seem crucial that the counselor be viewed by his potential clientele not only as a caring and helping individual, but equally important, as one who does not have, and does not represent, the authority of the institution. The counselor should represent the highest level of security in the institution, he should be an individual with whom another person can correctly feel, "I can be totally honest with this person, and I will not have to pay a price." Surely that statement cannot be made to the administrator if he has accepted any level of responsibility for the operation of the institution.

c. If there is no particular difference in the functions and the responsibilities of the counselor and the administrator, then it is not unreasonable to assume, as do many administrators, that there is no need for any special training or education for the counselor. If the counselor does not have a specialized function, quite different from those of the teacher and administrator, then obviously there is no need for a special program of education for counselors.

A professional individual, of course, in a school as elsewhere, does not ask his employer, "What do you want me to do?" It is not a case of the individual being fitted to the job, but rather the particular skills and capacities of the individual being such that he can be effective in a certain task. If they are, he might consider accepting the position; if they are not, he obviously should not accept the position even if it were offered to him. It is difficult for me to believe that any professional school counselor, if asked by a potential employer, "Do you accept the responsibility of utilizing your authority to compel certain students to change their behavior?" would answer any other way than "No, I do not." On the other hand, it would seem equally logical that a school administrator, if asked the same question, might respond, "Well, I hope we never have to compel a student to do anything, but if his behavior is disruptive, and counter to school policy, then yes, I might have to compel him to change his behavior or leave the institution."

On this same point there is also the assumption that the counselor's professional knowledge, as well as his professional skills, are not in any way different from those of the teacher or the administrator. This again, of course, is totally counter to the position taken by APGA, ACES, and ASCA, and these positions represent the attitude of, literally, thousands of counselors and counselor educators. The counselor, obviously, as part of his professional education, should know the school, and the people who work in the school, and the culture and the environment that affect the school. But he should not be expected to be as expert in his knowledge of school building construction as is the superintendent; he should not be expected to be as knowledgeable about the costs and the staffing of the various curricular programs in the modern high school as the principal; he should not be expected to know as much about the latest in the "new math" as does the elementary teacher; he should not be expected to know as much about the history of Europe as the history teacher. He should, however, be expert in problems dealing with human communication; he should know much about people and their behavior; he

415

should have diagnostic capacities and skills; he should know much about the nonschool world of work and further education; above all he should be capable of relating in a positive way with individuals who resist and resent any attempt at human communication and closeness. In effect, his knowledge and his capacities must be different from those of the teacher and the administrator if he is going to have any right to the name of counselor.

d. With the continuing uncertainty as to what the counselor does in the school, it is not surprising to find that it is difficult to find much evidence as to the uniqueness of either the counselor or his task. The question here is not so much whether what the counselor does is unimportant, but rather whether it can be done just as well by other school personnel. In the 1969 issues of the *School Counselor*, for example, there were some eighty-two features and articles, twenty-three of them being written by school counselors. Four years later, in the 1973 issues, there were thirty-seven featured articles. Of these, three were written by guidance administrators, none at all by school counselors! There were more suggestions for change in the later issues, but it is disheartening to note that practically none of these suggestions of change regarding school counselors came from school counselors!

Thus one must at least wonder if the school counselor actually, functionally, does perform a unique service for which he is specially educated and trained, or if he is actually a teacher performing functions that are primarily those of the teacher or the administrator.

When Dahlem stresses the need for better public relations so that popular misconceptions about the functions of the counselor might be erased,[58] the embarrassing fact is that at least three of his five "misconceptions,"—namely, the counselor as a disciplinarian, the counselor as a giver of advice, and the counselor as a clerical assistant to students—are still being performed assiduously by a significant number of counselors. One may well wonder if Rosner's guess will be shown to be correct:

> *My guess is that guidance and counseling as it is currently defined and practiced will disappear, but the disappearance will be gradual. Some counselors may . . . move into the field of interpersonal relations. Some may elect administration. Some may return to teaching or leave the school for other social service agencies or enter industry. I would like to suggest that some may take advantage of the information-processing capa-*

58. Glenn G. Dahlem, "Popular Misconceptions of Guidance—A Danger," *School Counselor*, 16:223–227 (January, 1969).

bilities of the computer, and become supervisors of school-community information centers.[59]

The professional literature gives the impression that counselors do not want to write about what they do, and that when they do write, it would appear that their functions are primarily those of teachers or administrators. In addition to this, however, there is little in the way of research by counselors as to the effects of what counselors do. Thus not only is one hard pressed in trying to answer the question "Just what's so special about what counselors do?" but it is even more difficult to react to the question "Just exactly what difference does it make when counselors do what they say they do?" Most members of other professional groups would be rather startled to find out that the great majority of school counselors, in terms of the actual tasks they perform, have little or no evidence to indicate that it would make any significant difference whether or not these tasks were continued. On the contrary, the evidence that is available raises serious doubts about the effectiveness, in terms of achieving stated objectives, of the activities of school counselors.

e. The logical question that follows any suggestion that the counselor *does* have a unique function is: "Well, what is it?" It is interesting to follow the changes of one who might be called the father of school counseling in the United States, C. Gilbert Wrenn. In 1957 he felt that any discussion of the counselor role should be based on the following assumptions:

1. *The school counselor is an educator with special professional training at the M.A. level and beyond.*
2. *The school counselor is a generalist in a number of school functions and may be a specialist in at least one type of service. The nature of this specialization may vary with each counselor's unique personal qualification and with the specific emphasis on his professional education.*
3. *The school counselor's clients include teachers, parents, and administrators as well as students.*
4. *The school counselor's skills should include not only those necessary for the individual counseling relationship but those essential to working effectively with groups.*
5. *The school counselor is concerned primarily with the normal growth needs of students, more with personality development than with problem crises.*

59. Benjamin Rosner, "A Different Problem and a Different Solution," *Personnel and Guidance Journal*, 48:108–110 (October, 1969).

6. *The school counselor, because of the expectations of student, teacher, administrator, must have a fairly high level of
psychological sophistication in his professional education
and in-service development . . . .*[60]

Five years later, one of his four recommendations dealing with
the counselor was as follows:

*That the professional job description of a counselor specify
that he perform four major functions: (a) counsel with students; (b) consult with teachers, administrators, and parents as
they in turn deal with students; (c) study the changing facts
about the student population and interpret what is found to
school committees and administrators; (d) coordinate counseling resources in school and between school and community.
From two-thirds to three-fourths of the counselor's time, in either elementary or high school, should be committed to the first
two of these functions. Activities that do not fall into one of
these four areas neither should be expected nor encouraged as
part of the counselor's regular working schedule.*[61]

A decade later, Wrenn felt that these functions were still valid,
but he put them in terms of the person of the counselor rather than
in terms of the program, in terms of the counselor's expectations of
himself that bring about certain behaviors. Thus he sees the counsel-
or's major goals as helping students indirectly by contributing to the
improvement of the learning environment of the school; helping students directly, both individually and through groups; and keeping
the counselor as a person in constant touch with the surrounding
changing world.[62]

There is no question that the major current debate concen-
trates on the extent to which the counselor should be involved as an
active agent of social change. In considering this issue, we should be
careful not to confuse the very real and desperate need for social
change with actions that might diminish the effectiveness of the
counselor *as a counselor.* The counselor must seriously consider the
extent to which the open identification with social and political
causes may alienate many of those who need to be helped. I would
not think of this as a cop-out, or a running away, but rather a facing
of the reality of the situation. The identification of a counselor with
the human needs and problems of an individual or a group or a com-

60. C. Gilbert Wrenn, "Status and Role of the School Counselor," *Personnel and
Guidance Journal,* 36:175–183 (November, 1957).
61. C. Gilbert Wrenn, *The Counselor in a Changing World* (Washington, D.C.:
American Personnel and Guidance Association, 1962), p. 137. Copyright 1962 by
the American Personnel and Guidance Association. Reprinted by permission.
62. C. Gilbert Wrenn, *The World of the Contemporary Counselor* (Boston: Houghton
Mifflin, 1973). p. 271.

munity is quite different from identification with a social or political cause.

The question is not whether the counselor should be involved in change, but rather how he can best utilize his particular knowledge and skills and human understandings to help individuals to change in ways that will be best for them, and thus for their society. No one could argue with Goldman when he says, ". . . maybe we should be . . . aiming for change rather than stability,"[63] or with Caldwell, who says that "the counselor must reassess his role as an agent of change in the student body, the campus, the curriculum and the community."[64] The counselor, as one who works with those who have been hurt by their in- and out-of-school experiences, cannot ignore his preventive role.

His primary professional function, however, and his particular professional expertise would be in the counseling involvement with individuals or with small groups of students, or teachers, or parents. Nurses and psychiatrists and social workers and psychologists work with teachers and school administrators and parents, but they bring with them their professional identity and their professional expertise. They never forget their primary function, and I see no rationale as to why counselors should operate in a different manner in this regard. Since, as Zerface and Cox point out, "school counselors in general do not counsel,"[65] the most radical suggestion for change might be that counselors become more involved in counseling. Social change is the product of individual action, and the counselor may be doing the best he can do by helping young individuals to become the sort of people who can stand up for justice and honesty and decency, and thus have a marked impact on their society. Lewis and Lewis may well be being "new-fashioned," not old-fashioned, when they say that "primary to the counselor's role, of course, must be direct counseling contact with individual students, providing an avenue aiding the student to explore himself and his potential and freeing him to face a challenging future openly and less defensively."[66] May, too, may be suggesting a radical change in the counselor's function when he states that "by offering psychological coun-

63. Leo Goldman, *op. cit.*

64. Edson Caldwell, "Counseling in Context," *Personnel and Guidance Journal,* 49:271–278 (December, 1970).

65. James P. Zerface and Walter H. Cox, "School Counselors, Leave Home," *Personnel and Guidance Journal,* 49:371–375 (January, 1971).

66. Michael Lewis and Judith A. Lewis, "Relevant Training for Relevant Roles: A Model for Educating Inner City Counselors," *Counselor Education and Supervision,* 10:31–38 (Fall, 1970).

seling, counselors are in a unique position to help people improve their self-concepts and develop more of their potentials."[67]

Of interest, too, is a comment made by Walz in presenting his view of the perception of counseling held by the U.S. Office of Education. He indicated that there is not enough association or linkage made between counselor involvement in such areas as counseling with the culturally distinct or youth alienation and drug abuse. He expressed the feeling that if counseling is to get more support it will be because it is seen as relevant and helpful in specific critical problem areas; counseling is not seen as a tool to bring about improvement in school and community situations.[68] I would think of these comments as being supportive of the above concepts regarding counselor function. More than anyone else in the school, it is the counselor whose *professional responsibility* it is to be close and understanding and helpful with those individuals who may have stresses and problems because of their minority position or their general youthful alienation or their drug involvement. Any such young people in a school should know the counselor as a person; they should have warm feelings because of the understanding, the compassion, and the helpfulness of this person. It is to the shame of counselors and the counseling profession that, far too often, these young people have either never heard of the counselor, or if they have, they react with "Man, you must be crazy" when one asks them why they didn't go and see him.

f. If, for the moment, we accept the face-to-face involvement with individuals or small groups as the primary professional function of the counselor, there is still the more specific question of just what the purpose of this relationship might be. The basic difference here is whether we see the counselor as an academic and vocational adviser or teacher, or as a counselor in a psychological and therapeutic sense. A study by Ginzberg indicts counselors as having failed to have any impact,[69] but it is important to note that Ginzberg sees counselors as being responsible for vocational and academic guidance. Since counselors have been ineffective in this role, one might reason that the job should be given to those to whom it rightly belongs, namely, teachers and advisers. This lack of discrimination between counseling, on the one hand, and advising and teaching on the other, is evident in a paper by Meskill and Sheffield. These men, who happen to be a vice-president and a dean, discuss a new plan in

---

67. Eugene P. May, "Quantity or Quality in Dealing with Human Problems," *Personnel and Guidance Journal*, 49:376–382 (January, 1971).

68. Gary R. Walz, "Director's Print Out," *Capsule*, 4:18 (Winter, 1971).

69. Eli Ginzberg, *Career Guidance: Who Needs It, Who Provides It, Who Can Improve It* (New York: McGraw-Hill, 1971).

which they have a number of full-time "academic counselors," who deal with expressed problems as "I can never find my adviser" and "I was not aware that I was eligible for the pass/fail option" and "I did not know that I needed that course to graduate" and "When will Psychology 40 be offered again?"[70] Again, these people are individuals who function as advisers and teachers, and, indeed, much of what they do could be done away with by a modification of the system and/or the use of better technology. It is interesting to note that when Loughary suggest that counselors give up "the myth of face-to-face counseling," he is talking about counseling as perceived above, and he correctly suggests that it be replaced by a more effective computer-based system.[71]

Thus the evidence at least suggests that counselors as academic and vocational advisers have failed to have any positive effect, and that what they have done ineffectively can be done better by the use of computers. It would seem reasonable, then, that counselors accept as their professional responsibility the functions of the psychological counselor, who works primarily with individuals or small groups of individuals. His task is both therapeutic and preventive, helping individuals to attain a higher level of individual freedom and dignity and pride in self, and thus to become contributing rather than destroying members of the society of which they are a part.

THE ALIENATED COUNSELOR[72]

What the counselor does is obviously related to his perception of his culture as well as his perception of himself, and it would probably be fair to say that a significant number of school counselors, possibly the majority, have always been alienated from a significant part of the school population. Such counselors, and those counselor educators who feel the same way, see themselves as an arm of the school system and see little difference in their behavior from that of the teacher or administrator. They hold, fairly rigidly, to a middle-class value structure, not only for themselves but also for all the children in the school. Indeed, along with teachers and administrators, they

70. Victor P. Meskill and Wesley Sheffield, "A New Specialty: Full-Time Academic Counselors," *Personnel and Guidance Journal*, 49:55–58 (September, 1970).

71. John W. Loughary, "The Computer Is In," *Personnel and Guidance Journal*, 69:185–191 (November, 1970).

72. Dugald S. Arbuckle, "The Alienated Counselor," *Personnel and Guidance Journal*, 48:18–24 (September, 1969). Copyright 1969 by the American Personnel and Guidance Association.

see the inculcation of these values as the basic responsibility of the school. They tend to get along fairly well with children who are of the same pattern, children who do what they feel children should do, and children who represent what they feel children should represent.

They view with some hostility, suspicion—and, possibly, fear—those children who stand for something different. They *know* the correct moral attitudes, they *know* what is good and what is bad, they *know* a good American as compared with a not-so-good American. A teacher or counselor committee on problems of sex, drugs, and alcohol often sounds remarkably like a committee from the attorney general's office, or a committee of policemen. They do not sound like a committee of mental health personnel or therapists.

Individuals of this nature find it difficult, if not impossible, to relate effectively with a significant number of children. But it should be stressed that as far as the counseling relationship is concerned, the real alienation is that of the counselor from the client. The pattern of behavior of the alienated client should be not only clinically understandable but totally acceptable to any professional counselor worthy of the name. The apathetic, sullen, and hostile ghetto adolescent who faces the counselor makes no claim to professional understanding and skill and compassion, and his alienation and all that goes with it can be taken for granted. Too frequently, however, not only is his alienation matched by an equal alienation of the counselor from the client, but the counselor, in addition, wishes to impose his version of values on the client. Thus we find that a supposedly neurotic client may hate the counselor in a rather clean sense but does not wish to impose upon him, while the professional counselor abhors the client's way of life and in addition attempts to impose his particular version upon the client.

This alienation of the counselor and his value system from the client and his value system is sometimes subtle, and sometimes almost brutally clear. While the counselor may be honestly horrified at the thought of imposing his values upon the client, he nevertheless sees his goal as trying to help the client to learn the better way of life—the counselor's way of life.

Sometimes the imposition is only implied in statements which are coldly and clinically correct. Thompson, for example, describes the responsibilities of counselors, and then goes on to say, "Only then will much of our client's behavior become meaningful, and only then can we help develop a sound basis for giving him the necessary help."[73] But the implication is that it is meaningful to the counselor,

73. "Psychological Bases for Career Planning and Development," Albert S. Thompson in Charles G. Morehead and Frank G. Fuller (eds.), *Career Planning and Development* (Raleigh, N.C.: State Dept. of Public Instruction, 1966), p. 11.

and that the counselor is then able to help the client to become the sort of person the counselor thinks he should be. When, at a counselors' conference, Busfield stated, "We do have an acute need in Michigan in the area of health technology,"[74] he was clearly imply ing that counselors should "counsel" more students to become health technicians. At another workshop, where, presumably, counselors were learning to become more effective as counselors, DuVal left no doubt about his version of the counselors' role when he stated: "You as counselors, school counselors, can do a great deal in assisting the person to establish good work habits, such as being on time and doing the work assigned."[75] Gross comments on the tendency of counselors, including those who "understand," to try to get the client to give up his ethnic identity,[76] while in another paper Mealy and Perrone comment that once the client can become involved in self-disclosure there will be, among other things, "an incorporation of 'more acceptable' values—such as delaying gratification."[77] The client, in other words, takes on an aspect of the middle-class value system, and this is what makes him acceptable, even though this is not acceptable in his own milieu. This is a loss of ethnic identity—or is it? In a somewhat similar manner, Leacock indicates that one cannot expect to help a socially disadvantaged child to simply conform, but then she goes on to say, "The counselor must instead help him to learn that certain forms of rebellion are pointless and self-destructive, whereas other forms are meaningful."[78] But, again, this is meaningful to the counselor but not to the client. Most counselors would say that the burning of buildings in ghetto riots was pointless, but most of the young people who were involved in the burning of buildings did not feel that way. The majority of student activists on American campuses in the 1960's were among the most intelligent and creative of our students, and they did not feel that their sit-ins and demonstrations and violent behavior were pointless and senseless, although most college administrators may have felt this way. There is a communication gap, and the key and crucial role of the counselor is to somehow bridge that gap, so

74. Roger M. Busfield, "Counseling the Technically Oriented Student," *School Bulletin,* 44:33 (September, 1967).

75. Marshal DuVal, "Implications for School Counselors of the Manpower Development and Training Act," in Charles G. Morehead and Frank G. Fuller (eds.), *op. cit.,* p. 67.

76. Edward Gross, "Counseling Special Problems," *Employment Service Review,* 5:14–19 (January/February, 1968).

77. John J. Mealy and Philip A. Perrone, "A Case Approach in Madison," *Employment Service Review,* 5:11–13 (January/February, 1968).

78. Eleanor Leacock, "The Concept of Culture and Its Significance for School Counselors," *Personnel and Guidance Journal,* 46:844–851 (May, 1968).

that there can once again be meaningful communication between black and white, young and old, employee and employer, the "have-not" and the "have." And this can only be done by one who might be known as the "nonalienated counselor."

The nonalienated counselor must surely be one who is sharply aware that he has a unique professional function quite unlike that of most other humans, and in a school setting his responsibilities are quite unlike those of teachers and administrators. It is not a case of being better or worse, or more effective or less effective than other school personnel, but it is simply a matter of being different, and until the counselor accepts his unique and different function he is going to remain alienated from a significant proportion of the youthful population of the land, black and white. The position of the counselor must be nonauthoritarian, so that he cannot make decisions regarding punishments or rewards. There may be some point in trying to manipulate a teacher or a principal or a policeman or a judge or a boss, but there should obviously be no point in trying to manipulate a counselor, since he is not the one who "can do things for you."

Even more important, however, is the attitude of the counselor, and this is really the critical issue. Is it not possible for a human being, who also happens to be a counselor, to feel deeply that he need not impose his version of life and living on the other person in order to have that person become acceptable to him? Bingham is all too correct when he says, "Counselors are often uncomfortable with the notion of permitting unsophisticated people to make choices,"[79] but such a person, surely, simply should not be a counselor. This need not mean, of course, that the counselor necessarily likes what the client does, or that he would want to be like the client. An honest answer to the question "Well, would you like to live in the ghetto?" might be "Hell, no," but the counselor should be able to be equally honest when he answers the question "Do you think I should really make an effort to get out of the ghetto?" by feeling, if not saying, "Well, I don't know—that must depend on you." In this sense, I would agree with Vontress when he says, "Essentially, the problem is one of perception: how the counselor perceives the counselee and vice versa,"[80] although the perception of the counselor must be a deep and basic part of his being, and it must reflect a trust and a confidence in the ability of the other person to determine the direction of his life.

"Nondemanding" and "acceptance" and "love" are often con-

79. William C. Bingham, *Counseling Services for Unemployed Youth* (New York: New York University Center for the Study of Youth, (Summer, 1967). p. 32.
80. Clemment E. Vontress, "Counseling Negro Adolescents," *School Counselor,* 15:86–91 (November, 1967).

sidered to be meaningless clichés, and they probably are for many counselors. But the nonalienated counselor does not enter into a counseling session feeling that the client *must* come to open up and look at himself, that he *must* come to trust the counselor, that he *must* come to feel free to talk about his mistakes and problems and fears. This is to be determined by the client, not the counselor. Why should one try to impose on a client the behavior of getting to a job on time? Why not try to help the client to look at the relationship between not getting to the job on time and not having a job for very long? The choice is his, not the counselor's.

Regardless of the issue, major or minor, many young people, black and white, male and female, need desperately to talk and relate with someone who not only does not possess institutional authority, but also does not personally feel the need for authority and so can thus comfortably, at times, accept direction from others.

The world of work for the young, after all, is the school, and responsibility for what happens in their formal education can only come if they have an active involvement in their educational experience. The law may force the child to go to school, but the law does not force the school to impose an irrelevant education upon the child, and by the time an individual is at the post–high school level, every possible step should be taken to make him responsible for the direction of his education. The laws that govern the behavior of the student should be the same as the laws that apply to any other adult citizen, and the rewards and penalties that accrue as a result of responsible or irresponsible behavior should be the same for students as for any other individuals.

The counselor must also be involved in the development of a more meaningful and relevant curricular experience, since the irrelevance of much of what goes on in the classroom today shows a high level of irresponsibility on the part of the school. Much of what happens in the classrooms of high schools and colleges is medieval and anti-intellectual, to some degree in the matter of content, but even more in methodology and procedures and techniques. Basically, the youth of today are being taught in very much the same manner as they were a century or more ago. While it may be true that all of the past and the planned-for future cannot be tied in to the present, the educational job that is being done today could be vastly improved. A few years ago a number of us in a graduate seminar in counseling watched out of a seventeenth-story window as a disruption flared on the campus below us. Student and police heads were being bloodied, and eventually twenty-four screaming and shouting students were carted off to the police station. Many would say that one cannot be related to the other, but surely none of us can afford the luxury of

sitting and meditating in a classroom about theories of human behavior (or about chemistry or history or biology), ignoring totally the
fact that blood is flowing in the streets outside. Counselors and
schools must become cognizant of the society in which they live,
since their existence depends on this society, and they ignore it at
their own peril. An old accepted dictum in any psychology of learning class is that one starts where the learner is, and that one accepts
the concept of individual differences. If this is so, then both counselor and teacher must surely start with the intense "now" involvement of the young, and from there, possibly, see if the past makes
any sense, and if it is possible to prepare for an unknown future. For
the young the old adage that "eventually you will see the wisdom of
doing what you now think is nonsense" is no longer acceptable. The
student of today is increasingly resistant to the idea of putting up
with nonsense now for the hoped-for benefits of a doubtful future.
The counselor, whether working individually with clients, or as a
consultant with teachers, should have as his objective helping individuals to look at the reality of their selves and their society now, so
that they may become capable of rational consideration of a rational
future. And rational consideration is only possible when individual
members of a society become capable of accepting and understanding both their feeling and their intellect.

A basic therapeutic tenet of operation is the acceptance and
compassionate understanding, in a nonjudgmental sense, of the feelings of an individual. A primary function of the counselor would
appear to be to bring more of this therapeutic atmosphere into the
school so that the vast majority of the students will not have to
reflect either the passive hostility of the majority of the students or
the more overt acting-out hostility of a minority of students. The use
of force to prevent destruction is too frequently the natural response
of an unlistening adult population who were not sensitive to the feelings of frustration and rage and anger. Usually, by the time one gets
to the street, it is force against force, and each side becomes the
victim rather than the master of his passion, and all reason is lost.
When one has been personally involved in violence, on the campus
or on the street, the futility of it is all too obvious. For those individuals whose feelings ride roughshod over their intellect, the counselor
may provide an atmosphere in which they can come again to think
as well as feel. The counselor must exert himself so that the majority
of the young who are in educational institutions can be accepted as
individuals whose feelings do count, rather than being considered as
bloodless and faceless intellectual machines.

The counselor should be a model, but not so much a model to
be imitated as a model from whom one can learn to develop his own

self, since far too many people are but clay imitations of others. On the other hand, the counselor must clearly be one with whom the young person can feel there is at least some possibility of communication.

Very simply, then, the counselor in his counseling relationship must become involved rather than aloof, he must be aware and understanding and acceptant of the values of the youth culture, rather than trying to proselytize for an adult culture. He should be able to help the young to look at tomorrow by living with them in their today. He should be capable of accepting their feelings so that they may be helped to develop a type of living in which neither feeling nor intellect is repressed, but both are part of a high-living human being. As a consultant he must do all he can to see that these precepts also become part of the classroom atmosphere, so that we may actually come to have a society in which change comes as a natural outgrowth of love and living rather than as a product of hatred and violence.

Chapter 15

The Professional Education
of the Counselor

Reference has already been made to the involvement of professional organizations and the federal government in the field of counseling in the decade of the 1960's. Part of this involvement included attempts to describe an adequate program of counselor education and means by which such programs could be approved or certified.

THE PROFESSIONAL VERSION OF COUNSELOR EDUCATION

Historically, there was no such thing as a carefully planned program of counselor education prior to the 1960's, although a few institutions were involved in the education of counselors many years prior to that. It was the National Defense Education Act of 1958, which made available federal funds, that really spurred the development of counselor education programs. The implementation of Title VB of the National Defense Education Act soon made it painfully clear that very few institutions had actually developed effective programs for counselor education. The number of institutions applying for contracts to conduct guidance and counseling institutes dropped off drastically when the U.S. Office of Education instituted a policy of requesting each institution that applied for a contract to present also an "Inventory of Institutional Resources." A perusal of these inventories made it clear that there were surprisingly few institutions that had more than one full-time staff member totally employed in the

428

education of the school counselor. The answers to questionnaires sent out by the U.S. Office of Education indicate an interesting institutional interpretation of the request for courses offering "specific preparation for guidance and student personnel."[1] Some of the courses mentioned by various institutions were, for example, "Correctional Arithmetic," "Parent Counseling in Speech," "Research in Education," "Theories of Language," "Intercultural Relations," "Modern American Family," "Introduction to Social Work," "Labor Problems," "Contemporary Problems in Education," and so on. Practically every course that one could think of in the area of education, psychology, measurement, sociology, and social service work was mentioned, and almost as many from almost every other area that might come under the heading of social sciences. Thus, institutionally, there was little agreement as to just what constituted the education of the counselor, although it is probably true that those institutions which might be regarded as the best known in the preparation of counselors had some similarity of experiences for their students.

There is no doubt that the National Defense Education Act of 1958 and the Education Professions Development Act of 1968 had a major impact on the education of counselors. Earlier in the decade, as an increasing proportion of NDEA Title VB funds began to be diverted to academic-year institutes (later to be changed by the U.S. Office of Education despite professional recommendations to the contrary), it became obvious that there were very few institutions in the country that could offer even an effective one-year program at the master's level. There is no question that there are more and better programs of counselor education now than a decade ago because of federal involvement, but a vast amount of federal seed money was wasted in a futile attempt to build up inadequate programs. On the whole, the good programs became bigger and better, but the poor ones, after the federal money was removed, remained pretty much as they were.

Federal legislation also spurred the American Personnel and Guidance Association to greater action in providing some indication of just what did constitute an effective program of counselor education. With the U.S. Office of Education, and the American people, ready to provide tens of millions of dollars for the more effective education of school counselors, it was rather embarrassing to discover that the professional organizations representing counselors

---

1. *Preparation Programs and Course Offerings in School and College Personnel Work, 1959-60* (Washington, D.C.: U.S. Department of Health, Education and Welfare, Office of Education).

429

and counselor educators apparently did not know just what constituted an effective program of counselor education. Eventually, however, these organizations did press for action, and the acceptance of
various policy statements in 1964 and 1967 did represent a real
achievement. The three major organizations that were involved in
these policy statements were the American Personnel and Guidance
Association, the "parent" body, and two of its divisions, the American School Counselors Association and the Association for Counselor Education and Supervision.

In many ways, these policy statements are elaborations of the
seven basic recommendations regarding counselor education presented in the Wrenn report in 1962:

1. *That state certifying agencies for counselors and graduate
   faculties in counselor education specify that, in addition to
   essential professional courses and experiences, two other
   major cores be required in the counselor education curriculum; one major core is in the field of psychology, another in
   the social and other behavioral sciences, the two combined
   to represent a minimum of from one-third to one-half of the
   course work required for certification.*
2. *That the minimal two-year graduate program in counselor
   education include: (a) two major cores in psychology and
   the social sciences as described in Recommendation 1; (b)
   adequate orientation in educational philosophy and school
   curriculum patterns; (c) applied or professional courses as
   described in the text to the extent of not more than one-
   fourth of the total graduate programs; (d) supervised experience in both counseling and planned group leadership to the
   extent of not less than one-fourth of the total graduate programs; (e) an introduction to the understanding and utiliza-
   tion of changing research concepts; (f) an introduction to
   the problems of ethical relationships and legal responsibilities in counseling.*
3. *That the graduate courses in counselor education be taught
   by faculty qualified in the respective areas involved, i.e.,
   psychology courses by psychologists; counseling theory and
   technique courses by faculty who are both qualified in psychology and experienced in counseling; social science
   courses by social scientists; occupational information, psychological measurement, and research courses by qualified
   scholars in the areas involved.*
4. *That supervised counseling experience be required in every
   pattern of counselor certification; that certification be*

granted only upon the satisfactory completion of this experience and the recommendation of the graduate faculty involved.[2]

A decade later Wrenn stressed the sort of person who was to be admitted to the program as much as the program itself. He considered the ability to listen as being crucial, and doubted that this was something that could be taught to anyone. His suggested basic change in the curriculum was to provide students with early contact with people, so that student counselors would see clients from the first month on, and that ideas about people would be presented parallel with flesh-and-blood realities.[3]

This still, however, represents a rather traditional program of the so-called helping professions. There has been and there still is difficulty in distinguishing programs of education and training for school psychologists, school social workers, and school counselors. Thus we can hardly go into any school, pick out a counselor, a psychologist, a social worker and refer to the differences in the functions of the three professional groups on the basis of the differences in the education of these three individuals.

Let us assume, for the purpose of comparison, that each of the three is a graduate of a two-year program from an approved institution—one from a school of social work, one from a department of counselor education, and one from a department of psychology or a department of education. Would their professional education have been such as to definitely equip them for *different* professional tasks? Many, probably most, of the professional educators in each of the three areas would probably answer this question in the affirmative, but one may wonder.

Casework, for example, is usually considered to be the special something that the social worker has that nobody else possesses. And yet, what is this mysterious casework:

. . . when casework is employed to help the individual achieve better social functioning it becomes a form of psychosocial therapy. It relies mainly on rational procedures closely allied to psychoanalytic techniques, augmented by methods of direct influence when diagnosis indicates that these will be more effective. Focus is always upon the person-situation gestalt, which is

2. C. Gilbert Wrenn, *The Counselor in a Changing World* (Washington, D.C.: American Personnel and Guidance Association, 1962), p. 161. Copyright 1962 by the American Personnel and Guidance Association. Reprinted by permission.
3. C. Gilbert Wrenn, *The World of the Contemporary Counselor* (Boston: Houghton Mifflin, 1973), pp. 274–276.

431

seen as an interacting balance of forces between the needs of the person and the influence upon him of the environment.[4]

A psychologist (or a counselor) might take this to say that the social worker is really a psychologist (or counselor) who helps individuals or families by a therapeutic involvement with them, or by a modification of the outer environment, usually the home, if this is the major cause of the problem. On the other hand, the social worker might feel that the current movement in the education of both the psychologist and the counselor to increase their involvement in the total environment of the child, including the home, is trespassing on territory which she has considered as her own. Then too, we may note that the scope and standards of preparation in psychology for school counselors often read almost like the complete educational program at the doctoral level of one who might be called a school counseling psychologist.

Thus it would appear that the education and training of the psychologist, counselor, and social worker in the schools are not too far apart, and those graduates of at least minimal two-year programs in approved institutions function on the job in a somewhat similar manner. Their functions may differ but this is due less to the fact that they are a counselor or a social worker or a psychologist, than it is because they work with a different population, their own personal interests and motivations and personality patterns are different, and the clinical and practicum aspect of their professional education may have been in a different milieu with a different kind of population. Actually, even in a two-year program, and certainly in a doctoral program, while we could assume that there would be a particular base core of skill and knowledge, the population with whom the individual would work and the milieu in which he would work would be the major factors determining the possible differences in professional education, rather than the occupational title of the individual. One student might see his professional future in an occupation in which he would be working in a therapeutic relationship with developmental problems; another student might see himself working primarily in the area of clinical diagnosis and appraisal of atypical children; another might see himself as involved primarily with parents, and the milieu in which they live. Each one of these individuals could be called a psychologist, a counselor, or a social worker and still remain within the framework of function as recommended by his professional organization.

Traditionally, however, all three have minimized the humanness of both the counselor and the client. Skill and knowledge are

4. Florence Hollis, *Casework: A Psychosocial Therapy* (New York: Random House, 1964), pp. 29–30.

what characterize the counselor or therapist, and sickness and incapability are the measures of the client or patient! The real revolution in the helping professions is just beginning to stir, and it will stress the common core of humanness that binds all of us—including client and counselor.

WHO IS BEING EDUCATED FOR WHAT

One of the greatest misnomers that has ever been accepted by the American public is the term "mental health." The human condition described by this term is, and has been, well entrenched under the wing of medicine.[5] It is interesting to note, however, that medical men are becoming increasingly involved in nonmedical problems, away from the hospital, or they are converting part of the hospital into something that bears a great resemblance to a school. Medical control is as much as anything else an historical accident. We might wonder what would have happened if Freud had been a Ph.D. professor in a university, instead of a medical doctor working with a hospital. Freud made clear his feeling that the fact that he was a medical man had little to do with his involvement with the human psyche. Those who followed him accepted the medical man in a hospital concept when dealing with individuals whose difficulties were either primarily of the mind and the emotions or of the physical body.

While the ideas as to what should be done for the oft-quoted 19,000,000 Americans who suffer from poor mental health are changing rapidly, psychotherapy would still appear to be the major kingpin as far as treatment is concerned. A report of the Joint Commission on Mental Health makes it clear that psychotherapy is the realm of the medical doctor, although some room is left for the psychologist.[6] One might say that if you have "bad" mental health you go to a hospital, see a doctor, and "get" psychotherapy! What has happened, however, is that man, with certain kinds of human difficulties, has been asked to fit into an already established profession, medicine, and he has naturally been regarded as a fellow with a disease. Psychology, in trying to break into the circle, has imitated

5. See Dugald S. Arbuckle, "Psychology, Medicine and the Human Condition Known as Mental Health," *Community Mental Health Journal*, 2:129–134 (Summer, 1966). Parts of the following section in this chapter were first printed in that article.

6. Joint Commission on Mental Illness and Health, *Action for Mental Health* (New York: Basic Books, 1961).

medicine, the only difference being that it insists on viewing man as a set of behavioral problems rather than a disease. The words of Blanck would appear to be appropriate for the current situation:

Considered and objective study of the question should involve the complete resources of all of the relevant departments of a university, both in the social and physical sciences. The best thinking of educators might lead, not to a decision in favor of either contender, medicine or psychology, but to the creation of a new discipline with undergraduate and postgraduate curricula appropriate to its specific goals.[7]

Many voices, from medicine, from psychology, and from various other areas have been raised questioning the traditional "You have a disease and you must go to the hopsital for treatment" concept. The medical practitioners, however, while they overtly accept the need for change, are actually often recommending a slightly different concept of medical treatment for an ill patient, while the clinical psychologist too frequently tries to get more control for himself by doing pretty much what his medical colleague has suggested. Mainord, for example, states that "teaching the patient to believe that he is sick is to encourage him to become a passive recipient of whatever treatment the physician recommends," and he describes a different approach.[8] We might wonder, however, if a person is not sick, why he is in a "hospital" being "treated" by a "physician."

Eysenck has been probably the consistent gadfly in the side of both medical and psychological psychotherapists. He feels that what little movement and change may have resulted from various treatments, in and out of hospitals, has had a learning-theory basis, and has nothing to do with sickness.[9] Szasz is another who argues that those who are called mental patients are not sick in a medical sense, but they have learned a certain style of living, and it is this that must be changed if they are to change.[10]

The disquiet with the current situation is expressed in many ways. Adams, for example, speaks against the current confusing terminology when he says:

If behavior can be systematically described in behavioral terms, there is no need for the confusing non-psychological analogies

7. Gertrude Blanck, *Education for Psychotherapy* (New York: The Institute for Psychoanalytic Training, 1962).
8. W. A. Mainord, *A Therapy* (Ft. Steilacoom, Washington, D.C.: Mental Health Research Institute Bulletin, 1962), pp. 85–92.
9. H. Eysenck, *Behavior Therapy and the Neurosis* (New York: Pergamon Press, 1960).
10. T. S. Szasz, *The Myth of Mental Illness* (New York: Hoeber-Harper, 1961).

and metaphors which have long plagued the mental-health professions. It becomes unnecessary to borrow words from medicine, engineering, or electronics, to describe human relationships. This approach makes it possible to clarify fundamental principles which have long been concealed by inappropriate, misleading jargon.[11]

Albee comments somewhat along the same line when he says:

In many ways, too, clinical psychologists, like well-treated slaves in other empires, have unconsciously adopted the values, the language and the manners of their owners' masters. . . . The depth of brain washing to which the present generation of clinical psychologists has been exposed is evidenced by the degree to which our thinking accepts without resistance the medical model and the primacy of medicine's responsibility for the field of mental disorder.[12]

It may be, of course, that Adams voices the desire of the clinical psychologist to replace the disease orientation of medicine with the sets of behaviors orientation of clinical psychology. Bugental indicates an equal skepticism about the medical treatment concept when he says:

Certainly the point is that we cannot follow a pattern of esoterically diagnosing our patient's difficulties and writing prescriptions in Latin and an illegible scrawl, which the patient dutifully carries to the pharmacist for compounding and then takes with complete ignorance of the preparation or its intended effects. We are recognizing more and more that essential to the psychotherapeutic course is the patient's own responsible involvement in the change process.[13]

On the other hand, he shows a much greater understanding of the gestalt man, and even suggests the heresy that "psychology can turn again to its parents, the humanities and philosophy, and from these take new strength to meet the challenge of our day."

The medical man shares the quandary of the psychologist, and each, to some degree, is bound by his own professional shackles. Switzer, a psychiatrist, for example, refers to mental health as a public health problem, and stresses the thought that the best public health efforts are those that prevent illness. He refers to his own

11. H. B. Adams, "Mental Illness of Interpersonal Behavior," *American Psychologist*, 19:191–197 (March, 1964).
12. G. Albee, "A Declaration of Independence for Psychology," *Bulletin of Psychologists Interested in the Advancement of Psychotherapy* (November, 1964).
13. J. F. T. Bugental, "Humanistic Psychology: A New Breakthrough," *American Psychologist*, 18:563–567 (September, 1963).

position as being in a residential treatment center. Yet at the same time the "dream" program that he advocates shows no relationship whatsoever to illness or medicine or hospitals except for the last few words, which actually contradict the rest of his statement:

> It would be a program composed of three intimately related areas of function: home, classroom, school activities, and guidance and counseling, parents, teachers, guidance and counseling personnel—all in constant communication with each other, all devoted to ever increasing understanding of what is needed for promotion of psychological growth, all striving for considerate action, all keenly aware of their own role, all respectful of the contributions of the others, all dedicated to the individual child within the group, all committed to conscious, conscientious, and organized effort toward prevention of mental and emotional illness. [14]

Glasser is another medical psychotherapist who, while dissatisfied with current psychiatric practice, still at least appears to feel that the people with whom he works are patients in need of medical treatment. He says that "mental hygiene is stalled because our present psychiatric approach emphasizes mental illness rather than responsibility." But he apparently feels that the right approach is still "psychiatric." Again, he states, ". . . assuming . . . that the schools were willing to participate in a mental hygiene program, conventional psychiatric concepts would be totally inadequate for the job."[15] Yet, interestingly enough, when he talks about his program, it would seem that he is functionally casting aside not only conventional *psychiatric* approaches, but conventional *medical* and *psychological* approaches as well.

Even while medicine and psychology argue over who is most effective in the helping relationship, heartening (or disheartening) evidence continues to accumulate indicating that a high level of medical or psychological knowledge and skill may not be necessary in order to be helpful in providing the human relationship to allow those individuals who are hospitalized as mentally ill to show growth and improvement. A study by Carkhuff and Truax describing the effects of lay group counseling on 80 hospitalized patients, is typical. They state:

> The evidence points to uniformly significant improvement in the patients treated by lay group counseling when compared to control patients. The suggestion is that a specific but relatively

14. R. E. Switzer, Guidance and Counseling as a Force in the Prevention of Mental Illness," paper read at the convention of the Minnesota Counselors Association, Minneapolis, February, 1962.
15. W. Glasser, *Reality Therapy* (New York: Harper and Row, 1965), p. 155.

*brief training program, devoid of specific training in psychopa-
thology, personality dynamics, or psychotherapy theory, can
produce relatively effective lay mental health counselors.*[16]

The obvious implication here is that people count more than
their so-called training, and that more of the same kind of training
makes one worse rather than better. Braginsky and Braginsky note
the absolute failure of mental health professionals to see patients
and hospitals for what they are. They cannot see

*because between them and a clear view of the patients 'stands a
conceptual wall which consists of three dominant models—the
medical model, the behavioral model, the imprisonment model.*
*Thus the patient is viewed as the victim of disordered intra-
psychic processes, disordered learning circuits, or disordered
societies. He is an ineffectual, inept, impotent creature unable
to control his own life.*[17]

Thus, we are now in a situation where the new elite, the witch
doctors, the high priests, have convinced millions of people, who
might previously have been considered to have their ups and downs,
that they are ill and that they need to go to a hospital for medical
treatment, by medical doctors, so that their illness might be cured.
Their illness, usually referred to as the lack of mental health, might
thus be categorized as mental unhealthiness. It is generally considered to be basically the same as other diseases: measles, smallpox,
syphilis—and the treatment is basically the same. The criticism of
many psychologists is not so much aimed at the pattern of treatment
as it is at the fact that it is medical doctors rather than psychologists
who determine what should be done. In the meantime, a small fringe
group of heretics, both medical doctors and psychologists, as well as
representatives of other disciplines, feel that what must be done is
something quite different from the diesase or problem orientation of
either medical personnel or psychologists.

It would seem to me that a crucial factor is our basic view of
the human person. Most of us tend to view the human being in a
broad and definable way, and it is this perception that vitally affects
our relations with our fellow members of the human species.[18] The
composite human of Heidegger, Kierkegaard, Jaspers, De Chardin,

16. R. R. Carkhuff and C. B. Truax, "Lay Mental Health Counseling," *Journal of
     Consulting Psychology,* 29:426–431 (November, 1965).

17. Benjamin M. Braginsky and Dorothea D. Braginsky, "Stimulus Response: Mental
     Hospitals as Resorts," *Psychology Today,* 6:22–100 (March, 1973).

18. See Dugald S. Arbuckle, "Educating Who for What?" *Counselor Education and
     Supervision,* 11:41–49 (September, 1971).

May, Rogers, van Kaam, and Maslow is not quite the same fellow who is viewed by Pavlov, Watson, Tolman, Hull, and Skinner. The person who is described in an existential-humanistic, phenomenological manner is not the same as one described in psychoanalytic, rational or behavioristic terms. As we noted in chapter 4, a behavioristic model is described as follows by Hitt:

> *Man can be described meaningfully in terms of his behavior; he is predictable; he is an information transmitter; he lives in an objective world; he is rational; he has traits in common with other men; he may be described in absolute terms; his characteristics can be studied independently of one another; he is a reality; and he is knowable in scientific terms.*[19]

And he describes the phenomenological model in the following manner:

> *Man can be described meaningfully in terms of his consciousness; he is unpredictable; he is an information generator; he lives in a subjective world; he is irrational; he is unique alongside millions of other unique personalities; he can be described in relative terms; he must be studied in a holistic manner; he is a potentiality; and he is more than we can ever know about him.*[20]

It is unfortunate that some members of the helping professions are personally uncertain enough that they cannot live easily with uncertainty, and thus they make a dogma which *must* be adhered to out of either of the above models. The phenomenological dogmatist usually sees the behaviorist as a nonhuman scientist, callous and unconcerned about the welfare of man. The behavioristic dogmatist, on the other hand, views those in the phenomenological camp as unscholarly sentimentalists, totally out of touch with reality, rarely saying anything other than "uh-huh . . ." For those who are more open, however, the dilemma remains, and while they may not blindly walk one path, they will tend nonetheless to hold to one model rather than the other and thus see both the purpose and, to a lesser degree, the practice of counseling in a somewhat different light. Actually, in terms of practice, the behavioral counselor is eclectic, in that if he finds that one technique will not work, he will try another.[21] The phenomenological counselor might be equally

19. William D. Hitt, "Two Models of Man," *American Psychologist,* 24:651–658 (July, 1969).
20. *Ibid.*
21. John D. Krumboltz and Carl E. Thoresen, *Behavioral Counseling: Cases and Techniques* (New York: Holt, Rinehart and Winston, 1969), p. 3.

eclectic, but what he would do would differ in obvious and subtle ways *because he viewed man in a different light.*

Thoresen, who views himself as a behavioral counselor, states: "This advent of counseling as an applied behavioral science concerned with empirically established effectiveness and efficiency in all of its areas seems manifestly appropriate to the contemporary context of change."[22] He then goes on to describe as the appropriate approach the systems approach, which "Is designed to achieve explicitly stated performance objectives. The key concept here is that the goals are performance goals, objectives stated in terms of the desired behavior of the counselor candidate."[23]

But Shoben is not quite so certain, and he comments that

although there is great warrant for the faith, our attitude toward science is precisely that—a faith, a more or less uncritical acceptance of the belief that because doing what scientists do has solved so many problems, doing what they do in wider and wider arenas will solve still more, including those problems bound up with counseling. Like all faiths, this one may be a bit misplaced or overdone, a trifle anachronistic, or a little short of fully adequate.[24]

Rosner would see the computer of tomorrow taking over from the counselor of today:

In sum, the school-community information system would be the operational definition of accountability. As such the system would assist boards of education and school administrators with their planning, programming and budgeting decisions and would provide the means whereby such decisions are rendered intelligible to the community at large. The system would assist teachers and students in designing instructional strategies, in selecting curricular materials, and, more generally, in diagnosing and prescribing individualized instructional treatments.[25]

He goes on to describe the training of the necessary personnel by saying that they "will need to become thoroughly conversant with the capabilities of computers, highly knowledgeable about educational measurement, familiar with the problems and processes of

---

22. Carl E. Thoresen, "The Systems Approach and Counselor Education," *Counselor Education and Supervision,* 9:3–17 (Fall, 1969).

23. *Ibid.*

24. Edward J. Shoben, Jr., "Comment," *Personnel and Guidance Journal,* 48:198–200 (November, 1969).

25. Benjamin Rosner, "Comment," *Personnel and Guidance Journal,* 48:108–110 (October, 1969).

curriculum development, and sensitive to school-community relations."[26]

Maslow reflects the unease of many, when, in talking about the literature dealing with the future, he says:

A good 95% of it deals entirely with purely technological changes, leaving aside completely the question of good and bad, right and wrong. Sometimes the whole enterprise seems almost entirely amoral . . . it is itself a sign of blindness to the real problems that are involved, that practically all of the people who get involved in these conferences are non-personal scientists . . . the psychologists and sociologists who occasionally are chosen to speak on this problem are characteristically technologists, "experts" committed to a value free conception of science.[27]

Argyris makes a pertinent comment when he states: "Perhaps one reason that Maslow's humanistic psychology has not been so readily accepted is that it is based on a universe that is rarely available for empirical research. Also, humanistic psychology would alter the presently acceptable criteria for rigorous research."[28]

It would appear, then, to be more appropriate, and empirically effective, to react to man in a more gestalt and in a more humanistic fashion. Man is a total being, and while it is questionable enough to treat a physically ill person as primarily a damaged heart, rather than as a human being suffering from a damaged heart, it is surely even more questionable to react to a person who has an overabundance of fears, anxieties, loneliness, as a paranoid or a schizophrenic or a manic-depressive, or as one who lacks mental health. Basically, then, man is neither a disease nor a problem; he is a total person, and we should surely react to an anxious man as a man who suffers from anxiety, to a lonely woman as one who suffers from loneliness, not to conditions known as anxiety and loneliness.

The vast majority of the people who fall into the category of mental unhealthiness have nothing wrong with them mentally, nor are they unhealthy in a physiological sense. Nor is the answer to their human difficulty a cure in the sense that you are sick if you have measles, and you are not sick when you are cured of measles. In fact, without the human traits that make up the "mentally un-

26. *Ibid.*
27. A. H. Maslow, "Toward a Humanistic Biology," *American Psychologist,* 24:724–735 (August, 1969).
28. Chris Argyris, "The Incompleteness of Social-Psychological Theory: Examples from Small Group, Cognitive Consistency, and Attribution Research," *American Psychologist,* 24:893–908 (October, 1969).

healthy" person there would be no human person. One could not live without experiencing varying levels of fear and anxiety and loneliness and hostility. Man's human problem is not so much to cure a person of such feelings, but to help him to come to live so that they are parts of his living that tend to be more appropriate to his experiencing of the moment. One is hardly guilty of disproportionate feelings if he experiences fear when he feels he might die; his anxiety is hardly irrational if he is awaiting word as to whether or not he might get the job he has sought; a mother who has just lost her son would rather naturally be experiencing a feeling called grief.

Thus help is needed, but the help is not in the form of medicines or treatments, but rather help in learning to be someone who is not quite the same sort of person that he might be. The process one must go through is a process of learning, a process of learning to be one who can experience and live with and change one's feelings, rather than allowing himself to be mastered by one's feelings.

Currently, the center for the "treatment" of the mentally ill is a hospital, although the movement is to change the center of treatment from the hospital to a more community-centered mental health center. Unfortunately, however, the change may be more of location than of attitude, and illness and treatment and disease are still the terms that are used in the supposed new centers. Actually, of course, the logical institution to house what are currently called mental health services is a school rather than a hospital, since we are concerned with human behavior and learning rather than with diseases, human organs and medicines. It is interesting to note that in the current stress on mental health the school has been given only a cursory glance. There is a sort of "Oh yes, it might fit in here somewhere" attitude. Even those school personnel who are most closely concerned with the children who may have problems and difficulties and tensions, developmental and otherwise, the school counselors, the school psychologists, the remedial services personnel, the school social worker, the school nurse—these individuals too are treated as if they are generally quite incapable of working with and helping those individuals who suffer from "mental illness." What is needed, instead of a mental health unit which operates on the hospital philosophy of disease and sickness and medical treatment, is an expansion of the school, mostly in the way of an expansion of the current pupil personnel services, and a greater understanding among teachers of what is involved in the development of personal difficulties among children, and what they can do about it.

Actually, if school social workers, psychologists and counselors have the professional competence organizations describe them as possessing, and all are rapidly approaching this stage, they are able to work quite effectively in a preventive and a helping manner with the vast majority of the children who will eventually make up the population described currently as being mentally ill. Even the current population of the mentally ill are more in need of reeducation than they are in need of medical treatment, and the center which houses services for them should also be a school, but one which would be geared to an adult population whose learning is centered in doing something about their own behavior and attitudes and feelings. It would, in a sense, be a self-actualization center, and one of its units might well be a hospital to which those individuals who were medically sick would be sent for the appropriate medical treatment.

One of the reasons for the lack of capacity of many adults who are currently hospitalized as mentally ill is not what they had when they came in, but what they have experienced, and thus learned, since they have been in the institution. Many state institutions, even today, are fearfully depressing places, peopled by depressed individuals, both staff and patients. It is easy to see how one could become sick after living for a while in such an environment. Glasser is talking about the reversing of this sort of thing when he says, *"It is the whole ward attitude, where everyone is involved, but where mental illness is not accepted, that brings the understanding home to them."*[29] Glasser, in effect, is talking about making at least a part of the hospital a learning center, staffed with concerned, compassionate and competent professional workers, who are there to help individuals who are not sick to learn how to become more effective and more responsible members of a community. But he still refers to doctors and patients and hospitals and medicine. Why not go the whole way? Why wait until people become classified as mentally ill and are sent to a hospital for treatment, even if the treatment is that described by Glasser? Why not start where we should start, with an institution known as a school, albeit an expanded one, housing learning and growth services rather than mental health services, since they are for people who are well rather than sick. There would be available, in the pupil personnel services department of the school, the services of a variety of specialists, and the entire school program would be geared to the prevention of excessive personal difficulties rather than to the development of them. This would obviously mean the involvement of all school personnel, including teachers and administrators. Attached to the school would be an adult unit, which would gradually decrease in size as the number of adults coming into it would decrease because of the earlier attention they had re-

29. W. Glasser, *op. cit.,* p. 113.

ceived. A third unit in the complex would be a hospital, which would correctly be for those individuals for whom there was at least some question as to the likelihood of their suffering from a disease, although even here, of course, these individuals would be treated as *humans* suffering from a disease. Switzer talks along the same line when he says:

> *The model would be an enlightened, considerate, action-oriented program of prevention, of joint and positive impingement on the child by parent, classroom teacher, guidance and counseling personnel, and school administrator, within a group-oriented, broad program that would keep a school building buzzing until long after dark.*[30]

More specifically, in the field of counselor education, there continue to be several areas of difference:

1. Although differences continue among counselor educators, as well as between counselor educators and school administrators, the model of man to which one adheres *need not* be a cause of conflict. Woody, who feels that the best approach is the integrative use of conditioning-based behavior modification procedures and insight-oriented procedures, states that "there seems virtually no reason to question whether the provision of mental health services is appropriate for schools; the schools should provide the full range of mental health services, from preventive to therapeutic to follow-up."[31] On the other hand, Aubrey suggests that counselor educators "would be well advised to examine the sociological structure of the school before suggesting counseling frameworks directly antithetical to institutional norms and expectations. The school is simply not a guidance clinic or a mental health center."[32] And Dey comments that the school "usually reflects to its members and consumers certain concepts, values, and attitudes which reflect the currently held values of dominant powers on the local or national level" and that "rarely does the school provide a condition where adequately functioning individuals are allowed to explore the behavioral forms which are manifestations of . . . rules for eligibility for membership in the human family."[33] As has been stated, these differences need not reflect

---

30. Switzer, *op. cit.*
31. Robert H. Woody, "Psychobehavioral Therapy in the School: Implications for Counselor Educators," *Counselor Education and Supervision,* 8:258–269 (Summer, 1969).
32. Roger R. Aubrey, "Misapplications of Therapy Models to School Counseling" *Personnel and Guidance Journal,* 48:273–278 (December, 1969).
33. Glen R. Dey, "Philosophers, Counselor Educators, and Relevant Questions," *Counselor Education and Supervision,* 8:135–142 (Winter, 1969).

a difference in one's model of man, but it would appear that the behavioral picture of man does appeal to those who need more structure, those who yearn for certainty, those who want to know, and those who see reality as here and now. This may be part of the current appeal of behavioral counseling, but be this as it may, this is one area where counselor educators, regardless of their model of man, should be able to communicate with each other. The basic question here is whether the counselor is to be viewed as the discrete heretic who works for the individual, thus helping to change the milieu surrounding him, or whether he is the arm of the milieu assisting in the conditioning of the individual to reality as it exists. In both cases, of course, an understanding of the milieu and an ability to work with the people in it are essential.

2. There would appear to be increasing agreement among counselors and counselor educators that the functions of counselors can no longer be limited, as recommended by various committees of APGA, ASCA and ACES in the past decade, to individual and small group counseling. Indeed, if one is to stress the preventive as well as—and, hopefully, ultimately instead of—the remedial, one must get to the cause of the problems and difficulties of the young—the world of the school and the home and the community. The difference comes in the extent to which the counselor retains his identity as one who is concerned with the welfare of the individual and works with others because the welfare of the client necessitates such involvement. The counselor who holds to a phenomenological view of man would be more likely to work with the client to attempt to change some of the school or home or community experiences that impinge upon him, since he would put his individual client first, whereas the counselor holding to a behaviorist point of view would be more likely to try to help the client to adjust to the reality of society as it exists. An example might be seen in the drug scene in high schools. One counselor, working with students, might place major stress on trying to communicate to teachers and parents and the community the feeling of many students about *their* reality in terms of the seriousness of the use of marijuana and the laws about it. Another counselor might see his function as trying to communicate to students the reality of the community in terms of their views about the use of marijuana, and the penalties that might accrue from its use. One counselor too, would likely see his involvement with students and with others in a much more personal sense, whereas another counselor would function as the adult consultant or teacher. One would likely stress the "How do you feel—how do you think—what can you maybe do," while the other would stress the reality of what is.

Boy and Pine argue for a new position, that of a school sociologist, to perform the newer functions described above.[34] I would question this, since this would make it even more likely that the young person would be abandoned for the welfare of the organization. The child, the adolescent, the young adult, has been conditioned and prodded and pushed to do what is best for the establishment for his entire life, and he needs the help of someone to achieve responsibility for his own actions, and to get the establishment to at least recognize *his* reality, and even, possibly, to adjust and modify and change itself to fit his reality. Such a person would be more likely to be a counselor holding to a phenomenological point of view than to the behavioristic model of man.

3. Another area of difference between counselor educators concerns their perception of counselor function, and this, in turn is directly related to the model of man to which they hold. On the one hand, some counselor educators prefer a psycho-medical model of education, a sort of a case-study approach, in which diagnosis and prognosis are stressed. The counselor appears as a consultant, a manipulator, a behavioral engineer who has minimal *personal* involvement with those with whom he works. Self-understanding of the counselor by the counselor is of little importance, but the cognitive knowledge and skills of the counselor are considered to be crucial. The counselor is considered to be an expert in behavior modification, and he will utilize any means to bring about the desired change in behavior. To some degree, the counselor would represent the authority of the institution, and he would likely be viewed by others as a part of the system. All of this obviously fits the behavioristic model of man.

On the other hand, there are those counselor educators who would see the primary purpose of counselor education as helping the student counselor to become more of a human, to achieve a higher level of individual freedom, of self-actualization. Such are Kell and Mueller, who say that "we think of good training as being the sort which leads counselors to be most human."[35] These counselor educators are skeptical of the psycho-medical model, feeling that it might be adequate when dealing with things and diseases and problems, but not very pertinent for the gestalt human being. They would see the counselor as being very personally involved with all those with whom he would work, and thus a self-understanding of the

34. Angelo V. Boy and Gerald J. Pine, "A Sociological View of the Counselor's Role: A Dilemma and a Solution," *Personnel and Guidance Journal*, 47:736–740 (April, 1969).

35. Bill L. Kell and William J. Mueller, *Impact and Change: A Study of Counseling Relationships* (New York: Appleton-Century-Crofts, 1966), p. 65.

counselor by the counselor would be a crucial aspect of counselor education. Counseling would be viewed as an intimate human involvement of two individuals rather than a somewhat aloof, doctor-patient, consultant-like relationship. Change in behavior would be seen as a likely goal, but the counselor would not *know,* for the client, what the direction of that change should be. His only power would be in himself as a person, and he would carry no institutional authority on his shoulders. Such a person would fit the phenomenological model of man.

These two views need not, of course, be polarized to become a sort of either-or kind of situation, but it is likely that if a hundred counselor educators were chosen at random, one would find a significant number close to the behavioristic model, while another group would be close to the existential-humanistic model. Whether these two groups could ever agree on a desired program of counselor education is a most important question.

4. While there is general acceptance of the idea that change in behavior and the results of that change are a more valid measure of the effectiveness of counseling than change in feelings, the behaviorist camp is probably more enthusiastic about this than are the humanists. The issue, really, is the question of a value judgment. Take, for example, the young man who has been caught smoking marijuana and given a suspended sentence, sees the counselor for a number of sessions, and then indicates he feels much better about himself and what he is going to do. The boy feels good because he is now quite certain that he has found a way to smoke with minimal chance of ever being picked up by the police. Or the girl, a straight-A student throughout high school, accepted by six top universities, who has been seeing a counselor because of her feelings of stress and disillusionment with education generally. After a number of sessions, she feels relaxed and happy. She has decided that she will be a waitress at a ski resort, and maybe a ski instructor during the winter. She is not concerned about whether she ever goes to college. Or the high school boy, a straight-A student, participant in many activities, known to all the students and teachers, who has been seeing the counselor because of his tension and anxiety. He becomes more relaxed, feels much better, and appears to be a much happier person, pleased with himself. His next quarterly grades drop to B's and C's, and he has withdrawn from most of his activities. Teachers and parents are worried. Are these examples of successful or unsuccessful counseling?

The behavioral counselor, feeling more certain about *knowing* and *reality,* would likely feel fairly sure about correct behavior for

446

the client, because he would know more about the situation than the client. Schell and Daubner use different terms, but they describe this situation when they say:

> The realist counselor should help his client perceive his prob- lem situation as it "really" is and as it appears to others. The phenomenalist counselor cannot do this; instead, he can only try to enter the client's subjectivity and to help him deepen and enrich his unique perception of the problem situation.[36]

The confidence in the "I know what is reality for the other person" approach is expressed by Styles:

> When I see an emotional reaction that seems overly strong, I do not seek a description of the feelings, but instead a description of the facts. I then try to line up the facts and ask the counselee for his judgment on them. This is frequently tangential to his emotional reaction and gets us on the safer ground of using reason rather than feelings in dealing, for instance, with a per- sonality clash. I have noticed, however, that the duller the stu- dent mentally, the more persistent he is in clinging to his emo- tional hangup.[37]

Another interesting and quite different view on this issue is expressed by Deese:

> Behavior as the goal in the study of thought is wrong, and the characteristic emphasis of the psychological laboratory on the measurable response and the controlling independent variable is responsible for the sterility of the study of thought.[38]

Thus the model that one holds of man becomes a factor in this difference in a point of view. While any professional counselor would surely accept man as a creature of mind and emotion, the behavioral counselor, like the physical scientist, tends to be more certain about knowledge and facts and reality. The counselors hold- ing to a more phenomenological view of man are not so certain about their ability, or their right, to determine, to diagnose, and to prescribe regarding the desired behavior of others.

36. Edith Schell and Edward Daubner, "Epistemology and School Counseling," *Per- sonnel and Guidance Journal,* 47:506–513 (February, 1969).

37. F. R. Styles, "Guidance Counseling from the Right," *Personnel and Guidance Journal,* 48:349–354 (January, 1970).

38. James Deese, "Behavior and Fact," *American Psychologist,* 24:515–522 (May, 1969).

THE GROWTH OF THE COUNSELOR[39]

In most occupations the "growth" of the worker refers, reasonably enough, to his improvement in his occupational skills and capacities. If a surgeon goes through a "growth experience" it likely means that he can perform better operations, a farmer who has "grown" will probably produce better crops, a horserace bookie provides better and more accurate odds as a result of his "growth," and a postman may "grow" in that he devises some more effective way to deliver mail. So, one might say, it is obvious that the growth of a counselor or therapist is related to his improvement as a therapist—the only catch being that it is rather difficult to come to any general conclusion as to who a therapist is and what he does. Each therapist, once he gathers the necessary degrees, diplomas, and certificates, becomes a law unto himself, and usually he is the one who determines who he is, what he is supposed to do, and what would be acceptable as evidence of his professional growth. Self-evaluation is of course, the mark of any truly professional worker, but the therapist who believes that he, and only he, can measure his own effectiveness is surely playing with the lives of clients and patients.

A significant body of research raises at least serious doubts as to the very existence of "psychotherapy" as a discrete and definable professional discipline, as contrasted with the obvious existence of "therapists" who have gone through the necessary training, education, indoctrination, suppression of the spirit, flattening of the soul, or whatever it might be, in order to achieve the mark which says, "You are now a so-and-so." Probably the majority of psychiatrists still see themselves as basically Freudian-oriented and operate on the apparent assumption that the rather select few individuals with whom Freud worked long ago were no different from the current population. Those who do not, find that their greatest struggle comes in extricating themselves from what they learned they were supposed to be and supposed to do. One author even suggests that psychiatrists never really recover from their own analysis—as one inner-city youth told me, "Man, those guys are really screwed up."

Then, too, the success of lay therapists sometimes becomes acutely embarrassing. The programs that train (an all-too-correct term) therapists, of either the medical or psychological model, become more selective, using invalid criteria of selection, and more rigid, and thus tend to perpetuate what is rather than acting vigorously to change what is. The evidence at least suggests that if you

39. Dugald S. Arbuckle, "Growth for What?" *Voices*, 5:52–57 (Fall-Winter, 1969). Reprinted from VOICES: the Art and Science of Psychotherapy. Journal of the American Academy of Psychotherapists.

are a certain kind of person, you need very little in the way of professional training to become effective as a therapist, but at the same time we pile on more of the same and pay little attention to the *kind of people* we select as the future chosen few. An oddity of the whole business is that a therapist would appear to be a rather conservative person who finds it difficult to change his own behavior, but spends his working day encouraging other people to change *their* behavior!

Some psychiatrists are trying to break away from their medical mold and think in terms of well individuals rather than sick patients, learning and developmental difficulties rather than diseases and injuries, self-actualization centers rather than hospitals, growth rather than treatment. At the same time, however, most psychologically oriented therapists try as much as possible to be like their medical counterparts. They ape as much as possible the medical jargon which some psychiatrists are trying to discard, and they even try to look like them. The much-revered title "Dr." is probably more important to the ego of the psychological therapists than it is to the ego of the medical therapists. It might be interesting to check at a psychological or psychiatric convention and find out who reacts with the most hostility to being addressed as "Mr."—the M.D.'s or the Ph.D.'s!

It is difficult to speak for anyone other than oneself when one asks the question: What do I see as the basic quandaries and questions in looking at this question of therapist growth? This is my answer for me:

1. Growth is movement and change, and the growth of the therapist, since he is a human and he works with other humans, is directly related to his perception and his view of man. What is the therapist trying to do with man, or for man, or to man? A devoutly dogmatic religious therapist who viewed this life as a rather brief preparation for the one that lies on the other side, would probably consider growth in a different manner than would a humanist therapist who, not knowing about life on the other side, would likely feel that growth must be measured in terms of the life that we currently experience. A deterministically oriented therapist might view growth in terms of the development of better and more effective skills of manipulation and conditioning, whereas an existentialist therapist would likely think in terms of enlarging the area of individual human freedom so that one can be as one is, not as one should be.

Some therapists appear to view humans as being primarily diseased organs, others see them as complex sets of problems and disjointed behaviors. Their perception of therapist growth would be

449

quite different from those therapists who view man as a complex gestalt human being, whose parts cannot be separated and isolated from one another. The former would think in terms of treatment of parts (as in the medical model), the latter in terms of the development of the whole being (as in the development and learning model). The same difference would appear in those who separate sharply, and tend to see man predominantly as a cognitive, rational thinking creature, or an emotive and feeling creature. The former usually see growth in terms of greater knowledge, and such therapists tend to be predominantly teachers. Their growth is measured in terms of knowing more about themselves and their clients. Content is their holy grail. The process or affective therapists, on the other hand, tend to consider feeling to be of more importance than knowing. There are others, of course, who think and feel that one should certainly *know* why he feels as he does, and that one should *feel* about what he knows, but the two must go together so that there is some hope that one's knowledge might develop into wisdom.

2. Therapist growth is also reflected in one's ability to divorce oneself from a method or technique so that one has to accept personal responsibility for one's behavior. It is surely ridiculous to seek refuge from the question "Why do you do that?" by saying, "Because I am a Freudian" (or Rogerian, or Adlerian or Ellisian or Whitakerian), but there are therapists who seem to use this as the sole rationale for their behavior. On the other hand, this does not mean that one should be seduced by the siren song of eclecticism, which generally tends to communicate that the therapist, particularly when in difficulty, should do what comes easiest and is the most comfortable for the therapist.

3. Therapist growth too, means that the therapist must be as sensitive to his own behavior as he is to that of the client. In fact, growth of the therapist might be better measured by the degree to which the therapist is aware of what the client is doing to him, rather than his awareness of what he is doing to the client. It is fairly clear, of course, that if the therapist accepts the doctor or teacher role he is going to have little concern with the effect of the client on him, since he would most likely see counseling and psychotherapy as a one-way street in which the therapist (who has) gives and tells to the client (who does not have). If the relationship between the two humans, however, is considered to be the crucial factor of psychotherapy, then "What is he doing to me? must be related to "What am I doing to him?"

4. The therapist who is open to growth is one who recognizes the differences in people and times and places. It is unfortunate that the typical patient or client is still as atypical of the population at

large as he was in the days of Freud, or possibly even more so. The inadequacy of therapy and therapists with a significant proportion of the population is painfully obvious, and it is essential that therapists take for granted the need to devise new ways and new means and new approaches for a group of people to whom the standard concepts of psychotherapy are quite foreign. The young black men and women of the inner city represent one large group of Americans who have been helped very little, and who can be helped very little, by what might be called the standard procedures of psychotherapy. Psychotherapy should not be the preserve of the white upper-middle-class society.

5. Finally, in the long run, it would seem that growth must be directly related to the development of a higher level of individual freedom in the therapist. The therapist who has not experienced individual freedom must surely have difficulty in helping others to grow and to develop and to expand so that they can deeply feel, "I can never be caught—I can never be chained—I am the determiner, possibly not of all *aspects* of my existence, but totally of the *meaning* of my existence." The ability to live deeply and positively, day by day—this is the direction of growth for the counselor.

SUPERVISION OF THE STUDENT COUNSELOR

The counselor possibly does well, in a "learning" sense, when he is involved in a therapeutic relationship with a client, but what happens when the counselor becomes a "teacher" of student counselors? The major difficulty arises, I think, because some counselor educators have a problem in distinguishing between a client and a student, and they have difficulty in perceiving their function as a teacher as different from their function as a counselor. They may have the same broad general objectives in terms of the development of the human individual, but the student-teacher relationship is quite different from the client-counselor relationship.

I have been greatly impressed over the years by the extreme reluctance—almost inability—of graduate students to overcome years of disciplining in the matter of satisfying the instructor, and to arrive at a point where there is a high level of honesty in their expressions both about the instructor and his ideas and about themselves and their ideas. Even when formal evaluation is removed from a course, and the students know that their grades depend solely on what they want to give themselves, they find it difficult to believe that they are working to satisfy only themselves, not the instructor. The extent to which this is so varies greatly with different student counselors, of course, and Kemp describes the situation well when he says:

> *The more closed-minded, the greater the possibility that the counselor-in-training will stimulate change in accordance with the expectancies of the situation. This change is likely to be phenotypical, "party-line" change rather than integrated concepts and new directions for action.*[40]

As I try to identify some of the thoughts and feelings about the problems of the counselor as an "instructor," three points seem to stand out:[41]

Even a modestly insightful counselor must surely very soon come to question the apparent contradictions between his behavior toward that fellow human being known as a client and his behavior toward the other person known as a student counselor. Research would tend to indicate, and most counselors, overtly at least, would appear to agree, that client growth and movement is facilitated when the counselor indicates self-congruence, genuineness and honesty; when he feels an unconditional positive regard toward the client; when he is capable of establishing a high level of empathic understanding. Here, it would seem, the counselor as a supervisor finds his first quandary. Can he function as a counselor when he is a supervisor? Is he the same person when he is either a counselor or a supervisor? Must he, basically, being the same human being, be the same person, or can he be the same person but function in a different way because of the different function and responsibility he may have?

The problem of self-congruence, honesty and genuineness should not prove to be too much of a problem, since this is something that is an entirely personal business, within the control of the counselor or supervisor, although the extent to which his idea of genuineness and honesty will be viewed as genuineness and honesty by another will, of course, vary. Nevertheless, I would think of this as a personal problem; this is my struggle, and the basic question is the degree to which I am honest with *me*. Whether others view honesty as I do is, on this particular issue, of secondary importance. Empathic understanding, however, is something else again, and the door that must be opened *is* opened by both student counselor and

40. C. G. Kemp, "Influence of Dogmatism on the Training of Counselors," *Journal of Counseling Psychology,* 9:155–157 (Summer, 1962).

41. *See* Dugald S. Arbuckle, "Supervision: Learning, Not Counseling," *Journal of Counseling Psychology,* 12:90–94 (Spring, 1965). Copyright 1965 by the American Psychological Association. Reprinted by permission.

supervisor, not just by one of them. This, in turn, is obviously related to the extent to which the supervisor feels toward the student counselor a high level of positive regard, and, even more important, the extent to which the student feels that this is the way the supervisor feels toward him. It is at this point, I would think, that the supervisor begins to be somewhat entrapped in the world of illusion; it is real to him, but illusion to the other people.

The counselor can, with self-congruence, with honesty, and with genuineness, say to the client, "The extent to which I am a threat to you can be determined by you, because in no overt, action-taking manner do I see me posing a threat to you. I will not do anything to you that may be hurtful or damaging." Can any supervisor, with honesty, say the same to the student counselor?

Peters and Hansen comment: "The practicum provides learning situations which can facilitate the optimal growth of the person by freeing his potentialities to be himself."[42] Indeed it does, but unlike a counseling relationship, it has limitations, and these limitations sometimes do not appear to be recognized by some supervisors.

Patterson would appear to be somewhat contradictory when he says, "Supervision, like counseling, must provide a non-threatening, accepting and understanding atmosphere," and then, on the same page, comments, "The supervisor does evaluate, must evaluate, and should evaluate."[43] In attempting to combine these two impossibles, the supervisor may become even more enmeshed in his illusion.

Some counselors feel that another aspect of the relationship which tends to reduce the evaluative element, and therefore the threat, is when the supervisor's reaction is an honest expression of a personal feeling rather than a judgment. In commenting on an article, for example, Rogers says:

> It is stated that the supervisor has said, in effect, "You are defensive as indicated by the use of your words," To me a more accurate summary of the supervisor's expression is, "My feeling about this is that you are using words to cover up, to hide behind." This may seem like a small difference, but the difference between a judgment *rendered by a person in authority*, and a personal feeling *which is contributed to the interaction*

42. Herman J. Peters and James C. Hansen, "Counseling Practicum: Bases for Supervision," *Counselor Education and Supervision*, 11:82–85 (Winter, 1963).
43. C. H. Patterson, "Supervising Students in the Counseling Practicum," *Journal of Counseling Psychology*, 11:47–53 (Spring, 1964).

as a part of the existing personal reality is, I believe, very great indeed.[44]

I would hope, with Rogers, that the level of self-actualization of all supervisors would be such that their expressions generally would be those of personal feelings, rather than pontifical judgments. The determination of the judgmental level of a statement, however, is often determined more by the degree of self-actualization of the recipient of the statement than by the one who makes the statement. The white racist may say contemptuously, to a black man, "You are nothing but a dirty nigger." One black man may cringe at this "judgment"; another may react with violence and hatred; another may smile with sympathy and wonder how he might help this unfortunate, ignorant, and fearful white man. If I am in the position of authority, namely, if I am the supervisor, my expression of personal feeling with regard to a certain action of the student counselor is viewed, to a greater or lesser degree, as a "judgment." The self-actualization of the student counselor has reached a high level if he can, in effect, expose himslf, with risk, without being threatened. This would mean that he would no longer view "risk" as something external, which he could not control, but rather as something internal, which he could control. The risk, of course, might come from either the supervisor or his fellows in the practicum. Many student counselors view their peers as a greater threat than the supervisor. Indeed, if I am to be honest, is not my expression of feeling, to all extents and purposes, a judgment? Later on, a director of guidance may ask for my opinion regarding the effectiveness of a counselor I have had in a practicum, who is now applying for a job. If I reflect this personal feeling in some way in a statement about the student counselor, then surely I am being judgmental. The extent to which a statement is threatening is probably less dependent on how it is put than it is on the relationship of the one who utters the statement to the other person, and the way in which the other person views the statement. I may say to a driver, "It is my feeling that you were going too fast." Exactly the same statement may be made by a traffic officer, but surely the statement will be regarded in a vastly different manner. The supervisor *is* a supervisor, and as such he carries the weight and the responsibility of judgment and evaluation on his shoulders. I have heard supervisors discussing the effectiveness of student counselors who, in turn, appear to believe that their counseling practicum is an unconditional positive acceptance, no-risk sort of human relationship. Is a supervisor being self-congruent

44. Carl R. Rogers, "Comment," *Journal of Counseling Psychology,* 2:195 (Fall, 1955).

when he develops in students the feeling of absolute freedom without risk, and later helps to determine the sorts of position that they will obtain by his statements about their counseling effectiveness, or lack of it?

There is another aspect of this problem of self-congruence and genuineness, which appears when a supervisor feels that a student counselor is ineffective in many ways, and will discuss this ineffectiveness with others, sometimes to the point of being involved in the removal of a student from a program, and yet, in the name of "unconditional positive regard," will never reveal his feelings to the student counselor himself. Is one being congruent if he *feels*, "Gosh, I get the feeling that you were scared stiff of the client when he made that statement," and he *says*, "It is your feeling that you were warm and comfortable with the client," because this is what the student counselor has verbalized to the supervisor. Is, possibly, the need to be loved so strong with some supervisors that they cannot risk loss of approbation and acceptance by the student counselor by expressing their negative feelings about his behavior? Or would some say that the supervisor, who is also a counselor, should never have any negative feelings toward anyone?

Probably no one would take issue with Anderson and Bown when they say that "maximum therapeutic growth occurs within the context of free communication," but when they say that as the second stage of their supervision "the supervisors *evaluate the recording* in terms of the facilitating or inhibiting factors in the communication,"[45] they are referring to an inhibiting, but a very real, factor as far as the communicative ability and the growth of the student counselor is concerned. Supervisory comments are regarded as evaluative because the person who is making them is, sooner or later, very likely going to be involved in an evaluation of the student counselor. If one can be totally honest and say, as he can as a counselor, "I cannot see myself ever involved in a judgmental role regarding this other person," then, of couse, we have a different story. Are there any supervisors who can say this about student counselors in a counseling practicum, and at the same time be consistent with their concept of their responsibility as supervisors?

A somewhat different method of reducing the evaluative function of the supervisor is reported by Truax, Carkhuff, and Douds. They describe how the evaluation of the trainee's behavior would be based upon "research measuring scales which have proven adequately reliable and valid rather than upon the supervisor's subjec-

45. Robert A. Anderson and Oliver H. Brown, "Tape Recordings and Counselor-Trainee Understandings," *Journal of Counseling Psychology*, 2:189–194 (Fall, 1955).

tive reaction." They then go on to say that this "would also tend to remove that barrier to the communication between trainee and supervisor by removing the supervisor from the realm of evaluation."[46] Here, instead of giving their personal feelings about the effectiveness of the student counselor (what does one do, by the way, with these feelings?), they present more objective evidence. But even if it is some instrument that, in effect, says to the student counselor that he is not indicating much ability in providing a warm and acceptant environment for the client, can the supervisor really remove himself from this evaluation? The student counselor would likely wonder, with some justification, if the supervisor agreed with the picture as presented by the evaluation scale. No matter what scales are used, the supervisor, in his human relationship with the student counselor, has an evaluative role. The stress should be on helping the student counselor to learn to be able to live, and to be honest, and to be free, in a human relationship that is therapeutic, but in which there is also an element of risk. The supervisor may be compassionate, and warm, and understanding, but openness and honesty with him *is* more risky. Self-congruence on the part of the supervisor surely demands that he not deliberately lull the student counselor into a comfortable, but false, sense of security.

When we think of the relationship between the counselor and the client, as compared with that between the teacher and the student, in the first case the verb that applies is "counseling," while in the latter case it is "teaching." The more important verb in both relationships, however, is learning, and learning occurs best in a therapeutic milieu that is acceptant and nonthreatening. The supervisor, however, like the teacher, has an assessment responsibility, and this tends to lessen the security and increase the potential threat in the relationship, so that the "other person" is seen possibly more like the student than the client. The supervisory relationship should be as nonthreatening as possible, but some student counselors may need to experience the less threatening counseling relationship so that they will be able to be genuine, and grow, in the more threatening supervisory relationship.

Actually, the feeling of the threat in evaluation may reflect the uneasiness of the supervisor rather than the student counselor. The results of a study by Kinney on the effects of grading on the supervisory relationship showed no significant differences in student reaction to supervisors who graded them as contrasted with supervisors who did not grade them. Nor were there any significant differences

46. Charles B. Traux, Robert R. Carkhuff, and John Douds, "Toward an Integration of the Didactic and Experiential Approaches to Training in Counseling and Psychotherapy," *Journal of Counseling Psychology*, 11:240–247 (January, 1961).

in student reaction to those individuals who functioned only as graders and those who had a supervisory relationship. The supervisors who graded students, however, did have a different perception of their relationship than did those who did not grade the students.[47]

Another major supervisory issue is related to the "cognitive-didactic" approach as contrasted with the "experiencing-feeling" approach. Advocates of both would be likely to agree that they were concerned with growth and learning and self-actualization, but they did not approach it in the same manner. A study by Walz and Roeber indicated that the usual supervisory response was cognitive and information-giving, with negative overtones, and that the supervisors appeared to be more concerned with what the counselor said than with what he did, and more concerned with the content of a counselor's statement than with the relationship to the client.[48] This might be considered as the telling approach, and would fit in rather reasonably with the supervisor who saw himself as an authority-figure teacher rather than as a counselor. For the supervisor who is a counselor; however, the cognitive-didactic-telling approach would appear to be somewhat contradictory, since most counselors, at least at a talking level, see counseling as a warm, human relationship, with the stress on process and the movement of the client toward freedom and self-actualization. Here again, however, the supervisor gets into some difficulties when he tries to function, in his supervising, as a counselor. Demos, for example, points out the necessity for supervisory stress on process rather than content, and suggests as typical desirable supervisory questions such comments as, "Were you aware of the feelings and attitudes you were experiencing?"; "Were you able to experience positive attitudes toward the client?"; "Were you really listening to what the client was saying?" These questions are certainly more process- and student-counselor-centered than such statements as "Why didn't you question him about his father?" and "You sounded pretty nervous to me," but are they so different, from the viewpoint of the student counselor? One supervisor might say to the student counselor, "Were you permissive?" as above; another supervisor might have said, "I gather you have noticed that the scale tends to indicate that you were not very permissive," and another might have said "I got the feeling as I listened that you were sort of resisting this fellow."[49] These are all process-, student-coun-

47. Peter Kinney, The Effects of Grading on the Supervisory Relationship (unpublished doctoral dissertation, Boston University, 1969).

48. Gary W. Walz and Edward C. Roeber, "Supervisors' Reactions to a Counseling Interview," Counselor Education and Supervision, 2:2–7 (Fall, 1962).

49. George D. Demos, "Suggested Uses of Tape Recordings in Counselor Supervision," Personnel and Guidance Journal, 42:704–705 (March, 1964).

selor-centered comments, but to the student counselor the person who is uttering these words has some feelings about the "goodness" and "badness" of his statements. Sooner or later the supervisor is going to make use of his particular set of goods and bads to determine just how good or bad the student counselor might be. This vision, of course, may be dimmed or exaggerated by the person of the supervisor, but it is there. The supervisor, in a way, makes content out of process. The counselor does not, since this is not his function.

The counselor can say, with a high level of honesty, "And your feeling right now is that it is predominantly your wife who is to blame for this difficulty." The emphasis is on the client, and the client's feelings, and this is real, since the frame of reference is that of the client, not that of the counselor. A crucial difference in the supervisory relationship, however, is that in the long run the frame of reference of the supervisor, not that of the student counselor, is going to be used in an evaluative manner. The supervisor may say, with honesty, "And your feeling right now is that it is the anxiety of the client rather than your anxiety that is causing this apparent stiffness between you," but in the total supervisory relationship, over a period of time, the supervisor is going to evaluate the student counselor on the basis of *his* frame of reference, which possibly sees the basic difficulty as the anxiety of the student counselor rather than the anxiety of the client. A few months ago I saw an example of this where the supervisor, in observing a videotape with a student counselor, indicated in a cognitive fashion that it was his impression that the student counselor was still trying to overpower the client rather than be acceptant of him. My impression of the supervisor was that he was warm and compassionate, and concerned, but by being congruent and honest he was also indicating that he did not have the much-quoted "total positive regard" for the student counselor, or at least the student counselor almost certainly did not get the impression of total positive regard. When a person feels hurt, he does not usually view the one who inflicts the hurt as one who also provides "total positive regard." The supervisor could have taken the safer, but less congruent, less honest, and basically less acceptant way, by continuing to operate in the student counselor's frame of reference until the end of the year, then failing him in the practicum!

The increasing use of videotapes and movies in counseling supervision adds another dimension to the cognitive-experiencing issue. The supervisor can, like the counselor, operate almost entirely within the client's frame of reference, and it makes little difference whether he is reacting with the client to the client's experience, which he has neither seen or heard, which he has seen and heard via a one-way mirror, which he has heard on a tape, or which he has seen and heard on a videotape or movie. However, the moment the supervisor begins to present his frame of reference, evaluative or no, cognitively or experientially, content or process, I would think that it tends to be interpreted by the student counselor in a content, cognitive sense. When the supervisor says, as he and the student counselor watch a movie or a videotape, "I wonder why you frowned at that moment" or "I have the feeling you were resisting the client when he made that comment," this is the supervisor's frame of reference, it is his reality. He is *thinking,* and he is likely thinking more than "I wonder why" and "I have the feeling."

A study by Yenawine and me of the use of audiotape and videotape in the counseling practicum produced some interesting results. While initially more anxious about the prospects of taping, students using videotape ultimately carried out this responsibility with demonstrably more enthusiasm than did their fellow students using audiotape. Self-disclosure and self-evaluation in relation to the analysis of taped interviews was found to be more pronounced, consistent and frank in the video group. In this group the focus of discussion in reviewing tapes typically centered on the counselor, dynamic aspects of the counselor-client relationship, and manifestations of non-verbal communication. In contrast, comparable discussion in the audio group typically focused on the client, his problems, and counselor techniques related to problem solution. Generally, students using videotape perceived these discussions to be more "objective" and "constructive," and depended less on the practicum supervisor for leadership than students using audiotape. The general feeling was that videotape placed more "cards on the table" than audiotape, and as a result, was a more effective stimulant for learning.[50]

A third issue is the personal bias and orientation of the supervisor as a counselor. The study by Walz and Roeber indicated that no two supervisors reacted to the same pattern of counselor/client statements or used similar wording or meaning in their statements.[51] The reviewers' reactions to the cases presented in Evraiff's book[52] made it abundantly clear that "good" counseling was not perceived in the same way by the different reviewers, and that each reviewer had his own perception of both the content and the process of the

50. Gardner D. Yenawine and Dugald S. Arbuckle, "Study of the Use of Videotape and Audiotape as Techniques in Counselor Education," *Journal of Counseling Psychology,* 18:1–6 (January, 1971).

51. Walz and Roeber, *op. cit.*

52. William Evraiff, *Helping Counselors Grow Professionally* (Englewood Cliffs, N.J.: Prentice-Hall, 1963).

459

counseling sessions. This situation does not present too much of a problem if one views counseling in a methodological sense, and sees as the purpose of the student counselor to learn the particular method of the master. One could then agree with Patterson that the student counselor should choose the supervisor whose methodology he wishes to learn,[53] or even with Ekstein and Wallerstein that the experiencing of several different methodologies might be "nihilistic in its effect."[54] If, however, one considers counselor self-congruence and genuineness, warm, nonpossessive regard, and empathic ability as basic counselor characteristics that transcend any theoretical positions, then it would seem that experience with counselors with different theoretical positions is most crucial. Only in this way could the student counselor be helped to determine just what theoretical position made most sense to him, or, indeed, whether he was able to function effectively as a counselor under any theoretical position. If a student counselor is exposed to only one theoretical position, he is very likely to adopt what is actually a most superficial position, and become quite parochial in his attitude. This has been one of the difficulties in the past in the "training" of the psychiatrist, and there are many psychiatrists who are astonishingly parochial, principally because of the "one-school-of-thought" that they have experienced in their training.

Unfortunately, the same parochialism exists in many of the newer therapies, such as those discussed in Chapter 7. The "I have found the way" therapist too frequently has absolute faith in *what* is being done, without paying too much attention to *why* it is being done.

On the other hand, the existential-humanistic supervisor does have a certain perception of humanity that is not likely held by a behaviorial supervisor. Thus while such a supervisor is open to the use of various methods and techniques, there is no doubt that there are some to which the behavioral supervisor might react positively and some to which he would react negatively. In the long run it would seem that the honest, and the best, reaction of the supervisor to the student counselor would be to indicate that he did have a certain philosophy about human beings and did believe in the effectiveness or lack of effectiveness of certain procedures and methods. Hopefully, such supervisors could also indicate that there was nothing sacred about their views, and they were continually open to the possibility that there were other and better ways. But the reality is that since "effectiveness" is also a relative term, their measure of

53. Patterson, *op. cit.*
54. R. Ekstein and R. S. Wallerstein, *The Teaching and Learning of Psychotherapy* (New York: Basic Books, 1958), p. 64.

student counselor effectiveness would, very possibly, not be the same as that of, say, a more behaviorally oriented supervisor.

THE CLIENT

The counselor is not one who is capable of doing everything for everybody, although the claims made on the counselor would sometimes seem to deny this obvious fact. It is equally obvious that the education of the counselor, if it is to be effective, must show some awareness of the people who make up the professional clientele of the counselor. Who then, are these people? Who is the person who, for a brief period of time, may be called "client"?

In the school milieu, the *potential* clientele should include not only the students in the school, but the personnel who work in the school, the parents of the children, and other members of the community, since the difficulties of one person are seldom isolated and remote from all others.

In some schools a real attempt is made to help all children who need help, but the counselor is rendered somewhat ineffective because he has to do everything, and thus does nothing very well. Too frequently the school takes literally the idea that if a counselor "has" five hundred students, then he must see five hundred students; or when school people read about an ideal situation with a counselor responsible for about two hundred children, they visualize the counselor spending an equal amount of time with all two hundred of those children. The counselor should *know* all his children, and they should know him, or at least know who he is and what he does, but some children he will see very often, and others he will see not at all. I cannot go along with the idea of the counselor's seeing all of the children for compulsory interviews so that they can get to know him, since very frequently they have no real reason to see him, nor do they want to see him.

Ryan and Gaier stress this point in discussing a study which indicated that the socioeconomic status of the student was a significant factor for both the frequency with which he was referred to the counselor and the problem areas discussed. They suggest that, counter to the usual we-see-every-student-once-a-year philosophy, unequal attention possibly should be paid to certain social classes.[55]

55. Doris W. Ryan and Eugene L. Gaier, "Student Socio-Economic Status and Counselor Contact in Junior High School," *Personnel and Guidance Journal*, 46:466–472 (January, 1968).

This would simply seem to be another way of saying that the children who need the most attention should get the most attention.

In many schools most of the counseling will be of a cognitive, information-providing nature for those students who are college bound. In other schools most of the counseling will be of a cognitive, information-providing nature for those students who are seeking a job. Too frequently, however, more time is spent on the college bound youth, even though those seeking a job are in greater numbers and have greater needs. In all schools, too, there will be some students whose difficulties are such that they will not be alleviated by the simple presentation of information, educational, vocational or personal. If there is only one counselor in the school, all he can do is allocate his time the best way he can so that the most children possible will benefit from his services. If there are two or more counselors, a division of labor would result in more efficiency. In any school with three counselors, for example, it does seem a bit ridiculous for all three to be doing everything, when there could be a very natural division of labor.

I see the provision of information as being a teaching function rather than a counseling function, but it is likely that for some years to come, many school counselors will spend much of their time being involved with information. It is to be hoped that an existential-humanistic counselor would not be expected to do what he did not see as his primary function as a counselor.

All counselors should, of course, coordinate their efforts, and all would work closely with the teaching staff. The relationship of the therapeutic counselor to the teacher might pose something of a problem, however, since his effectiveness as a counselor with the children depends, as has been mentioned, to some extent at least on their concept of his relationship with the administration and the teaching staff. He must be seen by the children as one who will work *for them* rather than for the teachers or the administration. On the other hand, it is essential that the teachers particularly do not feel that in working for the children the counselor is working *against them*. Some teachers may feel, correctly, that the counselor spends too much of his time with individual children, and not enough of his time with teachers, parents, and other members of the community. The counselor should remember that the best way to help *children* may be to work with individuals other than children.

In many schools there is a lack of communication between counselors and students as to counselor function. Many students would never consider coming to see a counselor about a personal problem because they view them as being concerned with the provision of academic and vocational information. In fact, many students

462

see the counselor as a teacher whose subject area is academic and vocational information. A study by Bigelow and Humphreys could have been duplicated in many schools. They found the major discrepancy in student and counselor perceptions was that counselors felt responsible for personal problems, while students felt they were concerned primarily with vocational and school-related problems.[56]

At the same time, many of the counselors who feel they are capable of working with individuals with personal problems do have a preferred kind of client. In a study by Thompson, for example, it was found that counselors indicated a preference for clients having characteristics pointing to higher school success as related to achievement, future aspirations, problem types, and problem causes. The nonpreferred client was found to be experiencing more emotional problems largely stemming from conflict with others such as parents, school authorities, and peers, and he was usually not achieving up to par.[57] Thus the student who would most likely to be referred for counseling would have the misfortune to be the least preferred by the counselor!

Many students who need counseling, of course, do not come to the counseling office, while other students who do not appear to have as much need for counseling want to spend most of the school day there. If counseling is effective, the client who wants to while away his time in the counselor's office can be helped to see why he does so; and he might then leave the counselor's office, or he might enter into counseling in a more beneficial way. In any counseling situation where the client seems to be actually doing nothing but wasting his own time and that of the counselor, we must, among other things, question the effectiveness of what has gone on in the counselor's office.

The client who does not come in, however, poses a different and a more difficult problem. Although it may not be the responsibility of the individual counselor, it is the responsibility of the counseling or guidance office at least to see if something can be done. The office certainly cannot pursue the client, but neither can it shrug its shoulders and watch an individual disintegrate without trying in some way to help him. Certainly the counseling office, and the individual counselors, and the teachers, can all do an effective job of helping children to feel that they are always welcome; but even so, there will always be children who will be wary of anything that

56. Gordon S. Bigelow and Ray A. Humphreys, "What Kinds of Problems Do They Bring? Student, Counselor Perceptions Vary," *School Counselor*, 14:157–160 (January, 1967).
57. Charles L. Thompson, "The Secondary School Counselor's Ideal Client," *Journal of Counseling Psychology*, 16:69–74 (January, 1969).

smacks of authority or control, or who may be unable or unwilling to face up to their problems, or who may have learned from their parents and their culture that when you are in trouble, you keep quiet so that you won't get into more trouble. Understanding and educated teachers can often help a child to reach the point of going to see a counselor; and sometimes the teacher or principal might even make himself the "fall guy" by telling the child that he has to see a counselor—while being very careful in no way to implicate the counselor in the "you have to" deal. Thus the child may arrive at the counselor's office full of hostility toward the teacher and the school, and, possibly, the counselor. Although this is not the best situation, at least the child is in the counselor's office, and then there is a possibility that something positive might happen. The counselor may help the child to dissociate him from the authority that has commanded, "You have to see the counselor," but he cannot hold an unwilling client, and the prognosis will not be good if the client continues to feel that he is with the counselor only because he has to be there.

On the other hand, counseling with the unwilling client may not be quite so impossible as some believe it to be. I was involved in a study where junior high school boys who were disciplinary cases were, as an experiment, put into three groups. One group received the usual disciplinary action, one group had nothing at all happen to them, and the third group was required to appear before a counselor for a minimum number of counseling sessions. Various measures were used before and after to determine differences. One of the conclusions of the study was that even when students are forced to appear for counseling, *some* of them benefit with *certain counselors.*[58]

A study by Grosz also indicated that positive client expectations for counseling did not have to be present before an effective counseling relationship could be established between the client and the counselor.[59]

Another example of the effectiveness of a nontherapeutic method of getting individuals into what eventually develops into a therapeutic relationship is seen in a research study in which delinquent children were paid to come to see a counselor. Practically all came with the feeling that this was a good deal, and that the counselors were really a prime lot of suckers to be taken advantage of. Yet,

58. Dugald S. Arbuckle and Angelo Boy, "An Experimental Study of the Effectiveness of Client-Centered Therapy in Counseling Students with Behavior Problems," *Journal of Counseling Psychology,* 8:136–139 (Summer, 1961).

59. Richard D. Grosz, "Effect of Client Expectations on the Counseling Relationship," *Personnel and Guidance Journal,* 46:797–800 (April, 1968).

after a while, at least some of the children became voluntary clients in a real counseling relationship.[60]

In the long run, the crucial question regarding the unwilling client is whether or not the counselor can, with total honesty, say to the client, if need be, "I am not the one who said you *had* to be here, and you may leave here at any time if you feel that that is what you really want to do." No counselor should be placed in a position where he must, in effect, say to the client, "I am sorry that I cannot allow you to leave, even though this is your wish." At the very least, every counselor should be able to say, with total honesty, "*I* had nothing to do with your having to come down here to see me." We can assume that he might also add, "But I'm glad to see you, and if there is anything that I might be able to do. . . ."

A person becomes a client for a variety of reasons. Tyler, in a recent book, stresses the uniqueness of the individual as determining the reasons for becoming a client,[61] while in an earlier edition of the same work, she had stated that "he must deal with a situation, or situations, for which there is some doubt as to the appropriateness of his reponse."[62] Bordin states that clients are likely to be looking for help, and for reassuring signs that help will be forthcoming. He also points out that almost all clients consider coming to the counselor a reflection upon their adequacy as individuals.[63]

Whitaker and Malone, on the other hand, look at this question in a somewhat different light. They point out, for example, that in seeking therapy the client tacitly blames his culture for its failure to provide him with adequate "growth nutritional," i.e., with therapy.[64] Thus the very act of coming to the therapist points up many of the deficiencies of the community in which the patient lives. More particularly, it implicates those members of the community who live in close relationship with him.

Sheen states a theological point of view that might be unacceptable to some theologians:

The person who seeks help with the psychiatrist considers himself "ill." He wants a cure and not a sermon. His doing of what

60. Charles W. Slack, "Experimental Subject Psychotherapy: A New Method of Introducing Intense Office Treatment for Unreachable Cases," *Mental Hygiene,* 44:238–256 (April, 1960).
61. Leona Tyler, *The Work of the Counselor* (New York: Appleton-Century-Crofts, 1969), pp. 53–58.
62. Leona Tyler, *The Work of the Counselor* (New York: Appleton-Century-Crofts, 1953), p. 69.
63. Edward Bordin, *Psychological Counseling* (New York: Appleton-Century-Crofts, 1955), pp. 186–187.
64. Carl A. Whitaker and Thomas P. Malone, *The Roots of Psychotherapy* (New York: Blakiston, 1953), p. 71.

*he ought not to have done he regards as a symptom. Hence
there is no sense in telling him that he sins; either he knows
this, and "cannot help it," or he does not admit it and is scared
away because he came to seek out the physician and not the
moralist.* [65]

Rogers gives an excellent picture of the expectancies of the
client:

*The client may have expected the counselor to be a parental
figure who will shield him from harm and who will take over
the guidance of his life. He may have expected the therapist to
be a psychic surgeon who will probe to the roots of his difficulties, causing him great pain and making him over against his
will. He may have expected him to be an advice-giver, and this
advice may be genuinely and dependently desired, or it may be
desired in order that the client can prove the advice wrong. He
may, due to unfortunate previous experiences with psychiatric
or psychological counselors, look upon this new experience as
one where he will be labeled, looked upon as abnormal, hurt,
treated with little respect, and thus may deeply dread the relationship. He may look upon the counselor as an extension of
the authority which referred him for help—the dean, the Veterans Administration, the court. He may, if he has some knowledge of client-centered therapy, view the counseling interview
as a place where he will have to solve his own problem, and this
may seem to him a positive or a very threatening possibility.* [66]

In a later article, in discussing the necessary conditions for
personality change, Rogers describes the client when he says, "The
first [of two persons] whom we shall term the client, is in a state of
incongruence, being vulnerable or anxious."[67] Rogers thinks of incongruence as referring to a discrepancy between the actual experience of the organism and the self picture of the individual, insofar as
it represents that experience.

Another description of the client is given by Ellis. In a symposium on marriage counseling, he referred to the neuroticizing ideas
to be found in the client as:

1. *The notion that it is a dire necessity for an adult human
being to be approved or loved by almost everyone for almost
everything he does.*

65. Fulton Sheen, *Peace of Soul* (New York: McGraw-Hill, 1959), pp. 147–148.
66. Carl R. Rogers, *Client-Centered Therapy* (Boston: Houghton Mifflin, 1951), p. 66.
67. Carl R. Rogers, "The Necessary and Sufficient Conditions of Therapeutic Personality Change," *Journal of Consulting Psychology,* 21:95–103 (April, 1957).

2. *The notion that a human being should be, or must be perfectly competent, adequate, talented, and intelligent in all possible respects; and that he is utterly worthless if he is incompetent in any way.*

3. *The notion that one should severely blame oneself and others for mistakes and wrongdoings; and that punishing oneself or others for errors will help prevent future mistakes.*

4. *The notion that it is terrible, horrible, and catastrophic when things are not the way one would like them to be; that others should make things easier for one, help with life's difficulties; and that one should not have to put off present pleasures for future gains.*

5. *The notion that most human unhappiness is externally caused or forced on one by outside people and events, and that, since one has virtually no control over one's emotions, one cannot help feeling bad on many occasions.*[68]

There are those counselors too, of course, who apparently never see the client as a total living person. Some of them see the client as a set of behaviors or a combination of problems. Some do not even see the client as a "problem," but only as a symbol of a problem! Weitz, for example, points out:

It is important to note that (except in unusual circumstances) the counselor can never participate in or deal directly with the client's problem, or the events which initiated it, or the client's anxiety. He can deal only with the symbols abstracted from these events.[69]

Esper investigated the differences between junior high school students of three categories—those referred to counselors, those who were self-referrals, and those who had no contact with counselors. He found that the self-referral counselees tended to reflect a higher frequency of problems; the noncontact group seemed to get the better grades, while the referral group got the poorest grades; the self-referred group were the most intelligent, the referred group the least; both referral groups displayed a higher incidence of problems in counseling regarding school; adolescent girls were more apt to be self-referred and boys were more likely to be referred for counseling.[70]

68. Albert Ellis, "Symposium on Neurotic Interaction in Marriage Counseling: Neurotic Interaction between Marital Partners," *Journal of Counseling Psychology*, 5:24–26 (Spring, 1958).

69. Henry Weitz, "Counseling as a Function of the Counselor's Personality," *Personnel and Guidance Journal*, 35:276–280 (January, 1957).

70. George Esper, "Characteristics of Junior High School Students Who Seek Counseling," *Personnel and Guidance Journal*, 42:468–472 (January, 1964).

In comparing college freshmen who utilized counseling facilities with those who did not, Mendelsohn and Kirk found that the students who seek counseling score less toward the judging side, more toward the intuitive side, less toward the feeling side, and more toward the introversion side. It was suggested that the customary attention to subjective experiences characteristic of the intuitive type and the greater tolerance for or enjoyment of ambiguity characteristic of the perception type predisposes such individuals to make use of the counseling approach.[71]

There is evidence too, that certain kinds of students take up a larger share of the counselor's time. Barnard, Clarke, and Gelatt, for example, found in their study that the clients were mostly boys, were typical of the community with regard to socioeconomic level, appeared to come from fairly stable homes, and were above the school average in academic aptitude. They also had adjustment problems, the major manifestations of which were poor academic achievement and overt nonconformity to classroom behavior and school rules.[72] It is interesting to note that in this paper, as in so many others, the proposed solution for these difficulties is more counseling. Some consideration might be given to the modification of the school experience that causes the problems, rather than an intensification of the attempts to "adjust" the students to an unrealistic and oppressive environment.

Goetz and Leach reported some interesting evidence in a study of the attitudes of withdrawees and continuers in college. They found no difference in attitudes toward facilities, teachers, and counselors. While one might assume that students who dropped out would be more in need of counseling than those who stayed in college, this study indicated that the few differences that did exist showed that continuers had more negative feelings than withdrawees.[73]

Class structure is also a determiner of clients. Tseng and Thompson, for example, found that counseling tends to attract clients who are more affluent, more ambitious, and more success oriented, and that counseled students more nearly reflect the middle class ideals and value structure. Students who did not seek counsel-

71. Gerald A. Mendelsohn and Barbara A. Kirk, "Personality Differences Between Students Who Do and Do Not Use a Counseling Facility," *Journal of Counseling Psychology*, 9:341–352 (Winter, 1962).

72. Marjorie L. Barnard, Robert Clarke, and H. B. Gelatt, "Students Who See Counselors Most," *School Counselor*, 16:185–190 (January, 1969).

73. Walter Goetz and Donald Leach, "The Disappearing Student," *Personnel and Guidance Journal*, 45:883–887 (May, 1967).

ing were less certain about their occupational plans than those who did seek counseling.[74]

Occupational goals also have some relationship to the potential clientele of counselors. Thus Holland, for example, found that arts and sciences students in college were more amenable than business students to long-term counseling.[75] Segal found that writers were freer, more willing to express emotion, and more willing to deal with ambiguity than were accountants, and they were thus a better bet as clients.[76]

Critics of school counseling, the "the kids are in school to study" type, do not always appear to realize that the personal problems that may become the business of the counselor are very much related to academic achievement in school. Taylor, for example, after a survey of the literature, came to the following conclusions:

1. *The degree to which a student is able to handle his anxiety is directly related to his level of achievement.*
2. *The value the student places upon his own worth affects his academic achievement.*
3. *The ability to conform and/or accept authority demands will determine the amount of academic success.*
4. *Students who are accepted and have positive relationships with peers are better able to accept themselves.*
5. *The less conflict over independence-dependence relationships a student copes with, the more effort he places on achievement.*
6. *Activities which are centered around academic interests are more likely to produce successful achievement.*
7. *The more realistic the goal the more chance there is of successful completion of that goal.*[77]

In a somewhat more psychological vein, Gowan states that

achievement is an indication that the individual has successfully transferred a large enough portion of his libidinal drives to areas of cultural accomplishment so that he derives a significant portion of his gratifications from them. We need always

74. Michael Tseng and Donald L. Thompson, "Differences Between Adolescents Who Seek Counseling and Those Who Do Not," *Personnel and Guidance Journal,* 47:333–336 (December, 1968).
75. J. L. Holland, "A Theory of Vocational Choice," *Journal of Counseling Psychology,* 6:35–45 (Spring. 1959).
76. S. J. Segal, "A Psychoanalytic Analysis of Personality Factors in Vocational Choice," *Journal of Counseling Psychology,* 8:202–210 (Fall, 1961).
77. Ronald G. Taylor, "Personality Traits and Discrepant Achievement: A Review," *Journal of Counseling Psychology,* 11:76–82 (Spring, 1964).

to consider how an individual is to receive psychological pay for tasks accomplished.[78]

The reasons why one must become a "client" have been discussed, one might presume, since man has existed. Jung comments that "a psycho-neurosis must be understood as the suffering of a human being who has not discovered what life means for him."[79]

In an interesting discussion of Freud and Marx, Fromm points out that alienation was, for Marx, *the* sickness of man.[80] Man is independent only when he is free *to* as well as free *from,* and Freud saw the independent man as one who had emancipated himself from the dependence on mother, while Marx saw the independent man as one who had emancipated himself from dependence on nature.[81]

Mowrer, who feels that it is somewhat sinful not to be acceptant of the reality of sin, asks, "Is it any wonder that we are suffering from what Frankl calls an 'existential vacuum,' that is, *meaninglessness?*"[82]

Levitsky contrasts the two sets of forces that, he believes, exist within all of us, "as growth forces which motivate us to face anxiety and learn new ways of handling it to our satisfaction, and non-growth forces which motivate us to avoid anxiety, not to grow, or to make compromise solutions."[83]

Self-descriptions such as the following have been used by clients, child and adult, in school and out. Positive self-statements would be:

I am a responsible person.

I usually like people.

I express my emotions freely.

My hardest battles are with myself.

I am optimistic.

I am sexually attractive.

I can usually make up my mind and stick to it.

I am satisfied with myself.

I am relaxed, and nothing really bothers me.

78. J. C. Gowan, "Factors of Achievement in High School and College," *Journal of Counseling Psychology,* 7—91-95 (Summer, 1960).

79. C. G. Jung, *Modern Man in Search of a Soul* (New York: Harcourt, Brace and World, 1933), p. 225.

80. Erich Fromm, *Beyond the Chains of Illusion* (New York: Pocket Books, 1962), p. 50.

81. *Ibid.,* pp. 70-72.

82. O. Hobart Mowrer, "Science, Sex and Values," *Personnel and Guidance Journal,* 42—746-753 (April, 1964).

83. A. Levitsky, "An Approach to a Theory of Psychotherapy," *Journal of Existential Psychiatry,* 4:134 (Fall, 1963).

Self-statements on the negative side would be:

I put on a false front.
I often feel humiliated.
I doubt my sexual powers.
I usually feel driven.
I feel helpless.
I don't trust my emotions.
I have a feeling that I am just not facing things.
I am no one. Nothing seems to be me.
I just don't respect myself.
I am confused.
All you have to do is just insist with me, and I give in.

These are descriptions that most of us could likely say are "pretty much like me" or "not very much like me." Probably few of us could say to any of them, "No—never—absolutely not!"

High school and junior high school counselors describe the client in the following ways:

"He is a person who is unloved and has retaliated by involving himself in norm-violating behavior."

"He is a person whose viewpoints have not been taken seriously because people have not taken the time to be interested enough in him to listen."

"He is a person whose functional effectiveness is impaired because of a lack of congruence between what he is and what he would like to be."

"He is a person who has become a victim of our societal institutions, which do not take the time to be sensitive to his needs."

"He is a person whose emotional development has been unattended because of increasingly automated human relations."

"He is a person whose individuality is usually in conflict with the demands of the group."

"He is a person who has bottled up his feelings because he feels that people will not be perceptive or understanding of his views of life."

"He is a person whose needs have been sacrificed because of the larger needs that the group has imposed on him."

"He is a person who would like to be emotionally free but has not acquired the inner conviction that he should be free."

471

It cannot be stressed too much that the children who are being described here, and in the pages that follow, are basically "normal," "ordinary" schoolchildren. They are not "queer" or "strange" or "deviate." They are the schoolchildren with whom the counselor works, and they are representative of the children with whom the teacher works, in a somewhat different way, with somewhat different objectives. Some self-referred junior high school children speak in this manner about themselves:

"I thought I'd explode if I didn't talk to you."

"Keeping things inside prevented me from doing my best work in school."

"I don't like to be singled out for ridicule and sarcasm."

"Nobody seems to respect me or my opinions."

"I feel discriminated against."

"I don't have any friends—none at all."

"I get nervous during a test—I go blank."

"My parents favor my younger sister."

"My parents are separated—and their separation just rips me inside."

"I'm a pawn for people who use me."

"I want to be a plumber . . . but when I mentioned it at home, all hell broke loose."

"I'm fed up with the double standards that surround me."

"I'm angry about the rumors that have been spread about me."

"Every time I try to express an opinion, he just cuts me off."

"I wanted to develop an inner strength . . . something that would sustain me in life—and not be washed away in the first rainstorm."

In somewhat more detail, here are some reactions of other clients to the question, "Why are you a client?":

In thinking back on why I entered counseling as a client, it is difficult for me to actually point to a particular factor or any one reason. Generally speaking, it appears that the main overall reason for entering the counseling relationship was that I was becoming continually less able to cope with the problems encountered in everyday living; this seemingly was brought about as I began to take stock of myself, trying to find meaning and purpose in living. Actually, it seems as if a course in Mental Hygiene and a course in English Literature were the things that helped me to see the type of life I was living and the neu-

rotic trend that seemed to be associated with it. In looking around me I could, and still can see a society that has lost sight of its end and has become painfully entangled in its means; I felt that there must be more to life than this hopeless entanglement of means, and that in reality the fulfillment of means utilized as ends are insatiable needs that form the vicious circle which is so characteristic of neurosis. . . .

I'm a client because I could no longer control my actions or emotions. This was leading to excessive use of alcohol accompanied by hysteria and no knowledge of what had happened the following day. I became very depressed, because my sense of morals and a strict upbringing made me aware things had gone far beyond any sense of decency I might still have. . . .

I felt that I was becoming excessively concerned with myself and my troubles and withdrawing further and further into myself and away from society. It became absolutely necessary to seek immediately some means of finding out what was wrong and to take necessary steps, at all costs, to remedy the situation. . . .

I am a client because my anxieties about my work in my academic program were becoming so intense that they were interfering with my work. The study materials—books, etc.—were becoming the stimuli for so much anxiety—being, of course, a constant reminder of the subject matter—that I could hardly sit down to read, or to write papers, but would become tense and fidgety—to the point of not being able to study at all. Also, my experience with some of my diagnostic test courses was stirring up a great deal of anxiety, so that I was beset by recurring thoughts of a sexual, and at times abnormal nature, which I could not inhibit. I concluded that some of my defenses were crumpling, and that the time had come to get some help. I was particularly concerned that my difficulties might affect my wife and my children, because I was also becoming irritable at. home. . . .

One of the main reasons I sought help was that I was (and still am, to a degree) very sensitive; had many fears and superstitions, problems with religion, and sex. I have tried to help myself with the help of Dr. Del and tried to analyze my behavior. . . .

Because in recent years I have become a very miserable, despondent person within myself—very despondent, envious, lonely, inefficient and feel that I don't have a mind of my own any more. Always looking at everyone else and always thinking *what I need, what I should do, being very unhappy generally. Everything I attempt to do is a chore and I am completely dissatisfied with life in general. I feel that I make mistakes in everything I shop for, plan for and just cannot feel at ease any more. I feel that making decisions has become a task—a real one. Knowing that having an interest, other than being the mother, wife, daughter, and homemaker has become one of my greatest thoughts. And from that I just flounder and flounder around—what do I want to do, what will keep me "occupied in thought" as well as time. . . .*

I felt that at this time, when there are a few things about me that are disturbing, that now would be a good time to try to do something about it. This in contrast to waiting several years, when such disturbances might grow into something really serious. I also felt this to be the best opportunity—at the University, while I'm studying, early in my life and early in marriage. . . .

I thought I would find a magic formula that would enable me to sleep. Since I was eighteen years old, it has been difficult to relax, and six nights out of seven I would get three to five hours a night. Basically I felt uneasy about myself—thought I was a fake and did not form relationships with people easily, although I was friendly (I thought). . . .

I'm a client because I know my emotional immaturity is creating many problems for me that I wouldn't have if I could find a way to grow up. I hope that in therapy I will gain a better understanding of myself. . . .

As a client I have undergone approximately twenty sessions. I feel very fortunate in having matriculated at the University, for I feel that I might not have had the opportunity to undergo counseling therapy. I spent a rather difficult first semester debating whether or not I should expose myself to therapy. After all, wasn't this admitting I was sick and unable to help myself? As I think back on this hectic period, my problems mounted increasingly; the tensions and anxieties of daily living became extremely difficult to cope with. Defense mechanisms were structured; yet nothing seemed to alleviate the fears and the tensions. One crutch after another failed; each exit became a dead end. There seemed but one unopened door—my religion. This became the only answer, this had to be it! Unfortunately, or perhaps fortunately, I twisted this excellent means to a desperate end. Consequently, more anxieties were being produced, till in complete frustration I chose to enter psychotherapy. . . .

474

How then, can the human being who for a time is called "client" be described? For whom do we educate the student counselor to a high degree of professional competence? Here are a few of my observations:

1. The client is *not* a sick person who needs medical treatment in a hospital. The client *is* a human being—like the counselor—who, for a variety of reasons, has developed attitudes and beliefs which in turn have produced behaviors which produce negative results both for the person of the client and for those around the client.

2. Clients are sometimes considered to be people who are crazy, and crazy people are usually thought of as individuals whose behavior makes it difficult or impossible for them to live with us. Craziness, however, cannot be divorced from society. Indeed, it is fairly clear that craziness is, to a great extent, the direct product of our society.

In talking about insane people, Krim, who has been considered one of them, says that "the majority had lost confidence in their own ability to survive in the world outside . . . but positively no serious effort was being made to equip them to become free and independent adults."[84] Percival, another "mad" person, in an article that first appeared in 1848 but would be quite appropriate today, wrote, "The lunatic doctors appear to think that patients do not feel their position; now I know that many lunatics are extremely sensible [sic] to ridicule; this sensitiveness is, indeed, one of the phenomena of an unsound mind."[85] Another patient, Mary MacLane, says, "Madness, compared to nothingness, is beautiful."[86]

Well over a century ago Emily Dickinson wrote words that would have been directed at today's society:

> *Much Madness is divinest Sense*
> *To a discerning Eye–*
> *Much sense–the starkest Madness–*
> *'Tis the Majority*
> *In this, as All, prevail–*
> *Assent–and you are sane–*
> *Demur–you're straightway dangerous–*
> *And handled with a Chain–*[87]

84. Bert Kaplan, *The Inner World of Mental Illness* (New York: Harper and Row, 1964), p. 67.
85. *Ibid.*, p. 248
86. *Ibid.*, p. 279
87. Thomas H. Johnson (ed.), *The Complete Poems of Emily Dickinson* (Boston: Little, Brown, 1960), p. 209.

Most of us have likely asked ourselves the question, "Just who is crazy anyway?" and some more open souls have probably wondered sometimes, "Am I crazy?" I can remember, during the years of the great campus unrest, coming into a men's room and being greeted by a beautiful but somewhat hostile young woman who informed me that the room had been liberated. I said, "Fine," then proceeded to utilize the facility. The young lady gave me a withering look, muttered, "You're crazy," and hurriedly left. When I mentioned the incident to another professor, he muttered, "Those crazy freaky hippies—real crazy people."

Reading through some of the material in *The Inner World of Mental Illness* (the products of mad people), then some of the products of R. D. Laing[88] and Fritz Perls (two eminent psychiatrists), one may well wonder, "Who's crazy—them, Laing and Perls, me—or maybe all of us!"

I returned once from a trip to find that a friend, whom we shall call Martha, had been taken to a "mental hospital." Her husband was away, and she had many children. I went to the hospital and eventually managed to get through several locked and barred doors and past several large grim-looking people, including the psychiatrist in charge, who I mistakenly assumed was being looked after by the other large grim-looking people. Martha was lying in bed, looking tired and wan and sad. I said to her, "Martha, what in hell are you doing here?" She said, "Well, I just got so tired and exhausted that I didn't know what I was doing, and the first thing I knew, I was here." I knew Martha, and I knew that she was an overworked and tired woman who was emotionally and physically drained. What she needed was tender loving care for a few days in a bright, cheerful place, with happy, kindly people around her. Instead, she was surrounded by depressing facilities and depressing people, all of whom communicated to her that she was "crazy."

In our current society, "crazy" is more likely to be a perception that others have of me rather than a perception that I have of myself. Rationally, the perceptions that make a person officially crazy are the really crazy things. "Peaceniks" are generally considered to be crazier than "warniks." To advocate making love instead of war is definitely crazier than the reverse. A long-haired youth would score higher on a "crazy scale" than would a crew-cut youth. Nudity is a condition strongly suggesting craziness, but violence is part of the American tradition. To use any word to describe the sex act is bad, but some words are worse than others—even though they all

88. Such as R. D. Laing, *Knots* (New York: Pantheon Books, 1970) and Frederick S. Perls, *In and Out of the Garbage Pail* (Lafayette, Ind.: Real People Press, 1969).

describe the same act. In a certain state if I am caught drinking liquor standing up I am subject to a fine and a jail sentence, but if I am seated I am being legal and proper. An "unnatural" sex act will likely result in confinement in the nearest mental institution for a psychiatric examination if committed between unmarried partners. The marriage vow, however, immediately changes the unnatural to the natural. In many states I am subject to a jail sentence if I am found with someone in the possession of marijuana. This makes college teaching a risky business, since it is likely that in most classes there will be some students who have the drug on their person. One cannot belong to certain "fraternal" organizations if his skin happens to be black. A powerful church considers the removal of a small amount of material called an embryo from the body of a woman to be murder, but the birth of a new child, unwanted, unloved, and doomed before birth, is quite acceptable.

And so it goes. We do indeed live in a crazy world, and one might hypothesize that one has to be at least somewhat crazy in order to exist comfortably in it. The counselor or therapist lives a somewhat schizophrenic existence, in that he works with people considered by the outside world to be high on the crazy scale, but he usually lives with the outside people who are the creators of the crazy people with whom he works. To be empathic with those with whom he works, the counselor must be able, to some degree at least, to live in their world, and this, in turn, may make some outside people uncomfortable with him.

A social perception of therapy, accepted by many therapists, is that the purpose of therapy is to help the person to adjust to the society in which he lives so that he will be a happier member of it. A healthier perception, both for the individual and for society, is to help the individual to accept some of this difference with society as an important part of his individuality, and indeed, as being quite crucial for any development of existential freedom. Such a person would assume that a certain price would have to be paid for these differences, and he would accept this as part of the price of the free life. At the same time, however, he would do his best to change societal conditions so that the next generation might be able to have his level of freedom without paying such an excessive price. In the mid-1970's no better examples can be found of this sort of person than certain poets and novelists in Russia. They set a shining example.

3. Clients are often lonely people, and loneliness is probably more related to the degree of dehumanization of life than it is to the extent to which one lives alone. As our current society crowds us closer and closer together, it is likely that we will move further and

further apart, and become *more* alone. Some of the most lonely of people are continually with others, often in a vain attempt to hide their loneliness from themselves.

Many people, too, feel that if someone prefers to be alone he must be at least slightly crazy. I have known more than one teacher who was worried about a child in her class because he sometimes preferred to be alone rather than with other children. We are taught that there is something wrong with being alone, and the implication is that being surrounded by people is the cure for loneliness. This is anything but the case, and being alone should not be confused with loneliness. Aloneness is a part of life and living, and the healthy personality is one who is able to accept his aloneness without being lonely. Indeed, the person who can live alone without the destructive thrusts of loneliness is likely to be the one who can live with others in a contributing way, since he does not have a desperate need for others. The therapist should be such a person, otherwise it is very likely that his effectiveness in a helping sense is going to be negated by his need for clients as a means of assuaging his loneliness.

Aloneness, then, is a way of life, and the goal is to be able to face it without loneliness. For all of us the final journey is the last, and major, test. Whether we die physically alone, or surrounded by people, on this journey we must travel by ourselves. We can't take "it" with us, nor can we take "them" with us. One of the major comforts of religion is that in life as in death, "*He* is with you," and the nonbeliever who faces death calmly and with dignity may be made of stouter stuff than the one who *must* believe.

The very thought of living, let alone dying, alone, fills many people with fear and panic. A client often views loneliness as a condition forced upon him because of his lack of opportunity to be with others. He sees it as an outer, imposed condition rather than an inner, developed state of mind. He hopes, in vain, that change will come from the outside to his center, but any positive change must come from the center to the outside. A person, regardless of his outer condition, *can* live his life without loneliness, but he cannot achieve this if he must depend on others to keep him from being lonely.

4. A client is often an anxious person—anxious about failing courses in school; anxious about doing well on a job; anxious about his lack of capacity as a husband, anxious about being able to live in a new environment, anxious about deviations that he does not want to modify but that are unacceptable to society. Although anxiety, of course, is common to all human beings, the relationship between the anxiety and the object or event producing it may often be a measure of one's disturbance. Thus anxiety prior to a championship tennis

match might be expected, but an equal state of anxiety before playing a friendly match with a friend might be considered unusual. A mother might be considered to be reasonably anxious about a child who is failing in all of his schoolwork, but a similar degree of anxiety because her son received one B instead of all A's would be a somewhat different story. Then, too, the event or situation producing the anxiety may be something that will change, and so reduce the anxiety, whereas an event or situation that will remain means that the individual's reaction to it must be changed. Thus a man who is somewhat fearful for his life during a hurricane has anxiety of a short duration, but the homosexual who is anxious over the reaction of the culture to him is going to have to adjust to such a culture if his anxiety is to decrease, or else he must change himself so that the reaction of the culture to him will change. Neither of these choices will be easy.

Then, too, having no anxiety might be considered more abnormal than having some anxiety. I remember an episode from Air Force days when I shared some anxiety with Air Force personnel because it appeared that the aircraft on which we were passengers was going to explode; and I can remember the irritation I shared with the others at another passenger, a fighter pilot, who actually went to sleep on the floor of the plane, with the philosophical comment, "We can't do anything about it anyway, so why worry?"

Clients are often extremely anxious, too, about what others would call very little or trivial things. "Will I look right?" "What will I do if I can't answer that question?" What if it snows and I don't have my rubbers?" "What will I do if Joe doesn't meet me?" "What will I buy for Don's dinner?" Although such anxiety is out of proportion as far as the rest of the world is concerned, it is not out of proportion as far as the client is concerned. Far too often we hear a comment like "Oh, I wouldn't worry about a little thing like that." The trouble with this statement is that "that" is "little" only to the person who makes the comment, not to the anxious one. It is surely, at best, a doubtful procedure to reject a client's feelings that something is big enough and important enough to cause anxiety with an airy "Why, that isn't anything to worry about at all." The most likely reaction to this sort of comment would be a resigned "Oh, well, I guess you can't blame him. He's just like the rest of them—just doesn't understand me."

The anxiety and fearfulness of the client are very real. The fact that what is not a threat to nearly everyone else is a threat to him means that there has to be a modification and change in the client. The dark room remains dark, but to the child who has grown, that same darkness is no longer a threat. Two of my children were once given a basement room as a bedroom when relatives were visiting, but the night was not far along before they were squeezing into bed with father and mother. The new room was too "spooky," they felt, and the fact that it was the same room where they played all day did not alter the fact that it was spooky. Their fear might even have been contagious, since neither father nor mother took their place, but all four spent the night in the one bed!

Whatever the anxiety may appear, overtly, to be about, any continuing stage of anxiety usually reflects an anxiety about one's self. This anxiety may also be shown by an "I cannot understand you" or "I cannot hear you." What these very often mean is that the person does not want to understand or to hear because of the implications of what might be being said, and the easiest way to avoid anxiety about doing something is to avoid understanding or hearing, for then one can hardly be expected to do anything.

5. The client is often hostile, and his hostility may be shown in a variety of ways. He may be overtly aggressive and contemptuous, unable to accept any ideas or suggestions that might contradict his own, or that might imply that someone else knows more than he does. This is a difficult person to work with, particularly if one is in a supervisory position, since he will react with sensitivity to any sort of criticism, no matter how gentle (if criticism can be gentle) or constructive. As a member of a class, he will often feel that the instructor's comments are personalized, that a criticism of some idea of his is a personal attack upon him. Similarly, he makes a difficult boss or teacher, since he can brook no opposition or suggestions that a job might be done in a different or better way than that suggested by him. No matter what his position or role might be, he will find it difficult to relate closely with almost anyone—other than a counselor. Other people seldom have the patience or the understanding to attempt to relate with such a person, a fact which in turn accentuates the difficulties, since these hostile individuals are often correct in their feeling that people do not agree with them. As with other clients, it is usually only in a therapeutic relationship that the client begins to feel there is no need for the elaborate defenses he has built up. He finds, for the first time, someone who is acceptant—in a secure manner, not in a weak and passive way—of him and his hostilities.

There are many ways, of course, in which a man may express his hostility in a more socially acceptable manner; often an individual may be consciously unaware of the fact that what he is expressing is really a deeply rooted hatred or hostility toward someone. Because a woman soon learns that a mother who hates her child is an awful person, she may show her hatred by being one who loves and loves and loves her child, and indicates to all her great love for her dear darling. The philanthropist, of either the twenty-five-cent or the million-dollar variety, may be sneering at people by his donation. The comic may show his veiled contempt for his audience by getting it to laugh at him and to pay him for the privilege of laughing.

Overt or not, our hostility is usually related to our own anxiety about ourselves. Even the little child, when he says, "I hate you," to his mother, is also probably feeling, "And I hate me too." It is generally easier to assert our disdain and contempt for others than for ourselves, and perhaps to express a feeling of "I hate me" by saying, "I hate you."

Much of man's prejudice, indeed, is self-rejection rather than rejection of others. When someone else is doing something that is obviously bigger and better and superior, it is only the solid and stable individual who can say, without any twinges or negative feelings, "He is a better person than I," or "He won because he was better." Minority groups are often tolerated when they are small and pose no threat to the majority; only when they become more potent in strength and numbers, and begin to challenge the status of the majority, do they become a threat. At the same time the members of the minority group cannot afford to show their hostility, and may develop a passive aggressiveness, so that their hatreds are expressed by their meekness and humility.

6. The client often feels guilty; the more the socioreligious pressures upon him, the greater the likelihood of feelings of guilt. Much of our cultural behavior would appear to be controlled by the guilt concept, and even advertisements stress the fact that the potential purchaser would not want to be guilty of various things. The more one learns that he "should not" do and feel, the more likely it is that he will have many feelings of guilt, since he will continue to do and feel, and it is the feelings about what has been done that cause the trouble and tension rather than the actual doing. Thus a client may feel guilty about wanting to marry someone of a different religion; he may feel guilty about speaking and acting harshly toward his children; he may feel guilty because he does not think kindly of his parents; he may feel guilty about masturbation; he may feel guilty about cheating; he may feel guilty about having sexual relations with a girl; and so on. Some would say that this is the voice of one's conscience, and that if we did not have any control by guilt we would have no social order. The trouble is that the guilt feeling itself is a contagious sort of thing that seldom change one for the better. If an individual felt guilty only about some act that most people would agree was questionable—such as brutal treatment of one's chil-

dren—and then moved ahead to a more stable attitude, and thus more positive behavior toward the children, this would be fine. That, however, is not usually what happens. If an individual is restrained from striking his children only because he feels guilty about it, then there is every likelihood that this same attitude toward his children will be expressed in an equally questionable, but possibly not equally guilt-producing manner. Thus, although guilt may repress or change or modify the act or the behavior, it does not change the attitude that produces the behavior.

7. Low self-esteem is another overt characteristic of many clients. Such a lack of respect for oneself may show itself in statements to this effect, or by depression or general unhappiness, or it may be shown by the contempt or ridicule that the client directs toward others. Low self-esteem is also shown by a discrepancy between the individual's ideal self-concept and his actual self-concept. This discrepancy has been brought sharply into focus in research studies by Rogers and Dymond, where the ideal self-concept was described as the organized conceptual pattern of characteristics and emotional states that the individual consciously holds as desirable (and undesirable) for himself. The greater the discrepancy, the more poorly he feels about himself.[89]

8. All of these items are, of course, related, although the inability to make a choice might be thought of as another characteristic of some clients. Of course, making a choice is a problem for all individuals, but a disturbed person may be completely unable to accept the responsibility for making a choice—and thereby a decision—which would then leave him subject to question and criticism. If one never makes a decision, one will never get into trouble or be blamed or criticized for making a choice.

9. It is increasingly obvious that counselors and therapists are unfamiliar and ineffective with a significant proportion of the population who might be described as members of minority groups.[90] Such people are unfamiliar with, and understandably suspicious of, counselors and counseling. Mealy and Perrone, in describing the youth who come into a Youth Opportunity Center, refer to them as having an intense distrust and suspicion of adults in general, particularly adults in positions of authority; they are extremely sensitive to criticism; they have an overwhelming need for self-gratification, with little in the way of long-term goals.[91] Gross sees the disadvan-

89. Carl R. Rogers and Rosalind F. Dymond, *Psychotherapy and Personality Change* (Chicago: University of Chicago Press, 1954).
90. See Dugald S. Arbuckle, "The Alienated Counselor," *Personnel and Guidance Journal*, 48:18–24 (September, 1969). Copyright 1969 by the American Personnel and Guidance Association.
91. John J. Mealy and Philip A. Perrone, "The Case Approach in Madison," *Employment Service Review*, 5:11–13 (October, 1968).

taged youth as being quite the opposite of most clients in that they are not voluntary clients, they do not want help and are usually either passively or overtly hostile, they are unwilling to accept the authority of the counselor, they are usually the sort of person who is unacceptable to most counselors, and they do not come in to have their attitudes, points of view, and skills changed.[92] In a report of the National Conference on Education of the Disadvantaged, one speaker said, "In the Negro ghettos you often hear the people say of themselves, 'The nigger ain't nuthin.' The disadvantaged youngster cannot identify with the world outside the ghetto." Another speaker commented, "We are dealing with the child who expects to fail, who has no confidence." The same speaker felt, as did most others, that the "lower class child needs immediate and tangible rewards."[93]

Vontress feels that the black client sees the white counselor as the enemy, and the black counselor as the collaborator with the enemy. He also feels that there is a good deal of self-hatred in the Negro, that he is reluctant to disclose himself psychologically to anyone, including the counselor, and that he tends to be suspicious of anyone who talks a lot.[94] Miller has referred to the focal concerns of the lower-class community as being trouble, toughness, smartness, excitement, fate, and autonomy.[95] Peterson comments that "the more divergent the original social-cultural environment is from the new, the greater the need for individual motivation for change on the part of the client."[96]

Bingham reported a study of unemployed men which indicated that while there was no difference in motivation to work between employed and unemployed men, there was a difference in motivation to avoid work.[97] On the other hand, a study by Gettlieb tends to suggest that "lower income youth do in fact seek a better life, a life that has the dimensions of what we have come to identify

92. Edward Gross, "Counseling Special Populations," *Employment Service Review,* 5:14–19 (October, 1968).

93. "A Report of a National Conference," *National Conference on Education of the Disadvantaged* (Washington, D.C.: U.S. Department of Health, Education, and Welfare, 1966) July 18–20, E-37004.

94. Clemment E. Vontress, "Counseling the Culturally Different in Our Society," *National Conference of State Employment Service Counseling Supervisors* (Detroit, April 5, 1968).

95. W. Miller, "Lower Class Culture as a Generating Milieu of Gang Delinquency," *Journal of Social Issues,* 14:5–19 (Fall, 1958).

96. Ronald A. Peterson, "Rehabilitation of the Culturally Different: A Model of the Individual in Cultural Change," *Personnel and Guidance Journal,* 45:1001–1007 (June, 1967).

97. William C. Bingham, *Counseling Services for Unemployed Youth* (New York: New York University Center for the Study of Youth, Summer, 1967), p. 37.

with the middle class."[98] Finally, reporting on a study of socially and economically disadvantaged individuals, Johnson and Gutsch found that the majority of their problems, as they perceived them, were related to personal financial difficulties.[99]

This is probably a fair reflection of what the literature and the research says about the disadvantaged, the underprivileged, the culturally deprived, the alienated.

What is particularly interesting, however, is the fact that such individuals should pose a problem for counselors, who are, after all, supposed to be experts in human communication and the professional understanding of human behavior. Johnston and Seales may be all too correct when they say, "The shift in concern and direction being given to counseling the disadvantaged is relatively new; the student is not,"[100] and this statement reveals the melancholy fact that for a long time counselors have apparently been unaware of the presence of a significant part of the young population of the school, just as psychiatrists have been generally unaware of the existence of a significant proportion of the troubled population of the country. If counselors find it difficult, if not impossible, to relate effectively with the sort of person described above, one might wonder what sort of people they are, professionally and personally, and just how they perceive their professional function known as counseling. The picture that comes out, in a way, is one of an alienated counselor working with a clientele from whom he has alienated himself. An effective program of counselor education will include in its ranks individuals who are representative of various segments of the population. Student counselors, in an experiential manner, will be helped to understand and accept the reality of the differences in human beings, so that they will not assume that "their way" is "*the* way."

10. Finally, we may hope that increasingly the client may be one who is in good psychological health, who is relatively untroubled, but who is attempting to make his life even more meaningful, and to prevent the development of attitudes and behaviors which might, in the future, tend to make life more meaningless. The more counseling assumes a preventive role, the more likely it is that the above statement will describe the potential client. Counselors and therapists may face the increasing, uncomfortable possibility that

98. David Gottlieb, "Poor Youth Do Want to Be Middle Class but It's Not Easy," *Personnel and Guidance Journal,* 46:116–122 (October, 1967).

99. Jerome Johnson and Kenneth Urial Gutsch, "The Unskilled Worker: Toward an Understanding of Poverty," *Journal of Employment Counseling,* 5:36–41 (June, 1968).

100. W. E. Johnston and Eldridge E. Seales, *Counseling the Disadvantaged* (New York: Associated Educational Services Corporation, 1967), p. 105.

clients may have proceeded further along the road to self-actualization than they have!

CHANGES IN PROGRAMS OF COUNSELOR EDUCATION

The last decade has seen many changes in programs of counselor education, but it is not easy to determine whether these changes at a relatively few institutions are indicative of any national trend. Then, too, the changes would sometimes appear to be somewhat artificial, with the basic philosophy, objectives, and procedures of the program remaining intact. We must also keep in mind that change can be regression into the past rather than movement into the future.

An immediate question would be, "Are the kinds of students who are being admitted into programs of counselor education *sharply* different from those of a decade ago?" I would say, "No."

Admissions criteria to counselor education programs continue to be based on such things as grade-point averages. Graduate Record Examinations, and the Miller Analogies Test, none of which show much of a relationship with effective counseling. While Matulef and Rothenberg were talking about programs in clinical psychology, they could be referring to counselor education when they say:

> Under the guise of objectivity, we use GRE's, Miller Analogies and grade point averages in determining admissions. . . . Although clinicians claim to and do evaluate personalities every day, they dare not apply their own skills to selecting trainees. We are not talking about screening out pathology as much as looking at professional attributes like empathy, positive regard and congruence. [101]

It is doubtful if most counselor education programs do much to help to humanize their student counselors, and this may tend to reflect the lack of concern in counselor education programs about the level of humanization and self-actualization of their graduates. It may be that they are more concerned with training highly skilled diagnosticians, whose concern and compassion about humanity may be considered to be of minor importance. Indeed, programs of counselor education, like other forms of human conditioning, tend all too frequently to enlarge the student's area of alienation. A student's professional program frequently teaches him that there is a great

101. Norman J. Matulef and Peter J. Rothenberg, "The Crisis in Clinical Training: Apathy and Action," *Special Bulletin of the National Council on Graduate Education in Psychology,* 2:8 (1968).

deal that he must not believe, very little that he can believe. Rather than helping him to open and enlarge his area of potential experiencing, it restricts him even further. Dreyfus expresses this feeling when he says:

> In many ways schools of psychotherapy tend to reinforce man's alienation from man. The therapist, like the physician, keeps his therapeutic armamentarium between himself and the patient, preventing real interhuman contact. . . . Helping would-be therapists to be more human with freedom to respond should be the goal.[102]

Clark is thinking along much the same line when he comments:

> What is also needed in the literature are some creative ideas on how to implement a self-actualization model in graduate education. Most graduate schools are run on a behavioristic model in that they require much immediate feed-back of reward and punishment and other manipulatory practices.[103]

An excellent example of this restricting of the freedom of the student counselor, and the pressure on the student *not* to experience and *not* to question, but rather to think as he is told to think, is indicated by this comment, written by a counselor-educator of some renown, on the paper of a student:

> Crap . . . your first big problem will be to bury this self concept junk on the high school level particularly in the educational-vocational level. Counselors should be expected to know, offer alternatives based on accurate and current information. They can save the foot-and-mouth game of reflection for those students who need support and can't be hurt too much by ineptness in training and technique.

The attitude behind this comment is very clearly "Do it my way, because my way is the right way." It is little wonder that the students who are the products of such programs are alienated not only from other differing professional ideologies and values, but probably from most of their fellow humans who do not think as they think. They in a sense then become the conditioning agents of the culture, and the repression of the individual, under the guise of a professional relationship, is continued.

102. Edward A. Dreyfus, "Humanness: A Therapeutic Variable," *Personnel and Guidance Journal*, 46:573–578 (February, 1967).
103. Donald L. Clark, "The Counseling Educator and His Own Teaching Approach," *Counselor Education and Supervision*, 6:166–169 (Spring, 1967).

Van Kaam points out a major weakness in the current methods of educating psychologists, counselors, psychotherapists, and social workers, when he asks:

Do they all take into account the fact that these therapists are being trained for a pluralistic society? How many seminars are dedicated to the understanding of the varied cultural, subcultural, and religious projects of existence which underlie the lives of their patients? Is there a sufficient number of group therapeutic sessions in which the students can work through their own unconscious hostilities and defensive misunderstandings of religions or cultures which are not their own?[104]

But there is change and there is movement in programs of counselor education. For example:

1. It is now taken for granted that a clinical practicum or some actual counseling involvement is the essential core around which any program of counselor education must be built.

2. There is increasing stress on the necessity for the humanizing of counselor education. A U.S. Office of Education brochure, for example, refers to the need for schools to be dedicated to the task of developing human potential rather than measuring and grading students on a competitive basis and then classifying them as successes and failures.[105] It also describes the counselor as one who "focuses his attention to the needs of individual students as opposed to the expectations society has for these students."[106]

Island sees the dehumanization of persons in schools continuing unless "we adopt an alternative model for counselor education which consists of a clinical consciousness process and a personalized intellectual process to help create in counselors the capability we desperately need: the ability to see."[107]

Graduate students in counselor education have stressed the need for a more personal and human relationship between staff and students, suggesting that they should be experiencing what they are supposed to learn.[108] Other students have indicated that they feel that this is what is happening in certain institutions.[109]

---

104. Adrian van Kaam, *The Art of Existential Counseling* (Wilkes-Barre, Pa.: Dimension Books, 1966), p. 125.

105. "Careers in Education," *National Center for Information in Careers in Education* (Washington, D.C.: U.S. Office of Education, 1973), p. 17.

106. *Ibid.*, p. 46.

107. David Island, "An Alternative for Counselor Education," *Personnel and Guidance Journal*, 50:762–766 (May, 1972).

108. "Graduate Student's Forum," *School Counselor*, 20:387–388 (May, 1973).

109. "Speakout," *School Counselor*, 21:84–86 (November, 1973).

Psychological education is a more humanistic viewpoint of education, and its importance was stressed by an entire issue of the *Personnel and Guidance Journal* (May, 1973) and one of the *School Counselor* (May, 1973) being devoted to this subject.

3. In a few institutions the traditional practicum has been greatly expanded so that the basic clinical learnings are experiential. Boston University, for example, has developed a field model with five teams—a Community Consultation team, and Identity Development team, a Persons, Groups and Organizations team, a Psychological Education team, and an Existential-Humanistic team. Each team is made up of a number of master's, advanced certificate, and doctoral students and a group of staff members. The learnings of the team are centered on their clinical experience.

4. A few institutions are beginning to stress competencies rather than courses. At each level of education a number of competencies are developed, and students must prove that they have satisfied these competencies. Traditionally a course supposedly indicated competency in a certain area, but a "competency-based" program allows for a much wider means by which the student might achieve competency. There are no "required" courses per se, but rather an expectation of proof of competency. Needless to say, this allows for a much greater creativity on the part of the student, who can, if he wishes, develop his own methods of achieving competency.

The development of competencies that are acceptable to a group of staff members is a difficult task, which is surpassed only by the difficulty of developing creative methods of evaluating the achievement of these competencies. Stanford University, Boston University, and Governors State University are institutions that are experimenting with a competency-based program of counselor education.

Changes such as these are difficult, and they require much effort and dedication and responsibility on the part of both students and faculty. Whether they represent a pattern of counselor education that will be commonplace in the decade of the 1980's or ones which will be remembered as experiments that failed remains to be seen.

AN EXISTENTIAL-HUMANISTIC PROGRAM OF COUNSELOR EDUCATION

The trouble with traditional programs for the education of counselors is that they train individuals who have already been trained, rather than helping individuals to develop their humanness so that they might be more effective in a human relationship. We can assume that the traditional criteria for admission to a professional program such as academic qualifications and scores on measures such as the Graduate Record Examination and the Miller Analogies Test have little relationship with future effectiveness as a counselor. If admission to a program must be on this basis, it possibly should be for the purpose of first trying to find out if one can become effective as a counselor. Then, if one passes this hurdle, he can become more involved in his education for counseling effectiveness. Any core of knowledge should be related to, and built around, actual clinical practice, in which the major immediate question asked by the counselor is "Who am I?" rather than "Who is he?" The student counselor, and his teachers and supervisors should surely believe that each client is a unique individual who is to be helped to grow and develop his own potential rather than being bludgeoned into someone else's mold. If this is so, then it would seem reasonable that the student counselor should also be helped to develop so that he too could determine how he could be most effective as a counselor, if, indeed, he can be effective as a counselor. This is a question that most student counselors have not as yet answered when they enter a counseling program, unless they have had some previous intimate human experiences that have provided them with some insight as to their potential as counselors. We might assume that many of the unknown lay therapists who may not possess the proper academic qualifications would be much better candidates for a counselor education program than would many of those in the program.

Those who are concerned with the professional education of counselors should be equally involved in the process of self-development, and the "Who am I" question should apply equally to supervisor, to student counselor and to client. We might theoretically assume that the level of self-actualization and humanness should be higher for the student counselor than for the client, and higher for the supervisor than for the student counselor. If the supervisor is not sensitive to, and acceptant of the hostility of the student counselor, then we might wonder if he can help the student counselor to become more acceptant and understanding of the hostility of the client.

Boy and Pine stress the uselessness of any so-called theory that is not practiced when they say:

When the counselor educator rebukes the school counselor who says that he is unable to implement a particular counseling theory because of the administrative attitudes within his school, and then in turn rejects student-centered teaching be-

489

cause of the limitations he feels are imposed upon him by a
university setting, that counselor exhibits a shallowness in his
own personal theory. . . . When one achieves a personal rele-
vancy regarding anything, he then develops a commitment to
translate that relevancy into a viable modus operandi that is
functional within the context of limitations.[110]

Chenault proposes what she sees as a humanistic model for
counselor education; it is based on nine value premises. These are:
(1) The goal for the education of students in counselor education is
growth, as differentiated from learning. (2) Growth is a creative process. (3) A humanistic counselor education program focuses upon
the person as an organic entity rather than as a receptacle for learning. (4) The highest form of morality, personal and professional, is
the encouragement of the individual's growing in his own values (5)
Counseling effectiveness is not a function of technique. (6) A necessary condition for growth is the subjective involvement of the student. (7) The highest educational goal is the student's search for
meaning, his search for himself. (8) The purpose of a humanistic
counselor education program is to facilitate growth as a process. (9)
The nature of the growth potential is and should be different for each
student.[111]

My only disagreement with Chenault would be a semantic
one, since I tend to view growth as the very essence of learning, and
I cannot see any true learning other than as an inside-out process
rather than an outside-in process. The latter, of course, does describe
the greater part of formal education, which I would tend to view as
neither growth nor learning.

Assessment and evaluation are a part of the counselor's education, but the student counselor should be involved in this assessment and evaluation. The purpose of counselor education is to help
to develop a genuine, self-actualized empathic individual, and if the
counselor is not this sort of person, then, as Olsen says, "he can only
fall back upon authoritarian behavior or the carrying out of an accepted technique. A sense of *being* someone has not been an outcome of his counselor education program."[112]

The student counselor, however, should be at such a point in
his own development that he can be open, rather than highly defen-

---

110. Angelo V. Boy and Gerald J. Pine, *The Counselor in the Schools* (Boston:
Houghton Mifflin, 1968), pp. 321–322.

111. Joann Chenault, "A Proposed Model for a Humanistic Counselor Education
Program," *Counselor Education and Supervision*, 8:4–11 (Fall, 1968).

112. LeRoy C. Olsen, "Success for New Counselors," *Journal of Counseling Psychology*, 10:350–355 (Winter, 1963).

sive toward evaluation of himself—by himself, by his peers, and by his supervisor. If he is not, one may question whether or not he belongs in a counselor education program. If the insecurity of the counselor is deeper than that of the client, the outlook for the client is surely not too hopeful!

An existential-humanistic attitude toward people comes from many sources other than counseling and psychology. I like the following examples. T. S. Eliot answers the question, "To what does this lead?"

> *To finding out*
> *What you really are. What you really feel.*
> *What you really are among other people.*[113]

Gibran's Prophet, speaking about teaching, says:

> *No man can reveal to you aught but that which already lies asleep in the dawning of your own knowledge. . . .*
> *. . . For the wisdom of one man lends not its wings to another man. . . .*[114]

Cicero also had some feelings on this question when he said, "The authority of the teacher is generally prejudicial to those who desire to learn.[115]

Somerset Maugham, on being asked what advice he gave young people, said:

> *Really, you know, there's only one thing to do, and that's follow your own nose and make your own mistakes. By following one's nose one can't go too far astray.*[116]

Pasternak was speaking about learning when he said:

> *When I hear people speak of reshaping life it makes me lose my self control and I fall into despair. Reshaping life!*
>
> *People who can say that have never understood a thing about life—they have never felt its breath, its heartbeat, however much they may have seen or done. They look on it as a lump of raw material that needs to be processed by them, to be enno-*

113. T. S. Eliot, "The Cocktail Party" in *The Complete Poems and Plays* (New York: Harcourt Brace, and World, 1952), p. 307.

114. Kahlil Gibran, *The Prophet,* Alfred A. Knopf, 1923, pp. 64–65.

115. Cicero, *De Fisibus, 1,* quoted by Montaigne in *Essays,* Chapter 26, Vol. 1, Emil Julius Trechmann, trans. "Of the Education of Boys," letter addressed to Diane de Faix, Comtesse de Gurson (Oxford: Oxford University Press, 1935).

116. Joel Lieber, "Somerset Maugham Talks about Life," *This Week* (January, 1961).

bled by their touch. But life is never a material, a substance to be molded. . . . Life is constantly renewing and remaking and changing and transfiguring itself. . . .[117]

Let us now look at what I would consider to be the basic ingredients of an existential-humanistic program of counselor education:

1. The involvement of staff and students is with fellow human beings, whom we do not see as sick people needing medical care in a hospital, but as people who are troubled, sometimes to the point of destruction, by negative learnings and experiences, and by cultural oppression. Counseling is viewed as a human involvement rather than a clinical investigation. The traditional methods of treatment—medical and psychological—are no longer suitable for the people, the times, and the culture. The existential-humanistic counselor is involved, in an individual, group, and community sense, with the prevention and modification of those experiences, personal and cultural, which produce trouble and pain. He is also aware of the need for remedial action for those individuals who are the victims of such experiences, and need immediate help if they are to survive.

There is an awareness of the cultures of which we are a part, but the individual is accepted as taking precedence over the culture. We change the culture by changing the individuals who make up the culture. Thus the counselor is involved and committed to social action for the betterment of the individual and the culture in which he exists. Functionally, this means that counseling is not just for the benefit of any one ethnic, religious, sexual, or national group, but rather for all human beings who make up the culture.

2. The core of the program will be experiential, and while most programs refer to experiencing as being crucial for the development of the counselor, little is done to provide the means by which the student can "experience." Most of the time he studies and reads and memorizes and takes examinations and writes papers, but only infrequently, as part of his formal program, does he live and experience deeply.

A crucial part of the program for the development of the existential-humanistic counselor is the provision of a series of kinds of experiences in which the sensitivities of the student become more finely honed—experiences in which feeling and imagination can run free, experiences in which all of a human's person can be more intimately felt and experienced. Nor should experiences be strictly "rational," since if we are to live comfortably, we should be understand-

---

117. Quoted by H. Salisbury in "The Triumph of Boris Pasternak," *Saturday Review* (November 8, 1958), p. 22.

ing of important aspects of our life that may be sensed and felt but remain cognitively unknown.

Experiences will also develop a heightened awareness of the body, what it actually is, and what it can do for us as a part of us. Many counselors would appear to be almost totally unaware of the existence of their body, other than as a thing that performs certain essential functions. An outdoor, physical experience of the Outward Bound type, correlated with the emotional and intellectual components, will be a part of an existential-humanistic program in counselor education. We become more aware of our body when our continued existence begins to obviously depend upon it. The awareness that you have actually walked, or staggered, half a mile beyond the point that was your absolute limit, the feeling of aloneness, with nothing but your person, deep in the woods or high on a mountain peak, the battle in a frail canoe with surging water—these are experiences that will be part of a program of existential-humanistic counselor education.

3. Stressing experiencing does not mean that knowledge is relegated to a minor position. Rather, it assumes a more important place, in that it becomes functionally meaningful to the individual person. Indeed, when we no longer seek knowledge as a necessary but rather uninteresting academic pastime, but rather as something which will become an integrated part of our being, then it is possible that we might even be on the right road to wisdom, a rare experience for most individuals in "helping" professions. It means that in terms of a human relationship, the counselor will be able to say not "Yes, I *know about* John . . ." but rather "Yes, I have sensed—experienced—touched John—I am aware of him." This, in turn, will mean that John will be sharply aware that he is perceived as a unique, potentially creative human being, not as a hapless and helpless disease or thing or object or problem or soul.

4. The goal will be student and staff learning, rather than staff teaching, and the extent of learning will be measured in terms of competencies rather than courses or hours. Students will be expected to demonstrate competencies rather than "pass" courses, and if a student can demonstrate competency in a certain area, then he will have satisfied that particular requirement. Competencies will be determined by staff and students, and while there will be a basic core at certain levels, there will also be individual differences that will be determined by the particular professional and human needs of the student. It is obvious, too, that the competencies considered to be crucial by an existential-humanistic team may be somewhat different from those of a behavioral or analytic team. Students, for example, will not be drilled in the merits of any one methodology or

technique or method, but rather exposed to many methods and theories, and helped, as creative human beings, to develop those methods
and procedures which will help them to be more effective with other
human beings.

5. The student counselor will be considered to be a responsible and creative person, quite capable of determining *how* he
wants to learn, and since the human relationship of the counselor is
considered to be the central element of counseling, it is essential that
the counselor have an awareness of self. This self-awareness of the
counselor by the counselor is of prime importance in an existential-
humanistic program of counselor education, and it takes precedence
over an understanding of the client by the counselor. The latter is
very important, of course, but the counselor who is unaware of who
he is, is not likely to be very helpful with another individual who is
trying to find a similar answer for himself. The goal is to help the
student counselor better understand himself, just as the counselor's
goal is to help the client better understand himself.

Stress is placed on the person of the counselor and the client
as a gestalt whole, a combination of the mental, emotional, and
physical. An existential-humanistic program accepts the reality of
the union of the mind, body and spirit, and helps in the total development of the person.

6. There is an awareness that each one of us is part of the
culture that surrounds us, and we impinge upon it as it impinges
upon us. The counselor's world does not just consist of students, nor
even of students and all of the staff of a school, but rather any person
or aspect of the culture that may be having an impact on the life of
the individual or individuals with whom the counselor is working. In
a sense, any place in the community, or even out of the community,
may become the "office" of the counselor.

7. There is an acceptance of realities rather than reality, and
the inner world of the person is considered to be a more adequate
measure of the functioning individual than our outer perception of
him. An important aspect of counseling is the attempt to understand
the inner perception of the individual rather than impose our outer
perception upon him, and the person of the counselor cannot be removed from the process of counseling any more than can the person
of the client.

8. The expanding of our conscious awareness is a crucial aspect of counseling, and this expansion of consciousness is a significant part of an existential-humanistic program of counselor education. Newer therapies will be explored and investigated as means by
which the boundaries of human development may be expanded.

9. The person of the student counselor will be a crucial item in admissions, and as such, there will be subjective elements in evaluation. Since "humanness" can be expanded, but hardly taught, the humanness of the student applying to the program is of great importance. The goal of the program is not to develop skilled technicians, but rather to expand the humanness, as well as the skills and knowledge, of the student counselor.

10. Since the program is an experiential field model, the students will spend the major portion of their time in schools, clinics, mental health centers, community agencies, and other institutions. The goal will be to develop a high level of of competence in human relationships, and in the skills and knowledge that are essential to the achievement of that relationship. Graduates of the program should be not only competent professional counselors, but compassionate and capable human beings.

Index